The Art of English Poesy

The Art of English Poesy

by George Puttenham

A CRITICAL EDITION

Edited by
Frank Whigham
and **Wayne A. Rebhorn**

Cornell University Press

ITHACA AND LONDON

Publication of this book was made possible, in part,
by a University Cooperative Society Subvention Grant
awarded by The University of Texas at Austin.

First published 2007 by Cornell University Press
First printing, Cornell Paperbacks, 2007

Printed in the United States of America

Library of Congress Cataloging-in-Publication Data

Puttenham, George, d. 1590.
  [Arte of English poesie]
  The art of English poesy : contrived into three books : the first of poets and
poesy, the second of proportion, and the third of ornament (London, 1589) / by
George Puttenham ; edited by Frank Whigham and Wayne A. Rebhorn. —
A critical ed.
    p. cm.
  Generally attributed to George Puttenham; has also been attributed to Richard
Puttenham and to John, Baron Lumley.
  Includes bibliographical references and index.
  ISBN 978-0-8014-3758-8 (cloth : alk. paper) — ISBN 978-0-8014-8652-4 (pbk. :
alk. paper)
  1. Poetry—Early works to 1800. 2. English poetry—History and criticism.
I. Puttenham, Richard, 1520?–1601? II. Lumley, John Lumley, Baron,
1534?–1609. III. Whigham, Frank. IV. Rebhorn, Wayne A., 1943– V. Title.

PN1031.P8 2007
821.009—dc22   2007021946

Cloth printing   10 9 8 7 6 5 4 3 2 1
Paperback printing   10 9 8 7 6 5 4 3 2 1

For Jo Anne
and
Marlette

Contents

Contents

Acknowledgments

This edition has been very much a communal project. Our principal debt is to our predecessors Gladys Doidge Willcock and Alice Walker, editors of the Cambridge edition of 1936, whose intelligence, industry, and sophistication have been a constant humbling inspiration to us. We owe similar thanks to other editors whose work has supported our own, especially Peter Medine, Hyder Edward Rollins, G. Gregory Smith, Brian Vickers, and Gavin Alexander.

Several members of our personal scholarly community deserve special recognition for years of shared labor on this edition, without whose aid it would have been unrecognizably different: David Armstrong, Steven W. May, David Harris Sacks, and Charles M. Young. Many other scholars worldwide have been very generous with their help. We thank J. D. Alsop, Harry Berger Jr., Mary Blockley, Carol Blosser, T. V. F. Brogan, Douglas Bruster, Gideon Burton, Lisa Carroll-Lee, Mary Hill Cole, Joseph Dane, Douglas Eskew, Robert C. Evans, Justin Flint, Cliff Frohlich, James Garrison, Jackie Henkel, Carol Kaske, Lois Kim, Theodore Leinwand, Jason Leubner, Brian P. Levack, Eric N. Lindquist, Arthur Marotti, John Martin, Emily McNee, David Lee Miller, Paul Allen Miller, John Monfasani, Louis Montrose, Vimala Pasupathi, Suzanne Penuel, Ingrid Rowland, Erika Rummel, John Rumrich, Liz Scala, Debora Shuger, Richard Strier, Paul Sullivan, Brian Vickers, Retha Warnicke, Stanley Wells, Brett Wilson, and Stanislav Zimic. We also thank the many scholars who participate in the SHAKSPER, Sidney-Spenser, and H-Albion on-line discussion groups (notably Hardy Cook), whose responses to our many queries have been too numerous to itemize. Finally, we want to express our gratitude to our research assistants Laura Neible, Tim Turner, and Brad Irish for their indispensable work for on the project.

We owe many debts to staff members of the Bodleian Library, Oxford, the British Library, the Folger Shakespeare Library (especially Gail Kern Paster and Georgianna Ziegler), the Harry Ransom Humanities Research Center and the Perry-Castañeda Library of the University of

Texas (especially Gera Draiijer), and to Andrew Ball of the *Oxford English Dictionary.* We also owe a special debt to Charles Willis, who first brought us news of the newly discovered and invaluable cache of data concerning Puttenham's life in the Hampshire Record Office.

It is a pleasure to acknowledge the financial support of the Arthur J. Thaman and Wilhelmina Doré Thaman and the Celanese Centennial Professorships of English, and the Graduate School of The University of Texas at Austin. We also wish to acknowledge a University Co-operative Society Subvention Grant awarded by The University of Texas at Austin. Without the aid provided by these supporters our task would have been vastly more difficult.

We would also like to say how much we appreciate the careful copy-editing our manuscript received at the hands of Amanda Heller and the generous editorial help we got from Ange Romeo-Hall, senior manuscript editor at Cornell University Press. We are especially grateful for the enthusiastic support our project has had from Bernhard Kendler, who was executive editor at Cornell when we began our work and is now retired, and from Peter Potter, who is currently editor in chief at the Press.

Finally, we wish to acknowledge how profound a shared experience it has been for us to work together for many years on this edition of Puttenham's extraordinary book. All of it belongs to both of us, flowers and weeds alike.

Abbreviations

We have employed the following abbreviations for titles cited frequently, when either (1) several versions of a work make confusion possible; (2) we cite from works taken from collections (Smith's *Elizabethan Critical Essays*, for instance); or (3) the abbreviation used would not immediately lead the reader to the appropriate alphabetical listing in the Bibliography (e.g., Croft's edition of Elyot's *Governor*).

1589	*The Art of English Poesy*, 1589 (Da Capo facsimile, 1971)
Croft	Elyot, *The . . . Governour*, 1883
CSP	*Calendar of State Papers*
CWE	*Collected Works of Erasmus*
EE	Turberville, *Epitaphes, Epigrams, Songs and Sonets*, 1567
Fraser and Rabkin	*Drama of the English Renaissance*
HMC	Historical Manuscripts Commission
Hoby	Castiglione, *The Book of the Courtier*, trans. Thomas Hoby
HRO	Hampshire Record Office
L&P	*Letters and papers, foreign and domestic, of the reign of Henry VIII*
LB	Erasmus, *Opera Omnia*, 1703–1706
LION	Literature Online
LN	Longer Notes
ODNB	*Oxford Dictionary of National Biography*
OED	*Oxford English Dictionary*
Partheniades	*Partheniades*, in *Ballads from Manuscripts*, 1873
PRO	Public Record Office
Smith	*Elizabethan Critical Essays*, ed. G. Gregory Smith, 1904
SP	State Papers
STC	*Short Title Catalogue*
Taverner	Erasmus, *Proverbs*, 1569
Tilley	*A Dictionary of the Proverbs in England in the Sixteenth and Seventeenth Centuries*, 1950

Tottel   *Tottel's Miscellany*, rev. ed. 1965
Udall   Erasmus, *Apophthegmes*, 1564
Vickers   *English Renaissance Literary Criticism*, 1999
Whiting   *Proverbs, Sentences, and Proverbial Phrases from*
                                   English Writings Mainly before 1500, 1968
Willcock and Walker   *The Art of English Poesy*, 1936
Williams   *A Glossary of Shakespeare's Sexual Language*, 1997
Wilson   *The Art of Rhetoric*, 1994

The Art of English Poesy

Introduction

When George Puttenham reviews his accomplishment at the end of *The Art of English Poesy*, he does so with characteristic density. By referring to "the poetical ornament consisting chiefly in the beauty and gallantness of *his* language and style" (conflating the poet and his art), Puttenham enables the promotion to courtly status of both ambitious man and aesthetic practice. He then voices the core fantasy of the book, of having

> appareled him [both art and courtier] to our seeming in all his gorgeous habiliments, and pulling him first from the cart to the school, and from thence to the court, and preferred him to your Majesty's service, in that place of great honor and magnificence to give entertainment to princes, ladies of honor, gentlewomen, and gentlemen, and by his many modes of skill to serve the many humors of men thither haunting and resorting. (3.25.378)[1]

This extraordinary digest combines richly disparate ingredients. The "apparel" metaphor celebrates a sumptuous joy in gorgeous clothing, poetic dress fit for the court as both entrée and reward, imitating and reflecting the ecstatic dress worn by Henry VIII and his children.[2] At the same time, and partly by this metaphorically sartorial means, the author's art enables a radical social mobility.[3] The incipient courtier and

---

1. References to passages in our text of Puttenham consist of book, chapter, and page numbers. Citations of printed sources refer to the works and editions listed in the Bibliography.

2. Not excluding the prim and priggish Edward VI. Sometimes the model was so intense as to be disabling, as we know from Henry and Elizabeth, but even Edward's favored color, violet, was "so prized by him that no one else dared wear a hat of this shade" (Jordan, *Edward VI: The Threshold of Power* 420).

3. Puttenham might be thought hyperbolic here, but lowborn commoners did in fact rise high socially thanks to their education, especially after the Dissolution—a success that forced the aristocracy and the gentry to start sending their own sons to school as well. One result was that the latter began to take the places usually occupied by commoners in the schools. As

his art are to be pulled "from the cart," Puttenham's recurrent alliterative term for the court's socially base opposite[4]—a locution rich enough to pause over. This usage, according to the *OED*, appears to embrace two social meanings. First, the two-wheeled farm cart; for its rustic social reference we may recall Polonius's oath: "If he love her not . . . / Let me be no assistant for a state, / But keep a farm and carters" (*Hamlet* 2.2.164–66). Second, the cart used "for conveying convicts to the gallows . . . [and] also for the public exposure and chastisement of offenders, esp. lewd women."[5] This figure of the cart might thus carry a multivalent and near-sulfuric energy. When Edmund Bonner sought to blacken Sir Thomas Wyatt's embassy to Charles V in 1538, he wrote to the Lord Chancellor, Thomas Cromwell, claiming that Wyatt had said,

---

early as 1540, when the Dissolution commissioners were setting terms for the new Canterbury Cathedral grammar school and it was proposed that admission be limited to sons and younger brothers of gentlemen, Cranmer objected, saying, "[P]oor men's children are many times endued with more singular gifts of nature . . . eloquence, memory, apt pronunciation, sobriety, and such like; and also commonly more apt to apply their study, than is the gentleman's son delicately educated" (Strype, *Cranmer* 1:129). On how the sons of the privileged competed with the sons of commoners for places in English schools, see, for a start, Hexter's classic study "The Education of the Aristocracy in the Renaissance."

4. The contrastive alliterative pairing of these terms is not solely Puttenham's, though his pairing is the best known, and he uses it at crucial moments. Steven W. May cites two uses of the pair to similar effect, from little-known companion poems to "My Mind to Me a Kingdom Is" (traditionally ascribed to Dyer): "To be a king thy care would much augment, / From Courte to Carte the fortune were but bare"; and "The Court ne Cart I like ne loath" (see May, "Authorship" 389). A LION search finds only three other period uses: in Austin Saker's euphuistic *Narbonus* (1580): "better for thee to leaue the Court, and followe the Cart, then to forsake thy substance, & forgoe thy friends" (230); in Thomas Lodge's *A Margarite of America* (1596): "From height of throne to abiect wretchednesse, / From woonderous skill to seruile ignorance: / From court to cart, from rich to rechlesnesse, / The ioyes of life haue no continuance" (9); and in George Chapman's *Monsieur D'Olive* (1606): "softnes and modestie sauors of the Cart, / tis boldnes boldnes does the deed in the Court" (scene 1).

5. *OED* does not cite the usage for capital felons explicitly before 1682, but, in addition to Wyatt's words cited below, the *Chronicle of the Grey Friars of London* records the usage as early as 1524: on February 20 "the lady Alys Hungrford was lede from the tower un to Holborne and there put into a carte at the church-yard with one of her servanttes, and so caryed unto Tyborne, and there both hongyd" for having murdered her husband (31). Wriothesley's *Chronicle* notes, as one of its final entries, that on June 27, 1556, "were 13 persons carried from Newgate in three carrs to the end of the towne of Stratford the Bowe, and there brent" (2.135). And Henry Machyn's *Diary* specifies (in his characteristically wild spelling) "rod in a care v. unto Tyborne" (five were ridden in a car, i.e., a cart) on July 2, 1556 (109). (*OED* cites "car" as "carriage, chariot, cart, wagon, truck, etc." from 1382 on.) In the fourteenth century, however, the term "car" was sometimes "extended to a sleigh or hurdle without wheels." "Hurdle" here means (from 1412 till very late) "[a] kind of frame or sledge on which traitors used to be drawn through the streets to execution." Apparently the terms "sled/ge," "hurdle," "car," and "cart" overlapped to varying degrees, wheels being inessential, such that, perhaps, being "drawn in a hurdle" and being "carted" were less distinct than they seem to modern ears. Puttenham's words here in 3.25 both accentuate the distance between the courtly poet's cartly origins and his eventual height and bridge the gap by alliteration. Puttenham resorts to the word "cart" repeatedly in the *Art*; as an intensive figure of social depth it reaches its simultaneous zenith and nadir, as a *tapinosis*, in 3.22, where one Sergeant Bendlowes halts the queen's coach at progress time and commits a near-disastrous faux pas by saying, "Stay thy cart, good fellow, stay thy cart, that I may speak to the Queen" (345).

most outrageously, "By goddess bludde, ye shall see the kinge our maister cast out at the carts tail, and if he soo be serued, by godds body, he is well serued."[6] The *OED* defines *cart's-tail* as "the hinder part of a cart, to which offenders were tied to be whipped through the streets," citing an example from Foxe in 1563. Cromwell (Wyatt's ally) suppressed the letter, but after Cromwell's death in 1540 Bonner managed to get the charge taken up again, and Wyatt was, on this and related grounds, investigated—and imprisoned—for treason. Wyatt presented a detailed linguistic defense, which survives. What Bonner took the phrase to mean Wyatt makes clear in his furious and frightened denial: "that by throwinge owte of a cartes ars I shulde mene that vile deathe that is or-dained for wretchede theves."[7] In this construction the insult was grave. Given such a range of associations, from manual labor to vile criminal-ity, Puttenham's courtly poet appears to begin his career at an extreme social depth indeed.

On his way from the cart to the court Puttenham also acknowledges the "school," evincing a matter-of-fact respect for the achievement of gentry status through institutional education. The "entertainment" his poet will then be equipped to supply appears to entail both unserious amusement and perhaps some form of "holding court."[8] And such per-formance embraces both feminizing and erotic service, to judge by its specified audience: three of the four top layers of what Puttenham seems to envision here as a "stepped" pyramid are female: "gentle-women," "ladies of honor," and his prince, Elizabeth. For the gentle-men, Puttenham offers an insistently elastic, perhaps superserviceable, ensemble of enchanting talents fit for satisfying the many desires of other powerful and ambitious males—both the great and those who haunt them.[9] He hastens to specify that these services offer solace, seri-ous advice, pleasant and honest profit. "No offense i'th' world," as Hamlet has it.

One finally decisive attribute of the courtly poet and his art receives separate and arresting attention: cunning dissembling. Puttenham judges his task complete, he says,

> so always as we leave him not unfurnished of one piece that best beseems that place of any other and may serve as a principal good lesson for all

6. See Muir, *Life and Letters* 67, cited from *L&P* 1538: XIII.2, no. 270. (Muir provides a useful context for the remark, sputteringly repeated by Bonner. The poet's fascinating and successful defense of his coarse speech appears at 196–200.)

7. Muir, *Life and Letters* 197.

8. Cf. Whigham, *Ambition and Privilege* 36–37, on Kenneth Burke's notion of the "per-former-audience dialectic." The urbane artist may be socially inferior to his audience, profes-sionally superior to them, yet bound to woo them. Each side of the dialectic confers both power and abjection. The performative life at court is above all a *predicament*.

9. For a rich and relevant treatment of the freight of "superserviceable" villainy in *King Lear*, see Strier, "Faithful Servants."

good makers to bear continually in mind in the usage of this science: which is, that being now lately become a courtier, he show not himself a craftsman, and merit to be disgraded, and with scorn sent back again to the shop or other place of his first faculty and calling, but that so wisely and discreetly he behave himself as he may worthily retain the credit of his place and profession of a very courtier, which is, in plain terms, cunningly to be able to dissemble. (3.25.378–79)

It is not clear whether this final condition amounts to achieving a durable disposition or enduring the ceaseless hazard of contemptible disgrace. Puttenham's maker, it seems, has but lately become a courtier, and remains anxiously at risk of showing himself a craftsman, deserving degradation to the shop. The way to avoid such humiliation, to maintain courtly place, is to enact oneself in accord with the "profession of a very courtier, which is, in plain terms, cunningly to be able to dissemble."

The objects of this dissembling are catalogued in striking detail: disguising the body with new fashions, the face with many countenances; disguising one's ideas and one's actions, "the better to win his purposes and good advantages" (3.25.379). Such disguising includes false illnesses and journeys and other absences from court, false health and wealth and poverty and busyness and idleness and religion and churlishness, and, of course, false courtesy. These disguisings, he then tells us, having so richly inventoried them, are typical of foreign courtiers, among whom he was raised and whom he knows better than English ones. However reality-based it may be, such deceit is not to be allowed to the English maker, who is to be an honest man and not a hypocrite, and who may dissemble only in the subtleties of his art, where *sprezzatura* may legitimately reign. The many cited disguisings linger for the reader nonetheless, as a rich anthology of "poems of conduct," to match the many examples of courtly poetry and conduct that enliven Book 3.

Puttenham goes on to explore the subtleties of poetic art, leaving behind without explanation the catalogue of courtly dissembling he has been at such pains to detail and then deny. Twice over, in fact: "I speak of the English," he essentially claims, "not foreigners, and of poetry, not conduct." This culminating gesture of *occupatio*, however, exactly epitomizes Puttenham's densely realized art of courtly *conduct*: an aggressively weird fan dance mixing supplication, anxiety, scorn, envy, the undisguised espousal of dissembling, and proud, even exhibitionist, display—all of these exposed, flaunted, coyly bared, and marked "to be concealed," by turns and all at once. The claims of insider expertise and the wincing fears of life (or worse) at the cart horse's tail together invite a view of the author as well acquainted with both precious place and loss, whether in personal memory, by report, or in avid fantasy. Whatever Puttenham may be felt to be doing here, crawling or prancing or insinuating or sneering, *sprezzatura* is far away: he struggles to shape and control a particular and strong view of himself—both ours and his own—as a designer of courtly promotion. Such emotional density now seems the most distinctive feature of the *Art*.

1. The Documentary Life

Birth, education, marriage.   The sources of Puttenham's complex hungry attitude are mostly lost to us, but many of the surviving details of his life must bear some relation to it. He was a younger son, born to parents on the fringe of Henry VIII's court in 1529 or 1530, one of eight children.[10] His paternal grandfather, Sir George, was present at the Field of the Cloth of Gold in 1520.[11] Puttenham's father, Robert, a Hampshire gentleman, marched with Sir Thomas Elyot, Wyatt's John Poyntz, John Cheke, Fulke Greville (the poet's grandfather), Sir Anthony Rous (a client of the duke of Norfolk mentioned in 3.18 and 3.24), Sir Andrew Flamock (Henry VIII's standard-bearer, mentioned in 3.23), and many others in the ill-fated parade of welcome for Anne of Cleves in 1539.[12] Puttenham's mother, Margery, was the sister of Sir Thomas Elyot, prince-advising author of *The Boke named the Governour* (1531), and Henry's disastrously unpaid ambassador to Charles V for a few months of "unthankfull travayle" in 1531–32.[13]

Puttenham matriculated at Christ's College, Cambridge, in November 1546; Cambridge was then the seedbed of English humanism, numbering Roger Ascham, Sir John Cheke, Thomas Wilson, and Sir Thomas Smith among its faculty. Taking no degree there, Puttenham was admitted to the Middle Temple, one of London's four law schools, on August 11, 1556 (at about age twenty-seven). Such enrollment was becoming typical for younger sons of elite families, who, without substantial inheritance, had their way to make. Sir Thomas Elyot had been a Templar before Puttenham. There he also met his future brother-in-law John Throckmorton.

Puttenham's legal expertise emerges later in a variety of offensive and defensive contexts, but in 1559 or so, when he was around thirty, he left the study of the law to marry Elizabeth, Lady Windsor (1520–ca.

10. Puttenham states in a letter of late 1578 (preserved in two drafts) that he is "now apon the point of fyftie yeares of age" (PRO, SP 12/126/17 and SP 12/126/18). According to heraldic visitation records, Robert and Margery Elyot Puttenham's children are listed as follows: (1) Richard, (2) George, (3) Francis, (4) William, then Rose, Anne, Mary, and Margaret. (Only the sons' birth order is recorded.) See "Pedigrees" 17–18.
11. *L&P* 1519: III.1, no. 704. The Field of the Cloth of Gold was a famous meeting between Henry VIII and Francis I of France in June 1520, arranged to confirm the bond between the two kings specified by the Anglo-French treaty signed in 1518. In fact each king sought to outshine the other in elaborate displays of clothing, feasting, and games.
12. *L&P* 1539: XIV.2, no. 572.
13. See the records from this period in Elyot's *Letters*; p. 13 is quoted here.

1588), who was some ten years his senior. She was the daughter and co-heir of Peter Cowdray of Hampshire, and widow first of Richard Paulet (will probated February 6, 1552) and then of William, second Baron Windsor (who died August 20, 1558).[14] Baron Windsor had been a bencher of the Middle Temple when Puttenham was admitted, and he captured Windsor's wealthy widow, who had been raised in the same part of Hampshire as Puttenham, inside two years. Puttenham thus not only followed the educational curriculum of a typical late Tudor gentleman, but also exemplified Lawrence Stone's dictum that "for a young man of gentle birth, the fastest ways of moving up the social scale were the lotteries of marriage with an heiress, Court favor, and success at the law. The first of the three is usually neglected or ignored by social historians, but it was probably the commonest method of upward movement for gentlemen."[15] Lady Windsor had retained the Herriard property (her sizable dowry) and her jointure from Baron Windsor (three manors).[16] Their estate was sufficiently impressive that in 1574 they lodged the queen—or at least some of her progress entourage—at Herriard.[17]

Travels. Puttenham's life experience was not restricted to England. He speaks at least nine times in the *Art* of his foreign travel: (1) "I myself, seeing this conceit so well allowed of in France and Italy . . ." (2.12.197). (2) "I myself, having seen the courts of France, Spain, Italy, and that of the Empire, with many inferior courts . . ." (3.23.356). (3) "[T]he Prince of Orange . . . looked aside on that part where I stood a beholder of the feast" (probably in Brussels in 1566; see 3.23.356). (4) "In the time of Charles IX, French King [ruled 1560–74], I being at the Spa waters . . ." (3.24.362). (5) "And was some blemish to the Emperor Ferdinand [ruled 1558–64], a most noble-minded man, yet so careless and forgetful of himself in that behalf, as I have seen him run up a pair of stairs so swift and nimble apace, as almost had not become a very mean man, who had not gone in some hasty business" (3.24.377). (6) "I have observed it in the court of France" (3.25.380). (7) "[A]s I have observed

---

14. Data otherwise unidentified here and elsewhere derive from Steven W. May's *ODNB* essay "Puttenham, George (1529–1590/91)" and from many personal communications from May, as well as from his forthcoming essay on Puttenham's life records, "George Puttenham's Lewd and Illicit Career," which he has shared with unparalleled generosity. Much of this work derives from the Jervoise of Herriard papers, deposited at the Hampshire Record Office in the 1960s but only now receiving attention. We owe our initial knowledge of this cache of data to Charles Willis, a descendant of Puttenham who discovered these records and generously shared his work on them with us. A more particular debt to Willis regarding the library inventories found among Puttenham's papers is noted below.

15. Stone, "Social Mobility" 34–35.

16. Collins, *Peerage* 4.76.

17. Chambers, *The Elizabethan Stage* 4.90: Chambers lists Herriard for September 14–16. Puttenham alludes in the *Art* to Elizabeth's supposed insistence on paying her own way at progress time (see 3.24.375).

in many of the princes' courts of Italy . . ." (3.25.381). (8) "[A]s I have seen of the greatest podestates and gravest judges and presidents of parliament in France . . ." (3.25.381). (9) "[E]specially in the courtiers of foreign countries, where in my youth I was brought up and very well observed their manner of life and conversation . . ." (3.25.381).

Documents in the Hampshire archive show that Puttenham was abroad in 1563 and possibly in 1565 or 1566. In 1578 he deposed that he had gone "beyonde the seaes . . . aboute the vth yeare of her Majestyes raigne."[18] He signed papers in Antwerp on February 5 and 8, 1563.[19] He seems also to have traveled to Flanders in 1565 or 1566, according to Richard Hartilpoole, who sued Puttenham in Chancery in April 1567 for back wages, having spent "six wekes and more" with him there.[20] The archive also preserves a later passport, issued on May 5, 1567, to "our welbeloued George Puttenham," entitling him "to returne to the baines [baths] of the spaw or other place requisite for his health."[21] These documents do not positively confirm Puttenham's presence at the banquet in Brussels or at Spa mentioned in the *Art* (3.23.356 and 3.24.362), but they are consistent with such travels. There is thus no reason to doubt his claims of travel abroad, and he may have gained experience of courts there, as he says. In addition to the dates suggested by the cited documents, he may also have traveled (indeed, been "brought up") abroad in the ten years between his matriculation at Cambridge in 1546 and his (late) admission to the Middle Temple in 1556.

Family relations and social violation. Most of the historical data about George Puttenham suggest an injured, bellicose, and, it must be said, vicious nature. He resembles in confusing and disturbing ways *King Lear*'s Gloster and his bastard younger son, Edmund. Legal records concerning Puttenham document numerous charges and counter charges of crimes against persons and property. He was repeatedly assaulted (suffering murder attempts four times, he claims), sued, countersued, arrested, imprisoned (at least six times), kidnapped, and excommunicated (four times). He was sued for assaulting a parson in his church, and was charged with subornation of murder and with treason (though he was eventually cleared), and with several varieties of what we would now call sexual predation (on which more below). Although it was a litigious and violent age, Puttenham's habits of life were extraordinarily unruly.

---

18. PRO, SP 12/127/27, f. 48v; SP 12/127/30, ff. 54v–55.

19. HRO, 44M69/f3/1, f. 8. For another possible clue to Puttenham's activities on the continent at this time, see LN 22.

20. PRO, C 3/90/84, m. 1.

21. For a facsimile of this document, see Willis, *Shakespeare and George Puttenham's "Arte of English Poesie"* 397. The passport grants Puttenham a year's absence from England at any time over the next two years.

Most of his collisions with the law occurred in connection with two main problems: his protracted quarrel from 1562 until 1584 with his niece and her husband over the paternal manor of Sherfield, and his deeply hostile divorce from Lady Windsor at some point after 1566. The data are sketchy and uneven, and derive largely from his enemies. We should proceed cautiously. Nonetheless, we must probably discern in Puttenham's struggles some profound failure of settled social and psychological construction within two of the most profound (if hardly unflawed) structures of obligation and identity on which Elizabethan culture rested: the experience of the primogenitural birth family—in Puttenham's case, that of a resentful younger brother[22]—and the cultural matrix of marriage. In this second and better-documented dysfunction, two factors are central. He married, apparently for sheerly instrumental reasons, an older and much richer woman, from whom most of the upward mobility he managed was derived. And he was relentlessly unfaithful and exploitive to his wife and, much more disturbingly to modern eyes, habitually violated a string of poor women and servants whom he misused as smoothly (at least initially) and grossly as he did Lady Windsor.

It should be said at the outset that judging the weight of these actions for reading *The Art of English Poesy* is difficult. For some, they may be so toxic as to render further reading intolerable, confirming Puttenham as a limit case of Renaissance misogyny. In this regard it is as well to recall that such disturbing conjunctions of literary intelligence and moral turpitude are not unique in early English literature. Geoffrey Chaucer was charged with rape (whether sexual assault or abduction we do not know), though eventually cleared. Sir Thomas Malory was also charged with assault and rape. Edmund Spenser, some would argue, welcomed the solution of genocide by famine for the Elizabethan Irish problem.[23] To some, these matters may seem extraliterary, irrelevant, unsightly, or adequately explained; to others, explained away, or worse, passed by in guilty silence. Perhaps, so far as the sexual crimes go, we should speak of a larger cultural pathology, of some volcanic transformation of the ownership logic of cuckoldry panic about the proper "use" of women, a panic only partly intelligible now. Perhaps instead there was a family pathology: Puttenham's elder brother, Richard, was convicted of rape in 1561. As editors we have no illusion of having produced a finally satisfactory frame for the confluence of Puttenham's troubling life and his art as we can know them now.

The conflict with his brother.   Of Puttenham's relationship with his brother, Richard, we know the least, and indeed, not enough to withhold

---

22. Cf. Thirsk's famous study of discontented younger sons and the English Civil War.

23. On Chaucer and Malory, see the series of articles by Cannon. For Spenser, see *A View of the State of Ireland* xv–xvi, xix–xx, 101–5.

confidently the sincere sympathy appropriate to abandoned and embittered younger sons in the period. These young men too often suffered the fate of redundant functional backstops in the primogenitural system. Once the heir achieved his majority and inherited, they were unneeded, unwanted, and unprovided for.[24] Richard Puttenham, the heir, had moved to the continent in 1560, probably to avoid the consequences of the rape for which he was convicted the next year.[25] In 1578 George deposed that he had journeyed there around 1562–63 to buy Sherfield from Richard, who had inherited it in 1550 (having already inherited his uncle Elyot's property in 1546).[26] George signed purchase agreements with Richard in Antwerp on February 5 and 8, 1563,[27] and occupied Sherfield until 1567, when Richard came home secretly and, breaking whatever deal had been made earlier, conveyed the manor to Anne and Francis Morris, who then took the house from Puttenham by force.

In the meantime, Puttenham was sued on a separate matter in London in 1565, and in 1569 the sheriffs in London and Middlesex were ordered by the courts to arrest him for contempt in regard to the suit, and for a variety of other crimes.[28] When he was selected to serve as a justice of the peace in 1569, the reforming Robert Horne, bishop of Winchester, wrote to Elizabeth's principal secretary William Cecil praying "that it be not true[,] for his evil life is well known, and also that he is a 'notorious enemye to God's Truthe.' "[29] By June 1570 Puttenham was being held in the Fleet prison, owing, it seems, to a deposition by a Julio Mantuano that Puttenham had slandered the queen and incited him to murder the bishop of London.[30] The divorce testimony records that he "was comytted to the fflete vppon matter of highe Treason,"[31] and in the same year was accused of suborning the assassination of Secretary Cecil.[32] Nevertheless, he seems to have cleared himself from these charges, successfully suing the warden of the Fleet, Brian Annesley, for

24. See, e.g., Lawrence Stone: "Under such a system [of primogeniture], both the elder and the younger children suffered. The latter normally inherited neither title nor estate, unless one of them happened to be heir to his mother's property, and they were therefore inevitably downwardly mobile, until they had made their own fortunes in some profession or occupation. Some were kept hanging around on or near the estate, as a kind of walking sperm-bank in case the elder son died childless and had to be replaced" (*The Family, Sex and Marriage* 88).

25. *CSP Domestic, 1547–1580*, 175: SP 12/16/61 (document of April 25, 1561).

26. PRO, SP 12/127/27, f. 48v; SP 12/127/30, ff. 54v–55.

27. HRO, 44M69/f3/1, f. 8.

28. PRO, REQ 2 219/25. These included both property crimes and at least two instances of assault.

29. HMC Salisbury 1.392–3, Horne to Cecil, January 21, 1568/69. Horne appears to have succeeded; Puttenham's name does not appear on a list of thirty Hampshire JPs who subscribed to the Act of Uniformity in November 1569, nor is he mentioned among those who failed to sign the document (SP 12/59/46, ff. 160–62).

30. This was Edmund Grindal, translated to York May 22, 1570. Mantuano's April 7 deposition (PRO, SP 70/111/627, *olim* 795) alleges that the idea was proposed five months before.

31. HRO, 44M69/F2/14/1.

32. PRO, SP 12/66/118.

funds given Annesley to pay Puttenham's debts during his imprisonment.[33] Meanwhile, Puttenham's normal life, such as it was, continued. His men seized the mill at Sherfield in April 1571, but Morris once
again recovered it by force. At this time Puttenham was residing there
with a Margaret Marriner, whose house, she averred, Morris and his
men had pulled down; she and Puttenham rebuilt it, and Morris once
again demolished it. The conflict finally came to an end in 1581, when
Morris was arrested for harboring the Jesuit Edmond Campion; he died
in prison in 1584.

The conflicts with his wife.   Puttenham's divorce battles aggravated
these other tensions. Lady Windsor later deposed that she had accepted
Puttenham "onlye by the perswasion of Sr Iohn Throckmorton," and
that he then lacked "any porcon of livinge."[34] According to her relations,
she had already become alienated from him by the early 1560s, having
decided very soon after their marriage in 1559 that he had "maried the
Landes and the liuinge and not the woman."[35] Things had apparently
gone very bad rather quickly, for in the fall of 1562 Thomas Paulet, Lady
Windsor's brother-in-law, assaulted Puttenham at Sherfield, later admitting that he wounded him in the head with his dagger, and "then agayne
with the blade of the said dagger gave unto the said complainant one
other litle Stroke."[36] Lady Windsor finally left Puttenham in 1575, and
for her later divorce proceedings prepared an elaborate documentation of
her reasons for so doing, consisting of depositions from seventeen witnesses (preserved in the Jervoise of Herriard archive, which documents
this rehearsal generally). She concluded that she was "prohibyted by the
lawes of god to keepe felowship wth so incestyous [i.e., adulterous] and
vnsatyable a man wth diuerse lewd women wherof one at that instant
she tooke from his house whose examynacon wth diuerse others of his
beastlyke demeanures remayneth most true of Record in tharches [the
London Court of Arches]."[37] Several documents affirm Puttenham's
physical abuse of Lady Windsor. She addressed him in a written complaint, saying: "Caule to yor remembrance how vildlie you haue in all re-
spectes delt wth me more like a kytchin slaue then like a wyfe. Consider
also how Latelie ye haue most wickedlie attempted not onlie to impeach
my rybbes but rather to spoile me of my life." Two servants also deposed
that he injured his wife's back by throwing her against a door.[38]

33. Annesley is otherwise familiar in literary studies for his youngest daughter, Cordelia,
his senility in old age, and the possibility that his experience influenced Shakespeare's rendi-
tion of *King Lear.*
34. HRO, 44M69 F2/14/1, bundle 1.
35. HRO, 44M69/F2/14/1, p. 3.
36. PRO, STAC 5, P66/2.
37. HRO, 44M69 F2/14/1, bundle 1.
38. HRO, 44M69/F2/14/1, p. 1; HRO, 44M69/F2/14/1, bundle 2, no. vii, ff. 2, 4.

According to more of Lady Windsor's witnesses, Puttenham conducted numerous adulteries with her servants, living (perhaps like
Gloster) the life of a brutal but persuasive sexual predator.[39] He
arranged a marriage for the pregnant Izard Cawley, "the better to geave
Colloure to his incontinente Dealinges wth her."[40] With another maid-
servant, Mary Champneys, he dealt as follows:

> to Wynne his vngodly purpose he firste practized wth faire wordes and re-
> wardes who neverthelesse resisted the same of a verie godly Mynde dis-
> posed But sith he cold not so wynne her he did dayly so beate her from
> tyme to tyme in suche sorte that the Maiden shold wax wery of her Ser-
> vice/After wch practize he . . . assaulted the said Maiden in moste wicked
> Maner and there wth all shewed her what thraldome and misery she
> shold sustayne and therefore the next way was to assente vnto him in his
> Carnall desires And that then she shold lyve in the estate of a gentle-
> woman in greate quietnes and in no lesse wealeth and felicitie.

When Champneys became pregnant, he took her to Flanders to give
birth, and then abandoned her there "in grete misery."[41]

Three more such cases are documented by the testimony of neighbors
and servants, specifying pregnancies and also financial payouts, which
might have been either "hush money" or child support. Puttenham's
bailiff, James Kirby, testified that he "dyd at [Puttenham's] Comaunde-
mente paye for the nursinge of the sayde children and also apparell whoe
gaue this deponente money allwayes to paye from tyme to tyme as the
sayde woman did demaunde of this deponente."[42] These corruptions, so
distasteful to modern sensibilities, may seem less disturbing than his
treatment of the last of the documented victims, Elizabeth Johnson,
whose abuse by Puttenham many local witnesses confirm. Johnson herself deposed in detail how Puttenham had one of his servants abduct her
in London as a teenager, luring her with the prospect of a place in service
with a lady. She was taken to a house in Paddington, where Puttenham
came, and "wthin an howre or twoe after he came thither he the sayde
Mr Puttenham *with muche adoe* had his pleasure carnallye wth her"
(emphasis added): surely what we would call rape is meant.[43] For three

---

39. This is, anyway, one obvious construction—that Gloster was a sexual predator—of
Edgar's cruel line, "The dark and vicious place where thee he got cost him his eyes" (*King
Lear* 5.3.175–76).

40. HRO, 44M69/F2/14/1, bundle 1, no. viii.

41. HRO, 44M69/F2/14/1, bundle 1, no. ii.

42. HRO, 44M69/F2/14/1, bundle 2, no. vii, f. 9. Middleton's characterization of the maid
Diaphanta in *The Changeling* (1622) suggests the possibility that such actions were not always simply gross and one-sided exploitation. She performs a sexual service for her mistress
that will net her enough gold to serve as a promising dowry: "I'm for a justice now, / I bring a
portion with me; I scorn small fools" (4.1.126–27). Whether such fictions resembled many
real-life cases is not at all clear.

43. HRO, 44M69/F2/14/1, bundle 2, no. vii, f. 3v.

years Puttenham moved Johnson from one place to another, setting her up in custodial housing with the aid of cooperative servants. This arrangement came to an end when Lady Windsor seized Johnson at her husband's farm of Upton Gray, writing to him, "I haue in my custodie a damsell chosen by you as she confessethe for yor owne toothe." Puttenham demanded that she be set free, but his wife replied, "Only yow Longe for her retorne to yor owne person," and felt herself "aucthoryzed . . . to answere for her kepinge."[44]

These disturbing materials are, it should be noted, both ambiguous and confusing. Puttenham's exploitation of his victims seems unmistakable, but much of Johnson's relation to the experience is opaque. Her testimony was summoned, possibly suborned or extracted, by Lady Windsor for her own explicitly hostile purposes, which may or may not have coincided with Johnson's. The custodial housing was probably captivity, but may have been concealment (from exposure or rescue) or even an initially imposed but perhaps then accepted "living." Johnson's so-called confession of sexual relations may be guilty, shamefaced, or triumphantly vengeful, or may simply amount to a matter-of-fact legal affirmation of what had happened. Lady Windsor may have liberated her, or locked her up in a different house, feeling "authorized" to do so by Johnson's fear of Puttenham, but Lady Windsor's actions would also have been motivated by her own sense of injury and vengeful spousal self-righteousness, actions possibly quite high-handed, enabled as such by her local clout as county magnate. While Puttenham's gross misconduct seems clear enough, it is equally clear that a great deal of the story is obscure, and was probably driven as much by the energies of status and honor as by those of what we would call gender politics.

In Easter Term of 1575,[45] Lady Windsor left Puttenham, moved in with her children, and reapplied herself to divorce proceedings at the Court of Arches in London, the ecclesiastical court under the jurisdiction of the archbishop of Canterbury. Puttenham had been bound to provide her with £100 annually for her upkeep, but had failed to honor the bond after 1572. Although the Court of Arches required him in the fall of 1575 to begin paying her £3 a week, he continued to default. The Privy Council then intervened, requiring the alimony on her behalf in 1576, and simultaneously investigating her charge (eventually shown to be true) that Puttenham had illegally transferred the Herriard estate to his brother-in-law Sir John Throckmorton. Puttenham had fraudulently persuaded her to sign the relevant transfer papers, assuring her that they would enable her daughter Elizabeth to inherit Herriard in re-

---

44. HRO, 44M69/F2/14/1, pp. 1, 2.
45. See the unaddressed copy of Throckmorton's letter dated March 18, 1579, HRO, 44M69/ f2/13/3.

version and without crown fees.[46] Instead, the documents disinherited her children.[47]

Incensed by these crimes and by his refusal to obey their summons, in June the Privy Council sent two royal pursuivants (officers empowered to execute warrants) to bring Puttenham before them:

> [T]he saide George caused the said two persons by vi. or vij others to be holden in the Churcheyarde of Herryard . . . soe as the said George then and there wth a weapon called a bastynadoe beatte the said persons in very contemptuous maner and brake one of their hedes very sore, for wch cause . . . he rested excommunycated ipso facto, and vnder the danger of the losse of one of his eares.[48]

Puttenham's excommunication from the Anglican Church for failure to pay his alimony was the first of four times he suffered this legal penalty, which had been strengthened by the 1563 Parliament: the statute observed that "diuers persons offendyng in many great crymes and offences apperteynyng meerely to the iurisdiction and determination of the Ecclesiastical courtes and iudges of the Realme, are manye tymes vnpunished for lacke and want of the good and due execution of the wryt *de Excommunicato capiendo*."[49] Enforcement was stiffened, and fines for failure to respond increased. As we see, Puttenham's beating of the pursuivants made him liable to the loss of an ear, and he may also have been branded, according to another suit (undated).[50] (Whether he actually underwent either of these mutilations remains unclear.)

In 1577 Puttenham left Herriard and became a permanent fugitive. His neighborhood of residence at this time is revealing: the precinct of London called Whitefriars, named for the church of the White Friars, or Carmelites, built in 1241 and torn down at the Dissolution of the Monasteries. The attached privilege of legal sanctuary remained unrevoked until 1697, however, and the tenements there thus attracted "a lawless community of fraudulent debtors, refugees from justice, and women of the streets . . . who defied the officers of the Law and governed themselves."[51] (Such dispossessed "hideout" habitation might remind us of Shakespeare's Edmund, who "hath been out nine years,"

---

46. Dasent, *Acts of the Privy Council* 9.148.

47. The young Elizabeth died before May 1576, and Lady Windsor's heir, John Paulet, sued Puttenham to recover the lands.

48. HRO, 44M69 F2/14/1, bundle 1, Lady Windsor's account, docketed as the "Answere to the allegatons made by georg Putenham to the Lords of the cownsell." A bastinado is a cudgel, though perhaps the phrasing suggests a special kind.

49. *A Table to al the Statutes* (STC 9546), 1570, sig. K5–6v.

50. One William Bethell seems to have affirmed in a suit that Puttenham "for his evell mysdemenor hath byn latley burned in the hande" (PRO, C3 205/14, m. 1). This punishment would probably have been for a different crime (not for his beating of the pursuivants, which carried a potential penalty of branding on the cheek, not the hand).

51. Sugden, *Topographical Dictionary* 564.

and soon "away he shall again," his father determines. In a play so profoundly concerned with outcasts and casting out, this first, curiously
undefined use of the word "out," regarding its most lawless refugee, has
an implicit reach well beyond the neutral gloss "abroad.") In 1578 the
divorce became final, and Lady Windsor's petitions for financial support resumed. In October Puttenham wrote the council that he could
not appear before them owing to fear of her children, whom he accused
of having assaulted him. On February 3 they had, he claimed, broken
into his rooms in Whitefriars with an armed band, served him with another writ *excommunicato capiendo*, and carried him away "without
any cappe, hatt or carchiffe bare heded" to prison in Middlesex, after ri-
fling through his chests and desks, where, he said, bonds of £11,000 or
more were held.[52] John Paulet, Lady Windsor's son by her second marriage, was seeking possession of Herriard, which should, he thought,
have come to him from his father (as part of Lady Windsor's dowry), but
which Puttenham had been using as his main residence while married
to her. The raid aimed to secure the records needed to recapture the
manor.

Puttenham was released from prison in June by collusion with the un-
dersheriff and resumed his fugitive life; the Privy Council then issued
another warrant for his arrest on sight to all mayors, sheriffs, and
bailiffs.[53] He complained to the council loudly by letter: "[Y]our Lordships haue me in great yll oppinion and displeasure. . . . I shall not be
able to lyue in my country (nor anye wherels free from euery mans
spoile and invation. for who will forebeare to offer me wronge that shall
behollde yowr good Lordships apon privat cawses so extraordynaryly
and sharply to persecute me with yowr displeasures?"[54] In response to
his claimed danger, the council issued letters of protection for his appearance, and arrested him on December 20 "with some difficulty."[55] By
July 13, 1579, he had agreed to provide Lady Windsor with six servants,
four suits, a coach, and £20 yearly (according to a document partly
drafted by Puttenham, completed and revised in more stringent terms in
the hand of William Cecil, Lord Burghley).[56] By November he was again,
predictably, in arrears, as the course of the law steadily eroded his in-
come, the great bulk of which derived from his access to Lady Windsor's
properties. He was imprisoned and excommunicated twice more (as late
as 1588). By 1589 Lady Windsor was deceased,[57] and Puttenham soon

---

52. PRO, STAC 5 P9/4, P3/3. The documents then seized constitute most of the Jervoise of
Herriard archive on which this narrative is based.

53. Dasent, *Acts of the Privy Council* 10.260.

54. PRO, SP 12/126/16, an unsigned holograph, endorsed in another contemporary hand,
"A long lettere drawne to the lords of the Councel. from Mr Georg Puttenham."

55. Thus Throckmorton to Burghley, December 21, 1578, HMC Salisbury 2.222.

56. PRO, PC 2/2, p. 540.

57. PRO, STAC 5 P33/22.

followed her, ending his life nearly indigent. Litigious to the end, he brought suit in that year against Henry, Lord Windsor, Lady Windsor's stepson, for an annuity that in fact had lapsed many years before when she and Puttenham became legally separated. Windsor denied all Puttenham's claims but reported that "the said plaintiff hath ben an importunant Sutor to him for some Anuytie or yearelie Rente as allso for money for the Relievinge of his poore estate . . . vppon which greate and earneste suite of the said plaintiff this defendent hath furnished the said plaintiff as by the waye of Loue with one Hundred poundes or more in ready money at sondry times."[58] In September 1590 Puttenham's nuncupative will left all his possessions to Mary Simmes, his servant. He was buried in London on January 6, 1591.

2. Puttenham's Writings

The wildness of Puttenham's personal life did not prevent a significant literary output. Only the *Art* and the *Partheniades* have survived, but numerous lost works are mentioned in the *Art*.

Partheniades.   This work, a set of seventeen poems totaling 555 lines in praise of Queen Elizabeth, is cited at least eleven times in the *Art*. It survives only in manuscript (BL, Cotton Vesp. MS E.8, fols. 169–78), and was not printed until 1811.[59] Its headnote labels it "The principall addresse in nature of a New yeares gifte." Its final poem, comparing Elizabeth to Pallas, says of her, "O now twenty yeare agon, / Forsaking Greece for Albion, / Where thow alone dost rule" (470–72).[60] This passage roughly dates at least this poem to around 1579. More exact dating is impossible. The first poem's opening lines suggest the presence of royalty at the New Year's celebration: "Gracious Princesse, Where princes are in place / To geue you gold, and plate, and perles of price, / It seemeth this day, saue your royall aduice, / Paper presentes should haue but little grace" (1–4). No royalty attended that celebration in 1579–80, but Elizabeth's suitor, the duke of Alençon, was present in 1581–82, and he is mentioned obliquely at 211 as having "bidd [invited] repulse" at the queen's hands (see Morfill's notes). As Willcock and Walker observe (xxxii),[61] there is also some reason to suppose that the seventeen poems were written at different times. Finally, there is no record that the poems were actually presented to the queen; perhaps the headnote is a literary fiction.

---

58. PRO, C2/Eliz/P17/50, m. 2.
   59. In Haslewood, *Ancient Critical Essays* 1.xvii–xxviii.
   60. *Partheniades*, in *Ballads from Manuscripts*, ed. Morfill, 2:72–91. All citations of the *Partheniades* are taken from this edition.
   61. Henceforth references to Gladys Doidge Willcock and Alice Walker's 1936 edition of the *Art* will appear parenthetically in the text.

Lost works. At various points in the *Art* Puttenham names the following lost works:

1. *Hierotechnē* (1.12.119), apparently a work on religion: the title seems to mean "On the Art of the Sacred," or perhaps "On the Power of the Gods."

2. "[A] little brief romance or historical ditty in the English tongue of the Isle of Great Britain in short and long meters" (1.19.131).

3. His "*Triumphals* written in honor of her Majesty's long peace" (1.23.135, 3.19.305 and 323).

4. A work titled *Philocalia*, wherein, he says, he has "strained to show the use and application of this figure [*exergasia*] and all others mentioned in this book [the *Art*]" (3.20.333–34; see also 2.12.186 and 3.20.335).

5. A comedy called *Ginecocratia* (2.18.218), about a king ruled by women.

6. His "books of the originals and pedigree of the English tongue" (3.4.228).

7. An eclogue titled *Elpine* (3.13.253), "which [he] made being but eighteen years old, to King Edward VI, a prince of great hope" (perhaps a coronation gift?).

8. An interlude called *Lusty London* (3.15.256, 3.19.282).

9. An interlude called *The Wooer* (3.19.287 and 311).

10. "[A] hymn written by us to the Queen's Majesty entitled 'Minerva'" (3.19.322).

11. A courtesy book called *De decoro* (On Decorum), perhaps in Latin, treating of both words and behavior (3.24.360).

Self-quotations. Puttenham cites from his own unnamed writings at least twenty-three times. Many of these passages were surely composed expressly as examples for the *Art*. He does not always identify them as his own; on one occasion (2.18.217) he identifies lines as his own which he elsewhere introduces by saying, "as one replied . . ." (3.19.288). This shifting attribution (along with common sense) suggests that more of his own material appears among the many unidentified passages the book contains (both versified translations and possibly original English verse). We have marked with an asterisk all of his identified self-citations from lost works.

The Justification. Puttenham is also the anonymous author of one overtly political work, *A Justificacion of Queene Elizabeth in Relacion to the Affaire of Mary Queene of Scottes*, unpublished until the Camden Society edition of Allan J. Crosby and John Bruce (1867) but well known in manuscript form at the time. Two of seven contemporary manuscripts (BL, Add. 48027, Harl. 831) ascribe it to him; no other attributions are known (Willcock and Walker xxiii). Its free and open discussion of the queen's ideas, attitudes, and actions, along with its frequently implied eyewitness acquaintance with the highest powers (see 73–75, 79, 84, etc.), suggests the possibility that it was an official commission.[62] This idea has seemed reasonable because public ventilating of such a risky matter without authorization had cost John Stubbes his hand at the time of the Alençon affair a decade before. Yet there is reason to doubt the "official commission" idea. Just when Parliament began to deal with the affair of Mary's execution (on November 4, 1586), Puttenham was excommunicated and soon thereafter imprisoned by the Privy Council. It therefore seems more likely that he wrote the *Justification* on his own initiative, while imprisoned, as a bid for the council's good graces. The council probably welcomed the *Justification*'s extenuation of their sneaking the death warrant into action on February 8, 1587, past the queen's known opposition. The fact that Robert Beale, clerk of the council, owned a copy he earmarked "It is thoght that this book was made by George Puttenham"[63] documents this link.[64]

Surely in recompense, Puttenham received the award of two leases in reversion (i.e., when they became available) in May 1588, by the hand of the queen via Thomas Windebank, Burghley's agent and a Clerk of the Signet.[65] The possible commission of this work and Puttenham's reward for it constitute the pinnacle of Puttenham's approach to Queen Elizabeth. Such a gift was, generally speaking, "very much a personal grant from the Queen."[66] The probable intermediation of Beale and Windebank, however, make it equally likely that the *Justification* was submitted to Burghley—in effect to the council—and that Burghley arranged for the gift of the leases. Such a route might explain why the *Art* is dedicated to Burghley, not well known as a reader of poetry. It must also be noted that the leases in reversion constituted no great reward. Elizabeth awarded outright leases of crown land, more valuable because they could pay dividends immediately, to many quite minor figures of her household.

62. This is the view of Willcock and Walker, though Steven May strongly questions this possibility in his forthcoming publication, "George Puttenham: Predator, Felon, and Fugitive," that shapes the objections cited here.

63. British Library, MS. Add. 48027, f. 451.

64. Willcock and Walker believe (xxiii) that the Bodleian MS. Add. C. 83 copy contains corrections in Puttenham's own hand, but May disputes this judgment.

65. The leases were for the parsonage of Marten, Wiltshire, and the parsonage of St. Botolph without Aldgate in London, both for forty years at a total fine of £40 per annum.

66. Thomas, "Leases in Reversion" 67.

3. The Authorship of the *Art*

The Art of English Poesy was published anonymously.[67] Ever since
Willcock and Walker argued in 1936 that George Puttenham was its author, their attribution has gone uncontested. (The recent discovery of
several inventories of his personal library somewhat strengthens this
view.) The evidence is as follows.

Contemporary references suggest that a man named Puttenham wrote
the *Art*. The book was published anonymously by Richard Field, who
said it came to his hands "with his bare title without any author's
name or any other ordinary address" (Dedication 90). Whoever the author may have been, he was engaged with its publication, altering the
text in press and referring in it to many of his other works. Field cannot
have been ignorant of the author's identity. The first recorded reference
to the *Art*, a slighting one, appears in Sir John Harington's *Brief Apology of Poetry*, the preface to his translation of the *Orlando Furioso*
(1591), also published by Field. Harington does not propose, he says, to
"trouble [the reader] with the curious definitions of a Poet and Poesie,
& with the subtil distinctions of their sundrie kinds; nor to dispute
how high and supernatural the name of a Maker is, so christned in English by that vnknowne Godfather, that this last yeare saue one, viz.
1589. set forth a booke called the Art of English Poetrie." After referring
in a bruised way to that author's view of translators as mere versifiers
(see 1.1.93), Harington goes on to say:

> [T]hough the poore gentleman laboreth greatly to proue, or rather to make
> Poetrie an art, and reciteth as you may see in the plurall number, some plu-
> ralities of patterns, and parcels of his owne Poetrie, with diuerse pieces of
> Partheniads and hymnes in praise of the most praisworthy; yet whatsoeuer
> he would proue by all these, sure in my poore opinion he doth proue noth-
> ing more plainly, then that which M. Sidney and all the learneder sort that
> haue written of it, do pronounce, namely that it is a gift and not an art, I say
> he proueth it, because making himselfe and manie others so cunning in the
> art, yet he sheweth himselfe so slender a gift in it. (2)

Harington does not name Puttenham here, but a surviving manuscript
note addressed to Field, concerning the publication of his own book, appears to confirm that Harington refers to the *Art*: "Mr. Field, [. . .] I
would have the allegory, as also the apology and all the prose that is to
come, except the table, in the same print that Putnams books is."[68] The

---

67. For extended consideration of this fact and the practice it instantiates, see North, *The
Anonymous Renaissance* 104–8 and passim.

68. Cited by Hughes ("Puttenham's 'Arte of English Poesie'" 404) from BM Add. MS.
18,920. The typeface for Harington's allegory, apology, and prose is indeed the same as the
one that Field used in the *Art*: further evidence that Field's ignorance of the identity of the
Art's author was a fiction.

second edition of Camden's *Remains* concerning Britain (1614) contains an essay by Richard Carew, "The Excellency of the English Tongue," which cites Puttenham by name: "And, in a word, to close up these proofs of our copiousness, look into our Imitations of all sorts of verses afforded by any other language, and you shall finde that Sir *Philip Sidney*, Maister *Puttenham*, Maister *Stanihurst*, and divers more have made use how farre wee are within compasse of a fore imagined impossibility in that behalfe" (43). Finally, in 1614 or so, Edmund Bolton speaks in his unpublished *Hypercritica* of "the elegant, witty, and artificial book of the *Art of English Poetrie*, (the work as the fame is) of one of [Elizabeth's] Gentleman Pensioners, Puttenham"[69] (2.250). These are the early modern recognitions; taken together, they confirm a clear early modern view that the *Art*'s author was named Puttenham.

In addition to George Puttenham, two other candidates for the authorship have been proposed: Richard Puttenham (ca. 1520–97 or later), George's elder brother and heir to both Robert Puttenham and Sir Thomas Elyot; and John, first Baron Lumley (ca. 1533–1609), the noted book and art collector, heir to Arundel, and participant in the Ridolfi plot to assassinate Elizabeth and put Mary, Queen of Scots, on the throne.

Richard Puttenham, as we have seen, was convicted of rape in 1561, having fled to the continent the preceding year. Like George, he married unhappily, probably went back and forth between England and the continent several times in flight from his troubles, and spent significant time in the King's Bench Prison for debts he blamed clamorously on his wife.[70] There is little evidence of literary activity.[71] H. H. S. Croft, however, the Victorian editor of Elyot's *Governour* (1883), argued for his authorship of the *Art*, first, on the basis of what he thought to be evidence that Richard could have witnessed the dinner that Arundel attended with Margaret of Parma and William of Orange, while George could not have; and second, because Richard was imprisoned for debt at the time the *Art* was licensed for publication and might have sought to relieve his difficulties by having it printed (anonymously).[72]

Lumley was the candidate of B. M. Ward.[73] Dismissing George out of hand in a footnote (289) and arguing at length against Croft's case for Richard, Ward contended (among other things) that:

69. First printed in Haslewood, *Ancient Critical Essays* 2.221–54.

70. See Stretton, *Women Waging Law* 143, 146–48, 191–92, 222.

71. He did collect an annuity at Chaucer's tomb, as Willcock and Walker note (xvii): see PRO, C. 54/743, no. 40.

72. See Croft 1.clxiii–clxxxix. Richard was born ca. 1520, and was thus too old to have written *Elpine* at age eighteen for Edward VI in 1547 or after (see 3.13.253), but Croft claims (clxxxvii) that it was not unheard of to address Edward as "the Sixth" while his father was alive.

73. See Ward, "The Authorship of the *Arte of English Poesie*."

1. Unlike Richard, Lumley was the right age to have written *Elpine* (see 3.13.253).

2. Lumley was present at the opening of Parliament in 1553 (see 3.2.223).

3. As Arundel's son-in-law and the eventual inheritor of his estate, Lumley had traveled with him to Brussels and Spa in 1566 (see 3.23.356 and 3.24.362).

4. He gave New Year's gifts to the queen on several occasions, including 1579, when the *Partheniades* may have been presented, while no record of a gift from any Puttenham can be found.

5. He was a courtier and man of rank.

6. He had a notable library.

7. Between the 1589 publication of the *Art* and the 1614 appearance of Carew's essay, many men published essays on poetry (Harington, Harvey, Nashe, Meres, Camden), but none mentioned Puttenham until Carew.

8. Given the specificity of the Harington attribution (to "Putnam"), Lumley must have plotted with Field to have his book printed anonymously and have it given out in rumor that it was the work of "a fellow called Putnam, or something of the sort" (294), since, as a courtier, he would have wished to conceal his authorship.

Willcock and Walker dispose heartlessly of most of Ward's case, arguing among other things (xiii) that as Arundel's son-in-law Lumley is unlikely to have "stood" (3.23.356) at the banquet in Brussels (instead of being seated), and that Lumley's library (which specialized in science, medicine, geography, and music) and his own writings seem quite at variance with the *Art*'s basic characteristics. His library contains many of his own writings, including juvenilia, they note, but none of the numerous missing works by the *Art*'s author. Lumley was a notable art and book collector as well as a "display" builder who designed the remarkable Grove of Diana, an allegorical garden, at Nonsuch Palace in Surrey. He shows little sign, however, of what we would now recognize as a literary life, though he did translate, at age seventeen (in 1550), Erasmus's *Education of a Christian Prince*.[74] Finally, Lumley was a committed Catholic, a supporter of Mary, Queen of Scots, and a conspirator in the Ridolfi plot, for which he was imprisoned at length in the Tower. Such zeal seems at variance with the views of the author of the *Art*, the *Justification*, and the *Partheniades* (see below).

George Puttenham's case, like his brother's, rests centrally on the name that Harington and those who followed him gave to the *Art*'s author. Both external and internal evidence for George link him to *The Art of English Poesy*: (1) his age, (2) his cosmopolitan continental asso-

74. British Library, Royal MS 17 A.xlix.

ciations, (3) his Cambridge humanist training, (4) his Middle Temple legal education, (5) his family of origin (in both its intellectual and courtly-historical aspects) and his humanist library, (6) his authorship of the *Justification* (possibly commissioned, definitely rewarded, externally recognized), (7) his relations to various significant courtly figures and families as well as his externally attested friendship with Sir John Throckmorton, and (8) the possible relationship between the *Art* and *Partheniades*. Let us take these points in greater detail.

1. George was about eighteen when Edward came to the throne in 1547 and could have written *Elpine* for him then (see 3.13.253). (Richard was some ten years older.)

2. The author says he was brought up in foreign courts (3.25.381). We know little of George's youth, but many Englishmen were abroad during the 1550s, and there are signs of continental connections of various kinds: he had an Italian servant in 1569 (the Julio Mantuano mentioned earlier), and, as Willcock and Walker report, "when he was attempting to avoid arrest in 1578 'a lytell frenche boye' acted as a messenger between him and his servants and it was 'in the frenche house' that he lay in hiding" (xxvi).[75] He visited the continent at least twice between 1563 and 1578 (Willcock and Walker xxvii, and May, "George Puttenham: Predator, Felon, and Fugitive"). His handwriting is also predominantly Italic in character, unlike that of most gentlemen of his generation.[76]

3. George's probable education at the Cambridge of Cheke and Ascham fits with the humanist mode of the *Art*, as does the surviving page from his translation of Suetonius and the many Latin and some Greek works in his library lists.

4. The *Art* refers many times to legal matters. George studied at the Middle Temple starting in 1556. He was related to eminent lawyers (Sir James Dyer, Elyot's widow's second husband, and the Throckmortons). His nephew Francis Morris, like others of his enemies at law, treats him as a habitual legal twister.[77] Puttenham tangled with the criminal justice system repeatedly, and he was the privately known author of the anonymous *Justification*, a text steeped in legality. Finally, there are numerous volumes concerned with English law in Puttenham's library lists. (Puttenham's brother Richard also experienced a good deal of legal trouble; the case for his authorship resembles George's on these grounds.)

75. Cited from SP 12/127/28, item 2. Willcock and Walker note (xxvi) that Richard Puttenham also had a foreign servant in 1558 (c.2 Eliz./R 10/27).

76. Renaissance humanists eventually made Italic script, derived from Carolingian minuscule, the "standard" cursive script throughout western Europe, but this process was not well advanced in England when Puttenham was being educated.

77. In 1571 Morris deposed that Puttenham was "full of brables of subtyll practyses and slanderous devyses . . . overconnynge in defacinge of truthe by wordes & speache eloquente and in invencon of myscheiffe verie perfytte" (PRO, STAC 5 P5/10).

5. By his own account the author of the *Art* wrote many other manuscript and lost works. George grew up around books (just as, presumably, did Richard, whose case is equally entitled by what follows in this
paragraph). In 1522 the brothers' maternal grandfather, Sir Richard
Elyot, willed all his English books to George's mother, Margery Elyot
Puttenham.[78] They had the example of their uncle Sir Thomas Elyot
generally before them, and the relationship may have been close. In
1533, when George was about four years old, Elyot dedicated his tract
The Education or bringinge up of children (adapted from Plutarch) to
"his only entierly beloved syster Margery Puttenham."[79] Later in life
(ca. 1580), George owned a substantial library of some 180 books (nothing like the 3,000 that Lumley amassed, but Lumley was a very wealthy
magnate). Many of them were specifically literary, and, as we will see,
would have played a significant role in the composition of the *Art*.
(Lumley's books play a similar role in Ward's argument.)

6. George was also the (anonymous) author of the *Justification*. Such
a touchy commission (if it was one) would normally have been given
only to an experienced writer skilled in rhetoric and legal reasoning.
These features fit the profile of the author we derive from the *Art* and
the Jervoise of Herriard papers, though he had till then no positive public reputation for such skill.

7. Many occasions referred to in the *Art* suggest an author directly, if
distantly, acquainted with notables of the court, including four English
monarchs. As we have seen, George and Richard's parents were in a position to report firsthand anecdotes about the Henrician court, and
George had marital connections, though not invariably genial ones,
with eminent lawyers and statesmen: Sir John Throckmorton, George's
brother-in-law; Throckmorton's brother Sir Nicholas, Elizabeth's ambassador to France and Scotland; Sir William Paulet, marquess of Winchester and Lord Treasurer; and many lesser but well-connected figures
among the Paulet and Windsor families. Puttenham's knowledge of manuscript writings of Dyer, Ralegh, Sidney, and Oxford (a distant marital
connection) also argues a degree of acquaintance with the aristocratic
world. If the *Partheniades* were actually presented at a New Year's celebration, that would suggest a connection with the court, as does the
overnight entertainment of the queen's party on progress at Herriard in
1574. Finally, George's authorship of the *Justification*, with its implicit
knowledge of events in Parliament and the Privy Council, not to mention the reward he received for his labors, including recorded thanks
from the queen herself (though such thanks may have been merely a
verbal formula),[80] all suggest what Puttenham would have experienced

---

78. According to Croft: Elyot, *Gouernour* 1, Appendix A, 312.
79. Elyot, *Letters* 43.
80. PRO, C. 66/1315, m. 7.

as a meaningful relation to the court, even if the historical documents suggest that his public reputation was, in the eyes of most established courtiers, mainly a spectacle of disgrace.

In particular, the *Art* refers specifically and lovingly to Sir John Throckmorton (see 3.17.263). Throckmorton was a Middle Temple friend of George's as well as being his brother-in-law, having married Puttenham's sister Margaret in 1565. They maintained a friendship, often strained by Puttenham's bad behavior, from the late 1550s until Throckmorton died in 1580. Throckmorton was the principal go-between for Puttenham in both his marriage and his divorce dealings with Lady Windsor and her soon aggrieved and pugnacious family, and mediated the Privy Council's interventions in the affair. (Richard was of course also allied to Throckmorton; indeed, he wrote George in reproach for his abuse of Throckmorton's friendship: see Willcock and Walker xxviii–xxix.)

8. Finally, Willcock and Walker argue at some length (xxxi–xliv) that the *Justification*, known to be from George's pen, exhibits several parallels with the *Art* and the *Partheniades*: a concern with the practical maintenance of civil society by a flexible relation to moral absolutes, guided by natural law; a copious vocabulary; a concern with linguistic exactitude; and an oft-stated devotion to Elizabeth. The first of these arguments must now seem ironic when juxtaposed to the attested records of Puttenham's personal misconduct. He certainly had a flexible relation to moral absolutes. Still, the new information we have about Puttenham's personal life does not disable Willcock and Walker's argument for authorship. Personal goodness is hardly a sine qua non for powerful literary and cultural criticism.

There are thus several loci of data that link George Puttenham to the *Art*. The family of origin and the Throckmorton connection (in Richard's case) and the library (in Lumley's) do not exclusively argue for George's authorship. Nonetheless, taken in sum, and in conjunction with the early references to the name Puttenham, these several kinds of data indicate fairly strongly that George Puttenham was the author of *The Art of English Poesy*.

4. Puttenham's Archive

George Puttenham shares with his contemporaries many literary, philosophical, social, and political interests, but more than most of them, he puts what he knows on extravagant display. In *The Art of English Poesy* he parades his classical learning in quotations, allusions, and anecdotes; he borrows from, cites, and argues with contemporary authors; he quotes poetry extensively, frequently his own; and he offers many opinions about issues, people, and what we would call current events. This ensemble of efforts constitutes most of what readers have known of him for centuries, and by means of it, we believe, he constructed his identity—for himself, for his readers, and for us. For himself especially, such an identity might help displace that other, decidedly historical one which external forces such as the Privy Council (perfectly justly, it will now seem) were stamping upon him for all to see, with what must have been such excruciating vigor.

The *Art* is many things—a poetics and a rhetoric, a theoretical treatise on prosody and a manual of courtly trifles, a work on education and a courtesy book—but it is also an effort at self-fashioning, which labors to constitute its author as a consummate Renaissance intellectual, that is, as a brilliant, learned, cosmopolitan courtier and poet. This image serves his complicated social, economic, and political ambitions, to pull himself, just as his book may serve to pull its readers, "from the cart to the school, and from thence to the court," and ultimately to prefer himself "to [her] Majesty's service" (3.25.378). This striking image of the cart (with which we began) may seem, after what we have learned from the historical archive, to bear a much more concrete relevance to Puttenham's own career than has been apparent. If Wyatt claimed that his frightening phrase about Henry VIII's being cast out at the cart's tail actually just meant "left behind" or "left out," his accuser Bonner managed quite successfully (changing "tail" to "arse") to make it seem instead as if the poet had likened the king to a deservedly condemned criminal being carted to Tyburn. Puttenham himself had literally been a fugitive and was repeatedly imprisoned; perhaps he had actually been branded, even suffered the loss of an ear. These experiences would have made the hated cart a particularly vivid image for him. All told, he had extraordinarily strong motives to put this cart behind him (rather than himself behind it).[81]

If the *Art* suggests that he hoped to come to rest near the very top of the social and political world in which he lived, the very height of the ambition may itself be not so much a matter of hubris as something like a screen behind which to shove his hateful "record" and the desperate cultural impoverishment it surely entailed. Recall La Rochefoucauld:

> [W]e . . . come to form our own best audience. . . . Our efforts to hoodwink the rest of the world amount to a prolonged essay in self-deception. . . . Life [is] a delusion imposed on the actor by himself; a desperate tactic by which he tries to foist a certain sense of himself onto himself, with whom he is far more likely to succeed than with others who lack his reasons for cooperating, and who are engrossed in similar designs on their own selves.[82]

81. For what it is worth, his unusual verb for social transformation—"pulling" his poet from the cart to the court—seems attracted from the cart's locomotion. All of the verb's uses in the *Art* concern either carts or pulling down a man's heart or house.

82. Cited in Jonas Barish's paraphrase from *The Antitheatrical Prejudice* (213).

If Machiavelli, hopelessly out of office, dressed in courtly clothing each night and conferred with the ancients, and exactly there, he told Vettori, wrote of self-determination, which he famously characterizes in *The Prince* as conquering a female by force,[83] it is perhaps not so hard to imagine Puttenham in hiding, carrying his library and manuscripts (and Elizabeth Johnson) with him, constructing the *Art* as the vessel of his "real" life. His highly conspicuous labors and claims in the *Art*, not to mention what we now can see of him at law, mark him as unsatisfied and unsuccessful. Nonetheless, the networks of his birth and marriage, however ragged, and his social contact with such figures as Arundel, Bacon, Margaret of Parma, William of Orange, and the emperor Ferdinand, even if entirely specular, suggest that his fantasy was not altogether counterfactual. By parading his enormous learning in the *Art*, Puttenham creates an identity for himself that is as profoundly dependent on the books he has read as it is willfully *in*dependent of the violent lived experience recorded for us in the Hampshire archive.

The library lists. When John Paulet and his posse raided Puttenham's lodgings in Whitefriars in 1578 and confiscated his belongings, they seized more than one hundred books. An inventory was subsequently made of those books. In addition, among the books were two notebooks composed by Puttenham himself, the first sometime between the mid-1560s and the early 1570s, and the second in 1576, both of which also contain additional inventories of his library. Finally, there is a brief list of his books in a letter he wrote to Richard Paulet in October 1580.[84] Although these four inventories do not agree entirely with one another—only a few titles appear in all of them—they nevertheless seem clearly to be authentic. One often cannot decipher just what book is meant by the references, which are sometimes illegible and often vague (e.g., "Plato"), but something over half of the 180 can be identified.

---

83. See Machiavelli's letter to Vettori: "When evening arrives, I return home and go into my study, and at the threshold, I take off my everyday clothes, full of mud and filth, and put on regal and courtly garments; and decorously dressed anew, I enter the ancient courts of ancient men, where, lovingly received by them, I feed myself on the food that is mine alone and for which I was born" (151). In *The Prince* he tells us, "Fortune is a woman, and it is necessary, if you wish to keep her down, to beat her and knock her about" (107).

84. Our work on Puttenham's library has benefited from the research of Charles Willis, who discovered these records and first told us of them, and who has written several books arguing that Puttenham was the real author of some of Shakespeare's works. While we cannot agree with these theories, we have profited from the first of Willis's books, which presents useful transcriptions of Puttenham's three library inventories and the list of books in Puttenham's letter to Paulet; see *Shakespeare and George Puttenham's "The Art of English Poesie"* 167–86. (Willis also provides photocopies of some of the originals.) For further discussion of these lists, see Steven W. May's life of Puttenham in *ODNB*, and his "George Puttenham's Lewd and Illicit Career." We are also indebted to Eric Lindquist of the University of Maryland, who kindly shared with us his unpublished paper on the lists, "An Elizabethan Writer and His Books."

Although much can be inferred about Puttenham's reading from what he says in the *Art*, the titles of the books he owned also tell us a great deal about his interests. The absence of a book from these lists does not mean that Puttenham had not read it, however. Indeed, as we shall detail below, various books important to the *Art* do not appear in the lists. Three explanations for such lacunae suggest themselves. The lists may have been fragmentary and incomplete even when they were compiled. Furthermore, since they all predate 1580, they would not include books he acquired and read after that year (and used when writing the *Art*, which appeared in 1589). In addition, as his financial fortunes plummeted after 1577, he may well have sold books for cash to live on. In general, it is reasonable to believe that Puttenham had read not only many of the 180 or so titles listed in the four inventories but a great many more as well.

Puttenham's library was both eclectic and very "intellectual." There were literary volumes, of course, both ancient (works by Cicero, Ovid, and Horace) and more contemporary (Giovanfrancesco Pico della Mirandola's *La strega*, Jacopo Sannazaro's *Arcadia*, and Pierre de Ronsard's *Elegies*). Yet, there were also many works of history, such as Jean Froissart's *Chronicles*, and travel books such as the account by Nicolas de Nicolay, a French geographer and ambassador to the Ottoman Empire, of his voyages in Turkey and the Middle East. There were volumes on medicine and mathematics, and quite a few on law, politics, and philosophy. The library was stacked with the works of Renaissance luminaries such as Petrarch, Castiglione, Machiavelli, and Erasmus. Generally, one is struck by the unusual breadth of Puttenham's reading, a breadth reflected in the *Art* as well. In it he provides many examples of poetry in English, Latin, Greek, French, and Italian, but he also cites philosophers, rehearses historical anecdotes about both ancient and Renaissance figures, argues a theory of prosody based on a mathematical concept (proportion), and includes bits and pieces of medical, psychological, and other sorts of proto-scientific lore.

Religion. The only field obviously underrepresented in Puttenham's library—especially in light of the supreme importance it had in the early modern period—is religion. His library lists contain no Bibles, biblical commentaries, or sermons, nor is there any evidence to suggest significant interest in the debates then raging among Catholics and Protestants. On the one hand, a few anti-prelatical remarks in the *Art* (see 1.7.102 and 1.27.142) suggest he was no papist.[85] On the other hand, to judge by *Partheniades* 11, he may have hated puritans. That poem, canvassing various theories of the creation, speaks of "a secte of

---

85. Puttenham uses this opprobrious term in the *Justification* when speaking against those who favor Mary, Queen of Scots (99).

men, somewhat precise" (257), whose creator will one day "in his rage" (265) crush the created world like a wicker cage. Such pungent, even violent language seems to be hostile code for puritans—a "sect precise" worshipping (he seems to say) a vengeful God who will damn all else in saving them. He then goes on to speak quite neutrally of the atomism of Democritus and the νουσ of Anaxagoras, and finishes by saying,

> O bootlesse carke
> Of mortall men searching to knowe,
> Or this or that, since he must rowe
> The dolefull barke
> Which Charon guides,
> Fraught ful of shadows colde and starke,
> That ferrye to the coontryes darke. . . .
> (288–94)

This discussion of religion seems both to exhibit a notable freethinking (especially striking in a gift meant for the queen) and to argue for the pointlessness of putting much faith in such schemes of organization (never mind salvation), when we must all float away into unrelieved dark, alone in fear.[86] Nowhere does Puttenham propose a kinder view of Christianity, when he might easily have done so, to dull the jagged edge of the critique of the puritans, who were, whatever else they might have been, Christians. Indeed, there may be some alignment between the vengeful God of the puritans crushing the world and Puttenham spurning the confident certainties of faith. It may thus be true that the inventories' deficiency of religious titles manifests Puttenham's personal hostility to Christianity. Willcock and Walker judge that what they see as *Partheniades* 11's "unmistakable preference" for atomism "expresses as openly heterodox a criticism of popular Christian teaching as is to be found in Elizabethan literature" (xxxiii). These concerns seem to echo Debora Shuger's summation of the development of prose style during the late Renaissance into one "capable of expressing the libertine, skeptical, individualist, and rationalistic impulses that define modern consciousness."[87]

Two documents from Puttenham's life may support this sense of hostility to religion, as we have seen: the charge (from which he was cleared) that he plotted the assassination of Edmund Grindal, bishop of London, and the letter of Robert Horne, bishop of Winchester, decrying Puttenham's evil life and hostility to "God's Truthe" and seeking to block his appointment as justice of the peace. Nevertheless, we really don't know enough about the assassination charge to judge it, and

---

86. Cf. his similar poem cited in the *Art*, "The good is geason" (3.19.299).
87. Shuger, "Conceptions of Style" 178.

Horne's hostility to Puttenham may well derive from Hampshire politics of the time. Fighting off the influence of the conservative politico-
religious party and John Paulet, Winchester's son and a central figure in
that party, Horne "managed to prevent the addition of more associates
of the Paulets to the commission of the peace in 1569."[88] That was the
year of Horne's attack on Puttenham, whom he may have seen as a
Paulet adherent (though this would by 1569 have been quite wrong). A
milder form of the hostility to religion hypothesis might stand on the
fact that both Horne and Grindal were Marian exiles: Puttenham's
aversion may well have focused on the reformed church.

Whatever Puttenham's religious views, in the *Art* he manifests a fairly
conventional piety in one poem he himself wrote and cites in Book 3 (see
"Our Christ, the son of God," 3.19.283).[89] Moreover, as we noted above,
the absence of a title from the library lists does not in itself prove much.
It is quite probable that Puttenham possessed—and read—the Bible, as
well as other religious books. Nevertheless, the relative numbers of
books in one field or another in his library do intimate where his interests and sympathies lay, and they suggest that his concerns were more
secular, social, and political than religious. Puttenham's copies of Machiavelli's *Prince* and Castiglione's *Courtier*, of Dante's *De monarchia* and
the republican Francesco Patrizi's *De Regno et Republica*, were probably
dearer to his heart than Giacopo Riccamati's brief *Dialogo* (1558) concerning the Last Judgment, one of the few religious books he owned.

Classical sources.   Works by classical authors are especially well
represented in Puttenham's library. His Latin authors include Vergil,
Ovid, Lucretius, Catullus, Tibullus, Propertius, Horace, and Cicero,
as well as minor figures such as Quintus Curtius Rufus and Marcus
Manilius. He owned Greek authors as well: Theocritus, Plato, and several volumes of Aristotle (these last two in Latin translation). Likewise,
the *Art* frequently refers to Roman poets (Vergil, Horace, Ovid) and the
sayings of famous Romans (Augustus, Cato the Elder, Scipio Africanus).
Puttenham's easy familiarity with Latin literature and culture should
not be surprising. Latin was the language of formal education in the Renaissance, and we know that he was enrolled at Christ's College, Cambridge, in the mid-1540s and studied law at the Middle Temple in the
mid-1550s. A single page survives from his translation of Suetonius'
Life of Tiberius. He may have dreamed, probably when young, of Englishing a Latin classic, as had Stanyhurst and Phaer. The ripe details of
Suetonius may have attracted him because of his general fascination
with celebrity, whether classical or modern.

---

88. Ralph Houlbrooke, "Horne, Robert (1513x15–1579)," *ODNB* http://www.oxforddnb
.com.content.lib.utexas.edu:2048/view/article/13792, accessed August 10, 2006.
89. This poem he says he wrote in his "younger years" (3.19.283).

Puttenham also puts his knowledge of Greek on display in the *Art*. He occasionally uses Greek terms such as φαντάστικος (1.8.109) and πῦρ (2.12.184), cites the first line of Homer's *Iliad* in the original (3.24.371), and renames Greek rhetorical terms in English throughout Book 3. Nevertheless, he cites passages in Latin far more often than in Greek; he uses the Latin forms of Greek words, such as *anthropopathis* (1.12.118: "characterized by human feelings"); and he seems to have read many Greek texts, such as Aristotle's *De anima* (On the Soul), not in the original but in Renaissance Latin translations. His library contains no books solely in Greek, though he did have two bilingual volumes in Greek and Latin. Still, he owned a Greek-Latin lexicon, which suggests he may have studied the language with some seriousness. It seems likely that although Puttenham's use of Greek in the *Art* may have been justified at times by his need for a theoretical term or an apt illustration from an ancient text, its main function was intellectual display. To cite the opening line of the *Iliad* in Greek gave Puttenham a kind of distinction that Latin alone could never confer on him, and it was thus an important move in his fashioning of himself in his book.

In general, Puttenham's mastery of Latin and his more limited, though real, acquaintance with Greek show him to be a typical product of a humanist education. That form of education had made its appearance in the late fifteenth century in England, and by the middle of the sixteenth had become more or less a requirement for membership in the ruling elite. Puttenham's uncle Sir Thomas Elyot was one of the most famous humanists of his day, and his *Book named the Governour* (1531) argued for the central value of such education for those who would be the rulers (the "governors") of the country.[90] Focused on the study of the classics, humanist education presented itself not merely as a means of personal cultivation but as a set of tools for social and political advancement. It gave young men the intellectual skills they needed to serve in bureaucratic positions or as personal secretaries to the powerful, equipping them to produce documents and conduct negotiations about trade or diplomacy in Latin. It also provided the cultural literacy they needed to display their merit for elevated position. Twice over, then, humanist education enabled the social advancement of those who, like Puttenham, had mastered what it had to offer.

Continental sources. Puttenham's learning was not restricted to the culture of antiquity. Most of the books he owned were actually written after the fall of Rome, and practically all of those during the Renaissance. He says he was brought up in foreign countries (3.25.381), and cites poems as well as sayings and aphorisms in French, Italian, and

90. For introductions to this matter, see Hexter, "Education of the Aristocracy," and Simon, *Education and Society.*

Spanish. Although he owned a substantial number of books in French and Italian and at least one in Spanish, however, texts in Latin far outnumber them. Moreover, while many of these were the works of the ancients, the lion's share of his Latin books, including most of those concerned with philosophy, political theory, and what we would call science, date from the Renaissance, not antiquity. Finally, although English-language texts are conspicuous by their near-absence from the inventories, Puttenham had obviously been reading them as well. He clearly possessed a wide knowledge of English poetry from Chaucer up to his own time; he mentions by name or cites from the works of dozens of English poets in the *Art*, and presents a brief history of English poetry in the last chapter of Book 1. The booklists, however, contain no identifiable mention of *Tottel's Miscellany*, where all of the Wyatt and Surrey poems he cites can be found, nor of the available published work of Gascoigne and Turberville.

Puttenham was also interested in Renaissance Neoplatonism. His library contained several dialogues by Plato, some works by the Florentine Neoplatonist Marsilio Ficino, and even a copy of the works attributed to "Hermes Trismegistus," "Thrice-great Hermes," a collection of writings on magic and alchemy dating from the second and third centuries CE, published by Ficino in 1471 and seen as containing a mysterious ancient wisdom thought to be anterior to Christianity. Puttenham never mentions Ficino in the *Art*, but he does refer to certain nameless "Platonics" when dismissing the notion that some version of the Platonic Ideas may have provided God with models for creating the world (1.1.93). In the next paragraph, however, he goes on to embrace the Neoplatonic conception of the *furor poeticus*, the divine inspiration that allowed poets access to celestial truths (a notion developed by Ficino), and he later refers to Hermes Trismegistus as "the holiest of priests and prophets" (1.8.112). This recondite interest may also lie behind his extensive discussion of emblems and *imprese* (2.12).

Historical writing.   Much of Puttenham's library could be described as historical-biographical. To judge by the *Art*, he was almost as interested in the actions and sayings of classical and Renaissance figures as he was in the literature of the two periods. Such an interest was quite usual among the heirs of humanism, who loved stories about Vergil and Cato the Elder, Charles V and Julius II, as readily as new poems by Ronsard or Spenser. Contemporary scholars fed this interest by producing not just biographical and historical works but also compendia of notable sayings. The great Dutch humanist Erasmus, for instance, collected classical maxims, idioms, and metaphors in his ever-expanding and enormously successful *Adages* (which eventually numbered over four thousand sayings, annotated in enormous detail), and he combed through countless ancient writers to compile the famous sayings and quips of philosophers, generals, and rulers in his *Apophthegmata* (pithy sayings). Although the *Adagia* does not appear in Puttenham's library lists, it is quite likely that he had recourse to it at a number of points in the *Art*. He did, however, own a copy of the *Apophthegmata*, and it is virtually certain that he used this book, rather than track down original sources, for many of the sayings and stories of classical figures he records, especially in Book 3. (Some thirty-four passages in the *Art* appear in the *Apophthegmata*.) Puttenham may also have read Nicholas Udall's translation of the *Apophthegmata*, although Udall could not have been Puttenham's main source, since his *Apophthegmes* contains only the third and fourth books of Erasmus's work, and some of the sayings Puttenham rehearses come from its other books.

Celebrity tales. The *Art* also presents a wide array of stories and sayings concerning Renaissance celebrities, both English and continental. Since Puttenham says he has seen or lived at "the courts of France, Spain, Italy, and that of the Empire, with many inferior courts" (3.23.356), and claims personal knowledge of English courtly notables of his own and his father's generation, he may have seen them himself, or heard eyewitness accounts of many of the things he reports. Still, some half-dozen of the stories and quips Puttenham records involving French rulers appeared in a single literary source, Gilles Corrozet's *Les divers propos memorables des nobles & illustres hommes de la Chrestienté* (The Various Memorable Sayings of the Noble and Illustrious Men of Christendom), originally published in Paris in 1557. Puttenham owned a copy of this often reprinted work, and probably cribbed a number of stories from it. Moreover, this book was not the only one of its kind; Puttenham may have taken some of his other stories from such texts, as yet unidentified.

Travel narratives. Matters farther afield also fascinated Puttenham. His library contained a number of books concerned with the world beyond the boundaries of Europe, including Nicolas de Nicolay's *Navigations, peregrinations et voyages faicts en la Turquie* (Sea Voyages, Wanderings, and Journeys in Turkey) of 1568; Simon Grynaus's *Novus orbis regionum ac insularum veteribus incognitarum* (New World of Regions and Islands Unknown to the Ancients) of 1555; and a book titled *De regionibus orientalibus* (On the Regions of the East) by a certain Paulus Venetus. This may very well be Marco Polo's *Il milione*, which was in wide circulation during the Renaissance.[91] Puttenham

---

91. Paulus Venetus is probably "Polo [or Paolo] the Venetian." Another title on a different list—"descriptio Geographique des Provinces de Inde orientale bound in black leather"—is most likely Polo's work: a 1556 edition of his book in French was titled *La Description geographique des prouinces & villes de l'Inde orientale.*

does not cite these books in the *Art*, but he does mention Attila the Hun (1.6.101, 2.12.194) and Tamerlane (2.12.194), and explores the motto and liveries of the "king of China in the farthest part of the Orient" (2.12.194), noting the general love of his subjects for the king and his nobles.

Equally notable is Puttenham's discussion of patterned poems in 2.12. He begins with the famous poem by Simias of Rhodes from the Greek Anthology, in the shape of an oval, which Puttenham mistakenly calls "Anacreon's egg" (180). Then he turns to two figure poems outside the Western tradition, in the shape of lozenges, one sent by a lady named Kermesine to a "great emperor in Tartary . . . surnamed Timur Cutlu" (182). The latter is certainly Tamerlane, and the other lozenge poem is his reply. This pair is then followed by two more love poems, triangular in shape, exchanged by a Persian sultan named Ribuska and his beloved, Selamour. The sentiments expressed in these poems are, in European terms, highly conventional, and since all the other patterned poems that follow are Puttenham's own creations, it seems entirely possible that he is the actual author of the Eastern poems he attributes to Tamerlane, Ribuska, and their beloveds (especially since we have been unable to identify any of the persons save Tamerlane). Moreover, Puttenham's account of how he came by these patterned poems is also slightly suspect. His source was a "gentleman" he had met in Italy "who had long traveled the oriental parts of the world, and seen the courts of the great princes of China and Tartary." This gentleman supposedly described the genre for him and then gave him a few examples, which Puttenham tells us he has "translated word for word and, as near as [he] could, followed both the phrase and the figure, which is somewhat hard to perform" (180) because of the limitations imposed by the shapes of the poems.

What Puttenham may be claiming here is that the anonymous "gentleman" gave him poems written in the languages of the Tartars and the Persians, which Puttenham has himself translated, demonstrating a linguistic competence notably beyond that of his peers. Perhaps, however, the "gentleman" just composed a few examples for him in Italian. Puttenham is vague about this unidentified Italian "gentleman," and when we consider that, according to A. L. Korn, the patterned poetry of the Persians and the Turks is very different from the examples Puttenham supplies, we should probably conclude that he had heard about the existence of such patterned poems in non-Western traditions while on his European travels, and is simply producing his own versions of them here.[92] Nevertheless, including such poems in his book suggests his keen interest in what European explorers and traders were doing as they effectively expanded the geographical and intellectual boundaries

92. Korn, "Puttenham and the Oriental Pattern-Poem" 289–303, esp. 294–96.

of Europe in the period. Thus, Puttenham shapes an image of himself that capitalizes on the prestige granted not just to those who had traveled the European continent and visited the courts of France and Spain and the Holy Roman Empire, as he says he has done, but to such celebrated figures as Hernán Cortés, Vasco da Gama, and Francis Drake, the last of whom makes a silent appearance in an anecdote Puttenham tells earlier in this chapter about the sacking of Cartagena in the West Indies (see 2.12.193).

Self-fashioning texts. If Puttenham shared Renaissance Europeans' fascination with the Other, he also conspicuously shared their interest in a newly prominent notion of the self, of human identity, as not only inherited or received but also shaped and fashioned. The Renaissance concern with self-fashioning produced a flood of educational and self-help materials—Latin and Greek grammars and dictionaries, sample dialogues and colloquies, treatises, courtesy books—that began as a trickle in Italy during the fifteenth century and inundated Europe in the sixteenth. In addition to a Greek-Latin dictionary and many editions of classical texts, Puttenham owned a copy of the *De morali disciplina libri quinque* (Five Books of Moral Philosophy) by the prince-pleasing courtly poet and Italian humanist Francesco Filelfo (1398–1481), in a Venetian edition of 1552. He also owned Erasmus's *Colloquies*, dialogues the Dutch humanist wrote as school exercises, small works of art, really, that taught students not only how to speak correct Latin but also how to speak in different roles—preparing them for both life in a literate elite and the role-playing that had come increasingly to characterize that elite life. The library also contained a book describing one of the most famous and radical instances of self-fashioning in the Renaissance, namely, the *Arrest mémorable du Parlement de Tholose* (The Memorable Decision by the Parlement of Toulouse), by the French jurist Jean de Coras (Paris, 1572). Republished many times, this book is the account of the trial of Arnaud du Tilh, who for four years succeeded in passing himself off as Martin Guerre, who had disappeared some eight years earlier, taking his place in his village, his family, and even his wife's bed. Puttenham's possession of Coras's little tome speaks volumes about the ultimate fantasy of social and personal mobility that he shared with his culture.

Puttenham also owned copies of the works of the two writers who determined most decisively what self-fashioning meant to the Renaissance: Machiavelli and Castiglione. The first defined his would-be princes as engaging in a continuous masquerade, shaping and controlling the image of the self in order to achieve and maintain political power. Machiavelli also wrote of figures such as Hieron of Syracuse, who began at the bottom of the social order and rose to rule his city-state. Puttenham seems to have shared Machiavelli's perspective when insisting on the need for his courtier-poet to use indirection, to dissemble, even to lie. That said, however, nowhere does the *Art* seem to have been specifically impacted by the thought of the great Florentine. By contrast, when Puttenham was composing 3.25, the chapter arguing "That the good poet or maker ought to dissemble his art" (378), he was almost certainly thinking about Castiglione, whose *Book of the Courtier*, in French translation, was in Puttenham's library. Like Castiglione, Puttenham writes of using art to hide art, in dissembling one's body, face, actions, and ideas, as well as "the subtleties of [one's] art" (382). And also like Castiglione, Puttenham seems to worry that the art of his courtier-poet may appear morally suspect, and he goes to great lengths in defending its legitimacy, insisting that it not be confused with the dissimulation practiced by hypocrites and "base-minded men" (382)—though he himself has just produced, with a grim smile, perhaps, exactly that confusion, by so richly detailing so many uncomfortable dissimulations of conduct, as we have seen. This maneuver, so typically oblique, may well seem a Machiavellian presentation of the complexities of Castiglione, designed to critique and enable effective prince-pleasing at one and the same time. Here he founds his "defense" on the separation of conduct and aesthetics, while more often he might be said to conflate the two categories. He appears to dissemble artfully his position on dissembling conduct, a perfect amalgam of Machiavelli and Castiglione.

Rhetorical and literary writings. The two arts of rhetoric and poetry were seen throughout the Renaissance as being profoundly similar. Both were fundamentally concerned with eloquence; both had the same goal, moving or persuading the audience or reader; rhetoric books frequently used examples from poetry (just as Puttenham versified a number of the prose examples he found in Susenbrotus); and both arts claimed the same mythical civilizing progenitors, Amphion and Orpheus. The difference between rhetoric and poetry was discussed, if only occasionally, but little more was usually said than that poetry, constrained by meter, was less free than the orator's prose. Thus, the Florentine humanist Coluccio Salutati, in a letter written near the beginning of the Renaissance (1374), claims that eloquence "can be treated under two heads, for either it flows forth free and relaxed in melodious prose, or it is confined continually within the narrow straits of meter," and Jean-François Le Grand, writing near the end of the period (1658), says that "poetry is nothing other than the most constrained and strictly observed part of the art of oratory."[93] For these writers, as for virtually everyone else, the most important characteris-

---

93. For the quotation from Salutati, see Rebhorn, *Renaissance Debates* 21; for that from Le Grand, see 287.

tic defining both oratory and poetry was their *power*, namely, their ability to possess and move their audience in whatever direction they wished. As Henry Peacham puts it memorably, the orator's command of rhetoric makes him "in a maner the emperour of mens minds & affections, and next to the omnipotent God in the power of persuasion."[94] Sidney thinks the very same thing about poetry, stressing how the poet's words will "strike, pierce, . . . [and] possess the sight of the soul," and how his "enchanting skill" is so great that it "holdeth children from play and old men from the chimney corner."[95] Puttenham, of course, agrees with such evaluations, insisting on the "great force" (3.2.226) eloquence displays when moving people. Revealingly, he makes this claim right after he has told the story not of a poet but of the orator Hegesias, whose eloquent arguments about the futility of life actually persuaded people, he says, to commit suicide.

Scaliger and the Italians.   There is no question that Puttenham knew Italian, although he may not have spoken it as readily as he did French. His library lists include a number of works, both literary and nonliterary, in Italian, including Machiavelli's *Prince*, a volume of Luigi Alamanni's poems, and Carlo Sigonio's commentary on Aristotle's *Rhetoric* (although Puttenham's copy of Castiglione's *Courtier* was in French). He also apparently owned an Italian grammar. In the *Art* Puttenham refers to Dante, Petrarch, and Ariosto, the great poets of the Italian Renaissance. He mentions *canzoni* (songs), a word he may be using as the label for the specific poems of Petrarch with different rhyme schemes, or as the title for Petrarch's entire sonnet sequence, which is more usually called the *Canzoniere* (Songbook). He also writes (in a confusing way) about Petrarch's use of a form Puttenham calls the *seizino*. This is perhaps a mistake for "sestina," but Puttenham offers a definition different from that of the sestina, which we have been unable to trace (see 2.11.176). Finally, Puttenham occasionally cites bits of Italian in the *Art*, albeit in forms that are not entirely accurate (see, for example, 3.24.370). Nevertheless, he seems to have little awareness—with one very significant exception—of the vast number of treatises on poetics that were produced in Italy during the century before the publication of the *Art* in 1589.

Starting with the 1482 Latin commentary of the Florentine Cristoforo Landino on Horace's *Ars poetica*, Italian humanists produced a steady stream of editions, commentaries, translations, and vulgarizations of classical works concerned with poetics. Although they were continuing a long tradition of using Horace, whose poem was well known throughout the Middle Ages, as a guide to their thinking on

94. Peacham, *The Garden of Eloquence* (1593), AB3v.
95. Sidney, *The Defence of Poesy* 222, 227 (hereafter cited in the text).

poetics, they also recovered and published the Platonic corpus, thus allowing them to reinforce their defenses of poetry by developing Plato's
notion of divine inspiration, or *furor poeticus*, which they found in the
Phaedrus (254a, 265b) and the *Ion* (534). At the same time, Plato forced
them to counter his criticisms of poetry (see *The Republic*, Books 3 and
10) as a pale imitation of reality and as morally suspect and dangerous
to the state. The greatest impulse to the production of works on poetics
in the Italian Renaissance, however, was the rediscovery of Aristotle's
Poetics. Although Averroës's medieval Arabic translation of the *Poetics*
had been turned into Latin in the late fifteenth century, that version of
Aristotle's work was seriously defective and did not have much of an
impact. Inspired by the humanist enthusiasm for antiquity, Giorgio
Valla produced a new and much superior Latin translation in 1498, and
the Aldine press in Venice published the Greek original in 1508. Nevertheless, only in 1536, when Alessandro de' Pazzi published a better
Greek text with a new Latin translation, did Aristotle become a major
figure in the landscape of Italian—and European—literary theory. That
position was reinforced by the publication of Francesco Robortello's
lengthy commentary on the work in 1548 (*In Librum Aristotelis de
Arte Poetica Explicationes* [Annotations of Aristotle's "Poetics"]), by
its first vernacular translation in 1549, and, most important, by Lodovico
Castelvetro's *Poetica d'Aristotele vulgarizzata et sposta* (Aristotle's
"Poetics" Translated and Expounded) of 1570, which famously proclaimed the doctrine of the unities of time, place, and action that would
come to dominate the drama in the later seventeenth century. By the
second half of the sixteenth century, according to Bernard Weinberg,
Aristotle's *Poetics* had moved from the scholar's study into the acade-
mies of Italy; it had become an essential part of ongoing public debates
about poetry.[96]

Motivated in part by the humanist passion for all things classical,
Italians were especially interested in Horace, Plato, Aristotle, and classical poetics generally because of a desire to justify poetry in the modern world and to defend vernacular poetry in comparison with that of
the ancients. To justify it, they had recourse to the Horatian formula
that poetry should be *dulce et utile*, "sweet and useful."[97] In other
words, poetry should aim to provide the reader with pleasure, which
they usually imagined as a matter of style, and with utility, which they
usually imagined in moral and political terms. Moreover, pleasure was
almost always seen either as independent of, but consistent with,
moral instruction, or as subordinate to it. As Weinberg has noted, from

---

96. For the material in this paragraph, see Weinberg, *History of Literary Criticism*
1.349–404, 502–10.

97. *Ars poetica* 343: *omne tulit punctum qui miscuit utile dulci* (he has won the vote who
has mixed the useful with the sweet).

the beginning of the Renaissance to the end, this interpretation of Horace was itself shaped by the dominant rhetorical thinking of the period that defined the *officia*, or functions (and ends), of that art as *movere* (to move), *delectare* (to delight), and *docere* (to teach).[98] Even though the recovery of Aristotle led some thinkers to speculate about other questions, such as the place of the marvelous in poetry, the *Poetics* was read in ways that largely made it consistent with this rhetoricized, ethical, and un-Aristotelian Horace. Revealingly, Aristotle's notion of imitation was seen as instrumental in the teaching of virtue, and his concept of purgation as the response to tragedy was often interpreted in moralistic terms as a diminishing of the passions of the audience in order to produce ethically superior citizens. This moralizing view of poetry could justify it in the face of Plato's desire to expel the art from his Republic, just as did critics' Plato-inspired notions that the poet's *furor* was divinely inspired and that what he imitated was not mere external reality but Ideas in the mind of God.

Italian critics also sought to defend modern poetry in comparison with that of the admired ancients. They did so in part by adapting Aristotle's discussions of the genres of tragedy and epic to those genres he did not treat, thus attempting to theorize in classical terms comedy, satire, epigram, and the various subgenres of the lyric, many of which, such as the love sonnet and the madrigal, were simply unknown in antiquity. Nevertheless, the need to defend the value of modern poetry—which led some actually to proclaim its superiority—was occasioned by the attacks that were made on a number of important vernacular Italian authors or works, especially after mid-century. For instance, although Dante was criticized for his difficult language as early as Pietro Bembo's *Prose della volgar lingua* (Dialogue on the Vernacular) of 1525, the entire *Divina commedia* was proclaimed deficient when judged according to such Aristotelian categories as unity and verisimilitude by Ridolfo (or Anselmo) Castravilla, manuscript copies of whose critique circulated widely after 1572 and provoked a host of replies. Similarly, Ariosto's *Orlando furioso* was attacked for combining features of romance and epic, although those attacks remained partial and fairly tentative between 1549 and 1584, in which year Camillo Pellegrino published *Il Carrafa, o vero della poesia epica* (Carrafa, or of Epic Poetry), a dialogue that reviews ancient and contemporary epics, compares Ariosto's work with Tasso's recently published *Gerusalemme liberata* (The Liberation of Jerusalem [1581]), and comes to the conclusion that Tasso's work is superior to all except the poems of Homer and Vergil for a variety of reasons, especially because of the unity of its plot.

---

98. Weinberg, *History of Literary Criticism* 2.806–7. Weinberg says that there was a strong desire throughout the sixteenth century to "reduce poetics to a kind of rhetoric," with its goals of teaching, delighting, and moving (1.463).

Pellegrino's work in its turn incited further attacks and defenses of both Ariosto and Tasso that went on until the end of the century.[99]

Like Sidney, Puttenham shares many of the general views of the Italians—which resemble those of most medieval and Renaissance theorists. Both, for instance, defend the dual aims of poetry to provide pleasure and moral instruction. Puttenham does not, however, mention Aristotle's key notion of purgation in tragedy, nor does he complain in Aristotelian terms, as Sidney does, about the failure of the drama to maintain the unities or about how it violates decorum by "mingling kings and clowns" (*Defence* 244). Puttenham says he had been to Italy, just as Sidney had been, but the latter seems far more sensitive to developments there than Puttenham was. Neither man, however, betrays the slightest awareness of the debates about Dante and Ariosto, although since those debates mainly went on during the last three decades of the sixteenth century, it is understandable that the two English writers, both of whom were dead by 1591, would have missed them. Nevertheless, even though Italian critics such as Robortello, Castelvetro, and Pellegrino seem to have been unknown to Puttenham, there was one writer on poetics who was originally from the peninsula—though he lived virtually all of his adult life in France—whose comprehensive, original work on poetics Puttenham not only read but also seems to have made direct use of in the *Art*. That writer was Julius Caesar Scaliger (1484–1558), whose *Poetices Libri Septem* (Seven Books on Poetry) was published posthumously in 1561.[100]

Scaliger's enormous work treats nearly every aspect of classical poetry, from genre to style to meter to figures of speech to the relative merits of various poets writing in Greek and Latin, both classical and contemporary. There can be little doubt, we think, that Puttenham actively used Scaliger in composing the *Art*, especially in Books 1 and 2. Less important in this regard is the fact that there are many general parallels between Puttenham's theories and Scaliger's. Both share, for instance, an emphasis on representation and on the genres of poetry, and both stress the didactic function of the poet, Puttenham doing so not just at the outset of his book, when he claims that poets were the first philosophers, orators, rulers, and so on, but also when he identifies

---

99. On the debate over Dante, see Weinberg 2.819–911, esp. 2.820–23 and 2.831–34; for that on Ariosto and Tasso, see 2.954–1073, esp. 2.991–97. Weinberg also describes the debates over the drama precipitated by Sperone Speroni's *Canace* (written ca. 1554, pub. 1597) and Battista Guarini's *Pastor fido* (1590); see 2.912–53 and 2.1074–1105

100. Puttenham's library lists do not include this work by Scaliger, although they do mention another work by him, his *Exotericarum exercitationum liber de Subtilitate adversus Hieronymum Cardanum* (Book of Exoteric Exercises Written in Opposition to the *Subtlety* of Jerome Cardano [1557]; *Subtlety* is Cardano's 1550 work *De subtilitate rerum*, "On the Subtlety [i.e., Fine Discriminations] of Things," which concerned natural phenomena). Since Puttenham owned this rather obscure and specialized work by Scaliger, it is hard to imagine that he was not also acquainted with the *Poetices*.

the specific moral and political functions of the various poetic genres. Scaliger also classifies poetry as one of the "pleasurable" arts (see 1.1), and although Puttenham does not make a comparable classificatory gesture, he does say the same thing in so many words by emphasizing that such aspects of poetry as rhythm and figures of speech involve a sensory appeal to the ear (see our discussion of this topic in the section "Poetics in the *Art*"). More revelatory of Puttenham's debt to Scaliger are the many specific details in the *Art* that can be traced back to Scaliger's work. For example, Puttenham divides the epithalamium into three subspecies, just as Scaliger does (see 1.26, note 8); he mentions the same two examples of *dirae* (curses) that Scaliger does (see 1.29, note 4); when defining the metrical unit of the foot, he plays on the literal meaning of the word in the same way that Scaliger does (see 2.3, note 4); and he takes the highly technical terms *penthemimeris* (a group of five half-feet) and *hephthemimeris* (a group of seven half-feet) directly from Scaliger (see 2.17, note 4). The inevitable conclusion: Puttenham kept a copy of the *Poetices Libri Septem* close to hand when writing the *Art*.

There is, however, a major difference between the ways the two men order the various genres of poetry. Scaliger says (1.3) that there are two principles for arranging them. One can focus on their *nobilitas*, by which he appears to mean the degree of elevation of their subject matter, and move from high forms, such as hymns, down to low ones, such as satyr plays, wedding poems, and epigrams. Alternatively, one can arrange the genres in historical sequence. He then declares that he will use the second method, starting with the oldest genre, the pastoral poem, and moving, just as nature does, from this simple form to more complex genres such as comedy and tragedy. Puttenham actually does something similar. He never says that he is following the "historical" method, but it soon becomes clear that he is. Thus, in 1.12 he starts by discussing hymns to the gods as the very "first" (117) poetic genre. "First" here might mean something like "most excellent," but the temporal meaning is reinforced at the start of the following chapter: he rejects the opinion that "*next* after the praise and honoring of their gods should *commence* the worshippings and praise of good men," arguing instead that "*before that came to pass*, the poets or holy priests chiefly studied the rebuke of vice" and "made certain poems in plain meters . . . like to sermons or preachings" (120, emphasis added).

Nevertheless, though Puttenham arranges the genres in historical sequence, his version of that sequence is not identical to Scaliger's. He openly disagrees with the view that the oldest genre is the pastoral, not identifying Scaliger by name but attributing this incorrect opinion instead to "[s]ome" who think that "pastoral poesy . . . should be the first of any other" (1.18.127). He then argues his own view that "the poet devised the eclogue long after the other dramatic poems" in order to use the speeches of "homely persons" to "insinuate and glance at greater matters . . . such as perchance had not been safe to have been disclosed in any other sort" (128). Scaliger may have been Puttenham's chief source for the discussion of poetic genres, but he does not follow his predecessor slavishly.

   French Renaissance writers.   Puttenham's thinking on poetry was also probably shaped by what was happening in France in the middle of the sixteenth century—that is, by the poetry and theory of the Pléiade. That Puttenham possessed fluent French can hardly be in doubt. He owned many books on many subjects in that language, and his probable continental travels would have taken him to places where French was the native language or was used by members of the social elite with whom he would have sought to spend his time. He owned at least one volume of poetry by Ronsard, the leading writer of the Pléiade, and the *Art* seems to indicate that he had read the group's major theoretical statement, Joachim Du Bellay's *La Deffence et illustration de la langue françoyse* (The Defense and Illustration of the French Language) of 1549. The evidence for this indebtedness appears in 2.12, in which Puttenham is discussing anagrams. Not only does he follow Du Bellay's lead in defining the form, but also he supplies as specific examples two anagrams on the names of French kings that he found in Du Bellay's text (see 2.12, note 96). Nevertheless, the *Deffence* seems to have had only a very general influence on Puttenham's thinking in the *Art*. Du Bellay stresses the worth of the French language while urging writers to enrich it with Greek and Latin words; he also argues for writing in classical genres, allowing only one modern one, the love sonnet. Puttenham may well have been inspired by Du Bellay to defend the English language as a suitable vehicle for poetry. Yet the organization of Puttenham's treatise and most of the material he covers in it have no precedent in Du Bellay's work.

   Perhaps Puttenham also read the treatises of other French writers, such as Thomas Sébillet's *Art poétique français* (1548), which anticipates many of Du Bellay's arguments but makes a stronger case for the vernacular, as opposed to the classical, tradition; Jacques Peletier's *Art poétique* (1555), which does review a few of the genres Puttenham discusses in Book 1 of the *Art*; and Ronsard's *Abrégé de l'Art poétique français* (1565), which includes a discussion of alexandrine verse that may have impacted Puttenham's thinking on the topic (see 1.19, note 29).[101] These texts, however, are much less certain influences on him

   101. For Sébillet's view of vernacular French poetry, see *Art poétique français* 1.1.51–54; though generally indebted in many ways to his predecessor, Du Bellay specifically rejects Sébillet's view of vernacular French poetry in *La Deffence* 2.2. Peletier discusses poetic genres in chapters 3–8 of the second book of his work.

than Du Bellay's, although Du Bellay was much less important than Scaliger in determining Puttenham's general approach to poetry and his actual structuring of the *Art*.

Rhetorical texts.   That Puttenham was knowledgeable about rhetoric can hardly be in doubt. His library included Plato's *Gorgias*, several unnamed works by Cicero, Aristotle's *Rhetoric*, and the *Partitiones oratoriae* (listed as by Aristotle in Puttenham's inventories, but really Cicero's). There is no certain evidence from either the library or the *Art* that Puttenham knew Quintilian's *Institutio oratoria*, though it is extremely likely; a great many items in Book 3 appear there. Puttenham also owned a copy of Petrus Ramus's *Dialectique*. This work is not directly concerned with rhetoric, but its presence in the library suggests that he may have been aware of Ramus and his attempts to reform rhetoric and dialectic. So far as English forebears go, it is likely that Puttenham had read Richard Sherry's *A Treatise of Schemes and Tropes* (1550). He follows Sherry generally in naming many figures of speech, especially those considered defects or "vices." (On this score Sherry himself was following Petrus Mosellanus, whose work Puttenham probably knew as well.) Puttenham specifically adopts Sherry's neologism *bomphiologia*, a word meaning "pompous speech." There is, however, no firm evidence that he knew the works of Thomas Wilson (1560) and Henry Peacham (1577), though he may well have.[102] Most important of all, as we will show, Puttenham relied extensively on Joannes Susenbrotus's rhetorical style manual of 1540, the *Epitome troporum ac schematum* (A Compendium of Tropes and Schemes), when presenting figures of speech in Book 3 of the *Art*. In general, though the evidence is uneven, it seems clear that Puttenham had studied a fair number of rhetoric books from both antiquity and the Renaissance.

The early Elizabethan perspective.   Although Puttenham's attention is wide-ranging and his knowledge of many sources elaborate, most of the *Art*'s engagement with literature dates from well before the Elizabethan High Renaissance. His sourcebook is *Tottel* (1557), his English humanism that of Elyot and Ascham. His vigorous interest in highly figured language exhibits no awareness of the linguistic energies of Euphuism (dating from 1578). Similarly, he mentions but does not quote, nor even seems to have read, *The Shepheardes Calender* (1579),

---

102. We learn in the Hampshire archive that at some time before 1582 Puttenham sued for letters patent for the disputed Sherfield estate to be issued for him. According to a letter he wrote to the queen, his petition had been presented to her by Wilson, who was then the queen's secretary and (after 1572) a Privy Councilor. If this statement is true, we may imagine a meeting (a relationship?) between two of the most notable authors of English Renaissance rhetorics, whose different career trajectories suggest the range of fates awaiting the lettered. (See HRO, 44M69/F2/14/1, bundle 1, "To her moste excellent Maiestie.")

nor does he know the author's name. (By contrast, Webbe's 1586 *Discourse* uses Spenser's poem as extensively as Puttenham does *Tottel*.) Moreover, the *Art* is essentially silent on the Elizabethan sonnet vogue, which did not really begin in earnest until the publication of *Astrophil and Stella* in 1591. Puttenham cites poems from the *Old Arcadia* (completed by late 1580) and *Certain Sonnets* (ca. 1582) but exhibits no manuscript access to *Astrophil and Stella* (the composition of which Ringler dates to 1581–83). He mentions the form among six or seven other forms of amatory poetry (1.22.134) and cites three Wyatt adaptations of Petrarch, but otherwise the sonnet has no special visibility for him. His drama consists of interludes, and he treats the word *theater* as a foreign term in need of glossing (1.17.126: *theatrum*), though James Burbage's Theater had opened in 1576. The plays of Peele, Lyly, Kyd, and *The Famous Victories of Henry V* are all invisible, as is the puritan antitheatrical attack that arose with Gosson (1579) and Stubbes (1583). (The freethinking author of the *Partheniades* is unlikely to have read such works and remained silent.)

Despite the general mid-Tudor emphasis, some portions of the *Art* seem datable to the 1580s. Willcock and Walker propose a useful, if speculative, temporal stratification of the book's composition (xliv–liii) that makes some sense of this. Chapters 1 to 30 of Book 1 seem the earliest, and language at the end of 1.30 suggests that Book 2 is to follow next. The rehearsal of English poets in 1.31, however, contains a list of "courtly makers" who are "her Majesty's own servants" (000), and Sidney, Ralegh, Dyer, and Greville are named. These authors together suggest a date of the early 1580s for the chapter, which is thus to be seen as a later addition. Book 2 as we now have it may be divided roughly into thirds. The initial subject, metrics, seems to end at 2.11.179 ("To finish the learning of this division . . ."), about a third of the way through. This may once have been the ending of Book 2. The middle third (2.12) examines quite different and perhaps more recent material (Willcock and Walker judge it "fire-new from the mint of the mid- and latter-eighties" [xlviii]).[103] This section examines shaped poems, anagrams, *imprese*, and so on, said to be "fittest for the pretty amorets in court to entertain their servants and the time withal, their delicate wits requiring some commendable exercise to keep them from idleness" (2.12.180). A further addition was inserted into this middle body during printing (that is, in 1589), consisting of eight unnumbered pages concerning the "posie transposed," now preserved only in Ben Jonson's copy (on which see 71 below). After these two nested additions follows the final third of

---

103. Gabriel Harvey, however, in his *Letter-Book* (material dated roughly to 1573–80) speaks of a contemporary fashion for shaped poetry "of late foolishely revivid by sum, otherwise not unlernid, as Pierus, Scaliger, Crispin, and the rest of that crue" (100). Such material need not be seen as "fire-new" a decade later.

Book 2, five more chapters (2.13–18) on the possibilities of classical and English quantitative verse. They seem consistent with the early 1580s, when Spenser and Harvey published their initial Familiar Letters on "reformed versifying" (1580) and Stanyhurst his *First Foure Bookes of Virgil his Aeneis* in quantitative meters (1582). Book 3, twice the size of the other two combined, shows highly intermixed signs of composition and amplification over a long period of time (including what seem to be various small failures of editing, discussed in the notes), and notably expands the orbit of the first two books to engage with courtly concerns.[104]

5. Poetics in the *Art*

For his foundational treatment of the cultural origins of poets and poetics, Puttenham resorts to the familiar idea that poets were the originators of all the arts, indeed, the originators of human society itself, having been the first priests, prophets, legislators, philosophers, astronomers, historiographers, orators, and musicians in the world (see 1.3 and 1.4). Such foundational claims are common to the Horatian-rhetorical tradition of poetics. Horace says that poets were the first lawgivers, whose powers of speech, like the magic of Orpheus and Amphion, enabled them to tame men who, beast-like, were still living in the woods (*Ars poetica* 391–401). Cicero rehearses the myth at the start of his *De inventione* (1.2.2–3); it goes back to Isocrates' *Antidosis* (254–56), and is picked up again by Quintilian in his *Institutio oratoria* (2.16.9). This story, usually involving some mention of Orpheus and Amphion, was widely diffused in the period, especially in the works of Renaissance rhetoricians.[105] Sidney adopts the same posture, defending the value of poetry as "the first light-giver to ignorance," which possessed the power to compel "wild, untamed wits" to embrace knowledge and civilization (*Defence* 213), and he claims both Orpheus and Amphion as mythical prototypes of the poet. When Puttenham retells the tale at the beginning of his *Art*, he is thus reworking material he could have found in treatises on rhetoric as easily as in treatises on poetry. What differentiates his version of the story is not that he claims for the poet, as distinguished from the orator, the title of "founder of civilization." Rather, what he does in the third and fourth chapters of his first book is

---

104. Ben Jonson supposedly said, according to William Drummond's record of their conversations in 1619, that "[t]he old book yt goes about (the art of English Poesie) was done 20 yeers since & Kept Long in wrytte as a secret" (see the Herford and Simpson edition of Jonson 1.144). Willcock and Walker suggest (li) that this might mean that the *Art* was composed around 1569 and published twenty years later.

105. See Rebhorn, *Emperor* 25. Elyot, for one, cites Plato's proposition in the *Protagoras* (see 322c–d) imputing the civilizing moment to Mercury's intervention with sapience and eloquence (*The Governour* 45–46).

to *amplify*, as Renaissance treatises on both poetry and rhetoric would have put it, the originary functions of the poet-orator. Identifying the poet as the first orator (1.4.98), Puttenham elevates him beyond what most Renaissance theorists would have claimed, and credits him not just with bringing a "rude and savage people to a more civil and orderly life" (1.3.96), but with having invented a host of the most important basic features defining civilization, from religion and law to astronomy and music. Such an elevation of the poet implies a similar elevation of the poet who composed the *Art* itself and studded it with countless examples of his own verse. Something of the same effect is then produced by other means in the winks and nods of the catalogue in 1.8 concerning past poets who were richly rewarded by their princes.

If Puttenham repeats the commonplace Horatian-rhetorical defense of poetry and the poet on moral and political grounds, he also follows that tradition in stressing the pleasure that poetry affords. That pleasure is fundamentally defined by the fact that it is an aural art, one whose appeal to the ear gets repeated attention in Puttenham's work. Poetry is better than prose, he says near the start of the *Art*, because it is "more current and slipper upon the tongue, and withal tunable and melodious, as a kind of music, . . . which cannot but please the hearer very well." This appeal to the ear is crucial, for in Puttenham's conception, the ear is the essential gateway to the mind. As he puts it a little later, unlike our "daily talk," poetry "is decked and set out with all manner of fresh colors and figures, which maketh that it sooner inveigleth the judgment of man and carrieth his opinion this way and that, whithersoever the heart by impression of the ear shall be most affectionately bent and directed" (1.4.98). The last quotation contains a contradiction that is deeply revelatory of Puttenham's conception of the sensual nature of poetry: although he speaks of it as being "decked and set out" with figures of speech, the visual conception of poetry implied here leads him to talk of its appeal not to the *eye*, as one might expect, but rather to the *ear*, which is imagined as moving the heart by means of the emotions ("affectionately").

A similar slippage from the sense of sight to that of hearing also occurs in Book 3, most of which is devoted to the figures of speech, which are initially defined in elaborately visual terms as the "kindly clothes and colors" (3.1.222) of discourse. The visual nature of poetical ornamentation seems confirmed in a later chapter when Puttenham says it must have what Quintilian called *enargeia*, that is, distinctness or vividness (*evidentia* in Latin). This word, says Puttenham, comes from the Greek word *argos*, which means "bright" or "shining," and describes the way ornamentation "giveth a glorious luster and light" (3.3.227) to a poem. Nevertheless, although Puttenham clearly understands what *enargeia* signifies, he really thinks of it not at all in terms of the eye, but rather in terms of the ear: this sort of ornamentation, he says, aims "to satisfy and delight the ear only by a goodly outward show set upon the matter with words and speeches smoothly and tunably running" (227).[106] Later, he divides all figures of speech into three kinds: those that appeal to the ear; those that appeal to the mind; and those that appeal to both. That first group of figures, which he dubs the "auricular figures," have what he once again calls *enargeia* (3.10.245), deliberately redefining the term to apply to the auditory rather than the visual.

In conceiving poetry thus in aural terms, Puttenham reinforces the rhetorical nature of the art: it subordinates pleasure to utility, using the delight provided by musical, ornamented language in order to move the auditor; and what the auditor is moved to do is embrace the useful lessons that the poet is teaching. For no one, he says elsewhere, can beat reason "so well into the ignorant head as the well-spoken and eloquent man" (3.2.225). Appropriately, in the last of the opening chapters of Book 1 that are devoted to celebrating the poet as the source of civilization, Puttenham says that "the poets were . . . from the beginning the best persuaders and their eloquence the first rhetoric of the world" (1.4.98). He then ends this chapter by identifying Orpheus, Amphion, and King David, among others, as the archetypes of the poet, singers who used "a delectable music . . . to delight their hearers and to call the people together by admiration to a plausible and virtuous conversation [mode of living together]." Poets were thus, he concludes, "the first philosophers ethic and the first artificial musicians of the world" (99).

In addition to giving the poet originary status, defending his art on moral and political grounds, and arguing for the moral utility of poetry's appeal to the sense of hearing, Puttenham offers a defense of the imagination itself. Plato and Neoplatonic philosophy make a modest appearance in this context—especially in the notion of *furor poeticus*, the divine inspiration that allowed poets to access celestial truths—but Puttenham's theories in the *Art* more frequently reflect Aristotelian notions, which he may have obtained by way of Scaliger. For example, like Aristotle and Scaliger (and like Sir Philip Sidney as well) Puttenham stresses the representational nature of poetry. Thus, in the eighth chapter of Book 1, Puttenham defends poetry from the charge of being "fantastical," that is, "superfluous . . . and vain" (109), by citing Aristotle (in Latin) on the essential role that the imagination, or "fantasy," plays in mental operations and, in particular, in the representation—and the management—of the external world. Puttenham goes on to compare the fantasy to a mirror, distinguishing good fantasy, which

---

106. Although Puttenham focuses on the ear rather than the eye throughout the *Art*, he does recognize the visual appeal of poetry in Book 2, where he talks about the shaping of stanzas, which he draws for us, and where he presents an extensive treatment of figure poems in a wide variety of shapes. It is not clear how one would reconcile such a presentation with his general insistence on the aural nature of poetry. On Puttenham's confusing use of *enargeia* in connection with the ear, see Galyon, "Puttenham's *Enargeia*."

represents beautiful things "according to their very truth," from bad fantasy, which produces "chimeras and monsters in man's imaginations, and not only in his imaginations, but also in all his ordinary actions and life which ensues." Like the latter, the former also contains but exceeds the strictly defined limits of art: "[O]f this sort of fantasy are all good poets, notable captains stratagematic, all cunning artificers and enginers, all legislators, politicians, and counselors of estate, in whose exercises the inventive part is most employed and is to the sound and true judgment of man most needful" (110).

After defining the ur-poet and describing his fundamental faculty, Puttenham turns to the equally familiar subject of classification, outlining the subjects and genres of poetry. He had the example of Scaliger before him but developed his own complex classificatory scheme. He speaks, richly if none too systematically, of several kinds of organizational categories: *function*, detailing poems of praise and reprehension (heroic genres, comic and tragic drama, satire, pastoral, epigram, *dirae*). He also cites poems for comparatively institutionalized *occasions* of rejoicing and lamentation (*genethliaca*, *epithalamia*, elegy). In some cases he organizes by *address* (poems to gods, great men, and ordinary men). In some cases he imagines the historical (or "prehistorical") *origin* of certain forms (eclogue and satire). He ends Book 1 (in 1.31, a later addition) with a chronological review of English poets, preceded in English only by Webbe (1.239–47), though he could have modeled his account after Du Bellay's *Deffence* (2.2).

In Book 2 Puttenham explores the harmonious arrangement of the formal materials of English poetry, which he calls "proportion," a mathematical concept that has serious metaphysical consequences—everything in the universe "stand[s] by proportion" (2.1.153)—and that he could have found elaborated in the works of contemporaries such as in Henry Billingsley's *Elements of Geometry* (1570).[107] "We may truly affirm," Puttenham says with modest pride, "to have been the first devisers thereof ourselves, as αὐτοδιδακτοι, and not to have borrowed it of any other by learning or imitation, and thereby trusting to be holden the more excusable if anything in this our labors happen either to mislike or to come short of the author's purpose" (1.30.146–47). He discusses the complex interactions of stanza (which he calls "staff"), measure or quantity, syllabic concerns such as accent (which he calls "stir"), line length,[108] the caesura, rhyme, and what he calls "situation"

---

107. In *The English Renaissance Stage*, Henry S. Turner argues that geometry, mathematics, and other "practical arts" had a shaping influence on English Renaissance poetics generally and on Puttenham's *Art* specifically; for his discussion of the latter, see 118–26. Such concerns may underlie Puttenham's occasional use of building-trade terms such as "band," "rabate," and so on.

108. He touches briefly on related matters in 1.19: the Greek and Latin hexameter and the alexandrine.

(the distances that separate rhyme words within stanzas) and "band" (the connective or unifying force that repetitive structural elements, such as rhyme scheme, refrain, or sestina repetition, impart to stanzas or to entire poems). He excoriates variations by "false" orthography. He explores the visual aspect of forms we now know as "shaped" poems, emblems and "devices," and anagrams. And he explores classical and English quantitative metrics. As we have seen, some of these materials are influenced by the French,[109] and by Scaliger's treatment of classical prosody in his Book 2, but Puttenham may also have read Gascoigne's *Certayne Notes of Instruction* (1575) and Webbe's *Discourse of English Poetrie* (1586), each of which may have offered him guidance in Book 2, despite his claim to inaugurate the study of English "proportion." He cites Gascoigne's poetry extensively, and would have found *Certayne Notes* appended to *The Posies* (1575), where he may have found the poems. If, however, he wrote 2.1–11 before 1575, or 2.13–18 before 1580 (when Spenser and Harvey began their public correspondence on quantitative verse in the *Familiar* and *Commendable Letters*), he may indeed justly claim to be the first in the field, as he says in 1.30.

Book 3, Puttenham's masterwork, nominally concerns "ornament." It displays his intricately shaped and layered knowledge of the tropes of classical rhetoric, his exploratory arrangement of tropes and schemes by sound and meaning (the "auricular" and the "sensible"), his celebration of conspicuous figuration, his sophisticated curiosity about language, his ideas about style and decorum in both speech and writing as well as in courtly behavior. His specific debts and originalities in these regards receive detailed attention below, when we treat of Puttenham's ambitions. Suffice it to say for the moment that his most original work appears when these literary and rhetorical categories come together in what for him are the most interconnected spheres of language and social agency: here his extraordinary sensitivity to the intricacies of artful courtly performance, to the "poetry of conduct," as C. S. Lewis called it,[110] is unsurpassed in the period.

Before turning to Puttenham's ambitions, we should conclude this review of his literary-oratorical poetics with his own generalizations concerning conspicuous artfulness. Just as he begins his *Art* (as he believes civilization began) with the founding conceptual elevation of the poet, he closes it in 3.25 with a meditation on the relations between Art and Nature. His enclosing frame here is the topic of poetic dissimulation, derived from the archetypal courtly virtue of *sprezzatura*, the art that hides art. He begins where our introduction began, by summarizing his accomplishments in articulating the elements of his *Art*, and

109. Du Bellay writes about rhythm and unrhymed verse in 2.7.148–53, and about rhyme in 2.8.153–57. Sébillet talks about such matters in 1.5.62–1.9.98, as does Peletier (2.1.285–2.2.292).
110. Lewis, *The Allegory of Love* 351.

moves forward then by stages: from the "one piece [of the courtly poet's praxis yet unsummarized] that best beseems" (378) the court, namely, his cunning dissembling; through the remarkable *occupatio* of his catalogue of particular dissembling actions; and finally, abjuring the vile mystery of these lovingly presented tactics, to an account of the courtly poet's proper dissimulations "in the subtleties of his art." And yet even these, he immediately says, are not all to be hidden, but only those that may "discover his grossness or his ignorance by some scholarly affectation."[111] For indeed, the courtier-poet may sometimes "both use and also manifest his art to his great praise" (382).

These permissible exhibitions of art Puttenham articulates by a series of distinctions and analogies. In some cases art is an "aid and coadjutor" to nature, he says, supplying her defects as the physician does, furthering her actions as does the gardener when he "seasons his soil by sundry sorts of compost, as muck or marl, clay or sand, and many times by blood, or lees of oil or wine, or stale, or perchance with more costly drugs." In these cases the physician and gardener deserve no small praise as "good and cunning artificers" (383). In other cases art may *alter* nature, as the physician prolongs life unnaturally and the gardener creates double gillyflowers, stoneless plums, pears without cores, and the like.[112] These actions are most singular (i.e., notable) when most artificial. In yet other cases art is only a bare *imitator* of nature, counterfeiting her effects as the marmoset does man's. Among these imitative arts are painting, carving, alchemy, and lapidary art, none of which is demeaned by calling its effects highly artificial. Finally, "in another respect art is, as it were, an encounterer and contrary to nature," producing effects "altogether strange [that is, foreign] and diverse" (384) in form (nature always supplying the unshaped matter). Among these effects are, first, such things as houses and furniture, garments, locks and keys; then such activities as dancing by measures, singing by note, playing on the lute. All these are products of study and discipline, impossible without humanly instituted rules and precepts.

Some actions, however (seeing, hearing, feeling), are so natural to man that excellence may be acquired in them without any art or imitation at all. To be artful in these would be as absurd as for one with perfect sight to use spectacles, to hear by an ear horn, to feel with gloves on. Art in these matters earns scorn and pity. But are language and discourse and persuasion unlike these, Puttenham asks? Such products are, when achieved through instinct, inspiration, and pleasure, far superior to those earned *invita Minerva*, against nature. Art may repair when nature is wanting but cannot be superior. And yet, says Putten-

---

111. Such affectation thus echoes the grossness and ignorance of the cart.

112. The gillyflower example looks forward to Shakespeare's famous treatment of art and nature in *The Winter's Tale* 4.4, which may well be indebted to this passage.

ham, the poet is to play many parts: to devise his "plat" (385), or subject, to fashion his poem, to use meter and proportion, and to utter with delight. *Poetry is thus both like and unlike the crafts.* The poet's relation to measure links him to the craftsman, who is artful, even unnatural. When he speaks of another man's doings, as Homer did of Priam, he works in a foreign material, as Puttenham says the painter and carver do. When he uses figures, argues subtly, persuades copiously and vehemently, he works like the cunning gardener, coadjutor with nature, furthering her conclusions, making them strange. By contrast, in that part which "rests only in device" and issues from invention, aided by fantasy and imagination, he is unlike the painter (who achieves similar effects to nature), unlike the gardener (who furthers nature and supplies her wants), unlike the carpenter (who works utterly different effects), but instead most like nature herself, "working by her own peculiar virtue and proper instinct and not by example or meditation or exercise as all other artificers do" (386). In this case he is most admired when most natural and least artificial—yet *to be honored for both* (since language is both suggested by nature and polished by art), but more for avoiding unseasonable artfulness, dissembling it well, than for grossly affecting and indiscreetly displaying it, "as many makers and orators do" (386).

Whether this ensemble of analogies be seen as miscellaneous or capacious, unrigorous or curious, it is clear that Puttenham strives to frame his poetics not finally with elegance but with suppleness, simultaneously welcoming and resisting many relations of analogy. Moreover, he ends harshly—perhaps unable to help himself, perhaps in some kind of self-knowledge—not with celebration but with bad art, with grossly affected and indiscreet poets and orators. Though ideally entitled to honorable self-exhibition, these failures clutter the aesthetic landscape, unable to see (or acknowledge) their disentitlement . . . like, perhaps, the self-divided author of the *Art* himself.[113]

6. Puttenham's Ambitions

Puttenham's literary, social, and political ambitions shape practically every aspect of *The Art of English Poesy*. By writing it, as he says over and over, for courtiers and ladies, he seeks to align himself with the social and intellectual elite of early modern England, to establish himself as a leading theorist of poetry, and to exhibit his own accomplishments as a poet. The *Art* further reveals Puttenham's ambitions in its dedications.

113. Strictly speaking, the *Art* ends not with the discussion of Art and Nature (which concludes its intellectual architecture), but with the complimentary close addressed to Elizabeth, in which Puttenham modestly dismisses the importance of poetry and his trifling book about it, while still noting that he remains available as a candidate for patronage.

The first one, to William Cecil, was possibly composed by the printer, Richard Field, though Puttenham would certainly have welcomed approval from this dedicatee, the dominant figure of Elizabeth's Privy Council and the most powerful man in the land, who granted Puttenham his greatest reward, for the *Justification*, and who oversaw much of Puttenham's plummeting legal fortunes (and whom Puttenham had supposedly plotted to kill in 1570). The authorial dedicatee of the work, however, is identified when the printer explains how the *Art* was "chiefly devised" for the "recreation and service" of the queen (90). Her importance to the work is underscored by a large engraving of her, with crown and scepter, that appears on a page of its own (AB4v) immediately following the dedication of the work to Cecil and across the fold from the start of the first chapter. Above the engraving stand the words *A colei*, and below it, *Che se stessa rassomiglia e non altrui* (To her who resembles herself and no one else). This emblem, with its figure and *subscriptio*, constitutes the real dedication of the *Art*.

From this point on there is no mention of Burghley, but the queen is a constant locus of adulation, mentioned and addressed dozens of times. Puttenham cites her famous and much reprinted poem of 1571,[114] "The doubt of future foes," going on to praise this "ditty of her Majesty's own making" as being "passing sweet and harmonical," having been composed by a queen who is "herself . . . the most beautiful, or rather beauty, of queens" (3.20.334). For the most part, however, Puttenham cites poems in praise of her, usually his own from the *Partheniades*. He also addresses her directly in the second person on several occasions. For instance, in 1.23, a chapter devoted to "poetical rejoicings," he speaks of public celebrations of peace, wherein (he says to her, in a late addition) "your Majesty (my most gracious Sovereign) have showed yourself to all the world for this one and thirty years' space of your glorious reign above all other princes of Christendom" (134). And as we have seen, near the end of Book 3 he presents the summary claim that his purpose in writing is to have pulled the courtier-poet from the cart to "your Majesty's service" and that writing his book has been an act of "duty" done for "your Majesty" (3.25.378). He also says, in the final chapter, that he has written it for "the pleasure of a Lady and a most gracious Queen" (3.Conclusion.387). The final words of his work stress the service he offers the queen: "I presume so much upon your Majesty's most mild and gracious judgment, howsoever you conceive of mine ability to *any better or greater service*, that yet in this attempt ye will allow of my loyal and good intent, always endeavoring to do your Majesty the best and greatest of those services I can" (387, emphasis added). Puttenham most ostentatiously wrote from a position of

---

114. On the date, see May, "Queen Elizabeth's 'Future Foes'" 4. Puttenham was the first to print the poem (in a quite corrupt form, as May shows).

modest and dutiful attendance upon the queen—not just as a servant but as a ready candidate for preferment.

It must nonetheless be observed that this subservient attendant posture sometimes appears to have felt suddenly degrading, arousing in Puttenham an occluded but iconoclastic response to the queen's social authority. Many readers have observed the occasional upsurge of something like sadism in the *Art*: see, for instance, Puttenham's detailed and hand-rubbing account of the rituals of the epithalamium in 1.26, simultaneously concealing and quoting the "screaking" of the virgin bride (139); his nurse's bawdy riddle ("I have a thing and rough it is / And in the midst a hole iwis," 3.18.273); his decried, erased, yet still coyly reported tale of Sir Andrew Flamock's soiling of Henry VIII's sweetheart (who "pist full sower, & let a fart": see 3.23, note 38); his suggestion that the fistula *in ano* is a useful courtly disease to profess, such "as the common conversant can hardly discover, and the physician either not speedily heal, or not honestly bewray" (3.25.380). Puttenham insists he is just honestly conveying (or bewraying?) the stories he tells, but they carry a strong charge of hostility that seems directed, over and over, at the very Virgin Queen and reader before whom he must abase himself in hopes of being raised.

Puttenham's desire to rise is served not only by what he openly displays in the *Art* but also by what he deliberately conceals in it. As we have noted, he elides the wide array of sources for most of the vast weight of information that renders his book so heavy. He recounts dozens of stories about classical figures, from the well known to the obscure, no source for which is ever provided. Though scattered throughout the *Art*, they come thick and fast in chapters 23 through 25 of Book 3, which are devoted to the courtly poet's behavior. The barrage of data announces relentlessly that Puttenham was widely and deeply learned in classical culture. He was certainly a widely read intellectual packrat, so it is possible that he had actually worked his way through Plutarch and other ancient writers to collect lore about Alexander, Cato, Maximinus, Cleomenes, and a score of others. A very large number of the anecdotes Puttenham recounts, however, are conveniently assembled in Erasmus's *Apophthegmata*, available in several editions in the sixteenth century, which helpfully arranged its sayings by the names of their authors and sat close to hand on a shelf in Puttenham's library. The *Apophthegmata* equipped its reader to trot out time after time both familiar and notably obscure quotations from the ancients, confirming a strong impression of dusty learning. By speaking as if he had direct access to the vast and shadowy realm of ancient knowledge, and hushing any presence of what seem exceedingly likely intermediaries such as Erasmus, Puttenham displays an apparently matter-of-fact, even nonchalant, mastery of antiquity that bespeaks a kind of scholarly *sprezzatura*. If sometimes he seems to show us not heavy learning worn lightly but the reverse, the pattern as a whole may exhibit only a somewhat journalistic period fascination with the "wit and wisdom" of classical figures, both famous and obscure. Save for the soldier's sword, Puttenham seems to aspire, like so many, to some version of Hamlet's courtier's scholar's eye and tongue.

Puttenham further augments his image with a ready store of anecdotes about figures from more recent history. He may indeed have been an eyewitness to many of them, or heard of them by word of mouth. Like his father and grandfather before him, he had at least some courtly "access." Nevertheless, we know that Puttenham owned a copy of Corrozet's *Les divers propos*, and he probably had read other books of "famous sayings." Again, what Puttenham does not tell his readers about his sources plays to his advantage, creating an impression of cosmopolitanism reinforced by his various statements about court-hopping in Europe. Like the modern world, the Renaissance had its cult of the rich and famous—and, almost always, the titled. For readers who had yet to move from the cart through the school to the court, let alone into the personal presence of the queen, Puttenham writes as a seeming insider, recounting intimate "eyewitness" experience of the great, and offering his readers a tantalizing glimpse of what might be seen privately in such public places.

The most obtrusive examples of Puttenham's silence about sources occur in Book 3, when he discusses the figures of speech. To illustrate them, he frequently cites his own self-identified poetry, but he also quotes from a host of other contemporary poets. Some of these he read in manuscript: various poems by Oxford, Sidney, Ralegh, Gorges (or Dyer), and others were not published until after the *Art* appeared.[115] Nevertheless, many of the poems that he includes in Book 3 can be found in *Tottel's Miscellany*, so it is very likely that he owned a copy of that much reprinted collection, which had begun to constitute something like the "canon" of poetry by this time. Silence about *Tottel* may function as a kind of inverted name-dropping, indicating a connoisseur's personal, non-print-mediated intimacy with English poetry in the sixteenth century.[116] Puttenham probably also owned the printed works of Gascoigne and of Turberville, whom he quotes nine and eleven times, respectively.

An equally crucial unacknowledged source in Book 3 is Joannes Susenbrotus's Latin *Epitome troporum ac schematum* (1540). Previous editors of the *Art* have tentatively argued that Puttenham used Susenbrotus in Book 3, but our comparison of the two works shows conclusively that Puttenham must have had Susenbrotus's book right at his elbow. First, there is the sheer weight of the numbers. Of the 121 fig-

---

115. On the so-called stigma of print, see the works cited in 1.8, note 57.
116. This idea owes a general debt to Marcy North's work.

ures identified by name in the *Art*, all but six appear in the *Epitome*, nor can this full list be found in any other classical or Renaissance rhetorical handbook. Moreover, of those six figures missing in Susenbrotus, five occur in the chapter Puttenham devotes to what he calls "vices," that is, figures one should avoid. This is a category Susenbrotus simply omits. It can be found, however, in the rhetorics of both Petrus Mosellanus (1527) and his derivative Richard Sherry (1550). Probably Sherry, and possibly Mosellanus as well, served as the basis for this category of Puttenham's figures.

Puttenham also organizes the figures the way Susenbrotus had—who was himself merely following the lead of the ancients. Among Greek and Latin rhetoricians there was a fair consensus on the subject, which the Renaissance inherited. To put it simply, all figures of speech were divided into *tropes*, which involve changes in the meaning of words, and *schemes* (also, confusingly, called *figures*), which involve changes in their form and arrangement but not their meaning. These two large categories were then subdivided in different ways by different rhetoricians. This is precisely what Susenbrotus and Puttenham, following in Susenbrotus's footsteps, do.[117]

At first glance, however, Puttenham's *Art* seems to organize the figures of speech quite differently from Susenbrotus and the classical tradition. Puttenham too divides them into three large groups, but labels those groups idiosyncratically, as the auricular, or figures that are pleasing to the ear; the sensable, or those that affect the mind and not the ear; and the sententious, or those that affect both. Willcock and Walker have suggested that Puttenham names the categories as he does in order to stress the sensory quality of poetry; they also applaud him for his daring in not simply following tradition as he does so (lxxviii). Nevertheless, it turns out that Puttenham's categories are precisely those of Susenbrotus and the classics, albeit in a different order and with different

117. The anonymous *Rhetorica ad Herennium* divided all the figures into two groups, figures of words and figures of thought (4.12.18), both of which were called "schemes" (*schemata*) in Greek, and were defined as involving changes in the form and arrangement of words. The *Rhetorica*, however, also separated out ten figures of words, including such things as metaphor and metonymy, from the rest because they involved changes in the meaning of words; the Greeks referred to this group of figures as "tropes" (from *tropos*, "turn"). Summing up the situation in his *Institutio oratoria*, Quintilian starts with tropes, defining them as involving the artistic alteration of a word's meaning (8.6.1–3), and then goes on to oppose them to *figurae*, "figures," which he says is the Latin equivalent of the Greek word *schemata*, and which, like his predecessors, he subdivides into figures of words (*verba*) and figures of thought (*sententiae*) (9.1.1–18). Susenbrotus generally follows Quintilian's lead but makes further distinctions: tropes are divided into those of single words and those of units of speech (*orationes*); schemes are first divided into those of grammar and those of rhetoric; and the grammatical are then further subdivided into the orthographical and the syntactical, while the rhetorical are turned into those of words, those of units of discourse, and those of amplification. Since Susenbrotus initially presents an overview of his system in the form of a tree diagram (4), it is likely that he was influenced by the thinking of Peter Ramus, who pioneered such visualizable schematization.

names. Thus, Puttenham's sensable figures are Susenbrotus's tropes, and just as the latter subdivided them into those involving individual words and those involving larger units of discourse, so does Puttenham, devoting a chapter to sensable figures in "single words" (3.17.262) and a second one to those involving "whole clauses or speeches" (3.18.270). Similarly, Puttenham's auricular figures are identical with Susenbrotus's first grand division of the schemes, which he calls the grammatical, and again, just as Susenbrotus subdivides grammatical schemes into two parts, so does Puttenham, although he covers the first part in just one chapter, 3.11, while devoting five chapters, 3.12 through 3.16, to the other. Finally, Puttenham composes the longest chapter of his work, 3.19, about the "sententious figures," which he also labels "rhetorical" (280), using exactly the same name for them that Susenbrotus gave to his second grand division of the schemes.

When we examine the sequences of individual figures Puttenham treats in the chapters of Book 3, we also see that in most of them he simply follows the arrangement his predecessor used. Even in chapter 19, in which Puttenham goes out of his way to rearrange the order he found in Susenbrotus, there are sets of related figures that closely resemble what one finds in the *Epitome*. Specifically, Puttenham begins with the same six figures that Susenbrotus does, albeit arranged differently, and he ends with four of Susenbrotus's last five, this time keeping them in exactly the same order.[118] What is more important, these two groupings of figures have no precedents among the ancients, thus offering additional evidence that Susenbrotus, rather than Cicero or Quintilian, was Puttenham's chief source here.

Finally, Puttenham's indebtedness to Susenbrotus is revealed by his retention of some of the specific examples, and sometimes the very words, he found in the *Epitome*. For example, for *asyndeton* both men have Julius Caesar's "I came, I saw, I conquered," and for *antiphrasis* both use the example of calling a dwarf a giant. Even more revealing is an example Puttenham provides for *sententia*: "Nothing sticks faster by us as appears, / Than that which we learn in our tender years" (3.19.321)—a verse recasting of Susenbrotus's "Nothing sticks more tenaciously than what we learn as boys" (91). Finally, in his discussion of *synecdoche* Puttenham lifts a bit of text in Latin straight out of his predecessor's work. Susenbrotus provides this example for *synecdoche*: *Virgineam soluit zonam, id est, devirginavit* (8: "he loosened her virginal zone, that is, he deflowered her"). Puttenham cites the same text, explaining it as he does so: "[I]n the old time, whosoever was allowed to

---

118. Susenbrotus's first six rhetorical figures are *anaphora, epanalepsis, epizeuxis, anadiplosis, antistrophe,* and *symploche.* Puttenham's first six in 3.19 (on sententious, or rhetorical, figures) are *anaphora, antistrophe, symploche, anadiplosis, epanalepsis,* and *epizeuxis.* Susenbrotus's very last figure is *digressio,* but before that he has these four: *similitudo, icon, parabola,* and *paradigma.* Puttenham's last four are identical with these.

undo his lady's girdle, he might lie with her all night; wherefore, the taking of a woman's maidenhead away was said to undo her girdle. *Virgineam dissoluit zonam*, saith the Poet" (3.18.280).[119]

In muffling his indebtedness to Scaliger and Du Bellay, to Tottel and Susenbrotus, Puttenham works to reinforce his image as a Renaissance polymath (though common period practice by no means required detailed citation of indebtedness). What he does with the Susenbrotus material, however, requires more comment, for he does not merely repeat what he found in the *Epitome*. He renames and rearranges Susenbrotus's major categories, and he alters the specific order of many of the figures he found within those categories, especially in 3.19. An obvious explanation for Puttenham's deliberate transformation is concealment. Indeed, since Susenbrotus's organization of his book is generally consistent with what one finds in Quintilian and other classical rhetoricians, Puttenham's reorganization works to disguise his dependence on the classical tradition as well.

Yet Puttenham's unusual arrangement of the figures can be viewed in a more positive light as part of a general attempt to rethink them, and fashion a distinctive image for himself as an original theorist, although that originality involves both deference to the classics which are his chief "sources" and his deliberate reworking and even criticism of them.[120] Consider how Puttenham defines all figures of speech as *deceptions*, that is, as deliberate attempts by the writer or speaker to "make our talk more guileful and abusing" (3.7.238) in order to produce a double sense that heightens the emotional response the figures are designed to elicit. Although he is following Quintilian's lead here, the latter merely claims that figures are "errors" (9.3.3), whereas Puttenham stresses the deliberate act of duplicity they require. By aggressively calling attention to the courtier-poet's duplicity, Puttenham creates a moral problem for him (and for himself), underscoring it by recalling how the Athenian court of the Areopagus forbade figurative speeches for just this reason, as corrupters of upright judgment. He defends his courtier-poet, but oddly, by diminishing the importance of poetry and limiting its audience, which he says does not include sour and severe

119. The "Poet" in question here is Homer, who uses this expression to describe Neptune's deflowering of the nymph Tyro in the *Odyssey* (11.245). That Puttenham cites the phrase using Susenbrotus's Latin, rather than Homer's Greek, suggests his particular indebtedness to Susenbrotus here.

120. In his *Origin and Originality in Renaissance Literature*, David Quint argues that the Renaissance is defined by a fundamental conflict, or contradiction, about originality. On the one hand, it still sees the work of art in traditional terms as being "original" insofar as it is authorized by and connected to its "origin," whether in the divine or in some other unimpeachable, authoritative work, such as the ones produced in classical antiquity. On the other hand, it sees the work's "origin" as being in the mind and talent of its creator, whose "originality" is thus its true source. For Quint, the Renaissance anticipates, without ever fully embracing, the Romantic notion that simply dispenses with any authorizing external source for poetry and assigns originality entirely to the artist.

"judges," just the less serious "princely dames, young ladies, gentle-women, and courtiers" (3.7.239). He also insists that he is talking about decent figures of speech here, not indecent ones, reinforcing their supposed inoffensiveness for that conspicuously gendered audience. Puttenham's argument here, however, contradicts his repeated, indeed ambitious, insistence throughout the *Art* on the fundamental magnitude of poetry and the poet.

In fact, there is something complexly disingenuous in Puttenham's "reduction" of the courtier-poet's address to an audience of trivialized (or at least tolerant, playful, unthreatening) "princely dames, young ladies, gentlewomen, and courtiers." His treatise was dedicated to the decidedly severe Lord Burghley, and addressed to that singular "princely dame," Elizabeth herself, who could never be rendered fully unserious. Puttenham's fundamental and highly un-Sidneyan conception that figures—and poets—are deliberately deceitful and abusive keeps before readers' eyes (at some level surely intentionally, out of a satisfying urge to threaten) a sense of poets as disturbing, morally dubious, potent, and worth watching. Such a notion of the poet stresses the distance between the poet and his audience, even if that distance is one he keeps struggling to undo (or, rather, control). It is very far from the dignity and calm of the comparatively mutually transparent *compact* that seems to obtain between Sidney's poet and his reader, who will never mistake the former's fictions for lies, since he "nothing affirmeth" (*Defence* 235). There is little that more firmly marks Sidney's confident sense of his born entitlement to speak his mind, as poet and servant of the state. Similarly, Puttenham's authorial address—by turns aggressive, slavish, hostile, in all cases slightly occluded—bespeaks his complex but abiding sense of disenfranchisement and unregarded desert. Restricting the courtly poet's arch-trait of cunning dissembling to the subtleties of his art does not really block the author's own (partial and leaky) self-dissembling. Indeed, such leakage is one of the most arresting qualities of his book.

Puttenham may also be attempting (as perhaps only a scholar would) to dramatize his independence as a theorist through his idiosyncratic conceptualization of the tropes and schemes. As we noted above, he places the former in between two distinct subsets of the latter, and he names them, in order, the auricular, the sensable, and the sententious.[121] He exhibits a certain discomfort with this "innovation," and certainly fears the scorn of "busy carpers," but also thinks that the novelty itself has direct attractions, especially for denizens of the court, for

121. Willcock and Walker praise Puttenham repeatedly for his independence and refusal simply to submit to authority. Not only do they admire his "daring" in renaming the figures, but also they say that although he "knew full well that the best rhetorical tradition restricted to prose the so-called rhetorical or 'sententious' figures," he claimed them for poetry anyway (lxxviii).

whom "new devices are ever dainty and delicate" (3.10.244). He is wrestling with a problem that consistently bedeviled ancient theorists: that the division of figures of speech into tropes, which alter the meanings of words, and schemes, which alter their arrangement, is anything but clear-cut. Quintilian himself tries to establish a firm boundary between them, but his attempt falters in important places, as with such figures as *hyperbole* and especially *irony*, which he admits can be classified both ways (9.1.1–7). Puttenham is responding to this conceptual problem by making his third group of figures consist of those that can be seen as both tropes and schemes. If he does not exactly "solve" the conceptual problem, at least he acknowledges it by building it into his analytical framework.

Puttenham also occasionally attempts to improve the ordering of some of the figures he found in Susenbrotus. Near the end of the *Epitome*, for example, Susenbrotus presents a series of rhetorical schemes that all focus on the idea of similarity or comparison (*similitude, icon, parable*, and *paradigma*). At the very end, however, he leaps to quite a different figure, *digressio*, which has nothing in common with its predecessors and thus seems something of an afterthought—indeed, a kind of digression—where it occurs. By contrast, Puttenham discusses *digressio* much earlier in his long chapter on "figures sententious," placing it just after a series of clearly related figures that involve moving rapidly through a topic (*paralepsis*), departing from it (*metastasis*), or dwelling on it insistently (*commemoratio*). In other words, by relocating *digressio* Puttenham attempts to make its placement more rational than in Susenbrotus. This rationalizing impulse may also explain why, after having finished his review of all the tropes and schemes, Puttenham devotes an entire chapter, 3.20, to the "last and principal figure of our poetical ornament," which he calls *exergasia*, or *expolitio*, or "the Gorgeous." He defines this figure by comparing it to the polishing of marble or the adorning of a body with beautiful clothing: it means the endowing of speech with "copious and pleasant amplifications and much variety of sentences." Here, he says, he may not be talking about a single figure so much as a "mass of many figurative speeches, applied to the beautifying of our tale or argument" (333). Puttenham thus nicely rounds off his presentation of all the figures of speech by presenting "the Gorgeous" as a kind of climax: the figure of figures, it embraces all the tropes and schemes that have come before it. Puttenham's arrangement here corrects Susenbrotus, since he, like Quintilian and the entire rhetorical tradition before him, confusingly placed this figure in the midst of all the other schemes.

Puttenham improves on Susenbrotus in yet another way. After treating "the Gorgeous," Puttenham writes two chapters about faulty or indecorous figures of speech that should be avoided by the courtier-poet (moving the book more and more into the territory of courtesy).

Susenbrotus's *Epitome* not only lacks this category (thus failing to distinguish good and bad figures clearly from each other) but also further muddies the waters by placing a few figures it says are faulty right in the middle of the ones it recommends. Thus *tapinosis*, the use of a mean word for something worthy, is set among such approved figures as *hendiadys* and *asyndeton*. Moreover, Puttenham also improves on Susenbrotus—and on much of the rhetorical tradition—by following his chapters on faulty figures with several more on the topic of decorum, for decorum, the judging of what is and is not appropriate, is really the principle by means of which one separates good figures from bad ones. Puttenham thus consciously seeks in these final chapters to broaden and deepen his analysis, concluding in the penultimate chapter with an even more general consideration, that of the relationship between art and nature. In other words, Puttenham has structured his third book so that it builds up to several substantial considerations of the general principles underlying everything he has been saying. Such a movement is largely unprecedented in rhetorical theory before him.

Perhaps the most generally memorable aspect of Puttenham's treatment of the figures of speech is his supplying original names for them in English, a move that is completely consistent with his invention throughout the *Art* of neologisms such as "predatory," "rotundity," and "insect," which often record the first use of those words in English.[122] Here again, as he is about to produce names in English for classical rhetorical figures, Puttenham waxes defensive (probably strategically) about what he is doing: he says he fears that his translations of Greek and Latin terms may "offend" the learned and that his new, English names for the figures "may move them to laughter." (As Gavin Alexander suggests, however, a certain courting of readerly smiles seems likely.)[123] Puttenham defends himself first by declaring that the strangeness of the new names is sheerly a byproduct of their novelty and will wear off in time. He then says that his retention of the original classical terms would have been a mistake, for it would have made his work "too scholastical," something fit for learned "clerks," not for poets. Finally, he defends himself by claiming not only that his translations of the Greek and Latin words are accurate—they are "as near as may be to their originals"—but also that they may "serve better to the purpose of the figure than the very original" (3.9.242). Like most Renaissance writers, Puttenham has deferred to the ancients throughout his treatise in many different ways, but his judgment about his names for the figures is anything but deferential: he regards them as superior in accuracy to the hallowed ancient terminology still in use today.

---

122. On Puttenham's coining of words, see Willcock and Walker xxxvii, and Lisak, "Le 'Poète épique.'"

123. For Alexander, see *Sidney's "The Defence of Poesy"* lxiv.

Indeed, the English names actually *do* more for him: they actively connect the courtier-poet's use of language to his behavior, to *agency*. Almost always, Puttenham's Englishings invite the reader to imagine a person actually uttering the figure to another in some sort of localized social context. Thus, *ironia* becomes "the Dry Mock" and *sarcasmus* "the Bitter Taunt": these are the kinds of remarks Puttenham and his readers might have been expected to make—or to suffer from another, especially a social superior, in the competitive arena of the Renaissance court (or in the dock). Two of the three examples Puttenham supplies for *ironia* are the "dry mocks" two kings supposedly made to gentlemen in their retinues, and rulers are the source of all three of the examples supplied for *sarcasmus*. Puttenham's use of personified renamings, however, connects language and behavior in the social world even more forcefully. Perhaps he is influenced by the fact that in Renaissance, as in modern, English, the word "figure" could mean both "figure of speech" and the "visual appearance" of a person. In any case, he transforms the vast majority of the tropes and schemes into *characters*: *etiologia* becomes "the Tell-Cause"; *prozeugma* "the Ringleader"; *prolepsis* "the Propounder"; *meiosis* "the Disabler"; and *paradoxon* "the Wonderer." Sometimes the personifications seem to identify actual social types, as when *protocatalepsis* is turned into "the Presumptuous" and *hyperbole* into "the Loud Liar, otherwise the Overreacher." This last example is famous, of course, for it provided Harry Levin with the title for his classic book about Marlowe, *The Overreacher: A Study of Christopher Marlowe*. What Levin does not quite say in his study, however, is what Puttenham's transforming of rhetorical terms into people clarifies completely: Marlowe's Tamburlaine and Doctor Faustus do not merely use hyperbole when they speak, but as "Overreachers" they themselves are essentially hyperboles in action.

If the Renaissance conceived of human beings as actors who perform not one but a host of different roles in the social world, Puttenham's Englishings of the figures of speech transform them into all the varied "figures"—that is, all the varied masks or personas or selves—that human beings might assume on the great stage of the world. Since the figures suggest that social interaction is always a matter of "counterfeiting" one role or another, Puttenham's personifications essentially turn life into a continual allegory, where thoughts and words are now by definition divergent from each other. Thus it should not be surprising that in 3.18 Puttenham gives pride of place in his work to allegory itself, declaring that "the courtly figure *allegoria*, which is when we speak one thing and think another," is so widely used and so essential that no one will ever "thrive and prosper in the world" without it (270). More important, he says allegory is *the* exemplary figure, identifying it as "the chief ringleader and captain of all other figures either in the poetical or oratory science."[124] (The two "sciences" here, as so often, merge into one praxis.) Finally, Puttenham first translates *allegoria* as "the Figure of False Semblant" (271), using a word of French origin that evokes the universe of romance allegory Spenser would shortly reanimate in his *Faerie Queene*. He then goes on to equate "False Semblant" with what he elsewhere (3.25.379) defines as the master feature of his courtier-poet—dissimulation. To use allegory and to be a courtier are, in essence, the very same thing.

Finally, Puttenham's *Art* is certainly original in its conspicuous generic merging of poetics and rhetoric manual, though as we have seen, the overlap between the categories, if not their merger in a single manual, was generally the case. A more genuine uniqueness derives, however, from the admixture of a third category: by the time he is done, Puttenham has merged his poetics and rhetoric manual with the core functions of a courtesy book. The *Art* becomes an unmistakable specimen of *genera mixta*, the combining of genres that Rosalie Colie has shown was typical of many of the greatest works of the Renaissance. Poems and speeches are forms of behavior, of course, but Puttenham takes the idea to at least one new logical conclusion. A sense of the social and political reference of English Renaissance rhetoric and poetry has become a commonplace, but Puttenham is the first contemporary writer to bind them together explicitly to that goal. If Milton would later argue that the poet hopeful of writing well of laudable things ought himself to be a true poem, "a composition and pattern of the best and honorablest things,"[125] it seems clear that Puttenham's courtly poet is an agent who will, in a spirit both similar and quite different, stage various particular acts of courtly conduct as themselves worthy of quotation, memorization, imitation—as acts of art. The many tales of deft, beautiful, or lethal courtly performance that he reports are themselves treated like his many quotations of verse, as "poems" by poets of conduct. (Furthermore, and more biographically, Puttenham himself seems to have combined great intellectual acumen with many of the worst features of character. He was therefore, by his own most un-Miltonic standard of cunning dissembling, himself a precisely true poem, if of a different genre—a composition and pattern founded on thoroughgoing, lifelong efforts at "brables of subtyll practyses," being "overconnynge in defacinge of

---

124. The first of these terms, "ringleader," has both negative and neutral senses during the period, though *OED* says that the negative antedates the neutral in print by forty-five years (1503, 1548). It cites a text that curiously and richly uses both of Puttenham's terms: "I dout not but . . . we shalbe able by good polici to distrii alle the captayns and ryngledres that be of yll and contrary mynde" (*Letters and papers illustrative of the reigns of Richard III and Henry VII* [Rolls series 1861–63]: 1.238).

125. Milton, *An Apology for Smectymnuus,* in *Complete Prose Works* 1.890. Cf. Quintilian 1.Proem.9 and 12.1.

truthe by wordes & speache eloquente," and a master of the "invencon of myscheiffe.")[126]

Filled with ambitions for the courtly poet that clearly reflect Puttenham's own, his book is animated by a core fantasy, as we have noted, that must have inspired countless English would-be gentlemen and courtiers. In 3.25 he defines this fantasy in spatial terms, as a movement from the cart to the school to the court and finally into the personal presence of the queen herself. A different and equally striking perspective on this fantasy appears in a remarkable passage that he locates just after his lengthy defense of the very idea of fantasy or imagination itself, in 1.8. This passage displays his very deeply conflicted feelings about the queen: his grateful dependence on her, his frustration and anger about that dependence, and his overwhelming desire to control her. Although Puttenham's disturbed feelings are still partly disguised here, as they are elsewhere in the *Art*, that disguise has become practically transparent.

In the chapter in question, he mounts on two fronts a defense of fantasy generally conceived, in the teeth of widespread scorn and derision, deriving, he says, from "the barbarous ignorance of the time, and pride of many gentlemen, and others, whose gross heads not being brought up or acquainted with any excellent art, nor able to contrive or in manner conceive any matter of subtlety in any business or science, they do deride and scorn it in all others as superfluous knowledges and vain sciences" (109). He then argues, as we have seen, that fantasy's critics condemn it only because they have failed to distinguish between good fantasy and bad. If they did, he insists, they would necessarily approve of an Apollonian good fantasy, without which "no man could devise any new or rare thing. . . . [O]f this sort of fantasy are all good poets, notable captains stratagematic, all cunning artificers and enginers, all legislators, politicians, and counselors of estate, in whose exercises the inventive part is most employed and is to the sound and true judgment of man most needful" (109–10). Such a rhetorical strategy maximizes the extension of the poetic faculty and recapitulates the originary civilizing process Puttenham has, following the literary-rhetorical tradition, founded upon poesy. The conflict that summons up this strategy, between those who honor the imagination and those who scorn it, also recapitulates one of the deepest and most abrasive fault lines in early modern English culture, between honoring the established structures of social hierarchy and honoring their porosity.

He then presents a second, intensive "argument," highly emotional and very revealing, for why no poet should ever hesitate to make use of fantasy. Poets should embrace it, he says,

the rather for that worthy and honorable memorial of that noble woman twice French queen, Lady Anne of Brittany, wife first to King Charles VIII

---

126. Francis Morris's accusing descriptions of Puttenham in 1571 from PRO, STAC 5 P5/10.

and after to Louis XII, who, passing one day from her lodging toward the king's side, saw in a gallery Master Alain Chartier, the king's secretary, an excellent maker or poet, leaning on a table's end asleep, and stooped down to kiss him, saying thus in all their hearings: "We may not of princely courtesy pass by and not honor with our kiss the mouth from whence so many sweet ditties and golden poems have issued." (110–11)

This "memorial" anecdote unaccountably (and anachronistically) substitutes Anne of Brittany (1477–1514) for Margaret of Scotland (1424–1445), who was clearly identified as its subject in Puttenham's likely source, Corrozet's *Les divers propos memorables*.[127] The tale expresses beautifully the core fantasy that drives Puttenham's ambitions and animates his entire work. That fantasy, one might say, is his desire to be "kissed by a queen." The poet's mouth, the source of his poetical utterances, compels the queen to confer the reward of her public and witnessed favor on him (an *anti-carting*, as it were) for his "sweet ditties and golden poems." The kiss actually involves a set of overlapping fantasies, all of which suggest that his Anne be read as a displaced version of Elizabeth.

The first layer of fantasy is a libidinal one: the kiss constitutes an erotic fruition so long sought from the poet's admired and admiring queen, whom he endlessly plied with the language of adoration so conspicuous in the poems of both Puttenham and so many of his fellow poets, all profoundly influenced by the tradition of Petrarchan longing.[128] It thus plays into the poetically eroticized politics Elizabeth used to manage relationships with so many of her courtiers, but it rewrites the most important rule and embodies the deepest fantasy they all had. In Puttenham's fantasy, it is the poet-subject, not the queen, who is in charge; his mouth and the "sweet ditties" it has produced force the

127. Chartier was sent to Scotland in 1428 by Charles VII of France to arrange Margaret's marriage to his son the future Louis XI (not Puttenham's Louis XII). It was there that the kiss supposedly took place. (Some authorities inaccurately allege that the incident was apocryphal because Margaret did not come to France until 1436, after Chartier died [in 1430].) The story made its first appearance nearly a century later, in Jehan Bouchet's *Les Annales d'Aquitaine* (1524; Poitiers, 1644). He says that Margaret saw Chartier sleeping on a bench and kissed him. Her (unidentified male) companion was shocked and asked her why she had kissed such an ugly man. She replied, "Ie n'ay pas baisé l'homme, mais la precieuse bouche, de laquelle sont yssuz & sortis tant de bons mots, & vertueuses parolles" (252: "I did not kiss the man, but the precious mouth from which have issued and come forth so many clever words and virtuous sayings"). Bouchet's anecdote was widely circulated by writers both in the Renaissance and afterwards. Modern scholarship suggests, however, that the tale was most likely made up by Bouchet, who wrote many years after the event and provided no source for the story, which is otherwise unconfirmed. (None of the French materials suggests that anyone other than Margaret of Scotland was the person who kissed the poet, so Puttenham's substitution of Anne of Brittany is hard to explain. Anne was, like Elizabeth, a queen; she was also famous for her patronage of poets and artists.) Puttenham's language in the passage closely tracks that of Corrozet, his probable direct source, who has suppressed the comment of Margaret's companion about Chartier's ugliness.

128. Puttenham's discussion of the kiss here, and especially the stress he places on its erotic nature, may well owe something to classical and Renaissance writers who produced

queen to stoop, even to bow, and kiss him.[129] The Petrarchan relationship attracted Elizabeth's investment because it both conferred power on a female figure and required of her no payment for it: the lovers' desire was to remain unfulfilled, or at least infinitely protracted (and motivating). By hinting at a further sort of erotic fulfillment—the food for hungry Desire, as Sidney has it—Puttenham begins to make the queen a "quean," a strumpet who will serve his desires.

Puttenham's fantasy about being kissed by a queen also displays a longing for "nourishment" from her. After all, it focuses on the mouth, through which the queen's sweets, her rewards, come to the poet in exchange for the "sweet ditties" he has composed for (and about) her. She figures not just as an erotic object but as a munificent mother figure, whose function is to serve and nurture her all-powerful, though seemingly dependent and needy, child.[130] The form that his nourishment will take is also implicit in what he suggestively calls his "golden poems," for which he will receive a "golden" reward: money or property, such as the leases in reversion that Puttenham got for the *Justification*. Indeed, the procreative quality of such payouts may also be discerned in the language Puttenham uses when he speaks at the very outset of the *Art* of the queen's near-magical "poetic" powers, which make her "the most excellent poet" of the time: "by your princely purse, favors, and countenance, making in manner what ye list, the poor man rich, the lewd well learned, the coward courageous, and vile both noble and valiant" (1.1.95). The queen's "creative" agency is her capacity to "make men," to confer wealth and promotion, but all three of its specified organs or instruments signify both erotics and capital, whether material or social: her princely "purse" (both money bag and sexual organ),[131] her "favors" (both specific approvals or gifts and appearance or face), and her "coun-

---

"kiss poems." Although long a topos in the courtly love tradition, the kiss achieved a particular salience in the Renaissance after the printing of Catullus' collection of poems in Venice in 1472. (Catullus was largely unknown before then, although several Italian scholars had seen manuscripts of his poems in Verona in the fourteenth century.) Two of Catullus' most famous poems (5 and 7) celebrate the kisses he exchanged with his mistress Lesbia. Inspired by these and other poems in Catullus' collection, the neo-Latin poet Joannes Secundus wrote an entire work, *Basia* (*Kisses*), exploiting the idea. Puttenham owned a copy of Catullus' poems, and in 1.26 he praises Catullus' two *epithalamia*. In the same passage he goes on to praise Secundus's *epithalamion* and his *Basia*: "in that [his epithalamion] and in his poem *De basiis* [Of Kisses], [Secundus] passeth any of the ancient or modern poets in my judgment" (141).

129. Had Puttenham known of Chartier's ugliness, he might well have used it as amplifying the distance the queen stoops to honor art (the original point). Perhaps he did, but felt too ugly to be able to stand using it.

130. Cf. the discussion by Montrose in "Shaping Fantasies" of the coincident erotic and maternal aspects of the queen.

131. For this extended meaning, cf. *The Merry Wives of Windsor* 1.3.61 and Williams's entry (*Glossary*). The same-sex equivalent is familiar from modern readings of Chaucer's Pardoner's demand of Harry Bailey ("unbokele anon thy purs," *Pardoner's Tale* 945) and Antonio's promise to Bassanio: "My purse, my person, my extremest means, / Lie all unlock'd to your occasions" (*The Merchant of Venice* 1.1.138–39).

tenance" (again, both goodwill and face). At this level the queen's kisses and her patronage merge to fill her subjects as from a breast.[132] In short, this kind of kiss captures the queen as an ideal version of the ruler-as-patron, the positive inversion of Faustus's words about "Helen of Troy": "Her lips suck forth my soul" (*Doctor Faustus* 4.5.111).

By being represented as she is here, Anne solves a problem, perhaps *the* problem, every courtier faced: how to get the desired reward of political favor and economic benefits from the ruler-patron. This problem is really two, however. First, it is the one created by rulers who should reward their courtiers without being asked, but who often fail to do so because of miserliness, indifference, forgetfulness, or ill will. For the courtier to ask would, at least partly, solve this problem—he would not be forgotten—but his asking would create a new one. For asking might make him seem ambitious and demanding, one of those "aspiring minds" (3.20.334) that Elizabeth, supposedly seconded by Puttenham himself, disliked and distrusted. By asking, in other words, the courtier could actually provoke ill will in the ruler and be denied his reward as a result. In short, for Puttenham's courtier it is a double bind.

Another anecdote reveals how Puttenham agonized over this dilemma, which might easily paralyze a needy aspirant. Puttenham returned obsessively to the many reasons that rulers always seemed to find to avoid giving rewards, no matter how meritorious the courtier. Among these returns he tells exactly the same story three times—the story of Sir Anthony Rous, who was reluctant to beg a reward from Henry VIII for services rendered. Rous's reluctance may exemplify the paralysis produced by the courtier's dilemma, although Puttenham attributes it instead to Rous's self-professed sense of shame. When an intermediary tells Henry of Rous's hesitation, Henry replies cuttingly, "If he be ashamed to beg, we are ashamed to give" (3.18.274, 3.24.361–62, and slightly varied at 3.24.375–76). Avoiding damnation for asking, Rous found himself damned for not asking, winding up as Henry's victim in an anecdote that must register Puttenham's own sense of helplessness, outrage, and urge to retaliate for being denied the rewards he must have felt he deserved. If the realities of monarchy prevented any retaliation in the real world, at least Puttenham could have satisfaction in the realm of the imaginary by telling this anecdote about Rous and Henry over and over again.[133] An alternative hypothesis, that the repetition derives from Puttenham's incomplete editing, mostly relocates the same energy. The story perhaps seemed so important that he tried it

---

132. Compare Puttenham's "special" roundel poem's treatment of the queen's breast, at 2.12.188, from which issue incessant streams of bounty (among other effects). He goes so far in 3.19 as to offer specific praise of her nipples (330).

133. Puttenham also seems to have identified Alexander the Great with this issue: he tells at least four stories of him that focus on his habits of princely reward (1.8.106 and 3.24.361 [twice], and 369–70).

out in several places, never managing to decide which one served him best. However we construe the repetition, Puttenham is clearly not going to let shame such as Rous's, to which he was so richly entitled, prevent him from begging.[134]

In the story about Anne's kiss, Puttenham finds a different, if also imaginary, solution to the courtier's dilemma. Anne's own words as she describes the impulse moving her to kiss Chartier are the key: "We may not of princely courtesy," she says, "pass by and not honor with our kiss the mouth from whence so many sweet ditties and golden poems have issued." One might read this as an expression of a free choice she has made to display "princely courtesy" in action: "Look," she declares, "this is how real princes behave, according to their prerogative." But her words, which give her agency when read this way, deprive her of it when read another way: "I am compelled," Puttenham's Anne may declare, "by the very sight of this poet, driven by a sense of duty imposed on princes, to bestow a kiss on him." Chartier has not commanded that she kiss him, to be sure, but totally passive—he is asleep, after all—he has not begged for it either, thereby risking refusal. His mere presence suffices to compel Anne to stoop down and kiss him, a gesture that she may rationalize as "princely courtesy" but that testifies to the power Chartier exercises over her. In fact, his sleeping presence not only forces her to kiss him but also in-spires her to breathe forth sentiments Puttenham and countless other English courtier-poets would have loved to hear from Elizabeth. In Puttenham's fantasy, the silent, deserving, potent courtier-poet need not even open his lips: he gets his golden reward, and hears (in his dreams?) the loving words that Puttenham himself has put in "Anne's" mouth. Such passivity—should we call it effortlessness?—is an ultimate form of control.

That Elizabeth herself is really at issue in this passage is revealed clearly by what Puttenham says next. Writing as if suddenly self-conscious about the kiss fantasy, he shifts to a register remarkable for its embarrassment and defensiveness:

> But methinks at these words I hear some smilingly say, I would be loath to lack living of my own till the prince gave me a manor of Ewelme for my rhyming. And another to say, I have read that the Lady Cynthia came once down out of her sky to kiss the fair young lad Endymion as he lay asleep; and many noble queens that have bestowed kisses upon their princes' paramours, but never upon any poets. The third methinks shrug-

134. Cf. Elyot's chapter (3.13) on "Patience deserved in repulse, or hindrance of promotion": "To a man having a gentle courage, likewise as nothing is so pleasant or equally rejoiceth him as reward or preferment suddenly given or above his merit, so nothing may be to him more displeasant or painful than to be neglected in his painstaking, and the reward and honour that he looketh to have, and for his merit is worthy to have, to be given to one of less virtue, and perchance of no virtue or laudable quality" (*The Governour* 192).

gingly saith, I kept not to sit sleeping with my poesy till a queen came and kissed me. (1.8.111)

Although the name "Elizabeth" does not sound here, it does not have to: her allegorical identification as Cynthia was widely known in Puttenham's culture, an identification John Lyly played on in his *Endimion, or the Man in the Moon*, staged in 1588, just before Puttenham's treatise was published.[135]

Several notable things appear in this striking follow-up. Puttenham makes himself clearly audible as a poet who longs for patronage, identifying himself with Chaucer, who, as he remarked earlier in this chapter (107), had received the manor of Ewelme from Richard II (it was thought).[136] The derisive second witness mocks Puttenham's conflation of "princes' paramours"[137] and poets, laying bare the direct eroticism of the moment, and indeed, imputing paramours to "many noble queens"—itself one of Puttenham's many caustic and perhaps resentful but deviously expressed needlings. For the third witness, like the first, royal patronage apparently involves a long wait. Most striking of all, by assigning these critical comments to others, Puttenham *stages himself* before them—and before his readers—as a figure of shame, whose barely concealed ambitions and desires make others smirk and shrug their shoulders in scorn and condescension.

These sentences might well function, at least momentarily, as Puttenham's way of censuring himself (for his potentially insolent "aspiring mind") before someone else does: a scolding prelude, perhaps, to a denial that he is actually talking about himself and Elizabeth in this passage. And yet, that is not what happens at all. Instead of apologizing, he goes on to say:

> But what of all this? Princes may give a good poet such convenient countenance and also benefit as are due to an excellent artificer, though they neither kiss nor cokes them, and the discreet poet looks for no such extraordinary favors, and as well doth he honor by his pen the just, liberal, or magnanimous prince, as the valiant, amiable, or beautiful, though they be every one of them the good gifts of God. (1.8.111)

All the sarcastic critiques are redirected and dismissed, as if they have been denying the prince's powers of reward. Princes can too award such favors, Puttenham seems to say, though they need not, nor does the discreet poet look for them. Nonetheless, the energies of the Chartier

---

135. See also the discussion in E. C. Wilson, *England's Eliza*.

136. On this erroneous view, see 1.8, note 11.

137. This phrase is complex. Are these *queens'* paramours, such as Lancelot? Men beloved by the queens' husbands? (The word is then presumably not erotically coded.) Those lovers worthy of themselves? *OED* recognizes no version of the word without either spiritual or erotic freight.

fantasy are revived in a new and equally ambiguous kiss here, dilated with a similarly libidinal partner, "cokes." But *who* kisses and coaxes here, we should ask: princes or poets? The pronouns are ambiguous. The queen kisses the poet in Puttenham's story; he does not coax her. The obvious reading is that princes may reward whom they like, even if (or especially if?) the discreet poet restrains his urge to flatter and wheedle, to "kiss" and "cokes," and only decently honors in verse the "just, liberal, or magnanimous" acts of his prince—even though these "be every one of them the good gifts of God," and thus, Puttenham may imply, personally undeserved. Perhaps, however, the agency is distributed in a more complex way.

The ambiguity of the passage exceeds that of its pronouns. The *OED* provides three related meanings of the verb "cokes": (1) *to make a "cokes" of, befool, "take in"*; (2) *to make a pet of; to fondle; to treat with blandishment*; (3) *to influence or persuade by caresses or flattery*. Moreover, the noun "cokes," meaning "gull," dates from 1567. These meanings encode two additional, remarkable ambiguities: one involving who is high and who is low in the power hierarchy, and another concerning the difference between "authentic" affection and devious manipulation. One may coax from above and below, and deviously or lovingly. Anne's loving affection for Chartier meets a kind of radical opposite in the far from silent, insinuating flattery of the English literary theorist for his still withholding queen, and yet again in another English fantasy, no sooner voiced than negated, of a "coaxing" queen and her excellent artificer, who seems to recoil in shock from having ever dreamed of such a thing. The kiss may be given, taken, bought, earned, or stolen, and this magical conjunction is at the core of Puttenham's dreamwork.

Perhaps this nexus lured all would-be poet-clients in Renaissance England. In *A Discourse of English Poetrie* (1586), William Webbe cites a 1584 French digest of Horace on cautions against such coaxing: "A Poet shoulde not bee too importunate, as to offende in vnseasonable speeches; or vngentle, as to contemne the admonitions of others; or ambicious, as to thinke too well of his owne dooinges; or too wayward, as to thinke reward enough cannot be gyuen him for his deserte; or, finally, too proude, as to desire to be honoured aboue measure" (1.300). Webbe sees an all too attractive array of demanding stances for the poet who seeks reward and reputation, one as full of intense agency as are Puttenham's names for tropes, though they are all presented as negative, risky, improvident. Together they also register, nearly as powerfully as Puttenham's kiss fantasy, the intensity of the courtier-poet's longing for high and honored place. The central difference between the two theorists is that Puttenham presents Anne's kiss as a defense of longing that is both poetic fantasy and social ambition; for Webbe, such a kiss is an object of desire surrounded by far too many motivations for toxic investment.

Puttenham is by no means unaware of the dangers Webbe cites, but the entire passage that started with Puttenham's fantasy about Anne—indeed, the entire chapter, if not the entire work—makes it clear that such "extraordinary favors" are precisely what this poet, at least, was looking for.

Perhaps Puttenham has lost control of his text here. Perhaps he is simultaneously appealing and seeming to rebuke and ridicule himself in the process. What is unmistakable, however, is that he wants the queen's kiss very badly. As he deploys the rhetorical strategy of *laudando praecipere*, of "teaching" her by "praising" her; as he tells her how poets such as himself write merely to honor the virtues that princes display; as he implies that if she wants that honor, she must be as "just, liberal, and magnanimous" as he says she is—so he embodies the courtier-poet's chief virtue, dissimulation, working to obscure his artful attempt to seize control of the relationship from below and bend it to his needs. As in the complex power dialectic of Anne of Brittany and Alain Chartier, he implicitly inverts the social hierarchy at least to the extent of reminding her that if he as a subject and client depends on her for his reward, she depends equally on him for the praise he would happily (but of course only honorably) give her.

Puttenham suggests daringly that the queen's good gifts *are* gifts, from God, and that it falls to her, if she is to be a proper prince, to distribute them further, to her deserving subjects. The excellent artificer will readily honor her with his excellent pen, without coaxing, if he can only cease to be "uncouthe, unkiste," as Spenser's shadowy interlocutor E.K. puts it when introducing the unknown poet Colin Clout to the world in 1579.[138] The artificer will then be able to leave the cart permanently behind and bask in the magical mythical Presence of the prince. Far from being an unschooled shepherd, Puttenham elaborately—perhaps somewhat too elaborately—presents himself in the *Art* as the consummate Renaissance intellectual, whose identity is defined by his classical erudition, his cosmopolitan knowledge of English and continental European society, his detailed grasp of both poetics and rhetoric, and his complex understanding of the deep connections between the ways we use language and the ways we behave on the great stage of the world. This is the fantasy that animates his book: that he will not merely pull himself, as he would pull his courtier-poet, from the cart to the school and then to the court, but that he will actually haul himself into the very Privy Chamber of the queen. There he will rule over and reward his ruler, and will finally reap the harvest of his own labors, the queenly kiss of royal countenance that he wrote *The Art of English Poesy*—and so much else—in order to obtain.

---

138. See the headnote to *The Shepheardes Calender* (ed. Oram et al.) 13.1; E.K. quotes Chaucer's *Troilus and Criseyde* 1.809, "Unknow, vnkist, and lost, that is unsought."

This, at any rate, is the fantasy George Puttenham. The "historical" George Puttenham is a different character, resembling, as we have said, both Shakespeare's sexual predator Gloster and his cruel wounded outcast bastard son. Like them, Puttenham was no stranger to dark and bitter places of the mind—nor to the tenements of Whitefriars. Yet as we imagine the royal kiss with him here, it is perhaps suggestive to end where Edmund ends, with the ambiguous fantasy satisfactions of "Yet Edmund was beloved."

7. Editorial Conventions

Modernization and regularization. Our aim has been to provide a readable modern text that makes Puttenham's complex and frequently obscure prose as clear as possible for modern readers. (For the unmodernized text, see Willcock and Walker.) We have modernized archaic printing conventions (i/j, u/v, vv/w, the ampersand), spelling, and punctuation throughout Puttenham's text; added paragraphs where it seemed useful; and broken up many of Puttenham's long sentences. We have often been guided by Stanley Wells's *Modernizing Shakespeare's Spelling*, but a word on modernizing punctuation is needed. Many irreducible obscurities accompany such efforts. A full framing of the problem, not mounted here, would have to consider at least the following problematic categories of authority and convention: early modern theories of punctuation and print culture's shifts on such questions in Puttenham's own time; theories of rhetorical versus "logical" structuring, and/or oral versus literate cognition; authorial specification versus changes—not to be assumed to be incompetent—by printers; notions of conventional or collective readerly expectation and individual authorial improvisation. Modern addressees also cast their retrospective shadows: "scholars" and "students," and historicizing editors and their modernizing adversaries. In light of both the increased availability of the 1589 text in digital facsimile and the presence of Willcock and Walker's fine original-punctuation text of 1936, our own conflation of all of these factors, inevitably unsatisfactory to many, has led us to identify the beginning graduate student in early modern literary studies as our chosen audience for this edition, and to modernize with this imaginary person in view.

Many miscellaneous decisions have been required. A few original spellings have been retained, where they seemed necessary to maintain rhyme or meter, or for some other reason. Also, we have retained Puttenham's capital for the word "Queen" whenever it refers to Elizabeth I, thus allowing it to remain as a gesture of deference in his text. Puttenham often (but not always) uses parentheses and square brackets for emphasis or exemplarity; these we have adjusted to modern format. We have, however, often cited early modern sources with original spelling in the notes when the editions used retain that spelling. In Renaissance

English *his* was often used where we would say *its*; we have not emended or annotated these instances, quite common in the *Art*. *Ne* has been regularly modernized to *nor*. The macron in all languages has been expanded, as have all Latin abbreviations; the ampersand in Latin has been turned into *et*. Mistakes in Puttenham's Latin have been corrected since they were more likely printer's errors than Puttenham's; mistakes in modern foreign languages have been corrected, except to preserve rhyme. The printing of many of Puttenham's short and long accent marks over vowels in Book 2 is highly defective and irregular. Many of the marks appear imperfect or damaged, and some expected ones are missing. Consequently, where we have thought it appropriate and were confident of our judgment, we have silently corrected the text. Finally, we have put Puttenham's side notes in Book 3 where they occur in *1589*, even though they seem slightly misplaced in some cases.

Source and analogue citations.   Puttenham's book is exceedingly heavy with references to other works and authors, as well as to historical and current events. We have attempted to provide the reader with guidance on these whenever possible. Many of his numerous examples, stories, and influences might have reached him by intermediate digests of earlier texts, by manuscript transmission, or by word of mouth. These mediations are impossible to trace exactly.

Our citations identify analogues or available versions of texts (which Puttenham may have used as sources, as he did with Susenbrotus), or the location of the text in the standard modern edition (e.g., Rebholz's Wyatt). A great many items clearly call for such annotation, but we have been unable to trace them all. Those left unidentified are marked with a dagger (†). Some complex items have received more extensive annotation; these we have grouped in the Longer Notes at the end of the text. Puttenham's self-identified citations to his own writings otherwise lost are marked with an asterisk.

Classical texts are cited from the Loeb Classical Library unless otherwise noted. We have tried to supply references to all of the major classical and English Renaissance rhetorical texts for possible sources and analogues to Puttenham's treatment of rhetorical tropes in Book 3. We mention medieval sources only in the rare cases when the trope appears not to have been coined until that period. Tropes sometimes have more than one name or overlap with other tropes, and a source or analogue will use a different name from Puttenham's. We have often turned to Gideon Burton's *Silva Rhetoricae* for help with such synonymy.

Citations from non-Shakespearean Renaissance drama are taken from *Drama of the English Renaissance*, ed. Fraser and Rabkin, unless otherwise noted. When we cite from Erasmus, we include the volume and column numbers for the Leiden edition (LB); the volume and page numbers from the Toronto *Collected Works of Erasmus* (*CWE*) where available; and, where useful, references to the Renaissance translations of Taverner and Udall. We cite works from Brian Vickers's *English Renaissance Literary Criticism* whenever they appear there unabridged, unless they are available in standard editions of the authors (e.g., Sidney, Spenser, Harington). Other such works are cited from G. Gregory Smith's *Elizabethan Critical Essays*. Note: Rollins's edition of *Tottel's Miscellany* and Pigman's edition of Gascoigne's *Adventures of Master F. J.*, frequently cited below, number all of the lines on a page, not the lines of individual poems on that page or poems that run on from one page to the next. We have set aside the matter of which edition(s) of *Tottel* Puttenham used; for exploration of this matter, see Doherty (Book 3, note 37ff.). Scaliger's 1561 edition misnumbers the chapters after 3.9 (skipping 3.10); we use his misnumbered references nonetheless, for ease of reference to the modern facsimile.

This Edition

References. All references to passages in our text of Puttenham take the form "1.2.24" (book, chapter, and page numbers).

The text. Puttenham's work appears in one edition, STC 20519. We have not produced a collated text; for bibliographical discussion, see Willcock and Walker's Bibliographical Note (ciii–cx). The present text is based on the Da Capo Press facsimile of the Bodleian Library's copy shelfmarked Douce PP 206, but we have sometimes resorted (see below) to the copy owned and annotated by Ben Jonson, preserved in the Scolar Press facsimile (BM, G. 11548). We have also consulted Jeffery Triggs's valuable SGML text of the *Art*, prepared for the *OED* North American Reading Program in 1993.

Three notable textual features.

1. Near the end of 2.12 (after *1589* p. 84, between the N and O gatherings) the Ben Jonson copy introduces eight unnumbered pages of text not present in other copies, concerning "the device or emblem" (after which the normal page numbering [85] resumes). These we print (2.12.190–98).

2. In some copies of the *Art* an anti-Flemish paragraph exemplifying *paradigma* appears at Eeiv, *1589* p. 206 (3.19.331–32 in this edition); in some presumably later copies this paragraph is replaced by a pro-Flemish passage. The content of both versions is of considerable interest as an *argumentum in utramque partem* demonstration of politically subtle *paradigma*. We have therefore printed both passages serially in the text proper, rather than relegating the earlier one to an appendix, as Willcock and Walker do. For the text of the earlier form we follow the Da Capo facsimile, which matches Willcock and Walker's use of

British Museum (hereafter BM), C. 71, c. 16. For the later text we follow the Ben Jonson copy of the *Art*, BM, G. 11548 (see the Scolar Press facsimile).

3. At the beginning of 3.20 a page appears (*1589* p. 207, sig. Ee2r) containing, in some copies, various minor corrections. We print the corrected version (from the Scolar Press facsimile of BM, G. 11548), and provide the uncorrected version (from the Da Capo Press facsimile of Douce PP 206, matching BM, C. 71, c. 16).

Paratext.   A variety of supporting materials follow the text proper.

1. Puttenham's list of chapter headings (the "Table of the Chapters in this Book") (389–93).

2. The uncorrected state of sig. Ee2r (395–96).

3. The Emendations (397–99). With four exceptions—see 1.11.115, 2.12.191, and 3.24.368 (twice)—we have not added any words to Puttenham's text.

4. The Longer Notes (401–20).

5. The Name Glossary (421–42). We provide biographical notes for all non-obvious proper names in the text (but not for those appearing only in the notes). In some cases, where information is immediately needed for local comprehension, such material appears in footnotes. All such names, whether unglossed, glossed in the text, or in the Name Glossary, are indexed.

6. The Word Glossary, of many frequently used but possibly obscure terms (443–48). These are marked in the text with the degree sign (°).

Bibliography

Unless otherwise noted, all references to classical texts are to the Loeb Classical Library editions, not listed here.

Works by George Puttenham

Puttenham, George. *The Arte of English Poesie*. 1589. (BM, G. 11548.) Menston: Scolar Press, 1968.

——. *The Arte of English Poesie*. 1589. (Bodleian, Douce PP 206.) New York: Da Capo Press, 1971.

——. *The Arte of English Poesie*. 1589. In Haslewood, *Ancient Critical Essays* 1:3–271.

——. *The Arte of English Poesie*. 1589. Ed. Edward Arber. English Reprints. London, 1869.

——. *The Arte of English Poesie* [selections]. 1589. In Smith, *Essays* 2:1–193.

——. *The Arte of English Poesie*. 1589. Ed. Gladys Doidge Willcock and Alice Walker. Cambridge: Cambridge University Press, 1936.

——. "George Puttenham's *The Arte of English Poesie*: A New Critical Edition." Ed. Stanley Joseph Doherty Jr. Ph.D. diss. Harvard University, 1983.

——. *The Arte of English Poesie* [selections]. 1589. In Vickers, *English Renaissance Literary Criticism* 190–296.

——. *The Art of English Poesy* [selections]. In Alexander, *Sidney's "The Defense of Poesy" and Selected Renaissance Literary Criticism*. London: Penguin, 2004. 55–203.

——. [Puttenham, George.] *A Justification of Queen Elizabeth in relation to the Affair of Mary Queen of Scots*. In *Accounts and Papers relating to Mary Queen of Scots*. Ed. Allan J. Crosby and John Bruce. Camden Society Publications [First Series]. Vol. 93. London, 1867. 67–134.

——. *Partheniades*. In Haslewood, *Ancient Critical Essays* 1:xix–xxxviii.

——. *Partheniades*. In *Ballads from Manuscripts*. Vol. 2. Part II: Ballads relating chiefly to the reign of Queen Elizabeth. Ed. W. R. Morfill. Hertford, 1873. 72–91.

Early Sources

Aquila Romanus. *De figuris sententiarum et elocutionis*. In Von Halm 22–37.

Aristotle. *Opera Latina*. Ed. Academia Regia Borussica. 16 vols. Berlin, 1831.

The Arundel Harington Manuscript of Tudor Poetry. Ed. Ruth Hughey. 2 vols. Columbus: Ohio State University Press, 1960.

Ascham, Roger. *English Works.* Ed. William Aldis Wright. Cambridge: Cambridge University Press, 1904. Contains *Toxophilus, Report of the Affaires and State of Germany,* and *The Scholemaster.*

Bacon, Francis. *The Advancement of Learning.* 1605. In *A Critical Edition of the Major Works.* Ed. Brian Vickers. Oxford: Oxford University Press, 1996. 120–299.

———. *Essays.* 1625. New York: Everyman, 1906.

———. *The History of the Reign of King Henry VII.* 1622. Ed. F. J. Levy. Indianapolis: Bobbs-Merrill, 1972.

Bale, John. *John Bale's Index of British and other writers (Index Brittaniae scriptorum quos ex variis bibliothecis non parvo labore collegit Ioannes Baleus cum aliis).* 1557. New York: AMS, 1989.

Bede, the Venerable. *De schematibus et tropis.* In Von Halm 607–18.

Bigges, Walter. *A Summarie and True Discourse of Sir Frances Drakes West Indian Voyage.* London, 1589.

Billingsley, Henry. *The Elements of Geometrie of the Most Auncient Philosopher Euclid of Megara.* London, 1570.

Bolton, Edmund. *Hypercritica.* Ca. 1614 (first printed 1722). In Haslewood, *Ancient Critical Essays* 2:221–54.

Bouchet, Jehan. *Les Annales d'Aquitaine.* 1524. Poitiers, 1644.

Calendar of State papers, Domestic series, of the Reigns of Edward VI, Mary, Elizabeth, 1547–1580. Ed. Robert Lemon. 1856.

Camden, William. *The History of the Most Renowned and Victorious Princess Elizabeth [Annales].* 1615. Trans. 1675.

———. *Remains Concerning Britain.* 1605. Ed. R. D. Dunn. Toronto: University of Toronto Press, 1984.

Campion, Thomas. *Observations in the Art of English Poetrie.* 1602. In *Works.* Ed. Walter R. Davis. New York: Norton, 1967. 287–317.

Carew, Richard. "The Excellency of the English Tongue." 1614. In Camden, *Remains* 37–44.

Castiglione, Baldassare. *The Book of the Courtier.* 1528. Trans. Sir Thomas Hoby. 1561. New York: Everyman, 1966.

Castiglione, Baldesar. *Il Libro del Cortegiano.* 1528. Ed. Bruno Maier. 2nd ed. Turin: Unione Tipografico-Editrice Torinese, 1964.

Cavendish, George. *The Life and Death of Cardinal Wolsey.* 1558. Ed. Richard S. Sylvester. Early English Text Society. London: Oxford University Press, 1961.

Chappell, William. *Old English Popular Music.* Rev. ed. H. Ellis Wooldridge. 1840. New York: Jack Brussel, 1961.

Chaucer, Geoffrey. *The Riverside Chaucer.* Gen. ed. Larry D. Benson. Boston: Houghton Mifflin, 1987.

The Chronicle of the Grey Friars of London. Ed. John Gough Nichols. Camden Society Publications [First Series]. Vol. 53. London, 1852.

The Chronicle of Queen Jane, and of Two Years of Queen Mary. Ed. John Gough Nichols. Camden Society Publications [First Series]. Vol. 48. London, 1840.

Corrozet, Gilles. *Les divers propos memorables des nobles & illustres hommes de la Chrestienté.* 1557. 4th ed. Paris, 1571.

Cotgrave, Randle. *A Dictionarie of the French and English Tongves.* London, 1611.

Daniel, Samuel. *"Poems" and "A Defence of Ryme."* Ed. Arthur Colby Sprague. 1930. Reprint. Chicago: Phoenix Books/University of Chicago Press, 1965.

Dasent, J. R. *Acts of the Privy Council of England.* New series (1542–1631). London: His Majesty's Stationery Office, 1890–1940.

Day, Angel. *The English Secretorie.* 1599. Facsimile reproduction. Intro. Robert O. Evans. Gainesville, Fla.: Scholars' Facsimiles and Reprints, 1967.

A Declaration of the Causes to Give aide in the lowe Countries. 1585. In *Elizabethan Backgrounds: Historical Documents of the Age of Elizabeth.* Ed. Arthur F. Kinney. Hamden, Conn.: Archon, 1975. 188–96.

De Commines, Philip. *The History of Commines.* 1596. Trans. and cont. Thomas Danett. Tudor Translations. 2 vols. London, 1897.

Desportes, Philippe. *Oeuvres.* Ed. Alfred Michiels. Paris: Delahaye, 1858.

Diomedes Grammaticus. *Artis grammaticae libri III.* In *Grammatici Latini.* Vol. 1. Ed. Heinrich Keil. Leipzig, 1857.

Donne, John. *John Donne.* Ed. Frank Kermode. The Oxford Authors. Oxford: Oxford University Press, 1990.

Drama of the English Renaissance. Ed. Russell A. Fraser and Norman Rabkin. 2 vols. New York: Macmillan, 1976.

Drayton, Michael. *The Barons Warres.* 1603. In *The Works of Michael Drayton.* Vol. 2. Ed. J. William Hebel. Oxford: Shakespeare Head Press, 1961.

Du Bartas, Guillaume De Salluste, seigneur. *Works.* Ed. Urban Tigner Holmes Jr., John Coriden Lyons, and Robert White Linker. 3 vols. Chapel Hill: University of North Carolina Press, 1935.

Du Bellay, Joachim. *La Deffence, et illustration de la langue françoyse.* Ed. Jean-Charles Monferran. Geneva: Droz, 2001.

Elizabeth I. *Collected Works.* Ed. Leah S. Marcus, Janel Mueller, and Mary Beth Rose. Chicago: University of Chicago Press, 2000.

Elyot, Sir Thomas. *The boke named The gouernour.* 1531. Ed. H. H. S. Croft. 2 vols. London, 1883.

——. *The Boke named The Governour.* 1531. Ed. S. E. Lehmberg. London: Dent, 1962.

——. *Four Political Treatises.* Gainesville, Fla.: Scholars' Facsimiles and Reprints, 1967.

——. *Letters.* Ed. K. J. Wilson. *Studies in Philology: Texts and Studies* 73 (1976). Also contains Elyot's *Prologues.*

Ennius, Quintus. *Poesis reliquiae.* Ed. Johann Vahlen. Leipzig: Teubner, 1903.

Erasmus, Desiderius. *Adages.* In *Collected Works of Erasmus.* Vols. 30–36 [incomplete; only vols. 31–34 available]. Trans. Margaret Mann Phillips et al. Annot. R. A. B. Mynors et al. Toronto: University of Toronto Press, 1982–1992.

——. *The Apophthegmes of Erasmus.* Trans. Nicolas Udall. 1564. Boston, Lincolnshire, 1877.

——. *Correspondence 1523–24 (Letters 1356–1534).* In *Collected Works of Erasmus.* Vol. 10. Trans. R. A. B. Mynors and Alexander Dalzell. Annot. James M. Estes. Toronto: University of Toronto Press, 1992.

——. *Literary and Educational Writings I: Antibarbari; Parabolae.* In *Collected Works of Erasmus.* Vol. 23. Ed. Craig R. Thompson. Toronto: University of Toronto Press, 1978.

——. *Opera omnia.* Ed. Jean Leclerc. 10 vols. Leiden, 1703–1706. London: The Gregg Press, 1962.

——. *Opus epistolarum.* Vol. 5. Ed. P. S. Allen and H. M. Allen. Oxford: Clarendon Press, 1924.

——. *Proverbs or Adages, Gathered out of the Chiliades and Englished by Richard Taverner.* 1539. Ed. DeWitt T. Starnes. 1569; Gainesville, Fla.: Scholars' Facsimiles and Reprints, 1956.

Fraunce, Abraham. *The Arcadian Rhetorike.* London, 1588. Reprint. Menston: Scolar Press, 1969.

Froissart, Jean. *The Chronicle.* Trans. Sir John Bourchier, Lord Berners. 1523–25. Intro. William Paton Ker. Tudor Translations. 6 vols. London, 1903.

——. *Chroniques: Livre I.* Vol. 3. Ed. George T. Dillon. Geneva: Droz, 1992.

Fuller, Thomas. *The History of the Worthies of England.* 1662. Ed. P. Austin Nuttall. 3 vols. London, 1840.

Furnivall, F. J., ed. *Ballads from Manuscripts: Ballads on the Condition of England in Henry VIII's and Edward VI's Reigns.* 2 vols. London, 1868–72.

Gascoigne, George. *A Hundreth Sundrie Flowres.* Ed. G. W. Pigman III. Oxford: Clarendon Press, 2000. Contains *The Adventures of Master F. J., The Devises of Sundrie Gentlemen,* additions from *The Posies,* and *Certayne Notes of Instruction.*

The Geneva Bible: A Facsimile of the 1560 Edition. Madison: University of Wisconsin Press, 1969.

Giovio, Paolo. *The Worthy tract of Paulus Iouius, contayning a Discourse of rare inuentions, both Militarie and Amorous called Imprese.* Trans. Samuel Daniel. London, 1585.

Gorges, Sir Arthur. *Poems.* Ed. Helen Estabrook Sandison. Oxford: Clarendon Press, 1953.

Goyet, Francis, ed. *Traités de poétique et de rhétorique de la Renaissance.* Paris: Librairie Générale Française, 1990.

Hall, Edward. *The Union of the Two Noble and Illustre Famelies of Lancastre and Yorke.* 1548. Reprint. London, 1809.

Harington, Sir John. *A Brief Apology of Poetry.* In Ludovico Ariosto. *Orlando Furioso.* 1532. Trans. Sir John Harington. 1591. Oxford: Clarendon Press, 1972. 1–15.

——, trans. Joannes de Mediolano. *The Englishmans Doctor. Or, The School of Salerne.* London, 1607.

Harvey, Gabriel. *Gabriel Harvey's Marginalia.* Coll. and ed. G. C. Moore Smith. Stratford-upon-Avon: Shakespeare Head Press, 1913.

——. *Letter-Book of Gabriel Harvey, 1573–1580.* Ed. Edward John Long Scott. Camden Society Publications. New series. Vol. 33. London, 1884.

Haslewood, Joseph, ed. *Ancient Critical Essays.* 2 vols. London, 1811.

Hayward, John. *The Life and Raigne of King Edward the Sixt.* Ed. Barrett L. Beer. Kent, Ohio: Kent State University Press, 1993.

Hearsey, Marguerite. *The Complaint of Henry Duke of Buckingham.* 1563. Yale Studies in English 86. New Haven: Yale University Press, 1936.

Henryson, Robert. *Poems.* Ed. Charles Elliott. Oxford: Clarendon Press, 1963.

Herberay, Nicolas de, Sieur des Essarts, trans. *Amadis de Gaule.* 4 vols. Paris, 1548–1559.

Herman, Peter C., ed. *Sir Philip Sidney's "An Apology for Poetry" and "Astrophil and Stella": Texts and Contexts.* Glen Allen, Va.: College Publishing, 2001.

Heywood, John. *The Proverbs, Epigrams, and Miscellanies of John Heywood.* Ed. J. S. Farmer. 1906. New York: Barnes & Noble, 1966.

Holinshed, Raphael. *Holinshed's Chronicles: England, Scotland, and Ireland.* 1587. Ed. Henry Ellis. 1807–8. 6 vols. Reprinted with a new intro. by Vernon F. Snow. New York: AMS, 1976.

Hoskins, John. *Directions for Speech and Style.* 1599–1600. Ed. Hoyt H. Hudson. Princeton: Princeton University Press, 1935.

Hucbaldus [Hucbald de Saint-Amand]. *Ecloga de laudibus calvitii.* In *Patrologia Latina.* Ed. J. P. Migne. Vol. 132. Paris, 1880. 1042.

Isidore of Seville. *Etymologiarum sive originum libri XX.* Ed. W. M. Lindsay. 2 vols. Oxford: Oxford University Press, 1911.

James I. *Ane schort Treatise, conteining some revlis and cautelis to be observit and eschewit in Scottis Poesie.* In *The Essayes of a Prentise, in the Divine Art of Poesie.* Edinburgh, 1584. In Smith, *Essays* 1:208–25.

Jonson, Ben. *Ben Jonson.* Ed. C. H. Herford, Percy Simpson, and Evelyn Simpson. 11 vols. Oxford: Clarendon Press, 1925–52.

Journal of the House of Lords. Vol. 1: 1509–1577. London, 1802.

Kinney, Arthur, ed. *Renaissance Drama: An Anthology of Plays and Entertainments.* Malden, Mass.: Blackwell, 1999.

Legh, Gerard. *The accedens of armory.* London, 1562.

Leo, Johannes [Africanus]. *A Geographical Historie of Africa.* 1550. Trans. John Pory. 1600. Amsterdam: Da Capo Press, 1969.

Letters and papers, foreign and domestic, of the reign of Henry VIII. Arr. and cat. J. S. Brewer et al. London, 1862–1910.

Leunclavius, Joannus. *Pandectes Historiae Turcicae.* Supplement to his *Annales Sultanorum Othmanidarum.* Frankfurt, 1588. In *Patrologia Graeca.* Ed. J. P. Migne. Vol. 159. Paris, 1866. 418–45.

"The Life of Henrye Fitz-Alan, last Earle of Arundell." Ed. J[ohn] G[ough] N[ichols]. *The Gentleman's Magazine* 103, pt. 2 (1833): 10–18, 118–24, 209–15.

Lily, William. *A Short Introduction of Grammar.* London, 1567.

Lipsius, Justus. *Politicorum, siue, Ciuilis doctrinae libri sex, qui ad principatum maxime spectant.* London, 1590.

——. *Six Bookes of Politickes or Civil Doctrine.* Trans. William Jones. 1594. New York: Da Capo Press, 1970.

Literature Online: English Poetry Full-Text Database. http://lion.chadwyck.com.

Literature Online: English Verse Drama Full-Text Database. http://lion.chadwyck.com.

Lodge, Thomas. *A Defence of Poetry, Music, and Stage Plays.* 1579. In Smith, *Essays* 1:61–86.

London Chronicle during the reigns of Henry the Seventh and Henry the Eighth. Ca. 1545. Ed. Clarence Hopper. *Camden Miscellany.* Vol 4. London: Camden Society, 1859.

Lydgate, John. *The Fall of Princes.* 1431–38. London, 1527.

Lyly, John. *Complete Works.* Ed. R. Warwick Bond. 3 vols. Oxford: Clarendon Press, 1902.

Machiavelli, Niccolò. *"The Prince" and Other Writings.* Trans. Wayne A. Rebhorn. New York: Barnes & Noble, 2003.

Machyn, Henry. *The Diary of Henry Machyn, Citizen and Merchant-Taylor of London, from A.D. 1550 to A.D. 1563.* Ed. John Gough Nichols. Camden Society Publications [First Series]. London, 1848.

Macrobe [Macrobius, Ambrosius Aurelius Theodosius]. *Les Saturnales.* Ed. and trans. Henri Bornecque. 2 vols. Paris: Garnier, 1937.

Marston, John. *The Malcontent.* Ed. George K. Hunter. London: Methuen, 1975.

May, Steven W. *The Elizabethan Courtier Poets: The Poems and Their Contexts.* 1991. Asheville, N.C.: Pegasus, 1999.

McCutcheon, Elizabeth, ed. *Sir Nicholas Bacon's Great House Sententiae.* *English Literary Renaissance,* Supplement no. 3 (1977).

Medieval English Political Writings. Ed. James M. Dean. Kalamazoo, Mich.: Medieval Institute Publications, 1996.

Meres, Francis. *Palladis Tamia.* 1598. In Smith, *Essays* 2:308–24.

Merrill, L. R. *The Life and Poems of Nicholas Grimald*. New Haven: Yale University Press, 1925.

Milton, John. *Complete Poems and Major Prose*. Ed. Merritt Y. Hughes. Indianapolis: Bobbs-Merrill, 1957.

——. *Complete Prose Works*. Gen. ed. Don M. Wolfe. 8 vols. New Haven: Yale University Press, 1953–82.

Mosellanus, Petrus [Peter Schade]. *Tabulae in schemata et tropos: In rhetorica Philippi Melanchthonis: Item In copiam duplicem Erasmi Roterodami. 1527.* Strasbourg, 1549.

Muir, Kenneth. *Life and Letters of Sir Thomas Wyatt*. Liverpool: Liverpool University Press, 1963.

Mulcaster, Richard. *The First Part of the Elementarie*. London, 1582.

Nashe, Thomas. *Works*. Ed. R. B. McKerrow. 5 vols. 1910. Oxford: Blackwell, 1966.

Nichols, John. *The Progresses and Public Processions of Queen Elizabeth*. 3 vols. London, 1823.

Original Letters relative to the English Reformation. Ed. and trans. Hastings Robinson. 2 vols. Cambridge: Parker Society, 1846.

Paradin, Claude. *Devises heroïques*. Lyons, 1557.

Paradin, Claudius, Canon of Beauvieu. *The Heroicall Devises, whereunto are added the Lord Gabriel Symeons and others*. Trans. P. S. London, 1591.

Peacham, Henry (the elder). *The Garden of Eloquence*. 1593. Facsimile reproduction, with selected pages from the 1577 edition and an introduction by William G. Crane. Gainesville, Fla.: Scholars' Facsimiles and Reprints, 1954.

Peacham, Henry (the younger). *The Compleat Gentleman*. 1622. New York: Da Capo Press, 1968.

Pedigrees from the visitation of Hampshire made by Thomas Benolt, Clarenceulx anno 1530: enlarged with the vissitation of the same county made by Robert Cooke, Clarenceulx anno 1575 both which are continued with the vissitation made by John Phillipott, Somersett (for William Camden, Clarenceux) in anno 1622 most part then done & finished in anno 1634. As collected by Richard Mundy in Harleian ms. no. 1544. Ed. W. Harry Rylands. Publications of the Harleian Society. Vol. 64. London: Harleian Society, 1913.

Peletier, Jacques. *Art poétique*. 1555. In Goyet 235–344.

Percy, Thomas. *Reliques of Ancient English Poetry*. Ed. Henry B. Wheatley. 3 vols. London, 1886.

Petrarch, Francis [Francesco Petrarca]. *Petrarch's Lyric Poems: The Rime Sparse and Other Lyrics*. Ed. and trans. Robert M. Durling. Cambridge: Harvard University Press, 1976.

The Phoenix Nest. 1593. Ed. Hyder E. Rollins. Cambridge: Harvard University Press, 1931.

The Pleasant History of the Life and Death of Will Summers. 1676. Reprint. London, 1794.

Priscian. *Institutiones grammaticae*. Basel, 1554.

Publilius Syrus. *Sententiae*. Ed. Otto Friedrich. Hildesheim: Georg Olms, 1964.

Ralegh, Sir Walter. *The Poems of Sir Walter Ralegh: A Historical Edition*. Ed. Michael Rudick. Tempe: Arizona Center for Medieval and Renaissance Studies in conjunction with Renaissance English Text Society, 1999.

Rebhorn, Wayne A., trans. and ed. *Renaissance Debates on Rhetoric*. Ithaca: Cornell University Press, 2000.

Rich, Barnaby. *Allarme to England*. London, 1578.

Ronsard, Pierre. *Abrégé de l'art poétique français*. In Goyet 465–87.

Rufinianus, Iulius. *De figuris sententiarum et elocutionis liber*. In Von Halm 38–62.

Rutilius Lupus. *Schemata Lexeos*. In Von Halm 3–21.

Sandys, George. *Ovid's Metamorphosis Englished, Mythologized, and Represented in Figures*. 1626. Ed. Karl K. Hulley and Stanley T. Vandersall. Lincoln: University of Nebraska Press, 1970.

Sargent, Ralph M. *The Life and Lyrics of Sir Edward Dyer*. 1935. Oxford: Clarendon Press, 1968.

Scaliger, Julius Caesar. *Poetices Libri Septem*. Lyon, 1561. Reprint. Stuttgart: Friedrich Frommann Verlag, 1964.

School of Salerno. *Conservandae bonae valetudinis praecepta*. Frankfurt, 1573.

Sébillet, Thomas. *Art poétique français*. In Goyet 37–183.

Servius. *In Vergilii carmina commentarii*. Ed. Georg Thilo and Hermann Hager. 3 vols. Leipzig, 1923.

Shakespeare, William. *The Complete Works of Shakespeare*. Ed. David Bevington. 5th ed. New York: Pearson/Longman, 1992.

Sherry, Richard. *A Treatise of Schemes and Tropes*. 1550. Delmar, N.Y.: Scholars' Facsimiles and Reprints, 1961.

Sidney, Sir Philip. *The Defence of Poesy*. In *Sir Philip Sidney*. Ed. Katherine Duncan-Jones. The Oxford Authors. Oxford: Oxford University Press, 1989. 212–50.

——. *Poems*. Ed. William A. Ringler. Oxford: Oxford University Press, 1962.

Skelton, John. *John Skelton's Complete Poems, 1460–1529*. Ed. Philip Henderson. 4th ed. London: Dent, 1964.

Smith, G. Gregory, ed. *Elizabethan Critical Essays*. 2 vols. Oxford: Oxford University Press, 1904.

Smith, Sir Thomas. *De Republica Anglorum*. Ed. Mary Dewar. Cambridge: Cambridge University Press, 1982.

——. "Sir Thomas Smith's orations for and against the Queen's marriage." 1561. In John Strype. *The Life of the Learned Sir Thomas Smith, Knight*. Oxford, 1820. Appendix III. 184–259. [Details regarding MS sources appear in Dewar 212–13.]

Southern, John. *Pandora*. London, 1584.

Southwell, Robert. *The Poems of Robert Southwell, S.J.* Ed. James H. McDonald and Nancy Pollard Brown. Oxford: Clarendon Press, 1967.

Spenser, Edmund. *Poetical Works*. Ed. J. C. Smith and E. de Selincourt. Oxford Standard Authors. Oxford: Oxford University Press, 1912.

——. *The Shepheardes Calender*. In *The Yale Edition of the Shorter Poems of Edmund Spenser*. Ed. William A. Oram et al. New Haven: Yale University Press, 1989. 12–213.

——. *Spenser-Harvey Correspondence*. 1580. In *Poetical Works*. Ed. J. C. Smith and E. de Selincourt. Oxford Standard Authors. Oxford: Oxford University Press, 1912. 609–12, 623–41.

——. *A View of the State of Ireland*. 1596–98. Ed. Andrew Hadfield and Willy Maley. Oxford: Blackwell, 1997.

Statutes of the Realm, from Magna Carta to the End of the Reign of Queen Anne . . . from original records and authentic manuscripts. London, 1810–28.

Sternhold, Thomas, John Hopkins, and others. *The Whole Book of Psalms, collected into English Metre*. 1562.

Strype, John. *Memorials of the most reverend father in God Thomas Cranmer*. 2 vols. London, 1853.

Surrey, Henry Howard, Earl of. *Poems.* Ed. Emrys Jones. Oxford: Clarendon Press, 1964.

Susenbrotus, Joannes. *Epitome troporum ac schematum et grammaticorum & rhetorum: ad autores tum prophanos tum sacros intelligendos non minus utilis quam necessaria.* Zurich, 1540.

Tottel's Miscellany. 1557. Ed. Hyder E. Rollins. 2 vols. 1928. Revised and reprinted. Cambridge: Harvard University Press, 1965.

Turberville, George. *Epitaphes, Epigrams, Songs and Sonets* and *Epitaphes and Sonnettes.* 1567, 1576. Intro. Richard J. Panofsky. Delmar, N.Y.: Scholars' Facsimiles and Reprints, 1977.

Two London Chronicles from the Collections of John Stow. Ed. Charles Lethbridge Kingsford. *Camden Miscellany.* Vol. 12. London: Camden Society, 1910.

Vaux, Thomas, Lord Vaux. *The Poems of Thomas, Lord Vaux . . . Edward, Earl of Oxford . . . Robert, Earl of Essex . . . and Walter, Earl of Essex.* Ed. Alexander B. Grosart. *Miscellanies of The Fuller Worthies' Library.* Vol. 4. Printed for private circulation, 1872. 349–93.

Vergil, Polydore. *An Abridgment . . . De Rerum Inventoribus.* Trans. Thomas Langley. London, 1546.

Vickers, Brian, ed. *English Renaissance Literary Criticism.* Oxford: Clarendon Press, 1999.

Victor, Sextus Aurelius. *De vita et moribus imperatorum romanorum.* Paris: Les Belles Lettres, 1999.

Vives, Juan Luis. *De ratione dicendi.* In *Opera omnia.* Vol. 2. Ed. Gregorio Majansio. Valencia, 1782. 87–237.

Von Halm, Karl Felix, ed. *Rhetores latini minores.* 1863. Frankfurt am Main: Minerva, 1964.

Wagner, Bernard M. "New Poems by Edward Dyer." *Review of English Studies* 11 (1935): 466–71.

Webbe, William. *A Discourse of English Poetrie.* 1586. In Smith, *Essays* 1:226–302.

Weldon, Sir Anthony. *The Court and Character of King James.* London, 1650.

Whetstone, George. *Dedication to "Promos and Cassandra."* 1578. In Vickers, *English Renaissance Literary Criticism* 172–74.

——. *The English Myrrour.* London, 1586.

Wilson, Thomas. *The Art of Rhetoric.* 1560. Ed. Peter E. Medine. University Park: Pennsylvania State University Press, 1994.

Wriothesley, Charles. *A Chronicle of England during the reigns of the Tudors from A.D. 1485 to 1559.* Ed. William Douglas Hamilton. 2 vols. Camden Society Publications [New Series]. London, 1875–77.

Wyatt, Sir Thomas. *The Complete Poems.* Ed. R. A. Rebholz. New Haven: Yale University Press, 1978.

Wyngaerde, Anthonis van den. *Wyngaerde's Panorama of London Circa 1544.* Ed. Howard Colvin and Susan Foister. London: London Topographical Society in association with the Ashmolean Museum, Oxford, 1996.

Later Sources

Atkins, J. W. H. "The Art of Poetry: Gascoigne, Harvey, 'E. K.,' Webbe, Puttenham." In *English Literary Criticism: The Renascence.* New York: Barnes & Noble/London: Methuen, 1947. 139–78.

Attridge, Derek. "Puttenham's Perplexity: Nature, Art, and the Supplement in Renaissance Poetic Theory." In *Literary Theory/Renaissance Texts.* Ed. Patricia Parker and David Quint. Baltimore: Johns Hopkins University Press, 1986. 257–79.

——. *Well-Weighed Syllables: Elizabethan Verse in Classical Metres*. Cambridge: Cambridge University Press, 1974.

Barish, Jonas. *The Antitheatrical Prejudice*. Berkeley: University of California Press, 1981.

Baroway, Israel. "The Accentual Theory of Hebrew Prosody: A Further Study in Renaissance Interpretation of Biblical Form." *ELH* 17 (1950): 115–35.

——. "Tremellius, Sidney, and Biblical Verse." *Modern Language Notes* 49 (1934): 145–49.

Beare, William. *The Roman Stage*. London: Methuen, 1964.

Bergeron, David. *English Civic Pageantry*. London: Edward Arnold, 1971.

Bindoff, S. T. *The House of Commons, 1509–1558*. 3 vols. London: Secker and Warburg, 1982.

Boyle, A. L. "Henry Fitzalan, 12th Earl of Arundel: Politics and Culture in the Tudor Nobility." Ph.D. diss. Oxford University, 2002.

Cannon, Christopher. "Chaucer and Rape: Uncertainty's Certainties." *Studies in the Age of Chaucer: The Yearbook of the New Chaucer Society* 22 (2000): 67–92.

——. "Malory's Crime: Chivalric Identity and the Evil Will." In *Medieval Literature and Historical Inquiry: Essays in Honor of Derek Pearsall*. Ed. David Aers. Cambridge: D. S. Brewer, 2000. 159–83.

——. "Raptus in the Chaumpiegne Release and a Newly Discovered Document Concerning the Life of Geoffrey Chaucer." *Speculum: A Journal of Medieval Studies* 68 (1993): 79–94.

Chambers, E. K. *The Elizabethan Stage*. 4 vols. Oxford: Clarendon Press, 1923.

Chaucer Life-Records. Ed. Martin M. Crow and Clair C. Olson. Oxford: Clarendon Press, 1966.

Cole, Mary Hill. *The Portable Queen: Elizabeth I and the Politics of Ceremony*. Amherst: University of Massachusetts Press, 1999.

Colie, Rosalie. *Paradoxia Epidemica: The Renaissance Tradition of Paradox*. Princeton: Princeton University Press, 1966.

Collins, Arthur. *The Peerage of England*. 4th ed. London, 1768.

Cook, Albert S. "Chaucerian Papers—I." *Transactions of the Connecticut Academy of Arts and Sciences* 23 (1919): 38–39.

Crewe, Jonathan V. "The Hegemonic Theater of George Puttenham." *English Literary Renaissance* 16 (1986): 71–85.

——. "Punctuating Shakespeare." *Shakespeare Studies* 28 (2000): 23–42.

Crum, Margaret, ed. *First-Line Index of English Poetry, 1500–1800, in Manuscripts of the Bodleian Library, Oxford*. Oxford: Clarendon Press, 1969.

Curtius, Ernst Robert. *European Literature and the Latin Middle Ages*. Trans. Willard R. Trask. 1953. New York: Harper and Row, 1963.

Dewar, Mary. *Sir Thomas Smith: A Tudor Intellectual in Office*. London: University of London Press/Athlone Press, 1964.

Dormer, Ernest W. *Gray of Reading: A 16th-Century Controversialist and Ballad Writer*. Reading: Bradley & Son, 1923.

Dunn, Alastair. *The Great Rising of 1381: The Peasants' Revolt and England's Failed Revolution*. Stroud: Tempus, 2002.

Eagle, Roderick L. " 'The Arte of English Poesie' (1589)." *Notes and Queries* 201 (1956): 188–90.

——. "The Authorship of *The Arte of English Poesie* (1589)." *Baconiana* 27 (1943): 38–41.

The Early Modern English Dictionaries Database. Ed. Ian Lancashire. http://www.chass.utoronto.ca/english/emed/emedd.html#dic.

European Literary Careers: The Author from Antiquity to the Renaissance. Ed. Patrick Cheney and Frederick A. de Armas. Toronto: University of Toronto Press, 2002.

Ferguson, Arthur B. *Utter Antiquity: Perceptions of Prehistory in Renaissance England.* Durham, N.C.: Duke University Press, 1993.

Finney, Gretchen. *Musical Backgrounds for English Literature, 1580–1650.* New Brunswick, N.J.: Rutgers University Press, 1962.

Fisher, John H. *John Gower, Moral Philosopher and Friend of Chaucer.* New York: New York University Press, 1964.

Fox, Adam. *Oral and Literate Culture in England, 1500–1700.* Oxford: Clarendon Press, 2000.

Franklyn, Charles A. H. *A Genealogical History of the Families of Paulet (or Pawlett), Berewe (or Barrow), Lawrence, and Parker.* Bedford: Foundry Press, 1963.

Freinkel, Lisa. "The Use of the Fetish." *Shakespeare Studies* 33 (2005): 115–22.

Galyon, Linda. "Puttenham's *Enargeia* and *Energeia*: New Twists for Old Terms." *Philological Quarterly* 60 (1981): 29–40.

Geyl, Pieter. *The Revolt of the Netherlands, 1555–1609.* 2nd ed. London: Benn, 1958.

Ghazvinian, John. " 'A certain tickling humour': English Travellers, 1560–1660." Ph.D. diss. Oxford University, 2003.

Gim, Lisa. "Blasoning 'the Princesse Paragon': The Workings of George Puttenham's 'False Semblant' in His *Partheniades* to Queen Elizabeth." *Modern Language Studies* 28 (1998): 75–89.

Greene, Roland. "Fictions of Immanence, Fictions of Embassy." In *The Project of Prose in Early Modern Europe and the New World.* Ed. Roland Greene and Elizabeth Fowler. Cambridge: Cambridge University Press, 1997. 176–202.

Harvey, I. M. W. *Jack Cade's Rebellion of 1450.* Oxford: Clarendon Press, 1991.

Hasler. P. W. *The House of Commons, 1558–1603.* 3 vols. London: History of Parliament Trust, 1981.

Hexter, J. H. "The Education of the Aristocracy in the Renaissance." In *Reappraisals in History.* Evanston: Northwestern University Press, 1961. 45–70.

Hillman, David. "Puttenham, Shakespeare, and the Abuse of Rhetoric." *Studies in English Literature, 1500–1900* 36 (1996): 73–90.

Hogrefe, Pearl. *The Life and Times of Sir Thomas Elyot, Englishman.* Ames: Iowa State University Press, 1967.

Hudson, Hoyt H. *The Epigram in the English Renaissance.* Princeton: Princeton University Press, 1947.

Hughes, Charles. "Puttenham's 'Arte of English Poesie.' " *Notes and Queries*, ser. 11, vol. 1 (1910): 404.

Ing, Catherine. *Elizabethan Lyrics: A Study in the Development of English Metres and Their Relation to Poetic Effect.* London: Chatto & Windus, 1951.

Jansen, Sharon L. *Dangerous Talk and Strange Behavior: Women and Popular Resistance to the Reforms of Henry VIII.* New York: St. Martin's, 1996.

——. *Political Protest and Prophecy under Henry VIII.* Rochester, N.Y.: Boydell & Brewer, 1991.

Javitch, Daniel. "The Impure Motives of Elizabethan Poetry." *Genre* 15 (1982): 225–38.

——. "Poetry and Court Conduct: Puttenham's *Arte of English Poesie* in the Light of Castiglione's *Cortegiano.*" *Modern Language Notes* 87 (1972): 865–82.

——. *Poetry and Courtliness in Renaissance England.* Princeton: Princeton University Press, 1978.

——. *Proclaiming a Classic: The Canonization of Orlando Furioso.* Princeton: Princeton University Press, 1991.

Jones, Richard F. *The Triumph of the English Language: A Survey of Opinions Concerning the Vernacular from the Introduction of Printing to the Restoration.* Stanford: Stanford University Press, 1953.

Jordan, W. K. *Edward VI: The Threshold of Power.* Cambridge: Harvard University Press, 1970.

Kegl, Rosemary. "The Rhetoric of Concealment: Figuring Gender and Class in Renaissance Literature." Ph.D. diss. Cornell University, 1990.

——. " 'Those Terrible Aproches': Sexuality, Social Mobility, and Resisting the Courtliness of Puttenham's *The Arte of English Poesie.*" *English Literary Renaissance* 20 (1990): 179–208.

Knauf, David M. "George Puttenham's Theory of Natural and Artificial Discourse." *Speech Monographs* 34 (1967): 34–42.

Korn, A. L. "Puttenham and the Oriental Pattern-Poem." *Comparative Literature* 6 (1954): 289–303.

Laroque, François. *Shakespeare's Festive World: Elizabethan Seasonal Entertainment and the Professional Stage.* Cambridge: Cambridge University Press, 1991.

Lausberg, Heinrich. *Handbook of Literary Rhetoric: A Foundation for Literary Study.* Foreword by George A. Kennedy; trans. Matthew T. Bliss, Annemiek Jansen, and David E. Orton; ed. David E. Orton and R. Dean Anderson. Boston: Brill, 1998.

Lehmberg, Stanford E. *Sir Thomas Elyot, Tudor Humanist.* Austin: University of Texas Press, 1960.

Leisher, John F. "George Puttenham and Emblemata." *Boston University Studies in English* 1 (1955): 1–8.

Levin, Harry. *The Overreacher: A Study of Christopher Marlowe.* Cambridge: Harvard University Press, 1952.

Lewis, C. S. *The Allegory of Love.* 1936. Reprint. Oxford: Oxford University Press, 1958.

Lezra, Jacques. " 'The Lady Was a Litle Peruerse': The 'Gender' of Persuasion in Puttenham's *Arte of English Poesie.*" In *Engendering Men: The Question of Male Feminist Criticism.* Ed. Joseph A. Boone and Michael Cadden. New York: Routledge, 1990. 53–65.

Lindquist, Eric. "An Elizabethan Writer and His Books: The Misadventures of George Puttenham's Library." Paper presented at the annual conference of the Society for the History of Authorship, Reading, and Publishing. London, 2002.

Lisak, Catherine. "Le 'Poète épique' de Puttenham: Une Étude Tudor de la théorie des genres." In *Après l'usure de toutes les routes: Retour sur l'épopée.* Ed. Jacques Darras. Brussels: Le Cri, 1997. 155–66.

Loades, D. M. *John Dudley, Duke of Northumberland, 1504–1553.* Oxford: Clarendon Press, 1996.

Luborsky, Ruth Samson, and Elizabeth Morley Ingram. *A Guide to English Illustrated Books, 1536–1603.* Tempe, Ariz.: Medieval and Renaissance Texts and Studies, 1998.

Marotti, Arthur F. *Manuscript, Print, and the English Renaissance Lyric*. Ithaca: Cornell University Press, 1995.

Masters, Betty R. "The Lord Mayor's Household before 1600." In *Studies in London History*. Ed. A. E. J. Hollaender and William Kellaway. London: Hodder & Stoughton, 1969. 95–114.

Mattingly, Garrett. *Renaissance Diplomacy*. Boston: Houghton Mifflin, 1955.

Matz, Robert. "Poetry, Politics, and Discursive Forms: The Case of Puttenham's *Arte of English Poesie*." *Genre: Forms of Discourse and Culture* 30 (1997): 195–213.

May, Steven W. "The Authorship of 'My mind to me a kingdom is.'" *Review of English Studies* 26 (1975): 385–94.

———. "George Puttenham's Lewd and Illicit Career." *Texas Studies in Literature and Language*. In press.

———. "Puttenham, George (1529–1590/91)." *Oxford Dictionary of National Biography*. http://www.oxforddnb.com.content.lib.utexas.edu:2048/view/article/22913, accessed 10 Aug 2006.

———. "Queen Elizabeth's 'Future Foes': Editing Manuscripts with the *First-Line Index of Elizabethan Verse* (a Future Friend)." *New Ways of Looking at Old Texts* 3, 1997–2001: 1–12.

———. *Sir Walter Ralegh*. Boston: Twayne, 1989.

———. "Tudor Aristocrats and the Mythical 'Stigma of Print.'" In *Renaissance Papers, 1980*. Ed. A. Leigh DeNeef and M. Thomas Hester. Raleigh: Southeastern Renaissance Conference, 1981. 11–18.

———, and William A. Ringler, eds. *Elizabethan Poetry: A Bibliography and First-Line Index of English Verse, 1559–1603*. 3 vols. New York: Thoemmes Continuum, 2004.

Mirbach, Lucia. *Form und Gehalt der substantivischen Reihungen in George Puttenhams "The Arte of English Poesie" (1589)*. Tübingen: Niemeyer, 1989.

Montrose, Louis Adrian. "Of Gentlemen and Shepherds: The Politics of Elizabethan Pastoral Form." *English Literary History* 50 (1983): 415–60.

———. "'Shaping Fantasies': Figurations of Gender and Power in Elizabethan Culture." *Representations* 1 (1983): 61–94.

Motley, John Lothrop. *The Rise of the Dutch Republic: A History*. 3 vols. Philadelphia: David McKay, n.d. [1856?].

Müller, Wolfgang. "Das Problem des Stils in der Poetik der Renaissance." In *Renaissance-Poetik/Renaissance Poetics*. Ed. Heinrich F. Plett. Berlin: de Gruyter, 1994. 133–46.

Nash, Walter. "George Puttenham." In *British Rhetoricians and Logicians, 1500–1600: Second Series*. Ed. Edward A. Malone. Detroit: Gale, 2003. 229–48.

The New Princeton Encyclopedia of Poetry and Poetics. Ed. Alex Preminger and T. V. F. Brogan. Princeton: Princeton University Press, 1993.

North, Marcy L. "Anonymity's Revelations in *The Arte of English Poesie*." *Studies in English Literature, 1500–1900* 39 (1999): 1–18.

———. *The Anonymous Renaissance: Cultures of Discretion in Tudor-Stuart England*. Chicago: University of Chicago Press, 2003.

Oxford Dictionary of National Biography. Oxford: Oxford University Press, 2004. http://www.oxforddnb.com.

Plett, Heinrich F. "Elisabethanische Hofpoetik: Gesellschaftlicher Code und ästhetische Norm in Puttenhams *Arte of English Poesie*." In *Europäische Hofkultur im 16. und 17. Jahrhundert*. Ed. August Buch, Georg Kauffmann,

Blake Lee Spahr, and Conrad Wiedemann. Vol. 2. Hamburg: Hauswedell, 1981. 41–50.

——. "The Place and Function of Style in Renaissance Poetics." In *Renaissance Eloquence: Studies in the Theory and Practice of Renaissance Rhetoric*. Ed. James J. Murphy. Berkeley: University of California Press, 1983. 356–75.

Powell, Jason. "Puttenham's *Arte of English Poesie* and Thomas Wyatt's Diplomacy." *Notes and Queries* 52 (2005): 174–76.

Quint, David. *Origin and Originality in Renaissance Literature: Versions of the Source*. New Haven: Yale University Press, 1983.

Rebhorn, Wayne A. *The Emperor of Men's Minds: Literature and the Renaissance Discourse of Rhetoric*. Ithaca: Cornell University Press, 1995.

——. " 'His tail at commandment': George Puttenham and the Carnivalization of Rhetoric." In *A Companion to Rhetoric and Rhetorical Criticism*. Ed. Walter Jost and Wendy Olmsted. Oxford: Blackwell, 2004. 96–111.

——. "Outlandish Fears: Defining Decorum in Renaissance Rhetoric." *Intertexts* 4 (2000): 3–24.

Roberts-Smith, Jennifer. "Puttenham Rehabilitated: The Significance of 'Tune' in *The Arte of English Poesie*." *TEXT Technology* 12 (2003): 75–91.

Rushton, William Lowes. *Shakespeare and "The Arte of English Poesie."* Liverpool: Young, 1909.

Saunders, J. W. "The Stigma of Print: A Note on the Social Bases of Tudor Poetry." *Essays in Criticism* 1 (1951): 139–64.

Scarisbrick, J. J. *Henry VIII*. Berkeley: University of California Press, 1968.

Scholz, Bernhard F. "Konstruktionen des Sichtbaren: Frühmoderne Regeln der Bedeutung, am Beispiel der Darstellung des Figurengedichts in den Poetiken Julius Caesar Scaligers und George Puttenhams." In *Regeln der Bedeutung: Zur Theorie der Bedeutung literarischer Texte*. Ed. Fotis Jannidis, Gerhard Lauer, Matias Martinez, and Simone Winko. Berlin: de Gruyter, 2003. 628–43.

Schuman, Sharo. "Sixteenth-Century English Quantitative Verse: Its Ends, Means, and Products." *Modern Philology* 74 (1977): 335–49.

Seznec, Jean. *The Survival of the Pagan Gods: The Mythological Tradition and Its Place in Renaissance Humanism and Art*. New York: Pantheon, 1953.

Shuger, Debora. "Conceptions of Style." In *The Cambridge History of Literary Criticism: The Renaissance*. Vol. 3. Ed. Glyn P. Norton. Cambridge: Cambridge University Press, 1999. 176–86.

Silcox, Mary V. " 'Ornament of Civill Life': The Device in Puttenham's *The Arte of English Poesie*." In *Aspects of Renaissance and Baroque Symbol Theory, 1500–1700*. Ed. Peter M. Daly and John Manning. New York: AMS Press, 1999. 39–49.

Silva Rhetoricae. Ed. Gideon O. Burton. http://humanities.byu.edu/rhetoric/silva.htm.

Simon, Joan. *Education and Society in Tudor England*. Cambridge: Cambridge University Press, 1967.

Skeat, W. W. *Chaucerian and Other Pieces: A Supplement to the Complete Works of Geoffrey Chaucer*. Oxford: Clarendon Press, 1892.

Sloane, Thomas O. *On the Contrary: The Protocol of Traditional Rhetoric*. Washington, D.C.: Catholic University of America Press, 1997.

Smith, Constance I. "Some Ideas on Education before Locke." *Journal of the History of Ideas* 23 (1962): 403–6.

Stanco, Michele. "Teoria, norma e canone poetico in *The Arte of English Poesie* (1589) di George Puttenham: L'elaborazione di una grammatica teorico-normativa e di un canone poetico in vista della formazione del poeta di corte e della fondazione di un'arte della poesia inglese." *Passaggi* 7 (1993): 103–35.

Stephens, Walter. *Giants in Those Days: Folklore, Ancient History, and Nationalism.* Lincoln: University of Nebraska Press, 1989.

Stone, Lawrence. *The Family, Sex and Marriage, 1500–1800.* London: Weidenfeld and Nicolson, 1977.

——. "Social Mobility in England, 1500–1700." *Past & Present* 33 (1966): 17–55.

Stretton, Tim. *Women Waging Law in Elizabethan England.* Cambridge: Cambridge University Press, 1998.

Strier, Richard. "Faithful Servants: Shakespeare's Praise of Disobedience." In *The Historical Renaissance: New Essays on Tudor and Stuart Literature and Culture.* Ed. Heather Dubrow and Richard Strier. Chicago, 1989: 104–33.

Sugden, Edward H. *A Topographical Dictionary to the Works of Shakespeare and His Fellow Dramatists.* Manchester: Manchester University Press, 1925.

Taylor, Barry. "'The Instrumentality of Ornament': George Puttenham's *Arte of English Poesie.*" In *Vagrant Writing: Social and Semiotic Disorders in the English Renaissance.* Toronto: University of Toronto Press, 1991. 127–50.

Thirsk, Joan. "Younger Sons in the Seventeenth Century." *History* 54 (1969): 358–77.

Thomas, David. "Leases in Reversion on the Crown's Lands, 1558–1603." *Economic History Review* 30 (1977): 67–72.

Tilley, Morris P. *A Dictionary of the Proverbs in England in the Sixteenth and Seventeenth Centuries.* Ann Arbor: University of Michigan Press, 1950.

Traci, Philip J. "The Literary Qualities of Puttenham's *Arte of English Poesie.*" *Renaissance Papers* (1957): 87–93.

Trousdale, Marion. "Puttenham's Figures of Decoration." In *Shakespeare and the Rhetoricians.* Chapel Hill: University of North Carolina Press, 1961. 81–94.

Turner, Henry S. *The English Renaissance Stage: Geometry, Poetics, and the Practical Spatial Arts, 1580–1630.* Oxford: Oxford University Press, 2006.

Van Hook, La Rue. "Greek Rhetorical Terminology in Puttenham's *The Arte of English Poesie.*" *Transactions and Proceedings of the American Philological Association* 45 (1914): 111–28.

Vickers, Brian. *Classical Rhetoric in English Poetry.* Carbondale: Southern Illinois University Press, 1989.

Walther, Hans. *Lateinische Sprichwörter und Sentenzen des Mittelalters.* Göttingen: Vandenhoeck and Ruprecht, 1963–67.

Ward, B. M. "The Authorship of the *Arte of English Poesie*: A Suggestion." *Review of English Studies* 1 (1925): 284–308.

Weinberg, Bernard. *A History of Literary Criticism in the Italian Renaissance.* 2 vols. Chicago: University of Chicago Press, 1961.

Weitzman, Francis W. "Notes on the Elizabethan Elegie." *PMLA* 50 (1935): 435–44.

Wells, Stanley. *Modernizing Shakespeare's Spelling.* Oxford: Clarendon Press, 1979.

Wels, Volkhard. "Imaginatio oder inventio: Das dichterische Schaffen und sein Gegenstand bei Puttenham, Sidney und Temple." *Poetica: Zeitschrift für Sprach- und Literaturwissenschaft* 37 (2005): 65–91.

Whigham, Frank. *Ambition and Privilege: The Social Tropes of Elizabethan Courtesy Theory.* Berkeley: University of California Press, 1984.

——. "Elizabethan Aristocratic Insignia." *Texas Studies in Literature and Language* 27 (1985): 325–53.

——. "A Lacuna in Puttenham's *Arte of English Poesie.*" *English Language Notes* 22 (1984): 20–22.

——. *Seizures of the Will in Early Modern English Drama.* Cambridge: Cambridge University Press, 1996.

Whiting, Bartlett Jere, with Helen Wescott Whiting. *Proverbs, Sentences, and Proverbial Phrases from English Writings Mainly before 1500.* Cambridge: Harvard University Press, 1968.

Williams, Gordon. *A Glossary of Shakespeare's Sexual Language.* London: Athlone, 1997.

Willis, Charles. *George Puttenham and the Authorship of Shakespeare's Sonnets.* St. Leonards-on-Sea, East Sussex: UPSO, 2005.

——. *Shakespeare and George Puttenham's "The Arte of English Poesie."* St. Leonards-on-Sea, East Sussex: UPSO, 2003.

Wilson, Elkin Calhoun. *England's Eliza.* 1939. Reprint. New York: Octagon Books, 1966.

Wilson, F. P. *The English Drama, 1485–1585.* Ed. with biblio., G. K. Hunter. Oxford: Oxford University Press, 1969.

THE ARTE

OF ENGLISH
POESIE.

Contriued into three Bookes: The first of Poets
and Poesie, the second of Proportion,
the third of Ornament.

AT LONDON
Printed by Richard Field, dwelling in the
black-Friers, neere Ludgate.
1589.

TO THE RIGHT HONO-
RABLE SIR WILLIAM CECIL,
KNIGHT, LORD OF BURGHLEY, LORD
HIGH TREASURER OF ENGLAND,

R. F.,[1] Printer, wisheth health and prosperity,

with the commandment and use of

his continual service

T*his book (right Honorable) coming to my hands, with his bare
title without any author's name or any other ordinary address,[2]
I doubted how well it might become me to make you a present
thereof, seeming by many express passages in the same at large,° that
it was by the author intended° to our Sovereign Lady the Queen, and
for her recreation and service chiefly devised, in which case to make
any other person her highness's partner in the honor of his gift, it could
not stand with my duty, nor be without some prejudice to her
Majesty's interest and his merit. Perceiving besides the title to purport
so slender[3] a subject, as nothing almost could be more discrepant
from[4] the gravity of your years and honorable function, whose contem-
plations are every hour more seriously employed upon the public administration and services, I thought it no condign[5] gratification, nor
scarce any good satisfaction for such a person as you. Yet when I considered that bestowing upon your Lordship the first view of this mine
impression[6] (a feat of mine own simple° faculty[7]), it could not cipher[8]*

1. **R. F.** Richard Field.
2. **ordinary address** identifying label.
3. **slender** insignificant.
4. **discrepant from** inconsistent with.
5. **condign** worthy.
6. **impression** printed copy.
7. **faculty** ability.
8. **cipher** diminish, evacuate.

*her Majesty's honor or prerogative in the gift, nor yet the author of his
thanks; and seeing the thing itself to be a device° of some novelty
(which commonly giveth every good thing a special grace) and a novelty so highly tending to the most worthy praises of her Majesty's most
excellent name (dearer to you I dare conceive than any worldly thing
besides), methought I could not devise to have presented your Lordship any gift more agreeable to your appetite, or fitter for my vocation
and ability to bestow, your Lordship being learned and a lover of
learning, my present a book and myself a printer always
ready and desirousto be at your honorable
commandment. And thus I humbly take
my leave from the Blackfriars,
this 28th of May, 1589.*

Your Honor's most humble
at commandment,

R. F.

A colei

Che se stessa rassomiglia,
& non altrui.

This image of Elizabeth may well have been created for the *Art*. Luborsky and Ingram list its first appearance there (no. 20519), and report later uses of it only in T.T.'s *True portraiture of the Kings of England* (1597: no. 23626) and (in an altered "second state") in Holland's translation of Livy's *Romane historie* (1600: no. 16613). Perhaps Field paid for it, with high hopes for the *Art*; maybe instead Puttenham funded the extra expense himself, as part of a possible campaign to recover court favor (probably begun earlier, around 1587, with the *Justification*). The Italian means "To her who resembles herself and no one else."

THE FIRST BOOK
Of Poets and Poesy

CHAPTER I

*What a poet and poesy is, and who may be worthily
said the most excellent poet of our time*

A poet is as much to say as° a maker. And our English name well
conforms with the Greek word, for of ποιεῖν, to make, they call
a maker *poeta*.[1] Such as (by way of resemblance and reverently) we
may say of God, who without any travail° to his divine imagination
made all the world of nought, nor also by any pattern or mold as the
Platonics with their Ideas do fantastically° suppose.[2] Even so the very
poet makes and contrives out of his own brain both the verse and matter of his poem, and not by any foreign copy[3] or example, as doth the
translator, who therefore may well be said a versifier, but not a poet.
The premises considered, it giveth to the name and profession no
small dignity and preeminence above all other artificers, scientific or
mechanical.[4] And nevertheless without any repugnancy[5] at all, a poet
may in some sort be said a follower or imitator, because he can express
the true and lively of every thing is set before him,[6] and which
he taketh in hand to describe; and so in that respect is both a maker

---

1. Cf. Sidney, *Defence* 215; he also explains the meaning of the word through its
etymology.

2. In Plato's view, everything we apprehend through sense perception is patterned
on and derives from eternal or immutable
essences, the "forms" or "ideas," invisible to
the senses but knowable by means of reason,
and including such ideas as those of the Good,
the Beautiful, and even Bed and Dog. The
Platonic notion of ideas was transmitted to
the Renaissance through various intermedi-

aries, including Neoplatonists such as Ploti-
nus (5.8.1), and Roman philosophers such as
Cicero (*Orator* 2.9–10) and Seneca (*Epistolae*
65.7).

3. **copy** pattern, original.

4. **artificers . . . mechanical** practitioners
of arts, whether involving knowledge and
learning or manual labor.

5. **repugnancy** inconsistency.

6. **the true . . . him** i.e., the true and living, lifelike image of everything that is set
before him.

and a counterfeiter,° and poesy an art not only of making, but also of imitation.[7]

And this science° in his perfection cannot grow but by some divine instinct[8]—the Platonics call it *furor*[9]—or by excellence of nature and complexion,[10] or by great subtlety[11] of the spirits and wit,° or by much experience and observation of the world and course of kind,° or peradventure° by all or most part of them. Otherwise how was it possible that Homer, being but a poor private man, and as some say, in his later age blind, should so exactly set forth and describe, as if he had been a most excellent captain or general, the order and array of battles,[12] the conduct of whole armies, the sieges and assaults of cities and towns? Or as some great prince's majordomo[13] and perfect surveyor[14] in court, the order, sumptuousness, and magnificence of royal banquets, feasts, weddings, and interviews? Or as a politician° very prudent, and much inured with[15] the private and public affairs, so gravely examine the laws and ordinances civil, or so profoundly discourse in matters of estate° and forms of all politic regiment?[16] Finally, how could he so naturally paint out the speeches, countenance, and manners° of princely persons and private, to wit, the wrath of Achilles, the magnanimity[17] of Agamemnon, the prudence of Menelaus, the prowess of Hector, the majesty of King Priam, the gravity of Nestor, the policies° and eloquence of Ulysses, the calamities of the distressed queens,[18] and valiance[19] of all the captains and adventurous knights in those lamentable wars of Troy?

It is therefore of poets thus to be conceived, that if they be able to devise and make all these things of themselves, without any subject of verity,[20] that they be (by manner of speech) as creating gods. If they do it by instinct divine or natural, then surely much[21] favored from above. If by their experience, then no doubt very wise men. If by any precedent or pattern laid before them, then truly the most excellent imitators and counterfeiters° of all others.

But you, Madam,[22] my most Honored and Gracious: if I should seem to offer you this my device° for a discipline° and not a delight, I might

---

7. Puttenham follows Scaliger (1.1), who defines poetry as being concerned with both real and imaginary things. Cf. Sidney, *Defence* 216.

8. **instinct** prompting.

9. *furor* inspiration, madness. For the original notion of *furor poeticus*, see Plato, *Phaedrus* 245a.

10. **nature . . . complexion** i.e., (the poet's) disposition or temperament.

11. **subtlety** acuteness.

12. **battles** battle formations.

13. **majordomo** steward or butler. Although the word originally applied to the chief official at the royal court of the Merovingian kings of France, by Puttenham's time it had

come to mean a person in charge of protocol in the household of a nobleman. Cf. 3.4.230–31.

14. **surveyor** an officer who superintended the preparation and serving of food.

15. **inured with** accustomed to.

16. **politic regiment** political rule, government.

17. **magnanimity** great-spiritedness.

18. **queens** Andromache and Hecuba, whose grief Homer records in *Iliad* 22.

19. **valiance** feats of valor.

20. **subject of verity** historically true subject matter.

21. **surely much** surely (they are) much. (And likewise in the following sentences.)

22. **Madam** Elizabeth I.

well be reputed of all others the most arrogant and injurious, yourself
being already, of any that I know in our time, the most excellent poet.
Forsooth, by your princely purse, favors, and countenance, making in
manner what ye list,°23 the poor man rich, the lewd° well learned, the
coward courageous, and vile24 both noble and valiant. Then for imitation no less, your person as a most cunning° counterfeiter° lively representing Venus in countenance, in life Diana, Pallas for government, and
Juno in all honor and regal magnificence.

23. **in . . . list** in whatever manner you
wish.

24. **vile** morally or socially base.

CHAPTER 2

That there may be an art of our English poesy,
as well as there is of the Latin and Greek

Then as there was no art in the world till by experience found out,
so if poesy be now an art, and of all antiquity hath been among
the Greeks and Latins, and yet were none until by studious persons
fashioned and reduced° into a method of rules and precepts, then no
doubt may there be the like with us. And if the art of poesy be but
a skill° appertaining to utterance, why may not the same be with us as
well as with them, our language being no less copious, pithy, and significative[1] than theirs, our conceits° the same, and our wits no less
apt to devise and imitate than theirs were?[2] If again art be but a certain order of rules prescribed by reason and gathered by experience,
why should not poesy be a vulgar° art with us as well as with the
Greeks and Latins, our language admitting no fewer rules and nice°
diversities[3] than theirs—but peradventure° more by a peculiar[4] which
our speech hath in many things differing from theirs, and yet in the
general points of that art, allowed to go in common with them? So as°
if one point perchance, which is their feet whereupon their measures°
stand, and indeed is all the beauty of their poesy, and which feet
we have not, nor as yet never went about to frame (the nature of
our language and words not permitting it),[5] we have instead thereof

1. **significative** capable of meaning.
2. Cf. Sidney, *Defence* 249, and R. F. Jones.
3. **diversities** variations.
4. **more by a peculiar** i.e., (our tongue admitting) more (rules and variations) owing to
its particular characteristics.
5. The quantitative verse of Greek and
Latin poetry, based on the length of syllables,

adapts poorly to use in English, though there
was a good deal of interest in such adaptation at this time: cf. Ascham, *Scholemaster*
289–92; Gascoigne, *Certayne Notes* 457;
Webbe 1.273ff.; the Spenser-Harvey correspondence; Sidney, *Defence* 248; Campion
287–317; and Daniel 125–58. Cf. Attridge,
"Puttenham's Perplexity"; Schuman.

twenty[6] other curious° points in that skill° more than they ever had, by reason of our rhyme and tunable° concords° or symphony,° which they never observed. Poesy therefore may be an art in our vulgar,° and that very methodical and commendable.

> 6. **So as if one point ... twenty** i.e., poetry) ..., we have instead thereof
> So that if (they have) one quality (in their twenty.

CHAPTER 3

*How poets were the first priests, the first prophets,
the first legislators and politicians° in the world*

The profession and use of poesy is most ancient from the beginning, and not, as many erroneously suppose, after, but before any civil society was among men. For it is written that poesy was the original cause and occasion of their first assemblies, when, before, the people remained in the woods and mountains, vagrant[1] and dispersed like the wild beasts, lawless and naked, or very ill clad, and of all good and necessary provision for harbor[2] or sustenance utterly unfurnished, so as° they little differed for their manner of life from the very brute beasts of the field. Whereupon it is feigned that Amphion and Orpheus, two poets of the first ages, one of them, to wit, Amphion, built up cities and reared walls with the stones that came in heaps to the sound of his harp, figuring thereby the mollifying of hard and stony hearts by his sweet and eloquent persuasion.[3] And Orpheus assembled the wild beasts to come in herds to hearken to his music and by that means made them tame, implying thereby how by his discreet and wholesome lessons uttered in harmony and with melodious instruments, he brought the rude° and savage people to a more civil and orderly life, nothing, as it seemeth, more prevailing or fit to redress[4] and edify the cruel and sturdy[5] courage° of man than it. And as these two poets, and Linus before them, and Musaeus also and Hesiod, in Greece and Arcadia, so by all likelihood had more poets done in other places and in other ages before them, though there be no remembrance left of them by reason of the records by some accident° of time perished and failing. Poets therefore are of great antiquity.

1. **vagrant** wandering.
2. **harbor** shelter.
3. In this passage Puttenham is recounting a version of the myth of the orator / poet-as-civilizer which occurs in a number of ancient texts, including Cicero, *De inven-* *tione* 1.2.2–3, Quintilian 2.16.9, and Horace, *Ars poetica* 391–401. Horace mentions Orpheus and Amphion. Cf. Peletier 240–44; Wilson 41–43; and Sidney, *Defence* 213.
4. **redress** amend.
5. **sturdy** fierce, violent.

Then forasmuch° as they were the first that intended° to the observation of nature and her works, and especially of the celestial courses, by reason of the continual motion of the heavens, searching after the first mover and from thence by degrees coming to know and consider of the substances separate and abstract, which we call the divine intelligences or good angels (*daemones*),[6] they were the first that instituted sacrifices of placation,[7] with invocations and worship to them as to gods, and invented° and established all the rest of the observances and ceremonies of religion, and so were the first priests and ministers of the holy mysteries. And because, for the better execution of that high charge and function, it behooved them to live chaste and in all holiness of life and in continual study and contemplation, they came by instinct divine and by deep meditation and much abstinence (the same assubtiling[8] and refining their spirits) to be made apt to receive visions both waking and sleeping, which made them utter prophecies and foretell things to come. So also were they the first prophets or seers (*videntes*), for so the scripture termeth them in Latin after the Hebrew word,[9] and all the oracles and answers of the gods were given in meter or verse, and published to the people by their direction.

And for that[10] they were aged and grave men, and of much wisdom and experience in the affairs of the world, they were the first lawmakers to the people and the first politicians,° devising all expedient means for the establishment of commonwealth, to hold and contain the people in order and duty by force and virtue of good and wholesome laws, made for the preservation of the public peace and tranquillity. The same peradventure° not purposely intended° but greatly furthered by the awe of their gods and such scruple of conscience as the terrors of their late invented° religion had led them into.[11]

---

6. This passage appears to combine two things: (1) Neoplatonic ideas about intermediate divine entities or *daemones* or angels, traceable to Iamblichus (d. ca. 330 CE) and Pseudo-Dionysus (ca. 500 CE, though in Puttenham's time believed to be Saint Paul's disciple Dionysus the Areopagite, mentioned in Acts 17:34); (2) notions of theological astrology deriving from Porphyry of Tyre (ca. 233–305 CE).

7. **placation** propitiation.

8. **assubtiling** rendering more subtle or fine.

9. The word *videns* (pl. *videntes*) occurs as a noun meaning "seer" in a few places in the Vulgate Old Testament; see, for example, 1 Samuel 9:9 and 2 Chronicles 19:2 and 29:30.

10. **for that** because.

11. Cf. Lodge 1.75; Webbe 1.231.

CHAPTER 4

How the poets were the first philosophers, the first
astronomers, and historiographers,
and orators, and musicians of the world

Utterance also and language is given by nature to man for persuasion of others and aid of themselves, I mean the first[1] ability to speak. For speech itself is artificial° and made by man, and the more pleasing it is, the more it prevaileth to such purpose as it is intended° for.[2] But speech by meter is a kind of utterance more cleanly° couched[3] and more delicate° to the ear than prose is, because it is more current° and slipper° upon the tongue, and withal° tunable° and melodious, as a kind of music, and therefore may be termed a musical speech or utterance, which cannot but please the hearer very well.

Another cause is, for that it is briefer and more compendious[4] and easier to bear away and be retained in memory, than that which is contained in multitude of words and full of tedious ambage° and long periods.[5] It is, beside, a manner of utterance more eloquent and rhetorical than the ordinary prose, which we use in our daily talk, because it is decked[6] and set out with all manner of fresh colors° and figures, which maketh that it sooner inveigleth° the judgment of man and carrieth his opinion this way and that, whithersoever the heart by impression of the ear shall be most affectionately[7] bent and directed. The utterance in prose is not of so great efficacy,° because not only it is daily used, and by that occasion the ear is overglutted with it, but is also not so voluble° and slipper° upon the tongue, being wide and loose and nothing numerous,° nor contrived into measures° and sounded with so gallant[8] and harmonical accents, nor, in fine,[9] allowed that figurative[10] conveyance° nor so great license in choice of words and phrases as meter is.

So as° the poets were also from the beginning the best persuaders and their eloquence the first rhetoric of the world, even so it became[11] that the high mysteries of the gods should be revealed and taught by a manner of utterance and language of extraordinary phrase,[12] and brief and compendious, and above all others sweet and civil as the metrical is. The same also was meetest to register the lives and noble gests° of

---

1. **first** original.
2. Cf., for instance, Wilson 35–36, 42; Sidney, *Defence* 247; Bacon, *Advancement of Learning* 138–39, 238–40.
3. **couched** expressed, arranged.
4. **it is . . . compendious** i.e., metrical speech can convey more with fewer words.
5. **periods** sentences, syntactical units.
6. **decked** decorated.
7. **affectionately** by the emotions.
8. **gallant** gorgeous, ornate.
9. **in fine** in the end, in short.
10. **figurative** using figures of speech.
11. **became** came to be.
12. **phrase** i.e., phrasing.

princes and of the great monarchs of the world, and all other the memorable accidents° of time, so as° the poet was also the first historiographer.

Then forasmuch° as they were the first observers of all natural causes and effects in the things generable[13] and corruptible, and from thence mounted up to search after the celestial courses and influences,[14] and yet penetrated further to know the divine essences and substances separate, as is said before, they were the first astronomers and philosophers and metaphysics.[15] Finally, because they did altogether endeavor themselves to reduce° the life of man to a certain method of good manners° and made the first differences between virtue and vice, and then tempered° all these knowledges and skills° with the exercise of a delectable music by melodious instruments, which withal° served them to delight their hearers and to call the people together by admiration° to a plausible° and virtuous conversation,° therefore were they the first philosophers ethic and the first artificial° musicians of the world. Such was Linus, Orpheus, Amphion, and Musaeus the most ancient poets and philosophers of whom there is left any memory by the profane writers. King David also and Solomon his son and many other of the holy prophets wrote in meters° and used to sing them to the harp, although to many of us ignorant of the Hebrew language and phrase, and not observing it,[16] the same seem but a prose.[17] It cannot be therefore that any scorn or indignity should justly be offered to so noble, profitable, ancient, and divine a science° as poesy is.

13. **generable** capable of being generated.

14. **courses and influences** i.e., of the planets.

15. **metaphysics** metaphysicians. The notion that all things beneath the moon are changeable and hence corruptible, while those above that sphere are unalterable, was widely diffused in the Middle Ages and the Renaissance. Ultimately, it goes back to Greek thought; see, for instance, pseudo-Aristotle, *On the Cosmos* 6.399a–400a.

16. **observing it** understanding its workings.

17. See 1.5.99–100 and LN 1.

CHAPTER 5

How the wild and savage people used a natural poesy in versicle[1] and rhyme as our vulgar° is

And the Greek and Latin poesy was by verse numerous° and metrical, running upon pleasant feet, sometimes swift, sometime slow (their words very aptly serving that purpose), but without any rhyme or tunable° concord° in the end of their verses, as we and all other nations now use. But the Hebrews and Chaldees, who were more ancient than

1. **versicle** verse (a term often associated with religious verse, as here).

the Greeks, did not only use a metrical poesy, but also with the same a manner of rhyme, as hath been of late observed by learned men.[2] Whereby it appeareth that our vulgar° rhyming[3] poesy was common to all the nations of the world besides, whom the Latins and Greeks in special[4] called barbarous.° So as° it was, notwithstanding, the first and most ancient poesy, and the most universal, which two points do otherwise give to all human° inventions° and affairs no small credit. This is proved by certificate[5] of merchants and travelers, who by late navigations have surveyed the whole world and discovered large countries and strange peoples wild and savage, affirming that the American, the Peruvian,[6] and the very Cannibal do sing and also say their highest and holiest matters in certain rhyming versicles and not in prose, which proves also that our manner of vulgar° poesy is more ancient than the artificial° of the Greeks and Latins, ours coming by instinct of nature, which was before art or observation, and used with the savage and uncivil, who were before all science° or civility, even as the naked by priority of time is before the clothed, and the ignorant before the learned. The natural poesy, therefore, being aided and amended° by art, and not utterly altered or obscured, but some sign left of it (as the Greeks and Latins have left none), is no less to be allowed and commended than theirs.

---

2. In the view of modern scholars (still subject to debate), Hebrew verse probably does not use rhyme, as has been argued since Josephus and Saint Jerome. See LN 1.

3. We emend "running" (*1589*) to "rhyming," since that is the point of Puttenham's argument. *OED*, however, cites "the running of their feet" from 2.3.159 to demonstrate the meaning "rhythmical flow of verse," and it is possible that "running" has some such technical force here.

4. **in special** particularly.

5. **certificate** testimony.

6. Printed as "Perusine" in *1589*; we emend to "Peruvian" for parallelism with the other tribal peoples (though Perusina was the Latin name for the Italian town Perugia).

CHAPTER 6

*How the rhyming poesy came first to the Greeks
and Latins, and had altered and
almost spilt[1] their manner of poesy*

But it came to pass, when fortune fled far from the Greeks and Latins, and that their towns flourished no more in traffic° nor their universities in learning as they had done, continuing those monarchies,[2] the barbarous° conquerors invading them with innumerable swarms of

---

1. **spilt** ruined, spoiled.

2. **continuing those monarchies** a Latinism: "those monarchies continuing" (i.e., while they continued to exist).

strange° nations, the poesy metrical of the Greeks and Latins came to be much corrupted and altered, insomuch as° there were times that the very Greeks and Latins themselves took pleasure in rhyming verses, and used it as a rare and gallant thing. Yea, their orators' proses[3] nor the doctors'° sermons were acceptable to princes nor yet to the common people, unless it went in manner of tunable° rhyme or metrical sentences,° as appears by many of the ancient writers about that time and since. And the great princes and popes and sultans would one salute and greet another—sometime in friendship and sport,° sometime in earnest and enmity—by rhyming verses, and nothing seemed clerkly° done but must be done in rhyme. Whereof we find diverse examples from the time of the emperors Gratian and Valentinian downwards, for thenabouts began the declination of the Roman Empire, by the notable inundations of the Huns and Vandals in Europe, under the conduct of Totila and Attila and other their generals.[4] This brought the rhyming poesy in grace, and made it prevail in Italy and Greece (their own long time cast aside and almost neglected), till after many years that the peace of Italy and of the Empire Occidental[5] revived[6] new clerks,° who recovering and perusing the books and studies of the civiler ages, restored all manner of arts, and that of the Greek and Latin poesy withal,° into their former purity and neatness.[7] Which nevertheless did not so prevail, but that the rhyming poesy of the barbarians remained still in his reputation, that one in the school, this other[8] in courts of princes more ordinary and allowable.[9]

---

3. **proses** compositions in prose.

4. Puttenham's sense of the dates here is confused; the figures named were active over some two hundred years (367–552 CE; see Name Glossary).

5. **Empire Occidental** Western Roman Empire.

6. **revived** (re)introduced.

7. **neatness** elegance, facility of expression, freedom from impurity.

8. **that one ... this other** i.e., classical quantitative verse ... vernacular rhyming verse.

9. For Puttenham, the historical eclipse of classical versification by the advent of rhyming verse was imposed on the Latins by conquering Gothic invaders. In his view, when Charlemagne revived the Western Roman Empire in 800 (see the next chapter), quantitative verse was recovered along with the other arts, and flourished among scholars, but rhyme still held sway at court. Ascham (*Scholemaster* 289) and Webbe (1.239–40) both lament the "barbarous" dominance of rhyme; Daniel applauds its universality (*Defence* 132–33).

CHAPTER 7

How in the time of Charlemagne and many years
after him the Latin poets wrote in rhyme

And this appeareth evidently by the works of many learned men who wrote about the time of Charlemagne's reign in the Empire Occidental,[1] where the Christian religion became, through the excessive authority of popes and deep devotion of princes, strongly fortified and established by erection of orders monastical, in which many simple° clerks° for devotion's sake and sanctity were received, more than for any learning; by which occasion and the solitariness of their life, waxing studious without discipline° or instruction by any good method, some of them grew to be historiographers, some poets, and following either the barbarous° rudeness° of the time, or else their own idle° inventions,° all that they wrote to the favor or praise of princes, they did it in such manner of minstrelsy,[2] and thought themselves no small fools, when they could make their verses go all in rhyme, as did the school of Salerno, dedicating their book of medicinal rules unto our king of England[3] with this beginning:

> *Anglorum Regi scripsit tota schola Salerni:*
> *"Si vis incolumem, si vis te reddere sanam,*
> *Curas tolle graves, irasci crede prophanum,*
> *Nec retine ventrem, nec stringas fortiter anum."*[4]

And all the rest that follow throughout the whole book more curiously° than cleanly,° nevertheless very well to the purpose of their art.[5]

In the same time King Edward III himself quartering[6] the arms of England and France, did discover° his pretence[7] and claim to the crown of France in these rhyming verses:

---

1. **Empire Occidental** Western Roman Empire.

2. **minstrelsy** rude or low poetry. See also Puttenham's remark about minstrels' music at 2.4.161.

3. The medical school in Salerno was the earliest and one of the greatest medical schools of the Middle Ages. The school dedicated this verse treatise to Edward III. Puttenham's uncle Elyot mentions it in the 1541 Prologue to his *Castel of Helth* (see *Letters* 58).

4. "The entire school of Salerno has written to the English king: 'If you want to make yourself safe and healthy, dispense with weighty cares, let the common people rage [i.e., do not be angry yourself], do not hold back your stomach, and do not strongly con-

strict your anus'" (School of Salerno, *Conservandae bonae valetudinis praecepta* [1573], ll. 1–3, 6; in the 1573 edition these lines are slightly different from what Puttenham cites here). Note that it was a central regulatory principle of Galenic medicine that humoral fluid balance be maintained, usually by regular vomits and purges. Sir John Harington translated the work into English as *The Englishmans Doctor. Or, The School of Salerne* (1608).

5. Presumably Puttenham means to acknowledge the medical sufficiency of the book while condemning its base use of rhyme.

6. **quartering** placing or bearing (separate) coats of arms quarterly upon a shield; adding (another's coat) to one's hereditary arms.

7. **pretence** assertion of a right or title.

Rex sum regnorum bina ratione duorum:
Anglorum regno sum rex ego iure paterno;
Matris iure quidem Francorum nuncupor idem;
Hinc est armorum variatio facta meorum.[8]

Which verses Philippe de Valois, then possessing the crown[9] as next heir male by pretext of the law Salic,[10] and holding out[11] Edward III, answered in these other of as good stuff:

Praedo regnorum qui diceris esse duorum
Regno materno privaberis atque paterno.
Prolis ius nullum ubi matris non fuit ullum.
Hinc est armorum variatio stulta tuorum.[12]

It is found written of Pope Lucius, for his great avarice and tyranny used over the clergy, thus in rhyming verses:

Lucius est piscis rex et tyrannus aquarum
A quo discordat Lucius iste parum.
Devorat hic homines, hic piscibus insidiatur.
Esurit hic semper hic aliquando satur.
Amborum vitam si laus aequata notaret,
Plus rationis habet qui ratione caret.†[13]

And as this[14] was used in the greatest and gayest[15] matters of princes and popes by the idle° invention° of monastical men then reigning all in their superlative,[16] so did every scholar° and secular clerk° or versifier, when he wrote any short poem or matter of good lesson, put it in rhyme, whereby it came to pass that all your old proverbs and common

---

8. "I am the king of two kingdoms for two reasons: I am the king over the kingdom of the English by paternal right; I am indeed called the same thing over the French by maternal right; for this reason my [coat of] arms has been made varied [with the arms of both kingdoms]." For the two Latin poems, see Corrozet 40v–41r (Puttenham's version of Philippe's reply to Edward differs somewhat from the text given in Corrozet's book). This example, like some others cited in this chapter, uses internal rather than end-rhyme.

9. I.e., of France.

10. Salic law excluded females from succession to the crown. It was adduced in favor of the succession of Philip V in 1316, and afterwards used to combat the claims of Edward III of England (and his successors) to the French crown (as here and in Shakespeare's *Henry V*). The precise meaning of the term "Salic" is disputed.

11. **holding out** excluding, resisting the claim of.

12. "You who are called the thief of two kingdoms will suffer the loss of your maternal and paternal kingdoms. The offspring has no right where the mother had none. For this reason, the variation in your coat of arms [i.e., the quartering of both kingdoms' arms in it] is foolish."

13. "Lucius [the pike] is the king of the fish and the tyrant of the waters, from whom this Lucius is little different. The latter devours men, the former lies in wait for fish. The latter is always hungry, the former is only sometimes sated. If balanced praise were assigned to the lives of both, the one lacking reason is the more reasonable [or: is more in the right]."

14. **this** i.e., this style of rhyming Latin.

15. **gayest** most brilliant or magnificent.

16. **then ... superlative** at the height of monastic power in both religious and secular realms.

sayings, which they would have plausible° to the reader and easy to remember and bear away, were of that sort as these:

> *In mundo mira faciunt duo: nummus et ira.*
> *Mollificant dura, pervertunt omnia iura.*[17]

And this verse in dispraise of the courtier's life following the court of Rome:

> *Vita palatina dura est animaeque ruina.*[18]

And these written by a noble learned man:

> *Ire redire sequi regum sublimia castra*
> *Eximius status est, sed non sic itur ad astra.*[19]

And this other which to the great injury of all women was written (no doubt by some forlorn lover, or else some old malicious monk), for one woman's sake blemishing the whole sex:

> *Fallere flere nere mentiri nilque tacere:*
> *Haec quinque vere statuit Deus in muliere.*[20]

If I might have been his judge, I would have had him for his labor served as Orpheus was by the women of Thrace: his eyes to be picked out with pins, for his so deadly belying of them, or worse handled if worse could be devised. But will ye see how God raised a revenger for the silly[21] innocent women, for about the same rhyming age came an honest civil courtier, somewhat bookish, and wrote these verses against the whole rabble of monks:

> *O Monachi, vestri stomachi sunt amphora Bacchi.*
> *Vos estis, Deus est testis, turpissima pestis.*[22]

Anon after came your secular priests as jolly rhymers as the rest, who being sore aggrieved with their pope Calixtus, for that he had enjoined them from their wives, and railed as fast against him:

> *O bone Calixte totus mundus perodit te*
> *Quondam Presbiteri poterant uxoribus uti*
> *Hoc destruxisti, postquam tu Papa fuisti.*[23]

---

17. "In the world two things produce marvels: money and anger. They soften what is hard and pervert everything that is right."

18. "Life on the Palatine [Hill] is harsh and the ruin of the soul."

19. "To go to and come back from and follow the lofty camps of kings is a grand condition [in life], but not thus does one journey to the stars."

20. "To deceive, to weep, to spin [fabrications?], to lie, and never to be silent: these five things God truly established in woman."

21. **silly** deserving of pity or sympathy, helpless, simple.

22. "O monks, your stomachs are Bacchus' jugs. You yourselves are, as God is my witness, the filthiest plague."

23. "O good Calixtus, the entire world loathes you. Before, priests had been able to enjoy their wives. You destroyed this after you became pope."

Thus, what in writing of rhymes and registering of lies, was the clergy of that fabulous° age wholly occupied.

We find some but very few of these rhyming verses among the Latins of the civiler ages, and those rather happening by chance than of any purpose in the writer, as this distich° among the disports[24] of Ovid:

> *Quot caelum stellas tot habet tua Roma puellas.*
> *Pascua quotque haedos tot habet tua Roma Cynaedos.*[25]

The posterity taking pleasure in this manner of symphony° had leisure, as it seems, to devise many other knacks[26] in their versifying that the ancient and civil poets had not used before, whereof one was to make every word of a verse to begin with the same letter, as did Hugobald the Monk who made a large poem to the honor of Carolus Calvus, every word beginning with C, which was the first letter of the king's name, thus:

> *Carmina clarisonae Calvis cantate camenae.*[27]

And this was thought no small piece of cunning,° being indeed a matter of some difficulty to find out so many words beginning with one letter as might make a just volume, though in truth it were but a fantastical° device° and to no purpose at all more than to make them harmonical to the rude° ears of those barbarous° ages.

Another of their pretty inventions° was to make a verse of such words as by their nature and manner of construction and situation° might be turned backward word by word and make another perfect° verse, but of quite contrary sense, as the gibing monk that wrote of Pope Alexander[28] these two verses:

> *Laus tua, non tua fraus, virtus, non copia rerum,*
> *Scandere te faciunt hoc decus eximium.*[†29]

Which if ye will turn backward they make two other good verses, but of a contrary sense, thus:

> *Eximium decus hoc faciunt te scandere rerum*
> *Copia, non virtus, fraus tua, non tua laus.*[†30]

And they called it verse lion.[31]

---

24. **disports** pastimes, i.e., light poems.

25. "Your Rome has as many girls as heaven has stars, and the pastures have as many young goats as your Rome has buggers." *Ars amatoria* 1.59, plus a spurious line. Writing against the use of rhyme in 1602, Thomas Campion says, "It was imputed a great error to Ovid for setting forth this one riming verse," citing the first of these lines (295).

26. **knacks** clever verbal tricks.

27. "Clear-sounding Muses, sing your songs about the bald." Hucbaldus (Hucbald de Saint-Amand), *Ecloga de laudibus calvitii* 1. Carolus Calvus was the French king Charles II, known as Charles the Bald. Cf. 3.22.341.

28. Probably Alexander VI.

29. "Your merit, not your trickery, your virtue, not the abundance of your possessions, cause you to mount up to this extraordinary glory [i.e., the papacy]."

30. "Your wealth, not your virtue, your trickery, not your honor, have caused you to rise up to this extraordinary glory."

31. **verse lion** i.e., leonine verse. See LN 2.

Thus you may see the humors and appetites of men how diverse and changeable they be in liking new fashions, though many times worse than the old, and not only in the manner of their life and use of their garments, but also in their learnings and arts and especially of their languages.

CHAPTER 8

In what reputation poesy and poets were in old time
with princes and otherwise generally, and how they
be now become contemptible and for what causes[1]

For the respects aforesaid, in all former ages and in the most civil countries and commonwealths, good poets and poesy were highly esteemed and much favored of the greatest princes.[2] For proof whereof we read how much Amyntas, king of Macedonia, made of the tragical poet Euripides, and the Athenians of Sophocles.[3] In what price the noble poems of Homer were held with Alexander the Great, insomuch as° every night they were laid under his pillow and by day were carried in the rich jewel coffer of Darius, lately before vanquished by him in battle.[4] And not only Homer, the father and prince of the poets, was so honored by him, but for his sake all other meaner° poets, insomuch as° Choerilus, one no very great good poet, had for every verse well made a Philip's noble[5] of gold, amounting in value to an angel English,[6] and so for every hundred verses (which a cleanly° pen could speedily dispatch) he had a hundred angels.[7] And since Alexander the Great, how Theocritus, the Greek poet, was favored by Ptolemy, king of Egypt, and

---

1. Cf., for instance, Elyot, *The Governour* 46–50, 199; Webbe 232–33; Sidney, *Defence* 240–42.

2. Cf. Webbe 1.232.

3. Euripides left Athens in 408 BCE to become the client not of Amyntas (ruled ca. 393–370 BCE) but of Archelaus (ruled 413–399 BCE), an earlier king of Macedonia. Sophocles (496–406 BCE), Athens's most distinguished playwright, won first prize in dramatic festivals anywhere from eighteen to twenty-four times; he was also a notable and honored public figure, serving as one of the ten commanders of the military in 440 BCE.

4. See Erasmus, *Apophthegmata* 4, "Alexander Magnus" 54 (LB 4.201C, Udall 229–30). For the original, see Plutarch,

Alexander 8.1–2. See also Plutarch's essay *On the Fortune or the Virtue of Alexander* 1 (*Moralia* 327F); and Pliny, *Natural History* 7.29.108. Cf. Sidney, *Defence* 238.

5. **Philip's noble** a gold coin bearing the image of Alexander's father, Philip II of Macedonia.

6. **angel English** an English coin with an angel on one face, worth ten shillings sixpence.

7. See Erasmus, *Apophthegmata* 4, "Alexander Magnus" 35 (LB 4.199F–200A, Udall 222). See also Horace, *Epistles* 2.1.233, *Ars poetica* 357. Note that Erasmus adds to Horace the consequences of bad verse: *pro malo colaphum*, which Udall translates as "for euery euill verse a good buffet."

Queen Berenice his wife,[8] Ennius likewise by Scipio, prince of the Romans,[9] Vergil also by the emperor Augustus.[10]

And in later times how much were Jean de Meun and Guillaume de Lorris made of by the French kings, and Geoffrey Chaucer, father of our English poets, by Richard II, who as it was supposed gave him the manor of Ewelme[11] in Oxfordshire. And Gower to Henry IV[12] and Hardyng to Edward IV. Also how Francis, the French king,[13] made Saint-Gelais, Salmoneus Macrinus, and Clement Marot of his privy chamber for their excellent skill° in vulgar° and Latin poesy. And King Henry VIII, her Majesty's father, for a few psalms of David turned into English meter by Sternhold, made him groom of his privy chamber, and gave him many other good gifts.[14] And one Gray, what good estimation did he grow unto with the same King Henry and afterward with the duke of Somerset, Protector, for making certain merry ballads,° whereof one chiefly was, "The hunt is up, the hunt is up."[15] And Queen Mary, his daughter, for one epithalamion or nuptial song made by Vargas, a Spanish poet, at her marriage with King Philip in Winchester, gave him during his life two hundred crowns pension.[16]

Nor this reputation was given them in ancient times altogether in respect that poesy was a delicate° art, and the poets themselves cunning° prince-pleasers, but for that also they were thought for their universal knowledge to be very sufficient men for the greatest charges in their com-

---

8. In fact, Theocritus' patron was Ptolemy II Philadelphus, the son of Ptolemy I Soter, a former general of Alexander's and husband to Berenice. He died in 282 BCE, while Theocritus is known to have been active in Egypt only in the 270s. Puttenham may have been misled by Idyll 17 (ca. 273 BCE), a plea for patronage to Ptolemy the son which begins with panegyrics of the elder Ptolemy and Berenice.

9. See Cicero, *Pro Archia* 9.22.

10. See Suetonius, *Vita Vergili passim*.

11. Puttenham's "new Holme" (here emended) is presumably a reference to the manor of Ewelme in Oxfordshire, which belonged to Thomas Chaucer (1367?–1434), the poet's elder son, to whom it came with other estates by his marriage. It thus had no actual connection with the poet.

12. Henry IV granted Gower two casks of wine per year for a compliment in one of his poems.

13. This is Francis I.

14. In fact Sternhold and his collaborators present translations of all 151 Psalms into English (hence the title of the published collection, *The Whole Book of the Psalmes*, 1562). Perhaps Puttenham composed this section of the *Art* prior to the appearance of

the *Whole Book*, or perhaps he was jealous. Sternhold received various grants of land during the Dissolution of the Monasteries, held several comfortable governmental posts, and received a bequest of one hundred marks in Henry VIII's will.

15. William Gray, known as Gray of Reading. This famous ballad begins, "The hunt is up, the hunt is up,/And it is well nigh day;/And Harry our king is gone hunting,/To bring his deer to bay." Given Henry's great pleasure in the hunt, his approval of Gray's ballad is easy to imagine, though its documentation seems to be recorded only here. For the text and music, as well as manuscript information, see Chappell 86–89. Gray's intimacy with Somerset went so far as to entail imprisonment with him, from about October 13, 1549, .till February 23, 1550 (Loades 140, 150). See LN 3.

16. Possibly the Balthasar de Vargas or Vergoza who wrote an *ottava rima* account of the duke of Alva's frightful conquest of the Low Countries, *Breve Relacion en octava Rima de la jornada que a hecho el . . . Duque d'Alua desde España hasta los estados de Flandres* (1568). Alva had attended Philip II at his marriage to Mary I in 1554.

monwealths, were it for counsel or for conduct, whereby no man need to doubt but that both skills° may very well concur and be most excellent in one person. For we find that Julius Caesar, the first emperor and a most noble captain, was not only the most eloquent orator of his time, but also a very good poet, though none of his doings therein be now extant.[17] And Quintus Catulus, a good poet,[18] and Cornelius Gallus, treasurer of Egypt,[19] and Horace, the most delicate° of all the Roman lyrics,[20] was thought meet and by many letters of great instance[21] provoked[22] to be secretary of estate° to Augustus the emperor, which nevertheless he refused for his unhealthfulness's sake, and being a quiet-minded man and nothing ambitious of glory: *non voluit accedere ad Rempublicam*, as it is reported.[23] And Ennius, the Latin poet, was not, as some perchance think, only favored by Scipio Africanus for his good making of verses, but used as his familiar[24] and counselor in the wars for his great knowledge and amiable° conversation.°[25] And long before that Antimenides and other Greek poets, as Aristotle reports in his *Politics*, had charge in the wars.[26] And Tyrtaeus the poet, being also a lame man and halting[27] upon one leg, was chosen by the oracle of the gods from the Athenians to be general of the Lacedaemonians' army, not for his poetry, but for his wisdom and grave persuasions and subtle stratagems whereby he had the victory over his enemies.[28] So as° the poets seemed to have skill° not only in the subtleties of their art, but also to be meet for all manner of functions, civil and martial, even as they found favor of the times they lived in, insomuch as° their credit and estimation generally was not small.

17. Julius Caesar was in fact assassinated while only *dictator perpetuus* and never became emperor. Cicero, not Julius Caesar, was actually considered by all accounts the best orator of his time. Puttenham's statement may thus be read as a reflection of his programmatic flattery of noblemen and rulers. Suetonius refers to a poem of Julius Caesar's, "The Journey," in *The Deified Julius Caesar* 55.5.

18. Puttenham appears to refer to Quintus Lutatius Catulus, Roman general and consul and author of light verse, admired by Cicero and introduced as a character into the *De oratore*, but also, as Erasmus reports, made a benchmark: Cicero swore that "he would ere he died make the name of Cicero more noble and famous, then was the name either of the Catons, or of the Catules" (Udall 337; cf. *Apophthegmata* 4, "M. Tullius Cicero" 1, LB 4.221D–E). Erasmus finds Cicero's name more common now "then are three hundred soch as the Catules," and Udall glosses the passage with a specific reference to Puttenham's Catulus. The much better known poet Quintus (or Gaius) Valerius Catullus had no "great charge

in the commonwealth" whatever. Note that Puttenham provides no nonliterary credential for this figure at all (a possible lacuna).

19. Gallus, a significant elegiac poet and subject of Vergil's *Tenth Eclogue*, served as the first prefect of Egypt after the fall of Cleopatra; see Suetonius, *The Deified Augustus* 66.

20. **lyrics** lyric poets.

21. **instance** earnest solicitation.

22. **provoked** called upon, summoned.

23. "He did not wish to enter into politics." A source for this quotation has not been identified; Puttenham may be using a well-known Ciceronian locution (see, e.g., *De officiis* 1.9.28, *De republica* 1.5.9). For the incident, see Suetonius, *Vita Horati* 461–63.

24. **familiar** intimate.

25. Though Ennius praised Scipio Africanus in verse, the general he accompanied to the wars was Fulvius Nobilior (see Cicero, *Pro Archia* 11.27).

26. See *Politics* 3.9.1285a–b.

27. **halting** limping.

28. See Pausanias, *Description of Greece* 4.15.6–4.16.7.

But in these days (although some learned princes may take delight in them) yet universally it is not so.[29] For as well poets as poesy are despised, and the name become of honorable infamous, subject to scorn and derision, and rather a reproach than a praise to any that useth it, for commonly whoso is studious in the art or shows himself excellent in it, they call him in disdain a "fantastical";° and a light-headed or fantastical° man (by conversion) they call a poet. And this proceeds through the barbarous° ignorance of the time, and pride of many gentlemen, and others, whose gross heads not being brought up or acquainted with any excellent art, nor able to contrive or in manner conceive any matter of subtlety in any business or science,° they do deride and scorn it in all others as superfluous knowledges and vain sciences,° and whatsoever device° be of rare invention° they term it "fantastical,"° construing it to the worst side; and among men such as be modest and grave, and of little conversation,° nor delighted in the busy life and vain, ridiculous actions of the popular,[30] they call him in scorn a philosopher or poet, as much to say as° a fantastical° man, very injuriously (God wot°) and to the manifestation of their own ignorance, not making difference betwixt terms.

For as the evil and vicious° disposition of the brain hinders the sound judgment and discourse of man with busy and disordered fantasies, for which cause the Greeks call him φαντάστικος,[31] so is that part,[32] being well affected,[33] not only nothing disorderly or confused with any monstrous imaginations or conceits,° but very formal,[34] and in his much multiformity uniform, that is, well proportioned, and so passing[35] clear, that by it, as by a glass or mirror, are represented unto the soul all manner of beautiful visions, whereby the inventive° part of the mind is so much helped, as without it no man could devise any new or rare thing. And where it is not excellent in his kind, there could be no politic[36] captain, nor any witty° enginer° or cunning° artificer, nor yet any lawmaker or counselor of deep discourse; yea, the prince of philosophers sticks° not to say *animam non intelligere absque phantasmate,*[37] which text to another purpose Alexander Aphrodisias well noteth, as learned men know.[38]

29. Such outcries were common in the period; see, for instance, Elyot, *The Governour* 40–41.

30. **the popular** the common people.

31. For a similar pejorative reference, see Sidney, *Defence* 236.

32. **that part** the imagination.

33. **affected** disposed.

34. **formal** sane.

35. **passing** surpassingly.

36. **politic** sagacious, prudent, shrewd.

37. Aristotle, *De anima* 3.7.431a15: "The soul does not understand without an image." See also *De memoria* 1.450a1. In a

Latin translation of the *De anima*, published in several different editions in the sixteenth century, by the Greek humanist John Argyropoulos (1415–1487), the phrase is close to, though not identical with, Puttenham's: *ipsa anima sine phantasmate numquam intelligit* (the soul itself never understands without an image); see *Opera Latina* 3.224.

38. See Alexander of Aphrodisias, *De anima* 12.19–24, where he is commenting on Aristotle's discussion of whether the faculties of the soul can exist without the body (in *De anima* 1.1.403a8–12).

And this fantasy[39] may be resembled to a glass, as hath been said, whereof there be many tempers° and manner of makings, as the perspectives do acknowledge,[40] for some be false glasses and show things otherwise than they be indeed, and others right as they be indeed, neither fairer nor fouler, nor greater nor smaller. There be again of these glasses that show things exceeding fair and comely, others that show figures very monstrous and ill-favored. Even so is the fantastical° part of man (if it be not disordered) a representer of the best, most comely, and beautiful images or appearances of things to the soul[41] and according to their very truth. If otherwise, then doth it breed chimeras and monsters in man's imaginations, and not only in his imaginations, but also in all his ordinary actions and life which ensues. Wherefore such persons as be illuminated with the brightest irradiations of knowledge and of the verity and due proportion° of things, they are called by the learned men not *phantastici* but *euphantasiote*,[42] and of this sort of fantasy are all good poets, notable captains stratagematic, all cunning° artificers and enginers,° all legislators, politicians,° and counselors of estate,° in whose exercises the inventive° part is most employed and is to the sound and true judgment of man most needful.

This diversity in the terms perchance every man hath not noted, and thus much be said in defense of the poet's honor, to the end no noble and generous[43] mind be discomforted in the study thereof, the rather for that worthy and honorable memorial[44] of that noble woman twice French queen, Lady Anne of Brittany, wife first to King Charles VIII and after to Louis XII, who, passing one day from her lodging toward the king's side,[45] saw in a gallery Master Alain Chartier, the king's secretary, an excellent maker or poet, leaning on a table's end asleep, and stooped down to kiss him, saying thus in all their hearings: "We may not of[46] princely courtesy pass by and not honor with our kiss the

---

39. **this fantasy** the imagination in general.

40. The sentence up to this point might be paraphrased as follows: "The category of 'glasses' consists of many kinds, as the variety of them demonstrates [acknowledges]—false, true, beautifying, etc." "Perspectives" are optical devices (mirrors, spectacles, "crystal balls"). Webster provides period examples of both negative and positive "perspective glasses"; see *The White Devil* 1.2.104–11 and *The Duchess of Malfi* 1.1.214–15.

41. **to the soul** i.e., to the soul of the viewer, or perhaps the things are represented "to [their] soul[s]," i.e., with accuracy and depth.

42. These are negative and positive terms, for corrupt and healthy imaginations: "busy and disordered" and "monstrous," as Puttenham calls them just above, versus "well proportioned and passing clear." Puttenham

derives the second term from Quintilian's discussion of how the orator must feel the emotions he hopes to make his auditor feel, and how the orator will generate those emotions within himself by vividly imagining things, people, and events. Everyone is subject to such vivid imaginings on occasion in the form of daydreams and the like, but the orator can train himself to experience them. Those vivid imaginings, says Quintilian, "the Greeks call *phantasíai*, and the Romans *visions*. . . . Some writers call the possessor of this power . . . by the Greek word *euphantasíotos*" (6.2.29–30).

43. **generous** wellborn.

44. **memorial** memory, story, monument, testament.

45. **the king's side** the king's apartments.

46. **of** with.

mouth from whence so many sweet ditties and golden poems have issued."[47]

But methinks at these words I hear some smilingly say, I would be loath to lack living of my own till the prince gave me a manor of Ewelme[48] for my rhyming. And another to say, I have read that the Lady Cynthia came once down out of her sky to kiss the fair young lad Endymion as he lay asleep;[49] and many noble queens that have bestowed kisses upon their princes' paramours, but never upon any poets. The third methinks shruggingly saith, I kept not[50] to sit sleeping with my poesy till a queen came and kissed me. But what of all this? Princes may give a good poet such convenient° countenance and also benefit as are due to an excellent artificer, though they neither kiss nor cokes[51] them, and the discreet poet looks for no such extraordinary favors, and as well doth he honor by his pen the just, liberal, or magnanimous prince, as the valiant, amiable,° or beautiful, though they be every one of them the good gifts of God.

So it seems not altogether the scorn and ordinary disgrace° offered unto poets at these days is cause why few gentlemen do delight in the art, but for that liberality is come to fail in princes, who for their largesse were wont to be accounted the only patrons of learning and first founders of all excellent artificers. Besides, it is not perceived that princes themselves do take any pleasure in this science,° by whose example the subject is commonly led and allured to all delights and exercises, be they good or bad, according to the grave saying of the historian: *Rex multitudinem religione implevit, quae semper regenti similis est.*[†52] And peradventure° in this iron and malicious age of ours, princes are less delighted in it, being over earnestly bent and affected[53] to the affairs of empire and ambition, whereby they are as it were enforced to endeavor themselves to arms and practices of hostility, or to intend° to the right policing of their states, and have not one hour to bestow upon any other civil or delectable art of natural or moral doctrine,° nor scarce any leisure to think one good thought in perfect° and godly contemplation, whereby their troubled minds might be moderated and brought to tranquillity. So as° it is hard to find, in these days, of noblemen or gentlemen any good mathematician or excellent musician or notable

---

47. According to Corrozet (167v–168r), the poet was kissed not by Anne of Brittany but by Margaret of Scotland, daughter of James I, who married the French Dauphin, later Louis XI, in 1436. See Introduction 62 and note 127.

48. See note 11.

49. Many writers in the period, such as Spenser, Ralegh, and Lyly, identified Elizabeth with Cynthia.

50. **I kept not** I did not care.

51. **cokes** *OED* provides three related meanings of the verb: (1) to make a "cokes"

of, befool, "take in"; (2) to make a pet of; to fondle; to treat with blandishment; (3) to influence or persuade by caresses or flattery. The noun *cokes* (meaning "gull") dates from 1567. Puttenham's passage allows suggestive uncertainty as to who might be coaxing/cokesing whom, so far as flattery and reward go.

52. "The king filled the multitude with religious awe, which is always just like ruling."

53. **affected** inclined.

philosopher or else a cunning° poet, because we find few great princes much delighted in the same studies.

Now also of such among the nobility or gentry as be very well seen[54] in many laudable sciences,° and especially in making or poesy, it is so come to pass that they have no courage° to write and if they have, yet are they loath to be acknown of[55] their skill.° So as° I know very many notable gentlemen in the court that have written commendably and suppressed it again,[56] or else suffered it to be published without their own names to it, as if it were a discredit for a gentleman to seem learned and to show himself amorous of any good art.[57]

In other ages it was not so, for we read that kings and princes have written great volumes and published them under their own regal titles. As, to begin with: Solomon, the wisest of kings; Julius Caesar, the greatest of emperors; Hermes Trismegistus, the holiest of priests and prophets; Evax, king of Arabia, wrote a book of precious stones in verse; Prince Avicenna, of physic[58] and philosophy; Alfonso, king of Spain, his astronomical tables;[59] Almansor, a king of Morocco, diverse philosophical works; and by their regal example our late sovereign lord, King Henry VIII, wrote a book in defense of his faith, then persuaded that it was the true and apostolic doctrine.°[60] Though it hath appeared otherwise since, yet his honor and learned zeal was nothing less to be allowed. Queens also have been known studious and to write large volumes, as Lady Margaret of France, Queen of Navarre in our time.[61]

But of all others the emperor Nero was so well learned in music and poesy, as[62] when he was taken by order of the Senate and appointed to die, he offered violence to himself and said, "*O quantus artifex pereo!*"[63] as much to say as,° "How is it possible a man of such science° and learning as myself should come to this shameful death?" The emperor Octavian, being made executor to Vergil, who had left by his last will and testament that his books of the *Aeneid* should be committed to the fire, as things not perfected° by him, made his excuse for infring-

---

54. **seen** educated.
55. **acknown of** known for.
56. **again** afterward.
57. Puttenham's discussion suggests that some early modern English gentlemen seem to have felt such reluctance on occasion, as if publishing were clerkly and status-degrading labor. For the founding discussion of the famous "stigma of print," see Saunders; see also, however, the strong contrary evidence cited in May, "Tudor Aristocrats" and *Elizabethan Courtier Poets*.
58. **physic** medicine.
59. The Alfonsine Tables, a set of astronomical tables prepared for King Alfonso X of Spain, were completed in 1252 and first printed in 1483.

60. His *Assertio Septem Sacramentorum* (*Defense of the Seven Sacraments*, 1521), proposed by Wolsey and written by Henry and others (including More, according to his son-in-law Roper) in reply to Luther's *Babylonian Captivity of the Church* (1520), some years before the English break with Rome. In return, Pope Leo X bestowed upon him the title of Defender of the Faith.
61. Margaret of Navarre's most famous work was her *Heptameron* (published posthumously in 1558).
62. **as** that.
63. "Oh, I die such a great artist!" Quoted in Erasmus, *Apophthegmata* 6, "Domitius Nero" 10 (LB 4.276D). For the original, see Suetonius, *Nero* 49.1.

ing the dead's will by a number of verses most excellently written, whereof these are part:

> *Frangatur potius legum veneranda potestas,*
> *Quam tot congestos noctesque diesque labores*
> *Hauserit una dies.*[64]

And put his name to them. And before him his uncle and father adoptive, Julius Caesar, was not ashamed to publish under his own name his commentaries of the French and Britain wars.

Since, therefore, so many noble emperors, kings, and princes have been studious of[65] poesy and other civil arts, and not ashamed to bewray° their skills° in the same, let none other meaner° person despise learning, nor (whether it be in prose or in poesy, if they themselves be able to write, or have written anything well or of rare invention°) be any whit squeamish to let it be published under their names, for reason serves it, and modesty doth not repugn.[66]

64. "The great power of the laws, which is to be venerated, should be broken rather than one day should have consumed what the poet's labors built up over so

many days and nights." Donatus, *Vita Vergilii* 15.58.
65. **studious of** devoted to.
66. **repugn** resist, object.

CHAPTER 9

How poesy should not be employed upon vain conceits,° or vicious,° or infamous

Wherefore the nobility and dignity of the art, considered as well by universality as antiquity and the natural excellence of itself, poesy ought not to be abased and employed upon any unworthy matter and subject, nor used to vain purposes, which nevertheless is daily seen, and that is to utter conceits° infamous and vicious,° or ridiculous and foolish, or of no good example and doctrine.° Albeit in merry matters (not unhonest) being used for man's solace and recreation it may be well allowed, for, as I said before, poesy is a pleasant manner of utterance varying from the ordinary of purpose to refresh the mind by the ear's delight.

Poesy also is not only laudable, because I said it was a metrical speech used by the first men, but because it is a metrical speech corrected and reformed by discreet judgments, and with no less cunning° and curiosity° than the Greek and Latin poesy, and by art beautified and adorned, and brought far from the primitive rudeness° of the first inventors;° otherwise it might be said to me that Adam and Eve's aprons were the gayest[1] garments because they were the first, and the

1. **gayest** finest.

shepherd's tent or pavilion the best housing because it was the most ancient and most universal; which I would not have so taken, for it is not my meaning, but that art and cunning° concurring with nature, antiquity, and universality in things indifferent° and not evil, do make them more laudable. And right so our vulgar° rhyming poesy, being by good wits brought to that perfection we see, is worthily to be preferred before any other manner of utterance in prose, for such use and to such purpose as it is ordained, and shall hereafter be set down more particularly.

CHAPTER 10

The subject or matter of poesy

Having sufficiently said of the dignity of poets and poesy, now it is time to speak of the matter or subject of poesy, which to mine intent[1] is whatsoever witty° and delicate° conceit° of man meet or worthy to be put in written verse, for any necessary use of the present time, or good instruction of the posterity. But the chief and principal is the laud,° honor, and glory of the immortal gods (I speak now in phrase of the gentiles°). Secondly, the worthy gests° of noble princes, the memorial[2] and registry of all great fortunes,[3] the praise of virtue and reproof of vice, the instruction of moral doctrines,° the revealing of sciences° natural and other profitable arts, the redress[4] of boisterous and sturdy[5] courages° by persuasion, the consolation and repose of temperate° minds, finally the common solace of mankind in all his travails° and cares of this transitory life. And in this last sort being used for recreation only, may allowably bear matter not always of the gravest, or of any great commodity or profit, but rather in some sort vain, dissolute, or wanton,° so it be not very scandalous and of evil example.

But as our intent is to make this art vulgar° for all Englishmen's use, and therefore are of necessity to set down the principal rules therein to be observed, so in mine opinion it is no less expedient to touch briefly all the chief points of this ancient poesy of the Greeks and Latins, so far forth as it conformeth with ours, so as° it may be known what we hold of them as borrowed, and what as of our own peculiar.[6] Wherefore now that we have said what is the matter of poesy, we will declare the manner and forms of poems used by the ancients.

1. **to mine intent** in my judgment.
2. **memorial** memory, story, monument, testament.
3. **fortunes** life histories.

4. **redress** restraint.
5. **boisterous and sturdy** rough and violent.
6. **our own peculiar** what is distinctively our own.

CHAPTER 11

Of poems and their sundry forms and how thereby
the ancient poets received surnames[1]

As the matter of poesy is diverse, so was the form of their poems and manner of writing, for all of them wrote not in one sort, even as all of them wrote not upon one matter. Neither was every poet alike cunning° in all as in some one kind of poesy, nor uttered with like felicity. But wherein anyone most excelled, thereof he took a surname, as to be called a poet heroic, lyric, elegiac, epigrammatist, or otherwise.

Such therefore as gave themselves to write long histories of the noble gests° of kings and great princes, intermeddling the dealings of the gods, half-gods, or heroes of the gentiles,° and the great and weighty consequences of peace and war, they called poets heroic, whereof Homer was chief and most ancient among the Greeks, Vergil among the Latins. Others who more delighted to write songs or ballads° of pleasure, to be sung with the voice, and to the harp, lute, or cithern,[2] and such other musical instruments, they were called melodious poets (*melici*), or by a more common name lyric poets, of which sort was Pindar, Anacreon, and Callimachus with others among the Greeks, Horace and Catullus among the Latins. There were another sort, who sought the favor of fair ladies and coveted[3] to bemoan their estates° at large° and the perplexities of love in a certain piteous verse called elegy, and thence were called elegiac; such among the Latins were Ovid, Tibullus, and Propertius.

There were also poets that wrote only for the stage, I mean plays and interludes,° to recreate° the people with matters of disport,[4] and to that intent did set forth, in shows [and] pageants[5] accompanied with speech, the common behaviors and manner of life of private persons and such as were the meaner° sort of men; and they were called comical poets, of whom among the Greeks Menander and Aristophanes were most excellent, with the Latins Terence and Plautus. Besides those poets comic there were other who served also the stage, but meddled not with so base matters, for they set forth the doleful falls of unfortunate and afflicted princes, and were called poets tragical. Such were Euripides and Sophocles with the Greeks, Seneca among the Latins.

There were yet others who mounted nothing so high as any of them both, but in base and humble style by manner of dialogue uttered the

1. **surnames** titles, epithets.
2. **cithern** guitar-like instrument.
3. **coveted** desired.
4. **disport** pastime, amusement.

5. **shows and pageants** emended from "shewes pageants" by Ben Jonson in his copy of the *Art*.

private and familiar talk of the meanest° sort of men, as shepherds, haywards,[6] and such like; such was among the Greeks Theocritus, and Vergil among the Latins; their poems were named eclogues or shepherdly talk. There was yet another kind of poet, who intended to tax the common abuses° and vice of the people in rough and bitter speeches, and their invectives were called satires,[7] and themselves satyrics. Such were Lucilius, Juvenal, and Persius among the Latins, and with us he that wrote the book called *Piers Plowman*.[8] Others of a more fine and pleasant° head were given wholly to taunting and scoffing at indecent° things, and in short poems uttered pretty merry conceits,° and these men were called epigrammatists.

There were others that for the people's good instruction and trial° of their own wits used in places of great assembly to say by rote numbers of short and sententious° meters,° very pithy and of good edification, and thereupon were called poets mimists, as who would say, imitable and meet to be followed for their wise and grave lessons.[9]

There was another kind of poem invented° only to make sport° and to refresh the company with a manner of buffoonery or counterfeiting° of merry speeches, converting all that which they had heard spoken before to a certain derision by a quite contrary sense. And this was done when comedies or tragedies were a-playing, and that between the acts when the players went to make ready for another, there was great silence and the people waxed weary, then came in these manner of

6. **haywards** cattle herdsmen.

7. Puttenham has "satyres" in his text. The Latin *satira*, originally *satura*, meant a dish composed of various ingredients, and hence a medley, stew, or hodgepodge. Later the word was spelled *satyra* because it was incorrectly believed that the genre was connected to the hairy, goat-footed satyrs of Greek mythology known for their roughness, and to the satyr plays that concluded Greek tragic trilogies. By the early modern period, *satyre* had come to mean: (1) bitter, rough, "satirical" speech; (2) a woodland god or demon in classical mythology, partly human and partly animal, and also, according to Puttenham, a fictional role or disguise formerly assumed by satiric social commentators (see 1.13 and 1.14); and (3) the hairy demons or monsters mentioned in the Old Testament as living in deserts (see, for example, Isaiah 13:21). The French scholar Isaac Casaubon disproved the existence of any connection between *satire* and *satyr* in *De satyrica Graecorum poesi et Romanorum satyra* (Paris, 1605). When Puttenham says "satyre," he means either "satire" or

"satyr" and never confuses the two; we have modernized his word accordingly. Cf. Lodge 1.80.

8. *Piers Plowman* a long allegorical poem attributed to William Langland.

9. Puttenham's "poets mimists" are probably Publilius Syrus and Decimus Laberius. Publilius (1st c. BCE) was a slave brought to Rome from Antioch who was freed because of his wit, became a writer and performer of mimes, and bested Laberius (ca. 106–ca. 43 BCE), a Roman knight who also wrote mimes, in a contest at the games sponsored by Julius Caesar in 46 BCE. Erasmus tells the tale in *Apophthegmata* 4, "C. Julius Caesar" 17 (LB 4.214E, Udall 301–2); in Udall's translation the story begins by referring to "Publius Mimus, a plaier of wanton enterludes," and describes Laberius as "a maker & a plaier as Publius was." Publilius' sayings, together with those of Marcus Porcius Cato (the *Catonis disticha*), became a popular schoolbook in the Middle Ages which was still being used in the early Renaissance. On the ancient mime, Puttenham could also have obtained information from Scaliger (1.10).

counterfeit° vices;[10] they were called *pantomimi*,[11] and all that had before been said, or great part of it, they gave a cross[12] construction to it very ridiculously. Thus have you how the names of the poets were given them by the forms of their poems and manner of writing.

10. **vices** originally, characters in medieval morality plays allegorically representing (often comically, like jesters or buffoons) some sin or evil. One of their number took on the generic name of "the Vice."

11. ***pantomimi*** the name, meaning "imitator of all things," given by the Romans to mimes.

12. **cross** contrary.

CHAPTER 12

In what form of poesy the gods of the gentiles° were praised and honored

The gods of the gentiles° were honored by their poets in hymns, which is an extraordinary and divine praise, extolling and magnifying them for their great powers and excellency of nature in the highest degree of laud,° and yet therein their poets were after a sort restrained, so as° they could not with their credit untruly praise their own gods, or use in their lauds° any manner of gross adulation or unveritable report. For in any writer untruth and flattery are counted most great reproaches. Wherefore, to praise the gods of the gentiles,° for that, by authority of their own fabulous° records, they had fathers and mothers, and kindred and allies, and wives and concubines, the poets first commended them by their genealogies or pedigrees, their marriages and alliances, their notable exploits in the world for the behoof of mankind, and yet, as I said before, none otherwise than the truth of their own memorials[1] might bear, and in such sort as it might be well avouched[2] by their old written reports, though in very deed they were not from the beginning all historically true, and many of them very fictions, and such of them as were true were grounded upon some part of a history or matter of verity, the rest altogether figurative and mystical,[3] covertly applied to some moral or natural sense, as Cicero setteth it forth in his books *De natura deorum*.[4]

1. **memorials** memories, stories, monuments, testaments.

2. **avouched** confirmed.

3. **mystical** allegorical.

4. Cicero interprets the pagan gods as allegorical, seeing them as divine gifts to humanity, such as grain, identified with the gods who supposedly gave them, in this case Ceres; representations of virtues and passions; departed human benefactors; or deified natural forces. See *De natura deorum* 2.23.60–2.27.69; for a modern interpretation, see Seznec; for a specifically English account, see Ferguson. Like Cicero (2.24.63–2.25.64), Puttenham is particularly concerned (in the next paragraph) with Saturn's gelding of his father.

For to say that Jupiter was son to Saturn, and that he married his own sister Juno, might be true, for such was the guise⁵ of all great princes in the oriental part of the world both at those days and now is. Again, that he loved Danaë, Europa, Leda, Callisto, and other fair ladies, daughters to kings, besides many meaner° women, it is likely enough, because he was reported to be a very incontinent person, and given over to his lusts,° as are for the most part all the greatest princes. But that he should be the highest god in heaven, or that he should thunder and lighten, and do many other things very unnaturally and absurdly; also that Saturn should geld his father Caelus⁶ to the intent to make him unable to get⁷ any more children, and other such matters as are reported by them, it seemeth to be some witty° device° and fiction made for a purpose, or a very noble⁸ and impudent lie, which could not be reasonably suspected by° the poets, who were otherwise discreet° and grave men, and teachers of wisdom to others.⁹ Therefore either to transgress the rules of their primitive records or to seek to give their gods honor by belying them (otherwise than in that sense which I have alleged) had been a sign not only of an unskillful° poet, but also of a very impudent and lewd° man, for untrue praise never giveth any true reputation.

But with us Christians, who be better disciplined° and do acknowledge but one God, almighty, everlasting, and in every respect self-sufficient (*autharcos*),¹⁰ reposed in all perfect° rest and sovereign bliss, not needing or exacting any foreign help or good: to him we cannot exhibit overmuch praise, nor belie him any ways, unless it be in abasing his excellency by scarcity of praise, or by misconceiving his divine nature, weening¹¹ to praise him if we impute to him such vain delights and peevish affections° as commonly the frailest men are reproved for.¹² Namely, to make him ambitious of honor, jealous and difficult in his worships, terrible, angry, vindictive, a lover, a hater, a pitier, and indigent of¹³ man's worships—finally so passionate¹⁴ as in effect he should be altogether *anthropopathis*.¹⁵ To the gods of the gentiles° they might well attribute these infirmities, for they were but the children of

5. **guise** custom, practice; the "ways" (of a country).

6. **Caelus** the Latin word for "sky" that Cicero uses in *De natura deorum* (2.23.63) as the equivalent for Uranus, Saturn's father in Greek mythology.

7. **get** beget.

8. **noble** notable.

9. Puttenham seems to be addressing Plato's concern in the *Republic* (2.17.377a–35.392c) over the immoral actions of the gods that are recorded in myths. Cf. Sidney, *Defence* 239–40.

10. **autharcos** Puttenham confuses *autarkes* (self-sufficient) with *autarchos* (auto-

cratic ruler). His spelling may be influenced by "author."

11. **weening** supposing.

12. A similar conception of the superiority of God to pagan deities as a subject for poets to praise can be found in Du Bartas's "L'Uranie ou muse céleste," a work Puttenham may have known. King James translated Du Bartas's poem, among other works, and published it in his youthful *Essayes of a Prentise* of 1584.

13. **indigent of** in need of.

14. **passionate** easily moved to anger.

15. **anthropopathis** characterized by human feelings.

men, great princes and famous in the world, and not for any other re-spect divine than by some resemblance of virtue they had to do good and to benefit many. So as° to the God of the Christians such divine praise might be verified; to the other gods, none but figuratively or in mystical[16] sense, as hath been said.

In which sort the ancient poets did indeed give them great honors and praises, and made to them sacrifices, and offered them oblations of sundry sorts, even as the people were taught and persuaded by such pla-cations[17] and worships to receive any help, comfort, or benefit to them-selves, their wives, children, possessions, or goods. For if that opinion were not, who would acknowledge any god? The very etymology of the name with us of the north parts of the world declaring plainly the na-ture of the attribute, which is all one as if we said good (*bonus*), or a giver of good things.[18] Therefore the gentiles° prayed for peace to the goddess Pallas; for war (such as thrived by it) to the god Mars; for honor and em-pire to the god Jupiter; for riches and wealth to Pluto; for eloquence and gain to Mercury; for safe navigation to Neptune; for fair weather and prosperous winds to Aeolus; for skill° in music and leechcraft[19] to Apollo; for free[20] life and chastity to Diana; for beauty and good grace, as also for issue and prosperity in love, to Venus; for plenty of crop and corn[21] to Ceres; for seasonable vintage to Bacchus; and for other things to others. So many things as they could imagine good and desirable, and to so many gods as they supposed to be authors thereof, insomuch as° Fortune was made a goddess, and the fever quartan[22] had her altars, such blindness and ignorance reigned in the hearts of men at that time; and whereof it first proceeded and grew, besides the opinion hath been given, appeareth more at large° in our books of *Hierotechnē*,[23] the matter being of another consideration than to be treated of in this work.

And these hymns to the gods was the first form of poesy and the highest and the stateliest, and they were sung by the poets as priests and by the people or whole congregation, as we sing in our churches the psalms of David, but they did it commonly in some shady groves of tall timber trees, in which places they reared altars of green turf, and bestrewed them all over with flowers, and upon them offered their oblations and made their bloody sacrifices (for no kind of gift can be

---

16. **mystical** allegorical.

17. **placations** actions of appeasement or propitiation.

18. A false etymology: "God" comes from the Old High German *got*, whereas "good" comes from *guot. Bonus* is Latin for "good."

19. **leechcraft** medicine.

20. **free** in a spiritual sense: not in bondage to (here, fleshly) sin.

21. **corn** in early modern English this word signified all cereals (wheat, rye, barley, oats, maize, and rice).

22. **fever quartan** a fever characterized by paroxysm every fourth day (in modern reck-oning, every third).

23. **Hierotechnē** a lost work by Putten-ham. The title appears to mean "On the Art of the Sacred," or perhaps "On the Power of the Gods."

dearer than life) of such quick cattle[24] as every god was, in their conceit,° most delighted in, or in some other respect most fit for the mystery.[25] Temples or churches or other chapels than these they had none
at those days.

24. **quick cattle** livestock.   25. **mystery** ritual.

CHAPTER 13

In what form of poesy vice and the common
abuses° of man's life was reprehended

Some perchance would think that next after the praise and honoring
of their gods should commence the worshippings and praise of good
men, and especially of great princes and governors of the earth, in sovereignty and function next unto the gods. But it is not so, for before
that came to pass, the poets or holy priests chiefly studied the rebuke
of vice, and to carp at the common abuses° such as were most offensive to the public and private; for as yet, for lack of good civility and
wholesome doctrines,° there was greater store° of lewd° lurdans[1] than
of wise and learned lords or of noble and virtuous princes and governors. So as° next after the honors exhibited to their gods, the poets,
finding in man generally much to reprove and little to praise, made certain poems in plain meters,° more like to sermons or preachings than
otherwise. And when the people were assembled together in those hallowed places dedicate to their gods, because they had yet no large halls
or places of conventicle,[2] nor had any other correction of their faults
but such as rested only in rebukes of wise and grave men, such as at
these days make the people ashamed rather than afeard, the said ancient poets used for that purpose three kinds of poems reprehensive,[3] to
wit: the satire, the comedy, and the tragedy. And the first and most bitter invective against vice and vicious° men was the satire: which, to the
intent their bitterness should breed none ill will, either to the poets or
to the reciters (which could not have been chosen if they had been
openly known), and besides to make their admonitions and reproofs
seem graver and of more efficacy,° they made wise as if[4] the gods of the
woods, whom they called satyrs or sylvans, should appear and recite
those verses of rebuke, whereas indeed they were but disguised persons
under the shape of satyrs, as who would say, these terrene[5] and base

1. **lurdans** sluggards, vagabonds: a general
term of reproach or abuse, implying either
dullness and incapacity, or idleness and ras-
cality.

2. **conventicle** meeting.
3. **reprehensive** containing reproof.
4. **made . . . . if** pretended that.
5. **terrene** earthly.

gods, being conversant with man's affairs and spyers out of all their secret faults, had some great care over man, and desired by good admonitions to reform the evil of their life and to bring the bad to amendment°
by those kind of preachings. Whereupon the poets, inventors° of the device,° were called satirists.[6]

6. Scaliger explains (1.17) how in their satire the ancients adopted certain *personae* (i.e., masks), including those of the gray-haired satyr, the bearded satyr, the young, beardless satyr, Silenus, Pappus (Daddy). Then he de-scribes the *satyricus ornatus*, the dress or adornment of the satirist (or satyr), which con-sisted of the skins of animals such as the mule, goat, or panther.

CHAPTER 14

*How vice was afterward reproved by two other manner
of poems, better reformed[1] than the satire,
whereof the first was comedy, the second tragedy*

But when these manner of solitary speeches and recitals of rebuke, uttered by the rural gods out of bushes and briars, seemed not to the finer heads sufficiently persuasive, nor so popular° as if it were reduced° into action of many persons, or by many voices lively represented to the ear and eye, so as° a man might think it were even now a-doing, the poets devised to have many parts played at once by two or three or four persons that debated the matters of the world—sometimes of their own private affairs, sometimes of their neighbors', but never meddling with any princes' matters, nor such high personages, but commonly of mer-chants, soldiers, artificers, good honest householders, and also of un-thrifty youths, young damsels, old nurses, bawds, brokers,[2] ruffians, and parasites,[3] with such like, in whose behaviors lieth in effect the whole course and trade[4] of man's life—and therefore tended altogether to the good amendment° of man by discipline° and example.[5] It was also much for the solace and recreation of the common people, by rea-son of the pageants and shows. And this kind of poem was called com-edy, and followed next after[6] the satire, and by that occasion[7] was somewhat sharp and bitter after the nature of the satire, openly and by express names taxing men more maliciously and impudently than became,[8] so as° they were enforced, for fear of quarrel and blame, to

1. **reformed** corrected.
2. **brokers** middlemen; secondhand deal-ers; pawnbrokers.
3. **parasites** flatterers.
4. **trade** manner (of life), occupation.
5. Cf. Elyot, *The Governour* 47–48; Whet-stone 172–74; Lodge 1.80; Sidney, *Defence* 229–30; Webbe 1.248–49.
6. **followed next after** closely resembled; came next in line of development.
7. **by that occasion** for that reason.
8. **became** was becoming.

disguise their players with strange° apparel and, by coloring their faces and carrying hats and caps of diverse fashions, to make themselves less known.

But as time and experience do reform everything that is amiss, so this bitter poem called the Old Comedy being disused and taken away, the New Comedy[9] came in place, more civil and pleasant a great deal and not touching any man by name, but in a certain generality glancing at every abuse,° so as° from thenceforth fearing none ill-will or enmity at anybody's hands, they left aside their disguisings and played bare-face, till one Roscius Gallus, the most excellent player among the Romans, brought up these vizards[10] which we see at this day used, partly to supply the want° of players when there were more parts than there were persons, or that it was not thought meet to trouble and pester princes' chambers with too many folks. Now by the change of a vizard one man might play the king and the carter,° the old nurse and the young damsel, the merchant and the soldier, or any other part he listed° very conveniently.° There be[11] that say Roscius did it for another purpose, for being himself the best *histrion*[12] or buffoon that was in his days to be found, insomuch as° Cicero said Roscius contended with him by variety of lively gestures to surmount the copy[13] of his speech,[14] yet because he was squint-eyed and had a very unpleasant countenance, and looks which made him ridiculous or rather odious to the presence,[15] he devised these vizards to hide his own ill-favored face.[16] And thus much touching the comedy.

---

9. Aristophanes (ca. 448–380 BCE) is the only surviving exemplar of the Old Comedy. His fellow Greek Menander (ca. 342–292 BCE) was the leading writer of the New Comedy, and the Romans Plautus (ca. 254–184 BCE) and Terence (ca. 190–159 BCE) developed this form.

10. **vizards** masks.

11. **there be** there are some.

12. **histrion** stage player, actor. In Latin a *histrio* is an actor, but not a buffoon; the word for the latter is *scurra*, and Puttenham uses it at 3.22.340, where he translates it correctly. His identification of *histrion* and buffoon in this passage may speak to the relatively low status of actors in the early Elizabethan period.

13. **copy** copiousness.

14. See Macrobius 3.14.12.

15. **the presence** those present; perhaps the royal presence.

16. The tradition identifying Roscius as the first to introduce the use of masks on the Roman stage dates back to the late antique grammarian Diomedes (or Diomedes Grammaticus, 4th or 5th c. CE). Cicero merely mentions that Roscius had a squint (*De natura deorum* 1.38.79), but Diomedes sees this as the reason for Roscius' having chosen to use masks (489). This tradition has been discredited; see Beare 303–5.

CHAPTER 15

In what form of poesy the evil and outrageous behaviors of princes were reprehended

But because in those days when the poets first taxed by satire and comedy, there was no great store° of kings or emperors or such high estates° (all men being yet for the most part rude° and in a manner popularly° equal), they could not say of them or of their behaviors anything to the purpose, which cases of princes are since taken for the highest and greatest matters of all. But after that, some men among the more[1] became mighty and famous in the world, sovereignty and dominion having learned[2] them all manner of lusts° and licentiousness of life, by which occasions also their high estates° and felicities fell many times into most low and lamentable fortunes. Whereas before, in their great prosperities, they were both feared and reverenced in the highest degree, after their deaths, when the posterity stood no more in dread of them, their infamous life and tyrannies were laid open to all the world, their wickedness reproached, their follies and extreme insolencies derided, and their miserable ends painted out in plays and pageants to show the mutability of fortune and the just punishment of God in revenge of a vicious° and evil life.

These matters were also handled by the poets and represented by action as[3] that of the comedies; but because the matter was higher than that of the comedies, the poets' style was also higher and more lofty, the provision[4] greater, the place more magnificent; for which purpose also the players' garments were made more rich and costly and solemn, and every other thing appertaining according to that rate.[5] So as° where the satire was pronounced by rustical and naked sylvans speaking out of a bush, and the common players of interludes,° called *planipedes*,[6] played barefoot upon the floor, the later comedies upon scaffolds,[7] and by men well and cleanly° hosed and shod. These matters of great princes were played upon lofty stages, and the actors thereof wore upon their legs buskins of leather called *cothurni*, and other solemn habits,[8] and for a special preeminence did walk upon those high corked shoes or pantofles, which now they call in Spain and Italy *choppini*.[9] And because those

1. **among the more** among the mass of people.
2. **learned** taught.
3. **as** such as.
4. **provision** advance preparation.
5. **according to that rate** proportionately.
6. *planipedes* "bare-footed" (Lat.), an alternative name for the ancient Roman performer of mimes or pantomimes who wore neither the comic *soccus* (slipper) nor the tragic *cothurnus*. See Scaliger 1.10.

7. **upon scaffolds** i.e., were performed upon scaffolds.
8. **habits** garments.
9. Buskins were half-boots, whereas *cothurni* were the thick-soled boots worn by the actors in ancient Greek tragedy; Horace mentions them in *Ars poetica* 80–82, as does Scaliger (1.10). *Pantofles* (Fr. *pantoufles*) meant slippers and was applied variously to all sorts of indoor slippers or loose shoes, especially to the high-heeled cork-soled *cioppini*.

buskins and high shoes were commonly made of goats' skins very finely tanned and dyed into colors, or for that as some say the best player's reward was a goat to be given him, or for that as other think, a goat was the peculiar sacrifice to the god Pan, king of all the gods of the woods— forasmuch° as a goat in Greek is called *tragos*—therefore these stately plays were called tragedies.[10] And thus have ye four sundry forms of poesy dramatic reprehensive, and put in execution by the feat and dexterity of man's body, to wit: the satire, Old Comedy, New Comedy, and tragedy, whereas all other kind of poems except eclogue—whereof shall be entreated° hereafter—were only recited by mouth or sung with the voice to some melodious instrument.

Cioppini is an Italianized form of the Spanish *chapin*; the more standard English word in Puttenham's day was *chopine* (*1589* reads "shoppini").

10. Horace provides such an etymological connection (see *Ars poetica* 220), and the matter was much discussed, but Puttenham is probably following Scaliger (1.6), who rehearses several etymologies for the word but prefers this one since, he notes, in ancient competitions among tragedians the winner was given a goat to sacrifice to a god, who was probably Pan. Cf. Lodge 1.80; Webbe 1.248.

CHAPTER 16

In what form of poesy the great princes and dominators of the world were honored

But as the bad and illaudable[1] parts of all estates° and degrees° were taxed by the poets in one sort or another, and those of great princes by tragedy in special (and not till after their deaths), as hath been before remembered, to the intent that such exemplifying (as it were) of their blames and adversities, being now dead, might work for a secret reprehension to others that were alive, living in the same or like abuses.° So was it great reason that all good and virtuous persons should for their well-doings be rewarded with commendation, and the great princes above all others with honors and praises, being for many respects of greater moment to have them good and virtuous than any inferior sort of men. Wherefore the poets, being indeed the trumpeters of all praise and also of slander (not slander, but well-deserved reproach), were in conscience and credit bound, next after the divine praises of the immortal gods, to yield a like rateable[2] honor to all such amongst men as most resembled the gods by excellency of function, and had a certain affinity with them by more than human° and ordinary virtues showed in their actions here upon earth.

---

1. **illaudable** unworthy of praise.   2. **rateable** proportional.

They were therefore praised by a second degree of laud°: showing their high estates,° their princely genealogies and pedigrees, marriages, alliances, and such noble exploits as they had done in the affairs of peace and of war to the benefit of their people and countries, by invention° of any noble science° or profitable art, or by making wholesome laws, or enlarging of their dominions by honorable and just conquests, and many other ways. Such personages among the gentiles° were Bacchus, Ceres, Perseus, Hercules, Theseus, and many other, who thereby came to be accounted gods and half-gods or goddesses (heroes)[3] and had their commendations given by hymn accordingly, or by such other poems as their memory was thereby made famous to the posterity forever after, as shall be more at large° said in place convenient.°[4] But first we will speak somewhat of the playing places and provisions which were made for their pageants and pomps representative[5] before remembered.

3. On Renaissance euhemerism, see Ferguson and (more generally) Seznec.

4. See 1.19.

5. **pageants and pomps representative** i.e., plays.

CHAPTER 17

Of the places where their interludes° or poems
dramatic were represented to the people

As it hath been declared, the satires were first uttered in their hallowed places within the woods where they honored their gods under the open heaven, because they had no other housing fit for great assemblies. The old comedies were played in the broad streets upon wagons or carts uncovered, which carts were floored with boards and made for removable stages to pass from one street of their towns to another, where all the people might stand at their ease to gaze upon the sights.[1] Their new comedies or civil interludes° were played in open pavilions or tents of linen cloth or leather half displayed,[2] that the people might see.

Afterward, when tragedies came up, they devised to present them upon scaffolds or stages of timber, shadowed with linen or leather as the other, and these stages were made in the form of a semicircle, whereof the bow served for the beholders to sit in, and the string or forepart was appointed for the floor or place where the players uttered, and had in it sundry little divisions by curtains as traverses[3] to serve for

1. See Horace, *Ars poetica* 275–77.

2. **half displayed** with curtains opened (?); in the form of a three-walled tent (?).

3. **traverses** curtains or screens placed in a hall or theater.

several rooms where they might repair unto and change their garments and come in again, as their speeches and parts were to be renewed. Also there was place appointed for the musicians to sing or to play upon their instruments at the end of every scene, to the intent the people might be refreshed and kept occupied. This manner of stage in half-circle the Greeks called *theatrum*, as much to say as° a beholding place, which was also in such sort contrived by benches and greces[4] to stand or sit upon, as no man should impeach[5] another's sight.[6]

But as civility and withal° wealth increased, so did the mind of man grow daily more haughty and superfluous[7] in all his devices,° so as° for their theaters in half-circle, they came to be, by the great magnificence of the Roman princes and people, sumptuously built with marble and square stone in form all round, and were called amphitheaters, whereof as yet appears one among the ancient ruins of Rome, built by Pompeius Magnus, for capacity able to receive at ease fourscore thousand persons as it is left written,[8] and so curiously° contrived as every man might depart at his pleasure without any annoyance to other. It is also to be known that in those great amphitheaters were exhibited all manner of other shows and disports[9] for the people, as their fence plays, or digladiations,[10] of naked men, their wrestlings, runnings, leapings, and other practices of activity and strength, also their baitings of wild beasts, as elephants, rhinoceroses, tigers, leopards, and others, which sights much delighted the common people, and therefore the places required to be large and of great content.[11]

4. **benches and greces** *grece* and *greces* both mean "a flight of stairs." As the theater shifted from Greece to Rome, the chorus was largely abandoned, and the orchestra where it had performed became part of the auditorium, eventually reserved for the elite, who seated themselves there on portable chairs and litters. Perhaps Puttenham alludes to some such seating distinction in referring to (front-row? floor-level?) benches and (raised? rising?) "greces" for sitting and standing.

5. **impeach** hinder.

6. Cf. Polydore Vergil, *De rerum inventoribus* f. lxxvii; Scaliger 1.21.

7. **superfluous** excessive, inordinate.

8. See Pliny, *Natural History* 36.24.115.

9. **disports** pastimes, amusements.

10. **fence plays, or digladiations** sword fights.

11. In early modern England baiting was the "sport" of setting on dogs to attack an animal such as a bear, boar, bull, or badger, usually chained or confined for this purpose. Such contests among beasts (a subset of *venationes*, Lat., "animal hunts") can be traced in Rome (in "circus" entertainments) at least to the second century BCE.

CHAPTER 18

Of the shepherd's or pastoral poesy, called eclogue,
and to what purpose it was first invented° and used[1]

Some be of opinion, and the chief of those who have written in this art among the Latins, that the pastoral poesy, which we commonly call by the name of eclogue and bucolic, a term brought in by the Sicilian poets,[2] should be the first of any other, and before the satire, comedy, or tragedy, because, say they, the shepherds' and haywards'[3] assemblies and meetings, when they kept their cattle and herds in the common fields and forests, was the first familiar conversation,° and their babble and talk under bushes and shady trees, the first disputation and contentious reasoning, and their fleshly heats growing of ease,[4] the first idle° wooings, and their songs made to their mates or paramours either upon sorrow or jollity of courage,° the first amorous musics. Sometime also they sang and played on their pipes for wagers, striving who should get the best game,[5] and be counted cunningest.°[6] All this I do agree unto, for no doubt the shepherd's life was the first example of honest fellowship, their trade the first art of lawful acquisition or purchase,[7] for at those days robbery was a manner of purchase. So saith Aristotle in his books of the *Politics*,[8] and that pasturage was before tillage, or fishing or fowling, or any other predatory art or chevisance.[9] And all this may be true, for before there was a shepherd keeper of his own or of some other body's flock, there was none owner in the world, quick cattle[10] being the first property of any foreign[11] possession. I say foreign, because always men claimed property in their apparel and armor and other like things made by their own travail° and industry. Nor thereby[12] was there yet any good town or city or king's palace, where pageants and pomps might be showed by comedies or tragedies.

But for all this, I do deny that the eclogue should be the first and most ancient form of artificial° poesy, being persuaded that the poet devised

---

1. Cf. Webbe 1.262–65.

2. **Sicilian poets** Theocritus, Moschus, and Bion, known as the inventors of pastoral poetry.

3. **haywards** cattle herdsmen.

4. **growing of ease** being produced by idleness.

5. **best game** victory.

6. See Scaliger 1.4. Note that Puttenham disagrees with Scaliger (who is possibly the one referred to as the "chief . . . among the Latins") about the antiquity of pastoral.

7. **purchase** procuring something.

8. On these matters, cf. Aristotle, *Politics* 1.3.1256a–b.

9. **chevisance** provision of what is wanted in life (from Fr. *chevir*, "to finish or bring to an end," and hence, to supply a want). In *The Shepheardes Calender* Spenser's E.K. glosses the term in "May" (92) as "sometime of Chaucer vsed for gaine: sometime of other for spoyle, or bootie, or enterprise, and sometime for chiefdome." (See also *Faerie Queene* 2.9.8, 3.7.45, and 3.9.24.)

10. **quick cattle** livestock.

11. **foreign** not one's own.

12. **thereby** besides. (Puttenham's text now returns abruptly from prehistoric anthropology to the question of the earliest genre.)

the eclogue long after the other dramatic poems, not of purpose to counterfeit° or represent the rustical manner of loves and communication, but under the veil of homely persons and in rude° speeches to insinuate and glance at greater matters, and such as perchance had not been safe to have been disclosed in any other sort, which may be perceived by the *Eclogues* of Vergil, in which are treated by figure[13] matters of greater importance than the loves of Tityrus and Corydon.[14] These eclogues[15] came after[16] to contain and inform° moral discipline,° for the amendment° of man's behavior, as be those of Mantuan and other modern poets.

13. **by figure** figurally, indirectly, allegorically.
14. Cf. Sidney, *Defence* 229.

15. **these eclogues** i.e., the genre.
16. **after** later.

Chapter 19

Of historical poesy, by which the famous acts of princes and the virtuous and worthy lives of our forefathers were reported

There is nothing in man of all the potential[1] parts of his mind (reason and will except) more noble or more necessary to the active life than memory, because it maketh most to a sound judgment and perfect° worldly wisdom, examining and comparing the times past with the present, and by them both considering the time to come, concludeth with a steadfast resolution what is the best course to be taken in all his actions and advices[2] in this world.[3] It[4] came upon this reason, experience to be so highly commended in all consultations of importance, and preferred before any learning or science°—and yet experience is no more than a mass of memories assembled, that is, such trials° as man hath made in time before. Right so, no kind of argument in all the oratory craft[5] doth better persuade and more universally satisfy than example, which is but the representation of old memories and like successes[6] happened in times past.[7]

1. **potential** potent.
2. **advices** deliberations.
3. Memory is one of the five traditional parts of rhetoric (along with invention, disposition, elocution or style, and delivery), and its importance is widely acknowledged. See, for instance, *Ad Herennium* 3.15.28, Cicero, *De oratore* 2.87.355–58, and Quintilian 11.2.1–10. See also Ascham, *Scholemaster*: memory "is so necessarie for learning, as

Plato maketh it a separate and perfite note of it selfe, and that so principall a note, as without it, all other giftes of nature do small seruice to learning" (195). (Ascham refers to *Republic* 7.25.535c; cf. also 6.2.487a.)
4. **it** i.e., this conclusion (?).
5. **oratory craft** art of rhetoric.
6. **successes** events.
7. This paragraph may combine several unreuised states of composition.

For these regards the poesy historical is of all other—next the divine—most honorable and worthy, as well for the common benefit as for the special comfort every man receiveth by it, no one thing in the world with more delectation reviving our spirits than to behold as it were in a glass the lively image of our dear forefathers, their noble and virtuous manner of life, with other things authentic, which, because we are not able otherwise to attain to the knowledge of by any of our senses, we apprehend them by memory, whereas the present time and things so swiftly pass away, as they give us no leisure almost to look into them, and much less to know and consider of them throughly.[8]

The things future, being also events very uncertain, and such as cannot possibly be known because they be not yet, cannot be used for example nor for delight otherwise than by hope. Though many promise the contrary, by vain and deceitful arts taking upon them to reveal the truth of accidents° to come, which, if it were so as they surmise, are yet but sciences° merely[9] conjectural, and not of any benefit to man or to the commonwealth where they be used or professed. Therefore, the good and exemplary things and actions of the former ages were reserved only to the historical reports of wise and grave men; those of the present time left to the fruition[10] and judgment of our senses; the future as hazards and uncertain events utterly neglected and laid aside for magicians and mockers[11] to get their livings by, such manner of men as by negligence of magistrates and remissness of laws every country breedeth great store° of.

These historical men nevertheless used not the matter so precisely to wish that all they wrote should be accounted true, for that was not needful nor expedient to the purpose, namely to be used either for example[12] or for pleasure, considering that many times it is seen a feigned matter or altogether fabulous°—besides that it maketh more mirth than any other—works no less good conclusions for example than the most true and veritable, but oftentimes more, because the poet hath the handling of them to fashion at his pleasure, but not so of the other which must go according to their verity and none otherwise without the writer's great blame.[13] Again, as ye know, more and more excellent examples may be feigned in one day by a good wit,° than many ages through man's frailty are able to put in ure,[14] which made the learned

---

8. **throughly** thoroughly. The value of history was a commonplace among humanists. For instance, Elyot writes: "The knowledge of . . . Experience is called Example, and is expressed by history, which of Tully is called the life of memory. . . . There is no doctrine, be it either divine or human, that is not either all expressed in history or at the least mixed with history" (*The Governour* 228).

9. **merely** completely.

10. **fruition** enjoyment.

11. **mockers** confidence men.

12. **for example** i.e., to be imitated.

13. Cf. Sidney, *Defence* 219–26.

14. **in ure** in use or practice.

and witty° men of those times to devise many historical matters of no verity at all, but with purpose to do good and no hurt, as using them for a manner of discipline° and precedent[15] of commendable life. Such was the commonwealth of Plato and Sir Thomas More's *Utopia*,[16] resting all in device,° but never put in execution, and easier to be wished than to be performed.

And you shall perceive that histories were of three sorts, wholly true and wholly false and a third holding part of either, but for honest recreation and good example they were all of them. And this may be apparent to us not only by the poetical histories, but also by those that be written in prose, for as Homer wrote a fabulous° or mixed report of the siege of Troy and another of Ulysses' errors or wanderings, so did Musaeus compile a true treatise of the life and loves of Leander and Hero, both of them heroic, and to none ill edification. Also, as Thucydides wrote a worthy and veritable history of the wars betwixt the Athenians and the Peloponnesians, so did Xenophon, a most grave philosopher and well-trained courtier and counselor, make another (but feigned and untrue) of the childhood of Cyrus, king of Persia, nevertheless both to one effect, that is, for example and good information° of the posterity.[17]

Now because the actions of mean° and base personages tend in very few cases to any great good example—for who passeth[18] to follow the steps and manner of life of a craftsman, shepherd, or sailor, though he were his father or dearest friend; yea, how almost is it possible that such manner of men should be of any virtue° other than their profession requireth?—therefore was nothing committed to history but matters of great and excellent persons and things, that the same by irritation[19] of good courages° (such as emulation[20] causeth) might work more effectually, which occasioned the story writer to choose a higher style fit for his subject, the prosaic[21] in prose, the poet in meter.°

And the poet's was by verse hexameter[22] for his gravity and stateliness most allowable; neither would they intermingle him[23] with any other shorter measure,° unless it were in matters of such quality as became best to be sung with the voice and to some musical instrument, as were, with the Greeks, all your hymns and *encomia*[24] of Pindar and

---

15. **precedent** model.

16. **commonwealth of Plato** the ideal state imagined in Plato's *Republic*. *Utopia* was published in 1516 (in Latin), in 1551 in English translation (by Ralph Robinson).

17. Cf. Sidney, *Defence* 216–17: the poetic faculty "so far substantially . . . worketh, not only to make a Cyrus . . . but to bestow a Cyrus upon the world to make many Cyruses, if they will learn aright why and how that maker made him."

18. **passeth** cares, bothers.

19. **irritation** incitement.

20. **emulation** the urge to imitation or rivalry (for power or honors); often resentful or grudging.

21. **prosaic** prose writer.

22. **verse hexameter** dactylic hexameter was the standard verse form of Greek and Latin epic.

23. **him** it, i.e., the hexameter verse.

24. *encomia* (Gr.) poems of praise.

Callimachus, not very[25] histories but a manner of historical reports, in which cases they made those poems in variable measures,° and coupled a short verse with a long to serve that purpose the better. And we ourselves who compiled this treatise have written for pleasure a little brief romance or historical ditty in the English tongue of the Isle of Great Britain in short and long meters,° and by breaches° or divisions to be more commodiously sung to the harp in places of assembly, where the company shall be desirous to hear of old adventures and valiances[26] of noble knights in times past, as are those of King Arthur and his knights of the round table, Sir Bevis of Southampton, Guy of Warwick, and others like.[27]

Such as have not premonition[28] hereof, and consideration of the causes alleged, would peradventure° reprove and disgrace every romance or short historical ditty, for that they be not written in long meters° or verses alexandrine,[29] according to the nature and style of large histories, wherein they should do wrong, for they be sundry forms of poems and not all one.

25. **very** true.

26. **valiances** feats of valor.

27. On English Renaissance views of romance, cf. 2.10.173; Ascham, *Scholemaster* 230–31; Nashe, *The Anatomie of Absurditie, Works,* 1.11; and Daniel 132. There was an extensive debate in Italy about romance in connection with Ariosto's *Orlando furioso*; on this topic, see Javitch, *Proclaiming a Classic.*

28. **premonition** previous warning or knowledge.

29. **verses alexandrine** lines of verse twelve syllables, or six iambs, in length; the vernacular equivalent of the classical hexameter in English and French, and hence, heroic verse, called alexandrine (from Fr. *alexandrin*) from the verse line used in the twelfth-century French *Roman d'Alexandre.* Pierre Ronsard, in his *Abrégé de l'art poétique français* (1565), devotes a chapter to alexandrine verse, stressing its lofty character (480–81). Puttenham appears, say Willcock and Walker, to be the first English critic to note the name and French provenance of the term (here and at 2.4.162), though an introductory poem to the first edition of James I's *Schort Treatise* (1584) is labeled "A Qvadrain of Alexandrin Verse" (Smith 1.208).

CHAPTER 20

In what form of poesy virtue in the inferior[1] sort was commended

In every degree° and sort of men virtue is commendable, but not equally—not only because men's estates° are unequal, but for that also virtue itself is not in every respect of equal value and estimation. For continence in a king is of greater merit than in a carter,° the one having all opportunities to allure him to lusts° and ability to serve his appetites, the other, partly for the baseness of his estate° wanting° such means and occasions, partly by dread of laws more inhibited, and not so

1. **inferior** i.e., socially inferior.

vehemently carried away with unbridled affections,° and therefore deserve not in the one and the other like praise nor equal reward by the very ordinary course of distributive justice.[2] Even so parsimony and illiberality[3] are greater vices in a prince than in a private person, and pusillanimity[4] and injustice likewise, for to the one fortune hath supplied enough to maintain them in the contrary virtues, I mean fortitude, justice, liberality, and magnanimity, the prince having all plenty to use largesse by and no want° or need to drive him to do wrong; also all the aids that may be to lift up his courage° and to make him stout[5] and fearless (*augent animos fortunae*,[6] saith the Mimist),† and very truly, for nothing pulleth down a man's heart so much as adversity and lack. Again, in a mean° man prodigality and pride are faults more reprehensible than in princes, whose high estates° do require in their countenance, speech, and expense a certain extraordinary,[7] and their functions enforce them sometime to exceed the limits of mediocrity[8] not excusable in a private person, whose manner of life and calling hath no such exigence.[9] Besides, the good and bad of princes is more exemplary, and thereby of greater moment, than the private person's.

Therefore it is that the inferior persons with their inferior virtues have a certain inferior praise to guerdon[10] their good with and to comfort them to continue a laudable course in the modest and honest life and behavior. But this lieth not in written lauds° so much as in ordinary reward and commendation to be given them by the mouth of the superior magistrate. For histories were not intended to so general and base a purpose, albeit many a mean° soldier and other obscure persons were spoken of and made famous in stories, as we find of Irus the beggar and Thersites the glorious noddy,[11] whom Homer maketh mention of.[12] But that happened (and so did many like memories of mean° men) by reason of some greater personage or matter that it was long of,[13] which therefore could not be a universal case nor chance to every other good and virtuous person of the meaner° sort. Wherefore the poet, in praising the manner of life or death of any mean° person, did it by some little ditty or epigram or epitaph, in few verses and mean°

---

2. **distributive justice** one of the forms into which Aristotle divided justice, involving the distribution of things in shares equal to the merits of the individuals receiving them; see his *Nicomachean Ethics* 5.2.12–5.3.17 (1130b–1131b).

3. **illiberality** stinginess.

4. **pusillanimity** faintheartedness; from the Latin words for "tiny" and "mind, soul." Cf. the regal virtue of magnanimity, "greatness of soul."

5. **stout** brave, resolute.

6. *augent ... fortunae* "Goods [or possessions] increase one's courage." Since Puttenham's brief discussion of mime in 1.11 echoes Udall's Erasmus and may also draw on Scaliger (1.10), it is probable that the "Mimist" in question here is Publilius Syrus, although the Latin phrase Puttenham cites is not recorded as his.

7. **extraordinary** i.e., extraordinary quality.

8. **mediocrity** moderation.

9. **exigence** urgency, requirement.

10. **guerdon** reward.

11. **glorious noddy** vainglorious fool.

12. Irus appears in *Odyssey* 18, Thersites in *Iliad* 2.

13. **long of** on account of.

style conformable to his subject. So have you how the immortal gods were praised by hymns, the great princes and heroic personages by ballads° of praise called *encomia*,[14] both of them[15] by historical reports of great gravity and majesty, the inferior persons by other slight poems.

14. *encomia* (Gr.) poems of praise.

15. **both of them** Perhaps it is the "great princes" and "heroic personages" who receive not only shorter *encomia* but also epic report, thought historical by Puttenham. The epic poems of Homer and Vergil, however, contain plenty of "immortal gods," so perhaps "both" specifies gods and humans. The sentence structure inclines toward the latter: gods get hymns, humans *encomia*, both get epics.

CHAPTER 21

The form wherein honest and profitable
arts and sciences° were treated

The profitable sciences° were no less meet to be imported to the greater number of civil men for instruction of the people and increase of knowledge, than to be reserved and kept for clerks° and great men only. So as° next unto the things historical, such doctrines° and arts as the commonwealth fared the better by were esteemed and allowed. And the same were treated by poets in verse hexameter favoring the heroical, and for the gravity and comeliness of the meter° most used with the Greeks and Latins to sad° purposes. Such were the philosophical works of Lucretius Carus among the Romans, the astronomical of Aratus and Manilius—one Greek, the other Latin—the medicinal of Nicander, and that of Oppianus of hunting and fishes, and many more that were too long to recite in this place.

CHAPTER 22

In what form of poesy the amorous affections
and allurements were uttered

The first founder of all good affections° is honest love, as the mother of all the vicious° is hatred.[1] It was not therefore without reason that so commendable, yea, honorable a thing as love well meant, were it in princely estate° or private, might in all civil commonwealths be uttered in good form and order as other laudable things are. And

1. The apparently gendered contrast between honest love as the (male?) founder of good affections and hatred as the mother of vicious affections is striking.

because love is of all other human° affections the most puissant[2] and passionate, and most general to all sorts and ages of men and women, so as° whether it be of the young or old, or wise or holy, or high estate° or low, none ever could truly brag of any exemption in that case, it requireth a form of poesy variable, inconstant, affected,° curious,° and most witty° of any others, whereof the joys were to be uttered in one sort, the sorrows in another, and by the many forms of poesy, the many moods and pangs of lovers throughly[3] to be discovered;° the poor souls sometimes praying, beseeching; sometime honoring, advancing,° praising; another while railing, reviling, and cursing; then sorrowing, weeping, lamenting; in the end laughing, rejoicing, and solacing the beloved again, with a thousand delicate° devices,° odes, songs, elegies, ballads,° sonnets, and other ditties, moving one way and another to great compassion.

2. **puissant** powerful.   3. **throughly** thoroughly, from start to finish.

CHAPTER 23

The form of poetical rejoicings

Pleasure is the chief part of man's felicity in this world and also (as our theologians say) in the world to come. Therefore, while we may (yea always, if it could be) to rejoice and take our pleasures in virtuous and honest sort, it is not only allowable, but also necessary and very natural to man. And many be the joys and consolations of the heart, but none greater than such as he may utter and discover° by some convenient° means, even as to suppress and hide a man's mirth and not to have therein a partaker, or at leastwise a witness, is no little grief and infelicity.

Therefore, nature and civility have ordained (besides the private solaces) public rejoicings for the comfort and recreation° of many. And they be of diverse sorts and upon diverse occasions grown: one and the chief was for the public peace of a country, the greatest of any other civil good. And wherein your Majesty (my most gracious Sovereign) have showed yourself to all the world for this one and thirty years' space of your glorious reign above all other princes of Christendom not only fortunate, but also most sufficient virtuous and worthy of empire. Another is for just and honorable victory achieved against the foreign enemy. A third at solemn feasts and pomps of coronations and installments[1] of honorable orders. Another for jollity at weddings and marriages. Another at the births of princes' children. Another for private

1. **installments** acts of formally installing people in office.

entertainments in court, or other secret disports[2] in chamber and such solitary places.

And as these rejoicings tend to diverse effects, so do they also carry diverse forms and nominations,[3] for those of victory and peace are called triumphal, whereof we ourselves have heretofore given some example by our *Triumphals* written in honor of her Majesty's long peace.[4] And they were used by the ancients in like manner, as we do our general processions or litanies[5] with banquets and bonfires and all manner of joys. Those that were to honor the persons of great princes or to solemnize the pomps of any installment were called *encomia*;[6] we may call them carols of honor. Those to celebrate marriages were called songs nuptial, or epithalamies, but in a certain mystical sense as shall be said hereafter. Others for magnificence at the nativities of princes' children, or by custom used yearly upon the same days, are called songs natal,[7] or *genethliaca*. Others for secret recreation and pastime in chambers with company or alone were the ordinary musics amorous, such as might be sung with voice or to the lute, cithern,[8] or harp, or danced by measures° as the Italian pavane and galliard are at these days in princes' courts and other places of honorable or civil assembly, and of all these we will speak in order and very briefly.

2. **disports** pastimes, amusements.
3. **nominations** names.
4. Although Puttenham's work has been lost, it presumably resembled such works as *Verses of Prayse and Joye. Written Upon Her Majesties Preservation* (1586, celebrating her delivery from the Babington plot) and *Elizabetha triumphans. Conteyning the damned*

practizes, that the diuelish popes of Rome haue vsed . . . and . . . the ouerthrow had against the Spanish fleete (1588).
5. **litanies** public prayers, often performed in processions.
6. *encomia* (Gr.) poems of praise.
7. **natal** birthday.
8. **cithern** guitar-like instrument.

CHAPTER 24

The form of poetical lamentations

Lamenting is altogether contrary to rejoicing: every man saith so, and yet is it a piece of joy to be able to lament with ease and freely to pour forth a man's inward sorrows and the griefs wherewith his mind is surcharged.[1] This was a very necessary device° of the poet and a fine: besides his poetry to play also the physician, and not only by applying a medicine to the ordinary sickness of mankind, but by making the very grief itself (in part) cure of the disease. Now are the causes of man's sorrows many: the death of his parents, friends, allies, and children (though many of the barbarous° nations do rejoice at their burials and

1. See Scaliger 3.122.

sorrow at their births); the overthrows and discomforts[2] in battle; the subversions[3] of towns and cities; the desolations of countries; the loss of goods and worldly promotions, honor and good renown; finally, the travails° and torments of love forlorn or ill-bestowed, either by disgrace,[4] denial, delay, and twenty other ways that well-experienced lovers could recite. Such of these griefs as might be refrained[5] or helped by wisdom and the party's own good endeavor, the poet gave none order to sorrow them.[6] For first, as to the good renown, it is lost for the more part by some default of the owner and may be by his well doings recovered again. And if it be unjustly taken away, as by untrue and famous[7] libels, the offender's recantation may suffice for his amends°: so did the poet Stesichorus, as it is written of him, in his *Palinode* upon the dispraise of Helen, and recovered his eyesight.[8] Also, for worldly goods, they come and go, as things not long proprietary[9] to anybody, and are not yet subject unto fortune's dominion so, but that we ourselves are in great part accessary[10] to our own losses and hindrances[11] by oversight[12] and misguiding of ourselves and our things. Therefore, why should we bewail our such voluntary detriment?

But death, the irrecoverable loss, death, the doleful departure of friends that can never be recontinued by any other meeting or new acquaintance—besides our uncertainty and suspicion of their estates° and welfare in the places of their new abode—seemeth to carry a reasonable pretext of just sorrow. Likewise, the great overthrows in battle and desolations of countries by wars, as well for the loss of many lives and much liberty[13] as for that it toucheth the whole state, and every private man hath his portion in the damage. Finally, for love, there is no frailty in flesh and blood so excusable as it, no comfort or discomfort greater than the good and bad success° thereof, nothing more natural to man, nothing of more force to vanquish his will and to inveigle° his judgment.

Therefore, of death and burials, of the adversities by wars, and of true love lost or ill-bestowed, are the only sorrows that the noble poets sought by their art to remove or appease, not with any medicament of a contrary temper,° as the Galenists use to cure *contraria contrariis*, but as the Paracelsians, who cure *similia similibus*, making one dolor to expel another, and in this case, one short sorrowing the remedy of a

---

2. **discomforts** a common confusion for "discomfits," i.e., defeats.

3. **subversions** overthrows, demolitions.

4. **disgrace** one's own dishonor, but also the state of being out of grace or favor with the beloved.

5. **refrained** restrained.

6. **gave none order to sorrow them** i.e., felt no obligation to lament them (?). (This is probably not finished text).

7. **famous** infamous, notorious.

8. Scaliger also mentions this example in his chapter on the palinode (1.54).

9. **proprietary** held in private ownership.

10. **are . . . accessary** accede.

11. **hindrances** injuries, damages.

12. **oversight** inadvertent omission or error.

13. **liberty** unrestrained action or expression, license, pillage.

long and grievous sorrow.[14] And the lamenting of deaths was chiefly at the very burials of the dead, also at month's minds[15] and longer times, by custom continued yearly, whenas they used many offices of service and love toward the dead, and thereupon are called obsequies in our vulgar,° which was done not only by cladding the mourners, their friends, and servants, in black vestures of shape doleful and sad,° but also by woeful countenances and voices, and besides by poetical mournings in verse. Such funeral songs were called *epicedia* if they were sung by many, and *monodia* if they were uttered by one alone, and this was used at the interment of princes and others of great account, and it was reckoned a great civility to use such ceremonies, as at this day is also in some country used.

In Rome they accustomed to make orations funeral and commendatory of the dead parties in the public place called *Pro rostris*,[16] and our theologians,[17] instead thereof, use to make sermons, both teaching the people some good learning and also saying well of the departed. Those songs of the dolorous discomfits[18] in battle and other desolations in war, or of towns saccaged[19] and subverted,[20] were sung by the remnant of the army overthrown, with great screakings[21] and outcries, holding the wrong end of their weapon upwards in sign of sorrow and despair. The cities also made general mournings and offered sacrifices with poetical songs to appease the wrath of the martial gods and goddesses. The third sorrowing was of loves, by long lamentation in elegy[22]: so was their song called, and it was in a piteous manner of meter,° placing a limping pentameter after a lusty hexameter,[23] which made it go dolorously more than any other meter.°

---

14. Galen believed in humoral medicine, namely, that the body contained four humors or fluids, that disease was a product of an imbalance among them, and that to cure it one should supply some form of a humor contrary to the one out of balance (hence *contraria contrariis*, "contraries by contraries"). (Sometimes an excess humor was drained rather than counteracted.) By contrast, Paracelsus rejected Galenic medicine and believed that people could be cured by giving them small doses of what was making them sick (hence *similia similibus*, "like by like").

15. **month's minds** in pre-Reformation England, the commemoration of a deceased person by the celebration of masses etc. on a day one month from the date of the death.

16. **Pro rostris** (Lat.) "on or at the *rostra*." The *rostra* was the public platform on which speakers stood in the Forum and which was named for the ships' prows (*rostra*) of defeated enemies that were attached to it.

17. **theologians** i.e., preachers.

18. **discomfits** defeats.

19. **saccaged** sacked, plundered.

20. **subverted** overthrown.

21. **screakings** screams, shrieks.

22. On the love elegy, see Scaliger 1.50; Elyot, *The Governour* 47; Harington 9; Sidney, *Defence* 218, 236; Campion 306; Daniel 150.

23. A classical elegiac couplet consisted of a line in dactylic hexameter followed by one in dactylic pentameter.

CHAPTER 25

*Of the solemn rejoicings at the
nativity of princes' children*

To return from sorrow to rejoicing, it is a very good hap[1] and no unwise part for him that can do it. I say, therefore, that the comfort of issue and procreation of children is so natural and so great not only to all men but especially to princes, as duty and civility have made it a common custom to rejoice at the birth of their noble children and to keep those days hallowed and festival forever once in the year during the parents' or children's lives, and that by public order and consent. Of which rejoicings and mirths the poet ministered the first occasion honorable by presenting of joyful songs and ballads° praising the parents by proof,[2] the child by hope, the whole kindred by report,[3] and the day itself with wishes of all good success,° long life, health, and prosperity forever to the newborn. These poems were called in Greek *genethliaca*; with us they may be called natal or birth songs.[4]

---

1. **hap** chance, luck.
2. **by proof** for having successfully produced good results (i.e., a good child).

3. **report** reputation, fame.
4. See Scaliger 3.102. *Genethliaca* (Gr.) means "birthday songs."

CHAPTER 26

The manner of rejoicings at marriages and weddings

As the consolation of children well begotten is great, no less but rather greater ought to be that which is occasion of children, that is, honorable matrimony, a love by all laws allowed, not mutable nor encumbered with such vain cares and passions as that other love, whereof there is no assurance, but loose and fickle affection° occasioned for the most part by sudden sights and acquaintance of no long trial° or experience, nor upon any other good ground wherein any surety may be conceived. Wherefore the civil poet could do no less in conscience and credit than as he had before done to the ballad° of birth, now with much better devotion to celebrate by his poem the cheerful day of marriages as well princely as others, for that hath always been accounted, with every country and nation of never so barbarous° people, the highest and holiest of any ceremony appertaining to man: a match forsooth made forever and not for a day, a solace provided for youth, a comfort for age, a knot of alliance and amity indissoluble. Great rejoicing was therefore due to such a matter and to so gladsome a time. This was done in ballad-wise[1] as the natal song and was sung very sweetly by musicians at the chamber door of the bridegroom and bride at such times as shall be hereafter declared, and they were called epithalamies,[2] as much to say as° ballads° at the bedding of the bride, for such as were sung at the board° at dinner or supper were other musics and not properly epithalamies. Here, if I shall say that which appertaineth to the art and disclose the mystery[3] of the whole matter, I must and do with all humble reverence bespeak[4] pardon of the chaste and honorable ears, lest I should either offend them with licentious speech, or leave them ignorant of the ancient guise[5] in old times used at weddings, in my simple° opinion nothing reprovable.[6]

This epithalamie was divided by breaches° into three parts to serve for three several fits[7] or times to be sung.[8] The first breach° was sung at the first part of the night when the spouse and her husband were brought to their bed and at the very chamber door, where in a large outer room used to be (besides the musicians) good store° of ladies or gentlewomen of their kinfolk and others who came to honor the marriage, and the tunes° of the songs were very loud and shrill, to the intent there might no noise be heard out of the bedchamber by the screaking[9] and outcry of the young damsel feeling the first forces of her stiff and rigorous[10] young man, she being as all virgins tender and weak, and inexpert in those manner of affairs. For which purpose also they used by old nurses (appointed to that service)[11] to suppress the noise by casting of pots full of nuts round about the chamber upon the hard floor or pavement, for they used no mats nor rushes as we do now. So as° the ladies and gentlewomen should have their ears so occupied, what with music, and what with their hands wantonly° scambling[12] and catching after the nuts, that they could not intend° to hearken after any other

1. **ballad-wise** in the manner of a ballad.

2. **epithalamies** *epithalamia* (sing. *epithalamion*): poems "about the marriage chamber" (Gr.).

3. **mystery** this use combines two meanings: (1) a religious ordinance or rite, esp. one of the Christian religion; and (2) the knowledge and skills, often kept secret, of a craft or profession. The phrase "art . . . and . . . mystery" perhaps echoes the formula used in contractual indentures by means of which apprentices were bound to their trade.

4. **bespeak** beg.

5. **guise** fashion, manner.

6. **nothing reprovable** not at all to be reproached.

7. **fits** parts or sections of a poem.

8. Scaliger (3.101) describes the same three divisions of the epithalamium.

9. **screaking** At 1.24.137 this word clearly means "screaming." Here, given what some readers see as a playful or raucous context, it may instead mean "screeching" or even "squeaking." In Marston, an author sometimes tonally similar to Puttenham, we find a possible reference to this sort of sound, also in a sexual context: "He is even one of the most busy-fingered lords; he will put the beauties to the squeak most hideously" (*The Malcontent* 5.5.40–41).

10. **rigorous** unbending, stiff.

11. It is noteworthy that the official agents of this sexual ritual, i.e., the nurses, are female. Cf. the old nurse, herself a gentlewoman, to whom Puttenham later attributes a bawdy poem (3.18.273).

12. **scambling** scrambling indecorously.

thing.[13] This was, as I said, to diminish the noise of the laughing, lamenting spouse. The tenor[14] of that part of the song was to congratulate[15] the first acquaintance and meeting of the young couple, allowing of their parents' good discretions in making the match, then afterward to sound cheerfully to the onset and first encounters of that amorous battle, to declare the comfort of children and increase of love by that means chiefly caused, the bride showing herself every ways well disposed and still° supplying occasions of new lusts° and love to her husband by her obedience and amorous embracings and all other allurements.

About midnight or one of the clock, the musicians came again to the chamber door (all the ladies and other women as they were of degree°[16] having taken their leave and being gone to their rest). This part of the ballad° was to refresh the faint and wearied bodies and spirits, and to animate new appetites with cheerful words, encouraging them to the recontinuance of the same entertainments, praising and commending (by supposal)[17] the good conformities[18] of them both and their desire one to vanquish the other by such friendly conflicts, alleging that the first embracements never bred bairns[19] by reason of their overmuch affection° and heat, but only made passage for children and enforced greater liking to the late made match; that the second assaults were less rigorous, but more vigorous and apt to advance the purpose of procreation; that therefore they should persist in all good appetite with an invincible courage° to the end. This was the second part of the epithalamie.

In the morning when it was fair broad day and that by likelihood all turns were sufficiently served,[20] the last acts of the interlude° being ended, and that the bride must within few hours arise and apparel herself, no more as a virgin but as a wife, and about dinner time must by order come forth *Sicut sponsa de thalamo,*[21] very demurely and stately

---

13. Since Spenser has Colin Clout recall a game in which he and his companions "fell all for nuts at strife" (*The Shepheardes Calender,* "December" 35), it is likely that "scambling" for nuts was a common Elizabethan recreation. A differently suggestive parallel, also involving "scambling," occurs in Taverner's commentary on Erasmus's adage *simia, simia est, etiam si aurea gestet insignia* (1.7.11: LB 2.265A–C, CWE 32.72): "An ape is an ape, althoughe she [?] weare badges of golde." Taverner tells the story of an Egyptian king who dressed some apes in finery and taught them to dance. Then a merry fellow tossed "a good sort of nuttes . . . in the floor amonges the maskers." Here the apes "beganne to showe what they were . . . tearinge a sunder theyr visours and maskinge apparell [they] skambled and went together by the eares for the nuttes" (C5r).

14. **tenor** substance, purport; perhaps, tenor voice.

15. **congratulate** express joy about.

16. **as they were of degree** in order of rank, or "having" rank (i.e., of high rank).

17. **by supposal** it is thought.

18. **conformities** likenesses, harmonies.

19. **bairns** children.

20. **turns . . . served** goals . . . achieved.

21. *Sicut . . . thalamo* "as a bride from the marriage bed." Cf. Psalms 19:4–5 (Geneva Bible, 1576): "in [the heavens] hath he set a tabernacle for the sun. / Which cometh forth as a bridegroom out of his chamber, and rejoiceth like a mighty man to run his race." Geneva gives "chamber" this marginal note: "Or, veil. The manner was that the bride and bridegroom should stand under a veil together, and after come forth with great solemnity and rejoicing of the assembly."

to be seen and acknowledged of her parents and kinfolk whether she were the same woman or a changeling, or dead or alive, or maimed by any accident° nocturnal. The same musicians came again with this last part and greeted them both with a psalm[22] of new applausions,[23] for that they had either of them so well behaved themselves that night, the husband to rob his spouse of her maidenhead and save her life, the bride so lustily[24] to satisfy her husband's love and escape with so little danger° of her person, for which good chance that they should make a lovely truce and abstinence of that war till next night, sealing the placard[25] of that lovely league with twenty manner of sweet kisses, then by good admonitions informed them to the frugal and thrifty life all the rest of their days. The good man getting and bringing home, the wife saving that which her husband should get, therewith to be the better able to keep good hospitality according to their estates° and to bring up their children (if God sent any) virtuously, and the better by their own good example. Finally, to persevere all the rest of their life in true and inviolable wedlock. This ceremony was omitted when men married widows or such as had tasted the fruits of love before (we call them well-experienced young women) in whom there was no fear of danger to their persons or of any outcry at all at the time of those terrible approaches.

Thus much touching the usage of epithalamie or bedding ballad° of the ancient times, in which if there were any wanton° or lascivious matter more than ordinary, which they called *Fescennina licentia*,[26] it was borne withal° for that time because of the matter no less requiring. Catullus hath made of them one or two very artificial° and civil, but none more excellent than of late years a young nobleman of Germany, as I take it, Joannes Secundus, who in that and in his poem *De basiis*, passeth any of the ancient or modern poets in my judgment.[27]

Puttenham switches the genders from bridegroom (or possibly couple) to bride; Spenser does the same in *Epithalamion* 148–50.

22. **psalm** ritual song.
23. **applausions** applause.
24. **lustily** with pleasure, willingly.
25. **placard** public proclamation.
26. ***Fescennina licentia*** "Fescennine license" (Horace, *Epistles* 2.1.145; cf. Catullus 61.119–48). The Etruscan town of Fescennia was famous for sportive, jeering dialogues in verse which were named after it. For the Romans, a poet who wrote such verse was thus considered to be assuming a Fescennine license. Erasmus cites this practice in *Apophthegmata* 4, "Octavius Caesar Augustus" 33 (LB 4.209D–209E, Udall 273); Udall translates the term as a "ragmans rewe," and ex-

plains, "For so dooe we call a long ieste, that railleth on any persone by name, or toucheth a bodies honestee somewhat nere" (274). Such songs, he says, were originally invented "for makyng laughter and sporte at marriages, euen like as is now vsed, to syng songes of the Frere and the Nunne, with other semblable merie iestes, at weddynges, and other feastings."

27. Catullus' two *epithalamia* are nos. 61 and 62 in his collected lyrics. After the latter were printed in Venice in 1472, they were much imitated, including by Joannes Secundus, whose *Basia* (Kisses), which Puttenham calls *De basiis*, takes off from two of the most famous poems in Catullus' collection (nos. 5 and 7).

CHAPTER 27

*The manner of poesy by which they uttered their
bitter taunts, and privy[1] nips or witty°
scoffs, and other merry conceits°*

But all the world could not keep, nor any civil ordinance to the contrary so prevail, but that men would and must needs utter their spleens in all ordinary matters also, or else it seemed their bowels would burst.[2] Therefore the poet devised a pretty fashioned poem short and sweet (as we are wont to say) and called it epigram, in which every merry conceited° man might without any long study or tedious ambage° make his friend sport,° and anger his foe, and give a pretty nip, or show a sharp conceit° in few verses. For this epigram[3] is but an inscription or writing made as it were upon a table, or in a window, or upon the wall or mantel of a chimney in some place of common resort, where it was allowed every man might come, or be sitting to chat and prate, as now in our taverns and common tabling houses,[4] where many merry heads meet and scribble with ink, with chalk, or with a coal such matters as they would every man should know and descant upon.[5] Afterward, the same came to be put in paper and in books and used as ordinary missives, some of friendship, some of defiance, or as other messages of mirth. Martial was the chief of this skill° among the Latins, and at these days the best epigrams we find, and of the sharpest conceit,° are those that have been gathered among the relics of the two mute satyrs in Rome, Pasquil and Marphorius, which in time of *sede vacante*, when merry conceited° men listed° to gibe and jest at the dead pope or any of his cardinals, they fastened them upon those images, which now lie in the open streets, and were tolerated, but after that term expired they were inhibited[6] again.[7] These inscriptions or epigrams at their beginning had no certain author that would avouch them, some for fear of blame, if they were over saucy or sharp, others for modesty of the writer, as was that distich° of Vergil which he set upon the palace gate of the emperor Augustus, which I will recite for the briefness and

---

1. **privy** surreptitious, covert.

2. In the humoral medicine of the Renaissance, the spleen was the source of the humor called melancholy (black bile) and (specifying a psychological disposition as well as a physical condition) of the emotions of melancholy, mirth, and anger.

3. **epigram** (Gk.) "writing upon."

4. **tabling houses** places of resort where one played games such as "tables" (backgammon).

5. **descant upon** comment on, discourse about. This derivation of the epigram from

the premodern equivalent of graffiti suggests how far beyond the boundaries of nominally "high" art the specifically literary realm extended at this time, for courtly as well as popular authors.

6. **inhibited** prohibited.

7. Pasquil and Marphorius were "talking statues" on which people in Rome placed satirical poems *sede vacante* (Lat., "while the [pope's] seat was empty"), though after the election of a new pope the pasquinades were prohibited ("inhibited") again. See LN 4.

quickness° of it, and also for another event that fell out upon the matter worthy to be remembered. These were the verses:

> *Nocte pluit tota, redeunt spectacula mane:*
> *Divisum imperium cum Iove Caesar habet.*[8]

Which I have thus Englished:

> *It rains all night, early the shows return:*
> *God and Caesar do reign and rule by turn.*

As much to say, God showeth his power by the night rains; Caesar, his magnificence by the pomps of the day.

These two verses were very well liked and brought to the emperor's majesty, who took great pleasure in them and willed the author should be known. A saucy courtier proffered himself to be the man and had a good reward given him, for the emperor himself was not only learned, but of much munificence toward all learned men. Whereupon Vergil, seeing himself by his overmuch modesty defrauded of the reward that an impudent had gotten by abuse° of his merit, came the next night, and fastened upon the same place this half meter,° four times iterated. Thus:

> *Sic vos non vobis*
> *Sic vos non vobis*
> *Sic vos non vobis*
> *Sic vos non vobis*[9]

And there it remained a great while because no man wist° what it meant, till Vergil opened[10] the whole fraud by this device.° He wrote above the same half meters° this whole verse hexameter:

> *Hos ego versiculos feci tulit alter honores.*[11]

And then finished the four half meters,° thus:

> *Sic vos non vobis* *Fertis aratra boves.*
> *Sic vos non vobis* *Vellera fertis oves.*
> *Sic vos non vobis* *Mellificatis apes.*
> *Sic vos non vobis* *Nidificatis aves.*[12]

And put to his name Publius Vergilius Maro. This matter came by and by[13] to the emperor's ear, who, taking great pleasure in the device,° called for Vergil and gave him not only a present reward, with a good allowance

---

8. This poem was attributed to Vergil by his fourth-century biographer and commentator Donatus (*Vita Vergilii* 17.69).

9. "Thus you, (but) not for yourselves."

10. **opened** disclosed, revealed.

11. "I myself made the little verses, but someone else took away the prize" (Donatus, *Vita Vergilii* 17.70). Also quoted by Lodge (1.85).

12. "Thus you, [like] the ox, pull the plow, but not for yourselves. / Thus you, [like] the sheep, bear a fleece, but not for yourselves. / Thus you, [like] the bee, make honey, but not for yourselves. / Thus you, [like] the bird, make a nest, but not for yourselves."

13. **by and by** straightway.

of diet[14]—a bouche[15] in court, as we use to call it—but also held him forever after, upon larger trial° he had made of his learning and virtue, in so great reputation as he vouchsafed to give him the name of a friend (*amicus*), which among the Romans was so great an honor and special favor, as all such persons were allowed to the emperor's table or to the senators' who had received them (as friends), and they were the only men that came ordinarily to their boards° and solaced with them in their chambers and gardens, when none other could be admitted.

14. **diet** food.
15. **bouche** (Fr., "mouth") an allowance of

food given by a king to the members of his household.

CHAPTER 28

*Of the poem called epitaph used
for memorial[1] of the dead*

An epitaph is but a kind of epigram, only applied to the report of the dead person's estate° and degree,° or of his other good or bad parts, to his commendation or reproach, and is an inscription such as a man may commodiously write or engrave upon a tomb in few verses, pithy, quick,° and sententious,° for the passerby to peruse and judge upon without any long tarriance.[2] So as° if it exceed the measure° of an epigram, it is then (if the verse be correspondent)[3] rather an elegy than an epitaph, which error many of these bastard[4] rhymers commit, because they be not learned, nor (as we are wont to say) their craft's masters. For they make long and tedious discourses and write them in large tables° to be hanged up in churches and chancels over the tombs of great men and others, which be so exceeding long as one must have half a day's leisure to read one of them, and must be called away before he come half to the end, or else be locked into the church by the sexton, as I myself was once served reading an epitaph in a certain cathedral church of England. They be ignorant of poesy that call such long tales by the name of epitaphs; they might better call them elegies, as I said before, and then ought neither to be engraven nor hanged up in tables.° I have seen them nevertheless upon many honorable tombs of these late times erected, which do rather disgrace than honor either the matter or maker.[5]

1. **memorial** memory, story, monument, testament.
2. **tarriance** delay. See Scaliger 3.102. *Epitaph* means "upon stone."

3. **correspondent** in accord with.
4. **bastard** base.
5. On Tudor confusion regarding elegy, epigram, and epitaph, see Weitzman.

CHAPTER 29

A certain ancient form of poesy by which
men did use to reproach their enemies

As friends be a rich and joyful possession, so be foes a continual torment and canker to the mind of man, and yet there is no possible mean to avoid this inconvenience, for the best of us all, and he that thinketh he lives most blameless, lives not without enemies that envy° him for his good parts or hate him for his evil. There be wise men, and of them the great, learned man Plutarch, that took upon them to persuade the benefit that men receive by their enemies, which though it may be true in manner of paradox, yet I find man's frailty to be naturally such, and always hath been, that he cannot conceive it in his own case, nor show that patience and moderation in such griefs, as becometh the man perfect° and accomplished in all virtue, but either in deed or by word, he will seek revenge against them that malice[1] him or practice his harms, especially such foes as oppose themselves to a man's loves. This made the ancient poets to invent° a mean to rid the gall of all such vindictive men, so as° they might be awreaked[2] of their wrong, and never belie their enemy with slanderous untruths. And this was done by a manner of imprecation, or, as we call it, by cursing and banning of the parties, and wishing all evil to alight upon them, and though it never the sooner happened, yet was it great easement to the boiling stomach.[3] They were called *dirae*, such as Vergil made against Battarus, and Ovid against Ibis.[4] We Christians are forbidden to use such uncharitable fashions and willed to refer all our revenges to God alone.[5]

1. **malice** desire to injure.
2. **awreaked** revenged.
3. **stomach** often regarded as the source of anger or vexation. On invective epigram, see Hudson 49–70.
4. Donatus, following Suetonius (*Vita Vergilii* 18), attributes *Dirae* (*Curses*) to the sixteen-year-old Vergil. In the poem the speaker denounces a soldier who appropriated his farm, a situation recalling that of Vergil's *Eclogues* 1 and 9. The actual date and authorship of *Dirae* are uncertain, though it is clearly part of a tradition of "curse poetry" going back at least to the Hellenistic poet Callimachus. (Note that Lycurgus, not Battarus, is the name of the soldier in the *Dirae*.) At the end of his life in Tomis, a port on the Black Sea to which he had been banished by the emperor Augustus, Ovid wrote his *Ibis*, a long curse directed at its otherwise unidentified title character. On *dirae*, see Scaliger 1.53, which mentions both examples.
5. See Deuteronomy 32:35 and Romans 12:19.

CHAPTER 30

Of short epigrams called posies

There be also other like epigrams that were sent usually for New Year's gifts or to be printed or put upon their banqueting dishes of sugarplate,[1] or of marchpane,[2] and such other dainty meats[3] as by the courtesy and custom every guest might carry from a common feast home with him to his own house, and were made for the nonce.° They were called *nenia* or *apophoreta*,[4] and never contained above one verse, or two at the most, but the shorter the better. We call them posies[5] and do paint them nowadays upon the backsides of our fruit trenchers[6] of wood, or use them as devices° in rings and arms and about such courtly purposes.

So have we remembered and set forth to your Majesty very briefly all the commended forms of the ancient poesy, which we in our vulgar° makings[7] do imitate and use under these common names: interlude,° song, ballad,° carol, and ditty, borrowing them also from the French, all saving this word "song" which is our natural Saxon English word. The rest, such as time and usurpation by custom have allowed us out of the primitive Greek and Latin, as comedy, tragedy, ode, epitaph, elegy, epigram, and other more. And we have purposely omitted all nice° or scholastical° curiosities° not meet for your Majesty's contemplation in this our vulgar° art, and what we have written of the ancient forms of poems, we have taken from the best clerks° writing in the same art.

The part that next followeth, to wit, of proportion,°[8] because the Greeks nor Latins never had it in use, nor made any observation, no more than we do of their feet, we may truly affirm to have been the first

---

1. **sugarplate** a flat sheet of sugar used as a kind of dish for other sweetmeats or delicacies; since it could be eaten in its turn, it was also considered a sweetmeat. For a period account of the elaborations of this form of "show" food, see *The Honorable Entertainment Given to the Queen's Majesty in Progress, at Elvetham in Hampshire* (in Kinney, *Renaissance Drama* 152–53).

2. **marchpane** marzipan.

3. **dainty meats** delicacies.

4. ***nenia* or *apophoreta*** The term *nenia* (or *naenia*) identifies a range of different kinds of poems, including magical incantations and funeral, popular, and nursery songs; the last two are most appropriate here. *Apophoreta* (Gk., "to be borne away") were presents which guests received at table, especially during the Saturnalia, to take home with them, or which were given to people by political candidates. On *nenia*, see Scaliger 1.50.

5. There may be a punning relation in the *Art* between this smallest of poetic forms (the "posy") and the largest abstraction of "poesy." "Posy" is a contraction of "poesy"; it now means a bunch of flowers, but originally the "flowers" meant by the word were poems or even a single short poem. In the period, both poems and figures of speech were referred to as "flowers." In fact, the word "anthology" (Lat. *florilegium*) meant "a collection of flowers." Renaissance writers sometimes play with this sense of "posy" in the titles of their collections, as Gascoigne does with *A Hundreth Sundrie Flowres Bounde up in One small Poesie.*

6. **trenchers** platters.

7. **makings** poems.

8. Since proportion is the master term of Book 2, it is possible that chapter 30 was originally the last chapter of Book 1; the highly self-contained chapter 31 may be a later addition.

devisers thereof ourselves, as αὐτοδιδακτοι,[9] and not to have borrowed it of any other by learning or imitation, and thereby trusting to be holden the more excusable if anything in this our labors happen either to mislike[10] or to come short of the author's purpose, because commonly the first attempt in any art or engine° artificial° is amendable,° and in time by often experiences reformed. And so no doubt may this device° of ours be by others that shall take the pen in hand after us.

9. **αὐτοδιδακτοι** (Gk.) "self-taught persons."   10. **mislike** be displeasing.

CHAPTER 31

Who in any age have been the most commended writers in our English poesy, and the author's censure[1] given upon them[2]

It appeareth by sundry records of books both printed and written, that many of our countrymen have painfully[3] travailed° in this part,[4] of whose works some appear to be but bare translations, other some matters of their own invention° and very commendable, whereof some recital shall be made in this place, to the intent chiefly that their names should not be defrauded of such honor as seemeth due to them for having by their thankful[5] studies so much beautified our English tongue, as at this day it will be found our nation is in nothing inferior to the French or Italian for copy[6] of language, subtlety of device,° good method, and proportion° in any form of poem, but that they may compare with the most and perchance pass a great many of them. And I will not reach above the time of King Edward III and Richard II for any that wrote in English meter,° because before their times by reason of the late Norman conquest, which had brought into this realm much alteration both of our language and laws, and therewithal[7] a certain martial barbarousness,° whereby the study of all good learning was so much decayed, as long time after no man or very few intended° to write in any laudable science,° so as° beyond that time there is little or nothing worth commendation to be found written in this art.

1. **censure** judgment.
2. Puttenham's account of the history of English poetry is antedated only by Webbe (1.239–47) among English writers, though French treatises such as Du Bellay's (2.2.121–27) provided models. Cf. Sidney, *Defence* 242–46; Meres; and Peacham, *The Complete Gentleman* 94–96.
3. **painfully** painstakingly.
4. **part** matter.
5. **thankful** deserving of thanks.
6. **copy** copiousness.
7. **therewithal** in addition to that.

And those of the first age were Chaucer and Gower, both of them, as I suppose, knights.[8] After whom followed John Lydgate, the monk of Bury, and that nameless who wrote the satire called *Piers Plowman;*[9] next him followed Hardyng the chronicler; then in King Henry VIII's times Skelton (I wot° not for what great worthiness surnamed the Poet Laureate).[10] In the latter end of the same king's reign sprung up a new company of courtly makers, of whom Sir Thomas Wyatt the elder and Henry, Earl of Surrey, were the two chieftains, who, having traveled into Italy and there tasted the sweet and stately measures° and style of the Italian poesy, as novices newly crept out of the schools of Dante, Ariosto, and Petrarch, they greatly polished our rude° and homely manner of vulgar° poesy from that it had been before, and for that cause may justly be said the first reformers of our English meter° and style. In the same time or not long after was the Lord Nicholas Vaux,[11] a man of much facility in vulgar° makings.

Afterward in King Edward VI's time came to be in reputation for the same faculty[12] Thomas Sternhold, who first translated into English certain psalms of David, and John Heywood, the epigrammist, who for the mirth and quickness° of his conceits,° more than for any good learning was in him, came to be well benefited by the king. But the principal man in this profession at the same time was Master Edward Ferrers, a man of no less mirth and felicity that way, but of much more skill° and magnificence in this meter,° and therefore wrote for the most part to the stage in tragedy and sometimes in comedy or interlude,° wherein he gave the king so much good recreation, as he had thereby many good

---

8. Chaucer was elected a Knight of the Shire (an administrative office) in 1386 but was never actually dubbed a knight. See *Chaucer Life-Records* 364–66. The earliest records of Chaucer's retrospective promotion to this status appear in the 1540s, in Latin works by Leland and Bale; the English designation "Sir" begins to appear in the 1560s, in a manuscript record (ca. 1560) and Gerard Legh's *The Accedens of Armory* (1562: see f. 16, c1r), and in numerous works thereafter, including Gascoigne's *The Adventures of Master F. J.* (1573) (see 143). For more information, see Cook 38–39. John Gower was born into the gentry and lived and worked among them throughout his life, maintaining many relations, legal and financial, with London and court society, but was not a knight. See the Life Records discussion in Fisher (37–69). Webbe also thought Gower was a knight (1.241).

9. This work was often attributed to what we now regard as its title character: see, e.g.,

Webbe 1.242. In the expanded edition of his *Scriptorum Illustrium Majoris Brittanniæ* (1557; see 1.474), however, John Bale identified the author of the poem as "Robertus Langlande" (now identified as William Langland). Puttenham knows that the work is not eponymous but has not read Bale.

10. Skelton's title was an academic honor, as he tells us in one of the poems "Against Garnesche": "A King to mine habit gave: / At Oxford, the university, / Advanced I was to that degree; / By whole consent of their senate / I was made poet laureate" (*Poems*, pp. 161–62). The title was bestowed on any graduate who had distinguished himself in rhetoric and poetry, and does not imply a position comparable to the ones held by later poets laureate from Ben Jonson on. Puttenham's references to him (below in this chapter at 150, and at 2.10.173) are uniformly disrespectful.

11. A mistake for Thomas Vaux.

12. **faculty** ability.

rewards.[13] In Queen Mary's time flourished above any other Doctor Phaer, one that was well learned and excellently well translated into English verse heroical certain books of Vergil's *Aeneid*. Since him followed Master Arthur Golding, who with no less commendation turned into English meter° the *Metamorphoses* of Ovid, and that other Doctor[14] who made the supplement to those books of Vergil's *Aeneid*, which Master Phaer left undone.

And in her Majesty's time that now is are sprung up another crew of courtly makers, noblemen and gentlemen of her Majesty's own servants, who have written excellently well, as it would appear if their doings could be found out and made public with the rest. Of which number is first that noble gentleman Edward Earl of Oxford, Thomas Lord of Buckhurst, when he was young, Henry Lord Paget, Sir Philip Sidney, Sir Walter Ralegh, Master Edward Dyer, Master Fulke Greville, Gascoigne, Breton, Turberville, and a great many other learned gentlemen, whose names I do not omit for envy,° but to avoid tediousness, and who have deserved no little commendation.

But of them all particularly this is mine opinion, that Chaucer, with Gower, Lydgate, and Hardyng, for their antiquity ought to have the first place, and Chaucer as the most renowned of them all, for the much learning appeareth to be in him above any of the rest. And though many of his books be but bare translations out of the Latin and French, yet are they well handled, as his books of *Troilus and Cresseid*, and *The Romaunt of the Rose*, whereof he translated but one half, the device° was Jean de Meun's, a French poet.[15] *The Canterbury Tales* were Chaucer's own invention,° as I suppose, and where he showeth more the natural[16] of his pleasant wit° than in any other of his works; his similitudes, comparisons, and all other descriptions are such as cannot be amended.° His meter° heroical of *Troilus and Cresseid* is very grave and stately, keeping the staff° of seven and the verse of ten;[17] his other verses of *The Canterbury Tales* be but riding rhyme,[18] nevertheless very well becoming the

13. Smith suggests that this is an error for George Ferrers (1500?–1579), politician, dramatist, and "master of the king's pastimes" to Edward VI when the latter was sorrowing over the execution of his uncle Somerset (on January 22, 1552; for Ferrers here, see Holinshed 3.1032). He also served as Master of the Revels for Mary I during Christmas 1553. Puttenham refers to his tragedies below in this chapter (000). As a major figure in the team of authors who produced *The Mirror for Magistrates* (1559), he wrote the tragical poems on Thomas, duke of Gloucester (Richard II's uncle); the Edmund, duke of Somerset, who died in 1454; and perhaps others. His comedies do not survive, unless his possible contributions to the queen's entertainments at Kenilworth in 1575 count as such.

14. Thomas Twyne.

15. Cf. 3.19.293.

16. **natural** natural character.

17. I.e., the "staff," or stanza, has seven lines and the line of verse ten syllables; it was called rhyme royal. (Gascoigne was the first to use this term in English, in *Certayne Notes* 460.)

18. **riding rhyme** Renaissance writers used the expression in different ways (see Pigman 739–40 for many examples). It was often used for the rhyming couplets of Chaucer's *Canterbury Tales*. The reason for the name remains obscure, though some seem to have associated it with either the ambling movement of the verse form or the fact that Chaucer's pilgrims were riding to Canterbury.

matter of that pleasant pilgrimage in which every man's part is played
with much decency.°[19]

Gower, saving for his good and grave moralities,[20] had nothing in him
highly to be commended, for his verse was homely and without good
measure,° his words strained much deal[21] out of the French writers, his
rhyme wrested,[22] and in his inventions° small subtlety; the applications of his moralities are the best in him, and yet those many times
very grossly bestowed;[23] neither doth the substance of his works sufficiently answer the subtlety of his titles.[24] Lydgate, a translator only and
no deviser of that which he wrote, but one that wrote in good verse.
Hardyng, a poet epic or historical, handled himself well according to
the time and manner of his subject. He that wrote the satire of *Piers
Plowman* seemed to have been a malcontent of that time, and therefore
bent himself wholly to tax the disorders of that age, and especially the
pride of the Roman clergy, of whose fall he seemeth to be a very true
prophet; his verse is but loose meter° and his terms[25] hard and obscure,
so as° in them is little pleasure to be taken.[26] Skelton, a sharp satirist,
but with more railing and scoffery than became a poet laureate; such
among the Greeks were called *pantomimi*,[27] with us buffoons, altogether applying their wits to scurrilities and other ridiculous matters.

Henry Earl of Surrey and Sir Thomas Wyatt, between whom I find
very little difference, I repute them (as before) for the two chief lanterns
of light to all others that have since employed their pens upon English
poesy. Their conceits° were lofty, their styles stately, their conveyance°
cleanly,° their terms proper, their meter° sweet and well-proportioned,
in all imitating very naturally and studiously their master Francis Petrarch. The Lord Vaux his commendation lieth chiefly in the facility of
his meter° and the aptness of his descriptions such as he taketh upon
him to make, namely in sundry of his songs, wherein he showeth the
counterfeit° action very lively and pleasantly.

Of the later sort I think thus: that for tragedy, the Lord of Buckhurst
and Master Edward Ferrers for such doings as I have seen of theirs do
deserve the highest price.[28] The Earl of Oxford[29] and Master Edwards of
her Majesty's Chapel for comedy and interlude.° For eclogue and

19. For period judgments of Chaucer, see
Ascham, *Toxophilus*, in *English Works* 27–29
and *Scholemaster* 289–90; Gascoigne, *Certayne Notes* 454; E.K., Spenser, *The Shepheardes Calender*, Epistle 13; Sidney, *Defence*
213; Webbe 1.241.
20. **moralities** moral teachings.
21. **much deal** to a large extent.
22. **wrested** forced.
23. **grossly bestowed** clumsily applied.
24. Cf. Sidney, *Defence* 213; Webbe
1.240–41.

25. **terms** manner of speaking.
26. Cf. Webbe 1.242.
27. ***pantomimi*** Latin plural of the Greek
word meaning "imitator of all things," used
for the actor in comedy who performed
in dumb shows and mimicked others. Cf.
Scaliger 1.10.
28. Both Buckhurst and George, not Edward, Ferrers were contributors to *The Mirror for Magistrates*. For Puttenham's mistake
over Ferrers's first name, see note 12.
29. Edward de Vere.

pastoral poesy, Sir Philip Sidney and Master Chaloner and that other gentleman[30] who wrote the late *Shepheardes Calender*. For ditty and amorous ode I find Sir Walter Ralegh's vein most lofty, insolent,[31] and passionate. Master Edward Dyer for elegy most sweet, solemn, and of high conceit.° Gascoigne for a good meter° and for a plentiful vein. Phaer and Golding for a learned and well-corrected verse, especially in translation clear and very faithfully answering their authors' intent. Others have also written with much facility, but more commendably perchance if they had not written so much nor so popularly.°

But last in recital and first in degree° is the Queen, our Sovereign Lady, whose learned, delicate,° noble muse easily surmounteth all the rest that have written before her time or since, for sense, sweetness, and subtlety, be it in ode, elegy, epigram, or any other kind of poem heroic or lyric, wherein it shall please her Majesty to employ her pen, even by as much odds as her own excellent estate° and degree° exceedeth all the rest of her most humble vassals.

30. Edmund Spenser.
31. **insolent** swelling, exultant (in a positive sense).

THE SECOND BOOK
Of Proportion° Poetical

CHAPTER I

Of proportion° poetical

It is said by such as profess the mathematical sciences° that all things stand by proportion,° and that without it nothing could stand to be good or beautiful.[1] The doctors° of our theology to the same effect, but in other terms, say that God made the world by number, measure, and weight.[2] Some for weight say tune,°[3] and peradventure° better, for weight is a kind of measure° or of much conveniency° with it, and

1. **stand by ... stand to be** are as they are by ... have the capacity to be. Puttenham thinks of things, from various aspects of a poem or piece of music to the universe in general, as being arranged in a harmonious, mathematical way that relates individual entities to others systematically and regularly by what he calls *proportion*. Proportion thus defines the governing principle of the arrangement, and is synonymous with the qualities of harmony and mathematical regularity. Further, he uses the word to refer to the arrangement itself, so that a poem or the world may or be proportion. Finally, he uses the word to refer to particular units within or features of an arrangement that are related to one another harmoniously or mathematically, such as meter and line length, stanza length or form, rhyme, and visual shape. Puttenham's notion that everything in the universe depends on proportion echoes what Henry Billingsley (d. 1606) said in his popular *Elements of Geometrie of the Most Auncient Philosopher Euclid of Megara* (1570). In his introductory statement to Euclid's fifth book, which concerns proportion and analogy, Billingsley writes that proportionality concerns not just lines,

figures, and bodies in geometry but also sounds and voices in music, time and movement in astronomy, weights, and places. In effect, he comes close to saying, as Puttenham does, that everything can be understood in terms of proportion. We should perhaps mention here that John Dee (1527–1608), Elizabeth's astrologer, possibly wrote parts of Billingsley's Euclid, including its popular "Mathematical Preface."

2. Curtius traces the development of this idea from the Wisdom of Solomon 11:17 (Geneva), "Thou hast ordered all things in measure, number and weight," through Jerome and Augustine, to Rabanus Maurus, Anselm, and many others. See Excursus xv, "Numerical Composition" (501–9).

3. **tune** agreement in pitch or harmony. Puttenham goes on to say that "tune" is better than "measure" as a way of describing the nature of the universe. "Tune" is a better candidate for a member of the triad "number, measure, and weight" than "weight" is, because the triad ought to be a set of *different* ideas (i.e., nonredundant), and *weight* and *measure* are too closely linked ("weight is a kind of measure").

therefore in their descriptions be always coupled together *statica et metrica*,[4] weight and measures.[5] Hereupon it seemeth the Philosopher gathers a triple proportion,° to wit: the arithmetical, the geometrical, and the musical.[6] And by one of these three is every other proportion° guided of the things that have conveniency° by relation, as the visible by light, color, and shadow; the audible by stirs,° times, and accents; the odorable by smells of sundry temperaments;° the tasteable by savors to the rate;[7] the tangible by his objects in this or that regard.

Of all which we leave to speak, returning to our poetical proportion,° which holdeth of[8] the musical, because, as we said before, poesy is a skill° to speak and write harmonically; and verses or rhyme be a kind of musical utterance, by reason of a certain congruity in sounds pleasing the ear, though not perchance so exquisitely as the harmonical concents[9] of the artificial° music, consisting in strained[10] tunes,° as is the vocal music, or that of melodious instruments, as lutes, harps, regals,[11] records,[12] and such like. And this our proportion° poetical resteth in five points: staff,° measure,° concord,° situation,° and figure,[13] all which shall be spoken of in their places.

---

4. **statica et metrica** not a Latin phrase, but a translation or rough transliteration of Greek *statika kai metrika*, "the art of weighing and the art of measuring."

5. For the primacy of the musical figure, see, for instance, Gioseffo Zarlino, *Le istituzioni harmoniche* (1558), cited in Finney 35.

6. If, as so often, "the Philosopher" is Aristotle, then the author may be working here with *Nicomachean Ethics* 5.3–5 (1131a10–1134a24) (or some summary version of it), where Aristotle appeals to arithmetic, geometric, and reciprocal proportion to explain various types of justice. The element of music (not original with Aristotle)

probably derives from Pythagorean or Euclidean sources. See also Scaliger 2.2.

7. **savors . . . rate** tastes proportional to (typical of?) the different foods.

8. **holdeth of** corresponds to, derives from.

9. **concents** harmonies.

10. **strained** uttered in song, melodious. Spoken and written verse are here distinguished from song and from the sounds of musical instruments.

11. **regals** a small portable organ (common ca. 1550–1625).

12. **records** recorders.

13. **figure** shape (Puttenham discusses "shaped poems" in 2.12).

CHAPTER 2

Of proportion° in staff°[1]

Staff° in our vulgar° poesy I know not why it should be so called, unless it be for that we understand it for a bearer or supporter of a song or ballad,° not unlike the old weak body that is stayed up by his staff, and were not otherwise able to walk or to stand upright. The Italian

---

1. **staff** Gascoigne (461) and Webbe (1.269–74) employ the term in the same sense of a verse stanza. Webbe also appears uncertain of the term's etymology, saying "some [verses

consist] of many rymes in one staffe (as they call it)" (1.269). According to *OED*, "staff" does not become associated with musical notation until the early seventeenth century.

called it *stanza*, as if we should say, a resting place.[2] And if we consider well the form of this poetical staff,° we shall find it to be a certain number of verses allowed to go all together and join without any intermission,[3] and do or should finish up all the sentences of the same with a full period, unless it be in some special cases, and there to stay till another staff° follow of like sort.[4] And the shortest staff° containeth not under four verses, nor the longest above ten; if it pass that number, it is rather a whole ditty than properly a staff.° Also, for the more part the staves° stand rather upon[5] the even number of verses than the odd, though there be of both sorts.

The first proportion,° then, of a staff° is by quatrain or four verses. The second of five verses, and is seldom used. The third by sixain or six verses, and is not only most usual, but also very pleasant to the ear. The fourth is in seven verses, and is the chief of our ancient proportions° used by any rhymer writing anything of historical or grave poem, as ye may see in Chaucer and Lydgate, the one writing the loves of Troilus and Cresseida, the other of the fall of princes, both by them translated, not devised.[6] The fifth proportion° is of eight verses very stately and heroic,[7] and which I like better than that of seven because it receiveth better band.°[8] The sixth is of nine verses, rare[9] but very

2. *Stanza* means "room" in Italian, though it derives from *stare*, "to rest or stand": hence Puttenham's definition of it as "resting place." Cf. Donne's play on the word in "The Canonization": "We'll build in sonnets pretty rooms" (32).

3. Such binding together of numerous verses into a single staff or stanza may hint at a possible relation to barrel staves or the staves or rungs of a ladder (both given by *OED* for *stave*), plural linear shapes arranged in parallel into a single form.

4. The early modern notion of stanza is ultimately inseparable from rhyme, just as its opposite, blank verse, is insistently non-stanzaic, working (as in Milton) with verse paragraphs shaped by nonmetrical requirements. Puttenham uses *staff* and *stanza*, then, to mean by definition a group of rhymed lines. The references in this chapter to *intertanglement*, *band*, and *closure* are fully intelligible only on the presumption that stanzas are rhymed.

5. **stand . . . upon** consist of, depend on.

6. The seven-verse stanza of which Puttenham speaks was called rhyme royal (rhyming *ababbcc*). It appeared first in English in Chaucer (in *Troilus and Criseyde*, *The Parlement of Foules*, and four *Canterbury Tales*), and was used by many fifteenth-century poets. Lydgate's civic verse for royal entries sug-

gests a link between the form and honoring historical as well as fictional royalty. The term seems to have been first been used in English in Gascoigne's *Certayne Notes* (1575) to mark the form as fit for "grave discourses" (460). The "translations" by Chaucer and Lydgate of which Puttenham speaks are the former's *Troilus*, which reworked Boccaccio's *Il filostrato*, and the latter's *The Fall of Princes*, which reworked Boccaccio's *De casibus virorum illustrium* (On the Falls of Famous Men).

7. Given the emphasis on the heroic, the author probably means to name *ottava rima* (rhyming *abababcc*), the verse form of heroic adventure in Boccaccio's *Il filostrato* (1338?) and *Teseida* (1340–42), from which Chaucer took his *Troilus* and *Knight's Tale* narratives (though not their verse forms). See also Boiardo's *Orlando innamorato* (1483), Ariosto's *Orlando furioso* (1516), and Tasso's *Gerusalemme liberata* (1581), all of which the author might have known in Italian.

8. In this passage Puttenham regards the eight-line stanza as superior to the seven-line insofar as it allows somehow for better band, that is, for the stanzaic unity that results from the use of repeated structural elements such as rhyme. (See the Word Glossary definition of *band* and the crucial discussion at 2.11.178 on which it rests.) See LN 5.

9. **rare** splendid, excellent.

grave.[10] The seventh proportion° is of ten verses, very stately, but in many men's opinion too long; nevertheless of very good grace and much gravity. Of eleven and twelve I find none ordinary staves° used in any vulgar° language; neither doth it serve well to continue any historical report or ballad° or other song, but is a ditty of itself, and no staff,° yet some modern writers have used it, but very seldom. Then last of all have ye a proportion° to be used in the number of your staves,° as to a carol and a ballad,° to a song, and a round, or virelay.[11] For to a historical poem no certain number is limited, but as the matter falls out. Also, a distich° or couple of verses is not to be accounted a staff,° but serves for a continuance, as we see in elegy, epitaph, epigram, or such meters° of plain concord° not harmonically intertangled,[12] as some other songs of more delicate° music be.[13]

A staff° of four verses containeth in itself matter sufficient to make a full period or complement[14] of sense, though it do not always so, and therefore may go by divisions.[15] A staff° of five verses is not much used, because he that cannot comprehend his period[16] in four verses will rather drive it into six than leave it in five, for that the even number is more agreeable to the ear than the odd is. A staff° of six verses is very pleasant to the ear, and also serveth for a greater complement[17] than the inferior[18] staves,° which maketh him more commonly to be used. A staff° of seven verses, most usual with our ancient makers, also the staff° of eight, nine, and ten, of larger complement[19] than the rest, are

10. This description matches in both particulars the remarkable nine-line stanza of *The Faerie Queene* (first printed in 1590, and thus almost contemporary with Puttenham, but unmentioned in the *Art*). Spenser's stanza surely constitutes an attempt at the metrical "overgoing" of *ottava rima*, just as the poem itself aimed at the establishment of his English epic as equal or superior to those of his Italian models Ariosto and Tasso, whom he names in his Letter to Ralegh.

11. Puttenham appears here to move from describing the harmonies of particular *stanzas* of different lengths to a different aspect of harmony, that of appropriate *poem* length ("the number of your staves" in a given genre), attaching it to five forms or genres. Not all of these forms, however, have a normative number of stanzas. For a discussion of the generic terms, see LN 6.

12. **harmonically intertangled** To judge from the author's uses of "intertangled" in the final paragraph of this chapter, the sense appears to be "bound together by interlaced rhymes." Puttenham seems to assume that English elegies, epitaphs, and epigrams are

composed of rhyming couplets (i.e., not "intertangled").

13. Puttenham appears to be distinguishing between the couplets used in elegy etc. and the more complicated rhyme schemes of more delicate (intricately constructed) poems.

14. **complement** completion.

15. As (in Puttenham's view) the shortest stanza, the quatrain has room for a full and complete thought, but perhaps only barely. When a larger thought is at issue, Puttenham seems to allow here for enjambed quatrains, with the (divided) sense carried from one to the next stanza without a full grammatical stop. The "period" Puttenham refers to here was, for classical writers of prose, a rhythmical, rather than syntactic, unit that was usually a lengthy sentence or even a paragraph. Puttenham discusses it in more detail in 2.5.164–65.

16. **comprehend his period** complete his thought.

17. **serveth ... complement** provides more room to complete a unit of thought.

18. **inferior** i.e., shorter.

19. **complement** completeness, amplitude.

only used by the later makers, and unless they go with very good band,° do not so well as the inferior staves.°[20] Therefore if ye make your staff° of eight by two fours not intertangled, it is not a huitain[21] or a staff° of eight, but two quatrains. So is it in ten verses: not being intertangled, they be but two staves° of five.

20. Again, Spenser's nine-line *Faerie Queene* stanza exhibits an interlaced rhyme that certainly seems to constitute "very good band," rhyming *ababbcbcc*.

21. **huitain** a set of eight lines of verse (from Fr. *huit*, "eight").

CHAPTER 3

Of proportion° in measure°

Meter° and measure° is all one, for what the Greeks call μέτρον, the Latins call *mensura*,[1] and is but the quantity[2] of a verse, either long or short. This quantity with them consisteth in the number of their feet,[3] and with us in the number of syllables which are comprehended in every verse, not regarding his feet otherwise than that we allow in scanning our verse: two syllables to make one short portion (suppose it a foot) in every verse.[4] And after that sort[5] ye may say we have feet in our vulgar° rhymes, but that is improperly, for a foot by his sense natural[6] is a member of office and function, and serveth to three purposes, that is to say, to go,[7] to run, and to stand still; so as° he must be sometimes swift, sometimes slow, sometime unequally marching, or peradventure° steady. And if our feet poetical want° these qualities, it cannot be said a foot in sense translative[8] as here. And this cometh to pass by reason of the evident motion and stir,° which is perceived in the sounding of our words not always equal: for some ask longer, some shorter time to be uttered in, and so, by the Philosopher's definition, stir° is the true measure of time.[9]

1. "Meter" comes from the Greek word, "measure" from the Latin.

2. **quantity** length of syllables, determined by the time required to pronounce them; chiefly used with reference to Greek and Latin verse.

3. **feet** i.e., quantitative feet.

4. Puttenham's account of quantitative verse is generally based on Scaliger's. For instance, Puttenham's playing on the literal meaning of "foot" in this chapter develops what is found at the start of Scaliger's 2.2, while the names Puttenham supplies for feet having two or three syllables can be found in 2.3 as well as in the individual chapters

Scaliger later devotes to each of the feet. Puttenham's account of quantitative metrics is one of the earliest and most thorough in English, and the *OED* credits him as the first writer to use the words "bisyllable," "trisyllable," and "tetrasyllable."

5. **after that sort** in that sense.

6. **by . . . natural** anatomically.

7. **go** walk.

8. **translative** metaphorical.

9. Time is the subject of Aristotle's *Physics* 4.10–14, where he says, "Time defines motion by being its number, and motion defines time" (220b16–18). Puttenham is talking about the fact that in English we

The Greeks and Latins, because their words happened to be of many syllables and very few of one syllable, it fell out right with them to conceive and also to perceive a notable diversity of motion and times in the pronunciation of their words, and therefore to every bisyllable they allowed two times,[10] and to a trisyllable three times, and to every polysyllable more according to his quantity, and their times were some long, some short, according as their motions were slow or swift. For the sound of some syllable stayed the ear a great while, and others slid away so quickly as if they had not been pronounced. Then every syllable being allowed one time, either short or long, it fell out that every tetrasyllable had four times, every trisyllable three, and the bisyllable two, by which observation every word not under that size, as he ran or stood in a verse, was called by them a foot of such and so many times: namely, the bisyllable was either of two long times as the spondee; or two short, as the pyrrhichius;[11] or of a long and a short, as the trochee; or of a short and a long, as the iamb. The like rule did they set upon the word trisyllable, calling him a foot of three times: as the dactyl of a long and two short; the molossus of three long; the tribrach of three short; the amphibrachys of two long and a short; the amphimacer of two short and a long.[12] The word of four syllables they called a foot of four times, some or all of them either long or short, and yet not so content they mounted higher, and because their words served well thereto, they made feet of six times. But this proceeded more of curiosity° than otherwise, for whatsoever foot pass the trisyllable is compounded of his inferior, as every number arithmetical above three is compounded of the inferior numbers, as twice two make four, but the three is made of one number, *videl.*,° of two and a unity.

Now because our natural and primitive language of the Saxon English bears not any words (at least very few) of more syllables than one (for whatsoever we see exceed cometh to us by the alterations of our language grown upon many conquests and otherwise), there could be no such observation of times in the sound of our words, and for that cause we could not have the feet which the Greeks and Latins have in their meters.°[13]

---

do not have syllables that are regularly long or short (requiring regular amounts of time for their pronunciation), whereas the ancients did. Hence we cannot, properly speaking, talk about "feet" in English. Later in the chapter, however, he speaks of Anglo-Saxon, saying that it consisted of one-syllable words, all of which had the same quantity, so that its uniformity prevented it from developing a quantitative metrical system.

10. **times** units of time.

11. The *pes pyrrhichius* (pyrrhic foot) is a variant name for the dibrach (Gr.,

"two" + "beat"), a foot containing two short beats. Since this foot was commonly used in a dance known as the "pyrrhic war dance," it became known by this alternative name.

12. Puttenham has here switched the definitions of amphibrachys and amphimacer, while confusing the sequence of longs and shorts in both figures. He otherwise gets them right, both below in this chapter and at 2.10.207, 2.11.211, and 2.12.213.

13. For contemporary interest in quantitative verse in the English Renaissance, see 1.2, note 5.

But of this stir° and motion of their devised feet, nothing can better show the quality than these runners at common games,[14] who, setting forth from the first goal, one giveth the start speedily and perhaps before he come halfway to the other goal, decayeth his pace, as a man weary and fainting; another is slow at the start, but by amending° his pace keeps even with his fellow or perchance gets before him; another one while[15] gets ground, another while loseth it again, either in the beginning or middle of his race, and so proceeds unequally, sometimes swift, sometimes slow, as his breath or forces serve him; another sort there be that plod on, and will never change their pace, whether they win or lose the game. In this manner doth the Greek dactyl begin slowly and keep on swifter till the end, for his race being divided into three parts, he spends one, and that is the first, slowly, the other twain swiftly; the anapest his first two parts swiftly, his last slowly; the molossus spends all three parts of his race slowly and equally; bacchius his first part swiftly and two last parts slowly; the tribrach all his three parts swiftly; the antibacchius his two first parts slowly, his last and third swiftly; the amphimacer his first and last part slowly and his middle part swiftly; the amphibrachys his first and last parts swiftly but his middle part slowly; and so of others by like proportion.°

This was a pretty fantastical° observation of them, and yet brought their meters° to have a marvelous good grace, which was in Greek called ρυθμος: whence we have derived this word "rhyme," but improperly and not well, because we have no such feet or times or stirs° in our meters° by whose sympathy or pleasant convenience° with the ear we could take any delight. This *rithmus* of theirs is not therefore our rhyme, but a certain musical numerosity° in utterance, and not a bare number as that of the arithmetical computation is, which therefore is not called *rithmus* but *arithmus*.[16] Take this away from them, I mean the running° of their feet,[17] there is nothing of curiosity° among them more than with us nor yet so much.

---

14. The different paces at which runners run their races correspond to the length and shortness of the syllables inside the poetic feet; each foot (a measure of time through motion) amounts to a different style of running a race. The different racers, however, do not line up serially with the poetic feet discussed later in the paragraph. The parallel for the first runner, for instance (who "giveth the start speedily and perhaps before he come halfway to the other goal, decayeth his pace"), is not the dactyl but the bacchius: the "bacchius [runs] his first part swiftly, and two last parts slowly."

15. **another one while** at another time.

16. Puttenham is making two different distinctions here, one between *rithmus* and rhyme, and another between *rithmus* and *arithmus*. For clarification, see his more detailed discussion in 2.6 as well as our notes there.

17. **running . . . feet** i.e., rhythmical movement of their (quantitative) feet.

Chapter 4[1]

How many sorts of measures° we use in our vulgar°

To return from rhyme to our measure° again, it hath been said that according to the number of the syllables contained in every verse, the same is said a long or short meter,° and his shortest proportion° is of four syllables, and his longest of twelve; they that use it above pass the bounds of good proportion.° And every meter° may be as well in the odd as in the even syllable, but better in the even, and one verse may begin in the even, and another follow in the odd, and so keep a commendable proportion.°

The verse that containeth but two syllables, which may be in one word, is not usual: therefore many do deny him to be a verse, saying that it is but a foot, and that a meter° can have no less than two feet at the least.[2] But I find it otherwise as well among the best Italian poets as also with our vulgar° makers, and that two syllables serve well for a short measure° in the first place and middle and end of a staff;° and also in diverse situations°[3] and by sundry distances,[4] and is very passionate and of good grace, as shall be declared more at large° in the chapter of proportion° by situation.°

The next measure° is of two feet or of four syllables, and then one word tetrasyllable divided in the midst makes up the whole meter,° as thus:

> *Rēvē rēntlȳ.*

Or a trisyllable and one monosyllable, thus: "Sovereign God." Or two bisyllables, and that is pleasant, thus: "Restore again." Or with four monosyllables, and that is best of all, thus: "When I do think." I find no savor in a meter° of three syllables nor in effect in any odd, but they may be used for variety's sake, and especially being interlaced with others. The meter° of six syllables is very sweet and delicate,° as thus:

> *O God, when I behold*
> *This bright heaven so high,*
> *By thine own hands of old*
> *Contrived so cunningly.*°†

---

1. At this point the *Art* text begins misnumbering the chapters of Book 2, treating this chapter as a second chapter 3; we correct silently hereafter.

2. Cf. King James I: "tak heid . . . that your langest lynis exceid nochte fourteen fete, and that your shortest be nocht within foure" (1.214–15). (The context suggests that he means syllables here, not feet.)

3. **situations** different locations in the stanza.

4. **distances** Puttenham uses this term to denote (1) the distances that separate rhymes from one another, and (2) the relative distance between feet of different quantities or meters. See 2.11, "Of Proportion by Situation."

The meter° of seven syllables is not usual; no more is that of nine and eleven; yet, if they be well composed, that is, their caesura well appointed, and their last accent, which makes the concord,° they are commendable enough, as in this ditty where one verse is of eight, another is of seven, and in the one the accent upon the last, in the other upon the last save one:

> *The smoky sighs, the bitter tears*
> *That I in vain have wasted,*
> *The broken sleeps, the woe and fears*
> *That long in me have lasted*
> *Will be my death, all by thy guilt*
> *And not by my deserving,*
> *Since so inconstantly thou wilt*
> *Not love but still° be swerving.*[5]

And all the reason why these meters° in odd syllable are allowable is for that the sharp accent falls upon the penultimate, or last save one, syllable of the verse, which doth so drown the last as he seemeth to pass away in manner unpronounced, and so make the verse seem even. But if the accent fall upon the last and leave two flat[6] to finish the verse, it will not seem so, for the oddness will more notoriously appear, as for example in the last verse before recited, "Not love but still° be swerving," say thus, "Love it is a marvelous thing." Both verses be of equal quantity, *videl.,*° seven syllables apiece, and yet the first seems shorter than the latter, who shows a more[7] oddness than the former by reason of his sharp accent which is upon the last syllable, and makes him more audible than if he had slid away with a flat accent, as the word "swérving."

Your ordinary rhymers use very much their measures° in the odd, as nine and eleven, and the sharp accent upon the last syllable, which therefore makes him go ill-favoredly and like a minstrel's music.[8] Thus said one in a meter° of eleven, very harshly in mine ear, whether it be for lack of good rhyme or of good reason or of both, I wot° not:

> *Now suck child and sleep child, thy mother's own joy,*
> *Her only sweet comfort, to drown all annoy;*
> *For beauty surpassing the azured sky,*
> *I love thee my darling, as ball of mine eye.*[9]

---

5. **swerving** turning aside, wavering, forsaking. A close variant of poem no. 214.1–10 (Anonymous; 5–6 omitted) in *Tottel*.

6. **flat** unstressed.

7. **more** greater.

8. **minstrel's music** base music. Although in early use "minstrel" was a general designation for anyone whose profession was to entertain patrons, whether with singing, music, and storytelling, or with buffoonery or juggling, by the mid-sixteenth century, minstrels were thought of in particularly pejorative terms by those who insisted on a more elevated vision of poetry, as Puttenham does in the *Art*.

9. These lines are a version of the beginning of an anonymous poem found in MS Harl. 7392, f. 311.

This sort of composition in the odd I like not, unless it be helped by the caesura or by the accent, as I said before.

The meter° of eight is no less pleasant than that of six, and[10] the caesura falls just[11] in the middle, as this of the Earl of Surrey's:

> *When raging love, with extreme pain.*[12]

The meter° of ten syllables is very stately and heroical and must have his caesura fall upon the fourth syllable, and leave six behind him. Thus:

> *I serve at ease, and govern all with woe.*

This meter° of twelve syllables the Frenchman calleth a verse alexandrine,[13] and is with our modern rhymers most usual; with the ancient makers it was not so, for before Sir Thomas Wyatt's time they were not used in our vulgar.° They be for grave and stately matters fitter than for any other ditty of pleasure.

Some makers write in verses of fourteen syllables, giving the caesura at the first eight, which proportion° is tedious, for the length of the verse keepeth the ear too long from his delight, which is to hear the cadence° or the tunable° accent in the end of the verse. Nevertheless, that of twelve, if his caesura be just in the middle and that ye suffer him to run at full length, and do not as the common rhymers do, or their printer for sparing of paper, cut them off in the midst, wherein they make in two verses but half rhyme, they do very well, as wrote the Earl of Surrey, translating the book of the preacher[14]:

> *Solomon, David's son, king of Jerusalem.*

This verse is a very good alexandrine, but perchance would have sounded more musically if the first word had been a bisyllable or two monosyllables and not a trisyllable, having his sharp accent upon the antepenultimate as it hath, by which occasion it runs like a dactyl, and carries the two later syllables away so speedily as it seems but one foot in our vulgar° measure,° and by that means makes the verse seem but of eleven syllables, which oddness is nothing pleasant to the ear. Judge somebody whether it would have done better if it might have been said thus:

> *Robóham, David's son, king of Jerusalem.*

Letting the sharp accent fall upon *bo*, or thus:

> *Restóre king Dávid's són untó Jerúsalém.*

---

10. **and** if.

11. **just** exactly.

12. Surrey, *Tottel* no. 16.1 (Jones no. 1).

13. **alexandrine** line of verse twelve syllables, or six iambs, in length; see 1.19, note 29.

14. **the book of the preacher** Ecclesiastes (meaning "Preacher"); the passage paraphrases verse 1.1 (see Jones no. 43). Cf. Webbe on dividing long lines in two (1.267–68), and 2.6.167.

For now the sharp accent falls upon *bo*, and so doth it upon the last in *restóre*, which was not in the other verse.[15] But because we have seemed to make mention of caesura, and to appoint his place in every measure,° it shall not be amiss to say somewhat more of it, and also of such pauses as are used in utterance, and what commodity[16] or delectation they bring, either to the speakers or to the hearers.

15. Alexander argues that this sentence is corrupt and should possibly read: "for now the sharp accent falls upon 'restóre,' and so doth it upon the last in 'untó,' which was not in the other verse" (371, note 20).

16. **commodity** benefit, profit. "Commodity and delectation" is a version of Horace's "dulce et utile," the sweet and the useful (*Ars poetica* 343), which he specifies as the aims of poetry in general.

CHAPTER 5

On caesura[1]

There is no greater difference betwixt a civil and brutish utterance than clear distinction of voices,[2] and the most laudable languages are always most plain and distinct, and the barbarous° most confused and indistinct. It is therefore requisite that leisure be taken in pronunciation, such as may make our words plain and most audible and agreeable to the ear. Also the breath asketh to be now and then relieved with some pause or stay more or less; besides that the very nature of speech, because it goeth by clauses of several construction and sense, requireth some space betwixt them with intermission of sound, to the end they may not huddle one upon another so rudely° and so fast that the ear may not perceive their difference.

For these respects the ancient reformers of language invented° three manner of pauses, one of less leisure than another, and such several intermissions of sound to serve (besides easement to the breath) for a treble distinction of sentences or parts of speech, as they happened to be more or less perfect° in sense. The shortest pause or intermission they called *comma*, as who would say a piece of a speech cut off.[3] The second they called *colon*, not a piece but as it were a member for his larger

1. Puttenham derives much of his material in this chapter from Scaliger 4.25. Gascoigne discusses the caesura at *Certayne Notes* 459–60; cf. also James I 1.214–15.

2. **voices** articulate sounds, utterances.

3. *Comma* in Greek means a short clause (from *kopto*, "to cut off"). *Colon* in Greek means the limb or member of a body. And *period* (*periodos*) in Greek means a going around something, making a full circle, hence a completed thought in rhetorical terms; Aristotle defines it as "a sentence that has a beginning and end in itself and a magnitude that can easily be grasped" (*Rhetoric* 3.9.3 [1409a]). On these terms, see Quintilian 9.4.22. Commas, colons, and periods were the units of prose rhythm into which classical writers divided their speeches. In Puttenham's theory, the words are coming to mean the punctuation marks indicating stopping points or pauses of varying types, which is what they have meant since then.

length, because it occupied twice as much time as the comma. The third they called *period*, for a complement or full pause and as a resting place and perfection° of so much former speech as had been uttered, and from whence they needed not to pass any further unless it were to renew more matter to enlarge the tale.[4]

This cannot be better represented than by example of these common travelers[5] by the highways, where they seem to allow themselves three manner of stays or easements[6]: one a-horseback calling perchance for a cup of beer or wine, and having drunken it up, rides away and never lights;[7] about noon he cometh to his inn and there baits himself[8] and his horse an hour or more; at night when he can conveniently° travel no further, he taketh up his lodging and rests himself till the morrow, from whence he followeth the course of a further voyage, if his business be such. Even so, our poet, when he hath made one verse, hath as it were finished one day's journey, and the while[9] easeth himself with one bait[10] at the least, which is a comma or caesura in the midway, if the verse be even and not odd, otherwise in some other place, and not just[11] in the middle. If there be no caesura at all and the verse long, the less is the maker's skill° and hearer's delight. Therefore, in a verse of twelve syllables the caesura ought to fall right upon the sixth syllable; in a verse of eleven upon the sixth also, leaving five to follow; in a verse of ten upon the fourth, leaving six to follow; in a verse of nine upon the fourth, leaving five to follow; in a verse of eight, just in the midst, that is, upon the fourth; in a verse of seven, either upon the fourth or none at all, the meter° very ill-brooking any pause. In a verse of six syllables and under is needful no caesura at all, because the breath asketh no relief; yet if ye give any comma, it is to make distinction of sense more than for anything else, and such caesura must never be made in the midst of any word, if it be well appointed.

So may you see that the use of these pauses or distinctions is not generally with the vulgar° poet as it is with the prose writer because, the poet's chief music lying in his rhyme or concord° to hear the symphony,° he maketh all the haste he can to be at an end of his verse, and delights not in many stays by the way, and therefore giveth but one caesura to any verse. And thus much for the sounding of a meter.°

Nevertheless, he may use in any verse both his comma, colon, and interrogative point, as well as in prose. But our ancient rhymers, as Chaucer, Lydgate, and others, used these caesuras either very seldom,

---

4. Cf. Mulcaster's description of the three pauses, at *Elementarie* 148, which Nashe cites as a byword in *The Anatomie of Absurditie* (*Works* 1.48).

5. **travelers** both those who journey and those who labor.

6. **easements** periods of repose and refreshment.

7. **lights** alights.

8. **baits himself** stops for food and rest.

9. **the while** for a while, a moment.

10. **bait** pause.

11. **just** exactly, precisely.

or not at all, or else very licentiously, and many times made their me-
ters° (they called them riding rhyme)[12] of such unshapely words as
would allow no convenient° caesura, and therefore did let their rhymes
run out at length, and never stayed till they came to the end. Which
manner, though it were not to be misliked in some sort of meter,° yet
in every long verse the caesura ought to be kept precisely, if it were but
to serve as a law to correct the licentiousness of rhymers, besides that it
pleaseth the ear better, and showeth more cunning° in the maker by following the rule of his restraint. For a rhymer that will be tied to no
rules at all, but range as he list,° may easily utter what he will. But such
manner of poesy is called in our vulgar,° rhyme doggerel, with which
rebuke we will in no case our maker should be touched. Therefore, before all other things let his rhyme and concords° be true, clear, and
audible with no less delight than almost the strained[13] note of a musician's mouth, and not dark° or wrenched by wrong writing as many do
to patch up their meters,° and so follow in their art neither rule, reason,
nor rhyme.

Much more might be said for the use of your three pauses, comma,
colon, and period, for perchance it be not all a matter[14] to use many
commas, and few, nor colons likewise, or long or short periods, for it is
diversely used by divers good writers. But because it appertaineth more
to the orator or writer in prose than in verse, I will say no more in it
than thus, that they be used for a commodious[15] and sensible° distinction of clauses in prose, since every verse is, as it were, a clause of itself,
and limited with a caesura howsoever the sense bear, perfect° or imperfect,° which difference is observable betwixt the prose and the meter.°[16]

---

12. **riding rhyme** See 1.31, note 18.
13. **strained** sung, melodic.
14. **all a matter** all the same.
15. **commodious** convenient.

16. I.e., the three pauses in prose derive
from the sense (the meaning), whereas a verse
caesura derives from its place in the verse line,
whether the sense calls for a pause there or not.

CHAPTER 6

Of proportion° in concord,° called
symphony° or rhyme

Because we use the word *rhyme*, though by manner of abusion,[1] yet
to help that fault again we apply it in our vulgar° poesy another way
very commendably and curiously.°[2] For wanting° the currentness° of
the Greek and Latin feet, instead thereof we make in the ends of our

---

1. **abusion** misuse. Webbe also finds the
derivation of rhyme from *rhythmos* an abuse
(1.267).

2. Puttenham is referring to the fact that
in the English Renaissance *rhyme* and
rhythm, both derived from *rhythmos* (Gk.

verses a certain tunable° sound, which anon[3] after with another verse reasonably distant we accord together in the last fall or cadence,° the ear taking pleasure to hear the like tune° reported,[4] and to feel his return. And for this purpose serve the monosyllables of our English Saxons excellently well, because they do naturally and indifferently° receive any accent, and in them, if they finish the verse, resteth the shrill[5] accent of necessity, and so doth it not in the last of every bisyllable, nor of every polysyllable word.[6]

But to the purpose: *rhyme* is a borrowed word from the Greeks by the Latins and French, from them by us Saxon Angles, and by abusion, as hath been said, and therefore it shall not do amiss to tell what this *rithmos* was with the Greeks, for what is it with us hath been already said.[7] There is an accountable[8] number which we call arithmetical (*arithmos*), as: one, two, three. There is also a musical or audible number° fashioned by stirring[9] of tunes° and their sundry times in the utterance of our words, as when the voice goeth high or low, or sharp or flat, or swift or slow. And this is called *rithmos* or numerosity,°[10] that is to say, a certain flowing utterance by slipper° words and syllables, such as the tongue easily utters, and the ear with pleasure receiveth, and which flowing of words with much volubility° smoothly proceeding from the mouth is in some sort harmonical and breedeth to the ear a great compassion.[11]

This point grew by the smooth and delicate° running of their feet, which we have not in our vulgar,° though we use as much as may be

---

ῥυθμός), by way of Latin *rhythmus*, were often used to mean what we call *rhyme*, although that is not what the Greek term means. Puttenham will go on to explain this confusion in this chapter, drawing on such sources as Scaliger 2.2, Sébillet 1.2.54–57, and Du Bellay 2.8.153–57. Cf. Webbe 1.267. Puttenham pretty consistently identifies rhyme as *concord* or *symphony*.

   3. **anon** immediately.

   4. **reported** echoed.

   5. **shrill** sharp, strong.

   6. Both Gascoigne and James I (1.215) note what Puttenham observes, that monosyllables accept any accent. Gascoigne also warns against using too many polysyllables, because "the most auncient English wordes are of one sillable, so that the more monasyllables that you use, the truer Englishman you shall seeme, and the lesse you shall smell of the Inkhorne" (*Certayne Notes* 457–58). Cf. Sidney, *Defence* 248–49.

   7. In this passage Puttenham is distinguishing *arithmos* from *rithmos* (more properly transliterated from the Greek as *rhuthmos*, although he may be deliberately mis-transliterating to make the two words seem more closely related). Puttenham identifies *rithmus* (ῥυθμός, more accurately transcribed as *rhuthmos*) with "numerosity," and opposes it to *arithmus*, also called "bare number" (see 2.3.159). He seems to be distinguishing between the kind of counting involved in marking the rhythmical movement of music or poetry and the nonrhythmical counting of arithmetic. *Arithmos* is the Greek word for "number" (from *arithmeo*, "to count"). By contrast, *rhuthmos* means "measured motion, time," and hence "rhythm" (from *rheio*, "to flow"). Both "rhythm" and "rhyme" come from the Greek word *rhythmos*. "Rhyme" was originally spelled "rime," but its spelling was changed in the sixteenth century about the same time that "rhythm" was acquiring its modern meaning. (Puttenham first mentions this subject in 2.3.159.)

   8. **accountable** able to be counted.

   9. **stirring** uttering.

  10. Cf. Scaliger 2.2.

  11. **compassion** sympathy.

the most flowing words and slippery° syllables that we can pick out.
Yet do not we call that by the name of rhyme as the Greeks did, but do
give the name of rhyme only to our concords,° or tunable° concents[12]
in the latter end of our verses, and which concords° the Greeks nor
Latins never used in their poesy till by the barbarous° soldiers out of
the camp it was brought into the court and thence to the school, as
hath been before remembered.[13] And yet the Greeks and Latins both
used a manner of speech by clauses of like termination, which they
called ὁμοιοτέλευτον, and was the nearest that they approached to our
rhyme, but is not our right concord.°[14] So as° we in abusing this term
rhyme be nevertheless excusable applying it to another point in poesy
no less curious° than their rhythm or numerosity° which indeed
passed the whole verse throughout, whereas our concords° keep but
the latter end of every verse, or perchance the middle and the end in
meters° that be long.[15]

12. **concents** harmonies. Since *1589*
spells the word "consents," it is possible that
Puttenham may have meant that word
(meaning "agreements"); the two spellings
(and words) were interchangeable in the period, and both meanings are possible here.

13. See 1.6.100–1.

14. *Homoioteleuton* is a rhetorical figure
which Puttenham defines as "a manner of

speech or writing in their proses that
went by clauses, finishing in words of like
tune" (3.16.257–58). Puttenham misspells
the figure as ὁμιοτελυτον. On *homoioteleuton* and rhyme, cf. Du Bellay 2.8.154 and
Campion 294.

15. What is internal rhyme here may be
the end-rhymes of the "cut" long lines Puttenham mentions at 2.4.162.

CHAPTER 7

Of accent, time, and stir° perceived evidently in the
distinction of man's voice, and which
makes the flowing of a meter°

N ow because we have spoken of accent, time, and stir° or motion in
words, we will set you down more at large° what they be. The ancient Greeks and Latins, by reason their speech fell out originally to be
fashioned with words of many syllables for the most part, it was of necessity that they could not utter every syllable with one like and equal
sound, nor in like space of time, nor with like motion or agility, but
that one must be more suddenly and quickly forsaken, or longer paused
upon than another, or sounded with a higher note and clearer voice
than another. And of necessity[1] this diversity of sound must fall either
upon the last syllable, or upon the last save one, or upon the third,[2] and

1. **of necessity** i.e., because.

2. **the third** i.e., the third from the end,
the antepenultimate.

could not reach higher to make any notable difference.[3] It caused them to give unto three different sounds three several names: to that which was highest lifted up and most elevated or shrillest[4] in the ear, they gave the name of the sharp accent; to the lowest and most base, because it seemed to fall down rather than to rise up, they gave the name of the heavy accent;[5] and that other which seemed in part to lift up and in part to fall down, they called the circumflex, or compassed,° accent—and if new terms were not odious, we might very properly call him the Windabout, for so is the Greek word.[6] Then because everything that by nature falls down is said heavy, and whatsoever naturally mounts upward is said light, it gave occasion to say that there were diversities in the motion of the voice, as swift and slow, which motion also presupposes time, because time is *mensura motus*,[7] by the Philosopher. So have you the causes of their primitive invention° and use in our art of poesy.

All this by good observation we may perceive in our vulgar° words if they be of more syllables than one, but especially if they be trisyllables, as, for example, in these words *altitude* and *heaviness* the sharp accent falls upon *al-* and *hea-*, which be the antepenultimates; the other two fall away speedily as if they were scarce sounded. In this trisyllable *forsaken* the sharp accent falls upon *sa-*, which is the penultimate, and in the other two is heavy and obscure.[8] Again in these bisyllables, *endúre, unsúre, demúre, aspíre, desíre, retíre*, your sharp accent falls upon the last syllable, but in words monosyllable, which be for the more part our natural Saxon English, the accent is indifferent,° and may be used for sharp or flat and heavy at our pleasure. I say Saxon English, for our Norman English alloweth us very many bisyllables, and also trisyllables, as: *reverence, diligence, amorous, desirous*, and such like.

---

3. **could not . . . difference** i.e., could not be placed farther forward in the word because that would not distinguish it from a word having one of the other three accents (because the voice would naturally place an additional accent on one of the three last syllables?).

4. **shrillest** sharpest, strongest.

5. Puttenham's use of *heavy* here is counterintuitive, since it would seem to designate a strong accent but actually does just the opposite. In later chapters he uses *flat* (2.4.161, 2.14.208) and *low* (2.18.217) as synonyms for *heavy*, whereas for *sharp* he uses *shrill* (2.6.166) and *high* (2.14.207, 2.18.217).

6. Circumflex comes from *circumflexus*, a late Latin translation of the Greek *per spomenos*; both mean "drawn about or around." Cf. Gascoigne's discussion of the three stresses (*Certayne Notes* 456). Puttenham's description of the three kinds of accents in Latin and Greek reflects what he could have found in Latin grammars, such as in the section labeled "De Prosodia" (On Prosody) in Lily H11–v.

7. **mensura motus** the measure of motion; see Aristotle, *Physics* 4.11.220a24–25.

8. **obscure** indistinctly heard.

CHAPTER 8

*Of your cadences° by which your meter° is made
symphonical;° when they be sweetest
and most solemn in a verse*

As the smoothness of your words and syllables running upon feet
of sundry quantities make with the Greeks and Latins the body of
their verses numerous° or rhythmical, so in our vulgar° poesy—and of
all other nations at this day—your verses answering each other by couples, or at larger distances[1] in good cadence,° is it that maketh your me-
ter° symphonical.°[2] This cadence° is the fall of a verse in every last word
with a certain tunable° sound, which being matched with another of
like sound, do make a concord.° And the whole cadence° is contained
sometime in one syllable, sometime in two, or in three at the most: for
above the antepenultimate there reacheth no accent,[3] which is chief
cause of the cadence,° unless it be by usurpation in some English words,
to which we give a sharp accent upon the fourth, as, *hónorable, mátri-
mony, pátrimony, míserable*, and such other as would neither make a
sweet cadence,° nor easily find any word of like quantity to match
them.[4] And the accented syllable with all the rest under[5] him make the
cadence,° and no syllable above,[6] as in these words, *agílity, facílity, sub-
jéction, diréction*, and these bisyllables, *ténder, slénder, trústy, lústy*.
But always the cadence° which falleth upon the last syllable of a verse is
sweetest and most commendable; that upon the penultimate more
light, and not so pleasant; but falling upon the antepenultimate is most
unpleasant of all, because they make your meter° too light and trivial,
and are fitter for the epigrammatist or comical poet than for the lyric
and elegiac, which are accounted the sweeter musics.

---

1. **verses . . . couples, or at larger distances**
i.e., either adjacent verses that rhyme (couplets) or rhyming lines separated from one
another by intervening lines.

2. "Cadence" means the rhythmical flow
of language that marks the end of a line of
poetry. It comes from a Latin word meaning
"to fall," and in Italy by the end of the late
Middle Ages, *cadenza* referred to the falling
off of the voice in music at the end of a
phrase or song. According to the *OED*, this
Italian meaning became available in English
only at the start of the seventeenth century.
It appears, however, to underlie Puttenham's
use of the word in this chapter. Here and
elsewhere he uses it as something like a synonym for "rhyme" or "rhyming syllables."

3. **above the antepenultimate . . . accent**
i.e., there is no accent in the line of verse

more than three syllables before the last
one.

4. Puttenham's claim here seems to be
that although some English words do have
the accent on the fourth syllable from the
end, their pronunciation is a "usurpation,"
deriving unnaturally or non-natively from
foreign tongues such as French and Latin.
Moreover, there are few words available to
rhyme with them. For both reasons they
are not useful for English poetry. Puttenham
restates his claim more straightforwardly
in 2.9: "For some words of exceeding great
length, which have been fetched from the
Latin inkhorn or borrowed of strangers, the
use of them in rhyme is nothing pleasant"
(171–72).

5. **under** i.e., after.

6. **above** before.

But though we have said that to make good concord° your several verses should have their cadences° like, yet must there be some difference in their orthography, though not in their sound, as if one cadence° be *constrain*, the next *restrain*, or one *aspire*, another *respire*, this maketh no good concord,° because they are all one,[7] but if ye will exchange both these consonants of the accented syllable, or void but one of them away, then will your cadences° be good and your concord° too, as to say: *restrain, refrain, remain; aspire, desire, retire*—which rule nevertheless is not well observed by many makers for lack of good judgment and a delicate° ear.[8] And this may suffice to show the use and nature of your cadences,° which are in effect all the sweetness and cunning° in our vulgar° poesy.

7. **all one** i.e., all the same. Cf. James I 1.215–16.

8. For adventurous counterexamples of "good" "bad" rhyming, see 2.9, note 1.

CHAPTER 9

How the good maker will not wrench his word to help his rhyme, either by falsifying his accent, or by untrue orthography

Now there cannot be in a maker a fouler fault than to falsify his accent to serve his cadence,° or by untrue orthography to wrench his words to help his rhyme,[1] for it is a sign that such a maker is not copious in his own language, or (as they are wont to say) not half his craft's master.[2] As, for example, if one should rhyme to this word *restore*, he may not match him with *door* or *poor*, for neither of both are of like terminant,[3] either by good orthography or in natural sound. Therefore, such rhyme is strained. So is it to this word *ram* to say *came*, or to *bean, den*, for they sound not nor be written alike; and many other like

1. Webbe also inveighs against these faults (1.268, 273). Spenser is sometimes guilty of them, though uncertainty over flexible Renaissance pronunciation makes judgments about accent tricky. See, however, *Faerie Queene* 3.4.9, where *blowes* and *rowes* rhyme with *shallowes*, and 3.6.36, where *horrore* rhymes with *more* and *store*. Puttenham himself cites without complaint Kermesine's lozenge poem, which rhymes *eyes* with *enemies* (2.12.182), and writes Philo's odolet to Calia, which rhymes *flower* ("flour") with *honour* (2.12.186). He also cites Wyatt rhyming *color* with *therefore* as iambs (3.16.260). Orthographical manipulation can be seen in *Muiopotmos*, where Spenser writes *vow* for *vows* (237: "Ne may thee helpe the manie hartie vow") in order to rhyme it with *thou* and *now*.

2. Puttenham's "as they are wont to say" suggests an allusion to a proverbial saying, although we have not located it. Justice Shallow also remarks, "He is not his craft's master; he doth not do it right" (*Henry IV, Part Two* 3.2.278–79).

3. **terminant** termination.

cadences° which were superfluous to recite, and are usual with rude° rhymers who observe not precisely the rules of prosody. Nevertheless, in all such cases, if necessity constrained, it is somewhat more tolerable to help the rhyme by false orthography than to leave an unpleasant dissonance to the ear by keeping true orthography and losing the rhyme. As, for example, it is better to rhyme *dore* with *restore* than in his truer orthography, which is *door*, and to this word *desire* to say *fier* than *fyre*, though it be otherwise better written *fire*.[4] For since the chief grace of our vulgar° poesy consisteth in the symphony,° as hath been already said,[5] our maker must not be too licentious in his concords,° but see that they go even, just, and melodious in the ear, and right so in the numerosity° or currentness° of the whole body of his verse, and in every other of his proportions.°

For a licentious maker is in truth but a bungler and not a poet. Such men were in effect the most part of all your old rhymers, and especially Gower, who to make up his rhyme would for the most part write his terminant[6] syllable with false orthography, and many times not stick° to put in a plain French word for an English. And so, by your leave, do many of our common rhymers at this day, as he that by all likelihood, having no word at hand to rhyme to this word *joy*, he made his other verse end in *Roy*, saying very impudently thus:

> O mighty Lord of Love, dame Venus' only joy,
> Who art the highest God of any heavenly Roy.[7]

Which word was never yet received in our language for an English word.[8] Such extreme licentiousness is utterly to be banished from our school, and better it might have been borne with in old rhyming writers, because they lived in a barbarous° age, and were grave, moral men, but very homely poets, such also as made most of their works by translation out of the Latin and French tongue, and few or none of their own engine,° as may easily be known to them that list° to look upon the poems of both languages.

Finally, as ye may rhyme with words of all sorts, be they of many syllables or few, so nevertheless is there a choice by which to make your cadence° (before remembered)[9] most commendable. For some words of exceeding great length, which have been fetched from the Latin inkhorn[10]

---

4. This last example is unclear.

5. See 2.6.165.

6. **terminant** terminal.

7. These lines appear in Turberville, "The Louer to Cupid for mercie" (EE, leaves 45r–v: 1–4). They appear in a slightly different version in 3.22.338.

8. Smith says that "'Roy' is found in Northern writings, and is . . . a common word in Middle Scots" (*Essays* 2.416).

9. See 2.8.169.

10. The inkhorn was a portable container for ink and became a symbol of ostentatious learning and pedantry. Writers typically borrowed words from Latin and Greek, but also from other European languages, by means of which they sought not merely to display their knowledge but also, in many cases, to enrich the vernacular by importing foreign words into it. Since most Renaissance writers

or borrowed of strangers,° the use of them in rhyme is nothing pleasant, saving perchance to the common people, who rejoice much to be at plays and interludes,° and, besides their natural ignorance, have at all such times their ears so attentive to the matter, and their eyes upon the shows of the stage, that they take little heed to the cunning° of the rhyme, and therefore be as well satisfied with that which is gross,[11] as with any other finer and more delicate.°

---

shared some version of the goal of enriching the vernacular, what Puttenham is objecting to here is an *excessive* borrowing that shows too little respect for the properties of the ver-

nacular. Puttenham himself imports such words, but frequently supplies English glosses for them.

11. **gross** coarse, common.

CHAPTER 10

Of concord° in long and short measures,° and by near or far distances,[1] and which of them is most commendable

But this ye must observe withal,° that because your concords° contain the chief part of music in your meter,° their distances may not be too wide or far asunder, lest the ear should lose the tune° and be defrauded of his delight. And whensoever ye see any maker use large and extraordinary distances, ye must think he doth intend to show himself more artificial° than popular,° and yet therein is[2] not to be discommended, for respects[3] that shall be remembered in some other place of this book.[4]

Note also that rhyme or concord° is not commendably used both in the end and middle of a verse, unless it be in toys° and trifling poesies,[5] for it showeth a certain lightness either of the matter or of the maker's head, albeit these common rhymers use it much.[6] For, as I said before, like as the symphony° in a verse of great length is, as it were, lost by looking after him,[7] and yet may the meter° be very grave and stately, so on the other side doth the over-busy and too speedy return of one manner of tune° too much annoy and, as it were, glut the ear—unless

---

1. **distances** i.e., between lines that rhyme.
2. **is** i.e., the use of such distances is.
3. **respects** considerations.
4. Puttenham may be referring to his discussion in the following chapter of rhymes that occur four or more lines apart in a poem. He may instead be referring to his praise for carefully dissembled artifice in 3.25.
5. **poesies** Puttenham may be playing on the pun *poesy/posy*, a posy being a short,

light poem often inscribed on rings and armor. For Puttenham's own definition, see 1.30.146.
6. Internal rhyme was a feature of much English and French medieval verse, and of the rhymed Latin verse Puttenham decries in 1.7.
7. **by looking after him** i.e., having to find it because the line of verse is too long or because there are several unrhymed syllables that come after the rhyming syllable in it.

it be in small and popular° musics sung by these *cantabanqui*[8] upon benches and barrels' heads, where they have none other audience than boys or country fellows that pass by them in the street; or else by blind harpers or such like tavern minstrels that give a fit[9] of mirth for a groat,[10] and their matters being for the most part stories of old time, as *The Tale of Sir Topas*, the reports[11] of *Bevis of Southampton*, *Guy of Warwick*, *Adam Bell*, and *Clym of the Clough*, and such other old romances or historical rhymes, made purposely for recreation of the common people at Christmas dinners and bride-ales,[12] and in taverns and alehouses and such other places of base resort. Also they be used in carols and rounds and such light or lascivious poems, which are commonly more commodiously uttered by these buffoons or vices[13] in plays than by any other person. Such were the rhymes of Skelton; usurping the name of a poet laureate, being indeed but a rude,° railing rhymer, and all his doings ridiculous, he used both short distances and short measures,° pleasing only the popular° ear. In our courtly maker we banish them utterly.

Now also have ye in every song or ditty concord° by compass,° and concord° intertangled, and a mixt[14] of both. What that is and how they be used shall be declared in the chapter of proportion° by situation.°[15]

---

8. *Cantabanqui* (It., "sings-on-benches"; more accurately, *cantabanchi*) were itinerant ballad-singers and entertainers akin to the "blind harpers" and "tavern minstrels." Like the similarly named mountebanks (quack peddlers of medicine), they would mount a bench or stage in a town square and entertain crowds with popular songs, often on legendary or historical subjects, and with buffoonish antics. Puttenham's attitude toward them here is clearly condescending although in Book 1 he seems to have a more positive view of the part of their repertory that included such historical romances as *Bevis of Southampton* and *Guy of Warwick* (see 1.29.131). Sidney exhibits similar ambivalence: "Certainly, I must confess mine own barbarousness, I never heard the old song of Percy and Douglas that I found not my heart moved more than with a trumpet; and yet it is sung but by some blind crowder, with no rougher voice than rude style" (*Defence* 231).

9. **fit** division (usually larger than a stanza) of a poetical (or musical) composition.

10. **groat** silver coin worth four pence.

11. **reports** narratives.

12. The bride-ale was the wedding feast: when the bride and groom had returned from the church, they and the wedding party were presented with warm, sweet spiced ale.

13. **vices** See 1.11.117.

14. **mixt** mixture.

15. Puttenham distinguishes here among three kinds of rhymes: those that can be connected by vertical curved lines ("compass") not intersected by other such lines, such as couplets; those in which the curved lines drawn between the rhyme words intersect other such lines ("intertangled"), as they would in alternating rhyme; and those rhyme patterns involving both kinds, such as the rhyme royal stanza (*ababbcc*). See Puttenham's drawings of various kinds of rhyme schemes in 2.11.

Chapter 11

Of proportion° by situation°[1]

This proportion° consisteth in placing of every verse in a staff° or ditty by such reasonable distances as may best serve the ear for delight, and also to show the poet's art and variety of music. And the proportion° is double: one by marshalling the meters° and limiting their distances, having regard to the rhyme or concord,° how they go and return; another by placing every verse, having a regard to his measure° and quantity only, and not to his concord,° as to set one short meter° to three long, or four short and two long, or a short measure° and a long, or of diverse lengths with relation one to another. Which manner of situation,° even without respect of the rhyme, doth alter the nature of the poesy and make it either lighter or graver, or more merry or mournful, and many ways passionate[2] to the ear and heart of the hearer, seeming for this point[3] that our maker by his measures° and concords° of sundry proportions° doth counterfeit° the harmonical tunes° of the vocal and instrumental musics. As the Dorian because his falls, sallies, and compass°[4] be diverse from those of the Phrygian, the Phrygian likewise from the Lydian, and all three from the Aeolian, Mixolydian, and Ionian, mounting and falling from note to note such as be to them peculiar, and with more or less leisure or precipitation.[5] Even so, by diversity of placing and situation° of your measures° and concords,° a short with a long, and by narrow or wide distances, or thicker or thinner bestowing of them, your proportions° differ, and breedeth[6] a variable and strange° harmony not only in the ear, but also in the conceit° of them that hear it, whereof this may be an ocular example:

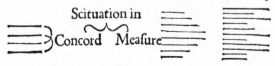

Where ye see the concord° or rhyme in the third distance, and the measure° in the fourth, sixth, or second distances,[7] whereof ye may devise as many other as ye list,° so the staff° be able to bear it. And I set you down

---

1. Puttenham's phrase refers to the different ways that rhymes can be arranged in the stanza of a poem.

2. **passionate** moving.

3. **point** purpose.

4. **falls, sallies, and compass** descending notes, rising (lit. "upward-leaping") notes, and the full range of connecting notes imagined as moving in an arc between the beginning and the end.

5. Puttenham names several different modes or scales of Greek music. Ancient au-

thors differ about their names and number: see Plato, *Republic* 3.10 (398d–399a); Plutarch, "On Music" 15–17, in *Moralia* 1136B–1137A; and Aristotle, *Politics* 8.7.1342a–b. None of these authorities mentions an Aeolian mode, but Scaliger (1.19) discusses all those here mentioned, so he may well be Puttenham's main source.

6. I.e., such diversity breeds.

7. The rhyme in "the third distance" appears to be the rhyme between lines 1 and 3 in the left diagram. Puttenham's diagram actu-

an ocular example, because ye may the better conceive it. Likewise, it so falleth out most times, your ocular proportion° doth declare the nature of the audible, for if it please the ear well, the same represented by delineation to the view pleaseth the eye well, and *e converso*.[8] And this is by a natural sympathy between the ear and the eye, and between tunes° and colors, even as there is the like between the other senses and their objects, of which it appertaineth not here to speak.

Now for the distances usually observed in our vulgar° poesy, they be in the first, second, third, and fourth verse, or if the verse be very short, in the fifth and sixth, and in some manner of musics, far above. And the first distance for the most part goeth all by distich° or couples of verses agreeing in one cadence,° and do pass so speedily away and so often return again, as their tunes° are never lost, nor out of the ear, one couple supplying another so nigh and so suddenly. And this is the most vulgar° proportion° of distance of situation,° such as used Chaucer in his *Canterbury Tales*, and Gower in all his works.

Second distance is, when ye pass over one verse, and join the first and the third, and so continue on till another like distance fall in, and this is also usual and common, as:

Third distance is, when your rhyme falleth upon the first and fourth verse, overleaping two. This manner is not so common, but pleasant and allowable enough.
In which case the two verses ye leave out are ready to receive their concords° by the same distance or any other ye like better.

The fourth distance is by overskipping three verses and lighting upon the fifth. This manner is rare and more artificial° than popular,° unless it be in some special case, as when the meters° be so little and short as they make no show of any great delay before they return. Ye shall have example of both:

And these ten little meters° make but one hexameter at length[9]:

‑‑ , ‑‑ , ‑‑ , ‑‑ , ‑‑ ، ‑‑ ، ‑‑ ، ‑‑ ،

There be larger distances also, as when the first concord° falleth upon the sixth verse, and is very pleasant if they be joined with other distances not so large, as:

ally represents rhyme in the second distance, as we can see from what he says about such rhyme just two paragraphs below. The middle and right diagrams suggest that "measure" here means "line length." How the phrase "in the fourth, sixth, or second distances" relates to the diagram remains obscure.

8. *e converso* contrariwise (Lat.).

9. Here Puttenham briefly drops the subject of the "fourth distance" of rhyme, turning to a garbled discussion of measure. The grouped dashes and commas presumably representing "ten little meters" make a pentameter, not a hexameter. Further, Puttenham normally uses "meter" to mean a particular poem or a line of verse; here the word seems to mean "syllable." Finally, the text reads logically if this single sentence and its diagram are ignored. An error has probably occurred, whether Puttenham's or his printer's.

There be also of the seventh, eighth, tenth, and twelfth distance, but then they may not go thick,[10] but two or three such distances serve to proportion[11] a whole song, and all between must be of other less distances, and these wide distances serve for coupling of staves,°[12] or for to declare high and passionate or grave matter, and also for art. Petrarch hath given us examples hereof in his *canzoni*,[13] and we, by lines of sundry lengths and distances, as followeth: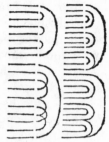

And all that can be objected against this wide distance is to say that the ear, by losing his concord,° is not satisfied. So is, indeed, the rude° and popular° ear, but not the learned, and therefore the poet must know to whose ear he maketh his rhyme, and accommodate himself thereto, and not give such music to the rude° and barbarous,° as he would to the learned and delicate° ear.

There is another sort of proportion° used by Petrarch called the *seizino*, not rhyming as other songs do, but by choosing six words out of which all the whole ditty is made, every of those six commencing and ending his verse by course, which restraint, to make the ditty sensible,° will try the maker's cunning.°[14] As thus:

Besides all this there is in situation° of the concords° two other points: one that it go by plain and clear compass,°[15] not entangled; another by interweaving one with another by knots,[16] or as it were by band,° which is more or less busy° and curious,° all as the maker will double or redouble his rhyme or concords,° and set his distances far or nigh, of all which I will give you ocular examples, as thus:

---

10. **they . . . thick** i.e., such use of widely separated rhymes should not be frequent in a stanza.

11. **proportion** make harmonious.

12. These widely spaced rhymes link together what would otherwise be separate stanzas.

13. Petrarch's lyric collection is usually referred to as the *Canzoniere* (*Songbook*); Puttenham may be referring, however, to Petrarch's "songs" or "poems," i.e., his *canzoni*.

14. Presumably Puttenham misnames (and misunderstands) Petrarch's sestina, a complex Provençal form consisting of six six-line stanzas in which the six words ending the lines of the first stanza are used as end-words in all subsequent stanzas, their order rearranged by the principle of retrograde inversion (*abcdef* becomes *faebdc*, etc.), plus a final three-line *envoi* using all six end-words. (See, for instance, *Canzoniere* 22.)

Puttenham's diagram of the *seizino* matches the definition he provides, however. It is possible that Puttenham had only heard of the sestina and had never read one. Cf. the related treatment of *anadiplosis* at 3.19.284 (which does not mention the *seizino*) and, for extension of the idea to linking by whole lines, the discussion of refrains and "band" in this chapter at 178 and of concatenation in *epimone* or *versus intercalaris* at 3.19.310 (see esp. note 225).

15. **plain and clear compass** i.e., the arc drawn between two rhyme words is not broken by an intervening arc drawn between two other rhyme words. By contrast, what Puttenham calls "intertangled" rhyme does have such intersecting arcs; it is now called crossrhyme.

16. **knots** crossing lines (that is, interlacing rhymes).

And first in a quatrain there are but two proportions,° for four verses in this last sort coupled are but two distichs,° and not a staff° quatrain or of four.[17]

The staff° of five hath seven proportions,° as:

whereof some of them be harsher and unpleasanter to the ear than other some be.

The sixain or staff° of six hath ten proportions,° whereof some be usual, some not usual, and not so sweet one as another.

The staff° of seven verses hath seven proportions,° whereof one only is the usual of our vulgar,° and kept by our old poets Chaucer and other in their historical reports and other ditties, as in the last part of them that follow next.[18]

The huitain,[19] or staff° of eight verses, hath eight proportions° such as the former staff,° and because he is longer, he hath one more than the settain.[20]

The staff° of nine verses hath yet more than the eight, and the staff° of ten more than the ninth, and the twelfth, if such were allowable in ditties, more than any of them all, by reason of his largeness receiving more compasses° and interweavings, always considered[21] that the very large distances be more artificial° than popularly° pleasant, and yet do give great grace and gravity, and move passion and affections° more vehemently, as it is well to be observed by Petrarch's *canzoni*.[22]

17. Puttenham is saying that one can truly rhyme a quatrain in only two ways: the first with the fourth line and the second with the third; or the first with the third and the second with the fourth—as in his first two diagrams. To rhyme the first with the second and the third with the fourth turns a "staff quatrain," that is, a four-line stanza, into two distichs or couplets.

18. Although Puttenham refers to "seven proportions," the diagram provides eight, the last of which describes rhyme royal.

19. **huitain** from Fr. *huit*, "eight."

20. **settain** from Fr. *sept*, "seven." Puttenham's spelling reflects the actual pronunciation of the French original, *septaine*.

21. **considered** i.e., bearing in mind.

22. See note 13. For "large distances" in Petrarch, see, for instance, *Canzoniere* 23.

Now ye may perceive by these proportions° before described that
there is a band° to be given every verse in a staff,° so as° none fall out
alone or uncoupled, and this band° maketh that the staff° is said[23] fast
and not loose: even as ye see in buildings of stone or brick the mason
giveth a band,° that is a length to two breadths, and upon necessity
divers other sorts of bands° to hold in the work fast and maintain the
perpendicularity of the wall. So, in any staff° of seven or eight or more
verses, the coupling of the more meters° by rhyme or concord° is the
faster[24] band;° the fewer, the looser band;° and therefore in a huitain,
he that putteth four verses in one concord° and four in another concord,° and in a dizain five, showeth himself more cunning,° and also
more copious in his own language. For he that can find two words of
concord° cannot find four or five or six, unless he have his own language at will. Sometime also ye are driven of necessity to close and
make band° more than ye would, lest otherwise the staff° should fall
asunder and seem two staves°—and this is in a staff° of eight and ten
verses—whereas without a band° in the middle, it would seem two
quatrains or two quintains,[25] which is an error that many makers slide
away with.[26] Yet Chaucer and others in the staff° of seven and six do almost as much amiss, for they shut up the staff° with a distich,° con-
cording° with none other verse that went before, and maketh but a
loose rhyme, and yet because of the double cadence° in the last two
verses serve the ear well enough. And as there is, in every staff,° band°
given to the verses by concord° more or less busy,° so is there in some
cases a band° given to every staff,° and that is by one whole verse running alone[27] throughout the ditty or ballad,° either in the middle or end
of every staff.° The Greeks called such uncoupled[28] verse *epimone*, the
Latins *versus intercalaris*.[29]

Now touching the situation° of measures,° there are as many or more
proportions° of them which I refer to the maker's fantasy and choice,
contented with two or three ocular examples and no more.

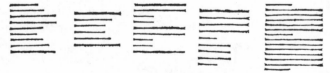

Which manner of proportion° by situation° of measures° giveth more
efficacy° to the matter oftentimes than the concords° themselves, and

23. **said** i.e., said to be.
24. **faster** firmer.
25. **quintains** five-line stanzas.
26. **slide away with** evade stealthily.
27. **alone** all one, i.e., unchanged. Puttenham speaks of a refrain.
28. **uncoupled** unrhymed.
29. In Greek rhetoric, *epimone* means a

dwelling upon a point or argument (*epi-*
"upon," *-mone* "tarrying"). Puttenham,
however, follows Susenbrotus (41), who defines it as the repetition of a verse in poetry
or of an opinion in an oration, and also identifies it with *versus intercalaris* (verse to be
inserted), that is, poetry that contains repeated elements or lines, or a refrain.

both proportions° concurring together as they needs must, it is of much more beauty and force to the hearer's mind.

To finish the learning[30] of this division,[31] I will set you down one example of a ditty written extempore with this device,° showing not only much promptness of wit° in the maker, but also great art and a notable memory. "Make me," saith this writer to one of the company, "so many strokes or lines with your pen as ye would have your song contain verses, and let every line bear his several[32] length, even as ye would have your verse of measure,° suppose of four, five, six, or eight or more syllables, and set a figure of every number at the end of the line, whereby ye may know his measure.° Then, where you will have your rhyme or concord° to fall, mark it with a compassed° stroke or semicircle passing over those lines, be they far or near in distance, as ye have seen before described. And because ye shall not think the maker hath premeditated beforehand any such fashioned ditty, do ye yourself make one verse, whether it be of perfect° or imperfect° sense, and give it him for a theme to make all the rest upon. If ye shall perceive the maker do keep the measures° and rhyme as ye have appointed him, and besides do make his ditty sensible° and ensuant to[33] the first verse in good reason, then may ye say he is his craft's master. For if he were not of a plentiful discourse, he could not upon the sudden shape an entire ditty upon your imperfect° theme or proposition in one verse. And if he were not copious in his language, he could not have such store° of words at commandment as should supply your concords.° And if he were not of a marvelous good memory, he could not observe the rhyme and measures° after the distances of your limitation, keeping with all gravity and good sense in the whole ditty."

30. **learning** teaching.
31. **division** chapter. We are at this point less than halfway through Book 2. This fossil ending suggests that the following chapter on shaped poems, anagrams, etc. (2.12) is a later addition, "fittest for the pretty amorets in court to entertain their servants and the time withal" (180).
32. **several** separate, distinct.
33. **ensuant to** appropriately following.

CHAPTER 12

Of proportion° in figure

Your last proportion° is that of figure, so called for that it yields an ocular representation, your meters° being by good symmetry reduced° into certain geometrical figures, whereby the maker is restrained to keep him within his bounds, and showeth not only more art, but serveth also much better for briefness and subtlety of device.°

And for the same respect are also fittest for the pretty amorets[1] in
court to entertain their servants and the time withal,° their delicate°
wits requiring some commendable exercise to keep them from idleness.° I find not of this proportion° used by any of the Greek or Latin
poets, or in any vulgar° writer, saving of that one form which they
call Anacreon's egg.[2] But being in Italy conversant with a certain
gentleman, who had long traveled the oriental parts of the world, and
seen the courts of the great princes of China and Tartary, I being
very inquisitive to know of the subtleties of those countries, and
especially in matter of learning and of their vulgar° poesy, he told me
that they are in all their inventions° most witty,° and have the use of
poesy or rhyming, but do not delight so much as we do in long tedious
descriptions, and therefore when they will utter any pretty conceit,°
they reduce° it into metrical feet and put it in form of a lozenge, or
square, or such other figure. And so, engraven in gold, silver, or ivory,
and sometimes with letters of amethyst, ruby, emerald, or topaz,
curiously° cemented and pieced together, they send them in chains,
bracelets, collars, and girdles to their mistresses to wear for a remembrance. Some few measures° composed in this sort this gentleman
gave me, which I translated word for word and, as near as I could,
followed both the phrase and the figure, which is somewhat hard
to perform, because of the restraint[3] of the figure from which ye
may not digress.[4] At the beginning they will seem nothing pleasant to
an English ear, but time and usage will make them acceptable
enough, as it doth in all other new guises, be it for wearing of apparel
or otherwise. The forms of your geometrical figures be hereunder
represented.[5]

---

1. **amorets** sweethearts, amorous women.

2. The *Greek Anthology* actually contained a number of pattern poems, including
one roughly in the shape of an egg lying on
its side. It is by Simias of Rhodes (ca. 300
BCE), not Anacreon. See LN 7.

3. **restraint** restriction, limitation.

4. According to Korn (291), this is probably the earliest mention of Chinese poetry in
English. Chinese merchants did travel to
Italy, and it is possible that Puttenham may
have encountered their poetry while traveling there.

5. For his geometrical figures, Puttenham
may well have used Billingsley's *Elements of*
Geometrie. Korn (296) has examined the possibility that Puttenham was influenced not
by Chinese but by Persian or Ottoman poetry, but concluded that the shaped poems
and forms Puttenham supplies and the
shaped poems of Persia and Turkey are really
very different, even though Puttenham's use
of names such as Timur Khan and Ribuska
allows one to entertain the possibility of
some, perhaps hearsay, knowledge of Middle
Eastern poetry. Note also that a number of
the names of Puttenham's pattern poems,
such as "spindle," "fuzee," and "triquet,"
were terms used in heraldry.

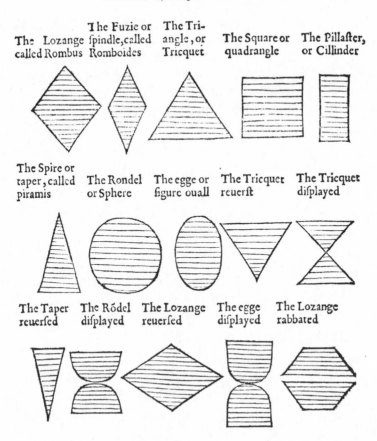

The Lozange called Rombus | The Fuzie or spindle, called Romboides | The Triangle, or Tricquet | The Square or quadrangle | The Pillaster, or Cillinder

The Spire or taper, called piramis | The Rondel or Sphere | The egge or figure ouall | The Tricquet reuerst | The Tricquet displayed

The Taper reuersed | The Rôdel displayed | The Lozange reuersed | The egge displayed | The Lozange rabbated

Of the Lozenge

The lozenge is a most beautiful figure, and fit for this purpose, being in his kind a quadrangle reversed, with his point upward like to a quarrel[6] of glass. The Greeks and Latins both call it rhombus, which may be the cause, as I suppose, why they also gave that name to the fish commonly called the turbot, who beareth justly that figure. It ought not to contain above thirteen, or fifteen, or one and twenty meters,° and the longest furnisheth the middle angle, the rest pass upward and downward still° abating their lengths by one or two syllables till they come to the point. The fuzee[7] is of the same nature but that he is sharper and slenderer. I will give you an example or two of those which my Italian friend bestowed upon me, which, as near as I could, I translated into the same figure, observing the phrase of the oriental speech word for word.

6. **quarrel** a square or, more usually, diamond-shaped pane.

7. **fuzee** a spindle-shaped figure (Fr. *fusée*, "a spindleful of tow," from Lat. *fusus*, "spindle").

A great emperor in Tartary, whom they call Khan, for his good fortune in the wars and many notable conquests he had made, was surnamed Timur Cutlu.[8] This man loved the lady Kermesine, who presented him returning from the conquest of Khorason (a great kingdom adjoining) with this lozenge made in letters of rubies and diamonds intermingled thus:

Sound,

O   Harp,

Shril   ly   out

Timur, the stout

Rider who with sharp

Trenching blade of bright steel

Hath made his fiercest foes to feel,

All such as wrought him shame or harm,

The strength of his brave right arm,

Cleaving hard down unto the eyes

The raw skulls of his enemies.

Much honor hath he won

By doughty deeds done

In   Khora   son

And all the

World

Round.

To which Khan Timur answered in fuzee, with letters of emeralds and amethysts artificially° cut and intermingled, thus:

8. Timur Cutlu is almost certainly Timur Khan, or Tamerlane. "Cutlu" is an Ottoman title meaning "lucky," and was given to Tamerlane because of his good fortune in his wars. On this point, see Korn (301–2), who is citing Joannus Leunclavius's *Pandectes Historiae Turcicae*. Korn also suggests (302) that while the lady Kermesine's name may be a corruption of the name for one of the branches of the Tartars, the Cheremissen Tartars, it is more likely related to the medieval Latin *kermesinus*, a word derived from the Persian *qirmiz* (cochineal), which becomes "crimson" in English. Finally, Korn suggests (300) that Puttenham's Corasoon is the Persian province of Khorasan (or Khurasan), which Tamerlane conquered between 1383 and 1385.

<pre>
                    Five
                Sore   battles
             Manfully   fought
          In   bloody   field
        With bright blade in hand
       Hath Timur won and forced to yield
      Many   a captain strong and stout
     And many a king his crown to vail,[9]
     Conquering large countries and land.
   Yet   nev   er   won   I   vic   to   ry,
    I   speak   it   t o   my   great   glory,
   So   dear   and   joyful   unto   me,
    As   when   I   did   first   conquer   thee,
    O   Kerme   sine,   of   all   mine   foes
    The most cruel, of all mine woes
     The   smartest,   the   sweetest,
       My   proud   conquest,
        My   richest   prey.
         O,   once   a   day
           Lend me thy sight
           Whose only light
              Keeps me
               Alive.
</pre>

Of the Triangle or Triquet

The triangle is a half square, lozenge, or fuzee parted upon the crossed angles, and so, his base being broad and his top narrow, it receiveth meters° of many sizes, one shorter than another. And ye may use this figure standing or reversed, as thus.

A certain great sultan of Persia called Ribuska entertains in love the lady Selamour, sent her this triquet reversed, piteously bemoaning his estate,° all set in marquetry with letters of blue sapphire and topaz artificially° cut and intermingled.[10]

---

9. **vail** lower in sign of submission.
10. Korn argues (302) that "Selamour" is probably a variant of the Turkish name "Selim."

Selamour, dearer than his own life
To thy distressed wretch captive,
Ribuska, whom late ly erst[11]
Most cru el ly thou pierced
With thy dead ly dart,
That pair of stars
Shi ning a far
Turn from me, to me,
That I may and may not see
The smile, the lour,[12]
That lead and drive
Me to die to live
Twice, yea thrice
In one
hour.

To which Selamour, to make the match equal, and the figure entire, answered in a standing triquet, richly engraven, with letters of like stuff:

Power
Of death
Nor of life
Hath Selamour.
With gods it is rife[13]
To give and bereave breath.
I may for pity perchance
Thy lost liberty re store,
Upon thine oath with this penance,
That while thou livest thou never love no more.

This condition seeming to Sultan Ribuska very hard to perform, and cruel to be enjoined him, doth by another figure in taper, signifying hope, answer the lady Selamour, which ditty for lack of time I translated not.

Of the Spire or Taper Called Pyramis

The taper is the longest and sharpest triangle that is, and while he mounts upward, he waxeth continually more slender, taking both his figure and name of the fire, whose flame, if ye mark it, is always pointed and naturally by his form covets to climb. The Greeks call him *pyramis*, of πύρ.[14] The Latins in use of architecture call him *obeliscus*. It holdeth the altitude of six ordinary triangles, and in metrifying his base cannot well be larger than a meter° of six. Therefore, in his altitude he will require divers rabates° to hold so many sizes of meters° as shall serve for his composition, for near the top there will be room little enough for a meter° of two syllables, and sometimes of one, to finish

---

11. **lately erst** just a short while ago.   14. Πύρ, or more accurately, πῦρ, (Gk.,
12. **lour** gloomy or sullen look.   "fire") is the root of *pyramis* (pyramid).
13. **rife** customary.

the point. I have set you down one or two examples to try how ye can digest the manner of the device.°

Her Majesty, for many parts in her most noble and virtuous nature to be found, resembled to the spire. Ye must begin beneath according to the nature of the device.°15

From God, the fountain of all good, are derived into the world all good things, and upon her Majesty all the good fortunes any worldly creature can be furnished with. Read downward according to the nature of the device.°

Sky.
———

Azured
in   the
assured,
———

And better,
And   richer,
Much greater,
———

Crown and empire
After   an   higher
For   to   aspire
Like flame of fire
In form of spire
———

To   mount   on   high,
Con   ti   nu   al   ly
With travail° and teen[16]
Most gracious queen,
Ye have made a vow,
Shows us plainly how
Not feigned but true,
To every man's view,
Shining clear in you
Of so bright a hue,
Even   thus   virtue
———

Vanished out of our sight,
Till his fine top be quite
To taper in the air
Endeavors soft and fair
By his kindly° nature
Of tall comely stature
Like as this fair figure

God
On
High
From
Above
Sends love,
Wis   dom,
Ju   stice,
Cou   rage,
Boun   ty,
And   doth   give
All   that   live,
Life and breath,
Heart's ease, health,
Children,   wealth,
Beauty,   strength,
Restful   age,
And   at   length
A   mild   death.
He   doth   bestow
All men's fortunes,
Both high and low,
And the best things
That earth can have
Or mankind crave,
Good queens and kings
Fi nally is the same.
Who gave you, Madam,
Season of this crown,[17]
With power sovereign,
Impug nable[18] *right,*
Redoubtable[19] *might,*
Most prosperous reign,
Eternal   re   nown,
And that your chiefest is
Sure hope of heaven's bliss.

15. I.e., the first spire poem reads from the bottom up.

16. **teen** vexation.

17. **Season of this crown** i.e., the period of your reign.

18. **Impugnable** unassailable.

19. **Redoubtable** formidable.

The Pillar, Pilaster, or Cylinder

The pillar is a figure among all the rest of the geometrical most beautiful, in respect that he is tall and upright and of one bigness from the bottom to the top. In architecture he is considered with two accessory parts, a pedestal or base, and a chapter[20] or head; the body is the shaft. By this figure is signified stay, support, rest, state,[21] and magnificence. Your ditty then being reduced° into the form of a pillar, his base will require to bear the breadth of a meter° of six or seven or eight syllables, the shaft of four, the chapter equal with the base. Of this proportion° I will give you one or two examples which may suffice.

Her Majesty resembled to the crowned pillar. Ye must read upward.

> Is bliss with immortality.
> Her trimmest top of all ye see
> Garnish the crown.
> Her just renown
> Chapter and head;
> Parts that maintain
> And womanhead,
> Her maiden reign
> In te gri ty;
> In ho nor and
> With ve ri ty,
> Her roundness[22] stand
> Strengthen the state.°
> By their increase
> With out de bate,
> Concord and peace,
> Of her sup port.
> They be the base
> With steadfastness.
> Virtue and grace,
> Stay and comfort,
> Of Albion's rest,
> The sound pillar
> And seen a far
> Is plainly expressed
> Tall, stately, and straight,
> By this no ble por trait,

Philo to the lady Calia[23] sendeth this odolet[24] of her praise in form of a pillar, which ye must read downward.

> Thy princely port and majesty
> Is my ter rene dei ty;
> Thy wit° and sense,
> The stream and source
> Of e lo quence
> And deep discourse;
> Thy fair eyes are
> My bright loadstar;
> Thy speech, a dart
> Piercing my heart;
> Thy face, alas,
> My loo king glass;
> Thy love ly looks,
> My prayer books;
> Thy pleasant cheer,
> My sunshine clear;
> Thy rue ful sight,
> My dark midnight;
> Thy will, the stent[25]
> Of my con tent;
> Thy glo ry, flour
> Of mine ho nour.[26]
> Thy love doth give
> The life I live;
> Thy life it is
> Mine earthly bliss;
> But grace and favor in thine eyes,
> My body's soul and soul's paradise.

20. **chapter** i.e., chapiter (the capital of a column).

21. **state** prosperous condition.

22. Puttenham is referring to the roundness of the pillar but punning on the meaning of the word as "uprightness."

23. *Philo* means "lover" in Greek, and *calia*, "beautiful." Presumably the poem is Puttenham's own, taken from his work *Philocalia*, referred to at 3.20.333–34.

24. **odolet** a diminutive form of "ode." Puttenham was the first to use the term.

25. **stent** limit, perhaps extent.

26. We have retained Puttenham's origi-

The Roundel or Sphere

The most excellent of all the figures geometrical is the round for his many perfections. First, because he is even and smooth, without any angle or interruption, most voluble° and apt to turn and to continue motion, which is the author of life, he containeth in him the commodious description of every other figure,[27] and for his ample capacity doth resemble the world or universe, and for his indefiniteness, having no special place of beginning nor end, beareth a similitude with God and eternity. This figure hath three principal parts in his nature and use much considerable[28]: the circle, the beam, and the center. The circle is his largest compass° or circumference; the center is his middle and indivisible point; the beam is a line stretching directly from the circle to the center, and contrariwise from the center to the circle. By this description our maker may fashion his meter° in roundel, either with the circumference, and that is circlewise; or from the circumference, that is, like a beam; or by the circumference, and that is overthwart and diametrally[29] from one side of the circle to the other.[30]

A general resemblance of the roundel to God, the world, and the Queen

> *All, and whole, and ever, and one,*
> *Single, simple,° each where,*[31] *alone,*
> *These be counted, as clerks° can tell,*
> *True properties of the roundel.*
> *His still° turning by consequence*[32]
> *And change do breed both life and sense.*
> *Time, measure of stir° and rest,*
> *Is also by his course expressed.*
> *How*[33] *swift the circle stir° above,*
> *His center point doth never move;*
> *All things that ever were or be,*
> *Are closed in his concavity.*
> *And though he be still° turned and tossed,*

---

nal spellings of "flower" and "honor" here in order to allow his poem to rhyme properly. (Rhyming by "falsely" accenting the second syllable of *honour* appears to flout Puttenham's own rule against this practice; see 2.9.170.)

27. **he containeth ... figure** i.e., every other figure can be "described," that is, traced or drawn, within the circumference of a circle.

28. **considerable** notable.

29. **overthwart and diametrally** crosswise and along the diameter.

30. Puttenham's supposed roundel poems following are not printed as shaped poems. For possible printing arrangements that this obscure passage may suggest, see Ing 93.

31. **each where** everywhere.

32. **consequence** sequential motion. This paradoxical union of circular form, sequential motion, and change, with stillness and eternity animates poems from Spenser's Mutability Cantos (*Faerie Queene* 7.58) and Donne's "A Valediction: Forbidding Mourning," to Eliot's *Burnt Norton* V ("a Chinese jar still / Moves perpetually in its stillness").

33. **How** however.

No room there wants,° nor none is lost.
The roundel hath no bunch[34] or angle,
Which may his course stay or entangle.
The furthest part of all his sphere
Is equally both far and near.
So doth none other figure fare
Where nature's chattels closed[35] are,
And beyond his wide compass,°
There is nobody nor no place,
Nor any wit° that comprehends,
Where it begins, or where it ends,
And therefore all men do agree,
That it purports eternity.
God above the heavens so high
Is this roundel; in world, the sky;
Upon earth, she who bears the bell[36]
Of maids and queens is this roundel:
All, and whole, and ever alone,
Single, sans peer, simple,° and one.

A special and particular resemblance of her Majesty to the roundel

First, her authority regal
Is the circle compassing° all,
The dominion great and large
Which God hath given to her charge,
Within which most spacious bound
She environs her people round,
Retaining them by oath and 'legiance
Within the pale of true obeisance,[37]
Holding imparked, as it were,
Her people like to herds of deer,
Sitting among them in the mids[38]
Where she allows, and bans,[39] and bids
In what fashion she list,° and when,
The services of all her men.
Out of her breast as from an eye
Issue the rays incessantly
Of her justice, bounty, and might,
Spreading abroad their beams so bright,
And reflect[40] not, till they attain

---

34. **bunch** protuberance.
35. **closed** enclosed.
36. **bears the bell** wins the prize, comes in first (from the fact that a leading cow or sheep in a herd typically had a bell around its neck).

37. **obeisance** obedience.
38. **mids** midst.
39. **bans** summons; curses.
40. **reflect** turn or bend back.

The farthest part of her domain,
And makes each subject clearly see,
What he is bounden for to be
To God, his prince, and commonwealth,
His neighbor, kindred, and to himself.
The same center and middle prick,[41]
Whereto our deeds are dressed so thick,[42]
From all the parts and outmost side
Of her monarchy large and wide,
Also from whence reflect these rays
Twenty hundred manner of ways,
Where her will is them to convey
Within the circle of her survey.
So is the Queen of Briton ground,
Beam, circle, center of all my round.

Of the Square or Quadrangle Equilater[43]

The square is of all other accounted the figure of most solidity and steadfastness, and for his own stay and firmity[44] requireth none other base than himself, and therefore as the roundel or sphere is appropriate to the heavens, the spire to the element of the fire, the triangle to the air, and the lozenge to the water, so is the square for his inconcussable[45] steadiness likened to the earth, which perchance might be the reason that the Prince of Philosophers, in his first book of the *Ethics*, termeth a constant-minded man, even equal and direct on all sides, and not easily overthrown by every little adversity, *hominem quadratum*, a "square man."[46] Into this figure may ye reduce° your ditties by using no more verses than your verse is of syllables, which will make him fall out square; if ye go above, it will grow into the figure trapezion,[47] which is some portion longer than square. I need not give you any example, because in good art all your ditties, odes, and epigrams should keep and not exceed the number of twelve verses, and the longest verse to be of twelve syllables, and not above, but under that number as much as ye will.

---

41. **prick** center of a target (from archery).
42. **dressed so thick** addressed, or aimed, in such great numbers.
43. **equilater** having equal sides.
44. **stay and firmity** support and stability.
45. **inconcussable** unshakable.
46. See Aristotle, *Nicomachean Ethics* 1.10.11 (1101a20–23). Puttenham probably read this work in a Latin translation, although which one he used is unclear. The saying appears in Erasmus's *Adagia* (4.8.35 [LB 2.1131B-D, *CWE* 36.378]) as well.
47. **trapezion** a quadrilateral with at least two parallel sides; probably a rectangle.

The Figure Oval[48]

This figure taketh his name of an egg, and also, as it is thought, his first origin, and is, as it were, a bastard or imperfect° round declining toward a longitude, and yet keeping within one line for his periphery or compass,° as the round. And it seemeth that he receiveth this form not as an imperfection° by any impediment unnaturally hindering his rotundity, but by the wisdom and providence of nature for the commodity[49] of generation in such of her creatures as bring not forth a lively[50] body (as do four-footed beasts), but instead thereof a certain quantity of shapeless matter contained in a vessel, which, after it is sequestered[51] from the dame's body, receiveth life and perfection,° as in the eggs of birds, fishes, and serpents. For the matter being of some quantity, and to issue out at a narrow place, for the easy passage thereof it must of necessity bear such shape as might not be sharp and grievous to pass, as an angle, nor so large or obtuse as might not assay some issue out with one part more than other, as the round; therefore, it must be slenderer in some part and yet not without a rotundity and smoothness to give the rest an easy delivery. Such is the figure oval whom for his antiquity, dignity, and use, I place among the rest of the figures to embellish our proportions.° Of this sort are divers of Anacreon's ditties, and those other of the Grecian lyrics,[52] who wrote wanton,° amorous devices° to solace their wits° withal,° and many times they would (to give it right shape of an egg) divide a word in the midst, and piece out the next verse with the other half, as ye may see by perusing their meters.°[53]

Of the Device° or Emblem, and that Other Which the Greeks Call Anagramma, and We, the Posy Transposed

And besides all the remembered points of metrical proportion,° ye have yet two other sorts of some affinity with them, which also first issued out of the poet's head, and whereof the courtly maker was the principal artificer, having many high conceits° and curious° imaginations, with leisure enough to attend his idle° inventions.° And these be the short, quick,° and sententious° propositions, such as be at these days all your devices° of arms and other amorous inscriptions which

48. In 2.25, devoted to poems composed of stanzas of different line lengths, Scaliger includes two oval ones when discussing poems whose first and last lines are the same length. This figure takes its name from "egg" (Lat. *ovum*).

49. **commodity** convenience.

50. **lively** living.

51. **sequestered** separated.

52. **lyrics** i.e., lyric poets.

53. At this point (p. 84 in *1589*) begin the Ben Jonson copy's unique, unnumbered, exactly eight pages of material (see Introduction 71), which end just before the final paragraph of the chapter ("When I wrote of these devices," 198). The first word of the Ben Jonson text ("And") is printed with a "drop cap," a feature otherwise reserved throughout the *Art* for the first word of chapters.

courtiers use to give and also to wear in livery for the honor of their ladies, and commonly contain but two or three words of witty° sentence° or secret conceit° till they [be] unfolded or explained by some interpretation.[54] For which cause they be commonly accompanied with a figure or portrait of ocular representation, the words so aptly corresponding to the subtlety of the figure, that as well the eye is therewith recreated as the ear or the mind. The Greeks call it *emblema*, the Italians *impresa*, and we, a device,°[55] such as a man may put into letters of gold and send to his mistresses for a token, or cause to be embroidered in escutcheons of arms, or in any border of a rich garment, to give by his novelty marvel to the beholder. Such were the figures and inscriptions the Roman emperors gave in their money and coins of largesse,[56] and in other great medals of silver and gold, as that of the emperor Augustus: an arrow entangled by the fish *remora*, with these words, *Festina lente*, signifying that celerity is to be used with deliberation, all great enterprises being for the most part either overthrown with haste or hindered by delay, in which case leisure in the advice[57] and speed in the execution make a very good match for a glorious success.°[58]

The emperor Heliogabalus, by his name alluding to the sun, which in Greek is *helios*, gave for his device° the celestial sun, with these words *Soli invicto*. The subtlety lieth in the word *soli*, which hath a double sense, *videl.*,° "to the sun," and "to him only."[59] We ourselves, attributing that most excellent figure, for his incomparable beauty and light, to the person of our Sovereign Lady, altering the mot,[60] made it far pass that of the emperor Heliogabalus both for subtlety and multiplicity of sense, thus: *Soli nunquam deficienti*, "to her only that never fails," *videl.*,° in bounty and munificence toward all hers that deserve; or else thus: "to her only (whose glory and good fortune) may never decay or wane." And so it inureth[61] as a wish by way of resemblance in *simile dissimile*,[62] which is also a subtlety likening her Majesty to the sun for his brightness, but not to him for his passion, which is ordinarily to go to glade[63] and sometime to suffer eclipse.

54. Puttenham also discusses such poems, which he calls posies, in 1.30.

55. **device** a combination of text and image composed of a motto and a visual representation presenting its subject. Some devices include explanatory texts or epigrams. Puttenham probably uses compilers here such as Giovio and Paradin.

56. **coins of largesse** commemorative coins or medals (?).

57. **advice** deliberation.

58. For Augustus' motto, see Giovio B2v; see also Aulus Gellius 10.11, Macrobius 6.8.9, Suetonius, *The Deified Augustus* 25, and Erasmus, *Adagia* 2.1.1 (LB 2.399B–399E, CWE 33.3–17). The remora is the sucking-fish (*echenesis remora*) described in Pliny's *Natural History* (32.1) and was believed by the ancients to have the power to stop the movement of any ship to which it attached itself. Augustus' motto could be translated more simply as "make haste slowly."

59. Heliogabalus' device could be translated as either "to the unconquered sun" or "to him alone who is unconquered."

60. **mot** word, motto (Fr. *mot*, "word").

61. **inureth** operates.

62. *simile dissimile* "similar dissimilar." I.e., Elizabeth is both similar to and dissimilar from the sun.

63. **go to glade** set.

King Edward III, her Majesty's most noble progenitor, first founder of the famous Order of the Garter, gave this posy with it: *Hony soit qui mal y pense,* commonly thus Englished, "Ill be to him that thinketh ill," but in mine opinion better thus, "Dishonored be he, who means unhonorably."[64] There cannot be a more excellent device,° nor that could contain larger intendment,° nor greater subtlety, nor (as a man may say) more virtue or princely generosity.[65] For first he did by it mildly and gravely reprove the perverse construction of such noblemen in his court, as imputed the king's wearing about his neck the garter of the lady with whom he danced to some amorous alliance betwixt them, which was not true. He also justly defended his own integrity, saved the noblewoman's good renown, which by licentious speeches might have been impaired, and liberally recompensed her injury with an honor, such as none could have been devised greater nor more glorious or permanent upon her and all the posterity of her house. It inureth[66] also as a worthy lesson and discipline° for all princely personages, whose actions, imaginations, countenances, and speeches should evermore correspond in all truth and honorable simplicity.

Charles V, Emperor, even in his young years showing his valor and honorable ambition, gave for his new order, the Golden Fleece, usurping it upon[67] Prince Jason and his Argonauts' rich spoil brought from Colchis.[68] But for his device° two pillars with this mot *Plus ultra,* as one not content to be restrained within the limits that Hercules had set for an uttermost bound to all his travails,° *videl.,*° two pillars in the mouth of the strait Gibraltar, but would go further. Which came fortunately to pass, and whereof the good success° gave great commendation to his device,° for by the valiancy of his captains before he died, he conquered great part of the West Indies, never known to Hercules or any of our world before.[69]

In the same time, seeming[70] that the heavens and stars had conspired to replenish the earth with princes and governors of great courage,° and most

<hr />

64. More accurately, the motto should be translated as "May he be ashamed who thinks ill of this." The quip was supposedly made by Edward III in 1347 and directed at his court, who laughed when they saw him with the countess of Salisbury's garter. Giovio discusses this motto on C11r–v.

65. **generosity** excellence, nobility of birth.

66. **inureth** operates.

67. **usurping it upon** taking it from.

68. The Order of the Golden Fleece was actually established by Philip the Good of Burgundy in 1429 or 1430. The "device," which Puttenham goes on to describe, was the motto not of the order but of Charles V. *Plus ultra* means "beyond the limit." The

phrase plays on the Latin expression *ne* (or *nec*) *plus ultra,* meaning "[there is] nothing beyond this," or "this is the height or limit." Giovio discusses Charles's motto on B8r and on B8v discusses the Order of the Golden Fleece. Giovio presents these two items as distinct, but Puttenham seems to have confused them.

69. A version of Charles V's device can be found in Paradin's 1557 *Devises heroïques* (29); in the *Heroicall Devises* (1591): "Plus oultre, Hee conceiueth hope to proceed further" (32). Puttenham owned a work by Claude's elder brother Guillaume, *L'Historie de Notre Temps.*

70. **seeming** i.e., it seeming.

famous conquerors, Selim, emperor of Turkey, gave for his device° a crescent or new moon, promising to himself increase of glory and enlargement of empire till he had brought all Asia under his subjection, which he reasonably well accomplished. For in less than eight years which he reigned, he conquered all Syria and Egypt, and laid it to his dominion. This device° afterward was usurped by Henry II, French king, with this mot *Donec totum compleat orbem*, "till he be at his full": meaning it not so largely[71] as did Selim, but only that his friends should know how unable he was to do them good, and to show beneficence until he attained the crown of France unto which he aspired as next successor.[72]

King Louis XII, a valiant and magnanimous prince, who because he was on every side environed with mighty neighbors, and most of them his enemies, to let them perceive that they should not find him unable or unfurnished (in case they should offer any unlawful hostility) of sufficient forces of his own, as well to offend as to defend, and to revenge an injury as to repulse it, he gave for his device° the porcupine with this posy *pres et loin*, "both far and near." For the porcupine's nature is, to such as stand aloof,[73] to dart her prickles from her, and if they come near her, with the same, as they stick fast, to wound them that hurt her.[74]

But of late years in the ransack of the cities of Cartagena and San Domenico[75] in the West Indies, manfully put in execution by the prowess of her Majesty's men, there was found a device° made peradventure° without King Philip's knowledge, wrought all in massive copper: a king sitting on horseback upon a *monde*, or world, the horse prancing forward with his forelegs as if he would leap off, with this inscription, *Non sufficit orbis*, meaning, as it is to be conceived, that one whole world could not content him.[76] This immeasurable ambition of

71. **not so largely** not to have so wide, or perhaps extravagant, an application.

72. We have found no specific source for Puttenham's association of the crescent with Selim I, but legend has it that Osman (1258–1326), founder of the Ottoman Empire, had a dream in which a crescent moon stretched to embrace the whole earth, so he took it for his emblem. When Mehmed II (1432–1481) conquered Constantinople in 1453, a crescent and star were said to have appeared in the sky. Thereafter the symbol was constantly associated with the Turks. For Henry II's use of the emblem, see Giovio C2r–v. A version of the device, with the link to Henry II, can be found in Paradin's *Devises heroïques* (20); in the *Heroicall Devises*, "Donec totum impleat orbem, Till he replenish the whole world" (21).

73. **aloof** at a distance.

74. For Louis XII's emblem, see Giovio C1v–C2r. A porcupine emblem for Louis XII

(with a different *mot, Ultus avos Troiae*) can also be found in Paradin's *Devises heroïques* (25); in the *Heroicall Devises*, 27.

75. I.e., Santo Domingo.

76. In 1585 Sir Francis Drake commanded a fleet of British ships that went to the West Indies, where, in the following year, they plundered the town of Cartagena (in present-day Colombia) and the Spanish colony of Santo Domingo on the island of Hispaniola. (At present the island is divided between Haiti and the Dominican Republic.) Drake then pillaged the coast of Florida before sailing to Virginia to rescue Sir Walter Ralegh's colony at Roanoke. Puttenham seems to have read the account of Drake's voyage written by Walter Bigges (d. 1586), which contains the tale of Philip's device. Puttenham's publisher, Richard Field, published Bigges's account in 1589; Puttenham may have read the book in the printinghouse. The discussion of Philip II's device appears at 27–28.

the Spaniards, if her Majesty, by God's providence, had not with her forces providently stayed and retranched,[77] no man knoweth what inconvenience might in time have ensued to all the princes and commonwealths in Christendom, who have found themselves long annoyed with his excessive greatness.

Attila, king of the Huns, invading France with an army of 300,000 fighting men, as it is reported, thinking utterly to abase the glory of the Roman Empire, gave for his device° of arms a sword with a fiery point and these words, *Ferro et flamma,* "with sword and fire." This very device° being as ye see only accommodate to a king or conqueror and not a cullion[78] or any mean° soldier, a certain base man of England, being known even at that time a bricklayer or mason by his science,° gave for his crest: whom it had better become to bear a trowel full of mortar than a sword and fire, which is only the revenge of a prince and lieth not in any other man's ability to perform, unless ye will allow it to every poor knave that is able to set fire on a thatched house. The heralds ought to use great discretion in such matters, for neither any rule of their art doth warrant such absurdities, nor though such a coat or crest were gained by a prisoner taken in the field, or by a flag found in some ditch and never fought for (as many times happens), yet is it no more allowable than it were to bear the device° of Tamerlane, an emperor in Tartary, who gave the lightning of heaven, with a posy in that language purporting these words, *Ira Dei,*[79] which also appeared well to answer his fortune. For from a sturdy[80] shepherd he became a most mighty emperor, and with his innumerable, great armies desolated so many countries and people, as he might justly be called "the wrath of God." It appeared also by his strange° end, for in the midst of his greatness and prosperity, he died suddenly and left no child or kindred for a successor to so large an empire, nor any memory after him more than of his great puissance[81] and cruelty.

But that of the king of China in the farthest part of the Orient, though it be not so terrible,[82] is no less admirable° and of much sharpness and good implication[83] worthy for the greatest king and conqueror; and it is two strange° serpents intertangled in their amorous congress, the lesser creeping with his head into the greater's mouth, with the words purporting[84] *ama et time,* "love and fear."[†] Which posy with marvelous much reason and subtlety implieth the duty of every subject to his prince, and of every prince to his subject, and that without either of them both, no subject could be said entirely to perform his alle-

---

77. **retranched** cut short, cut down. Puttenham refers to the destruction of the Spanish Armada in 1588.

78. **cullion** base or low person; originally, "testicle" (Fr. *couillon*).

79. *Ira Dei* (Lat.) "the wrath of God."

80. **sturdy** fierce, violent.

81. **puissance** power.

82. **terrible** inspiring terror or awe.

83. **of . . . implication** trenchant and suggestive.

84. **purporting** stating.

giance, nor the prince his part of lawful government. For without fear and love the sovereign authority could not be upholden, nor without justice and mercy the prince be renowned and honored of his subject. All which parts are discovered° in this figure: love by the serpent's amorous intertangling; obedience and fear by putting the inferior's head into the other's mouth, having puissance to destroy; on the other side, justice in the greater to prepare and menace death and destruction to offenders, and if he spare it, then betokeneth it mercy, and a grateful recompense of the love and obedience which the sovereign receiveth.

It is also worth the telling, how the king useth the same in policy.° He giveth it in his ordinary[85] liveries[86] to be worn in every upper garment of all his noblest men and greatest magistrates and the rest of his officers and servants, which are either embroidered upon the breast and the back with silver or gold or pearl or stone, more or less richly according to every man's dignity and calling. And they may not presume to be seen in public without them, nor also in any place where, by the king's commission, they use to sit in justice, or any other public affair, whereby the king is highly both honored and served; the common people retained in duty and admiration° of his greatness; the noblemen, magistrates, and officers every one in his degree° so much esteemed and reverenced, as[87] in their good and loyal service they want° unto their persons little less honor for the king's sake than can be almost due or exhibited to the king himself.

I could not forbear to add this foreign example to accomplish[88] our discourse touching devices,° for the beauty and gallantness of it, besides the subtlety of the conceit° and princely policy° in the use, more exact than can be remembered in any other of any European prince, whose devices° I will not say but many of them be lofty and ingenious, many of them lovely and beautiful, many other ambitious and arrogant, and the chiefest of them terrible and full of horror to the nature of man, but that any of them be comparable with it for wit,° virtue, gravity, and, if ye list,° bravery,[89] honor, and magnificence, not usurping upon[90] the peculiars[91] of the gods—in my conceit° there is none to be found.

This may suffice for devices,° a term which includes in his generality all those other, *videl.*,° liveries, cognizances,[92] emblems, ensigns, and *impresas.* For though the terms be divers, the use and intent is but one, whether they rest in color° or figure or both, or in word or in mute

---

85. **in his ordinary** in his regular practice.
86. **liveries** badges.
87. **as** that.
88. **accomplish** complete.
89. **bravery** excellence, splendor, showiness.
90. **not usurping** stopping short of trespass.

91. **peculiars** i.e., peculiar attributes.
92. **liveries, cognizances** Both of these terms meant a badge worn to indicate one's status and/or attachment to a gentleman or nobleman or to his house. "Livery" could also mean the particular garments one wore, whereas "cognizance" meant something more general, a "mark" of any sort.

show, and that is to insinuate some secret, witty,° moral, and brave[93] purpose presented to the beholder, either to recreate° his eye, or please his fantasy, or examine[94] his judgment, or occupy his brain, or to manage his will, either by hope or by dread, every of which respects be of no little moment to the interest and ornament of the civil life, and therefore give them no little commendation. Then, having produced so many worthy and wise founders of these devices,° and so many puissant[95] patrons and protectors of them, I fear no reproach in this discourse, which otherwise the venomous appetite of envy° by detraction or scorn would peradventure° not stick° to offer me.

Of the Anagram, or Posy Transposed[96]

One other pretty conceit° we will impart unto you and then trouble you with no more, and is also borrowed primitively of[97] the poet, or courtly maker. We may term him the posy transposed, or in one word a transpose, a thing, if it be done for pastime and exercise of the wit° without superstition,[98] commendable enough and a meet study for ladies, neither bringing them any great gain nor any great loss unless it be of idle° time. They that use it for pleasure is to breed one word out of another, not altering any letter nor the number of them, but only transposing of the same, whereupon many times is produced some grateful news[99] or matter to them, for whose pleasure and service it was intended. And because there is much difficulty in it, and altogether standeth upon haphazard, it is counted for a courtly conceit° no less than the device° before remembered. Lycophron, one of the seven Greek lyrics,[100] who when they met together, as many times they did, for their excellence and lovely concord were called the seven stars, *Pleiades*. This man was very perfect° and fortunate in these transposes, and for his delicate wit° and other good parts was greatly favored by Ptolemy, King of Egypt, and Queen Arsinoë, his wife. He after such sort called the king ἀπομελίτος, which is letter for letter Ptolomaeus, and Queen Arsinoë he called ἴον ἤρας, which is Arsinoë.[101] Now the subtlety lieth not in the conversion, but in the sense in this, that *apomelitos* signifieth

93. **brave** excellent, splendid.
94. **examine** test.
95. **puissant** powerful.
96. Puttenham paraphrases Du Bellay's discussion of anagrams (2.8.155–56), citing his examples of Lycophron of Chalcis, François I de Valois, and Henri II de Valois. The anagrams on the names of the two French kings were famous in the sixteenth century and appeared in many different texts. The Ptolemy and Arsinoë mentioned here are Ptolemy II Philadelphus and Arsinoë II Philadelphus.

97. **borrowed primitively of** i.e., taken from the ancients by.
98. **superstition** over-nicety, excessive care.
99. **grateful news** pleasing novelty.
100. **lyrics** lyric poets. Lycophron was one of the Pléiade, a group of seven (or eight) tragic poets (not lyric poets, as Puttenham says) from Hellenistic Alexandria.
101. To see how these anagrams work, it is necessary to know that in Greek, Ptolemy is Πτολεμαῖος, and Arsinoë is Ἀρσινοη.

in Greek "honey sweet"; so was Ptolemy the sweetest-natured man in the world both for countenance and conditions. And *iôneras* signifieth the "violet or flower of Juno," a style among the Greeks for a woman endowed with all beauty and magnificence, which construction, falling out grateful[102] and so truly, exceedingly well pleased the king and the queen, and got Lycophron no little thank and benefit at both their hands.

The French gentlemen have very sharp wits and withal° a delicate° language, which may very easily be wrested to any alteration of words sententious,° and they of late years have taken this pastime up among them, many times gratifying their ladies and oftentimes the princes of the realm with some such thankful[103] novelty. Whereof one made by° François de Valoys thus: *De façon suis royal*, who indeed was of fashion, countenance, and stature, besides his regal virtues, a very king, for in a world there could not be seen a goodlier man of person.[104] Another found this by° Henry de Valoys: *Roy es de nul hay*,[105] "a king hated of no man," and was apparent in his conditions and nature, for there was not a prince of greater affability and mansuetude than he.

I myself, seeing this conceit° so well allowed of in France and Italy, and being informed that her Majesty took pleasure sometimes in deciphering of names, and hearing how divers gentlemen of her court had essayed, but with no great felicity, to make some delectable transpose of her Majesty's name, I would needs try my luck, for cunning° I know not why I should call it, unless it be for the many and variable applications of sense, which requireth peradventure° some wit° and discretion more than of every unlearned man. And for the purpose I took me these three words (of any other in the world) containing in my conceit° greatest mystery[106] and most importing good to all them that now be alive under her noble government:

Elissabet Anglorum Regina.

Which orthography (because ye shall not be abused°) is true and not mistaken, for the letter *zeta* of the Hebrews[107] and Greek and of all other tongues is in truth but a double *ss* hardly uttered,[108] and *h* is but a

---

102. **grateful** pleasingly.

103. **thankful** deserving of thanks.

104. **of person** of his person, i.e., of his body. Note that *1589* has François de Vallois as the king's name, which does not make the anagram possible, so we have changed it to François de Valoys. This is the way the name is spelled in Puttenham's source for this anagram, Du Bellay's *Deffence*. We have also added *-al* to *roy* since that is what is in Du Bellay and is also necessary to make the anagram possible. The anagram means: "I am royal by my fashion, i.e., appearance."

105. Once again, Puttenham or his printer garbles what is found in Du Bellay. He has here "Henry de Vallois, *Roy de nulz hay*." We have replaced this with what is found in the source, to allow the anagram.

106. **mystery** secret knowledge, as of a craft or guild, or religious in character.

107. Puttenham sometimes names a language using a terminal *s*. Thus he says "Hebrews" for "Hebrew." Later he will speak of "Normans" and "Latins" (see 2.13.204).

108. **hardly uttered** i.e., as a voiced (as distinguished from voiceless) consonant.

note of aspiration only and no letter, which therefore is by the Greeks omitted. Upon the transposition I found this to redound:

Multa regnabis ense gloria.
By thy sword shalt thou reign in great renown.

Then, transposing the word *ense*, it came to be:

Multa regnabis sene gloria.
Aged and in much glory shall ye reign.

Both which results falling out upon the very first marshaling of the letters, without any darkness° or difficulty, and so sensibly and well appropriate to her Majesty's person and estate,° and finally so effectually to mine own wish (which is a matter of much moment in such cases), I took them both for a good boding and very fatality[109] to her Majesty, appointed by God's providence for all our comforts. Also I imputed it for no little good luck and glory to myself to have pronounced to her so good and prosperous a fortune, and so thankful news to all England, which though it cannot be said by this event[110] any destiny or fatal necessity, yet surely is it by all probability of reason so likely to come to pass, as any other worldly event[111] of things that be uncertain, her Majesty continuing the course of her most regal proceedings and virtuous life in all earnest zeal and godly contemplation of His Word, and in the sincere[112] administration of his terrene justice, assigned over to her execution as his lieutenant upon earth within the compass° of her dominions.

This also is worth the noting, and I will assure you of it, that after the first search whereupon this transpose was fashioned, the same letters being by me tossed and tranlaced[113] five hundred times, I could never make any other, at least of some sense and conformity to her Majesty's estate° and the case. If any other man by trial° happen upon a better omination,[114] or whatsoever else ye will call it, I will rejoice to be overmatched in my device° and renounce him[115] all the thanks and profit of my travail.°[116]

When I wrote of these devices,° I smiled with myself, thinking that the readers would do so too, and many of them say that such trifles as these might well have been spared, considering the world is full enough of them, and that it is pity men's heads should be fed with such vanities as are to none edification nor instruction, either of moral

---

109. **very fatality** true destiny.
110. **by this event** i.e., owing to this anagram's oracular force.
111. **event** outcome.
112. **sincere** correct, true.
113. **tranlaced** shuffled.
114. **omination** prognostication (from "omen").

115. **him** i.e., to him.
116. Here ends the eight-page section of material that appears only in the Ben Jonson copy of the *Art*. The original page numbering resumes on the next page in *1589* (p. 85).

virtue, or otherwise behooveful for the commonwealth, to whose service (say they) we are all born, and not to fill and replenish a whole world full of idle° toys.° To which sort of reprehenders, being either all holy and mortified to the world and therefore esteeming nothing that savoreth not of theology, or altogether grave and worldly and therefore caring for nothing but matters of policy° and discourses of estate,° or all given to thrift and passing[117] for none art that is not gainful and lucrative, as the sciences° of the law, physic, and merchandise[118]: to these I will give none other answer than refer them to the many trifling poems of Homer, Ovid, Vergil, Catullus, and other notable writers of former ages, which were not of any gravity or seriousness, and many of them full of impudicity[119] and ribaldry, as are not these of ours, nor for any good in the world should have been.[120] And yet those trifles are come from many former siecles[121] unto our times, uncontrolled or condemned or suppressed by any pope or patriarch or other severe censor of the civil manners° of men, but have been in all ages permitted as the convenient° solaces and recreations of man's wit.° And as I cannot deny but these conceits° of mine be trifles, no less in very deed be all the most serious studies of man, if we shall measure gravity and lightness by the wise man's balance, who, after he had considered of all the profoundest arts and studies among men, in the end cried out with this *epiphoneme*,[122] *Vanitas vanitatum et omnia vanitas*.[123] Whose authority, if it were not sufficient to make me believe so, I could be content with Democritus rather to condemn the vanities of our life by derision, than as Heraclitus with tears, saying with that merry Greek thus:

> *Omnia sunt risus, sunt pulvis, et omnia nil sunt,*
> *Res hominum cunctae, nam ratione carent.*[124]

117. **passing** caring.
118. **physic, and merchandise** medicine, and trade.
119. **impudicity** immodesty.
120. Puttenham is thinking of the following mock-serious poems incorrectly ascribed to the poets in question during the Renaissance: Homer's *Batrachomyomachia* (The Battle of the Frogs and the Mice), Vergil's *Culex* (The Gnat) and *Moretum* (the name of a rustic dish), and Ovid's *Nux* (The Nut). The poems of Catullus could indeed be characterized as containing "impudicity and ribaldry."
121. **siecles** centuries (Fr. *siècles*).
122. *epiphoneme* a concluding line (or lines) in a poem that sums up and rounds off everything in it. At 3.19.302, Puttenham identifies this as the figure of speech that the Latins called *acclamatio* and that

he dubs the Surclose or the Consenting Close.
123. Ecclesiastes 1:2: "Vanity of vanities, [and] all is vanity." This book of the Bible was conventionally ascribed to Solomon.
124. "All things are laughable, all are dust, and all are nothing, / For all things human are lacking in reason." Puttenham's translation, which follows, is a somewhat free version of this elegiac couplet, whose source is unknown, but which does seem an accurate reflection of the skeptical philosophy of Democritus. The latter was known as the "laughing philosopher" because he supposedly saw all human striving as folly; his ethics privileged the tranquillity of the soul, its indifference to humans' typical desires and sufferings. On Democritus, see, for example, Seneca, "On the Tranquillity of Mind" 15.2, and "On Anger" 2.10.5.

Thus Englished:

> *All is but a jest, all dust, all not worth two peason,*[125]
> *For why in man's matters is neither rhyme nor reason.*

Now passing from these courtly trifles, let us talk of our scholastical° toys,° that is, of the grammatical versifying of the Greeks and Latins, and see whether it might be reduced° into our English art or no.

125. **peason** peas.

CHAPTER 13

How, if all manner of sudden innovations were not very scandalous, especially in the laws of any language or art, the use of the Greek and Latin feet might be brought into our vulgar° poesy, and with good grace enough

Now, nevertheless, albeit we have before alleged that our vulgar° Saxon English, standing most upon[1] words monosyllable, and little upon polysyllables, doth hardly admit the use of those fine, invented° feet of the Greeks and Latins,[2] and that for the most part wise and grave men do naturally mislike with all sudden innovations, especially of laws (and this the law of our ancient English poesy)—and therefore lately before we imputed it to a nice° and scholastical° curiosity° in such makers as have sought to bring into our vulgar° poesy some of the ancient feet, to wit the dactyl into verses hexameters, as he that translated certain books of Vergil's *Aeneid* in such measures° and not uncommendably[3]—if I should now say otherwise, it would make me seem contradictory to myself. Yet for the information° of our young makers and pleasure of all others who be delighted in novelty, and to the intent we may not seem by ignorance or oversight to omit any point of subtlety material or necessary to our vulgar° art, we will in this present chapter and by our own idle° observations show how one may easily and commodiously lead all those feet of the ancients into our vulgar° language.[4] And if men's ears were not perchance too dainty, or their judgments over-partial, would peradventure° nothing at all misbecome our art, but make in our meters° a more pleasant numerosity° than now is. Thus far, therefore, we will adventure and not beyond, to

1. **standing . . . upon** being based on.
2. See 2.3.159.
3. Puttenham is thinking of Stanyhurst's

First Foure Bookes of Virgil his Aeneis (1582).
4. Cf. Stanyhurst's "Dedication" to his *Aeneis.*

the intent to show some singularity in our art that every man hath not heretofore observed, and (her Majesty's good liking always had) whether we make the common readers to laugh or to lour,[5] all is a matter,[6] since our intent is not so exactly to prosecute the purpose, nor so earnestly, as to think it should by authority of our own judgment be generally applauded at to the discredit of our forefathers' manner of vulgar° poesy, or to the alteration or peradventure° total destruction of the same, which could not stand[7] with any good discretion or courtesy in us to attempt.

But thus much I say, that by some leisurable travail° it were no hard matter to induce° all their ancient feet into use with us, and that it should prove very agreeable to the ear and well according with our ordinary times and pronunciation, which no man could then justly mislike, and that is to allow every word polysyllable one long time of necessity, which should be where his sharp accent falls in our own idiom most aptly and naturally, wherein we would not follow the license of the Greeks and Latins, who made not their sharp accent any necessary prolongation of their times, but used such syllable sometimes long, sometimes short, at their pleasure.[8] The other syllables of any word where the sharp accent fell not to be accounted[9] of such time and quantity as his orthography would best bear, having regard to himself or to his next neighbor word bounding him on either side, namely to the smoothness and hardness of the syllable in his utterance, which is occasioned altogether by his orthography and situation,° as in this word *dáily*, the first syllable for his usual and sharp accent's sake to be always long, the second for his flat accent's sake to be always short, and the rather for his orthography, because if he go before another word commencing with a vowel not letting him to be eclipsed,[10] his utterance is easy and current.° In this trisyllable *dāngĕrŏus*, the first to be long, the other two short for the same causes. In this word *dāngĕrŏusnēss*, the first and last to be both long, because they receive both of them the sharp accent, and the two middlemost to be short. In these words *remedy* and *remediless*, the time to follow also the accent, so as° if it please better to set the sharp accent upon *re* than upon *dy*, that syllable should be made long, and *e converso*,[11] but in this word *remediless*, because many like better to accent the syllable *me* than the syllable *less*, therefore I leave him for a common syllable to be able to receive both a long and a short time as occasion shall serve. The like law I set in these words

5. **lour** frown, scowl.
6. **all is a matter** it is all the same.
7. **stand** be consistent.
8. Puttenham is not entirely accurate here. A few words in Latin and Greek do have vowels that could be long or short, but the number is not great. He may be thinking of the metrical rule that short vowels become long in lines of poetry when they are followed by two consonants. (We are using the briefest formulation of this rule here.)
9. I.e., are to be accounted.
10. **not letting ... eclipsed** not preventing it from being elided.
11. *e converso* contrariwise.

revocable, recoverable, irrevocable, irrecoverable, for sometime it sounds better to say *rĕvŏ cāblĕ*[12] than *rĕ vōcăblĕ, rēcŏvĕr āblĕ* than *rĕcōvĕr ăblĕ*. For this one thing ye must always mark, that if your time fall either by reason of his sharp accent or otherwise upon the penultimate, ye shall find many other words to rhyme with him, because such terminations are not geason.[13] But if the long time fall upon the antepenultimate, ye shall not find many words to match him in his termination, which is the cause of his concord° or rhyme. But if you would let your long time by his sharp accent fall above the antepenultimate, as to say *cōvĕrăblĕ*, ye shall seldom or perchance never find one to make up rhyme with him unless it be badly and by abuse,° and therefore in all such long polysyllables ye do commonly give two sharp accents and thereby reduce° him into two feet, as in this word *rēmŭ nĕrātĭŏn*, which makes a couple of good dactyls, and in this word *cōntrībūtĭŏn*, which makes a good spondee and a good dactyl, and in this word *recāpĭtŭlātĭŏn*, it makes two dactyls and a syllable overplus to annex to the word precedent to help piece up another foot.

But for words monosyllables (as be most of ours), because in pronouncing them they do of necessity retain a sharp accent, ye may justly allow them to be all long if they will so best serve your turn, and if they be tailed one to another, or the one to a bisyllable or polysyllable, ye ought to allow them that time that best serves your purpose and pleaseth your ear most, and truliest answers the nature of the orthography, in which I would, as near as I could, observe and keep the laws of the Greek and Latin versifiers. That is, to prolong the syllable which is written with double consonants or by diphthong or with single consonants that run hard and harshly upon the tongue; and to shorten all syllables that stand[14] upon vowels, if there were no cause of elision, and single consonants, and such of them as are most flowing and slipper° upon the tongue, as *n, r, t, d, l*, and for this purpose to take away all aspirations and many times the last consonant of a word, as the Latin poets used to do, especially Lucretius and Ennius, as to say *finibu* for *finibus*.[15] And so would not I stick° to say thus *delite* for *delight*, *hye* for *high*, and such like, and doth[16] nothing at all impugn the rule I gave before against the wresting of words by false orthography to make up rhyme, which may not be falsified.[17] But this omission of letters in the midst of a meter° to make him the more slipper° helps the numerosity° and hinders not the rhyme.[18] But generally the shortening or prolonging

---

12. In placing the final two accent marks over this word, we have followed the Scolar Press edition of the *Art*.

13. **geason** rare.

14. **stand** are based.

15. *finibus* the dative or ablative of *fines* (Lat.), "limits, boundaries."

16. I.e., it doth.

17. See 2.9.170.

18. Cf. Harvey, *Spenser-Harvey Correspondence* 623.

of the monosyllables depends much upon the nature of their orthography, which the Latin grammarians call the rule of position, as, for example, if I shall say thus:

Nōt mănỹ dāys pāst.[19]

This makes a good dactyl and a good spondee, but if ye turn them backward, it would not do so, as:

Many days not past.

And the distich° made all of monosyllables:

Būt nōne ōf ūs trūe mēn ānd frēe,
Could find so great good luck as he.

Which words serve well to make the verse all spondaic or iambic, but not in dactyl, as other words, or the same otherwise placed, would do, for it were an ill-favored dactyl to say:

Būt nŏne ŏf ūs ăll trūe.

Therefore, whensoever your words will not make a smooth dactyl, ye must alter them or their situations,° or else turn them to other feet that may better bear their manner of sound and orthography, or if the word be polysyllable, to divide him, and to make him serve by pieces, that he could not do whole and entirely. And no doubt by like consideration did the Greek and Latin versifiers fashion all their feet at the first to be of sundry times, and the selfsame syllable to be sometime long and sometime short for the ear's better satisfaction, as hath been before remembered.

Now also, whereas I said before that our old Saxon English for his many monosyllables did not naturally admit the use of the ancient feet in our vulgar° measures° so aptly as in those languages which stood[20] most upon polysyllables, I said it in a sort truly, but now I must recant and confess that our Norman English, which hath grown since William the Conqueror, doth admit any of the ancient feet, by reason of the many polysyllables, even to six and seven in one word, which we at this day use in our most ordinary language; and which corruption hath been occasioned chiefly by the peevish affectation not of the Normans themselves, but of clerks° and scholars° or secretaries long since, who, not content with the usual Norman or Saxon word, would convert the very Latin and Greek word into vulgar° French, as to say *innumerable*

---

19. The original line cited here reads, "Nōt mănỹ dāys pāst. Twenty days after." The status of this second phrase is obscure. It comes some five spaces after "pāst" and is not in italics, as quoted lines usually are, but in Roman type, the normal typeface of the book. The phrase is probably a rejected draft alternative to the first phrase, printed by mistake, since Puttenham speaks next of "a good dactyl and a good spondee," a description that applies only to the first phrase.

20. **stood** were based.

for *innombrable, revocable, irrevocable, irradiation, depopulation,* and
such like, which are not natural Normans nor yet French, but altered
Latins,[21] and without any imitation at all,[22] which therefore were long
time despised for inkhorn[23] terms, and now be reputed the best and
most delicate° of any other, of which, and many other causes of corruption of our speech, we have in another place more amply discoursed.[24]
But by this mean we may at this day very well receive the ancient feet
metrical of the Greeks and Latins, saving those that be superfluous, as
be all the feet above the trisyllable, which the old grammarians idly° in-
vented° and distinguished by special names, whereas indeed the same
do stand compounded with[25] the inferior feet, and therefore some of
them were called by the names of *didactylus, dispondeus,* and *disi-
ambus.* All which feet, as I say, we may be allowed to use with good
discretion and precise choice of words and with the favorable approbation of readers, and so shall our plat[26] in this one point be larger and
much surmount that which Stanyhurst first took in hand by his hexameters dactylic and spondaic in the translation of Vergil's *Aeneid,* and
such as for a great number of them my stomach can hardly digest for
the ill-shaped sound of many of his words polysyllable and also his cop-
ulation of monosyllables, supplying the quantity of a trisyllable to his
intent.

And right so,[27] in promoting this device° of ours, being (I fear me)
much more nice° and affected, and therefore more misliked than his,
we are to bespeak favor, first of the delicate ears,[28] then of the rigorous
and severe dispositions, lastly to crave pardon of the learned and ancient makers in our vulgar,° for if we should seek in every point to
equal our speech with the Greek and Latin in their metrical observations, it could not possibly be by us performed, because their syllables
came to be timed, some of them long, some of them short, not by reason of any evident or apparent cause in writing or sound remaining
upon one more than another,[29] for many times they shortened the syllable of sharp accent and made long that of the flat; and therefore we
must needs say, it was in many of their words done by pre-election[30] in
the first poets, not having regard altogether to the orthography and

---

21. "Latins" means the Latin language, just as "Normans" means Norman French. For "Hebrews," meaning "Hebrew," see 2.12, note 107.

22. I.e., these words are not (properly speaking) imitations (of one language in another) but just uses of the same (Latin) word, and so not really French at all.

23. **inkhorn** ostentatiously learned, pedantic.

24. See 3.4.228.

25. **compounded with** made up of.

26. **plat** plan or scheme (of a literary work or system).

27. **right so** just so.

28. **delicate ears** i.e., of court ladies and the queen, unused to harsh inkhorn squabbles.

29. **by reason . . . another** i.e., because it was evident that one sound, whether written or spoken, lasted longer than another.

30. **pre-election** a preconscious, nonrational choice, or a prehistoric one, or perhaps both.

hardness or softness of a syllable, consonant, vowel, or diphthong, but at their pleasure, or as it fell out. So as° he that first put in a verse this word *Penelope*, which might be Homer or some other of his antiquity, where he made *pē* in both places long and *ně* and *lŏ* short, he might have made them otherwise and with as good reason, nothing in the world appearing that might move them to make such pre-election more in the one syllable than in the other, for *pe*, *ne*, and *lo*, being syllables vocals, be equally smooth and current° upon the tongue, and might bear as well the long as the short time. But it pleased the poet otherwise, so he that first shortened *ca* in this word *cano*, and made long *tro* in *troia*, and *o* in *oris*, might have as well done the contrary, but because he that first put them into a verse found, as it is to be supposed, a more sweetness in his own ear to have them so timed, therefore, all other poets who followed were fain to do the like, which made that Vergil, who came many years after the first reception of words in their several times, was driven of necessity to accept them in such quantities as they were left him, and therefore said:

> *ārmă vĭ rūmqūe că nō trŏ iĕ quī prīmŭs ăb ōrīs.*[31]

Neither truly do I see any other reason in that law (though in other rules of shortening and prolonging a syllable there may be reason), but that it stands[32] upon bare tradition. Such as the Cabalists[33] avouch in their mystical constructions theological, and others, saying that they received the same from hand to hand from the first parent Adam, Abraham, and others, which I will give them leave alone both to say and believe for me, thinking rather that they have been the idle° occupations, or perchance the malicious and crafty constructions, of the Talmudists and others of the Hebrew clerks° to bring the world into admiration° of their laws and religion. Now peradventure° with us Englishmen it be somewhat too late to admit a new invention° of feet and times that our forefathers never used nor never observed till this day, either in their measures° or in their pronunciation, and perchance will seem in us a presumptuous part to attempt, considering also it would be hard to find many men to like of one man's choice in the limitation of times and quantities of words, with which not one, but every ear is to be pleased and made a particular judge, being most truly said, that a multitude or commonalty[34] is hard to please and easy to offend. And therefore

---

31. This is the first line of the *Aeneid*: "Arms and the man I sing, who first from the shores of Troy...." Note that Puttenham has *trŏ iĕ* rather than the more correct *trŏ iāe*. His spelling is characteristically medieval and may suggest that Puttenham was citing from—or remembering—a medieval edition of the poem. One of the achievements of humanist scholarship was the restoration of the correct spelling of the Latin *-ae* ending. Also, the long sign over the *que* of *virumque* should be a short sign.

32. **stands** is based.

33. **Cabalists** adepts of the esoteric Jewish mysticism of the Kabbala (Heb., "tradition"), which arose in the twelfth century.

34. **commonalty** common people.

I intend not to proceed any further in this curiosity° than to show some small subtlety that any other hath not yet done, and not by imitation but by observation, nor to the intent to have it put in execution in our vulgar° poesy, but to be pleasantly scanned upon,[35] as are all novelties so frivolous and ridiculous as it.

35. **pleasantly scanned upon** i.e., viewed as a pastime.

Chapter 14

*A more particular declaration[1] of the metrical feet of
the ancient poets Greek and Latin,
and chiefly of the feet of two times*

Their grammarians made a great multitude of feet, I wot° not to what huge number, and of so many sizes as their words were of length, namely six sizes, whereas indeed, the metrical feet are but twelve in number, whereof four only be of two times, and eight of three times, the rest compounds of the premised two sorts, even as the arithmetical numbers above three are made of two and three.[2] And if ye will know how many of these feet will be commodiously received with us, I say all the whole twelve. For first, for the foot *spondeus*, of two long times, ye have these English words: *mōrnīng, mīdnīght, mīschānce*, and a number more whose orthography may direct your judgment in this point. For your trochee, of a long and short, ye have these words: *mănnĕr, brōkĕn, tākĕn, bōdў, mēmbĕr*, and a great many more if their last syllables abut not upon the consonant in the beginning of another word, and in these, whether they do abut or no: *wīttў,° dīttў, sōrrŏw, mōrrŏw*, and such like, which end in a vowel. For your iamb, of a short and a long, ye have these words: *rĕstōre, rĕmōrse, dĕsīre, ĕndūre*, and a thousand besides. For your foot *pyrrhichius*,[3] or of two short syllables, ye have these words: *mănў, mŏnĕy, pĕnnў, sīllў,°* and others of that constitution or the like.

For your feet of three times, and first your dactyl, ye have these words and a number more: *pātĭĕnce, tēmpĕrănce, wōmănhŏod, jŏllĭtў, dāngĕrŏus, dūtĭfŭl*, and others. For your molossus, of all three long, ye have a number of words also, and especially most of your participles active, as: *pērsīstīng, dēspōilīng, īndēntīng*, and such like in orthography. For your anapest, of two short and a long, ye have these words, but not many more, as: *mănĭfōld, mŏnĕylēss, rĕmĕnānt,[4] hŏlĭnēss*. For your foot

1. **declaration** explanation, exposition.
2. **two and three** i.e., twos and threes.
3. On this foot, see 2.3, note 11.
4. **remenant** i.e., remnant.

tribrachus, of all three short, ye have very few trisyllables, because the sharp accent will always make one of them long by pronunciation, which else would be by orthography short, as: *mĕrrĭlў̆, mĭnĭŏn*, and such like. For your foot *bacchius*, of a short and two long, ye have these and the like words trisyllables: *lămēntīng, rĕquēstīng, rĕnōuncīng, rĕpēntānce, ĭnūrīng*. For your foot *antibacchius*, of two long and a short, ye have these words: *fōrsākĕn, īmpūgnĕd*, and others many. For your *amphimacer*, that is a long, a short, and a long, ye have these words and many more: *ēxcĕllēnt, īmmĭnēnt*, and especially such as be proper names of persons or towns or other things, and namely Welsh words. For your foot *amphibrachus*, of a short, a long, and a short, ye have these words and many like to these: *rĕsīstĕd, dĕlīghtfŭl, rĕprīsăl, ĕnāuntĕr,*[5] *ĕnāmĕl*. So as° for want° of English words, if your ear be not too dainty and your rules too precise, ye need not be without the metrical feet of the ancient poets such as be most pertinent and not superfluous.

This is (ye will perchance say) my singular[6] opinion: then ye shall see how well I can maintain it. First, the quantity of a word comes either by pre-election[7] without reason or force, as hath been alleged,[8] and as the ancient Greeks and Latins did in many words, but not in all, or by election with reason, as they did in some, and not a few. And a sound is drawn at length either by the infirmity of the tongue, because the word or syllable is of such letters as hangs long in the palate or lips ere he will come forth, or because he is accented and tuned higher and sharper than another, whereby he somewhat obscureth the other syllables in the same word that be not accented so high; in both these cases we will establish our syllable long. Contrariwise, the shortening of a syllable is, when his sound or accent happens to be heavy and flat, that is, to fall away speedily and, as it were, inaudible, or when he is made of such letters as be by nature slipper° and voluble° and smoothly pass from the mouth. And the vowel is always more easily delivered than the consonant; and of consonants, the liquid more than the mute;[9] and a single consonant more than a double; and one more than twain coupled together. All which points were observed by the Greeks and Latins, and allowed for maxims in versifying.

Now if ye will examine these four bisyllables *rēmnānt, rĕmāin, rēndĕr, rĕnnĕt*, for an example by which ye may make a general rule, and ye shall find that they answer our first resolution.[10] First in *remnant, rem*, bearing the sharp accent and having his consonant abut upon another, sounds long. The syllable *nant*, being written with two conso-

---

5. **enaunter** in case that, lest by chance.
6. **singular** individual, unusual.
7. **pre-election** a preconscious, nonrational choice, or a prehistoric one, or perhaps both.
8. See 2.13.204–5.

9. The liquid consonants are *l*, *r*, *m*, and *n*; the mute or plosive ones are *k*, *p*, and *t*.

10. **first resolution** i.e., the first part of Puttenham's proposition (concerning bisyllables) that Latin prosody may be applied to English verse (?).

nants, must needs be accounted the same, besides that *nant* by his Latin
original is long, *videl.*,° *remanēns*. Take this word *remain*: because the
last syllable bears the sharp accent, he is long in the ear, and *re*, being
the first syllable, passing obscurely away with a flat accent, is short, besides that *re* by his Latin original and also by his orthography is short.
This word *render*, bearing the sharp accent upon *ren*, makes it long; the
syllable *der*, falling away swiftly and being also written with a single
consonant or liquid, is short and makes the trochee. This word *rĕnnĕt*,
having both syllables sliding and slipper,° make the foot *pyrrhichius*, because if he be truly uttered, he bears in manner no sharper accent upon
the one than the other syllable, but be in effect equal in time and tune,°
as is also the spondee. And because they be not written with any hard or
harsh consonants, I do allow them both for short syllables, or to be used
for common, according as their situation° and place with other words
shall be. And as I have named to you but only four words for an example,
so may ye find out by diligent observation four hundred, if ye will.

But of all your words bisyllables, the most part naturally do make the
foot *iambus*, many the *trocheus*, fewer the *spondeus*, fewest of all the
pyrrhichius, because in him the sharp accent (if ye follow the rules of
your accent as we have presupposed) doth make a little odds.[11] And ye
shall find verses, made all of monosyllables, and do very well, but
lightly[12]: they be iambics, because for the more part the accent falls
sharp upon every second word rather than contrariwise, as this of Sir
Thomas Wyatt's:

> *I fĭnd nŏ peāce, ănd yēt mў̆wār ĭs dōne,*
> *I fear and hope, and burn and freeze like ice.*[13]

And some verses where the sharp accent falls upon the first and third,
and so make the verse wholly trochaic, as thus:

> *Work not, no, nor wish thy friend or foes harm.*
> *Try, but trust not, all that speak thee so fair.*[†]

And some verses made of monosyllables and bisyllables interlaced, as
this of the Earl's:

> *When raging love, with extreme pain.*[14]

And this:

> *A fairer beast of fresher hue beheld I never none.*[15]

And some verses made all of bisyllables and others all of trisyllables,
and others of polysyllables equally increasing and of divers quantities

11. **odds** difference.
12. **lightly** The meaning of this word is
obscure.
13. *Tottel* no. 49.35–36 (Rebholz no. 17).

14. Surrey, *Tottel* no. 16.12 (Jones no. 1).
15. Surrey, *Tottel* no. 264.23 (not in
Jones).

and sundry situations,° as in this of our own, made to daunt the insolence[16] of a beautiful woman.

> *Brittle beauty, blossom daily fading,*
> *Morn, noon, and eve in age and eke[17] in eld[18]*
> *Dangerous,[19] disdainful, pleasantly persuading,*
> *Easy to grip, but cumbrous[20] to wield,*
> *For slender bottom, hard and heavy lading,[21]*
> *Gay[22] for a while, but little while durable,*
> *Suspicious, uncertain, irrevocable,[23]*
> *O, since thou art by trial° not to trust,*
> *Wisdom it is, and it is also just,*
> *To sound the stem before the tree be felled,*
> *That is, since death will drive us all to dust,*
> *To leave thy love ere that we be compelled.*[*24]

In which ye have your first verse all of bisyllables and of the foot
trocheus; the second all of monosyllables and all of the foot *iambus*;
the third all of trisyllables and all of the foot *dactylus*; your fourth of
one bisyllable and two monosyllables interlarded; the fifth of one monosyllable and two bisyllables interlaced; and the rest of other sorts and
situations,° some by degrees increasing, some diminishing. Which example I have set down to let you perceive what pleasant numerosity° in
the measure and disposition of your words in a meter° may be contrived by curious° wits. And these with other like were the observations[25] of the Greek and Latin versifiers.

16. **insolence** haughtiness.
17. **eke** also.
18. **eld** old age.
19. **dangerous** haughty, difficult to please, reluctant to comply.
20. **cumbrous** cumbersome.
21. **lading** loading, i.e., the cargo of a ship.

22. **Gay** mirthful; showy.
23. **irrevocable** obstinate (?).
24. Though he claims this poem as his own, Puttenham loosely adapts *Tottel* no. 9, which Rollins hesitantly attributes to (Thomas), Lord Vaux.
25. **observations** customs, rules.

CHAPTER 15

Of your feet of three times, and first of the dactyl

Your feet of three times by prescription of the Latin grammarians are
of eight sundry proportions,° for some notable difference appearing
in every syllable of three falling in a word of that size. But because above
the antepenultimate there was (among the Latins) none accent audible
in any long word, therefore to devise any foot of longer measure than of
three times was to them but superfluous, because all above the number
of three are but compounded of their inferiors. Omitting therefore to

speak of these larger feet, we say that of all your feet of three times, the dactyl is most usual and fit for our vulgar° meter,° and most agreeable to the ear, especially if ye overload not your verse with too many of them but here and there interlace an iamb or some other foot of two times to give him gravity and stay, as in this quatrain trimeter, or of three measures°:

> *Rēndĕr ăgaīn mў lībĕrtў,*
> *ănd sēt yoŭr cāptĭve frēe.*
> *Glōrĭoŭs īs thĕ vīctŏrў,*
> *Cōnquĕrŏrs ūse wĭth lēnĭtў.*[†]

Where ye see every verse is all of a measure,° and yet unequal in number of syllables, for the second verse is but of six syllables, where the rest are of eight. But the reason is for that in three of the same verses are two dactyls apiece, which abridge two syllables in every verse, and so maketh the longest even with the shortest. Ye may note besides by the first verse how much better some bisyllable becometh to piece out another longer foot than another word doth, for in place of *render*, if ye had said *restore*, it had marred the dactyl and of necessity driven him out at length to be a verse iambic of four feet, because *render* is naturally a trochee and makes the first two times of a dactyl. *Restore* is naturally an iamb and in this place could not possibly have made a pleasant dactyl.

Now again, if ye will say to me that these two words *liberty* and *conquerors* be not precise dactyls by the Latin rule, so much will I confess to, but since they go current° enough upon the tongue, and be so usually pronounced, they may pass well enough for dactyls in our vulgar° meters,° and that is enough for me, seeking but to fashion an art, and not to finish it, which time only and custom have authority to do, especially in all cases of language, as the poet hath wittily remembered in this verse:

> *—si volet usus*
> *Quem penes arbitrium est et vis et norma loquendi.*[1]

The Earl of Surrey upon the death of Sir Thomas Wyatt made among other this verse pentameter and of ten syllables:

> *What holy grave (alas), what sepulcher. . . .*[2]

But if I had had the making of him, he should have been of eleven syllables and kept his measure° of five still, and would so have run more pleasantly a great deal. For as he is now, though he be even, he seems

---

1. Horace, *Ars poetica* 71–72: "if usage wills it,/In whose hands lie the judgment and the force and norm of speaking." Puttenham misquotes Horace slightly here, substituting *vis* (force) for *ius* (right, rule).
2. *Tottel* no. 29.11 (Jones no. 31).

odd and defective for not well observing the natural accent of every word, and this would have been soon helped by inserting one monosyllable in the middle of the verse, and drawing another syllable in the beginning into a dactyl, this word *holy* being a good pyrrhichius and very well serving the turn, thus:

> *Whāt hŏlў grāve, ă lās whăt fīt sĕpūlchĕr.*

Which verse, if ye peruse throughout, ye shall find him after the first dactyl all trochaic and not iambic, nor of any other foot of two times. But perchance if ye would seem yet more curious,° in place of these four trochees, ye might induce other feet of three times, as to make the three syllables next following the dactyl the foot amphimacer, the last word *sepulcher* the foot *amphibrachus*, leaving the other middle word for an iamb, thus:

> *Whāt hŏlў grāve, ă lās whăt fīt sĕpūlchĕr.*

If ye ask me further why I make *what* first long and after short in one verse, to that I satisfied you before, that it is by reason of his accent sharp in one place and flat in another, being a common monosyllable, that is, apt to receive either accent. And so in the first place receiving aptly the sharp accent, he is made long; afterward, receiving the flat accent more aptly than the sharp, because the syllable precedent, *las*, utterly distains him,[3] he is made short and not long, and that with very good melody, but to have given him the sharp accent and plucked it from the syllable *las*, it had been to any man's ear a great discord. For evermore this word *alás* is accented upon the last, and that loudly and notoriously,[4] as appeareth by all our exclamations used under that term. The same Earl of Surrey and Sir Thomas Wyatt, the first reformers and polishers of our vulgar° poesy, much affecting[5] the style and measures° of the Italian Petrarch, used the foot dactyl very often, but not many in one verse, as in these:

> *Fūll mănў that in presence of thy līvelĭhĕad....*[6]
> *Shed Caesar's tears upon Pōmpĕĭūs' hĕad....*
> *Th'ēnĕmў to life, destroy er of all kind....*[7]
> *If āmŏ rŏus faith in an heart un feigned....*
> *Mine old dēar ĕnĕ my, my froward master....*
> *Thē fŭrĭ ous gun in his most ra ging ire....*[8]

And many more, which if ye would not allow for dactyls, the verse would halt, unless ye would seem to help it, contracting a syllable by

---

3. **distains him** makes it seem pale or colorless in comparison.
4. **notoriously** manifestly.
5. **affecting** admiring.
6. **livelihead** living form, life.

7. **kind** nature.
8. Puttenham cites six lines from different *Tottel* poems: nos. 30.24 and 30.26 (actually by Surrey: Jones no. 29), nos. 85.13, 98.22, 64.5, and 73.5 (Rebholz nos. 46, 13, 73, 43).

virtue of the figure *synaeresis*,[9] which I think was never their meaning, nor indeed would have bred any pleasure to the ear, but hindered the flowing of the verse. Howsoever ye take it, the dactyl is commendable enough in our vulgar° meters,° but most plausible° of all when he is sounded upon the stage, as in these comical verses showing how well it becometh all noblemen and great personages to be temperate° and modest, yea more than any meaner° man, thus:

> Lĕt nŏ nŏbīlĭtỹ, rīchĕs, ŏr hĕrĭtăge,
> Hōnŏr, ŏr ēmpĭre, ŏr eārthlỹ dŏmīnĭŏn
> Brēed ĭn yŏur heād ănỹ pēevĭsh[10] ŏpīnĭŏn
> Thāt yĕ mǎy sāfĕr ăvōuch[11] ănỹ ōutrāge.[†]

And in this distich° taxing the prelate symoniac, standing all upon perfect dactyls:

> Nōw mānỹ bỹ mōnēy pūrvĕy prŏmōtĭŏn,
> For money moves any heart to devotion.[†]

But this advertisement[12] I will give you withal,° that if ye use too many dactyls together, ye make your music too light and of no solemn gravity, such as the amorous elegies in court naturally require, being always either very doleful or passionate, as the affections of love enforce, in which business ye must make your choice of very few words dactylic, or them that ye cannot refuse, to dissolve and break them into other feet by such means as it shall be taught hereafter. But chiefly in your courtly ditties take heed ye use not these manner of long polysyllables and especially that ye finish not your verse with them, as *retribution, restitution, remuneration, recapitulation*, and such like, for they smatch[13] more the school of common players than of any delicate° poet lyric or elegiac.[14]

---

9. **synaeresis** The making of two vowels into a diphthong or a simple vowel (Gr., "a drawing together"). Probably because it is characteristic of Latin verse more than English, this figure does not appear in Book 3 of the *Art*, although Puttenham could have found it in his chief source, Susenbrotus (22), or in Peacham (E3r).

10. **peevish** foolish, perverse, malignant.

11. **avouch** acknowledge, sanction, confess.

12. **advertisement** admonition.

13. **smatch** taste of.

14. Puttenham may be right about the use of such polysyllabic words in the popular drama. Lewis Wager's *Marie Magdalene* (1566) rhymes on *ornature, conglutinate*, and *testification* (F. P. Wilson, *English Drama* 72). LION, however, records no occurrences of *retribution, remuneration*, or *recapitulation*, and only two of *restitution* (in Gascoigne and Marlowe), in plays before 1590.

Chapter 16

*Of all your other feet of three times, and how well
they would fashion a meter° in our vulgar°*

All your other feet of three times I find no use of them in our vulgar°
meters° nor no sweetness at all, and yet words enough to serve their
proportions.° So as,° though they have not hitherto been made artificial,°
yet now by more curious° observation they might be, since all arts grew
first by observation of nature's proceedings and custom. And first your
molossus, being of all three long, is evidently discovered° by this word
pērmĭttĭng; the anapest, of two short and a long, by this word *fŭrĭŏus*, if
the next word begin with a consonant; the foot *bacchius*, of a short and
two long, by this word *rĕsīstānce*; the foot *antibacchius*, of two long and
a short, by this word *ēxāmplĕ*; the foot *amphimacer*, of a long, a short,
and a long, by this word *cōnquĕrīng*; the foot of amphibrachys, of a short,
a long, and a short, by this word *rĕmēmbĕr*, if a vowel follow. The foot *tribrachus*, of three short times, is very hard to be made by any of our trisyllables, unless they be compounded of the smoothest sort of consonants or
syllables vocals,[1] or of three smooth monosyllables, or of some piece of a
long polysyllable, and after that sort we may with wresting of words
shape the foot *tribrachus* rather by usurpation than by rule, which nevertheless is allowed in every primitive art and invention.° And so it was by
the Greeks and Latins in their first versifying, as if a rule should be set
down that from henceforth these words should be counted all tribrachs,
ĕnĕmў, rĕmĕdў, sīllĭnĕss,[2] *mŏnĕylĕss, pĕnnĭlĕss, crŭĕllў*, and such like, or
a piece of this long word, *rĕcōvĕrăblĕ, innŭmĕrăblĕ, rĕădĭlў*, and others.

Of all which manner of apt words to make these stranger° feet of three
times, which go not so current° with our ear as the dactyl, the maker
should have a good judgment to know them by their manner of orthography and by their accent which serve most fitly for every foot, or else he
should have always a little calender[3] of them apart, to use readily when
he shall need them. But because in very truth I think them but vain and
superstitious observations,[4] nothing at all furthering the pleasant melody
of our English meter,° I leave to speak any more of them, and rather wish
the continuance of our old manner of poesy, scanning our verse by syllables rather than by feet, and using most commonly the word iambic, and
sometime the trochaic, which ye shall discern by their accents, and now
and then a dactyl, keeping precisely our symphony° or rhyme without
any other mincing measures,° which an idle,° inventive° head could easily devise, as the former examples teach.

1. **syllables vocals** i.e., vowels.
2. **silliness** happiness, simplicity.
3. **calendar** list, register.

4. **superstitious observations** excessive,
perhaps even idolatrously devoted, rules.

CHAPTER 17

Of your verses perfect° and defective, and that which the Greeks called the half-foot

The Greeks and Latins used verses in the odd syllable of two sorts, which they called catalectic and acatalectic, that is, odd under and odd over the just measure of their verse.[1] And we in our vulgar° find many of the like, and especially in the rhymes of Sir Thomas Wyatt, strained perchance out of their original, made first by Francis Petrarch, as these:

> *Like unto these immeasurable mountains,*
> *So is my painful life the burden of ire:*
> *For high be they, and high is my desire,*
> *And I of tears, and they are full of fountains.*[2]

Where in your first, second, and fourth verse, ye may find a syllable superfluous, and though in the first ye will seem to help it, by drawing these three syllables *īm mĕ sŭ* into a dactyl, in the rest it cannot be so excused, wherefore we must think he did it of purpose, by the odd syllable to give greater grace to his meter.° And we find in our old rhymes this odd syllable sometimes placed in the beginning and sometimes in the middle of a verse, and is allowed to go alone and to hang[3] to any other syllable. But this odd syllable in our meters° is not the half-foot as the Greeks and Latins used him in their verses, and called such measure° *penthemimeris* and *hephthemimeris*,[4] but rather is that, which they called the catalectic, or maimed verse. Their *hemimeris*, or half-foot, served not by license poetical or necessity of words, but to beautify and exornate[5] the verse by placing one such half-foot in the middle caesura and one other in the end of the verse, as they used all their pentameters elegiac, and not by coupling them together, but by account to make their verse of a just measure and not defective or superfluous.[6] Our odd syllable is not altogether of that nature, but is in a manner drowned and suppressed by the flat accent, and shrinks away, as it were, inaudible, and by that mean the odd verse comes almost to be an even in every man's hearing. The half-foot of the ancients was reserved purposely to a use, and

---

1. *Catalectic* (Gr. *katalegein*, "to leave off, stop") is used for a verse lacking a syllable at the end; *acatalectic* is used for a verse in which no syllable is missing in the last foot. Puttenham's second definition is clearly incorrect.

2. *Tottel* no. 97.6–9 (Rebholz no. 24).

3. **hang** attach.

4. A *penthemimeris* is a group of five half-feet, as in the first half of a pentameter line, or the first half of a hexameter if the caesura falls in the third foot. By *heph-*

themimeris Puttenham means a group of seven half-feet which constitute the first half of a hexameter line when the caesura falls in the fourth foot. *Hemimeris* in the next sentence means a half-foot. For these terms, see Scaliger 2.2.

5. **exornate** adorn.

6. In classical prosody, an elegiac couplet consisted of one regular line in dactylic hexameter, followed by a second such line in which the third and sixth feet, however, were replaced by catalectic half-feet.

therefore they gave such odd syllable, wheresoever he fell, the sharper accent, and made by him a notorious[7] pause, as in this pentameter:

Nīl mĭ hĭ rēscrībàs āttămĕn īpsĕ vĕ nì.[8]

Which in all make five whole feet, or the verse pentameter. We in our vulgar° have not the use of the like half-foot.

7. **notorious** conspicuous.
8. Ovid, *Heroides* 1.2: "Do not write back to me, but just come yourself." These are Penelope's words in an imaginary letter to her long-absent husband, Odysseus. Most modern editions have *attinet* (as far as I am concerned) for *attamen* (but just).

CHAPTER 18[1]

*Of the breaking your bisyllables and polysyllables,
and when it is to be used*

But whether ye suffer your syllable to receive his quantity by his accent or by his orthography, or whether ye keep your bisyllable whole or whether ye break him, all is one[2] to his quantity, and his time will appear the selfsame still° and ought not to be altered by our makers, unless it be when such syllable is allowed to be common and to receive any of both times, as in the dimeter, made of two syllables entire:

ēxtrēme dĕsīre

The first is a good spondee, the second a good iamb. And if the same words be broken thus, it is not so pleasant:

ĭn ēx trēme dĕ sīre

And yet the first makes an iamb, and the second a trochee, each syllable retaining still° his former quantities.

And always ye must have regard to the sweetness of the meter,° so as° if your word polysyllable would not sound pleasantly whole, ye should for the nonce° break him, which ye may easily do by inserting here and there one monosyllable among your polysyllables, or by changing your word into another place than where he sounds unpleasantly, and by breaking, turn a trochee to an iamb, or contrariwise, as thus:

*Hōllŏw vāllĕys ūndĕr hīghĕst mōuntăins,
Crāggў clīffs brĭng fōrth thĕ fāirĕst fōuntăins.*[3]

These verses be trochaic, and in mine ear not so sweet and harmonical as the iambic, thus:

1. This final chapter of Book 2 is erroneously numbered 13 in the original.
2. **all is one** it is all the same.

3. Perhaps a loose adaptation of Wyatt's "Like to these immeasurable mountains," cited at 2.17.214 (*Tottel* no. 97, Rebholz no. 24).

> *Thĕ hōllŏw'st vāles lĭe ūndĕr hīghĕst mōuntāins,*
> *Thĕ crāggĭ'st clīffs brĭng fōrth thĕ fāirĕst fōuntāins.*

All which verses be now become iambic by breaking the first bisyllables, and yet alters not their quantities though the feet be altered. And thus:

> *Restless is the heart in his desires,*
> *Raving after that[4] reason doth deny.*[†]

Which being turned thus makes a new harmony:

> *The restless heart renews his old desires,*
> *Ay raving after that reason doth it deny.*

   And following this observation, your meters° being built with polysyllables will fall diversely out, that is, some to be spondaic, some iambic, others dactylic, others trochaic, and of one mingled with another, as in this verse:

> *Hēavȳ īs thĕ būrdĕn of prĭncĕs' īre.*[†]

The verse is trochaic, but being altered thus, is iambic:

> *Fŭll hēavȳ īs thĕ pēise[5] ŏf prīncĕs' īre.*

And as Sir Thomas Wyatt sang in a verse wholly trochaic, because the words do best shape to that foot by their natural accent, thus:

> *Fārewĕll lōve, ănd āll thȳ lāws fŏr ēvĕr.*[6]

And in this ditty of the Earl of Surrey's, passing[7] sweet and harmonical, all be iambic:

> *When raging love, with extreme pain,*
> *So cruelly doth strain[8] my heart,*
> *And that the tears like floods of rain*
> *Bear witness of my woeful smart.*[9]

Which, being disposed otherwise or not broken, would prove all trochaic, but nothing pleasant.

   Now furthermore ye are to note that all your monosyllables may receive the sharp accent, but not so aptly one as another, as in this verse where they serve well to make him iambic, but not trochaic:

> *Gŏd grānt thĭs peāce mǎy lōng ĕndūre.*[†]

Where the sharp accent falls more tunably° upon *grant, peace, long, dure*, than it would by conversion, as to accent them thus:

> *Gōd grănt – thīs pĕace – māy lŏng – ēndŭre.*

4. **that** i.e., that which.
5. **peise** weight.
6. *Tottel* no. 99.3 (Rebholz no. 31).

7. **passing** surpassingly.
8. **strain** bind, constrain.
9. *Tottel* no. 16.12–15 (Jones no. 1).

And yet, if ye will ask me the reason, I cannot tell it, but that it shapes so to mine ear, and as I think, to every other man's. And in this meter° where ye have whole words bisyllable unbroken, that maintain (by reason of their accent) sundry feet, yet going one with another be very harmonical.

Where ye see one to be a trochee, another the iamb, and so intermingled not by election but by constraint of their several accents, which ought not to be altered, yet comes it to pass that many times ye must of necessity alter the accent of a syllable, and put him from his natural place. And then one syllable of a word polysyllable, or one word monosyllable, will abide to be made sometimes long, sometimes short, as in this quatrain of ours, played in a merry mood:

> Gìve mé mìne ówn, ànd whén I dó dèsíre,
> Give others theirs, and nothing that is mine,
> Nòr gíve mè thát, whereto all men aspire,
> Then neither gold, nor fair women, nor wine.*

Where in your first verse these two words *give* and *me* are accented one high, the other low. In the third verse the same words are accented contrary, and the reason of this exchange is manifest, because the maker plays with these two clauses of sundry relations, *give me* and *give others*, so as° the monosyllable *me*, being respective[10] to the word *others* and inferring a subtlety or witty° implication, ought not to have the same accent, as when he hath no such respect, as in this distich° of ours:

> Prōve[11] mĕ, Madam, ere ye rēprŏve.
> Meek minds should ēxcŭse, not āccŭse.*[12]

In which verse ye see this word *reprove*, the syllable *prove* alters his sharp accent into a flat, for naturally it is long in all his singles and compounds, *repròve*, *appròve*, *dispròve*, and so is the syllable *cuse* in *excuse*, *accuse*, *recuse*. Yet in these verses, by reason one of them doth, as it were, nick[13] another and have a certain extraordinary sense withal,° it behooveth to remove the sharp accents from whence they are most natural, to place them where the nick may be more expressly discovered.° And therefore in this verse, where no such implication is, nor no relation, it is otherwise, as thus:

> If ye rĕprōve my constancy,
> I will excūse you courteisly.†

For in this word *repróve*, because there is no extraordinary sense to be inferred, he keepeth his sharp accent upon the syllable *próve*, but in the former verses, because they seem to encounter each other, they do thereby merit an audible and pleasant alteration of their accents in those syllables that cause the subtlety.

10. **respective** logically parallel.   12. Also cited at 3.19.228.
11. **Prove** test.   13. **nick** match.

Of these manner of niceties° ye shall find in many places of our book, but especially where we treat of ornament, unto which we refer you, saving that we thought good to set down one example more to solace your minds with mirth after all these scholastical° precepts, which cannot but bring with them (especially to courtiers) much tediousness, and so to end. In our comedy entitled *Ginecocratia,**14 the king was supposed to be a person very amorous and effeminate,15 and therefore most ruled his ordinary affairs by the advice of women, either for the love he bore to their persons, or liking he had to their pleasant, ready wits and utterance. Comes me to the court one Polemon,16 an honest, plain man of the country, but rich, and having a suit to the king, met by chance with one Philino, a lover of wine and a merry companion in court, and prayed him, in that he was a stranger,°17 that he would vouchsafe to tell him which way he were best to work to get his suit, and who were most in credit and favor about the king, that he might seek to them to further his attempt.18 Philino, perceiving the plainness of the man, and that there would be some good done with him,19 told Polemon that if he would well consider him for his labor, he would bring him where he should know the truth of all his demands by the sentence° of the oracle. Polemon gave him twenty crowns. Philino brings him into a place where behind an arras cloth20 he himself spoke in manner of an oracle in these meters,° for so did all the Sybils and soothsayers in old time give their answers:

> Your best way to work—and mark my words well:
> Not money, nor many;
> Nor any, but any;
> Not weemen, but weemen bear the bell.

Polemon wist° not what to make of this doubtful° speech, and not21 being lawful to importune the oracle more than once in one matter, conceived in his head the pleasanter construction, and stuck to it; and having at home a fair young damsel of eighteen years old to his daughter, that could very well behave herself in countenance and also in her language, apparels her as gay22 as he could, and brought her to the court, where Philino, harkening daily after the event23 of this matter, met

---

14. **Ginecocratia** "The Rule of Women" (Gr.). This comedy has been lost.

15. **effeminate** self-indulgent, voluptuous; the term applies to someone either led by his passions (and hence womanish, since women were thought to be excessively passionate) or overly inclined to follow the dictates of women.

16. Puttenham may take this name from an anecdote he later quotes from Philostratus, at 3.23.350.

17. The pronouns are confusing here: Polemon is the "stranger" and is asking Philino for help.

18. *Polemon* means "warrior" (from Gk. *polemos,* "war"); *Philino* means "lover of wine" (Gr. *phil+oinos*).

19. **some good ... him** some gain gotten from him; some fun had with him.

20. **arras cloth** a tapestry hung on a wall for purposes of decoration, so called because many such tapestries came from the town of Arras in northern France.

21. **and not** i.e., and it not.

22. **gay** finely, showily.

23. **event** outcome.

him, and recommended his daughter to the lords, who perceiving her great beauty and other good parts, brought her to the king, to whom she exhibited[24] her father's supplication, and found so great favor in his eye, as without any long delay she obtained her suit at his hands. Polemon, by the diligent soliciting of his daughter, won his purpose; Philino got a good reward and used the matter so as,° howsoever the oracle had been construed, he could not have received blame nor discredit by the success,° for every ways it would have proved true, whether Polemon's daughter had obtained the suit, or not obtained it. And the subtlety lay in the accent and orthography of these two words *any* and *weemen*, for *any*, being divided, sounds *a ny*,[25] or near person to the king; and *we-men*, being divided, sounds *we men*, and not *wemen*. And so by this mean Philino served all turns and shifted himself from blame—not unlike the tale of the rattlemouse[26] who, in the wars proclaimed between the four-footed beasts and the birds, being sent for by the lion to beat his musters,[27] excused himself for that he was a fowl and flew with wings; and being sent for by the eagle to serve him, said that he was a four-footed beast, and by that crafty cavil[28] escaped the danger of the wars, and shunned the service of both princes. And ever since sat at home by the fire's side, eating up the poor husbandman's bacon, half lost for lack of a good housewife's looking to.

FINIS

24. **exhibited** presented.
25. **ny** i.e., nigh.
26. **rattlemouse** bat (a dialect word, perhaps based on the sound a bat's wings make when it flies).

27. **beat his musters** present himself for military service. *Beat* may allude to the drum summoning soldiers to muster; or it may be a typographical error for "be at."
28. **cavil** qibbling objection.

THE THIRD BOOK
Of Ornament

CHAPTER I
Of ornament poetical[1]

As no doubt the good proportion° of anything doth greatly adorn and commend[2] it, and right so our late-remembered proportions° do to our vulgar° poesy, so is there yet requisite to the perfection° of this art another manner of exornation, which resteth in the fashioning of our maker's language and style to such purpose as it may delight and allure as well the mind as the ear of the hearers with a certain novelty and strange° manner of conveyance,° disguising it no little from the ordinary and accustomed, nevertheless making it nothing the more unseemly or misbecoming,[3] but rather decenter° and more agreeable to any civil ear and understanding.[4] And as we see in these great madams of honor, be they for personage or otherwise never so comely and beautiful, yet if they want° their courtly habiliments,[5] or at leastwise such other apparel as custom and civility have ordained to cover their naked bodies, would be half-ashamed or greatly out of countenance to be seen in that sort, and perchance do then think themselves more amiable° in every man's eye when they be in their richest attire, suppose of silks or tissues[6] and costly embroideries, than when they go in cloth or in any other plain and simple apparel. Even so,[7] cannot our vulgar° poesy

---

1. The Latin word *ornamentum* meant the equipment of a soldier, his arms. It later acquired the meaning of the accouterments of a profession, such as the clothing of an actor, and, even later, that of mere decoration. As Puttenham presents the figures, his *poetical ornaments*, their definitions often reflect more than one of these meanings. *Exornation* (Lat. *exornatio*), which he uses in the first sentence of this chapter, means "adorn-

ment," but the other meanings of *ornamentum* are often present as well.
2. **commend** set off to advantage.
3. **misbecoming** unbecoming.
4. Cf. Quintilian's definition of figurative speech (9.1.14).
5. **habiliments** attire.
6. **tissues** rich kinds of cloth, often containing gold or silver threads.
7. **Even so** in the same way.

show itself either gallant[8] or gorgeous if any limb be left naked and bare and not clad in his kindly° clothes and colors,° such as may convey° them somewhat out of sight—that is, from the common course of ordinary speech and capacity of the vulgar° judgment—and yet, being artificially° handled, must needs yield it much more beauty and commendation.[9]

This ornament we speak of is given to it by figures and figurative speeches, which be the flowers, as it were, and colors[10] that a poet setteth upon his language by art, as the embroiderer doth his stone and pearl or passements[11] of gold upon the stuff of a princely garment, or as the excellent painter bestoweth the rich orient colors upon his table° of portrait. So, nevertheless, as if[12] the same colors° in our art of poesy (as well as in those other mechanical arts)[13] be not well-tempered,[14] or not well-laid, or be used in excess, or never so little disordered or misplaced, they not only give it no manner of grace at all, but rather do disfigure the stuff and spill[15] the whole workmanship, taking away all beauty and good liking from it; no less than if the crimson taint,[16] which should be laid upon a lady's lips, or right in the center of her cheeks, should by some oversight or mishap be applied to her forehead or chin,[17] it would make (ye would say) but a very ridiculous beauty. Wherefore the chief praise[18] and cunning° of our poet is in the discreet using of his figures, as the skillful° painter's is in the good conveyance° of his colors and shadowing traits of his pencil,[19] with a delectable variety, by all measure and just proportion,° and in places most aptly to be bestowed.

---

8. **gallant** attractive, showy (in a positive sense).

9. For a related defense of ornament, see *Partheniades* 14 ("Calliope"): 406–15.

10. *Flower* is a metaphor for rhetorical figure or device, whereas *color* is one for stylistic or rhetorical embellishments. Both metaphors were used from antiquity down through the Renaissance, although the latter was employed by both Greek and Latin authors, the former only by the Latins. For *flower*, see, for instance, Cicero, *De oratore* 3.25.96, and Quintilian 8.3.87. For *color* (Gk. *chroma*), see Plato, *Phaedrus* 239d; Dionysius of Halicarnassus, *De compositione verborum* 20; Cicero, *De oratore* 3.25.96; and Quintilian 12.10.71.

11. **passements** embroidery or trim.

12. **So, nevertheless, as if** In the same way, notwithstanding (the fact that figures make language beautiful), if. . . .

13. **mechanical arts** arts involving manual labor.

14. **well-tempered** well mixed (often referring to mortar).

15. **spill** spoil, damage.

16. **taint** stroke of color.

17. Such scrambling of the ingredients of female beauty was a trope. For a sample, see this typical line from Sidney's mock-blazon of Mopsa in *Old Arcadia* no. 3 (Ringler 12): "Her twinkling eies bedeckt with pearle, her lips of Saphir blew" (10). Perhaps the misogynist trope sometimes went beyond the literary. In *Ben Jonson's Conversations with Drummond of Hawthornden* (1619), Jonson is reported to have said that "Queen Elizabeth never saw her self after she became old in a true Glas. they painted her & sometymes would vermilion her nose" (Herford and Simpson 1.141–42: ll. 338–40).

18. **praise** praiseworthy quality.

19. **pencil** fine brush.

CHAPTER 2

How our writing and speeches public ought to be
figurative, and if they be not do greatly disgrace° the
cause and purpose of the speaker and writer

But as it hath been always reputed a great fault to use figurative speeches foolishly and indiscreetly, so is it esteemed no less an imperfection° in man's utterance to have none use of figure at all, especially in our writing and speeches public, making them but as our ordinary talk, than which nothing can be more unsavory and far from all civility. I remember in the first year of Queen Mary's reign a knight of Yorkshire was chosen Speaker of the Parliament, a good gentleman and wise in the affairs of his shire, and not unlearned in the laws of the realm, but as well for some lack of his teeth, as for want° of language nothing well spoken, which at that time and business[1] was most behooveful[2] for him to have been.[3] This man, after he had made his oration to the Queen—which ye know is of course to be done at the first assembly of both houses—a bencher of the Temple,[4] both well learned and very eloquent, returning from the Parliament house asked another gentleman his friend how he liked Mr. Speaker's oration. "Marry,"[5] quoth the other, "methinks I heard not a better alehouse tale told this seven years."† This happened because the good old knight made no difference between an oration or public speech to be delivered to the ear of a prince's majesty and state[6] of a realm, than he would have done of an ordinary tale to be told at his table in the country, wherein all men know the odds[7] is very great.[8]

And though grave and wise counselors in their consultations do not use much superfluous eloquence, and also in their judicial hearings do much mislike all scholastical° rhetorics, yet in such a case as it may be (and as this Parliament was), if the Lord Chancellor of England or Archbishop of Canterbury himself were to speak, he ought to do it cunningly° and eloquently, which cannot be without the use of figures, and nevertheless none impeachment[9] or blemish to the gravity of their persons or of the cause. Wherein I report me[10] to them that knew Sir Nicholas Bacon, Lord Keeper of the Great Seal,[11] or the now Lord Treasurer of

---

1. **time and business** busy season.
2. **behooveful** necessary.
3. On the identity of the old knight of Yorkshire, see LN 8.
4. **bencher of the Temple** lawyer; the four Inns of Court—the Inner and Middle Temples, Lincoln's Inn, and Gray's Inn—were the law schools of early modern England.
5. **Marry** a mild oath: "by Mary."
6. **state** rulers, government.

7. **odds** difference.
8. Cf. Elyot, *The Governour* 102.
9. **impeachment** detriment.
10. **report me** appeal for confirmation.
11. Puttenham seems to adduce Bacon here because his office as Lord Keeper was virtually identical with that of Lord Chancellor, mentioned just above. For the distinction between the two offices, see LN 9.

England,[12] and have been conversant with their speeches made in the Parliament house and Star Chamber. From whose lips I have seen to proceed more grave and natural eloquence than from all the orators of Oxford or Cambridge, but all is as it is handled, and maketh no matter whether the same eloquence be natural to them or artificial° (though I think rather natural), yet were they known to be learned and not unskillful° of the art when they were younger men. And as learning and art teacheth a scholar° to speak, so doth it also teach a counselor, and as well an old man as a young, and a man in authority as well as a private person, and a pleader[13] as well as a preacher, every man after his sort[14] and calling as best becometh.[15] And that speech which becometh one, doth not become another, for manners of speeches, some serve to work in excess, some in mediocrity,[16] some to grave purposes, some to light, some to be short and brief, some to be long, some to stir up affections,° some to pacify and appease them. And these common despisers of good utterance, which resteth altogether in[17] figurative speeches, being well used, whether it come by nature or by art or by exercise, they be but certain gross ignorants, of whom it is truly spoken, *scientia non habet inimicum nisi ignorantem.*[18] I have come to the Lord Keeper Sir Nicholas Bacon, and found him sitting in his gallery[19] alone with the works of Quintilian before him; indeed, he was a most eloquent man, and of rare learning and wisdom, as ever I knew England to breed, and one that joyed as much[20] in learned men and men of good wits.[21]

12. Puttenham probably refers to William Cecil, Lord Burghley, dedicatee of the *Art*, who had been Lord Treasurer since 1572, and was known for wisdom. It is possible (if he wrote this passage before 1572) that he means William Paulet, marquis of Winchester, his wife's first husband's grandfather and Lord Treasurer until 1572 (to whom he refers at 3.19.316). One surviving record, however, militates against citing Paulet for "grave and natural eloquence" here. In 1566 Elizabeth had released him from "performing the duties of speaker of the House of Lords, 'considering the Decay of his Memory and Hearing, Griefs accompanying hoary Hairs and old Age'" (*ODNB*, citing *Journal of the House of Lords* for 25 October 1566: 1.637).

13. **pleader** lawyer.

14. **sort** kind, rank.

15. **as best becometh** as is most appropriate.

16. **mediocrity** moderation.

17. **resteth . . . in** consists of.

18. Puttenham's contemptuous tone suggests that he is thinking of contemporary anti-intellectuals such as Heinrich Cornelius Agrippa von Nettesheim (1486–1535), whose treatise *Of the Vanitie and Uncertaintie of Artes and Sciences* (ca. 1530; trans. 1569)

aroused considerable irritation of this kind (and was in Puttenham's library). For instance, Barnaby Rich, in his *Allarme to England* (1578), speaks of this text as authorizing ignorant gentlemen who desire "to be curious in cauilling, propounding captious questions, thereby to shew a singularitie of their wisedomes" (H1v–H2r). In his *Brief Apology for Poetry* (the preface to his translation of Ariosto's *Orlando furioso*, 1591), Sir John Harington condemns such writing (and, separately, Puttenham's *Art*) (1). He also quotes there the Latin saying cited at the end of Puttenham's paragraph here: *scientia . . . ignorantem* ("knowledge has no enemy but an ignorant man"; source unknown; probably Renaissance Latin, often cited proverbially).

19. The walls of Bacon's gallery at Gorhambury were decorated with numerous *sententiae*, mostly derived from Cicero and Seneca. A manuscript record of these survives, edited by Elizabeth McCutcheon. Cf. Elyot's recommendation to similar decoration (*The Governour* 103).

20. **as much** i.e., very much, as much (as one could).

21. Bacon's fame as a model of eloquence was widespread. Nashe reported in 1592 that

A knight of the Queen's privy chamber once entreated a noblewoman of the court, being in great favor about her Majesty (to the intent to remove her from a certain displeasure, which by sinister[22] opinion she had conceived against a gentleman his friend), that it would please her to hear him speak in his own cause and not to condemn him upon his adversary's report. "God forbid," said she, "he is too wise for me to talk with. Let him go and satisfy such a man," naming him. "Why," quoth the knight again, "had your Ladyship rather hear a man talk like a fool or like a wise man?" This was because the lady was a little perverse[23] and not disposed to reform herself by hearing reason, which none other can so well beat into the ignorant head as the well-spoken and eloquent man.[†]

And because I am so far waded into this discourse of eloquence and figurative speeches, I will tell you what happened on a time, myself being present when certain doctors° of the civil law were heard in a litigious cause betwixt a man and his wife. Before a great magistrate who (as they can tell that knew him) was a man very well learned and grave, but somewhat sour and of no plausible° utterance, the gentleman's chance was to say, "My Lord, the simple° woman is not so much to blame as her lewd° abettors, who by violent persuasions have led her into this willfulness."[24] Quoth the judge, "What need such eloquent terms in this place?" The gentleman replied, "Doth your Lordship mislike the term *violent*? And methinks I speak it to great purpose, for I am sure she would never have done it but by force of persuasion. And if persuasions were not very violent to the mind of man, it could not have wrought so strange an effect as we read that it did once in Egypt"—and would have told the whole tale at large° if the magistrate had not passed it over very pleasantly.

Now to tell you the whole matter as the gentleman intended, thus it was.[25] There came into Egypt a notable orator whose name was Hegesias, who inveighed so much against the incommodities of this transitory life, and so highly commended death, the dispatcher of all evils, as a great number of his hearers destroyed themselves—some with weapon, some with poison, others by drowning and hanging themselves,

---

the French poet Guillaume Du Bartas celebrated "*Sir Nicholas Bacon*, Lord keeper" as one of the "chiefe pillars of our englishe speeche" (*Pierce Pennilesse his supplication to the Divell*, in *Works* 1.193–94). For the Du Bartas praise, see the *Seconde Sepmaine*, "Babylone" (1584): Du Bartas 3.141.619–26. Ben Jonson similarly praises the elder Bacon, comparing him to Cicero (*Timber, or Discoveries* in Herford and Simpson 8.591), and Camden, in his *Annales* (1615), finds him distinguished for "rare eloquence" (235).

22. **sinister** prejudicial, malicious.

23. **perverse** unreasonable, petulant, peevish.

24. On the identity of the litigious wife (possibly Puttenham's), see LN 10.

25. Puttenham's knowledge of what the gentleman would have said, the gentleman's self-conscious eloquence, and the husband-wife litigation all suggest that the gentleman was probably Puttenham himself. For his legal troubles, see Introduction 7–15.

to be rid out of[26] this vale of misery—insomuch as° it was feared lest
many more of the people would have miscarried by occasion of his persuasions, if King Ptolemy had not made a public proclamation that the
orator should avoid[27] the country, and no more be allowed to speak in
any matter.[28] Whether now persuasions may not be said violent and
forcible to simple° minds in special, I refer it to all men's judgments
that hear the story.

At leastways, I find this opinion confirmed by a pretty device° or emblem that Lucian allegeth he saw in the portrait of Hercules within the
city of Marseilles in Provence, where they had figured a lusty old man
with a long chain tied by one end at his tongue, by the other end at the
people's ears, who stood afar off and seemed to be drawn to him by the
force of that chain fastened to his tongue, as who would say, by force of
his persuasions.[29] And to show more plainly that eloquence is of great
force and not (as many men think amiss) the property and gift of young
men only, but rather of old men, and a thing which better becometh
hoary hairs than beardless boys,[30] they seem to ground it upon this reason: age (say they and most truly) brings experience, experience bringeth
wisdom, long life yields long use and much exercise of speech, exercise
and custom[31] with wisdom make an assured and voluble° utterance. So
is it that old men more than any other sort speak most gravely, wisely,
assuredly, and plausibly,° which parts are all that can be required in
perfect eloquence, and so, in all deliberations of importance where
counselors are allowed freely to opine and show their conceits,° good
persuasion is no less requisite than speech itself, for in great purposes
to speak and not to be able or likely to persuade is a vain thing. Now let
us return back to say more of this poetical ornament.

---

26. **rid out of** freed from.

27. **avoid** leave.

28. Puttenham's most likely source for
this anecdote is Cicero, *Tusculan Disputa-
tions* 1.34.83, although there is a similar,
briefer version of it in Valerius Maximus
8.9.3. In his translation of Erasmus's *Apophthegmata*, Nicholas Udall repeats the tale in
his marginal annotation for Diogenes' *Apoph-
thegme* no. 100 (Udall 125). Because Hegesias' dates are quite uncertain, the Ptolemy
in question may be either Ptolemy I Soter
(ruled 304–283 BCE) or his son Ptolemy II
Philadelphus (who ruled with his father
285–283 BCE and then alone 283–246 BCE).

29. In his *Herakles*, Lucian speaks of
the so-called Hercules Gallicus, who he says
was worshipped as Hermes, the god of eloquence, in a temple in Marseilles (1.63–71).

Puttenham may derive the image from an intermediate emblem ("device") book, and
Andrea Alciati's *Emblemata* (Augsburg,
1531), which included both a visual and written representation of the figure.

30. Others too saw eloquence as the
achievement of old men. George of Trebi-
zond argues that style, figures of speech, and
the like are fit subjects for boys, but that
the discovery and arrangement of one's
subject matter in a speech requires the wisdom, experience, and judgment of age; see
Five Books on Rhetoric, in Rebhorn, *Renaissance Debates* 28–29. Juan Luis Vives likewise thinks instruction in rhetoric given to
the young wasted because they lack the maturity of judgment necessary to achieve true
eloquence (90–91).

31. **custom** habitual use.

CHAPTER 3

How ornament poetical is of two sorts according to
the double virtue° and efficacy° of figures

This ornament then is of two sorts: one to satisfy and delight the ear only by a goodly outward show set upon the matter with words and speeches smoothly and tunably° running; another by certain intendments° or sense of such words and speeches inwardly working a stir° to the mind. That first quality the Greeks called *enargeia*,[1] of this word *argos*, because it giveth a glorious luster and light. This latter they called *energeia*[2] of *ergon*, because it wrought with a strong and virtuous° operation. And figure breedeth them both: some serving to give gloss only to a language, some to give it efficacy° by sense, and so by that means some of them serve the ear only, some serve the conceit° only and not the ear. There be of them also that serve both turns, as common servitors appointed for the one and the other purpose, which shall be hereafter spoken of in place.

But because we have alleged before that ornament is but the good or rather beautiful habit of language and style, and figurative speeches the instrument wherewith we burnish our language, fashioning it to this or that measure° and proportion,° whence finally resulteth a long and continual phrase or manner of writing or speech, which we call by the name of *style*: we will first speak of language, then of style, lastly of figure, and declare their virtue° and differences, and also their use and best application, and what portion in exornation[3] every of them bringeth to the beautifying of this art.

1. **enargeia** clarity, distinctness, vividness (from Gk. *enarges*, "visible, palpable, manifest," from *argos*, "bright, shining"). Although a nontechnical term in Plato and Aristotle, *enargeia* becomes one in Quintilian and, to a lesser degree, Cicero. Quintilian gives the Latin *evidentia* as a synonym (see 4.2.63, 6.2.32, 8.3.61–62, and 8.3.89–90). Cf. Cicero, *Academicae Quaestiones* 2.6.17, and *Topica* 26.97. Latin *descriptio* was also a synonym; see *Ad Herennium* 4.39.51. For the ancients generally, then, *enargeia* involved the use of ornamental figures to make the listener see something vividly in the mind's eye. Thus, Puttenham's declaration that *enargeia* is a matter of giving satisfaction and delight to the *ear* is either a misunderstanding of the term, or, since the etymology he presents here is quite clear, a deliberate transformation of it in keeping with his idiosyncratic conception of figures of speech as falling into three categories: those that affect the ear, those that affect the mind, and those that affect both. See also *Art* 3.10.245. For other Renaissance uses of *energeia*, see Peacham (1577) O2r and Day 97. On Puttenham's deliberate transformation of the meaning of *enargeia*, see Galyon.

2. **energeia** a technical term for Aristotle, variously translated as "activity" or "actuality" (see, for example, *Nicomachean Ethics* 1.8.8 [1098b33], *Rhetoric* 3.11.1–2 [1411b28], and *Metaphysics* 8.2.1 [1042b10] and 8.6.9 [1045b19]; *ergon* means "work" in Greek. Scaliger equates it with *efficacia*, or "force" (see 3.27). (Note also the use of "efficacy" in Puttenham's next sentence.) Cf. Sidney's use of the term (the first in English, according to *OED*, ca. 1581), which he translates as "forcibleness" (*Defence* 246).

3. **exornation** adornment.

CHAPTER 4

Of language

Speech is not natural to man saving for his only ability to speak, and that he is by kind° apt to utter all his conceits° with sounds and voices¹ diversified many manner of ways, by means of the many and fit instruments he hath by nature to that purpose: as a broad and voluble° tongue; thin and movable lips; teeth even and not shagged,² thick-ranged;³ a round-vaulted palate; and a long throat; besides an excellent capacity of wit° that maketh him more disciplinable° and imitative than any other creature. Then as to the form and action of his speech, it cometh to him by art and teaching, and by use or exercise.⁴ But after a speech is fully fashioned to the common understanding and accepted by consent of a whole country and nation, it is called a language, and receiveth none allowed alteration but by extraordinary occasions, by little and little, as it were, insensibly bringing in of many corruptions that creep along with the time; of all which matters we have more largely° spoken in our books of the originals and pedigree of the English tongue.⁵ Then, when I say language, I mean the speech wherein the poet or maker writeth, be it Greek or Latin, or, as our case is, the vulgar° English; and when it is peculiar unto a country it is called the mother speech of that people—the Greeks term it *idioma*⁶— so is ours at this day the Norman English. Before the conquest of the Normans it was the Anglo-Saxon, and before that the British, which, as some will, is at this day the Welsh, or, as others affirm, the Cornish.⁷ I for my part think neither of both as they be now spoken and pronounced.

This part in our maker or poet must be heedily⁸ looked unto, that it be natural, pure, and the most usual of all his country;⁹ and for the same purpose rather that which is spoken in the king's court or in the good towns and cities within the land, than in the marches¹⁰ and fron-

---

1. **voices** utterances.
2. **shagged** rough, jagged.
3. **thick-ranged** densely arranged.
4. In these opening sentences, what the author seems to be saying is that although we have all the right equipment, such as teeth and lips, to produce speech, that does not mean speech is natural to us in the same way that those bodily parts are, but rather that speech requires art and training for us actually to make it.
5. A lost work.
6. *idioma* (Gk.) specific property, style, idiom; by extension, the language peculiar to a people, region, or class.
7. Welsh and Cornish constitute, with

Breton, the so-called Brythonic branch of the "insular Celtic" language group, distinguished by modern linguistic historians from the Goidelic branch (Irish, Manx, and Scottish Gaelic). It is now thought that British separated out into Cornish and Welsh after 600 CE. Puttenham's use of the term "Anglo-Saxon" appears to be its first post–Old English vernacular use, though Camden's Latin *Britannia* uses it in 1586.

8. **heedily** heedfully.
9. Puttenham's concern with proper English here develops from prescriptions concerning correct Latinity in Cicero (*De oratore* 3.10.37–39) and Quintilian (8.1–2).
10. **marches** borders.

tiers, or in port towns, where strangers° haunt[11] for traffic's° sake; or yet in universities, where scholars° use much peevish[12] affectation of words out of the primitive languages;[13] or finally, in any uplandish[14] village or corner of a realm, where is no resort but of poor, rustical, or uncivil people. Neither shall he follow the speech of a craftsman or carter° or other of the inferior sort, though he be inhabitant or bred in the best town and city in this realm, for such persons do abuse° good speeches by strange° accents or ill-shaped sounds and false orthography.[15] But he shall follow generally the better-brought-up sort, such as the Greeks call *charientes*[16]: men civil and graciously behaviored and bred.

Our maker therefore at these days shall not follow *Piers Plowman* nor Gower nor Lydgate nor yet Chaucer, for their language is now out of use with us; neither shall he take the terms of northern men such as they use in daily talk—whether they be noblemen or gentlemen or of their best clerks,° all is a matter[17]—nor in effect any speech used beyond the river of Trent: though no man can deny but that theirs is the purer English Saxon at this day, yet it is not so courtly nor so current° as our southern English is; no more is the far western man's speech. Ye shall therefore take the usual speech of the court and that of London and the shires lying about London within sixty miles, and not much above. I say not this but that in every shire of England there be gentlemen and others that speak, but especially write, as good southern as we of Middlesex or Surrey do, but not the common people of every shire, to whom the gentlemen and also their learned clerks° do for the most part condescend;[18] but herein we are already ruled by the English dictionaries and other books written by learned men, and therefore it needeth none other direction in that behalf.[19]

Albeit peradventure° some small admonition be not impertinent,° for we find in our English writers many words and speeches amendable,°

---

11. **haunt** resort to frequently.

12. **peevish** silly, perverse, capricious, querulous, or vexing.

13. **primitive languages** i.e., Latin and Greek.

14. **uplandish** inland, remote.

15. **orthography** usually a term for spelling. Puttenham's references to "strange accents" and "ill-shaped sounds," however, suggest that the mispronunciations of the carters may sound to him like someone speaking *as if* from false spelling. For the requirements that the poet's speech be natural, pure, and usual, see, among others, Cicero, *De oratore* 3.10.37–39; Quintilian 1.5 and 8.1–2; and Aristotle, *Rhetoric* 3.2.1–2 (1404b).

16. **charientes** (Gk.) graceful, elegant, or witty ones; wealthy citizens, gentlemen.

Plato uses it for those who make witty and sarcastic remarks (*Republic* 5.452b), while Aristotle uses it for the wealthy members of the state (*Politics* 4.10.1297b10). At 3.18.276 Puttenham defines the trope he calls *charientismus* as the "privy nip, or a mild and appeasing mockery"; this word means "wit" in Greek and defines the essential quality possessed by those labeled *charientes*.

17. **all is a matter** it is all the same.

18. **condescend** lower oneself graciously (to speak with in their language); contempt is not implied.

19. There were at least six quasi-lexicographical works dealing with English to which Puttenham might be referring (printed before 1589): (1) John Palsgrave's *Lesclarcissement de la langue francoyse*

and ye shall see in some many inkhorn[20] terms so ill-affected,[21] brought in by men of learning, as preachers and schoolmasters, and many strange° terms of other languages by secretaries and merchants and travelers, and many dark° words and not usual nor well-sounding, though they be daily spoken in court.[22] Wherefore great heed must be taken by our maker in this point, that his choice be good.

And peradventure° the writer hereof be in that behalf[23] no less faulty than any other, using many strange° and unaccustomed words and borrowed from other languages, and in that respect himself no meet magistrate to reform the same errors in any other person; but since he is not unwilling to acknowledge his own fault and can the better tell how to amend° it, he may seem a more excusable corrector of other men's; he intendeth° therefore, for an indifferent° way and universal benefit, to tax himself first and before any others.

These be words used by the author in this present treatise.[24] *Scientific,*° but with some reason, for it answereth the word *mechanical,*[25] which no other word could have done so properly, for when he spake of all artificers which rest either in science° or in handicraft, it followed necessarily that *scientific* should be coupled with *mechanical,* or else neither of both to have been allowed but in their places: a man of science liberal[26] and a handicraftsman, which had not been so cleanly° a speech as the other.[27] *Majordomo:* in truth this word is borrowed of the Spaniard and Italian, and therefore new and not usual but to them that are acquainted with the affairs of court, and so for his jolly[28] magnificence (as this case is) may be accepted among courtiers, for whom this is especially written. A man might have said, instead of *majordomo,* the French word *maistre d'hostell,* but ill-favoredly, or the right English

---

(an English-French dictionary, 1530); (2) William Thomas's *Principal Rules of the Italian Grammar* (an Italian-English dictionary, 1550); (3) Thomas Thomas's *Dictionarium Linguae Latinae et Anglicanae* (a Latin-English dictionary, 1587); (4) Bartholomew Traheron's translation of Vigon, *The most excellent workes of Chirurgerye* (1543); (5) William Turner's *The Nature of herbes in Greke, Latin, Englishe, Duche & Frenche* (1548); and (6) Richard Mulcaster's full English word list in *The first part of the Elementarie* (1582). For further information about this complex subject, consult the Early Modern English Dictionaries Database.

20. **inkhorn** a portable container for ink that became a symbol of ostentatious learning and pedantry.

21. **ill-affected** affected.

22. Cf. Thomas Wilson's parodic letter of supplication (189). See 3.22.338–39 for a re-

lated discussion of John Southern's use of inkhorn terms.

23. **behalf** regard.

24. Of the neologisms that follow, most appear in the first five chapters of Book 1. *Idiom,* however, as well as the last seven terms Puttenham supplies (from *dimension* to *combatible*), appear only here (although he uses *attempt* at 1.30.147). Puttenham seems to have coined *scientific, majordomo, politician, placation, numerosity,* and *assubtiling.*

25. **mechanical** arts that involve work with the hands, as opposed to more purely intellectual arts, referred to as "scientific" (cf. 1.1.93).

26. **of science liberal** i.e., trained in the knowledge of the liberal arts.

27. Compare Puttenham's defense of foreign borrowings with Wilson's similar defense of borrowings from Greek and Latin (191.6–27).

28. **jolly** brilliant, admirable.

word *Lord Steward*. But methinks for my own opinion this word *majordomo*, though he be borrowed, is more acceptable than any of the rest; other men may judge otherwise.[29] *Politician*°: this word also is received from the Frenchmen, but at this day usual in court and with all good secretaries, and cannot find an English word to match him, for to have said a man politic had not been so well, because in truth that had been no more than to have said a civil person. *Politician*° is rather a surveyor of civility than civil, and a public minister or counselor in the state.[30] Ye have also this word *conduict*,[31] a French word, but well allowed of us, and long since usual; it sounds somewhat more[32] than this word "leading," for it is applied only to the leading of a captain, and not as a little boy should lead a blind man, therefore more proper to the case when he said, *conduict* of whole armies. Ye find also this word *idiom*, taken from the Greeks yet serving aptly when a man wanteth° to express so much unless it be in[33] two words,[34] which surplusage° to avoid, we are allowed to draw in other words single and as much significative.[35] This word *significative* is borrowed of the Latin and French, but to us brought in first by some nobleman's secretary, as I think, yet doth so well serve the turn, as it could not now be spared. And many more like usurped[36] Latin and French words, as: *method, methodical, placation*,[37] *function, assubtiling*,[38] *refining, compendious, prolix, figurative, inveigle*.° A term borrowed of our common

29. *Majordomo* derives from medieval Latin *major domus*, "the chief of the house," and although it originally meant the chief official of the royal household under the Merovingian kings of France, it came to mean the head servant in any wealthy household. In English it was applied to a steward or butler, and Puttenham's use of the word in this sense seems to be the first recorded. "Maistre d'hostell" (or *maître d'hôtel* in modern French) refers to the chief steward running a nobleman's house (his *hôtel*).

30. **surveyor . . . state** public or official supervisor concerned with social life and behavior ("civility") and a public minister or state counselor rather than (just) a citizen or, perhaps, civilized person ("civil"). Cf. Puttenham's notion that the poets were the first lawmakers and politicians at 1.3.97.

31. **conduict** Original spelling is retained to preserve the link with the French. Puttenham's stress on the primarily military meaning of this word may seem slightly eccentric. According to Randle Cotgrave's *Dictionarie of the French and English Tonges* (1611), the term had the more general meaning of "conducting" or "leading." The French word, however, derives from the Latin *conductus*, which had both the general meaning of "con-

ducting" and the more specific ones of "leading a military troop" and the "contractual payment" one received for that activity. In Italian the comparable term is *condotta*, which has both of those meanings and from which is derived *condottiere*, or "mercenary captain."

32. **sounds somewhat more** is both more specialized and more elevated.

33. **unless it be in** without using.

34. Puttenham seems to be saying that the word *idiom* deserves to be naturalized in English because what it means can be expressed only by using a circumlocution involving two words or perhaps more; it is unclear which two words he is thinking of here.

35. **significative** meaningful.

36. **usurped** taken, seized. In order to describe the borrowing of terms from foreign languages Puttenham uses a word that had a distinctly political meaning in the period and that underscored the illegitimacy of the seizure involved. His choice of this word seems consistent with his general theory of figures as being "abuses, or rather trespasses, in speech" (3.7.238).

37. **placation** propitiation.

38. **assubtiling** subtilizing, refining, making fine or thin.

lawyers—*impression*—also a new term, but well expressing the matter, and more than our English word. These words, *numerous*,° *numerosity*,° *metrical*, *harmonical*, but they cannot be refused, especially in this place for description of the art. Also ye find these words, *penetrate*, *penetrable*, *indignity*, which I cannot see how we may spare them, whatsoever fault we find with inkhorn[39] terms: for our speech wanteth° words to such sense so well to be used. Yet instead of *indignity*, ye have *unworthiness*; and for *penetrate*, we may say *pierce*, and that a French term also, or *broach*, or *enter into with violence*, but not so well-sounding as *penetrate*. Item, *savage*, for *wild*; *obscure*, for *dark*.° Item, these words, *declination*, *delineation*, *dimension*, are scholastical° terms indeed, and yet very proper. But peradventure° (and I could bring a reason for it) many other like words borrowed out of the Latin and French were not so well to be allowed by us, as these words: *audacious*, for *bold*; *facundity*, for *eloquence*; *egregious*, for *great* or *notable*; *implete*,[40] for *replenished*; *attemptat*,[41] for *attempt*; *compatible*,[42] for *agreeable in nature*, and many more. But herein the noble poet Horace hath said enough to satisfy us all in these few verses:

> *Multa renascentur quae iam cecidere cadentque*
> *Quae nunc sunt in honore vocabula si volet usus*
> *Quem penes arbitrium est et vis et norma loquendi.*[43]

Which I have thus Englished, but nothing with so good grace, nor so briefly as the poet wrote:

> *Many a word yfall'n shall eft*[44] *arise*
> *And such as now been held in highest prise*[45]
> *Will fall as fast, when use and custom will,*
> *Only umpires of speech, for force and skill.*[46]

---

39. **inkhorn** ostentatiously learned, pedantic.

40. **implete** full (from Lat. *implere*, "to fill up").

41. **attemptat** from Lat. *attemptare* (or *attentare*), "to strive for, to attempt."

42. **compatible** from Lat. *compati*, "to suffer together or mutually," hence "congruent or agreeable with."

43. Horace, *Ars poetica* 70–72; the last two lines are also cited at 2.15.210. Modern editions of Horace's poem have *ius* for *vis*.

44. **yfallen**, **eft** archaisms for "fallen" and "again." Such locutions were sometimes used (as frequently in Spenser) to convey the feel of ancient dignity.

45. **prise** both price and prize, both of which mean "worth or value."

46. **when . . . skill** whenever use and custom wish to do so, they being the only umpires of speech (i.e., they alone will decide whether words will survive) because of their (i.e., use and custom's) force and power.

CHAPTER 5

Of style

Style is a constant and continual phrase[1] or tenor of speaking and writing, extending to the whole tale or process of the poem or history, and not properly to any piece or member of a tale, but is of words, speeches, and sentences[2] together a certain contrived form and quality, many times natural to the writer, many times his peculiar[3] by election and art, and such as either he keepeth by skill° or holdeth on by ignorance, and will not or peradventure° cannot easily alter into any other. So we say that Cicero's style and Sallust's were not one, nor Caesar's and Livy's, nor Homer's and Hesiod's, nor Herodotus' and Thucydides', nor Euripides' and Aristophanes', nor Erasmus's and Budaeus's styles. And because this continual course and manner of writing or speech showeth the matter and disposition of the writer's mind more than one or few words or sentences can show, therefore there be[4] that have called style the image of man (*mentis character*),[5] for man is but his mind, and as his mind is tempered° and qualified,[6] so are his speeches and language at large,° and his inward conceits° be the mettle[7] of his mind, and his manner of utterance the very warp and woof of his conceits,° more plain, or busy° and intricate, or otherwise affected after the rate.°[8] Most men say that not any one point in all physiognomy is so certain as to judge a man's manners° by his eye, but more assuredly, in mine opinion, by his daily manner of speech and ordinary writing. For if the man be grave, his speech and style is grave; if light-headed, his style and language also light; if the mind be haughty and hot, the speech and style is also vehement and stirring;° if it be cold and temperate,° the style is also very modest; if it be humble or base and meek, so is also the language and style.

And yet peradventure° not altogether so, but that every man's style is for the most part according to the matter and subject of the writer, or so

1. **phrase** manner of speech.

2. **words ... sentences** i.e., individual words, phrases or clauses, and syntactic units (but also sayings: Lat. *sententiae*).

3. **peculiar** special or exclusive characteristic.

4. **there be** i.e., there are (those).

5. *mentis character* mark of the mind.

6. **tempered and qualified** composed and endowed with certain qualities.

7. **mettle** Elizabethans did not distinguish by spelling, as we do, the words for the material substance of *metal* and *mettle* as a quality of disposition or temperament. The *Art* spells this term "metall" here. In addition to the clear sense of "disposition," Puttenham may have meant to build a secondary meta-

phoric chain linked with how the mind is "tempered" (earlier in the sentence).

8. Both *style* and *character* have the same literal meaning at their origins: a pointed stake or stick, which later came to indicate the object used to write or engrave letters. Their meanings were then extended metaphorically to the letters themselves, and eventually to the particular mode of writing (*style*) of an individual or the type or nature (*character*) of a thing or a person. *Style* (Lat. *stilus*) only acquired this last meaning in the post-Augustan period in writers such as Sallust and Tacitus. *Character* (Gk. *kharacter*) was used to refer to the nature of a language or a person by the fifth century BCE. On this topic, see Scaliger 4.1.

ought to be, and conformable thereunto. Then again may it be said as well that men do choose their subjects according to the mettle of their minds, and therefore a high-minded man chooseth him high and lofty matter to write of; the base courage,° matter base and low; the mean° and modest mind, mean° and moderate matters after the rate.° Howsoever it be, we find that under these three principal complexions[9] (if I may with leave so term them), high, mean,° and base style, there be contained many other humors[10] or qualities of style, as the plain and obscure, the rough and smooth, the facile[11] and hard, the plentiful and barren, the rude° and eloquent, the strong and feeble, the vehement and cold styles, all which in their evil are to be reformed, and the good to be kept and used. But generally to have the style decent° and comely, it behooveth the maker or poet to follow the nature of his subject; that is, if his matter be high and lofty, that the style be so too; if mean,° the style also to be mean;° if base, the style humble and base accordingly. And they that do otherwise use it, applying to mean° matter high and lofty style, and to high matters style either mean° or base, and to the base matters the mean° or high style, do utterly disgrace° their poesy and show themselves nothing skillful° in their art, nor having regard to the decency,° which is the chief praise[12] of any writer.

Therefore, to rid all lovers of learning from that error, I will, as near as I can, set down which matters be high and lofty, which be but mean,° and which be low and base, to the intent the styles may be fashioned to the matters, and keep their decorum[13] and good proportion° in every respect. I am not ignorant that many good clerks° be contrary to mine opinion, and say that the lofty style may be decently° used in a mean° and base subject and contrariwise, which I do in part acknowledge, but with a reasonable qualification. For Homer hath so used it in his trifling work of *Batrachomyomachia*, that is, in his treatise of the war betwixt the frogs and the mice;[14] Vergil also in his *Bucolics* and in his *Georgics*, whereof the one is counted mean,° the other base, that is, the husbandman's discourses and the shepherd's.[15] But hereunto serveth a reason,

9. **complexions** combinations of qualities (originally, humors) defining a being.

10. **humors** characters, modes.

11. **facile** easy.

12. **praise** praiseworthy quality.

13. See Puttenham's discussion of decorum in 3.23.

14. The *Batrachomyomachia* is an anonymous burlesque of Homer thought authentic in Puttenham's time. It was attributed in antiquity to the semi-legendary Homeric parodist Pigres the Carian (ca. 480 BCE); modern scholarship, however, has argued that since it imitates Callimachus (d. ca. 260 BCE), and is mentioned by Plutarch, Martial, and Statius, all late first century CE, it was probably

composed sometime between 250 BCE and 50 CE.

15. Servius, the early and extremely influential commentator on Vergil, suggested that his *Eclogues*, *Georgics*, and *Aeneid* epitomized the base or simple, the middle, and the grand styles, a formulation that reappears throughout Renaissance discussions of poetic style and the poet's progress toward maturity (as in the beginning of *The Faerie Queene*). This triple distinction lies behind Puttenham's discussion here. For extended treatment of the career trope, see the essays in Cheney and de Armas. The Latin rhetorical tradition also imagined styles as base, intermediary, and grand; see Cicero, *Orator* 75–99, and Quintilian 12.10.58–72.

in my simple° conceit.° For first, to that trifling poem of Homer: though the frog and the mouse be but little and ridiculous beasts, yet to treat of war is a high subject, and a thing in every respect terrible and dangerous to them that it alights on, and therefore of learned duty asketh martial grandiloquence, if it be set forth in his kind° and nature of war, even betwixt the basest creatures that can be imagined. So also is the ant or pismire,[16] and they be but little creeping things, not perfect° beasts, but *insects*,[17] or worms; yet in describing their nature and instinct, and their manner of life approaching to the form of a commonwealth, and their properties not unlike to the virtues° of most excellent governors and captains, it asketh a more majesty of speech than would the description of any other beast's life or nature, and perchance of many matters pertaining unto the baser sort of men, because it resembleth the history of a civil regiment,[18] and of them all the chief and most principal, which is monarchy.

So also in his *Bucolics*, which are but pastoral speeches and the basest of any other poem in their own proper nature, Vergil used a somewhat swelling style when he came to insinuate the birth of Marcellus, heir apparent to the Emperor Augustus, as child to his sister, aspiring by hope and greatness of the house to the succession of the empire and establishment thereof in that family.[19] Whereupon Vergil could do no less than to use such manner of style, whatsoever condition the poem were of, and this was decent,° and no fault or blemish, to confound[20] the tenors of the styles for that cause. But now when I remember me again that this eclogue (for I have read it somewhere)[21] was conceived by Octavian the Emperor to be written to the honor of Pollio, a citizen of Rome and of no great nobility—the same was misliked again as an implicative nothing decent° nor proportionable° to Pollio's fortunes and calling[22]—in which respect I might say likewise the style was not to be such as if it had been for the emperor's own honor and

16. **pismire** ant.

17. Puttenham appears to be the first to have used "insect" in its modern sense in English. Although the *OED* cites this passage to exemplify the adjectival meaning of "insect" as "having the body divided into segments" (the term derives from the Latin *insectus*, meaning "segmented"), Puttenham's word here is a noun, and that noun appears in no other treatise earlier than 1601.

18. **regiment** system of government.

19. As nephew and heir apparent of Augustus, Marcellus was celebrated by many writers, especially by Vergil in a famous passage in the *Aeneid* (6.855–86). He was frequently identified with the wondrous newborn boy whose birth Vergil's *Fourth Eclogue* celebrates, though so too was the in-

fant son of Gaius Asinius Pollio, to whom the poet addresses the poem. Modern classical scholarship rejects the Marcellus identification.

20. **confound** confuse.

21. The author's uncertainly remembered story of Augustus' dislike does not seem to appear in a classical source. In an analogous case Horace warns a young nobleman to be wary of accepting praise fit only for Augustus (*Epistles* 1.16.25–40).

22. **implicative . . . calling** i.e., as an inaccurate and indecorous implied classification. Pollio was rich, powerful, and distinguished, but he was also provincial, and the first of his family to be raised to the patriciate. Such "new blood" was not entitled to quasi-imperial praise.

those of the blood imperial, than which subject there could not be among the Roman writers a higher nor graver to treat upon, so can I not be removed from mine opinion, but still methinks that in all decency° the style ought to conform with the nature of the subject.

Otherwise, if a writer will seem to observe no decorum at all, nor pass[23] how he fashion his tale[24] to his matter, who doubteth but he may in the lightest cause speak like a pope, and in the gravest matters prate like a parrot, and find words and phrases enough to serve both turns, and neither of them commendably? For neither is all that may be written of kings and princes such as ought to keep a high style, nor all that may be written upon a shepherd to keep the low, but according to the matter reported, if that be of high or base nature. For every petty pleasure and vain delight of a king are not to be accounted high matter for the height of his estate,° but mean° and perchance very base and vile;[25] nor so a poet or historiographer could decently° with a high style report the vanities of Nero, the ribaldries of Caligula, the idleness° of Domitian, and the riots of Heliogabalus. But well the magnanimity and honorable ambition of Caesar, the prosperities of Augustus, the gravity of Tiberius,[26] the bounty of Trajan, the wisdom of Aurelius, and generally all that which concerned the highest honors of emperors, their birth, alliances, government, exploits in war and peace, and other public affairs: for they be matter stately and high, and require a style to be lifted up and advanced by choice of words, phrases, sentences,° and figures, high, lofty, eloquent and magnific[27] in proportion.° So be the mean° matters to be carried with all words and speeches of smoothness and pleasant moderation; and finally the base things to be holden within their tether by a low, mild, and simple° manner of utterance, creeping rather than climbing, and marching rather than mounting upwards with the wings of the stately subjects and style.

---

23. **pass** care.

24. **tale** narration.

25. **vile** morally debased, as often with such rulers as Nero or Caligula.

26. The evil Renaissance reputation of Tiberius visible in Jonson's *Sejanus* is rejected by modern scholars, who regard the scandals of debauchery as later inventions, but the positive view was available to Puttenham: the emperor's Roman *gravitas* is not absent in Suetonius, and is clear in Taci-

tus, who thought him a good prince and an old-fashioned Roman until he retired to Capri and Sejanus took over. It should be noted, however, that Puttenham did at least a partial translation of Suetonius' *Life* of Tiberius, of which a single page survives (PRO, SP 12/126/67), and that page, which corresponds to chapters 58–61 (with omissions) of Suetonius' work, stresses Tiberius' wanton cruelty, not his *gravitas*.

27. **magnific** glorious, splendid.

CHAPTER 6

Of the high, low, and mean° subject

The matters therefore that concern the gods and divine things are highest of all other to be couched in writing; next to them the noble gests° and great fortunes of princes and the notable accidents° of time, as the greatest affairs of war and peace. These be all high subjects, and therefore are delivered over to the poets hymnic and historical who be occupied either in divine lauds° or in heroical reports. The mean° matters be those that concern mean° men—their life and business, as lawyers, gentlemen, and merchants, good householders and honest citizens—and which sound neither to[1] matters of state nor of war, nor leagues, nor great alliances, but smatch[2] all the common conversation,° as of the civiler and better sort of men. The base and low matters be the doings of the common artificer, servingman, yeoman, groom, husbandman,[3] day-laborer, sailor, shepherd, swineherd, and such like of homely calling, degree,° and bringing up.

So that in every of the said three degrees° not the selfsame virtues be equally to be praised, nor the same vices equally to be dispraised, nor their loves, marriages, quarrels, contracts, and other behaviors be like high nor do require to be set forth with the like style, but every one in his degree° and decency°: which made that[4] all hymns and histories and tragedies were written in the high style; all comedies and interludes° and other common poesies of loves and such like in the mean° style; all eclogues and pastoral poems in the low and base style. Otherwise, they had been utterly disproportioned.° Likewise, for the same cause, some phrases and figures be only peculiar to the high style, some to the base or mean,° some common to all three, as shall be declared more at large° hereafter when we come to speak of figure and phrase. Also some words and speeches and sentences° do become the high style that do not become the other two, and contrariwise, as shall be said when we talk of words and sentence.° Finally, some kind of measure° and concord° do not beseem the high style that well become the mean° and low, as we have said speaking of concord° and measure.°

But generally the high style is disgraced° and made foolish and ridiculous by all words affected, counterfeit,° and puffed up, as it were a wind-ball[5] carrying more countenance[6] than matter, and cannot be better resembled[7] than to these midsummer pageants in London, where to make the people wonder are set forth great and ugly giants marching as if they were alive and armed at all points,[8] but within they are stuffed

---

1. **sound neither to** do not have some connection with.
2. **smatch** taste of.
3. **husbandman** farmer.
4. **which made that** i.e., the foregoing have produced the result that.

5. **wind-ball** an inflated ball used in a game, struck to and fro with the fists.
6. **countenance** appearance, show.
7. **resembled** compared.
8. **at all points** fully.

full of brown paper and tow,[9] which the shrewd° boys underpeering do guilefully discover° and turn to a great derision.[10] Also all dark° and unaccustomed works, or rustical and homely, and sentences° that hold too much of the merry and light, or infamous and unshamefast,[11] are to be accounted of the same sort, for such speeches become not princes nor great estates,° nor them that write of their doings, to utter or report and intermingle with the grave and weighty matters.

9. **tow** the unworked stem or fiber of flax.

10. Castiglione uses this image to describe bad princes puffed up with self-love: "[T]hey are . . . like the Colosses that were made in Rome the last year upon the feast daye of the place of Agone, which outwardly declared a likeness of great men and horses of triumph, and inwardly were full of towe and ragges" (Hoby 263; for the original, see Castiglione 4.7.454). For discussion of such festivities and pageants, see Bergeron, Stephens, and Laroque. For data on the construction and operation of such pageant figures, see Nichols

1.489–90. This comparison stages a clash between a more traditional mentality in the Renaissance that expressed itself in such civic pageantry and a more skeptical, perhaps modern, mentality that is evident in the irreverent behavior of the "shrewd boys" as well as in the author's recounting of their activity. The passage also registers a play between the guile of the boys who undo or undercut the pageant and the pageant's beguiling the minds and eyes of the audience. For Puttenham's linked discussion of decorum, see 3.23.

11. **unshamefast** immodest.

CHAPTER 7

Of figures and figurative speeches

As figures be the instruments of ornament in every language, so be they also in a sort abuses,° or rather trespasses, in speech, because they pass the ordinary limits of common utterance, and be occupied of purpose to deceive the ear and also the mind, drawing it from plainness and simplicity to a certain doubleness, whereby our talk is the more guileful and abusing.[1] For what else is your *metaphor* but an inversion of sense by transport;[2] your *allegory* by a duplicity of meaning or dissimulation under covert and dark° intendments;° one while speaking obscurely and in riddle called *enigma*; another while by common proverb or adage called *paroemia*; then by merry scoff called *ironia*; then by bitter taunt called *sarcasmus*; then by paraphrase or circumlocution when all might be said in a word or two; then by incredible comparison giving credit, as by your *hyperbole*; and many other ways seeking to inveigle° and appassionate[3] the mind? Which thing made the

1. **abusing** deceiving. Cf. Quintilian 9.3.2–3; note that Quintilian says that figures would be errors (*vitia*) if they were intended by the speaker or writer and were not aesthetically pleasing to the hearer or listener.

2. **an inversion of sense by transport** a transposing or alteration of meaning by a change (from literal to figurative). Puttenham's

definition of metaphor contains a certain redundancy, since the word means literally a "bearing or transporting across (a boundary)." Puttenham examines metaphor in 3.17; see the discussion and notes there for his habitual odd usage of *inversion*. All of the other tropes mentioned here receive close treatment in 3.18.

3. **appassionate** impassion.

grave judges Areopagites (as I find written) to forbid all manner of figurative speeches to be used before them in their consistory of justice, as mere[4] illusions to the mind and wresters of upright judgment, saying that to allow such manner of foreign and colored° talk to make the judges affectioned° were all one[5] as if the carpenter, before he began to square his timber, would make his square crooked[6]: insomuch as° the strait[7] and upright mind of a judge is the very rule of justice till it be perverted by affection.°[8]

This no doubt is true and was by them gravely considered; but in this case—because our maker or poet is appointed not for a judge but rather for a pleader, and that of pleasant and lovely causes and nothing perilous, such as be those for the trial° of life, limb, or livelihood; and before judges neither sour nor severe, but in the ear of princely dames, young ladies, gentlewomen, and courtiers, being all for the most part either meek of nature, or of pleasant humor; and that all his abuses° tend but to dispose the hearers to mirth and solace by pleasant conveyance° and efficacy° of speech—they[9] are not in truth to be accounted vices, but for virtues, in the poetical science° very commendable. On the other side, such trespasses in speech (whereof there be many) as give dolor and disliking to the ear and mind by any foul indecency° or disproportion° of sound, situation,° or sense, they be called, and not without cause, the vicious° parts or rather heresies of language. Wherefore the matter resteth much in the definition and acceptance of this word *decorum*, for whatsoever is so, cannot justly be misliked. In which respect it may come to pass that what the grammarian setteth down for a viciosity° in speech may become a virtue and no vice; contrariwise, his commended figure may fall into a reproachful[10] fault, the best and most assured remedy whereof is, generally to follow the saying of Bias: *ne quid nimis*.[11] So as°

4. **mere** absolute, complete.
5. **all one** the same.
6. Cf. Aristotle, *Rhetoric* 1.1.5–6 (1354a).
7. **strait** strict.
8. The Areopagites were the earliest aristocratic council or court of ancient Athens; the name derives from the Areopagus (hill of Ares), a hill northwest of the Acropolis, where the court met. According to Aeschines (1.92), this court differed from other Athenian courts in its resistance to the wiles of rhetoric. Aristotle also alludes to the resistance of the Areopagus to emotional speeches; see *Rhetoric* 1.1.5 (1354a); cf. also Lucian, *Anacharsis* 19; Castiglione 4.23.475 (Hoby 277).
9. **they** i.e., figurative speeches.
10. **reproachful** worthy of reproach.
11. *ne quid nimis* "nothing too much," a Latin translation of the Greek μεδὲν ἄγαν,

one of the Sayings of the Seven Wise Men or Sages of Greece taught to ancient schoolboys. The Latin is cited by Erasmus, Puttenham's probable source, as *Adagia* 1.6.96 (LB 2.259B, *CWE* 32.63); Erasmus attributes it to Bias. According to modern scholars, the phrase was supposedly written on Apollo's temple at Delphi, and it is impossible to determine which ancient writer actually coined it. Gascoigne also uses the phrase (without attribution) in *Certayne Notes* (458). (The Seven Sages are substantially legendary, though some were actual people. Plutarch [*Solon* 12.4] provides this list: Bias of Priene, Chilon of Sparta, Cleobulus of Lindus, Periander of Corinth, Pittacus of Mytilene, Solon of Athens, and Thales of Miletus.) Bias, sometimes called Bion, should not be confused with the Greek bucolic poet Bion (fl. 100 BCE).

in keeping measure,° and not exceeding nor showing any defect in the use of his figures, he cannot lightly do amiss, if he have besides (as that must needs be) a special regard to all circumstances° of the person, place, time, cause, and purpose he hath in hand, which, being well observed, it easily avoideth all the recited inconveniences,° and maketh now and then very vice go for a formal[12] virtue in the exercise of this art.

12. **formal** essential, methodical, (perhaps) well formed.

CHAPTER 8

Six points set down by our learned forefathers for
a general regiment[1] of all good utterance
be it by mouth or by writing

But before there had been yet any precise observation made of figurative speeches, the first learned artificers of language considered that the beauty and good grace of utterance rested in no many[2] points, and whatsoever transgressed those limits, they counted it for vicious° and thereupon did set down a manner of regiment in all speech generally to be observed, consisting in six points.[3] First they said that there ought to be kept a decent° proportion° in our writings and speech, which they termed *analogia*.[4] Secondly, that it ought to be voluble° upon the tongue and tunable° to the ear, which they called *tasis*.[5] Thirdly, that it were not tediously long, but brief and compendious as the matter might bear, which they called *syntomia*.[6] Fourthly, that it should carry an orderly and good construction, which they called *synthesis*.[7] Fifthly, that it should be a sound, proper, and natural speech, which they called *cyriologia* Sixthly, that it should be lively and stirring,° which they called

1. **regiment** rule, government.
2. **no many** a few.
3. We have located no such consensus among classical authorities; it seems likely that Puttenham is attributing to them a synthesis that he has made himself or that he adapted from Sherry.
4. On *analogia*, see Mosellanus B3v; see also Aristotle, *Rhetoric* 3.2.9 (1405a); Sherry 37.
5. On *tasis* (Gk., "pitch"), see Mosellanus B4r; see also Dionysius of Halicarnassus, *De compositione verborum* 19.10; Sherry 37–38. See LN 11.
6. On *syntomia* (Gk., "brevity, conciseness"), see Mosellanus B4r; see also Aristo-

tle, *Rhetoric* 3.6.1 (1407b); Demetrius, *On Style* 7.
7. On *synthesis*, see Mosellanus B4v; see also Sherry 38–39. *Synthesis* was a common word among Greek grammarians and rhetoricians for stylistic composition.
8. On *cyriologia*, see Mosellanus B4r–v. *Cyriologia*, probably a variant on *kyria onomata* (Gk., "the use of the ordinary names for things"), is not a technical term in antiquity, although the word does appear in several relevant texts: Aristotle, *Poetics* 22 (1458a), *Rhetoric* 3.2 (1404b–1405a); Longinus 28.1; and Dionysius of Halicarnassus, *Lysias* 3.

tropus.[9] So as° it appeareth by this order of theirs that no vice could be committed in speech keeping within the bounds of that restraint.

But sir,[10] all this being by them very well conceived, there remained a greater[11] difficulty, to know what this proportion,° volubility,° good construction, and the rest were; otherwise we could not be ever the more relieved.[12] It was therefore of necessity that a more curious° and particular description should be made of every manner of speech, either transgressing or agreeing with their said general prescript. Whereupon it came to pass that all the commendable parts of speech were set forth by the name of figures, and all the illaudable parts under the name of vices or viciosities,° of both which it shall be spoken in their places.

9. On *tropus*, see Mosellanus B4v; see also Sherry 39–40. Longinus (12.1) speaks of three distinct styles, the sublime, the emotional, and the metaphorical (*tropon*).

10. **But sir** This remark is perhaps addressed to Burghley, the dedicatee, or possibly to the general reader, who is thus implicitly gendered as male. It is at odds,

however, with Puttenham's several explicit addresses elsewhere in this work to Queen Elizabeth (see Introduction 50).

11. **greater** greater, perhaps further.

12. **ever the more relieved** an obscure phrase, perhaps meaning "relieved fully from the risk of vicious speech."

Chapter 9

How the Greeks first, and afterward the Latins, invented° new names for every figure, which this author is also enforced to do in his vulgar°

The Greeks were a happy people for the freedom and liberty of their language, because it was allowed them to invent° any new name that they listed° and to piece many words together to make of them one entire, much more significative[1] than the single word.[2] So, among other things, did they to their figurative speeches devise certain names. The Latins came somewhat behind them in that point, and for want° of convenient° single words to express that which the Greeks could do by cobbling[3] many words together, they were fain to use the Greeks' still, till after many years that the learned orators and good grammarians among the Romans, as Cicero, Varro, Quintilian, and others, strained themselves to give the Greek words Latin names, and yet nothing so apt and fitty.[4]

1. **significative** meaningful.

2. A common feature of Greek: e.g., *batraxomuomaxia=batraxos+mus+mache=*frog+ mouse+battle=battle of frogs and mice. Cf. Sidney on the ability of English, like Greek, to form compound words (*Defence* 248).

3. **cobbling** joining. *Pace* OED's definition (which cites this passage), there is no pe-

jorative implication in Puttenham's use of this word.

4. **fitty** suitable; trim, neat. On the Romans' recognition of the difficulty involved in translating or matching Greek words with Latin ones, see *Ad Herennium* 4.7.10; Cicero, *Academica* 1.6.24; and Quintilian 1.5.70.

The same course are we driven to follow in this description, since we are enforced to cull out for the use of our poet or maker all the most commendable figures. Now to make them known (as behooveth) either we must do it by the original Greek name, or by the Latin, or by our own. But when I consider to what sort of readers I write, and how ill-faring[5] the Greek term would sound in the English ear; then also how short the Latins come to express many of the Greek originals; finally, how well our language serveth to supply the full signification of them both, I have thought it no less lawful, yea, peradventure,° under license of the learned, more laudable, to use our own natural,[6] if they be well chosen and of proper signification, than to borrow theirs. So shall not our English poets, though they be to seek of[7] the Greek and Latin languages, lament for lack of knowledge sufficient to the purpose of this art.

And in case any of these new English names given by me to any figure shall happen to offend, I pray that the learned will bear with me and to think the strangeness° thereof proceeds but of novelty and disaquaintance with our ears, which in process of time and by custom will frame[8] very well. And such others as are not learned in the primitive languages,[9] if they happen to hit upon any new name of mine (so ridiculous in their opinion) as may move them to laughter, let such persons yet assure themselves that such names go as near as may be to their originals, or else serve better to the purpose of the figure than the very original, reserving always that such new name should not be unpleasant in our vulgar° nor harsh upon the tongue; and where it shall happen otherwise, that it may please the reader to think that hardly any other name in our English could be found to serve the turn better. Again, if to avoid the hazard of this blame I should have kept the Greek or Latin still, it would have appeared a little too scholastical° for our makers, and a piece of work more fit for clerks° than for courtiers, for whose instruction this travail° is taken. And if I should have left out both the Greek and Latin name and put in none of our own neither, well perchance might the rule of the figure have been set down, but no convenient° name to hold him in memory. It was therefore expedient we devised for every figure of importance his vulgar° name, and to join the Greek or Latin original with them, after that sort much better satisfying as well the vulgar° as the learned learner, and also the author's own purpose, which is to make of a rude° rhymer a learned and a courtly poet.

---

5. **ill-faring** unwelcome.
6. **natural** native expressions.
7. **to seek of** unable to understand, deficient in.

8. **frame** adapt themselves.
9. **primitive languages** i.e., Latin and Greek.

CHAPTER 10

*A division of figures, and how they
serve in exornation[1] of language*

And because our chief purpose herein is for the learning of ladies and
young gentlewomen, or idle° courtiers, desirous to become skill-
ful° in their own mother tongue, and for their private recreation to
make now and then ditties of pleasure—thinking for our part none
other science° so fit for them and the place as that which teacheth *beau
semblant*,[2] the chief profession as well of courting as of poesy—since to
such manner of minds nothing is more cumbersome than tedious doc-
trines° and scholarly° methods of discipline,° we have in our own con-
ceit° devised a new and strange° model of this art, fitter to please the
court than the school, and yet not unnecessary for all such as be willing
themselves to become good makers in the vulgar,° or to be able to judge
of other men's makings. Wherefore, intending to follow the course
which we have begun, thus we say, that though the language of our
poet or maker, being pure and cleanly,° and not disgraced° by such vi-
cious° parts as have been before remembered in the chapter of language,[3] be sufficiently pleasing and commendable for the ordinary use
of speech, yet is not the same so well appointed[4] for all purposes of the
excellent poet as when it is gallantly arrayed in all his colors° which
figure can set upon it. Therefore we are now further to determine of
figures and figurative speeches.

Figurative speech is a novelty of language evidently[5] (and yet not absurdly) estranged from the ordinary habit and manner of our daily talk
and writing; and figure itself is a certain lively or good grace set upon
words, speeches, and sentences,[6] to some purpose and not in vain,
giving them ornament or efficacy° by many manner of alterations in
shape, in sound, and also in sense: sometime by way of surplusage,°
sometime by defect;° sometime by disorder, or mutation; and also by
putting into our speeches more pith and substance, subtlety, quickness,° efficacy,° or moderation; in this or that sort tuning and temper-
ing° them, by amplification, abridgment, opening, closing, enforcing,
meekening,[7] or otherwise disposing them to the best purpose. Whereupon the learned clerks° who have written methodically of this art in
the two master languages Greek and Latin have sorted all their figures
into three ranks, and the first they bestowed upon the poet only; the

---

1. **exornation** embellishment.
2. ***beau semblant*** beautiful appearance or
outward seeming. Cf. the treatment of *allegoria* as the similarly courtly figure of "False
Semblant" at 3.18.271.
3. See 3.4.

4. **appointed** equipped.
5. **evidently** vividly.
6. **speeches, and sentences** phrases or
clauses, and whole thoughts.
7. **enforcing, meekening** rendering force-
ful, rendering mild.

second upon the poet and orator indifferently; the third upon the orator alone. And that first sort of figures doth serve the ear only and may be therefore called *auricular*; your second serves the conceit° only and not the ear, and may be called *sensable*, not sensible nor yet sententious;[8] your third sort serves as well the ear as the conceit° and may be called *sententious° figures*, because not only they properly appertain to full sentences,° for beautifying them with a current° and pleasant numerosity,° but also giving them efficacy,° and enlarging[9] the whole matter besides with copious amplifications.[10]

I doubt not but some busy[11] carpers will scorn at my new devised terms *auricular* and *sensable*, saying that I might with better warrant have used in their steads these words, *orthographical* or *syntactical*, which the learned grammarians left ready made to our hands, and do import as much as the other that I have brought.[12] Which thing peradventure° I deny not in part, and nevertheless for some causes thought them not so necessary. But with these manner of men I do willingly bear, in respect of their laudable endeavor to allow[13] antiquity and fly innovation; with like benevolence I trust they will bear with me writing in the vulgar° speech and seeking by my novelties to satisfy not the school but the court, whereas,[14] they know very well, all old things soon wax stale and loathsome, and the new devices° are ever dainty[15] and delicate;° the vulgar° instruction requiring also vulgar° and communicable terms, not clerkly° or uncouth,[16] as are all these of the Greek and Latin languages primitively received, unless they be qualified or by much use and custom allowed and our ears made acquainted with them. Thus then I say that auricular figures be those which work alteration in the ear by sound, accent, time, and slipper° volubility° in utterance, such as for that respect was called by the ancients numerosity° of speech. And not only the whole body of a tale in poem or history

---

8. *Sensable* here means "consisting in an alteration of the sense of words," as distinguished from *sensible* (perceptible by the senses; evident) and *sententious* (meaningful; aphoristic).

9. **enlarging** developing.

10. On the division of figures into three categories by ancient as well as Renaissance writers, and on Puttenham's reformulation of that division, see Introduction 53–54. Although there is no precedent for Puttenham's claim that certain figures are granted to poets, others to orators, and yet others to both, Peacham does claim that orthographical schemes are "lawful only to poets" (1577: D1v).

11. **busy** meddlesome, restless.

12. In the section titled "De Figuris" (On Figures) in his *Short Introduction of Grammar*—a popular grammar textbook

Puttenham may well have known—William Lily distinguishes between what he calls "figurae dictionis" (figures of single words) and "figurae constructionis" (figures of syntax) (G4r–H1r). Following Lily's lead—and that of other grammarians—Susenbrotus says that one category of the schemes, which he calls "grammatical," is itself divided into the "orthographical" and the "syntactical" (19). This terminology reappears in Peacham's initial subdivision of Greek figures of speech, which begins, "A figure is deuided into Tropes & Schemates, Grammatical, Orthographical, Syntactical" (1577: B1r).

13. **allow** follow, approve.

14. **whereas** where.

15. **dainty** delightful, precious.

16. **uncouth** unknown.

may be made in such sort pleasant and agreeable to the ear, but also every clause by itself and every single word carried in a clause may have their pleasant sweetness apart. And so long as this quality extendeth but to the outward tuning of the speech, reaching no higher than the ear and forcing the mind little or nothing, it is that virtue° which the Greeks call *enargeia*,[17] and is the office of the auricular figures to perform. Therefore as the members of language at large° are whole sentences, and sentences are compact[18] of clauses, and clauses of words, and every word of letters and syllables, so is the alteration (be it but of a syllable or letter) much material to the sound and sweetness of utterance. Wherefore, beginning first at the smallest alterations which rest in letters and syllables, the first sort of our figures auricular we do appoint to single words as they lie in language; the second to clauses of speech; the third to perfect° sentences and to the whole mass or body of the tale, be it poem or history written or reported.

17. **enargeia** tuneful and delightful in sound; for Puttenham's deliberate redefinition of this term, see 3.3, note 1.
18. **compact** composed.

CHAPTER II

Of auricular figures appertaining to single words and
working by their divers sounds and audible tunes°
alteration to the ear only and not the mind

A word as he lieth in course of language is many ways figured, and thereby not a little altered in sound, which consequently alters the tune° and harmony of a meter° as to the ear. And this alteration is sometimes by adding, sometimes by rabating° of a syllable or letter to or from a word, either in the beginning, middle, or ending; joining or unjoining of syllables and letters, suppressing or confounding[1] their several sounds; or by misplacing of a letter; or by clear exchange of one letter for another; or by wrong ranging[2] of the accent.

And your figures of addition or surplus be three, *videl.*°: in the beginning, as to say *ydone* for *done*, *endanger* for *danger*, *embolden* for *bolden*. In the middle, as to say *renverse* for *reverse*, *meeterly* for *meetly*, *goldilocks* for *goldlocks*. In the end, as to say *remembren* for *remember*, *spoken* for *spoke*.[3]

And your figures of rabate° be as many, *videl.*°: from the beginning, as to say *twixt* for *betwixt*, *gainsay* for *againsay*, *ill* for *evil*. From the mid-

1. **confounding** mixing.
2. **ranging** placement.
3. Susenbrotus identifies these three "figures of addition" as *prothesis*, *epenthesis*, and *paragoge* or *proparalepsis* (20–21).

dle, as to say *peraunter* for *peradventure*,° *poorty* for *poverty*, *sov'reign* for *sovereign*, *ta'en* for *taken*. From the end, as to say *morn* for *morning*, *bet* for *better*, and such like.[4]

Your swallowing or eating up one letter by another is when two vowels meet, whereof the one's sound goeth into other, as to say for *to attain t'attain*, for *sorrow* and *smart sor* and *smart*.[5]

Your displacing of a syllable, as to say *desier* for *desire*, *fier* for *fire*.[6]

By clear exchange of one letter or syllable for another, as to say *evermare* for *evermore*, *wrang* for *wrong*, *gould* for *gold*, *fright* for *fraight*, and a hundred more, which be commonly misused and strained to make rhyme.[7]

By wrong ranging[8] the accent of a syllable, by which mean a short syllable is made long and a long short, as to say *sovéreign* for *sovéreign*, *gracíous* for *grácious*, *éndure* for *endúre*, *Solómon* for *Sólomon*.[9]

These many ways may our maker alter his words; and sometimes it is done for pleasure to give a better sound, sometimes upon necessity, and to make up the rhyme. But our maker must take heed that he be not too bold, especially in exchange of one letter for another, for unless usual speech and custom allow it, it is a fault and no figure; and because these be figures of the smallest importance, I forbear to give them any vulgar° name.

---

4. Susenbrotus identifies these three "figures of rabate" as *aphaeresis*, *syncope*, and *apocope* (20–21).

5. Susenbrotus identifies this figure as *synaloepha* (22).

6. Susenbrotus speaks of *diaeresis* (23).

7. Susenbrotus speaks of *antithesis* or *antistoechon* (23). In the examples cited in this sentence we have retained Puttenham's

spelling, by means of which he indicated a shift in pronunciation (rather than in meaning) of the words in question.

8. **ranging** placement.

9. Susenbrotus defines *systole* as the shortening of a naturally long syllable, and *diastole* as the lengthening of a naturally short syllable (21–22).

CHAPTER 12

Of auricular figures pertaining to clauses of speech,
and by them working no little alteration to the ear

As your single words may be many ways transfigured to make the meter° or verse more tunable° and melodious, so also may your whole and entire clauses be in such sort contrived by the order of their construction as the ear may receive a certain recreation,° although the mind for any novelty of sense be little or nothing affected.°[1] And therefore all your figures of grammatical construction, I account them but

---

1. These figures are what Susenbrotus denominates grammatical schemes of syntax (24).

merely[2] auricular, in that they reach no further than the ear. To which there will appear some sweet or unsavory point to offer you dolor or delight, either by some evident defect,° or surplusage,° or disorder,[3] or immutation[4] in the same speeches, notably altering either the congruity grammatical, or the sense, or both.

And first of those that work by defect,° if but one word or some little portion of speech be wanting,° it may be supplied by ordinary understanding and virtue° of the figure *eclipsis*.[5] As to say "so early a man," for "(are ye) so early a man"; "he is to be entreated," for "he is (easy) to be entreated"; "I thank God I am to live like a gentleman," for "I am (able) to live"; and the Spaniard said in his device° of arms, *acuerdo olvido*, "I remember I forget," whereas in right congruity of speech it should be, "I remember (that I do) forget."[6] And in a device° of our own *empechement pur a choison*,[7] "a let[8] for a furtherance,"* whereas it should be said "(use) a let for a furtherance"; and a number more like speeches, defective and supplied by common understanding.

Eclipsis,
or the Figure
of Default

But if it be to more clauses than one that some such word be supplied to perfect° the congruity or sense of them all, it is by the figure *zeugma*.[9] We call him the Single Supply because by one word we serve many clauses of one congruity, and may be likened to the man that serves many masters at once, but all of one country or kindred. As to say:

Zeugma,
or the Single
Supply

Fellows and friends and kin forsook me quite.[†10]

Here this word "forsook" satisfieth the congruity and sense of all three clauses, which would require every of them as much. And as we, setting forth her Majesty's regal pedigree, said in this figure of Single Supply:

---

2. **merely** purely.

3. **disorder** a deliberate rearranging of the order, not an absence thereof.

4. **immutation** mutation.

5. On *eclipsis*, see Susenbrotus 25; see also Quintilian 8.6.21, 9.3.58; Sherry 31; Peacham (1577) E3v; Day 81.

6. This phrase, apparently the translator's motto, can be found in large type on the title page of the first three volumes of Nicolas de Herberay's translation from Spanish into French of the *Amadis de Gaule* (Paris 1548–59). Puttenham might have seen it in one of these volumes.

7. ***empechement ... choison*** (Fr.) "(a) hindrance for an opportunity." With the verb "use" that Puttenham says is implied in his device, it means "to take a hindrance as an opportunity (to accomplish something)."

8. **let** hindrance.

9. On *zeugma*, see Susenbrotus 26–27; see also Rufinianus, *De schematis lexeos* 3; Sherry 29; Peacham (1577) E4v, K2v; Day 82. Puttenham is elaborating his definition on the basis of Susenbrotus, who says that *zeugma* has different names depending on its placement in a line, supplying the three Puttenham gives. Sherry and Peacham also offer a similar division.

10. The transition between Puttenham's prose and this verse is slightly confusing, owing to the fact that in the prose explanation he speaks (using a *figure*) of following masters (clauses) who are all of one country or kindred (responsive to a single word/verb); then he gives an example the *content* of which contains a set of terms of specifically country/kindred force ("fellows," "friends," "kin": *not* used figurally). This continuity is not logical, though the prose figure may have led Puttenham to compose the verse.

> *Her grandsires, father, and brother was a king,*
> *Her mother a crowned queen, her sister, and herself.*[11]

Whereas ye see this one word "was" serves them all, in that they require but one congruity and sense.

    Yet hath this figure of Single Supply another property, occasioning him to change now and then his name by the order of his supply, for if it be placed in the forefront of all the several clauses whom he is to *Prozeugma,* serve as a common servitor, then is he called by the Greeks *prozeugma,* *or the* by us the Ringleader.[12] Thus: *Ringleader*

> *Her beauty pierced mine eye, her speech mine woeful heart,*
> *Her presence all the powers of my discourse, etc.*[†]

Where ye see this one word "pierced," placed in the foreward,[13] satisfieth both in sense and congruity all those other clauses that follow him.

    And if such word of supply be placed in the middle of all such clauses *Mesozeugma,* as he serves, it is by the Greeks called *mesozeugma,* by us the Middle- *or the Middle-* marcher.[14] Thus: *marcher*

> *Fair maids'*[15] *beauty (alack), with years it wears away,*
> *And with weather, and sickness, and sorrow, as they say.*[16]

Where ye see this word "wears" serves one clause before him and two clauses behind him, in one and the same sense and congruity. And in this verse:

> *Either the troth*° *or talk nothing at all.*[17]

Where this word "talk" serves the clause before and also behind.

    But if such supply be placed after all the clauses, and not before nor in *Hypozeugma,* the middle, then is he called by the Greeks *hypozeugma,* and by us the *or the* Rearwarder.[18] Thus: *Rearwarder*

> *My mates that wont to keep me company,*
> *And my neighbors, who dwelt next to my wall,*
> *The friends that swore they would not stick*° *to die*
> *In my quarrel: they are fled from me all.*[†]

---

11. These lines do not appear in the *Parthe-niades*, though they closely resemble Puttenham's poetic style and subject matter there.

12. On *prozeugma*, see Susenbrotus 26; see also *Ad Herennium* 4.27.38; Sherry 29; Peacham (1577) K2v.

13. **foreward** vanguard.

14. On *mesozeugma*, see Susenbrotus 26; see also *Ad Herennium* 4.27.38; Sherry 29; Peacham (1577) K3r.

15. **maids'** Puttenham's text has "maids," which might also be taken as a possessive singular.

16. Puttenham is here reworking either an example the *Ad Herennium* supplies for this figure (4.27.38) or an example Susenbrotus gives (20).

17. Puttenham is translating one of Susenbrotus's examples of *zeugma* (26).

18. **Rearwarder** a member of the rear guard of an army. On *hypozeugma*, see Susenbrotus 26; see also *Ad Herennium* 4.27.38; Quintilian 9.3.62; Sherry 29; Peacham (1577) K3r.

Where ye see this word "fled from me" serve all the three clauses, requiring but one congruity and sense.

But if such want° be in sundry clauses, and of several congruities or senses, and the supply be made to serve them all, it is by the figure *syllepsis*,[19] whom for that respect we call the Double Supply, conceiving and, as it were, comprehending under one, a supply of two natures, and may be likened to the man that serves many masters at once, being of strange° countries or kindreds, as in these verses, where the lamenting widow showed the pilgrim the graves in which her husband and children lay buried:

> *Here my sweet sons and daughters, all my bliss,*
> *Yonder mine own dear husband buried is.*[†]

Where ye see one verb singular supplieth the plural and singular. And thus:

> *Judge, ye lovers, if it be strange or no:*
> *My lady laughs for joy, and I for woe.*[†]

Where ye see a third person supply himself and a first person. And thus:

> *Madam, ye never showed yourself untrue,*
> *Nor my deserts would ever suffer you.*[†]

Videl.,° to show. Where ye see the mood indicative supply himself and an infinitive. And the like in these other:

> *I never yet failed you in constancy,*
> *Nor never do intend until I die.*[†]

Videl.,° to fail.

Thus much for the congruity, now for the sense. One wrote thus of a young man who slew a villain that had killed his father and ravished his mother:

> *Thus valiantly and with a manly mind,*
> *And by one feat of everlasting fame,*
> *This lusty lad fully requited kind,*°
> *His father's death, and eke*° *his mother's shame.*[20]

Where ye see this word "requite" serve a double sense: that is to say, to revenge and to satisfy. For the parents' injury was revenged, and the duty of nature performed or satisfied by the child.

19. On *syllepsis*, see Susenbrotus 27–28; see also Isidore 1.36.5–6; Sherry 30; Peacham (1577) F1r; Day 82.

20. Puttenham's example resembles one he found in Susenbrotus for *syllepsis* (28), taken from the *Epitome* (3.1.9) of Justinus, an abridgment of the *Historiae Philippicae et* *totius mundi origines et terrae situs* (The History of Philip and the Origins of the Entire World and the Regions of the Earth) by Pompeius Trogus, now lost. Arthur Golding translated Justinus in 1570, so Puttenham possibly read him directly. The similarity to the *Hamlet* story is notable.

But if this supply be made to sundry clauses, or to one clause sundry times iterated, and by several words, so as° every clause hath *Hypozeuxis,* his own supply, then is it called by the Greeks *hypozeuxis.*[21] We call *or the* him the Substitute after his original, and is a supply with iteration, *Substitute* as thus:

> *Unto the king she went, and to the king she said,*
> *"Mine own liege lord, behold thy poor handmaid."*[†]

Here "went to the king" and "said to the king" be but one clause iterated with words of sundry supply. Or as in these verses following:

> *My lady gave me, my lady wist° not what,*
> *Giving me leave to be her sovereign:*
> *For by such gift my lady hath done that,*
> *Which whilst she lives she may not call again.*[†]

Here "my Lady gave" and "my Lady wist°" be supplies with iteration, by virtue of this figure.

Ye have another auricular figure of defect,° and is when we begin to speak a thing and break off in the middle way, as if either it needed no further to be spoken of, or that we were ashamed or afraid to speak it out. It is also sometimes done by way of threatening, and to show a *Aposiopesis,* moderation of anger. The Greeks call him *aposiopesis;* I, the Figure of *or the Figure* Silence, or of Interruption, indifferently.°[22] *of Silence*

If we do interrupt our speech for fear, this may be an example, where, as one durst[23] not make the true report as it was, but stayed half-way for fear of offense, thus:

> *He said you were—I dare not tell you plain:*
> *For words once out, never return again.*[24]

If it be for shame, or that the speaker suppose it would be indecent° to tell all, then thus, as he that said to his sweetheart, whom he checked for secretly whispering with a suspected person:

> *And did ye not come by his chamber door?*
> *And tell him that—go to, I say no more.*[†]

If it be for anger or by way of menace or to show a moderation of wrath, as the grave and discreeter sort of men do, then thus:

> *If I take you with such another cast,*[25]
> *I swear by God—but let this be the last.*[†]

21. On *hypozeuxis,* see Rufinianus, *De schematis lexeos* 4; Peacham (1577) K3r.

22. On *aposiopesis,* see Susenbrotus 25–26; see also *Ad Herennium* 4.30.41; Cicero, *De oratore* 3.53.205; Quintilian 9.2.54–55; Wilson 205.15–20, 223.10–23, and notes; Peacham (1577) E4r, N1v; Day 81. *Aposiopesis* means "becoming silent."

23. **durst** dared.

24. Cf. Horace, *Ars poetica* 390.

25. **If . . . cast** i.e., If I catch you playing another such trick.

Thinking to have said further, *videl.*,° "I will punish you." If it be for none of all these causes, but upon some sudden occasion that moves a man to break off his tale, then thus:

> He told me all at large°—lo, yonder is the man;
> Let himself tell the tale that best tell can.†

This figure is fit for fantastical° heads and such as be sudden[26] or lack memory. I know one of good learning† that greatly blemisheth his discretion[27] with this manner of speech: for if he be in the gravest matter of the world talking, he will upon the sudden for the flying of a bird overthwart[28] the way, or some other such slight cause, interrupt his tale and never return to it again.

Ye have yet another manner of speech purporting at the first blush a defect° which afterward is supplied. The Greeks call him *prolepsis*, we the Propounder, or the Explainer, which[29] ye will, because he works both effects.[30] As thus, where in certain verses we describe the triumphant enterview[31] of two great princesses thus:

Prolepsis, or the Propounder

> These two great queens came marching hand in hand
> Unto the hall, where store° of princes stand,
> And people of all countries, to behold:
> Coronis† all clad in purple cloth of gold;
> Celiar† in robes of silver tissue white,
> With rich rubies and pearls all bedight.*

Here ye see the first proposition in a sort defective° and of imperfect° sense, till ye come by division to explain and enlarge it, but if we should follow the original right, we ought rather to call him the Forestaller, for like as he that stands in the market way and takes all up before it come to the market in gross and sells it by retail, so by this manner of speech our maker sets down before all the matter by a brief proposition, and afterward explains it by a division more particularly.[32]

---

26. **sudden** hasty, rash.

27. **discretion** judgment.

28. **overthwart** across.

29. **which** whichever.

30. On *prolepsis*, see Susenbrotus 28–29; see also Quintilian 9.2.16; Sherry 28–29; Wilson 212.7–12, 213.12–25, and notes; Peacham (1577) F1v; Day 82.

31. **enterview** formal meeting between two princes or great persons. We retain Puttenham's spelling of this unusual word because the passage so distinctly describes a triumphant (i.e., ceremonial) entrance. Puttenham uses the word of princely encounter in the *Justification* (72). Speaking there of Elizabeth's initial disposition toward Mary, Queen of Scots, he describes his own queen as "mervelouslie desiringe to see her, and to

conferre with her personallie, and to solace them selves together with all amiable conversacion" (109). His lines here perhaps record a fantasy of (or preparation for?) such a meeting. They may also derive from Puttenham's lost *Triumphals*.

32. Puttenham is probably offering this passage as an example of *prolepsis* because the first three lines merely say that two queens came marching into a room, without specifying who they are. In other words, those lines are "defective," i.e., incomplete, until the rest of the poem supplies their names and a few details describing them. *Prolepsis* is involved because the first lines anticipate what will be explained by the later lines (in the "division," a technical rhetorical term for the dividing of a speaker's thesis into its component parts).

By this other example it appears also:

> *Then, dear lady, I pray you let it be,*
> *That our long love may lead us to agree:*
> *Me, since I may not wed you to my wife,*
> *To serve you as a mistress all my life;*
> *Ye, that may not me for your husband have,*
> *To claim me for your servant and your slave.*[†]

CHAPTER 13[1]

Of your figures auricular working by disorder

Hyperbaton, or the Trespasser

To all their speeches which wrought by disorder the Greeks gave a general name *hyperbaton*, as much to say as° the Trespasser.[2] And because such disorder may be committed many ways, it receiveth sundry particulars under him: whereof some are only proper to the Greeks and Latins and not to us,[3] other some ordinary in our manner of speeches, but so foul and intolerable as I will not seem to place them among the figures, but do range them as they deserve among the vicious° or faulty speeches.[4]

Parenthesis, or the Inserter

Your first figure of tolerable disorder is *parenthesis*, or, by an English name, the Inserter; and is when ye will seem for larger information° or some other purpose to piece or graft in the midst of your tale an unnecessary parcel of speech, which nevertheless may be thence[5] without any detriment to the rest.[6] The figure is so common that it needeth none example. Nevertheless, because we are to teach ladies and gentlewomen to know their school points and terms appertaining to the art, we may not refuse to yield examples even in the plainest cases, as that of master Dyer's very aptly:

> *But now, my dear (for so my love makes me to call you still),*
> *That love I say, that luckless love, that works me all this ill.*[7]

---

1. At this point the *Art* misnumbers a second chapter 12, corrected here to chapter 13.

2. On *hyperbaton*, see Susenbrotus 31; see also *Ad Herennium* 4.32.44; Quintilian 8.6.62–67; Longinus 22; Sherry 30; Peacham (1577) F3v. *Hyperbaton* means "transposition."

3. I.e., some figures of disorder function only in inflected languages.

4. See 3.22.

5. **thence** i.e., taken away.

6. On *parenthesis*, see Susenbrotus 33; see also Quintilian 9.3.23; Sherry 31; Peacham (1577) F4v, (1593) 198; Day 83.

7. These are lines 9–10 of "Before I dy, faire dame," preserved in Humphrey Coningsby's Elizabethan manuscript miscellany (BL, MS Harl. 7392), and published by Bernard M. Wagner in "New Poems by Edward Dyer" (467–68). This poem does not appear in Sargent, whose 1935 edition seems to have gone to press before Wagner's 1935 article appeared.

Also in our eclogue entitled *Elpine*,[8] which we made being but eighteen years old, to King Edward VI, a prince of great hope, we surmised that the pilot of a ship answering the king, being inquisitive and desirous to know all the parts of the ship and tackle, what they were, and to what use they served, using this insertion or parenthesis:

> *Sovereign Lord (for why[9] a greater name*
> *To one on earth no mortal tongue can frame;*
> *No stately style can give the practiced pen*
> *To one on earth conversant° among men). . . .* [10]

And so proceeds to answer the king's question:

> *The ship thou seest sailing in sea so large, etc.*

This insertion is very long and utterly impertinent° to the principal matter, and makes a great gap in the tale, nevertheless is no disgrace° but rather a beauty and to very good purpose. But you must not use such insertions often, nor too thick, nor those that be very long as this of ours, for it will breed great confusion to have the tale so much interrupted.

Ye have another manner of disordered speech when ye misplace your words or clauses and set that before which should be behind *et e converso*.[11] We call it in English proverb the cart before the horse—the Greeks call it *hysteron proteron*;[12] we name it the Preposterous°—and if it be not too much used is tolerable enough and many times scarce perceivable, unless the sense be thereby made very absurd. As he that described his manner of departure from his mistress said thus, not much to be misliked:

> *I kissed her cherry lip and took my leave.*[†]

Hysteron Proteron, or the Preposterous°

For "I took my leave and kissed her." And yet I cannot well say whether a man use to kiss before he take his leave, or take his leave before he kiss, or that it be all one business. It seems the taking leave is by using some speech, entreating license of departure; the kiss a knitting up of the farewell, and as it were a testimonial of the license without which here in England one may not presume of courtesy to depart. Let young courtiers decide this controversy.

---

8. A lost work, apparently dating ca. 1547–48, when Edward VI was some ten years old.

9. **for why** because.

10. Paralleling the grammar of the first two lines, the third line of this quatrain inverts the subject ("the practiced pen") and object ("No stately style") of the verb ("can give"). It is possible that Puttenham meant "ne" (nor) for "no" in this line.

11. *et e converso* and contrariwise (Lat.).

12. On *hysteron proteron*, see Susenbrotus 32–33; see also Sherry 31; Peacham (1577) F4r, (1593) 119, 141; Day 83. See also Puttenham's later discussion of the trope at 3.22.341. *Hysteron proteron* means literally "the latter, the former," thus miming the semantic disturbance it names.

One describing his landing upon a strange° coast said thus preposterously°:

> *When we had climbed the cliffs, and were ashore.*[13]

Whereas he should have said by good order:

> *When we were come ashore and climbed had the cliffs.*

For one must be on land ere he can climb. And as another said:

> *My dame that bred me up and bare me in her womb.*[14]

Whereas the bearing is before the bringing up. All your other figures of disorder, because they rather seem deformities than beauties of language, for so many of them as be notoriously indecent° and make no good harmony, I place them in the chapter of vices hereafter following.

---

13. Puttenham's example may be derived from Susenbrotus (32), who is citing a line of Vergil's *Aeneid* (3.662).

14. Puttenham appears to have made a fourteener out of an example he found in Susenbrotus (32).

CHAPTER 14

Of your figures auricular that work by surplusage°

Your figures auricular that work by surplusage°—such of them as be material and of importance to the sense or beauty of your language—I refer them[1] to the harmonical speeches of orators among the figures rhetorical, as be those of repetition and iteration or amplification. All others sorts of surplusage° I account rather vicious° than figurative, and therefore not melodious, as shall be remembered in the chapter of viciosities° or faulty speeches.[2]

---

1. **I . . . them** ambiguous: either "I refer interested readers to" or "I assign such auricular figures to." Puttenham discusses these matters in 3.19.

2. See 3.21.

CHAPTER 15

Of auricular figures working by exchange

Your figures that work *auricularly* by exchange were more observ- *Enallage,*
able to the Greeks and Latins for the braveness of their language, *or the Figure*
over that ours is,[1] and for the multiplicity of their grammatical acci- *of Exchange*
dents,[2] or verbal affects, as I may term them—that is to say, their divers
cases, moods, tenses, genders, with variable terminations—by reason
whereof they changed not the very word but kept the word, and
changed the shape of him only, using one case for another, or tense, or
person, or gender, or number, or mood. We, having no such variety of
accidents, have little or no use of this figure. They called it *enallage.*[3]

But another sort of exchange which they had, and very pretty, we do *Hypallage,*
likewise use, not changing one word for another by their accidents or *or the*
cases, as the *enallage,* nor by the places, as the Preposterous,° but *Changeling*
changing their true construction and application, whereby the sense is
quite perverted and made very absurd: as he that should say for "tell me
troth° and lie not," "lie me troth° and tell not"; for "come dine with me
and stay[4] not," "come stay with me and dine not."[5]

A certain piteous lover, to move his mistress to compassion, wrote
among other amorous verses this one:

Madam, I set your eyes before mine woes.†

For "mine woes before your eyes," spoken to the intent to win favor in
her sight.

But that was pretty of a certain sorry man of law that gave his
client but bad counsel and yet found fault with his fee, and said, "My
fee, good friend, hath deserved better counsel." "Good master,"
quoth the client, "if yourself had not said so, I would never have believed it, but now I think as you do." The man of law, perceiving his
error, "I tell thee," quoth he, "my counsel hath deserved a better
fee." Yet of all others was that a most ridiculous, but very true exchange, which the yeoman of London used with his Sergeant at the

---

1. **more observable ... over that ours is**
To paraphrase this difficult passage: auricular figures that work by exchange were more
capable of being used ("observable") by the
Greeks and Latins because of the excellence
("braveness") of their language beyond what
ours is (i.e., their languages were more excellent than ours).

2. **accidents** inflections.

3. On *enallage,* see Susenbrotus 34–35
(*antiptosis*), 41–44 (*alleotheta, alleosis*); see
also Longinus 23.1; Quintilian 8.6.28,
9.3.6–11 (but unnamed); Peacham (1577)
H3v–H4v. According to Susenbrotus, the

form of *enallage* (exchange) called *antiptosis*
occurs when one case is placed for another.
The forms of *enallage* called *alleotheta* and
alleosis are substitutions in number, tense,
gender, person, or mood, as when a plural
subject is joined to a singular verb or the present tense is substituted for the past. These
substitutions are frequent in Greek and
Latin, and usually cannot be duplicated in
English.

4. **stay** hesitate.

5. On *hypallage,* see Susenbrotus 34; see
also Cicero, *Orator* 27.93; Quintilian 8.6.23;
Day 83.

Mace, who said he would go into the country and make merry a day or two while his man plied his business at home.[6] An example of it[7] you shall find in our interlude° entitled *Lusty London*: the Sergeant, for sparing of horse-hire, said he would go with the carrier[8] on foot. "That is not for your worship," said his yeoman, whereunto the Sergeant replied:

> *I wot° what I mean, John: it is for to stay*
> *And company the knave carrier, for losing my way.*[9]

The yeoman, thinking it good manner to soothe his Sergeant, said again:

> *I mean what I wot,° Sir: your best is to hie,*
> *And carry a knave with you for company.*

Ye see a notorious exchange of the construction and application of the words in this: "I wot° what I mean," and "I mean what I wot,"° and in the other, "company the knave carrier," and "carry a knave in your company."[10]

The Greeks call this figure *hypallage*, the Latins *submutatio*. We in our vulgar° may call him the Underchange, but I had rather have him called the Changeling, nothing at all swerving from his original, and much more aptly to the purpose and pleasanter to bear in memory—especially for our ladies and pretty mistresses in court for whose learning I write, because it is a term often in their mouths, and allud-

---

6. The Sergeants at Mace were officers of the Lord Mayor of London whose main duties concerned functions of the court of the mayor and aldermen (summoning defendants and witnesses, confiscating goods, etc.). Their subordinate officers were called yeomen or valets (see Masters); Puttenham's initial reference to "his [the yeoman's] Sergeant" suggests that "yeoman" has this meaning here. There is, presumably, a bawdy joke in these lines deriving from the phallic shape of the mace and the pun on "country" (i.e., the female genitals): while the Sergeant is in the country, his yeoman is plying the Sergeant's business, i.e., sleeping with his wife, at home.

7. A new example seems to begin here, a fictional one from *Lusty London* different from the factual one that records a "very true exchange." If the Sergeant and his yeoman are the same in each story, then "true" means "lifelike."

8. **carrier** porter, bearer; perhaps carter.

9. **for . . . way** i.e., lest I lose my way.

10. This exchange is quite difficult to parse, but it seems to depend on a comic so-

cial competition among the Sergeant, his yeoman, and the carrier. The Sergeant's initial reply to his yeoman can be read as a rebuke (for presuming to tell his master that he should rent a horse because going on foot would be socially indecorous): "I know what I mean, John: I am going to accompany the knave carter lest I should lose my way." Perhaps the last phrase attempts to disguise comic tightfistedness or marks the Sergeant as a blockhead. The yeoman then attempts to soothe his master's ruffled feelings by emphasizing the latter's superior social standing, focusing on the potential social inversion suggested by the Sergeant's saying he would "company" the carrier. That statement could imply the social equality of the two men, or even the inferiority of the Sergeant, an inferiority reinforced by the idea that he depends on the carrier to keep from getting lost. What the yeoman says can be paraphrased as: I mean what I know, Sir: your best (course of action) is to get on with it ("hie thee") and to take a knave with *you* for company (companionship or entertainment).

ing to the opinion of nurses, who are wont to say that the fairies use to steal the fairest children out of their cradles, and put other ill-favored in their places, which they called changelings, or elves. So, if ye mark, doth our poet or maker play with his words, using a wrong construction for a right and an absurd for a sensible, by manner of exchange.

CHAPTER 16

Of some other figures which because they serve chiefly to make the meters° tunable° and melodious, and affect not the mind but very little, be placed among the auricular[1]

The Greeks used a manner of speech or writing in their proses that went by clauses, finishing in words of like tune,° and might be by using like cases, tenses, and other points of consonance, which they called *homoioteleuton*,[2] and is that wherein they nearest approached to our vulgar° rhyme, and may thus be expressed:

Homoioteleuton, or the Like Loose

> *Weeping, creeping, beseeching, I wan*[3]
> *The love at length of Lady Lucian.*†

Or thus, if we speak in prose and not in meter°[4]:

> *Mischances ought not to be lamented,*
> *But rather by wisdom in time prevented;*
> *For such mishaps as be remediless,*
> *To sorrow them it is but foolishness;*
> *Yet are we all so frail of nature,*
> *As to be grieved with every displeasure.*[5]

1. Puttenham abandons any attempt to define a coherent subspecies of auricular figures in this chapter. Most are taken from Susenbrotus's grammatical figures of syntax and follow roughly the same order. The first figure, however, *homoioteleuton*, is taken from Susenbrotus's rhetorical schemes of words.

2. On *homoioteleuton*, see Susenbrotus 54 (*similiter desinens*); see also Aristotle, *Rhetoric* 3.9.9 (1410b), although the term is mentioned only in passing here; *Ad Herennium* 4.20.28; Quintilian 9.3.77–80; Sherry 58; Wilson 226.22–227.84 and note; Peacham (1577) K1v, (1593) 54; Day 86. By "of like tune" Puttenham means "of like sound." This

figure is the ancient equivalent of rhyme, except that it is more a prose effect than a poetic one and is not as systematic as rhyme.

3. **wan** won.

4. These lines following appear to be prose printed as verse to foreground visually the quasi-rhyme of *homoioteleuton*.

5. These lines are the first of four passages, as Willcock and Walker point out (325–26), to which closely correspondent passages appear in MS. Harl. 6910, ff. 159v, 166r, and 166v. (The other three appear in 3.19: the two Crates and the Metrodorus poems "What life is the liefest" and "What life ye list to lead" [290, 290–91], and "Set the Giant deep in a dale" [329].)

The cracking[6] Scots, as the chronicle reports, at a certain time made this bald[7] rhyme upon the Englishmen:

> Long beards heartless,
> Painted hoods witless,°
> Gay coats graceless
> Make all England thriftless.[8]

Which is no perfect rhyme indeed, but clauses finishing in the self-same tune°: for a rhyme of good symphony° should not conclude his concords° with one and the same terminant syllable, as *less, less, less,* but with diverse and like terminants, as *les, pres, mes,* as was before declared in the chapter of your cadences.°[9] And your clauses in prose should neither finish with the same nor with the like terminants, but with the contrary, as hath been showed before in the book of proportions,°[10] yet many use it otherwise, neglecting the poetical harmony and skill.° And the Earl of Surrey with Sir Thomas Wyatt, the most excellent makers of their time, more peradventure° respecting the fitness and ponderosity[11] of their words than the true cadence° or symphony,° were very licentious in this point. We call this figure, following the original, the Like Loose, alluding to the archer's term, who is not said to finish the feat of his shot before he give the loose and deliver his arrow from his bow, in which respect we use to say "mark the loose" of a thing for "mark the end" of it.[12]

Paroemion, or the Figure of Like Letter

Ye do by another figure notably affect the ear when ye make every word of the verse to begin with a like letter.[13] As, for example, in this verse written in an epitaph of our making:

> Time tried his truth, his travails,° and his trust,
> And time too late tried his integrity. *[14]

6. **cracking** wisecracking, boasting.

7. **bald** bare of ornament and grace.

8. **Thriftless** unsuccessful. These lines derive originally from the account of Edward III's first campaign against the Scots in 1327, recorded in *The Brut* (often called *Caxton's Chronicle*; see 1.249) and frequently recycled in later chronicles. Holinshed reprints the lines, explaining, "Bicause the English souldiers of this armie were cloathed all in cotes and hoods embroidered with floures and branches verie séemelie [sic], and vsed to nourish their beards: the Scots in derision thereof made" this rhyme (Holinshed 2.595).

9. See 2.8.170.

10. It is not clear to which passage in Book 2 Puttenham refers.

11. **ponderosity** weightiness.

12. For this technical term, see Ascham, *Toxophilus* 105–6.

13. On *paroemion*, see Susenbrotus 36; see also Rutilius Lupus 2.12; Isidore 1.36.14; Peacham (1577) G3v, (1593) 49. The Greek original was spelled *paramoion* and meant "words of similar sound," or what we would call assonance. By the time the word arrived in Susenbrotus, however, its spelling had become *paroemion* and its meaning what we call alliteration; these changes go back at least to Isidore of Seville. *Paroemion* should not be confused with *paroemia*, or proverbial speech; for *paroemia*, see 3.18.273.

14. These lines may come from the epitaph for Sir John Throckmorton, so named and quoted at more length at 3.17.263–64; the work is no longer extant.

It is a figure much used by our common rhymers, and doth well if it be not too much used, for then it falleth into the vice, which shall be hereafter spoken of, called *tautologia*.[15]

Ye have another sort of speech in a manner defective° because it wants° good band° or coupling, and is the figure *asyndeton*[16]—we call him Loose Language—and doth not a little alter the ear.[17] As thus:

Asyndeton, or the Loose Language

> *I saw it, I said it, I will swear it.*[†]

Caesar the Dictator, upon the victory he obtained against Pharnax King of Bithynia, showing the celerity of his conquest, wrote home to the Senate in this tenor of speech, no less swift and speedy than his victory:

> *Veni, vidi, vici:*
> *I came, I saw, I overcame.*[18]

Meaning thus: I was no sooner come and beheld them but the victory fell on my side. The Prince of Orange, for his device° of arms in banner displayed against the Duke of Alva and the Spaniards in the Low Country, used the like manner of speech:

> *Pro Rege, pro lege, pro grege:*
> *For the king, for the commons, for the country laws.*[19]

It is a figure to be used when we will seem to make haste, or to be earnest, and these examples with a number more be spoken by the figure of Loose Language.

Quite contrary to this ye have another manner of construction which they called *polysyndeton*; we may call him the Couple Clause, for that every clause is knit and coupled together with a conjunctive.[20] Thus:

Polysyndeton, or the Couple Clause

> *And I saw it, and I say it, and I*
> *Will swear it to be true.*[†]

So might the poesy of Caesar have been altered, thus:

> *I came, and I saw, and I overcame.*

---

15. See 3.22.340–41.

16. On *asyndeton*, see Susenbrotus 36–37; see also *Ad Herennium* 4.30.41; Quintilian 9.3.53–54; Sherry 59; Peacham (1577) G4r, I4r, (1593) 52; Day 83.

17. **alter the ear** affect the sound.

18. This example occurs in Susenbrotus (37); for the original, see Suetonius, *The Deified Julius Caesar* 37.2. Caesar's defeat of Pharnax (or Pharnaces), son of Mithradates the Great, occurred in 47–46 BCE.

19. The Latin order actually reads: "For the king, for the law, for the common people." William of Orange affixed this motto (in the form *Pro lege, rege et grege*) as epigraph to

an appeal to his countrymen for funds to expel the Spanish, commonly called the *Waarschouwing* (i.e., the "admonition"; published August 31, 1568), and (until 1572) flew it on his battle banner in his struggles against the duke of Alva. The *pro rege* (for the king) element, which might seem puzzling for use in battle against the general Philip II certainly sent to subdue the Netherlands, affirmed the fiction that Orange and his allies were loyal and nonrebellious subjects of Philip, merely fighting against his evil agent.

20. On *polysyndeton*, see Susenbrotus 37; see also Quintilian 9.3.53–54; Peacham (1577) G4v, I4r, (1593) 53; Day 83.

One wrote these verses after the same sort:

> *For in her mind no thought there is,*
> *But how she may be true, iwis;*[21]
> *And tenders*[22] *thee and all thy heal,*[23]
> *And wisheth both thy health and weal;*[24]
> *And is thine own, and so she says,*
> *And cares for thee ten thousand ways.*[25]

Hirmos,
or the
Long Loose

Ye have another manner of speech drawn out at length and going all after one tenor[26] and with an imperfect° sense till you come to the last word or verse which concludes the whole premises[27] with a perfect° sense and full period. The Greeks call it *hirmos*; I call him the Long Loose.[28] Thus appearing in a ditty of Sir Thomas Wyatt where he describes the divers distempers° of his bed:

> *The restless state, renewer of my smart,*
> *The labor's salve, increasing my sorrow,*
> *The body's ease, and troubles of my heart,*
> *Quieter of mind, mine unquiet foe,*
> *Forgetter of pain, rememb'rer of my woe,*
> *The place of sleep wherein I do but wake,*
> *Besprent with tears, my bed I thee forsake.*[29]

Ye see here how ye can gather no perfection° of sense in all this ditty till ye come to the last verse, in these words, "my bed I thee forsake." And in another sonnet of Petrarch, which was thus Englished by the same Sir Thomas Wyatt:

> *If weaker care, if sudden pale color,*
> *If many sighs with little speech to plain,*[30]
> *Now joy now woe, if they my joys distain,*[31]
> *For hope of small, if much to fear therefore,*
> *Be sign of love, then do I love again.*[32]

---

21. **iwis** (lit. "I know") certainly, indeed (often used merely as a metrical tag, as here).

22. **tenders** regards favorably, treats with compassion.

23. **heal** health, well-being, prosperity.

24. **weal** wealth, well-being.

25. *Tottel* no. 278.22–25, 28–30. This anonymous poem is among those added to the second edition, of July 31, 1557; Hearsey (*Complaint of Buckingham* 119) suggests that it was composed by Thomas Sackville.

26. **tenor** course of meaning holding throughout a document; substance, drift.

27. **premises** the aforesaid. Puttenham is thinking in legal terms in this passage.

28. On *hirmos*, see Susenbrotus 38; see also Isidore 1.36.18; Peacham (1577) H11; Day 83–84.

29. Cf. *Tottel* no. 62 (Rebholz no. 117); indebted to Petrarch, *Canzoniere* 234. Turberville later paraphrased and amplified the poem (EE, leaves 35v–36v). Rollins suggests that Surrey echoes Wyatt's second phrase in *Tottel* no. 15 (13.41) (Jones no. 27.45).

30. **to plain** to complain; perhaps a pun on "too plain."

31. **distain** stain, impair; perhaps a pun on "disdain."

32. Cf. *Tottel* no. 44.22–25, 27 (Rebholz no. 85); indebted to Petrarch, *Canzoniere* 224. Turberville imitated this poem ("If banisht sleepe, and watchfull care," EE, leaves 39r–v).

Here all the whole sense of the ditty is suspended till ye come to the last three words, "then do I love again," which finisheth the song with a full and perfect° sense.

When ye will speak giving every person or thing besides his proper name a quality by way of addition,[33] whether it be of good or of bad, it is a figurative speech of audible alteration.[34] So is it also of sense,[35] as to say:

Epitheton, or the Qualifier

> Fierce Achilles, wise Nestor, wily Ulysses,
> Diana the chaste, and thou lovely Venus,
> With thy blind boy that almost never misses,
> But hits our hearts when he levels at us.[†]

Or thus commending the isle of Great Britain:

> Albion, hugest of western islands all,
> Soil of sweet air and of good store,°
> God send we see thy glory never fall,
> But rather daily to grow more and more.[†]

Or as we sang of our Sovereign Lady, giving her these attributes besides her proper name:

> Elizabeth, regent of the Great Britain isle,
> Honor of all regents and of queens.[*]

But if we speak thus, not expressing her proper name Elizabeth, *videl*.°:

> The English Diana, the great Briton maid.[†]

Then is it not by *epitheton*, or figure of attribution, but by the figures *antonomasia* or *periphrasis*.

Ye have yet another manner of speech when ye will seem to make two of one not thereunto constrained, which therefore we call the Figure of Twins, the Greeks *hendiadys*.[36] Thus:

Hendiadys, or the Figure of Twins

> Not you coy dame, your *lours*[37] nor your looks.[†]

For "your louring looks." And as one of our ordinary rhymers said:

> Of fortune, nor her frowning face,
> I am nothing aghast.[38]

---

33. **addition** a word or phrase annexed to a man's name to show his rank, occupation, or place of residence, or otherwise to distinguish him.

34. On *epitheton*, see Susenbrotus 39; see also Quintilian 8.6.40–43; Peacham (1577) H1r, (1593) 146; Day 84. See also Puttenham's second treatment of *epitheton* at 3.17.267.

35. **sense** meaning.

36. On *hendiadys*, see Susenbrotus 35; see also Peacham (1577) H4r; Day 83.

37. **lours** frowns.

38. Turberville, "That Louers ought to shunne no paines to attaine their Loue" (EE, leaves 132r–v: 80–81). Puttenham reverses the order of the lines.

Instead of "fortune's frowning face." One praising the Neapolitans[39] for good men at arms, said, by the Figure of Twins, thus:

> *A proud people and wise and valiaunt,[40]*
> *Fiercely fighting with horses and with barbs:*
> *By whose prowess the Roman Prince did daunt*
> *Wild Africans and the lawless Alarbes,*
> *The Nubians marching with their armed carts*
> *And slaying afar with venom and with darts.[†41]*

Where ye see this figure of twins twice used: once when he said "horses and barbs" for "barbed horses"; again when he saith with "venom" and with "darts" for "venomous darts."

39. Neapolis is the ancient name not only of the modern city of Naples but also of a city in what is now Tunisia. Which Neapolitans are meant here is uncertain.

40. **valiaunt** valiant (original spelling is preserved for the sake of the rhyme).

41. The Roman Prince remains unidentified, but the Alarbes are the Arabs, and the Nubians inhabited an ancient North African region that included parts of modern Egypt, Sudan, and Libya.

CHAPTER 17[1]

Of the figures which we call sensable,[2] because they
alter and affect the mind by alteration
of sense, and first in single words

The ear having received his due satisfaction by the auricular figures, now must the mind also be served with his natural delight, by figures sensable, such as by alteration of intendments° affect the courage° and give a good liking to the conceit.° And first, single words have their sense and understanding altered and figured many ways, to wit: by *Metaphor, or the Figure of Transport* transport, abuse,° cross-naming, new naming, change of name.[3] This will seem very dark° to you unless it be otherwise explained more particularly. And first of Transport.[4] There is a kind of wresting of a single

1. At this point the *Art* misnumbers a second chapter 16, corrected here to chapter 17.

2. See the distinctions made in 3.10 among *sensable* (consisting in an alteration of the sense of words), *sensible* (perceptible by the senses; evident), and *sententious* (meaningful; aphoristic).

3. Puttenham's list here identifies the first five figures he discusses in this chapter. Metaphor is later identified as the Figure of Transport; *catachresis* is that of Abuse; *metonymy*, though called "the Misnamer"

below, could actually be translated as the "cross-namer" (*meta-*, "across"; *nym-* from *onoma*, "name"); *antonomasia* is labeled "the Surnamer" below, but "new namer" identifies it as well (*anto-*, "instead"; *onomasia* from *onomazein*, "to name"); and "change of name" might be equated with *epitethon*, although Puttenham's phrase might be used for all the rest of the terms in this chapter.

4 *Metaphor* means literally a "bearing or transporting across (a boundary)." The normal Latin word for the Greek term was

word from his own right signification to another not so natural, but yet of some affinity or conveniency° with it; as to say, "I cannot digest your unkind words," for "I cannot take them in good part"; or as the man of law said, "I feel you not," for "I understand not your case," because he had not his fee in his hand. Or as another said to a mouthy[5] advocate, "Why barkest thou at me so sore?"[6] Or to call the top of a tree or of a hill, the crown of a tree or of a hill: for indeed "crown" is the highest ornament of a prince's head, made like a close[7] garland, or else the top of a man's head, where the hair winds about, and because such term is not applied naturally to a tree or to a hill, but is transported from a man's head to a hill or tree, therefore it is called by *metaphor*, or the Figure of Transport.

And three causes moves us to use this figure: one for necessity or want of a better word, thus:

> As the dry ground that thirsts after a show'r
> Seems to rejoice when it is well ywet,
> And speedily brings forth both grass and flow'r,
> If lack of sun or season do not let.[8]

Here, for want of an apter and more natural word to declare the dry temper° of the earth, it is said to thirst and to rejoice, which is only proper to living creatures, and yet, being so inverted, doth not so much swerve from the true sense but that every man can easily conceive the meaning thereof.

Again, we use it for pleasure and ornament of our speech, as thus in an epitaph of our own making to the honorable memory of a dear friend, Sir John Throckmorton, knight, justice of Chester, and a man of many commendable virtues:

> Whom virtue reared, envy° hath overthrown
> And lodged full low, under this marble stone:
> Nor never were his values so well known,
> Whilst he lived here, as now that he is gone.*

---

translatio, which means exactly what *metaphor* does. Although Puttenham identifies *metaphor* as the "Figure of Transport" at the start of this chapter, his preferred English equivalent for it is not "translation," which was common in the Renaissance, but "Inversion" (and the verb "invert"), which he uses in the sense not of turning something upside down but of transposing or altering, perhaps even perverting it. In this case, what is being "inverted," that is, transposed or altered, is the meaning of the word in question from its literal to a figurative sense. On *metaphor*, see Susenbrotus 7; see also Aristotle, *Rhetoric* 3.2.5–13 (1404b–1405b); *Ad*

Herennium 4.34.45; Quintilian 8.6.4–18; Sherry 40; Wilson 198.7–199.25; Peacham (1577) B3r, (1593) 3; Fraunce 1.7; Day 77; Hoskins 8.

5. **mouthy** railing.

6. These examples speak to Puttenham's unhappy legal experience.

7. **close** closed.

8. **let** hinder, prevent. In this poem Puttenham seems to be reworking rather freely two examples of metaphors he finds in Susenbrotus: *sitire agros* and *luxuriare segetes* (7: "the fields thirst," "the crops grow wantonly"). Cf. Quintilian: *sitire segetes* (8.6.6: "the crops thirst").

Here these words—"reared," "overthrown," and "lodged"—are inverted, and metaphorically applied not upon necessity, but for ornament only. Afterward again in these verses:

> No sun by day that ever saw him rest,
> Free from the toils of his so busy charge,
> No night that harbored rancor in his breast,
> Nor merry mood made reason run at large.[9]

In these verses the inversion or *metaphor* lieth in these words—"saw," "harbored," "run"—which naturally are applied to living things and not to insensible, as the sun or the night; and yet they approach so near, and so conveniently,° as the speech is thereby made more commendable. Again, in more verses of the same epitaph, thus:

> His head a source of gravity and sense,
> His memory a shop of civil art,
> His tongue a stream of sugared eloquence,
> Wisdom and meekness lay mingled in his heart.

In which verses ye see that these words—"source," "shop," "flood"[10] "sugared"—are inverted from their own signification to another, not altogether so natural but of much affinity with it.

Then also do we it sometimes to enforce a sense and make the word more significative,[11] as thus:

> I burn in love, I freeze in deadly hate,
> I swim in hope, and sink in deep despair.†[12]

These examples I have the willinger given you to set forth the nature and use of your figure *metaphor*, which of any other, being choicely made, is the most commendable and most common.

Catachresis, or the Figure of Abuse But if for lack of natural and proper term or word we take another, neither natural nor proper, and do untruly apply it to the thing which we would seem to express, and without any just inconvenience,°[13] it is not then spoken by this figure *metaphor* or of inversion as before, but by plain Abuse.°[14] As he that bade his man go into his library and fetch

---

9. **run at large** take flight (?).

10. **flood** presumably substituted for "stream" in l. 3 of the passage.

11. **significative** meaningful.

12. For an example of the conventional freezing-burning oxymoron in the courtly love tradition, see Petrarch, *Canzoniere* 153, translated by Wyatt as "Go, burning sighs, unto the frozen heart" (*Tottel* no. 103, Rebholz no. 3).

13. The double negative ("without . . . inconvenience") is probably an error: if *catachresis* is a figure of abuse, operating by

untrue application, it should be applied without any just *convenience*; also, it seems logical that the phrase ("without . . . inconvenience") would be introduced by an adversative conjunction ("yet" or "but"), not "and."

14. On *catachresis*, see Susenbrotus 11; see also *Ad Herennium* 4.33.45; Quintilian 8.2.6, 8.6.34–36; Sherry 41; Wilson 200.6–11; Peacham (1577) C4r, (1593) 16; Day 79; Hoskins 11. "Abuse" is Puttenham's Englishing of the Lat. *abusio*, which translates the Gk. *catachresis* (wrong use).

him his bow and arrows, for indeed there was never a book there to be found; or as one should in reproach say to a poor man, "thou rascal knave," where "rascal" is properly the hunter's term given to young deer, lean and out of season, and not to people; or as one said very prettily in this verse:

I lent my love to loss, and gaged my life in vain.[15]

Whereas this word "lent" is properly of money or some such other thing as men do commonly borrow for use, to be repaid again, and being applied to love is utterly abused,° and yet very commendably spoken by virtue of this figure. For he that loveth and is not beloved again hath no less wrong than he that lendeth and is never repaid.[16]

Now doth this understanding or secret conceit° reach many times to the only nomination[17] of persons or things in their names, as of men, or mountains, seas, countries, and such like, in which respect the wrong naming, or otherwise naming of them than is due, carrieth not only an alteration of sense but a necessity of intendment° figuratively.[18] As when we call love by the name of Venus, fleshly lust by the name of Cupid, because they were supposed by the ancient poets to be authors and kindlers of love and lust; Vulcan for fire, Ceres for bread, Bacchus for wine by the same reason; also if one should say to a skillful° craftsman known for a glutton or common drunkard, that had spent all his goods on riot and delicate° fare,

Metonymy, or the Misnamer

Thy hands they made thee rich, thy palate made thee poor.†

It is meant, his travail° and art made him wealthy, his riotous life had made him a beggar. And as one that boasted of his housekeeping said that never a year passed over his head that he drank not in his house every month four tuns of beer and one hogshead of wine, meaning not the casks or vessels but that quantity which they contained.[19] These and such other speeches, where ye take the name of the author for the thing itself, or the thing containing for that which is contained, and in many other cases do, as it were, wrong name the person or the thing, so,

---

15. See *Tottel* no. 195.30 (Anonymous).

16. The level of "abuse" in the first of the three examples of *catachresis* is greater by far than that in the others and renders the example obscure. The third example, which appears to make the reciprocation of desire obligatory, perhaps bespeaks Puttenham's owned checkered erotic life.

17. **only nomination** naming only.

18. **necessity of intendment figuratively** need to understand in a figurative manner. On *metonymy*, see Susenbrotus 8–9; see also *Ad Herennium* 4.32.43; Quintilian 8.6.23–27; Wilson 200.12–28; Peacham

(1577) C2r, (1593) 19; Fraunce 1.2–5; Day 78; Hoskins 10.

19. *Tuns* and *hogsheads* were terms for casks or barrels of specified (though variable) size. By one account, a tun was four hogsheads, and a hogshead 50 to 60 imperial (English) gallons (which were about 20 percent larger than modern American gallons). Puttenham's host thus claimed to serve roughly 8,000 modern American pints of beer and 325 modern bottles of wine a month. How boastful this claim may be depends on the size of the host's household.

nevertheless, as it may be understood, it is by the figure *metonymy*, or Misnamer.[20]

Antonomasia, or the Surnamer

And if this manner of naming of persons or things be not by way of misnaming as before, but by a convenient° difference, and such as is true esteemed and likely to be true it is then called not *metonymy*, but *antonomasia*, or the Surnamer (not the Misnamer, which might extend to any other thing as well as to a person).[21] As he that would say not King Philip of Spain, but "the Western King," because his dominion lieth the furthest west of any Christian prince; and the French King "the Great Valois," because so is the name of his house; or the Queen of England, "the Maiden Queen," for that is her highest peculiar[22] among all the queens of the world; or, as we said in one of our *Partheniades*, the "Briton Maid," because she is the most great and famous maiden of all Britain, thus:

> But in chaste style, am borne, as I ween,
> To blazon forth the Briton Maiden Queen.[23]

So did our forefathers call Henry I "Beauclerk," Edmund "Ironside," Richard "Coeur de Lion," Edward "the Confessor," and we, of her Majesty Elizabeth, "the Peaceable."

Onomatopeia, or the New Namer

Then also is the sense figurative when we devise a new name to any thing consonant, as near as we can to the nature thereof.[24] As to say: "flashing[25] of lightning," "clashing of blades," "clinking of fetters," "chinking of money"; and as the poet Vergil said of the sounding a trumpet, *ta-ra-tant, taratantara*;[26] or as we give special names to the voices of dumb beasts, as to say, a horse neigheth, a lion brays, a swine grunts, a hen cackleth, a dog howls, and a hundred more such new

---

20. **so ... Misnamer** i.e., so when, despite the "wrong naming," the meaning is apparent, the trope is called *metonymy*.

21. On *antonomasia*, see Susenbrotus 9–10; see also *Ad Herennium* 4.31.42; Quintilian 8.6.29–30; Sherry 44; Wilson 201.1-5 and note; Peacham (1577) C3v, (1593) 22; Day 79. Puttenham distinguishes *antonomasia* from *metonymy* in two ways: first, *antonomasia* involves a word that is appropriate as a substitute for the word it replaces, whereas a *metonymy* is unlike the word it replaces; and second, *antonomasia* applies only to persons, whereas *metonymy* can be used for both persons and things.

22. **peculiar** special or exclusive characteristic.

23. *Partheniades* 2 ("Clio"): 40–41.

24. On *onomatopoeia*, see Susenbrotus 10–11; see also *Ad Herennium* 4.31.42; Quintilian 8.6.31-33; Peacham (1577) C4r, (1593) 14; Day 79.

25. **flashing** at its origins, an onomatopoetic word for the splashing sound made by moving water; only in the second half of the sixteenth century did it begin to be applied to such things as lightning, although as Puttenham's series of phrases here suggests, it still retained an aural component rather than having the strictly visual meaning it does today.

26. Actually, this coinage is attributed to Ennius by the Roman grammarian Priscian in his *Institutiones grammaticae*; Ennius' line reads, *At tuba terribili sonitu taratantara dixit* (*Annales* 2, no. 18: "And the horn made the terrifying sound of *taratantara*"). Vergil does not use this word, although in his commentary on the *Aeneid*, Servius says that Vergil imitates the first part of Ennius' line in *Aeneid* 9.503: *At tuba terribilem sonitum....* Puttenham is here following Susenbrotus (10).

names as any man hath liberty to devise, so it be fitty[27] for the thing which he covets to express.

Your *epitheton* or Qualifier, whereof we spoke before, placing him among the figures auricular, now because he serves also to alter and enforce the sense, we will say somewhat more of him in this place, and do conclude that he must be apt and proper for the thing he is added unto, and not disagreeable or repugnant.[28] As one that said "dark disdain"[29] and "miserable pride,"[†] very absurdly, for disdain or disdained things cannot be said dark, but rather bright and clear, because they be beholden and much looked upon, and pride is rather envied° than pitied or miserable—unless it be in Christian charity, which helpeth not the term in this case. Some of our vulgar° writers take great pleasure in giving epithets and do it almost to every word which may receive them, and should not be so, yea though they were never so proper and apt, for sometimes words suffered to go single do give greater sense and grace than words qualified by attributions do.

Epitheton, or the Qualifier; otherwise, the Figure of Attribution

But the sense is much altered and the hearer's conceit° strangely entangled by the figure *metalepsis*, which I call the Far-fetched.[30] As when we had rather fetch a word a great way off than to use one nearer hand to express the matter as well and plainer. And it seemeth the deviser of this figure had a desire to please women rather than men, for we use to say by manner of proverb, things far fetched and dear bought are good for ladies.[31] So, in this manner of speech we use it: leaping over the heads of a great many words, we take one that is furthest off to utter our matter by, as Medea, cursing her first acquaintance with Prince Jason, who had very unkindly° forsaken her, said:

Metalepsis, or the Far-fetched

> Woe worth[32] the mountain that the mast bare
> Which was the first causer of all my care.[33]

Where she might as well have said, "Woe worth our first meeting," or "Woe worth the time that Jason arrived with his ship at my father's city in Colchis, when he took me away with him"; and not so far off as

---

27. **fitty** suitable, neat, trim.

28. On *epitheton*, see Susenbrotus 39; see also Aristotle, *Rhetoric* 3.2.14–15 (1405b), 3.3.3 (1406a–b); Quintilian 8.6.40–43; Peacham (1577) H1r, (1593) 146; Day 84. Puttenham "spoke before" of this figure at 3.16.261.

29. See Gascoigne, *The Devises of Sundrie Gentlemen* 36 (248.1 and note).

30. On *metalepsis*, see Susenbrotus 11; see also Quintilian 8.6.37–39; Sherry 41; Wilson 200.29–33; Peacham (1577) C4v, (1593) 23; Day 79.

31. This proverb dates from at least ca.

1450 (Whiting F58), and appears in Heywood (1546) 1.11.

32. **Woe worth** may woe befall. Wyatt uses this idiom in his first canzone; see *Tottel* no. 64 (1.48.20), Rebholz no. 73.139. Jane Grey used it to curse Northumberland (*Chronicle of Queen Jane* 25).

33. This is Puttenham's rather free rendering of the opening of a speech by the Nurse from Ennius' translation of Euripides' *Medea*. These lines are preserved in the *Ad Herennium* (2.22.34), and the first two also appear in Quintilian (5.10.84). Ennius' passage follows closely the lines in Euripides' play (3–6).

to curse the mountain that bore the pine tree, that made the mast, that bore the sails, that the ship sailed with, which carried her away.

A pleasant gentleman came into a lady's nursery and saw her for her own pleasure rocking of her young child in the cradle, and said to her:

> I speak it, Madam, without any mock,
> Many a such cradle may I see you rock.†

"God's passion, whoreson," said she, "would thou have me bear more children yet?" "No, Madam," quoth the gentleman, "but I would have you live long that ye might the better pleasure your friends." For his meaning was that as every cradle signified a newborn child, and every child the leisure of one year's birth, and many years a long life, so by wishing her to rock many cradles of her own, he wished her long life.†34

Vergil said:

> Post multas mea regna videns mirabor aristas.35

Thus in English:

> After many a stubble shall I come
> And wonder at the sight of my kingdom.

By "stubble" the poet understood years, for harvests come but once every year, at leastways36 with us in Europe. This is spoken by the Figure of Far-fetched, *metalepsis*.

Emphasis,
or the
Reinforcer And one notable mean to affect the mind is to enforce the sense of anything by a word of more than ordinary efficacy,° and nevertheless is not apparent, but as it were, secretly implied.37 As he that said thus of a fair lady:

> O rare beauty, O grace and courtesy.†

And by° a very evil man thus:

> O sin itself, not wretch, but wretchedness.†

Whereas if he had said thus, "O gracious, courteous, and beautiful woman," and "O sinful and wretched man," it had been all to one effect, yet not with such force and efficacy° to speak by the denominative as by the thing itself.

As by the former figure we use to enforce our sense, so by another we temper° our sense with words of such moderation, as in appearance it

---

34. The character of emotional investments in children among the elite has been a matter of extensive critical and historical debate. Puttenham's overt reference to maternal pleasure sits quite uncomfortably with the intensity of the lady's repudiation of what she takes to be a suggestion about having more children.

35. *Eclogues* 1.69. In modern editions the line reads slightly differently; Puttenham is citing it in the form it has in Susenbrotus (11).

36. **leastways** least.

37. On *emphasis*, see Susenbrotus 44–45; see also Quintilian 8.3.83–86; Wilson 205.21–32 and note; Peacham (1577) H2r, (1593) 178.

abateth it, but not in deed,[38] and is by the figure *litotes*, which therefore I call the Moderator, and becomes us many times better to speak in that sort qualified than if we spoke it by more forcible terms, and nevertheless is equipollent in sense.[39] Thus:

> *I know you hate me not, nor wish me any ill.*[†]

Meaning indeed that he loved him very well and dearly, and yet the words do not express so much, though they purport so much. Or if you would say, "I am not ignorant," for "I know well enough"; "Such a man is no fool," meaning indeed that he is a very wise man.

But if such moderation of words tend to flattery, or soothing, or excusing, it is by the figure *paradiastole*,[40] which therefore nothing improperly we call the Curry-Favel.[41] As when we make the best of a bad thing, or turn a signification to the more plausible° sense: as, to call an unthrift, a liberal gentleman; the foolish-hardy, valiant or courageous; the niggard, thrifty; a great riot or outrage, a youthful prank; and such like terms, moderating and abating the force of the matter by craft[42] and for a pleasing purpose. As appeareth by these verses of ours, teaching in what cases it may commendably be used by courtiers.[*43]

But if you diminish and abase a thing by way of spite or malice, as it were to deprave[44] it, such speech is by the figure *meiosis*, or the Disabler, spoken of hereafter in the place of sententious° figures.[45]

> *A great mountain as big as a molehill.*
>
> *A heavy burthen, perdie,*[46] *as a pound of feathers.*

But if ye abase your thing or matter by ignorance or error in the choice of your word, then is it by vicious° manner of speech called *tapinosis*, whereof ye shall have examples in the chapter of vices hereafter following.[47]

---

38. **in deed** not "indeed" but instead the opposite of "in appearance."

39. **equipollent in sense** equivalent in meaning. On *litotes*, see Susenbrotus 41; see also *Ad Herennium* 4.38.50; Sherry 61; Peacham (1577) H2v, (1593) 150; Day 84.

40. On *paradiastole*, see Susenbrotus 45–46; see also Quintilian 9.3.65; Peacham (1577) N4v, (1593) 168; Day 84. Susenbrotus speaks later, when discussing diminution or *meiosis*, of how we can extenuate a vice by giving it the name of a neighboring virtue; cf. also Castiglione 1.18.102 (Hoby 31). For a detailed discussion of this trope's operation in regard to courtly conduct, see Whigham, *Ambition and Privilege* 40–42.

41. "Curry-Favel" refers to the use of insincere flattery to gain some advantage. The word refers literally to the curry-combing of a fallow-colored horse, specifically the eponymous figure in the *Roman de Fauvel*

(1310: the Romance of the Fallow-Colored Horse), whose behavior made him synonymous with the trickster Reynard the Fox. (Although "fallow" may indicate an earthy red tone, the exact color is uncertain; the word survives only in "fallow deer," whose coat is pale yellow.)

42. **craft** skill, art.

43. Apparently an example from Puttenham's verse has dropped out here.

44. **deprave** disparage.

45. On *meiosis*, see Susenbrotus 75–77; see also Cicero, *De oratore* 3.53.202; Quintilian 8.3.50; Sherry 61; Wilson 206.4–9 and note; Peacham (1577) N4v, (1593) 168. *Meiosis* will be discussed again at 3.19.304–6.

46. **perdie** By God (a mild oath).

47. On *tapinosis*, see Susenbrotus 35; see also Quintilian 8.3.48; Sherry 34; Peacham (1577) G2r, (1593) 33, 168. For the discussion of this term in the chapter on vices, see 3.22.344–45.

Then again, if we use such a word (as many times we do) by which we
drive the hearer to conceive more, or less, or beyond, or otherwise than
the letter expresseth, and it be not by virtue of the former figures *meta-*
phor and Abaser, and the rest, the Greeks then call it *synecdoche*, the
Latins *subintellectio* or understanding.[48] For by part we are enforced to
understand the whole; by the whole, part; by many things, one thing;
by one, many; by a thing precedent, a thing consequent; and generally
one thing out of another by manner of contrariety to the word which is
spoken: *aliud ex alio*.[49] Which because it seemeth to ask a good, quick,°
and pregnant capacity, and is not for an ordinary or dull wit° so to do, I
chose to call him the figure not only of conceit° after the Greek original,[50] but also of quick° conceit.° As for example, we will give none because we will speak of him again in another place, where he is ranged
among the figures sensable appertaining to clauses.[51]

48. On *synecdoche*, see Susenbrotus 7–8;
see also *Ad Herennium* 4.33.44–45; Quintilian   8.6.19–22;   Sherry   42;   Wilson
199.26–200.5; Peacham (1577) C3r, (1593) 17;
Fraunce 1.8–11; Day 78; Hoskins 11. Cf. also
the discussion of the term at 3.19.315–16.
Contrary to Puttenham's assertion, the
Latins translated the Greek *synecdoche* not
as *subintellectio* but as *intellectio*, the word

also used by Renaissance rhetoricians such
as Susenbrotus and Peacham. *Subintellectio*
means "understanding a little."
    49. **aliud ex alio** one thing from some-
thing different.
    50. *Synecdoche* in Greek comes from
syn- (with) and *ekdoche* (sense, interpretation).
    51. See 3.18.279–80.

CHAPTER 18

Of sensable[1] *figures altering and affecting the*
mind by alteration of sense or intendments°
in whole clauses or speeches

As by the last remembered figures the sense of single words is altered, so by these that follow is that of whole and entire speech,
and first by the courtly figure *allegoria*, which is when we speak one
thing and think another, and that our words and our meanings meet
not.[2] The use of this figure is so large, and his virtue° of so great efficacy,° as it is supposed no man can pleasantly utter and persuade without it, but in effect is sure never or very seldom to thrive and prosper
in the world, that cannot skillfully° put in ure[3]—insomuch as° not
only every common courtier, but also the gravest counselor, yea, and

1. **sensable** generally, figures of speech
that alter the meaning of words or groups of
words; i.e., tropes.
    2. On *allegoria*, see Susenbrotus 12–14;
see also *Ad Herennium* 4.34.46; Quintilian

8.6.44–58,   9.2.46;   Sherry   45;   Peacham
(1577) D1r; Wilson 201.19–32; Day 79;
Hoskins 9.
    3. **ure** use.

the most noble and wisest prince of them all are many times enforced to use it, by example (say they) of the great emperor who had it usually in his mouth to say, *Qui nescit dissimulare nescit regnare.*[4] Of this figure, therefore, which for his duplicity we call the Figure of False Semblant[5] or Dissimulation, we will speak first, as of the chief ringleader[6] and captain of all other figures either in the poetical or oratory science.°

And ye shall know that we may dissemble, I mean speak otherwise than we think, in earnest as well as in sport;° under covert and dark° terms, and in learned and apparent[7] speeches; in short sentences, and by long ambage and circumstance[8] of words; and finally, as well when we lie as when we tell truth. To be short, every speech wrested from his own natural signification to another not altogether so natural is a kind of dissimulation, because the words bear contrary countenance to the intent. But properly, and in his principal virtue,° *allegoria* is when we do speak in sense translative[9] and wrested from the own[10] signification, nevertheless applied to another not altogether contrary, but having much conveniency° with it, as before we said of the *metaphor.*[11] As, for example, if we should call the commonwealth a ship, the prince a pilot, the counselors mariners, the storms wars, the calm and haven peace, this is spoken all in *allegory.*[12] And because such inversion[13] of sense in one single word is by[14] the figure *metaphor*, of whom we spake before, and this manner of inversion extending to whole and large speeches, it maketh the figure *allegory* to be called a long and perpetual *metaphor*.

A nobleman, after a whole year's absence from his lady, sent to know how she did, and whether she remained affected° toward him as she was when he left her:

> *Lovely Lady, I long full sore to hear*
> *If ye remain the same I left you the last year.*

Allegoria, or the Figure of False Semblant

4. "He who does not know how to dissimulate, does not know how to rule." Though in Latin, this saying is not classical and was usually credited to the French King Louis XI in the Renaissance. See LN 12.

5. **Semblant** outward aspect or appearance. Faus-Semblant is an allegorical character who appears in *The Romance of the Rose*, a thirteenth-century allegory by Guillaume de Lorris and Jean de Meun of which Chaucer produced a fragmentary translation. A Middle English text was first printed as Chaucer's in the Thynne edition of 1532 (though the larger part of it—the so-called Fragment B, written in a northern dialect—is now rejected by scholars as non-Chaucerian). Puttenham might also have read it in Stow's edition of

1561. He alludes to allegorical characters who appear in the *Romance* at 3.19.324.

6. **ringleader** often used in a neutral sense in the sixteenth century; see, for instance, Hoby 20, 277.

7. **apparent** clear.

8. **ambage, circumstance** roundabout or indirect speech.

9. **translative** metaphorical (*translatio* is Latin for the Greek *metaphora*).

10. **the own** i.e., its own.

11. See 3.17.262–63.

12. The allegory of the ship of state can be found in Quintilian (8.6.44), who takes it from Horace, *Odes* 1.14.

13. **inversion** transposition, transfer.

14. **by** i.e., effected by

To whom she answered in *allegory* other two verses:

> *My loving Lord, I will well that ye wist°*
> *The thread is spun that never shall untwist.†*

Meaning that her love was so steadfast and constant toward him as no time or occasion could alter it.

Vergil, in his shepherdly poems called *Eclogues*, used a rustical but fit *allegory* for the purpose thus:

> *Claudite iam rivos pueri sat prata biberunt.*[15]

Which I English thus:

> *Stop up your streams (my lads); the meads have drunk their fill.*

As much to say, "Leave off now, ye have talked of the matter enough." For the shepherd's guise in many places is by opening certain sluices to water their pastures, so as° when they are wet enough, they shut them again; this application is full allegoric.

Ye have another manner of *allegory*, not full, but mixed, as he that wrote thus:

> *The clouds of care have cover'd all my coast.*
> *The storms of strife do threaten to appear.*
> *The waves of woe, wherein my ship is tossed,*
> *Have broke the banks, where lay my life so dear.*
> *Chips of ill chance are fallen amidst my choice,*
> *To mar the mind that meant for to rejoice.*[16]

I call him not a full *allegory* but mixed, because he discovers° withal° what the "cloud," "storm," "wave," and the rest are, which in a full *allegory* should not be discovered,° but left at large[17] to the reader's judgment and conjecture.

Enigma,
or the
Riddle

We dissemble again under covert and dark° speeches when we speak by way of riddle (*enigma*), of which the sense can hardly be picked out but by the party's own assoil.[18] As he that said:

> *It is my mother well I wot,°*
> *And yet the daughter that I begot.*[19]

Meaning it by[20] the ice which is made of frozen water: the same, being molten by the sun or fire, makes water again.

---

15. *Eclogues* 3.111.
16. See Gascoigne, *The Adventures of Master F. J.* 161.25–30.
17. **at large** open.
18. **assoil** solution, explanation. This usage also appears in the *Partheniades*; Puttenham so labels the answer to the riddle of *Partheniades* 7 ("Euterpe"): 177–82, and the following

"assoile at large, moralized in three Dizaynes" (183–212). On *enigma*, see Susenbrotus 14; see also Quintilian 8.6.52–53; Sherry 45; Peacham (1577) D2r, (1593) 27–29; Day 80.
19. Cf. Susenbrotus 14.
20. **Meaning it by** In early modern English this phrase was syntactically nondistinct from the correlative "meaning by it."

My mother had an old woman in her nursery who in the winter nights would put us forth many pretty riddles, whereof this is one:

> *I have a thing and rough it is*
> *And in the midst a hole iwis;*[21]
> *There came a young man with his gin,*[22]
> *And he put it a handful in.*[23]

The good old gentlewoman would tell us that were children how it was meant by a furred glove. Some other naughty body would peradventure° have construed it not half so mannerly. The riddle is pretty but that it holds too much of the *cacemphaton*, or foul speech, and may be drawn to a reprobate sense.[24]

We dissemble after a sort when we speak by common proverbs,[25] or, as we use to call them, old said saws, as thus: *Paroemia, or Proverb*

> *As the old cock crows so doth the chick.*[26]
> *A bad cook that cannot his own fingers lick.*[27]

Meaning by the first, that the young learn by the old, either to be good or evil in their behaviors; by the second, that he is not to be counted a wise man, who, being in authority and having the administration of many good and great things, will not serve his own turn and his friends' whilst he may. And many such proverbial speeches, as "Totnes is turned French,"[28] for a strange° alteration; "Scarborough warning,"[29] for a sudden commandment, allowing no respect or delay to bethink a man of his business. Note nevertheless a diversity, for the two last examples be proverbs, the two first proverbial speeches.

Ye do likewise dissemble when ye speak in derision or mockery, and that may be many ways: as sometime in sport,° sometime in earnest, and privily, and apertly,[30] and pleasantly, and bitterly. But first by the figure *ironia*, which we call the Dry Mock.[31] As he that said to a bragging ruffian that threatened he would kill and slay, "no doubt you are a *Ironia, or the Dry Mock*

---

21. **iwis** indeed, truly (often with weakened sense as a metrical tag).

22. **gin** skill, cunning; tool, instrument (engine).

23. A version of these lines appears in Cambridge University Library MS. Dd.5.75, f. 63v.

24. **reprobate** morally corrupt. See Puttenham's discussion of *cacemphaton* at 3.22.340.

25. On *paroemia*, see Susenbrotus 14; see also Aristotle, *Rhetoric* 3.11.14 (1413a); Sherry 45; Peacham (1577) D2v, G3v, (1593) 49–50; Day 80. (*Paroemia*—proverbial speech—should not be confused with *paroemion*, which we normally call alliteration; see 3.16.258–59.)

26. Cf. Heywood's *Proverbs . . . concerning Marriage* 1.10.23.

27. Cf. ibid.1.8.89.

28. This proverb xenophobically contrasts a fundamentalist Englishry with offensive foreign corruption, as an "impossibility trope." See LN 13.

29. **"Scarborough warning"** i.e., no warning at all. Heywood says, in his "Brief Ballet [Ballad] touching the traitorous taking of Scarborough Castle": "This term . . . grew, (some say),/By hasty hanging, for rank robbery there" (313). Cf. also Tilley S128.

30. **privily . . . apertly** privately, among intimates, as opposed to openly in public.

31. On *ironia*, see Susenbrotus 14–15; see also Quintilian 8.6.54–55, 9.2.44–51; Sherry 45; Peacham (1577) D3r–v, (1593) 35–36; Fraunce 1.6; Day 80.

good man of your hands."[32] Or, as it was said by a French king to one that prayed his reward, showing how he had been cut in the face at a certain battle fought in his service: "Ye may see," quoth the king, "what it is to run away and look backwards."[33] And as Alfonso King of Naples said to one that proffered to take his ring when he washed before dinner, "This will serve another well": meaning that the gentlemen had another time taken them, and because the king forgot to ask for them, never restored his ring again.[34]

Sarcasmus,
or the
Bitter Taunt

Or when we deride with a certain severity, we may call it the Bitter Taunt, *sarcasmus*.[35] As Charles V Emperor answered the Duke of Aerschot, beseeching him recompense of service done at the siege of Renty against Henry the French king, where the Duke was taken prisoner and afterward escaped clad like a collier. "Thou wert taken," quoth the Emperor, "like a coward, and escapedst like a collier, wherefore get thee home and live upon thine own."[†36] Or as King Henry VIII said to one of his privy chamber[37] who sued for Sir Anthony Rous, a knight of Norfolk, that his Majesty would be good unto him, for that he was an ill beggar. Quoth the king again, "If he be ashamed to beg, we are ashamed to give."[†] Or as Charles V Emperor, having taken in battle John Frederick Duke of Saxony, with the Landgrave of Hesse and others, this duke being a man of monstrous bigness and corpulence, after the Emperor had seen the prisoners, said to those that were about him, "I have gone a-hunting many times, yet never took I such a swine before."[38]

---

32. **of your hands** in a fight. For such irony, cf. Vittoria's response to the knife thrust that kills her: " 'Twas a manly blow. / The next thou giv'st, murder some sucking infant, / And then thou wilt be famous" (John Webster, *The White Devil* 5.6.234–36).

33. Corrozet (62r) ascribes this comment to Louis XII, but the same tale is twice told of the Caesars by Erasmus in *Apophthegmata* 4, "Octavius Caesar Augustus" 19 (LB 4.207D–E, Udall 263) and in *Apophthegmata* 4, "C. Julius Caesar" 29 (LB 4.215D–E, Udall 307). For the first example, see Macrobius 2.4.7; for the second, see Quintilian 6.3.75.

34. Corrozet tells this story about Alfonso V, king of Aragon, and an unidentified servant (76v). Corrozet's version is clearer than Puttenham's. In it, the king wished to wash his hands before dinner and gave his rings to the servant without noting to whom he had given them. When the king did not ask for them back, the servant kept them. Some time later, when the king was again about to wash before dining, the servant stretched out his hands to take the king's rings. The king whispered to him: "Let it be enough for you to have had the first ones, for

these here will be good for another [person]" (*Suffise toy d'auoir eu les premiers: car ceux-cy seront bons pour vn autre*).

35. On *sarcasmus*, see Susenbrotus 15–16; see also Rufinianus, *De schematis dianoeas* 11; Sherry 46; Peacham (1577) D3v, (1593) 37–38; Day 80.

36. No source for this anecdote has been located. Renty was the site of a battle in Flanders, where the army of Henry II of France, led by the duke of Guise, routed the emperor's forces on August 12, 1554.

37. Probably Thomas Howard, third duke of Norfolk (1473–1554), Rous's lifelong family patron, and first among equals on the privy council after Cromwell's fall in 1540. Puttenham repeats this anecdote twice in 3.24, at 361–62 and 375–76. The passage should in all probability read "a knight of Norfolk's": Rous was from Suffolk, not Norfolk.

38. This tale refers to the capture of John Frederick by the forces of Charles V at the battle of Mühlberg on April 24, 1547; this battle gave Charles control over all of Germany. The succeeding interview between the rulers was unusually hostile. The emperor made some form of the "pig" remark immediately thereafter.

Or when we speak by manner of pleasantry or merry scoff, that is, by a kind of mock, whereof the sense is far-fetched, and without any gall or offense. The Greeks call it *asteismus*; we may term it the Civil Jest, because it is a mirth very full of civility and such as the most civil men do use.[39] As Cato said to one that had given him a good knock on the head with a long piece of timber he bare on his shoulder, and then bade him beware: "What," quoth Cato, "wilt thou strike me again?" For ye know, a warning should be given before a man have received harm, and not after.[40] And as King Edward VI, being of young years but old in wit,° said to one of his privy chamber who sued for a pardon for one that was condemned for a robbery, telling the king that it was but a small trifle, not past sixteen shillings' matter, which he had taken. Quoth the king again, "But I warrant you the fellow was sorry it had not been sixteen pound," meaning how the malefactor's intent was as evil in that trifle, as if it had been a greater sum of money.[†41] In these examples, if ye mark, there is no grief or offense ministered, as in those other before, and yet are very witty° and spoken in plain derision.

The Emperor Charles V was a man of very few words and delighted little in talk. His brother King Ferdinand, being a man of more pleasant discourse, sitting at the table with him, said, "I pray your Majesty be not so silent, but let us talk a little." "What need that, brother," quoth the Emperor, "since you have words enough for us both."[†42]

Or when we give a mock with a scornful countenance, as in some smiling sort looking aside or by drawing the lip awry or shrinking up the nose, the Greeks called it *micterismus*; we may term it a Fleering Frump.[43] As he that said to one whose words he believed not, "No doubt, Sir, of that." This Fleering Frump is one of the courtly graces of *Hick the Scorner.*[44]

Or when we deride by plain and flat contradiction, as he that saw a dwarf go in the street said to his companion that walked with him,

---

39. On *asteismus*, see Susenbrotus 16; see also Rufinianus, *De figuris* 4; Sherry 46; Peacham (1577) D4r, (1593) 33–34.

40. Erasmus records a version of this saying in his *Apophthegmata* 5, "Cato Senior" 49 (LB 4.263B). Castiglione tells another (2.77.301, Hoby 163). For its source, see Cicero, *De oratore* 2.69.279.

41. This tale chimes with many stories of the boy king as wise beyond his years. As Loades reports from a much-copied manuscript report of the Italian humanist Petruccio Ubaldini, a visitor in 1552, Edward's court was "bound by an extremely rigid etiquette and permeated by a 'contrived adulation' of the young king. Every ambassador and visitor was expected to comment on the boy's precocity in learning" (Loades 202).

42. Charles's comparative coldness and his younger brother Ferdinand's vivacity were proverbial.

43. **Fleering Frump** Both *fleer* and *frump* are synonyms for a mocking or sneering speech or action. On *micterismus*, see Susenbrotus 16; see also Sherry 46; Peacham (1577) D3v-4r, (1593) 38–39.

44. Udall uses the term to translate the following from Erasmus's *Preface* to the *Adagia*: "*Zeno* beeyng outright all together a Stoique, vsed to call *Socrates* the scoffer, or the Hicke scorner of the Citee of *Athenes*" (xxvi). A reference is possibly intended to the interlude *Hickscorner* (1513–16), whose title character is a scoffer. "Hick" is an early modern diminutive for Richard, used apparently of bumpkins.

"See yonder giant"; and to a Negro[45] or woman blackamoor, "In good sooth, ye are a fair one"—we may call it the Broad Flout.[46]

Or when ye give a mock under smooth and lowly words, as he that heard one call him all to naught[47] and say, "Thou art sure to be hanged ere thou die"; quoth the other very soberly, "Sir, I know your mastership speaks but in jest."[48] The Greeks call it *charientismus*; we may call it the Privy Nip, or a mild and appeasing mockery.[49] All these be soldiers to the figure *allegoria* and fight under the banner of dissimulation.

Nevertheless ye have yet two or three other figures that smatch[50] a spice of[51] the same False Semblant, but in another sort and manner of phrase, whereof one is when we speak in the superlative and beyond the limits of credit, that is, by the figure which the Greeks call *hyperbole*, the Latins *dementiens* or the lying figure.[52] I for his immoderate excess call him the Overreacher, right with his original, or Loud Liar, and methinks not amiss.[53] Now when I speak that which neither I myself think to be true nor would have any other body believe, it must needs be a great dissimulation, because I mean nothing less than that I speak. And this manner of speech is used, when either we would greatly advance or greatly abase the reputation of any thing or person, and must be used very discreetly, or else it will seem odious. For although a praise or other report may be allowed beyond credit, it may not be beyond all measure, especially in the proseman,[54] as he that was Speaker in a parliament of King Henry VIII's reign, in his oration—which ye know is of ordinary[55] to be made before the Prince at the first assembly of both houses—would seem to praise his Majesty thus: "What should I go about[56] to recite your Majesty's innumerable virtues,

Charientismus, or the Privy Nip

Hyperbole, or the Overreacher; otherwise called the Loud Liar

---

45. **Negro** here possibly a gendered term (given the contrastive "or"); cf. *OED* I.1: "An individual (esp. a male) belonging to the African race of mankind." Puttenham's "fair" is of course a derisive pun.

46. On *antiphrasis*, see Susenbrotus 12, 16–17; see also Quintilian 9.2.47–48; Sherry 46; Peacham (1577) C4v, (1593) 24–25, 35; Day 80.

47. **call . . . naught** abuse or decry vehemently.

48. This joke is obscure. The term *master* was often used by superiors to inferiors as a form of top-down deference: when Lorenzo in *The Spanish Tragedy* instructs his henchmen to hang Horatio, he says, "Quickly dispatch, my masters" (2.4.53). Perhaps Puttenham's reply is meant to combine such lexical deference with an implicit (hence "privy") sneer from above, politely addressing the other as a servant.

49. **Privy Nip** surreptitious or covert bite;

hence, a rebuke or a sharp, sarcastic remark. On *charientismus*, see Susenbrotus 17; see also Rufinianus, *De figuris* 3; Sherry 46; Peacham (1577) D4v, (1593) 36–37; Day 80. Cf. 3.4, note 16.

50. **smatch** taste of.

51. **a spice of** a kind of.

52. On *hyperbole*, see Susenbrotus 17–19; see also Aristotle, *Rhetoric* 3.11.15 (1413a–b); *Ad Herennium* 4.33.44; Quintilian 8.6.67–76; Sherry 71; Wilson 208.11–27; Peacham (1577) D4v-E1v, (1593) 31–33; Day 80–81. *Dementiens* (Lat.) means "insane"; Puttenham (or the printer) must have meant *mentiens*, "lying."

53. *Hyperbole* means literally a reaching beyond or over.

54. Compared to poetry, prose is presumably the more down-to-earth everyday medium, less fit for such amplification.

55. **of ordinary** customarily.

56. **go about** labor.

even as much as if I took upon me to number the stars of the sky, or to tell[57] the sands of the sea?"[58] This *hyperbole* was both *ultra fidem* and also *ultra modum*,[59] and therefore of a grave and wise counselor made the Speaker to be accounted a gross flattering fool. Peradventure° if he had used it thus, it had been better and nevertheless a lie too, but a more moderate lie and no less to the purpose of the king's commendation, thus: "I am not able with any words sufficiently to express your Majesty's regal virtues; your kingly merits also towards us your people and realm are so exceeding many, as your praises therefore are infinite, your honor and renown everlasting." And yet all this, if we shall measure it by the rule of exact verity, is but an untruth, yet a more cleanly° commendation than was Master Speaker's.

Nevertheless, as I said before, if we fall a-praising, especially of our mistress's virtue, beauty, or other good parts, we be allowed now and then to overreach a little by way of comparison, as he that said thus in praise of his lady:

> Give place ye lovers here before,
> That spent your boasts and brags in vain:
> My lady's beauty passeth[60] more
> The best of your, I dare well sayn,[61]
> Than doth the sun the candlelight,
> Or brightest day the darkest night.[62]

And as a certain noble gentlewoman, lamenting at the unkindness of her lover, said very prettily in this figure:

> But since it will no better be,
> My tears shall never blin[63]
> To moist the earth in such degree,
> That I may drown therein,
> That by my death all men may say,
> Lo, women are as true as they.[64]

Then have ye the figure *periphrasis*, holding somewhat of the dissembler by reason of a secret intent not appearing by the words, as when we go about the bush and will not in one or a few words express

Periphrasis, or the Figure of Ambage°

57. **tell** count.

58. This is probably Sir Richard Rich (1496/7–1567), whose opening speech for the Parliament of 1536 notably compared Henry to Solomon for prudence and justice, to Samson for strength and bravery, and to Absalom for beauty (Bindoff 3.193). Of Henry's other Speakers, Sir Nicholas Hare (ca. 1495–1557) was graciously noted by the king for an unusually florid closing speech in 1540 (Bindoff 2.296), and might also have spoken as Puttenham reports.

59. **ultra fidem ... ultra modum** beyond credit or belief ... beyond measure or propriety.

60. **passeth** surpasses.

61. **sayn** say (archaic).

62. See Surrey, *Tottel* no. 20.28–33 (Jones no. 12).

63. **blin** cease.

64. See *Tottel* no. 222.23–28 (Anonymous).

that thing which we desire to have known, but do choose rather to do it by many words.[65] As we ourselves wrote of our Sovereign Lady thus:

> *Whom princes serve, and realms obey,*
> *And greatest of Briton kings begot:*
> *She came abroad[66] even yesterday,*
> *When such as saw her, knew her not.[67]*

And the rest that followeth, meaning her Majesty's person, which we would seem to hide, leaving her name unspoken, to the intent the reader should guess at it; nevertheless upon[68] the matter did so manifestly disclose it, as any simple° judgment might easily perceive by whom it was meant, that is, by Lady Elizabeth, Queen of England and daughter to King Henry VIII, and therein resteth the dissimulation.

It is one of the gallantest figures among the poets, so[69] it be used discreetly and in his right kind,°[70] but many of these makers that be not half their craft's masters do very often abuse° it and also many ways. For if the thing or person they go about[71] to describe by circumstance be by the writer's improvidence otherwise bewrayed,° it loseth the grace of a figure, as he that said:

> *The tenth of March when Aries received*
> *Dan Phoebus'[72] rays into his horned head.[73]*

Intending to describe the spring of the year, which every man knoweth of himself, hearing the day of March named. The verses be very good, the figure naught worth if it were meant in *periphrasis*, for the matter—that is, the season of the year—which should have been covertly disclosed by ambage,° was by and by[74] blabbed out by naming the day of the month, and so the purpose of the figure disappointed. Peradventure° it had been better to have said thus:

65. On *periphrasis*, see Susenbrotus 39–40; see also *Ad Herennium* 4.32.43; Quintilian 8.6.29–30; Sherry 44; Wilson 201.6–18 and note; Peacham (1577) Hiv, (1593) 148–49; Day 84.

66. **abroad** into public view.

67. *Partheniades* 4 ("Thalia"): 59–62. Shakespeare's Antony and Cleopatra indulge in a similar practice of appearing disguised in public (1.1.54–56). The reference is, however, based at least in part on Plutarch, *Antony* 29 (where the fact of disguising clothing is specified, only being implied in Shakespeare and Puttenham). It might be argued that Partheniade 4 does not in fact imply disguise, but that the queen's unrecognizability flows from her "serpents head and angells face" (76).

68. Probably there is an omission here: "upon consideration" (?).

69. **so** so long as.

70. **in his right kind** in keeping with its true nature.

71. **go about** labor.

72. **Dan Phoebus'** Apollo's (the sun's). "Dan," meaning "Lord" or "Master" (from Lat. *dominus*), was applied to members of religious orders and extended to knights, squires, and distinguished men generally as an honorific title.

73. See Gascoigne, *The Devises of Sundrie Gentlemen* 25 (237.1–2).

74. **by and by** immediately.

*The month and day when Aries receiv'd
Dan Phoebus' rays into his horned head.*

For now there remaineth for the reader somewhat to study and guess upon, and yet the springtime to the learned judgment sufficiently expressed.

The noble Earl of Surrey wrote thus:

*In winter's just return, when Boreas gan[75] his reign,
And every tree unclothed him fast as nature taught them plain.[76]*

I would fain learn of some good maker, whether the Earl spake this in figure of *periphrasis* or not. For mine own opinion, I think that if he meant to describe the winter season, he would not have disclosed it so broadly as to say "winter" at the first word, for that had been against the rules of art and without any good judgment, which in so learned and excellent a personage we ought not to suspect. We say therefore that for "winter" it is no *periphrasis* but language at large.° We say, for all that, having regard to the second verse that followeth, it is a *periphrasis*, seeming that thereby he intended to show in what part of the winter his loves gave him anguish—that is, in the time which we call the fall of the leaf, which begins in the month of October and stands very well with the figure to be uttered in that sort, notwithstanding winter be named before, for winter hath many parts, such namely as do not shake off the leaf nor unclothe the trees as here is mentioned. Thus may ye judge as I do, that this noble earl wrote excellently well and to purpose. Moreover, when a maker will seem to use circumlocution to set forth any thing pleasantly and figuratively, yet no less plain to a ripe reader than if it were named expressly, and when all is done, no man can perceive it to be the thing intended, this is a foul oversight in any writer. As did a good fellow† who, weening[77] to show his cunning,° would needs by *periphrasis* express the realm of Scotland in no less than eight verses, and when he had said all, no man could imagine it to be spoken of Scotland; and did, besides many other faults in his verse, so deadly belie the matter by his description as it would pity any good maker to hear it.[78]

Now for the shutting up of this chapter, will I remember you farther of that manner of speech which the Greeks call *synecdoche*, and we the Figure of Quick° Conceit,° who for the reasons before alleged may be put under the speeches allegorical because of the darkness° and duplicity of his sense.[79] As when one would tell me how the French king was

75. **gan** began.
76. See *Tottel* no. 18 (1.16.15–16) (Jones no. 16).
77. **weening** thinking.
78. **pity ... maker** i.e., cause any good maker to grieve.

79. On *synecdoche*, see Susenbrotus 7–8; see also *Ad Herennium* 4.33.44–45; Quintilian 8.6.19–22; Sherry 42; Wilson 199.26–200.5; Peacham (1577) C31, (1593) 17; Fraunce 1.8–11; Day 78; Hoskins 11.

overthrown at St. Quentin, I am enforced to think that it was not the king himself in person, but the Constable of France with the French king's power.[80] Or if one would say the town of Antwerp were famished, it is not so to be taken but of the people of the town of Antwerp.[81] And this conceit° being drawn aside and, as it were, from one thing to another, it encumbers the mind with a certain imagination what it may be that is meant, and not expressed. As he that said to a young gentlewoman who was in her chamber making herself unready,[82] "Mistress, will ye give me leave to unlace your petticoat," meaning perchance the other thing that might follow such unlacing. In the old time, whosoever was allowed to undo his lady's girdle,[83] he might lie with her all night: wherefore the taking of a woman's maidenhead away was said "to undo her girdle." *Virgineam dissoluit zonam*,[84] saith the Poet, conceiving out of a thing precedent, a thing subsequent. This may suffice for the knowledge of this figure Quick° Conceit.°

80. A reference to the decisive battle of St. Quentin (August 18–27, 1557), where the Spanish forces of Philip II commanded by Emmanuel Philibert, duke of Savoy (1528–1580), defeated the forces of Henry II of France; this victory (with another at Gravelines in 1558), and civil religious struggle in France, brought about the Peace of Cateau-Cambrésis (1559), concluding Spain's sixty-five-year struggle with France for the control of Italy. The captured Constable of France was Anne, duke of Montmorency. As a consequence of Mary I's marriage to Philip II (July 25, 1554), the duke of Savoy's victory was celebrated in London with processions and bonfires.

81. Antwerp had recently fallen to the army of Alessandro Farnese, duke of Parma, on August 17, 1585, after one of the most famous sieges in military history. There had been considerable dearth and numerous popular riots for bread.

82. **making . . . unready**   getting . . . undressed.

83. **girdle** belt.

84. **Virgineam dissoluit zonam** a Latin translation of the Greek words λῦσε δὲ παρ–θενίην ζώνην, from *Odyssey* 11.245, used of Neptune seducing Tyro. The phrase (with *solvere* rather than *dissolvere*) was the common Latin expression for "to give up one's virginity," as in Catullus 2.13, 61.52, and 67.28. Puttenham probably took the example from the discussion of *synecdoche* in Susenbrotus (8).

CHAPTER 19

Of figures sententious,° otherwise called rhetorical

Now if our presupposal be true, that the poet is of all other the most ancient orator, as he that by good and pleasant persuasions first reduced° the wild and beastly people into public societies and civility of life, insinuating unto them under fictions with sweet and colored° speeches many wholesome lessons and doctrines,° then no doubt there is nothing so fit for him as to be furnished with all the figures that be rhetorical, and such as do most beautify language with eloquence and sententiousness.° Therefore, since we have already allowed to our maker his auricular figures, and also his sensable, by which all the words and clauses of his meters° are made as well tunable° to the ear as stirring° to the mind, we are now by order to bestow upon him those other figures which may execute both offices, and all at once to beautify and give sense and sententiousness° to the whole language at large.° So as° if we should entreat our maker to play also the orator, and whether it be to plead, or to praise, or to advise, that in all three cases he may utter and also persuade both copiously and vehemently.[1]

And your figures rhetorical, besides their remembered ordinary virtues—that is, sententiousness° and copious amplification, or enlargement of language[2]—do also contain a certain sweet and melodious manner of speech, in which respect they may after a sort be said auricular, because the ear is no less ravished with their current° tune° than the mind is with their sententiousness.° For the ear is properly but an instrument of conveyance° for the mind, to apprehend the sense by the sound. And our speech is made melodious or harmonical not only by strained[3] tunes,° as those of music, but also by choice of smooth words; and thus or thus marshalling them in their comeliest construction and order, and as well by sometimes sparing, sometimes spending them more or less liberally, and carrying or transporting of them farther off or nearer, setting them with sundry relations and variable forms in the ministry[4] and use of words, do breed no little alteration in man. For to say truly, what else is man but his mind? Which, whosoever have skill° to compass° and make yielding and flexible, what may not he command the body to perform? He therefore that hath vanquished the mind of man hath made the greatest and most glorious conquest. But the mind is not assailable unless it be by sensible° approaches, whereof the audible is of greatest force for instruction or discipline,° the visible for apprehension of exterior knowledges, as the Philosopher saith.[5] Therefore the well-tuning of your words and clauses to the delight of the ear maketh your information° no less plausible° to the mind than to the ear—no, though you filled them with never so much sense and sententiousness.° Then also must the whole tale (if it tend to persuasion) bear his just and reasonable measure, being rather with the largest than with the scarcest.[6] For like as one or two drops of water pierce not the flint stone, but many and often droppings do, so cannot a few words (be they never so pithy or sententious°) in all cases and to all manner of minds

---

1. Pleading, praising, and advising refer to the three kinds of rhetoric: judicial, epideictic, and deliberative.

2. Amplification was a fundamental goal of rhetorical education in the Renaissance. Erasmus's *De duplici copia rerum ac verborum* (On the Double Copiousness of [Subject] Matter and Words) not only taught students ways to amplify their style in Latin but also reinforced the principle that having "copie,"

or copiousness, was essential for writers in both Latin and the vernacular.

3. **strained** melodic.

4. **ministry** provision, management.

5. See Aristotle, *Sense and Sensibilia* 1.437b4–16.

6. **being . . . scarcest** being (grouped) with the copious rather than the scanty (as the next sentence makes clear).

make so deep an impression as a more multitude of words to the purpose, discreetly° and without superfluity uttered—the mind being no
less vanquished with large load of speech than the limbs are with heavy
burden. Sweetness of speech, sentence,° and amplification are therefore
necessary to an excellent orator and poet, nor may in no wise be spared
from any of them.

And first of all others, your figure that worketh by iteration or repetition of one word or clause doth much alter and affect the ear and also
the mind of the hearer, and therefore is counted a very brave[7] figure
both with the poets and rhetoricians. And this repetition may be in
seven sorts.

*Anaphora,
or the
Figure of
Report*

Repetition in the first degree we call the Figure of Report, according
to the Greek original, and is when we make one word begin, and, as
they are wont to say, lead the dance to many verses in suit.[8] As thus:

> *To think on death it is a misery;*
> *To think on life it is a vanity;*
> *To think on the world, verily it is*
> *To think that here man hath no perfect bliss.*[†]

And this written by Sir Walter Ralegh of his greatest mistress, in most
excellent verses:

> *In vain, mine eyes, in vain you waste your tears;*
> *In vain, my sighs, the smokes of my despairs,*
> *In vain you search the earth and heavens above;*
> *In vain ye seek, for fortune keeps my love.*[9]

Or as the buffoon in our interlude° called *Lusty London* said very knav-
ishly and like himself:

> *Many a fair lass in London town,*
> *Many a bawdy basket*[10] *borne up and down,*
> *Many a broker in a threadbare gown,*
> *Many a bankrupt scarce worth a crown—*
> > *In London.*[*]

---

7. **brave** splendid, gorgeously appareled,
showy (?).

8. On *anaphora*, see Susenbrotus 47–48;
see also *Ad Herennium* 4.12.19; Quintilian
9.3.30, 45; Sherry 47; Wilson 225.16–27;
Peacham (1577) H4v, (1593) 41–42; Fraunce
1.19; Day 84; Hoskins 13. *Anaphora* in Greek
means "carrying back." "Report," in music,
means a note that responds to or repeats another (from Fr. *reporter*, Lat. *reportare*: "to
carry back"). Puttenham's "in suit" metaphor derives from a company of followers
dressed "in suit," i.e., in (matching) livery.

9. See Ralegh 19: no. 15A.9–12. These
lines are from Ralegh's famous verse exchange with Queen Elizabeth (see May, *Elizabethan Courtier Poets* 316–21, for both
Ralegh's poem and her reply, "Ah, silly
pugg"). The quoted lines may be indebted to
a Sidney poem from the *Old Arcadia* (no. 14:
Ringler 38). Puttenham cites again from this
poem at 3.19.285, and from Elizabeth's at
3.19.321.

10. **bawdy basket** hawker of licentious
literature (or perhaps his container of merchandise).

Ye have another sort of repetition quite contrary to the former, when ye Antistrophe, make one word finish many verses in suit, and that which is harder, to or the finish many clauses in the midst of your verses or ditty (for to make Counterturn them finish the verse in our vulgar° it should hinder the rhyme). And because I do find few of our English makers use this figure, I have set you down two little ditties which ourselves in our younger years played upon the *antistrophe*, for so is the figure's name in Greek: one upon the mutable love of a lady, another upon the meritorious love of Christ our Savior.[11] Thus:

> *Her lowly looks, that gave life to my love;*[12]
> *With spiteful speech, curstness,*[13] *and cruelty,*
> *She killed my love. Let her rigor remove,*[14]
> *Her cheerful lights and speeches of pity*
> *Revive my love. Anon, with great disdain,*
> *She shuns my love, and after, by a train*[15]
> *She seeks my love, and saith she loves me most.*
> *But seeing her love so lightly won and lost,*
> *I longed not for her love, for well I thought,*
> *Firm is the love, if it be as it ought.* *

The second upon the merits of Christ's passion toward mankind. Thus:

> *Our Christ, the son of God, chief author of all good,*
> *Was he by his allmight*[16] *that first created man;*
> *And with the costly price of his most precious blood,*
> *He that redeemed man; and by his instance wan*[17]
> *Grace in the sight of God, his only father dear;*
> *And reconciled man; and to make man his peer*
> *Made himself very man. Brief, to conclude the case,*
> *This Christ both God and man, he all and only is:*
> *The man brings man to God and to all heaven's bliss.* *

The Greeks call this figure *antistrophe*, the Latins, *conversio*; I, following the original,[18] call him the Counterturn, because he turns counter in the midst of every meter.°

Take me the two former figures and put them into one, and it is that Symploche, which the Greeks call *symploche*, the Latins *complexio* or *conduplica-* or the *tio*, and is a manner of repetition, when one and the self word doth be- Figure of gin and end many verses in suit and so wraps up both the former figures Reply

11. On *antistrophe*, see Susenbrotus 50; see also *Ad Herennium* 4.13.19; Sherry 47; Wilson 225.28–34; Peacham (1577) I1v, (1593) 42–43; Fraunce 1.20; Day 85; Hoskins 13.

12. This line seems either corrupt or the conclusion of a sentence, the first part of which is not quoted.

13. **curstness** shrewishness.

14. **remove** depart.

15. **train** stratagem, trap.

16. **allmight** omnipotence.

17. **wan** won.

18. *Antistrophe*, in Greek, means literally a "turning around against."

in one.[19] As he that sportingly° complained of his untrusty mistress, thus:

> *Who made me shent[20] for her love's sake?*
>   *Mine own mistress.*
> *Who would not seem my part to take?*
>   *Mine own mistress.*
> *What made me first so well content?*
>   *Her courtesy.*
> *What makes me now so sore repent?*
>   *Her cruelty.*[†]

The Greeks name this figure *symploche*, the Latins *complexio*, perchance for that he seems to hold in and to wrap up the verses by reduplication, so as° nothing can fall out. I had rather call him the Figure of Reply.[21]

Anadiplosis,
or the
Redouble

Ye have another sort of repetition when, with the word by which you finish your verse, ye begin the next verse with the same.[22] As thus:

> *Comfort it is for man to have a wife,*
> *Wife chaste and wise and lowly all her life.*[†]

Or thus:

> *Your beauty was the cause of my first love;*
> *Love while I live, that I may sore repent . . . .*[†]

The Greeks call this figure *anadiplosis*; I call him the Redouble as the original bears.

Epanalepsis,
or the Echo
Sound;
otherwise,
the Slow
Return

Ye have an other sort of repetition when ye make one word both begin and end your verse, which therefore I call the Slow Return, otherwise the Echo Sound.[23] As thus:

> *Much must he be beloved, that loveth much.*
> *Fear many must he needs, whom many fear.*[24]

Unless I called him the Echo Sound, I could not tell what name to give him, unless it were the Slow Return.

19. On *symploche*, see Susenbrotus 50–51; see also *Ad Herennium* 4.14.20; Sherry 47; Peacham (1577) I1v–I2r, (1593) 43–44; Fraunce 1.21; Day 85; Hoskins 13. Both the Greek *symploche* and the Latin *complexio* mean literally an "entwining about."
20. **shent** disgraced, ruined.
21. "Reply" here may mean "folding back on itself" (from Fr. *replier*, "to fold").
22. On *anadiplosis*, see Susenbrotus 49–50; see also Quintilian 9.3.44; Peacham (1577) I3r; Fraunce 1.17; Day 85; Hoskins 12. The Greek word means a "doubling back."

This appears to be the effect specified in Puttenham's definition of the *seizino* at 2.11.176.
23. On *epanalepsis*, see Susenbrotus 30–31; see also Rutilius Lupus 1.11; Peacham (1577) F3r, I2v; Fraunce 1.22; Day 85; Hoskins 14.
24. The first line of Puttenham's pair may well be his own invention, but the second one is a translation of a quip that Macrobius reports the actor Laberius made when playing in a mime before Julius Caesar (2.7.4). Cf. Sidney, *Certain Sonnets* no. 14 (Ringler 143).

Ye have another sort of repetition when in one verse or clause of a verse ye iterate one word without any intermission. As thus:

It was Maryne, Maryne that wrought mine woe.[†]

And this bemoaning the departure of a dear friend:

The chiefest staff of mine assured stay,[25]
With no small grief, is gone, is gone away.[†]

And that of Sir Walter Ralegh's very sweet:

With wisdom's eyes had but blind fortune seen,
Then had my love, my love for ever been.[26]

The Greeks call him *epizeuxis,* the Latins *subjunctio;* we may call him the Underlay.[27] Methinks if we regard his manner of iteration and would depart from the original, we might very properly in our vulgar° and for pleasure call him the Cuckoo-Spell. For right as the cuckoo repeats his lay, which is but one manner of note, and doth not insert any other tune° betwixt, and sometimes for haste stammers out two or three of them one immediately after another, as *cuck, cuck, cuckoo,* so doth the figure *epizeuxis* in the former verses, "Maryne, Maryne," without any intermission at all.

Yet have ye one sort of repetition which we call the Doubler, and is as the next before, a speedy iteration of one word, but with some little intermission, by inserting one or two words between.[28] As, in a most excellent ditty written by Sir Walter Ralegh, these two closing verses:

Yet when I saw my self to you was true,
I loved my self, because my self loved you.[29]

And this spoken in common proverb:

An ape will be an ape by kind,° *as they say,*
Though that ye clad him all in purple array.[30]

---

25. **stay** prop, support.

26. See Ralegh 19: no. 15A.21–22 (the second quotation from his poem to the queen: see 3.19.282); for a citation from her reply, see 3.19.321.

27. On *epizeuxis,* see Susenbrotus 49; see also Quintilian 9.3.28; Wilson 207.31–208.4, 224.27–225.4, and notes; Peacham (1577) I3r–v, (1593) 47–48; Fraunce 1.16; Day 85; Hoskins 12. Whereas *epizeuxis* means a "yoking or fastening upon," its Latin equivalent, *subjunctio,* means a "yoking under," which may explain why Puttenham Englishes the figure as the "Underlay."

28. On *ploche,* see Susenbrotus 51; see also Aquila Romanus 28; Peacham (1577)

I2r–v, (1593) 44–45; Day 86. *Ploche* means "weaving."

29. See Ralegh 9: no. 9A.17–18. May notes a similarity in content to Gorges no. 6 (*Ralegh* 29). Line 18 adapts a line in Philippe Desportes, *Les Amours d'Hyppolyte,* sonnet 20 (*Oeuvres* 129). The entire poem was first printed in *The Phoenix Nest* (1593): 80.

30. From Erasmus, *Adagia* 1.7.11: *Simia simia est, etiam si aurea gestet insignia* (LB 2.265A–C, *CWE* 32.72), Englished by Taverner in 1539 (C4v in 1569 ed.) as "An ape is an ape, althoughe she weare badges of gold." Lucian is the original source of the proverb; see "The Ignorant Book-Collector" 4. In his adage Erasmus also cites a story told by

Or as we once sported° upon a fellow's name who was called Woodcock, and for an ill part he had played, entreated favor by his friend:

> I pray you entreat no more for the man;
> Woodcock will be a woodcock,[31] do what ye can.*

Now also be there many other sorts of repetition if a man would use
them, but are nothing commendable and therefore are not observed in
good poesy, as a vulgar° rhymer who doubled one word in the end of
every verse, thus:

> . . . adieu, adieu,
> . . . my face, my face.†

And another that did the like in the beginning of his verse, thus:

> To love him and love him, as sinners should do.†

These repetitions be not figurative but fantastical,° for a figure is ever
used to a purpose either of beauty or of efficacy;° and these last recited
be to no purpose, for neither can ye say that it urges affection,° nor that
it beautifieth or enforceth the sense, nor hath any other subtlety in it,
and therefore is a very foolish impertinence° of speech and not a figure.

Prosonomasia,
or the
Nicknamer

Ye have a figure by which ye play with a couple of words or names
much resembling, and because the one seems to answer the other by
manner of illusion,[32] and doth, as it were, nick[33] him, I call him the
Nicknamer. If any other man can give him a fitter English name, I will
not be angry, but I am sure mine is very near the original sense of
prosonomasia, and is rather a byname given in sport,° than a surname
given of any earnest purpose.[34] As, Tiberius the Emperor, because he was
a great drinker of wine, they called him, by way of derision to his own
name, "Caldius Biberius Mero" instead of Claudius Tiberius Nero;[35] and
so a jesting friar that wrote against Erasmus called him, by resemblance

---

Lucian about apes imitating human dancing
but reverting quickly to their simian nature
when someone tosses them a handful of
nuts; see "The Dead Come to Life" 36. Cf.
1.26.139–40 and Tilley A263.

31. **woodcock** The bird was proverbially
foolish or gullible.

32. **illusion** derision, mockery. The examples of *prosonomasia* Puttenham supplies
are all derisive nicknames, so (following
1589, Arber, and Willcock and Walker) we
print *illusion*. When Puttenham explains the
term, however, he says that the one (the
nickname?) "seems to answer" the other
(the name?); perhaps, then, *allusion* (a reference or likening) is the correct term. The discussion at the very end of his treatment of
prosonomasia combines both ideas: the pairs
of terms he adduces there "*mock* one another

by their much resemblance; and this is by
the figure *prosonomasia*, as well as if they
were men's proper names *alluding* to each
other" (3.19.288; emphasis added).

33. **nick** correspond to, suit exactly.

34. On *prosonomasia*, see Susenbrotus
54–55; see also *Ad Herennium* 4.21.29–22.32;
Fraunce 1.24; Wilson 206.10–27 and note;
Day 86; Hoskins 15.

35. **Caldius Biberius Mero** punning on
calidus (hot), *bibere* (to drink), and *merum*
(undiluted—with water—wine): i.e., Hot-
Drinker-StraightWine. Erasmus records this
pun in *Apophthegmata* 6, "Tiberius Caesar"
8 (LB 4.273C, Udall 359). Udall's text (359)
also inserts the joke in *Apophthegmata* 4,
"M. Tullius Cicero" 51 (which he numbers
as 50) (LB 4.225E); the passage he presents
there (along with his own discussion of the

to his own name, "Errans mus";[36] and are maintained by this figure *prosonomasia*, or the Nicknamer. But every name given in jest or by way of a surname, if it do not resemble the true, is not by this figure, as, the Emperor of Greece, who was surnamed Constantinus Copronymus, because he beshit the font at the time he was christened[37]: and so ye may see the difference betwixt the figures *antonomasia* and *prosonomasia*.[38]

Now when such resemblance happens between words of another nature, and not upon men's names, yet doth the poet or maker find pretty sport° to play with them in his verse, especially the comical poet and the epigrammatist. Sir Philip Sidney in a ditty played very prettily with these two words, "love" and "live," thus:

> And all my life I will confess,
> The less I love, I live the less.[39]

And we in our interlude° called *The Wooer*[40] played with these two words, "lubber" and "lover," thus: the country clown came and wooed a young maid of the city, and being aggrieved to come so oft and not to have his answer, said to the old nurse very impatiently,

---

nickname) does not appear in Erasmus's Latin. (Cicero died before Tiberius was born, as both Erasmus and Udall would have known; some error has supervened.) For the original, see Suetonius, *Tiberius* 42.

36. **Errans mus** "erring (or wandering) mouse." The source for this joke has not been traced, but Erasmus did write to Girolamo Aleandro, bishop of Brindisi, that "in Rome they call me Errasmus" ("You err, mouse"; *CWE* (*Correspondence*) 10.358 (no. 1482:53; September 2, 1524). (For the original, see *Opus epistolarum* 5.530.) In his critique of Erasmus's edition of the New Testament, published in Rome in 1522 and 1524, Diego López Zúñiga, who coined this nickname, suggested that "Arasmus" ("You plow, mouse," hence, "You are a plowman or peasant, mouse") would also be appropriate (*CWE* 10.358, note 28).

37. **Copronymus** "he whose name is dung," a byname given the emperor by theological enemies, who invented the story of the baptism to explain it. No source for Puttenham's knowledge of this matter has been traced.

38. On *antonomasia*, see Susenbrotus 9–10; see also *Ad Herennium* 4.31.42; Quintilian 8.6.29–30; Sherry 44; Peacham (1577) C3v, (1593) 22–23; Day 79. Puttenham's statement of the difference between "*antonomasia* and *prosonomasia*" is confusing, partly owing to the tropes' similarity,

and partly to his inversion of the order of the *terms* in his final summary phrase here, from that of the *examples* preceding. Technically speaking: (1) The Tiberius and Erasmus jokes *play on* the names (punningly, i.e., by *resemblance*: see "if it do not resemble the true," above), transforming them into insults. *Prosonomasia* (from Greek *pros*, "to," and *onomos*, "name") was usually assimilated to *paronomasia* (from Greek *para*, "alongside," and *onomos*, "name": "to alter slightly in naming"), normally a matter of using words that sound alike but that differ in meaning (punning). The first two insults, of Tiberius and Erasmus, are puns, *paronomasias*. (2) The Constantine insult *adds an epithet*, to be treated as part of, coextensive with, the name. *Antonomasia* (from Greek *anti*, "instead," and *onomos*, "name") usually consists of substituting a descriptive phrase for a proper name, or substituting a proper name for a quality associated with it. The third insult, of Constantine, is antonomastic, by *addition* (of the non-punning epithet) rather than by *substitution*.

39. From *Certain Sonnets* no. 27: "To the tune of a Neapolitan Vilanell" (Ringler 157: 39–40). This quotation appears to be the first occurrence of this poem in print; Puttenham would have seen it in manuscript sources.

40. We provide Puttenham's speech headings in their original marginal location.

Wooer

Ich[41] *pray you, good mother, tell our young dame*
Whence I am come and what is my name;
I cannot come a-wooing every day.

Quoth the nurse:

Nurse

They be lubbers,[42] *not lovers, that so use to say.* *

Or as one replied to his mistress's charging him with some disloyalty towards her:

Prove[43] *me, madam, ere ye fall to reprove;*
Meek[44] *minds should rather excuse than accuse.* *[45]

Here the words "prove" and "reprove," "excuse" and "accuse," do pleasantly encounter, and (as it were) mock one another by their much resemblance; and this is by the figure *prosonomasia*, as well as if they were men's proper names alluding to each other.

Traductio, or the Tranlacer

Then have ye a figure which the Latins call *traductio*, and I the Tranlacer: which is when ye turn and tranlace a word into many sundry shapes, as the tailor doth his garment, and after that sort do play with him in your ditty.[46] As thus:

Who lives in love, his life is full of fears
To lose his love, livelode,[47] *or liberty,*
But lively spirits, that young and reckless be,
Think that there is no living like to theirs.†[48]

Or as one who much gloried in his own wit,° whom Persius taxed in a verse very pithily and pleasantly, thus:

Scire tuum nihil est nisi te scire, hoc sciat alter.[49]

Which I have turned into English, not so briefly but more at large,° of purpose the better to declare the nature of the figure, as thus:

41. **Ich** I (dialectal).
42. **lubbers** louts.
43. **Prove** test.
44. **Meek** gentle, compassionate.
45. These lines are identified as Puttenham's own at 2.18.217.
46. On *traductio*, see Susenbrotus 52; see also *Ad Herennium* 4.14.20–21; Quintilian 9.3.42; Sherry 48; Peacham (1577) I3v–I4r, (1593) 49; Fraunce 1.25; Day 86. Citing this passage, *OED* defines the term *tranlace* as "to repeat a word in the shape of its various derivatives or cognates." Puttenham's term also suggests an effect of "lacing" the elements of the poem together (with the varied but repeated word), which corresponds with his frequent concern for "band."

47. **livelode** inheritance or livelihood; perhaps chosen for metrical reasons.
48. This poem perhaps bears some relation to Robert Southwell's "Lifes death, loues life," not printed till 1595 (see Southwell 54), but available in MS form (Crum W2120). It begins, "Who liues in loue, loues least to liue."
49. Persius 1.27: "Is your knowledge nothing unless someone else knows that you know it?" Quintilian cites this example in defining *traductio* (polyptoton), at 9.3.42. Nashe cites and translates Persius' line when condemning writers such as Philip Stubbes, who similarly glories in his own cleverness, but who actually makes "the Presse the dunghill" with such works as *The Anatomie of Abuses* (see Nashe's *Anatomie of Absurditie*, in *Works* 1.20–21).

Thou weenest[50] *thy wit° naught worth if other weet*[51] *it not*
As well as thou thyself, but one thing well I wot,°
Who so in earnest weens, he doth in mine advice[52]
Show himself witless, or more witty° than wise.

Here ye see how in the former rhyme this word "life" is tranlaced into "live," "living," "lively," "livelode"; and in the latter rhyme this word "wit"° is translated into "weet," "ween," "wot,"° "witless," "witty,"° and "wise," which come all from one original.

Ye have a figurative speech which the Greeks call *anthypophora*; I name him the Response, and is when we will seem to ask a question to the intent we will answer it ourselves, and is a figure of argument and also of amplification.[53] Of argument, because proponing[54] such matter as our adversary might object and then to answer it ourselves, we do unfurnish and prevent him of such help as he would otherwise have used for himself. Then, because such objection and answer spend much language, it serves as well to amplify and enlarge our tale. Thus, for example:

Anthypophora, or Figure of Response

Wily worldling, come tell me, I thee pray,
Wherein hopest thou, that makes thee so to swell?
Riches? Alack, it tarries not a day,
But where fortune the fickle list° to dwell.
In thy children? How hardly[55] *shalt thou find*
Them all at once good and thrifty and kind.°
Thy wife? O fair but frail metal to trust.
Servants? What thieves, what treachers[56] *and unjust!*
Honor, perchance? It rests in other men.
Glory? A smoke. But wherein hopest thou then?
In God's justice? And by what merit, tell?
In his mercy? O now thou speakest well.
But thy lewd° life hath lost his love and grace,
Daunting all hope to put despair in place.[57]

We read that Crates, the philosopher Cynic, in respect of the manifold discommodities of man's life, held opinion that it was best for man never to have been born or soon after to die—*Optimum non nasci vel cito mori*[58]—of whom certain verses are left written in Greek which I have Englished thus[59]:

<hr/>

50. **weenest** suppose.
51. **weet** know.
52. **advice** opinion.
53. On *anthypophora*, see Susenbrotus 57–60; see also *Ad Herennium* 4.23.33–4.24.34; Wilson 231.8–28 and note; Peacham (1577) L4v, (1593) 170; Day 87.
54. **proponing** proposing.
55. **hardly** with difficulty.
56. **treachers** deceivers, (sometimes) traitors.

57. The poem versifies, with a few differences, the third example that Susenbrotus gives for this figure (58). Since the example is not said to be taken from a particular source, one may assume that Susenbrotus himself invented it.
58. "The best thing is not to have been born or to die soon": from Erasmus, *Adagia* 2.3.49 (LB 2.503A–B, *CWE* 33.160).
59. Erasmus translated the following pair of poems in his annotation of this adage, in

What life is the liefest? The needy is full of woe and awe;
The wealthy full of brawl and brabbles[60] of the law.
To be a married man? How much art thou beguiled,
Seeking thy rest by cark[61] for household, wife, and child.
To till it is a toil, to graze[62] some honest gain,
But such as gotten is with great hazard and pain.
The sailor of his ship, the merchant of his ware,
The soldier in arms: how full of dread and care?
A shrewd° wife brings thee bate;[63] wive not and never thrive;
Children a charge, childless the greatest lack alive.
Youth witless is and frail, age sickly and forlorn.
Then better to die soon, or never to be born.

Metrodorus, the philosopher Stoic, was of a contrary opinion, reversing all the former suppositions against Crates, thus:

What life list° ye to lead? In good city and town
Is won both wit° and wealth. Court gets us great renown.
Country keeps us in heal[64] and quietness of mind,
Where wholesome airs and exercise and pretty sports° we find.
Traffic° it turns to gain, by land and eke[65] by seas.
The land-born lives safe, the foreign at his ease.
Householder hath his home, the rogue roams with delight,
And makes more merry meals, than doth the lordly wight.°
Wed and thou hast a bed of solace and of joy;
Wed not and have a bed of rest without annoy.
The settled love is safe, sweet is the love at large.°[66]
Children they are a store,° no children are no charge.

Adagia 2.3.49 (LB 2.503D–504C, *CWE* 33.160). *Tottel* contains different translations of them (nos. 151 and 152) by Nicholas Grimald. The poems originate in Greek epigrams of disputed authorship (see Rollins for further data; see also Merrill). The first was said by Erasmus to be the work of Posidippus (probably Posidippus of Pella, fl. 3rd c. BCE, to whom have been attributed some twenty epigrams in the *Greek Anthology* as well as a hundred others preserved in a third-century BCE papyrus) or Crates the Cynic. *Tottel* ascribes it to Posidonius (a Stoic philosopher, ca. 135–51 BCE), but probably mistakes the name. The second poem is associated with a Metrodorus, but though Puttenham calls him "Metrodorus the Philosopher Stoic," there is no certainty as to the identity or dates of the Metrodorus identified as the author of this and another epigram in the *Greek Anthology*. In fact, the same Metrodorus may not be the author of both epigrams, and he is certainly not to be confused with the Epicurean philosopher Metrodorus of Lampsacus. Why Puttenham calls him a Stoic is a mystery, especially in light of the sentiments expressed in the epigram.

60. **brabbles** paltry quarrels.

61. **cark** anxiety, the burden of responsibility.

62. **graze** pasture cattle.

63. **bate** discord.

64. **heal** health.

65. **eke** also.

66. **the love at large** premarital or extramarital love (cf. Puttenham's own life).

> *Lusty and gay is youth, old age honored and wise.*
> *Then not to die or be unborn is best in mine advise.*[67]

Edward Earl of Oxford, a most noble and learned gentleman, made in this Figure of Response an emblem of desire—otherwise called Cupid—which, for his excellence and wit,° I set down some part of the verses, for example:

> *When wert thou born, Desire?*
> In pomp and prime of May.
> *By whom sweet boy wert thou begot?*
> By good conceit,° men say.
> *Tell me who was thy nurse?*
> Fresh youth in sugared joy.
> *What was thy meat and daily food?*
> Sad sighs with great annoy.
> *What hadst thou then to drink?*
> Unfained[68] lovers' tears.
> *What cradle wert thou rocked in?*
> In hope devoid of fears.[69]

Ye have another figure which methinks may well be called (not much swerving from his original in sense) the Cross-Couple, because it takes me two contrary words and tieth them as it were in a pair of couples, and so makes them agree like good fellows, as I saw once in France a wolf coupled with a mastiff, and a fox with a hound.[70] Thus it is: *Syneciosis,
or the
Cross-Coupling*

> *The niggard's fault and the unthrift's is all one,*
> *For neither of them both knoweth how to use his own.*[71]

Or thus:

> *The covetous miser, of all his goods ill got,*
> *As well wants° that he hath, as that he hath not.*[72]

In this figure of the Cross-Couple we wrote for a forlorn lover[73] complaining of his mistress's cruelty these verses, among other:

---

67. **advise** advice.
68. **Unfained** undesired; authentic (unfeigned).
69. Lines 1–12 of Oxford no. 11 (May, *Elizabethan Courtier Poets* 277–78); written by December 1582 (quoted in Brian Melbancke's *Philotimus*, published that year).
70. On *syneciosis*, see Susenbrotus 79; see also Quintilian 9.3.81. It is not clear whether Puttenham is thinking of two animals sharing a leash or interbreeding.

71. This couplet translates Susenbrotus's first example of *syneciosis* (79).
72. Here Puttenham versifies an example in Susenbrotus (79), taken verbatim from Quintilian (8.5.6 and 9.3.64), who has taken it in turn from Publilius Syrus 486. Cf. Shakespeare, *The Rape of Lucrece* 134–40.
73. On such vicarious self-depiction, see Whigham, *Ambition and Privilege* 54–60 and 209, note 55.

> *Thus for your sake I daily die,*
> *And do but seem to live indeed.*
> *Thus is my bliss but misery,*
> *My lucre loss without your meed.**[74]

Antanaclasis,
or the
Rebound

Ye have another figure which by his nature we may call the Rebound, alluding to the tennis ball which, being smitten with the racket, rebounds back again, and where the last figure before played with two words somewhat like, this playeth with one word written all alike but carrying divers senses.[75] As thus:

> *The maid that soon married is, soon marred is.*†

Or thus better, because "married" and "marred" be different in one letter:

> *To pray for you ever I cannot refuse;*
> *To pray*[76] *upon you I should you much abuse.*°†

Or as we once sported° upon a country fellow who came to run for the best game, and was by his occupation a dyer and had very big swelling legs:

> *He is but coarse to run a course,*
> *Whose shanks are bigger than his thigh,*[77]
> *Yet is his luck a little worse,*
> *That often dyes before he die.**

Where ye see this word "course" and "dye" used in divers senses, one giving the rebound upon the other.

Climax,
or the
Marching Figure

Ye have a figure which, as well by his Greek and Latin originals,[78] and also by allusion to the manner of a man's gait or going, may be called the Marching Figure, for after the first step all the rest proceed by double the space, and so in our speech one word proceeds double to the first that was spoken, and goeth as it were by strides or paces; it may as well be called the Climbing Figure, for *climax* is as much to say as° a ladder.[79] As in one of our epitaphs showing how a very mean° man by his wisdom and good fortune came to great estate° and dignity:

---

74. **meed** recompense (i.e., the lady herself).

75. On *antanaclasis*, see Susenbrotus 55; see also Quintilian 9.3.68; Sherry 60; Peacham (1577) K2v, (1593) 56–57; Hoskins 44–45.

76. To make the play on words possible, we retain the same spelling in the second instance.

77. Puttenham's play on "dye" and "die" in this poem may be influenced by a line from one of Heywood's epigrams: "Dyers be ever dyeing, but never dead" (*Proverbs and Epigrams* no. 35, 247). There is, however, no evidence that Puttenham had read Heywood's 1562 collection. Also, the muscular

development of the dyer's shanks, like that of the strong-thighed bargeman imagined by Duke Ferdinand in *The Duchess of Malfi* (2.4.43), may be occupational, if he trod the cloth in the dye (though in Puttenham's poem dyeing and calf development may simply be paratactic, or driven by the rhyme).

78. *Climax* in Greek and *gradatio* in Latin both mean "stairway."

79. On *climax*, see Susenbrotus 77–78; see also *Ad Herennium* 4.25.34; Quintilian 9.3.54; Sherry 58; Wilson 226.13–21, 228.18–28, and notes; Peacham (1577) Q2v–Q3r, (1593) 133–34; Fraunce 1.18; Day 91, 94; Hoskins 12.

His virtue made him wise, his wisdom brought him wealth,
His wealth won many friends, his friends made much supply
Of aids in weal[80] and woe, in sickness and in health.
Thus came he from a low, to sit in seat so high. *[81]

Or as Jean de Meun, the French poet:

Peace makes plenty, plenty makes pride,
Pride breeds quarrel, and quarrel brings war;
War brings spoil, and spoil poverty,
Poverty patience, and patience peace:
So peace brings war, and war brings peace.[82]

Ye have a figure which takes a couple of words to play with in a verse, and by making them to change and shift one into other's place, they do very prettily exchange and shift the sense.[83] As thus:

Antimetabole, or the Counterchange

We dwell not here to build us bowers
And halls for pleasure and good cheer,
But halls we build for us and ours,
To dwell in them whilst we are here.†

Meaning that we dwell not here to build, but we build to dwell, as we live not to eat, but eat to live.[84] Or thus:

We wish not peace to maintain cruel war,
But we make war to maintain us in peace.†

Or thus:

If poesy be, as some have said,
A speaking picture to the eye,
Then is a picture not denied
To be a muet poesy.[85]

---

80. **weal** prosperity.

81. The subject of these lines is unknown, but he is certainly not the well-born Sir John Throckmorton, whose epitaph is cited at 3.17.263–64 and perhaps 3.16.258.

82. Gascoigne records this sentiment as an "olde sayde saw": "Princes pryde is cause of warre alway: / Plentie brings pryde, pryde plea, plea pine, pine peace, / Peace plentie, and so (say they) they never cease" (Additions from *The Posies*, "Dulce bellum inexpertis" 9.5–7; 401). See Tilley P139. Hughey records a variety of examples, the earliest from a fifteenth-century MS of Lydgate (see *Arundel Harington* 2.16). Lying somewhere behind this notion may be both the Wheel of Fortune commonplace, and Polybius' theory of cyclical history (see his

Histories, Book 6), later to influence Machiavelli's *Discourses*.

83. On *antimetabole*, see Susenbrotus 78–79; see also *Ad Herennium* 4.28.39; Quintilian 9.3.85–86; Wilson 228.29–229.9 and note; Peacham (1577) R2r, (1593) 164; Day 95; Hoskins 14.

84. This saying about eating to live is found in Susenbrotus (78), probably following Quintilian (9.3.85).

85. **muet** i.e., mute (original spelling retained for the sake of the meter). Susenbrotus has this example (78), which can be traced back to Horace, *Ars poetica* 361–65, to the *Ad Herennium* 4.28.39, and ultimately to Simonides (6th c. BCE), according to Plutarch, "On the Fame of the Athenians" (*Moralia* 3.346F).

Or as the philosopher Musonius wrote:

> *With pleasure if we work unhonestly and ill,*
> *The pleasure passeth, the bad it bideth still:*
> *Well if we work with travail°* and with pains,
> *The pain passeth and still the good remains.*[86]

A witty° fellow in Rome wrote under the image of Caesar the Dictator these two verses in Latin, which, because they are spoken by this Figure of Counterchange, I have turned into a couple of English verses very well keeping the grace of the figure:

> *Brutus, for casting out of kings, was first of consuls past;*
> *Caesar, for casting consuls out, is of our kings the last.**[87]

Cato, of any senator not only the gravest but also the promptest and wittiest in any evil scoff, misliking greatly the engrossing of offices in Rome that one man should have many at once, and a great number go without that were as able men, said thus by Counterchange:

> *It seems your offices are very little worth,*
> *Or very few of you worthy of offices.*[88]

Again:

> *In trifles earnest as any man can be,*
> *In earnest matters no such trifler as he.*[89]

Insultatio,
or the
Disdainful   Ye have another figure much like to the *sarcasmus* or Bitter Taunt we spake of before, and is when with proud and insolent words we do upbraid a man, or ride him, as we term it, for which cause the Latins also call it *insultatio*.[90] I choose to name him the Reproachful or Scorner, as, when Queen Dido saw that for all her great love and entertainments bestowed upon Aeneas, he would needs depart and follow the oracle of his destinies, she broke out in a great rage and said very disdainfully:

> *Hie thee, and by the wild waves and the wind*
> *Seek Italy and realms for thee to reign.*

---

86. Puttenham versifies a saying in Susenbrotus (79), which goes back to Aulus Gellius (16.1), who attributes it to the Roman Stoic philosopher Musonius. The saying was also translated by Nicholas Grimald in *Tottel* (no. 134).

87. See Erasmus, *Apophthegmata* 4, "C. Julius Caesar" 25 (LB 4.215C, Udall 305–6); for the original, see Suetonius, *The Deified Julius Caesar* 80.3.

88. See Erasmus, *Apophthegmata* 5, "Cato Senior" 20 (LB 261B); for the original,

see Plutarch, *Marcus Cato* 8.6 (340d) and his *Sayings of Romans*, "Marcus Cato" 20 (*Moralia* 199b).

89. See Erasmus, *Apophthegmata* 5, "Cato Senior" 18 (LB 4.261A); for the original, see Plutarch, *Sayings of Romans*, "Cato the Elder" 18 (*Moralia* 199A).

90. On *insultatio*, see Susenbrotus 61–62; Day 89. Susenbrotus also notes the closeness of this figure to sarcasm and gives the same example from Vergil.

> *If piteous gods have power amidst the main,*
> *On ragged rocks thy penance thou mayst find.*[91]

Or as the poet Juvenal reproached the covetous merchant, who for lucre's sake passed on[92] no peril either by land or sea, thus:

> *Go now and give thy life unto the wind,*
> *Trusting unto a piece of bruckle[93] wood,*
> *Four inches from thy death or seven good*
> *The thickest plank for shipboard that we find.*[94]

Ye have another figure very pleasant and fit for amplification, which to answer the Greek term, we may call the Encounter, but following the Latin name by reason of his contentious nature, we may call him the Quarreler, for so be all such persons as delight in taking the contrary part of whatsoever shall be spoken.[95] When I was a scholar° in Oxford they called every such one *Johannes ad oppositum*[96]:

Antitheton, or the Rencounter

> *Good have I done you much, harm did I never none,*
> *Ready to joy your gains, your losses to bemoan.*
> *Why therefore should you grutch[97] so sore at my welfare,*
> *Who only bred your bliss, and never caused your care?*[†]

Or as it is in these two verses, where one, speaking of Cupid's bow, deciphered thereby the nature of sensual love, whose beginning is more pleasant than the end, thus allegorically and by *antitheton*:

> *His bent is sweet, his loose is somewhat sour;*
> *In joy begun, ends oft in woeful hour.*[†98]

Master Dyer, in this quarrelling figure:

91. *Aeneid* 4.381–84.
92. **passed on** cared for.
93. **bruckle** fragile, brittle.
94. This example is in Susenbrotus (61–62); it ultimately derives from Juvenal, *Satires* 12.57–59. Puttenham seems to have misread Juvenal, whose poem praises the merchant Catullus precisely because he was *not* covetous.
95. On *antitheton*, see Susenbrotus 69–70; see also *Ad Herennium* 4.15.21; Quintilian 9.3.81; Sherry 56; Wilson 223.24–30 and note. The unspecified Latin term for *antitheton* is *contentio*, meaning a struggle or fight (as does *Rencounter*). *Encounter* could mean the same thing, but also has a neutral meaning.
96. **Johannes ad oppositum** "Contrary John." This sentence is ambiguous. In

modern English it would have a comma after either "scholar" or "Oxford." The former would suggest that Puttenham was probably not a student at Oxford University, the latter that he probably was. Some men studied at both universities. The *Art* seems more likely to derive from the classics-oriented Cambridge of Cheke and Ascham, who taught there in the 1540s, when Puttenham matriculated there (1546).
97. **grutch** murmur, complain.
98. Cf. *Ad Herennium* 4.15.21. The lines work by an archery figure. "Bent" refers to the drawn bow, that is, the initial powerfully extended state (of love); "loose" means the release of the arrow from the bow, and hence end. (Puttenham uses "loose" in this way at 3.16.258.)

> *Nor love hath now the force on me which it once had.*
> *Your frowns can neither make me mourn, nor favors make me glad.*[99]

Isocrates the Greek orator was a little too full of this figure, and so was the Spaniard that wrote the life of Marcus Aurelius, and many of our modern writers in vulgar° use it in excess and incur the vice of fond[100] affectation; otherwise, the figure is very commendable.[101]

In this quarrelling figure we once played this merry epigram of an importune and shrewd° wife, thus:

> *My neighbor hath a wife, not fit to make him thrive,*
> *But good to kill a quick° man, or make a dead revive.*
> *So shrewd° she is, 'fore God, so cunning° and so wise,*
> *To counter[102] with her goodman, and all by contraries.*
> *For when he is merry, she lurcheth[103] and she lours;[104]*
> *When he is sad,° she sings, or laughs it out by hours.*
> *Bid her be still, her tongue to talk shall never cease;*
> *When she should speak and please, for spite she holds her peace;*
> *Bid spare and she will spend; bid spend she spares as fast;*
> *What first ye would have done, be sure it shall be last.*
> *Say go, she comes; say come, she goes, and leaves him all alone.*
> *Her husband (as I think) calls her overthwart[105] Joan.* *

Erotema,
or the
Questioner
  There is a kind of figurative speech when we ask many questions and look for none answer, speaking indeed by interrogation which[106] we might as well say by affirmation. This figure I call the Questioner or

---

99. These lines are the first of Puttenham's four quotations from a poem, "But this and then no more," preserved in an important Elizabethan manuscript miscellany compiled by Humphrey Coningsby (BL, MS Harl. 7392; 22v–23r). For a transcription, see Wagner 468–69 (cf. no. 25 in the Sandison edition of Gorges). Puttenham ascribes the extract quoted here (19–20) to Dyer. He quotes three more times from this poem: 27–28 (at 312, attributing the passage to "Master Gorge"), 5–7 (at 322, attributed to Dyer), and 29–30 (at 323, unattributed). The MS poem, however, is subscribed "FY-NIS.GOR" in the MS, and it also appears in Gorges's own manuscript collection of his verse. We agree with Arthur Marotti and Steven W. May (in personal communications) that it is probably Gorges's. May suggests that perhaps Puttenham "confused the excerpts with Dyer's similar love lament beginning 'He that his mirth hath lost'" (Sargent poem 5, in the same verse form, poulter's measure).

100. **fond** foolish.
101. The Spanish author is no doubt Antonio de Guevara (1480–1545), whose work on Marcus Aurelius was translated twice into early modern English: a version titled the *Libreo Aureo de Marco Aurelio* (1528), as *The Golden Boke of Marcus Aurelius* (1535); and a fuller version, the *Libro del Emperador Marco aurelio con relox de principes* (1529), through an intermediate French version by René Berthault (1540), as *The Diall of Princes* (1557), by Thomas North, the translator of Plutarch's *Lives*. Puttenham might have known either version. Given Guevara's notoriously ornate style, John Lyly is the most obviously affected "modern writer" Puttenham may be referring to here.
102. **counter** dispute.
103. **lurcheth** sulks (?).
104. **lours** scowls.
105. **overthwart** cross-grained, contentious.
106. **which** i.e., that which.

Inquisitive.[107] As when Medea, excusing her great cruelty used in the murder of her own children which she had by Jason, said:

> *Was I able to make them, I pray you tell,*
> *And am I not able to mar them all as well?*[108]

Or as another wrote very commendably:

> *Why strive I with the stream, or hop against the hill,*
> *Or search that never can be found, and lose my labor still?*[109]

Cato, understanding that the Senate had appointed three citizens of Rome for ambassadors to the King of Bithynia, whereof one had the gout, another the megrim,[110] the third very little courage° or discretion to be employed in any such business, said by way of scoff in this figure:

> *Must not (trow*[111] *ye) this message be well sped,*
> *That hath neither heart, nor heels, nor head?*[112]

And as a great princess answered her servitor, who, distrusting in her favors toward him, praised his own constancy in these verses:

> *No fortune base or frail can alter me.*

To whom she in this figure repeating his words:

> *No fortune base or frail can alter thee.*
> *And can so blind a witch*[113] *so conquer me?*†

The Figure of Exclamation I call him the Outcry because it utters our mind by all such words as do show any extreme passion, whether it be by way of exclamation or crying out, admiration° or wondering, imprecation or cursing, obtestation[114] or taking God and the world to witness, or any such like as declare an impotent affection.°[115] As Chaucer of the Lady Cresseida by exclamation:

Ecphonesis, or the Outcry

107. On *erotema*, see Susenbrotus 56–57; see also *Ad Herennium* 4.15.21; Wilson 208.28–209.18 and note; Peacham (1577) L3v–L4r, (1593) 106; Day 87.

108. Susenbrotus, following Quintilian (8.5.6), cites this line from Ovid's lost play *Medea* (57).

109. See Gascoigne, "The complaint of the green Knight" 13–14 (Additions from *The Posies*, 442). "Strive against the stream" (Tilley S927) was an unusually popular phrase; Gascoigne used it no fewer than eight times, as did Daniel, Harington, Shakespeare, Spenser, and many others. Puttenham uses it again in the *Justification* (107).

110. **megrim** migraine.

111. **trow** believe, trust.

112. See Erasmus, *Apophthegmata* 5, "Cato Senior" 37 (LB 262D): when the Romans were sending three legates to Bithynia, Cato noticed that one had arthritis, the second had his head full of wounds, and the third was insane, and he quipped that "[t]he legation of the Roman people has neither feet, nor head, nor heart." For the original, see Plutarch, *Marcus Cato* 9.1. Bithynia's king at this time would have been Prusias I (ca. 228–180 BCE) or Prusias II (ca. 180–149 BCE).

113. **witch** i.e., Fortune.

114. **obtestation** solemn entreaty.

115. On *ecphonesis*, see Susenbrotus 60–61; see also *Ad Herennium* 4.15.22; Sherry 50; Peacham (1577) K4r, (1593) 62–64; Day 89.

> *O sop of sorrow sunken into care,*
> *O caitiff Cresseid, for now and evermare.*[116]

Or as Gascoigne wrote very passionately and well to purpose:

> *Ay me, the days that I in dole consume,*
> *Alas, the nights which witness well mine woe,*
> *O wrongful world which makest my fancy fume,*
> *Fie, fickle fortune, fie, fie, thou art my foe,*
> *Out and alas, so froward*[117] *is my chance,*
> *No nights nor days nor worlds can me advance.*[118]

Petrarch, in a sonnet which Sir Thomas Wyatt Englished excellently well, said in this figure by way of imprecation and obtestation, thus:

> *Perdie,*[119] *I said it not,*
> *Nor never thought to do;*
> *As well as I, ye wot°*
> *I have no power thereto.*
> *And if I did, the lot*
> *That first did me enchain*
> *May never slack the knot*
> *But strait*[120] *it to my pain.*
> *And if I did, each thing*
> *That may do harm or woe*
> *Continually may wring*
> *My heart whereso I go.*
> *Report may always ring*
> *Of shame on me for aye,*
> *If in my heart did spring*[121]
> *The words that you do say.*
> *And if I did, each star,*
> *That is in heaven above. . . .*[122]

And so forth, etc.

Brachylogia,
or the
Cutted Comma

We use sometimes to proceed all by single words without any close or coupling, saving that a little pause or comma is given to every word. This figure for pleasure may be called[123] in our vulgar° the Cutted Comma, for that there cannot be a shorter division than at every word's end. The Greeks in their language call it "short language."[124] As thus:

---

116. See Robert Henryson's *Testament of Cresseid* (407–8), regarded as Chaucerian in early modern England (see Skeat 340).

117. **froward** refractory, adverse.

118. See "The Fruite of Fetters" 25–30 (440).

119. **Perdie** By God (a mild oath).

120. **strait** tighten.

121. **spring** grow, flow forth.

122. See *Tottel* no. 91 (Rebholz no. 77.1–18), where the sentence ends "May frown on me to mar / The hope I have in love."

123. **for pleasure . . . called** i.e., we are pleased to call.

124. On *brachylogia*, see Susenbrotus 52–53; see also Quintilian 8.3.82, 9.3.50; Wilson 205.33–206.3 and note; Day 92.

> Envy,° malice, flattery, disdain,
> Avarice, deceit, falsehood, filthy gain.†

If this loose language be used not in single words but in long clauses, it is called *asyndeton*, and in both cases we utter in that fashion when either we be earnest or would seem to make haste.[125]

Ye have another figure which we may call the Figure of Even, because it goeth by clauses of equal quantity and not very long, but yet not so short as the Cutted Comma; and they give good grace to a ditty, but especially to a prose.[126] In this figure we once wrote in a melancholic humor these verses:

Parison, or the Figure of Even

> The good is geason,[127] and short is his abode,
> The bad bides long, and easy to be found;
> Our life is loathsome, our sins a heavy lode,
> Conscience a curst[128] judge, remorse a privy[129] goad.
> Disease, age, and death still° in our ear they round[130]
> That hence we must, the sickly and the sound:
> Treading the steps that our forefathers troad,[131]
> Rich, poor, holy, wise, all flesh it goes to ground.*[132]

In a prose there should not be used at once of such even clauses past three or four at the most.

Whensoever we multiply our speech by many words or clauses of one sense, the Greeks call it *synonymia*, as who would say, like or consenting names. The Latins having no fit term to give him called it by a name of event, for (said they) many words of one nature and sense, one of them doth expound another. And therefore they called this figure the Interpreter; I for my part had rather call him the Figure of Store,° because plenty of one manner of thing in our vulgar° we call so.[133] Aeneas,

Synonymia, or the Figure of Store°

Brachylogia is Greek for "short language." Puttenham's "Cutted Comma" is a redundancy, since *comma* in Greek comes from a verb meaning "to cut."

125. On *asyndeton*, see 3.16.259.

126. On *parison*, see Susenbrotus 53; see also *Ad Herennium* 4.20.27; Sherry 57; Wilson 227.35–228.6 and note; Peacham (1577) K1r–v, (1593) 58–59; Day 86.

127. **geason** rare, uncommon.

128. **curst** fierce, cross.

129. **privy** inward.

130. **round** whisper.

131. **troad** i.e., trod.

132. These unhopeful lines of Puttenham's bear comparison with similar ones from *Partheniades* 11, cited in the Introduction (27).

133. On *synonymia*, see Susenbrotus 67–68; see also *Ad Herennium* 4.28.38; Quintilian 9.3.45; Sherry 49; Peacham (1577)

P4r–v, (1593) 125, 149, 152, 193; Day 91. Puttenham's statement that the Latins had no word for the Greek *synonymia* appears correct, although none of his sources makes such a claim. Since *Ad Herennium* defines *interpretatio* in a way that makes it mean what we mean by "synonym," and Susenbrotus uses *synonymia* and *interpretatio* as equivalents, Puttenham's choice of "the Interpreter" seems explicable. His phrase "name of event" is puzzling, however. He may be saying that since a synonym is, in a sense, an *interpretation* or explanation of the word with which it is synonymous, then the synonym can be seen as a word (a noun or "name") that is the outcome ("event") of the word with which it is synonymous. We normally think of synonyms as being (simultaneous) equivalents, but Puttenham, like the rhetoricians he is dependent on here, is talking about one word explaining another *in succession*.

asking whether his captain Orontes were dead or alive, used this store°
of speeches all to one purpose:

> Is he alive,
> Is he as I left him, queaving[134] and quick,°
> And hath he not yet given up the ghost,
> Among the rest of those that I have lost?[135]

Or if it be in single words, then thus:

> What is become of that beautiful face,
> Those lovely looks, that favor amiable,°
> Those sweet features, and visage full of grace,
> That countenance which is alonely[136] able
> To kill and cure?[†]

Ye see that all these words—"face," "looks," "favor," "features," "visage," "countenance"—are in sense but all one. Which store° nevertheless doth much beautify and enlarge[137] the matter. So said another:

> My faith, my hope, my trust, my God, and eke my guide,
> Stretch forth thy hand to save the soul, what ere the body bide.[138]

Here "faith," "hope," and "trust" be words of one effect, allowed to us
by this Figure of Store.°

Metanoia,
or the
Penitent

　　Otherwhiles[139] we speak and be sorry for it, as if we had not well spoken, so that we seem to call in our word again and to put in another fitter for the purpose, for which respects the Greeks called this manner of
speech the Figure of Repentance; then, for that upon repentance commonly follows amendment,° the Latins called it the Figure of Correction, in that the speaker seemeth to reform that which was said
amiss.[140] I, following the Greek original, choose to call him the Penitent, or Repentant; and singing in honor of the Maiden Queen, meaning
to praise her for her greatness of courage,[141] overshooting myself, called
it first by the name of pride; then, fearing lest fault might be found
with that term, by and by[142] turned this word "pride" to "praise,"

---

134. **queaving** throbbing with life.
135. Puttenham here follows Susenbrotus in conflating two distinct passages
from the *Aeneid*. In one, Andromache asks
Aeneas about his son Ascanius (3.339);
in the other, one of Aeneas' followers
wonders if Aeneas is still alive (1.546–47).
Erasmus is the ultimate source of the
error (see *Ecclesiastae*, in LB 5.976A),
which derives from the fact that the second
halves of *Aeneid* 3.339 and 1.546 are identical.
136. **alonely** by itself alone.
137. **enlarge** develop copiously.

138. See *Tottel* no. 184.25–26 (Anonymous). "Eke" means also.
139. **Otherwhiles** on other occasions.
140. On *metanoia*, see Susenbrotus 73;
see also *Ad Herennium* 4.26.36; Quintilian
9.2.18, 9.3.89; Wilson 211.10–32; Peacham
(1577) R3r, (1593) 173; Day 94. *Metanoia*
means "repentance" in Greek.
141. **courage** Puttenham probably means
to allude here to Aristotle's *megalopsychia*
(greatness of spirit; *Nicomachean Ethics* 4.3
[1123a22–1125a38]), as well as to vigor,
pride, and bravery.
142. **by and by** immediately.

resembling[143] her Majesty to the lion, being her own noble armory,[144] which by a sly construction purporteth magnanimity. Thus in the latter end of a Partheniade:

> *O peerless you, or else no one alive,*
> *Your pride serves you to seize them all alone:*
> *Not pride, madam, but praise of the lion,*
> *To conquer all and be conquered by none.*[145]

And in another Partheniade thus insinuating her Majesty's great constancy in refusal of all marriages offered her, thus:

> *Her heart is hid, none may it see,*
> *Marble or flint folk ween*[146] *it be.*

Which may imply rigor and cruelty, then correcteth it thus:

> *Not flint, I trow,*[147] *I am a liar,*
> *But siderite,*[148] *that feels no fire.*[149]

By which is intended° that it proceeded of a cold and chaste complexion not easily allured to love.

We have another manner of speech much like to the Repentant, but doth not as the same recant or unsay a word that hath been said before, putting another fitter in his place, but having spoken anything to deprave the matter or party, he denieth it not, but as it were helpeth it again by another more favorable speech, and so seemeth to make amends, for which cause it is called by the original name in both languages, the Recompenser.[150] As he that was merrily asked the question whether his wife were not a shrew as well as others of his neighbors' wives, answered in this figure as pleasantly, for he could not well deny it:

Antanagoge, or the Recompenser

> *I must needs say that my wife is a shrew,*
> *But such a huswife*[151] *as I know but a few.*†

Another in his first preposition[152] giving a very faint commendation to the courtier's life, weening[153] to make him amends,° made it worse by a second proposition, thus:

> *The courtier's life full delicate° it is,*
> *But where no wise man will ever set his bliss.*†

---

143. **resembling** comparing.
144. **armory** armorial bearings.
145. *Partheniades* 12 ("Urania"): 340–43.
146. **ween** believe.
147. **trow** believe, trust.
148. **siderite** lodestone.
149. *Partheniades* 7 ("Uterpe"): 173–74.
150. On *antanagoge*, see Susenbrotus 59–60; see also Aquila Romanus 14. *Antanagoge* (leading up against, raising in

opposition) seems to be a coinage on Puttenham's part; Susenbrotus and Aquila Romanus have *anteisagoge*.
151. **huswife** This word had not yet decomposed into our modern words *housewife* and *hussy.*
152. **preposition** i.e., proposition. This usage comes from an early confusion of *pre-* and *pro-*; see *OED* n4.
153. **weening** thinking.

And another, speaking to the encouragement of youth in study and to become excellent in letters and arms, said thus:

> *Many are the pains and perils to be past,*
> *But great is the gain and glory at the last.*†

Our poet in his short ditties but especially playing the epigrammatist will use to conclude and shut up his epigram with a verse or two, spoken in such sort as it may seem a manner of allowance[154] to all the premises, and that with a joyful approbation, which the Latins call *acclamatio*; we therefore call this figure the Surclose or Consenting Close.[155] As Vergil, when he had largely° spoken of Prince Aeneas' success° and fortunes, concluded with this close:

> *Tantae molis erat Romanam condere gentem.*[156]

In English thus:

> *So huge a piece of work it was and so high,*
> *To rear the house of Roman progeny.*

Sir Philip Sidney very prettily closed up a ditty in this sort:

> *What med'cine then can such disease remove,*
> *Where love breeds hate and hate engenders love?*[157]

And we in a Partheniade written of her Majesty, declaring to what perils virtue is generally subject, and applying that fortune to herself, closed it up with this *epiphoneme*:

> *Then if there be*
> *Any so cankered heart to grutch*
> *At*[158] *your glories, my Queen, in vain*
> *Repining at*[159] *your fatal*[160] *reign,*
> *It is for that they feel too much*
> *Of your bounty.*[161]

As who would say, her own overmuch lenity and goodness made her ill-willers the more bold and presumptuous.[162]

Lucretius Carus, the philosopher and poet, inveighing sore against the abuses° of the superstitious religion of the gentiles,° and recounting

---

154. **allowance** praise, approval.

155. On *epiphonema* (*acclamatio*), see Susenbrotus 92; see also Quintilian 8.5.11; Peacham (1577) L2v–L3r, (1593) 104; Day 98; Hoskins 34–35. "Surclose" means "final close" (Puttenham's coinage).

156. This example (*Aeneid* 1.33) occurs in the passages in Quintilian and Susenbrotus cited in the preceding note.

157. These are the final lines of Sidney's

Old Arcadia no. 61, a sonnet (Ringler 85).

158. **grutch At** begrudge, complain of.

159. **repining at** expressing discontent with.

160. **fatal** destined.

161. *Partheniades* 6 ("Melpomene"): 119–24.

162. These lines may echo the Mary, Queen of Scots, affair: see 3.20.334–35 and the *Justification* 75–78.

the wicked fact[163] of King Agamemnon in sacrificing his only daughter Iphigenia, being a young damsel of excellent beauty, to the intent to please the wrathful gods, hinderers of his navigation, after he had said all, closed it up in this one verse, spoken in *epiphonema*:

> *Tantum religio potuit suadere malorum.*[164]

In English thus:

> *Lo what an outrage could cause to be done,*
> *The peevish scruple of blind religion.*

It happens many times that to urge and enforce the matter we speak of, we go still mounting by degrees and increasing our speech with words or with sentences° of more weight one than another, and is a figure of great both efficacy° and ornament, as he that, declaring the great calamity of an unfortunate prince, said thus:

Auxesis, or the Advancer

> *He lost, besides his children and his wife,*
> *His realm, renown, liege,*[165] *liberty, and life.*†

By which it appeareth that to any noble prince the loss of his estate° ought not to be so grievous as of his honor, nor any of them both like to the lack of his liberty, but that life is the dearest detriment[166] of any other. We call this figure by the Greek original the Advancer or Figure of Increase, because every word that is spoken is one of more weight than another.[167] And as we lamented the cruelty of an inexorable and unfaithful mistress:

> *If by the laws of love it be a fault*
> *The faithful friend in absence to forget,*
> *But if it be (once do thy heart but halt)*
> *A secret sin, what forfeit is so great,*
> *As by despite in view of every eye,*
> *The solemn vows oft sworn with tears so salt,*
> *And holy leagues fast sealed with hand and heart,*
> *For to repeal and break so willfully?*
> *But now (alas) without all just desert,*
> *My lot is for my troth° and much good will*
> *To reap disdain, hatred, and rude° refuse;*
> *Or if ye would work me some greater ill,*
> *And of mine earned joys to feel no part,*
> *What else is this (O cruel) but to use*
> *Thy murdering knife the guiltless blood to spill.**

---

163. **fact** crime.
164. Lucretius 1.101.
165. **liege** liegemen, followers.
166. **detriment** loss.

167. On *auxesis*, see Susenbrotus 68–69; see also Quintilian 8.4.3; Wilson 226.13–21; Peacham (1577) N4r, (1593) 167; Day 91.

Where ye see how she is charged first with a fault, then with a secret sin, afterward with a foul forfeit, last of all with a most cruel and bloody deed. And thus again in a certain lover's complaint made to the like effect:

> They say it is a ruth[168] to see thy lover need,
> But you can see me weep, but you can see me bleed,
> And never shrink nor shame, nor shed no tear at all.
> You make my wounds yourself and fill them up with gall.
> Yea, you can see me sound[169] and faint for want° of breath,
> And gasp and groan for life, and struggle still° with death.
> What can you now do more, swear by your maidenhead,
> Than for to flay[170] me quick,° or strip me being dead?[†]

In these verses you see how one cruelty surmounts another by degrees till it come to very slaughter and beyond, for it is thought a despite done to a dead carcass to be an evidence of greater cruelty than to have killed him.

Meiosis,
or the
Disabler

After the advancer followeth the abaser, working by words and sentences° of extenuation or diminution. Whereupon we call him the Disabler or Figure of Extenuation.[171] And this Extenuation is used to divers purposes: sometimes for modesty's sake and to avoid the opinion of arrogance, speaking of ourselves or of ours, as he that disabled[172] himself to his mistress, thus:

> Not all the skill° I have to speak or do,
> Which little is, God wot° (set love apart),
> Livelode,[173] nor life, and put them both thereto,
> Can counterpoise the due of your desert.[†]

It may be also done for despite, to bring our adversaries in contempt, as he that said by° one (commended for a very brave soldier), disabling him scornfully, thus:

> A jolly man (forsooth) and fit for the war,
> Good at handgrips, better to fight afar,
> Whom bright weapon in show, as it is said,
> Yea his own shade, hath often made afraid.[174]

---

168. **ruth** pity.
169. **sound** swoon.
170. The 1589 text prints "flea," an ambiguous word. Given the explicit parallelism with "strip me dead" (as of weapons, a dead warrior's hateful fate), the correct reading is probably "flay me quick" (skin me alive). But perhaps Puttenham meant "flee" (i.e., "forsake"), or perhaps he wrote "slea" (i.e., "slay"), misread by the printer as "flea." This last might echo *Tottel* no.

177 (Anonymous), where evil tongues "slea the quick, and eke the dead defame" (130.9).
171. On *meiosis*, see Susenbrotus 75–77; see also Cicero *De oratore* 3.53.202; Quintilian 8.3.50; Sherry 61; Wilson 206.4–9 and note; Peacham (1577) N4v, (1593) 168–69.
172. **disabled** disparaged.
173. **livelode** inheritance or livelihood; perhaps chosen for metrical reasons.
174. Puttenham versifies an example in Susenbrotus (76–77).

The subtlety of the scoff lieth in these Latin words, *eminus et cominus pugnare*.[175]

Also, we use this kind of extenuation when we take in hand to comfort or cheer any perilous enterprise, making a great matter seem small, and of little difficulty; and is much used by captains in the war, when they (to give courage to their soldiers) will seem to disable the persons of their enemies and abase their forces, and make light of everything that might be a discouragement to the attempt, as Hannibal did in his oration to his soldiers when they should come to pass the Alps to enter Italy, and for sharpness of the weather and steepness of the mountains their hearts began to fail them.[176]

We use it again to excuse a fault, and to make an offense seem less than it is, by giving a term more favorable and of less vehemence than the truth requires, as to say of a great robbery, that it was but a pilfry[177] matter; of an arrant ruffian that he is a tall fellow of his hands;[178] of a prodigal fool, that he is a kind-hearted man; of a notorious unthrift, a lusty youth; and such like phrases of extenuation, which fall more aptly to the office of the figure Curry-Favel before remembered.[179]

And we use the like terms by way of pleasant familiarity, and as it were for a courtly manner of speech with our equals or inferiors: as to call a young gentlewoman *Mall* for *Mary, Nell* for *Eleanor; Jack* for *John, Robin* for *Robert;* or any other like-affected[180] terms spoken of pleasure. As in our *Triumphals,* calling familiarly upon our Muse, I called her Mop:

> *But will you weet,*[181]
> *My little Muse, my pretty Mop:*
> *If we shall algates*[182] *change our stop,*
> *Choose me a sweet.**[183]

Understanding by this word "Mop" a little pretty lady, or tender young thing.[184] For so we call little fishes that be not come to their full growth mops, as whiting mops, gurnard mops. Also, such terms are used to be given in derision and for a kind of contempt, as when we say "lording" for "lord," and as the Spaniard that calleth an earl of small revenue *contadilio;*[185] the Italian calleth the poor man by contempt *poverachio,* or

---

175. That is, he is good at fighting hand to hand (*cominus,* from *cum,* "with," and *manus,* "hand"), but better at fighting out of reach—in the term's usual meaning, with missiles (*eminus,* from *ex,* "out of, away from," and *manus*).

176. Like Susenbrotus (76), Puttenham here summarizes a passage in Livy (21.30).

177. **pilfry** petty theft, pilfering.

178. **tall fellow of his hands** stout in combat or at fisticuffs.

179. See 3.17.269.

180. **like-affected** similarly affectionate.

181. **weet** know.

182. **algates** in any case.

183. The sense of these lines is obscure.

184. This is the earliest recorded such usage in *OED.*

185. **contadilio** "little count" (more accurately: *contadillo*).

poverino,[186] the little beast *animalculo* or *animaluchio*,[187] and such like diminutives appertaining to this figure, the Disabler, more ordinary in other languages than in our vulgar.°

This Figure of Retire holds part with the Propounder, of which we spake before (*prolepsis*),[188] because of the resumption[189] of a former proposition uttered in generality, to explain the same better by a particular division.[190] But their difference is, in that the Propounder resumes[191] but the matter only. This Retire resumes both the matter and the terms, and is therefore accounted one of the Figures of Repetition, and in that respect may be called by his original Greek name the Resound or the Retire, for this word *οδοσ* serves both senses, resound and retire.[192] The use of this figure is seen in this ditty following:

> *Love, hope, and death do stir*° *in me much strife,*
> *As never man but I lead such a life:*
> *For burning love doth wound my heart to death,*
> *And when death comes at call of inward grief,*
> *Cold ling'ring hope doth feed my fainting breath*
> *Against my will, and yields my wound relief,*
> *So that I live, but yet my life is such*
> *As never death could grieve me half so much.*[193]

Then have ye a manner of speech not so figurative as fit for argumentation, and worketh not unlike the *dilemma*[194] of the logicians, because he propones[195] two or more matters entirely and doth, as it were, set down the whole tale or reckoning of an argument and then clear every part by itself.[196] As thus:

> *It cannot be but niggardship or need*
> *Made him attempt this foul and wicked deed:*
> *Niggardship not, for always he was free,*
> *Nor need, for who doth not his riches see?*[197]

---

186. *poverachio ... poverino* "little poor one" in both cases, although the first ending is more pejorative (more accurately: *poveraccio*), the second more affectionate.

187. *animalculo ... animaluchio* "little animal" in both cases. The first one uses an Italian or Spanish form of the Latin *animalculus*; the second adds a Spanish (*-ucho*) or Italian (*-uccio*) suffix to make the diminutive.

188. See 3.12.251.

189. **resumption** recapitulation.

190. On *epanodos*, see Susenbrotus 79; see also Quintilian 9.3.35; Peacham (1577) S1r, (1593) 129 (the facsimile misprints as 125); Fraunce 1.23; Day 92; Hoskins 14.

191. **resumes** sums up, recapitulates.

192. *Epanodos* means a "return to a sub-

ject [lit., the way; in Gk. *odos*] from which one digressed or departed." Hence it can mean a Retire (return), in the sense of a return to a place from which one has departed, and a Resound, in the sense of an echoing of a sound already made.

193. See Gascoigne, *The Adventures of Master F. J.* 155.24–31.

194. **dilemma** technically, a form of argument involving a choice between two undesirable alternatives.

195. **propones** proposes, propounds.

196. On *dialysis*, see Susenbrotus 33; see also *Ad Herennium* 4.40.51; Sherry 55; Wilson 223.1–9 and note.

197. Puttenham is versifying an example from *Ad Herennium* 4.38.50.

Or as one that entreated for a fair young maid who was taken by the watch in London and carried to Bridewell to be punished:

> *Now gentle sirs, let this young maid alone,*
> *For either she hath grace or else she hath none:*
> *If she have grace, she may in time repent;*
> *If she have none, what boots her punishment!*[†198]

Or as another pleaded his deserts with his mistress:

> *Were it for grace, or else in hope of gain,*
> *To say of my deserts, it is but vain:*
> *For well in mind in case ye do them bear,*
> *To tell them oft, it should but irk your ear.*
> *Be they[199] forgot: as likely should I fail*
> *To win with words, where deeds cannot prevail.*[200]

Then have ye a figure very meet for orators or eloquent persuaders such as our maker or poet must in some cases show himself to be, and is when we may conveniently° utter a matter in one entire speech or proposition and will rather do it piecemeal and by distribution of every part for amplification sake.[201] As for example he that might say a house was outrageously plucked down will not be satisfied so to say, but rather will speak it in this sort: they first undermined the ground-sills,[202] they beat down the walls, they unfloored the lofts, they untiled it and pulled down the roof.[203] For so indeed is a house pulled down by circumstances,[204] which this Figure of Distribution doth set forth every one apart. And therefore I name him the Distributor according to his original. As wrote the Tuscan poet in a sonnet which Sir Thomas Wyatt translated with very good grace, thus:

Merismus, or the Distributor

> *Set me whereas[205] the sun doth parch the green,*
> *Or where his beams do not dissolve the ice;*
> *In temperate° heat where he is felt and seen,*
> *In presence pressed of people mad or wise;*
> *Set me in high or yet in low degree,°*

198. In light of his character as a sexual predator, it is easy to imagine Puttenham composing these verses in the Whitefriars neighborhood, perhaps with personal involvement.

199. **Be they** i.e., let them be.

200. This example, too, is from *Ad Herennium* 4.38.50.

201. On *merismus*, see Susenbrotus 87–89; see also *Ad Herennium* 4.35.47; Wilson 210.26–211.9; Day 97.

202. **groundsills** the foundation (usually of a wooden building).

203. Puttenham's decade-long quarrel with his niece Anne (daughter of Richard Puttenham) and her husband, Francis Morris, over possession of the family manor of Sherfield may have influenced this passage. One Margaret Marriner, in whose house in Sherfield Puttenham lived during 1571, reported being punished by Morris for her aid to Puttenham: Morris and his men evicted her and pulled down her house. She and Puttenham rebuilt it, only to have Morris pull it down a second time (see May, "Puttenham," *ODNB*).

204. **circumstances** components (possibly a conception from logic or rhetoric).

205. **whereas** where.

> In longest night or in the shortest day,
> In clearest sky, or where clouds thickest be,
> In lusty youth, or when my hairs are gray;
> Set me in heaven, in earth, or else in hell,
> In hill, or dale, or in the foaming flood;
> Thrall or at large,[206] alive whereso[207] I dwell,
> Sick or in health, in evil fame or good:
> Hers will I be, and only with this thought
> Content my self, although my chance be naught.[208]

All which might have been said in these two verses:

> Set me wheresoever ye will,
> I am and will be yours still.°

The zealous poet,[209] writing in praise of the Maiden Queen, would not seem to wrap up all her most excellent parts, in a few words them entirely comprehending, but did it by a distributor or *merismus* in the negative for the better grace, thus:

> Not your beauty, most gracious sovereign,
> Nor maidenly looks, maintained with majesty;
> Your stately port, which doth not match but stain,[210]
> For[211] your presence, your palace, and your train,
> All princes' courts mine eye could ever see;
> Not your quick° wits, your sober governance,
> Your clear foresight, your faithful memory,
> So sweet features in so staid countenance,
> Nor languages, with plenteous utterance
> So able to discourse and entertain;[212]
> Not noble race, far beyond Caesar's reign,
> Run in right line and blood of 'nointed kings;
> Not large empire, armies, treasures, domain,
> Lusty liv'ries of fortune's dear'st darlings;
> Not all the skills° fit for a princely dame,
> Your learned muse with use and study brings;
> Not true honor, nor that immortal fame
> Of maiden reign, your only own renown
> And no queen's else, yet such as yields your name
> Greater glory than doth your treble crown. . . .

And then concludes thus:

---

206. **Thrall or at large** enslaved or free.
207. **whereso** wherever.
208. In fact this imitation is Surrey's: see *Tottel* no. 12 (Jones no. 2); after Petrarch, *Canzoniere* 145 (in its turn indebted to Horace, *Carmina* 1.22, and Propertius, *Elegies* 2.15.29–36). Also translated in *The Phoenix*

Nest (1593), 90.
209. **zealous poet** Puttenham.
210. **stain** blemish by comparison ("All princes' courts").
211. **For** in regard to.
212. **entertain** i.e., entertain others.

Not any one of all these honored parts,
Your princely haps and habits that do move
And, as it were, ensorcell[213] all the hearts
Of Christian kings to quarrel for your love;
But to possess, at once and all, the good,
Art, and engine,° and every star above,
Fortune or kind,° could farce[214] in flesh and blood,
Was force enough to make so many strive
For your person, which in our world stood
By all consents the minion'st[215] maid to wive.[216]

Where ye see that all the parts of her commendation, which were particularly remembered in twenty verses before, are wrapped up in the two verses of this last part, *videl.°*:

Not any one of all your honored parts,
Those princely haps and habits, etc.

This figure serves for amplification, and also for ornament, and to enforce persuasion mightily. Sir[217] Geoffrey Chaucer, father of our English poets, hath these verses following in the Distributor:

When faith fails in priests' saws,[218]
And lords' hests[219] are holden for laws,
And robbery is ta'en for purchase,[220]
And lechery for solace,
Then shall the Realm of Albion
Be brought to great confusion.[221]

Where he might have said as much in these words: "when vice abounds and virtue decayeth in Albion, then," etc. And as another said:

When prince for his people is wakeful and wise,
Peers aiding with arms, counselors with advise,[222]
Magistrate sincerely using his charge,
People pressed to obey, nor let to run at large,°
Prelate of holy life, and with devotion

213. **ensorcell** enchant.
214. **farce** in cookery, to stuff (an animal, a piece of meat) with forcemeat, herbs, etc. *Farce* could simply mean "furnish." No inappropriate tone need be presumed; the sense is, the queen is furnished with all graces.
215. **minion'st** most favorite.
216. *Partheniades* 12 ("Urania"): 304–33. Puttenham's logic seems to have slipped his control, for he appears to say that no one of her excellencies "was force enough" to make her universally desirable. He presumably means the opposite.

217. See 1.31, note 8.
218. **saws** sayings, commands.
219. **hests** commands.
220. **purchase** livelihood; buying; originally, the hunt or chase.
221. The first of three "sayings" printed by Caxton, taken by early modern readers as Chaucerian (though not so ascribed by Caxton); see Skeat 450. Shakespeare's Fool varies it in *King Lear* 3.2.81–94.
222. **advise** advice.

> *Preferring piety before promotion,*
> *Priest still° preaching, and praying for our heal*[223]:
> *Then blessed is the state of a commonweal.*†

Epimone,
or the
Love-Burden All which might have been said in these few words: "when every man in charge and authorities doth his duty and executeth his function well, then is the commonwealth happy."

The Greek poets who made musical ditties to be sung to the lute or harp did use to link their staves° together with one verse running throughout the whole song by equal distance, and was for the most part the first verse of the staff,° which kept so good sense and conformity with the whole as his often repetition did give it greater grace. They called such linking verse *epimone*, the Latins *versus intercalaris*, and we may term him the Love-Burden[224] following the original, or, if it please you, the Long Repeat: in one respect because that one verse alone beareth the whole burden of the song according to the original; in another respect for that it comes by large distances to be often repeated.[225] As in this ditty made by the noble knight Sir Philip Sidney:

> *My true love hath my heart and I have his,*
> *By just exchange one for another given;*
> *I hold his dear, and mine he cannot miss,*[226]
> *There never was a better bargain driven.*
>   *My true love hath my heart and I have his.*
> *My heart in me*[227] *keeps him and me in one,*
> *My heart in him his thoughts and senses guides;*
> *He loves my heart, for once it was his own,*
> *I cherish his because in me it bides.*
>   *My true love hath my heart, and I have his.*[228]

---

223. **heal** health, well-being.
224. **Burden** refrain.
225. On *epimone*, see Susenbrotus 41; see also Longinus 12.2; Isidore 2.21.43. In Greek rhetoric, *epimone* means a dwelling upon a point or argument (*epi-* "upon," *-mone* "tarrying"). Puttenham, however, follows Susenbrotus (41), who defines it as the repetition of a verse in poetry or of an opinion in an oration, and also identifies it with *versus intercalaris* (verse to be inserted), that is, poetry containing repeated elements or lines, or a refrain. Puttenham's "Long Repeat" captures this sense of the term pretty well; his "Love-Burden" seems less legitimate, not only as a translation, but also—possibly—as an unnecessary confinement of the figure to the realm of amatory poetry.
226. **miss** be without.
227. A corruption: the hearts have been exchanged. Ringler prints "His" for "My."

228. These lines come from the song of Charita in the third book of the *Old Arcadia* (no. 45), a pair with no. 46 (Dametas's reply; Ringler 75–76). (The use of line 1 as a refrain in the version Puttenham supplies here, which is not in the *OA* version, suggests that Sidney's poem was set to music before 1589.) Such linkage of stanzas or poems by repeated lines or words falls generally under the rubric of concatenation or chaining (in rhetoric, *anadiplosis*, Gk. "doubled back"). The Sidney pair is a specimen of *rime serpentine* (see also Ovid, *Fasti* 2.235, and *OA* no. 72 and *Astrophil and Stella* no. 24 [Ringler 113–16 and 176–77]), where repeated lines or words bind stanzas or the beginning and end of a poem together. This pattern appears early in the Italian sonnet (in a series by Fazio degli Uberti, ca. 1305–ca. 1367) as a *corona* (a bound sonnet sequence), and famously in 1588 in Annibale Caro's nine-poem *corona* (perhaps known to

Many times our poet is carried by some occasion to report of a thing that is marvelous, and then he will seem not to speak it simply but with some sign of admiration.°[229] As in our interlude° called the *Wooer:*

Paradoxon, or the Wonderer

> *I wonder much to see so many husbands thrive,*
> *That have but little wit, before they come to wive,*
> *For one would easily ween,[230] who so hath little wit,*
> *His wife to teach it him, were a thing much unfit.* *

Or as Cato the Roman senator said one day merrily to his companion that walked with him, pointing his finger to a young unthrift in the street who lately before had sold his patrimony of a goodly quantity of salt marshes lying near unto Capua shore:

> *Now is it not a wonder to behold,*
> *Yonder gallant scarce twenty winter old,*
> *By might (mark ye) able to do more*
> *Than the main sea that batters on his shore?*
> *For what the waves could never wash away,*
> *This proper youth hath wasted in a day.[231]*

Not much unlike the Wonderer have ye another figure called the Doubtful, because oftentimes we will seem to cast perils and make doubt of things, when by a plain manner of speech we might affirm or deny him.[232] As thus of a cruel mother who murdered her own child:

Aporia, or the Doubtful

> *Whether the cruel mother were more to blame,*
> *Or the shrewd° child come of so curst[233] a dame,*
> *Or whether some smatch[234] of the father's blood,*
> *Whose kin were never kind° nor never good.*
> *Moved her thereto, etc.[235]*

This manner of speech is used when we will not seem, either for manner sake[236] or to avoid tediousness, to trouble the judge or hearer

Epitropis, or the Figure of Reference

Chapman and Donne). Gascoigne was the first English poet to thus bind sonnets together (in *The Devises of Sundrie Gentlemen* 61, the seven-sonnet sequence beginning "In haste, post haste, when first my wandring minde," 278); Chapman also wrote a *corona* (in 1595), but Donne's *La Corona* (ca. 1610) is the most famous English example.

229. On *paradoxon*, see Susenbrotus 63; see also Quintilian 4.1.40; Day 90.

230. **ween** know.

231. For this anecdote, see Erasmus, *Apophthegmata* 5, "Cato Senior" 21 (LB 4.261B). Two very similar versions exist in Plutarch: see "Cato the Elder" 21, in *Sayings*

of the Romans (*Moralia* 199B), and *Marcus Cato* 8.7. None of these versions specifies the selling of marshes near Capua.

232. **him** it. On *aporia*, see Susenbrotus 62; see also *Ad Herennium* 4.29.40; Quintilian 9.2.19, 9.3.88; Sherry 54; Wilson 210.13–25 and note; Peacham (1577) M1v, (1593) 109–10; Day 89.

233. **curst** fierce, shrewish.

234. **smatch** taste.

235. This passage may be a very free development of lines from Vergil (*Eclogue* 8.49–50) cited by Susenbrotus (62).

236. **for manner sake** for the sake of politeness.

with all that we could say, but having said enough already, we refer the rest to their consideration.[237] As he that said thus:

> Methinks that I have said what may well suffice,
> Referring all the rest to your better advice.[238]

Parrhesia,
or the
Licentious

The fine[239] and subtle persuader, when his intent is to sting his adversary, or else to declare his mind in broad[240] and liberal speeches, which might breed offense or scandal, he will seem to bespeak pardon beforehand, whereby his licentiousness may be the better borne withal.[241] As he that said:

> If my speech hap t'offend you any way,
> Think it their fault, that force me so to say.[242]

Anachinosis,
or the
Impartener

Not much unlike to the Figure of Reference is there another with some little diversity, which we call the Impartener because many times in pleading and persuading we think it a very good policy° to acquaint our judge or hearer or very adversary with some part of our counsel and advice, and to ask their opinion, as who would say they could not otherwise think of the matter than we do.[243] As he that had told a long tale before certain noblewomen, of a matter somewhat in honor touching the sex:

> Tell me, fair ladies, if the case were your own,
> So foul a fault would you have it be known?[244]

Master Gorges in this figure said very sweetly:

> All you who read these lines and scan of my desert,
> Judge whether was more good, my hap or else my heart.[245]

Paramologia,
or the Figure
of Admittance

The good orator useth a manner of speech in his persuasion and is when all that should seem to make against him being spoken by the other side, he will first admit it, and in the end avoid[246] all for his better advantage, and this figure is much used by our English pleaders in the Star Chamber and Chancery, which they call "to confess and avoid," if it be in case of crime or injury, and is a very good way. For when the

---

237. On *epitropis*, see Susenbrotus 63–64; see also *Ad Herennium* 4.29.39; Sherry 55; Wilson 230.1–5 and note; Peacham (1577) M4r, (1593) 112.

238. Puttenham may be versifying an example in Susenbrotus (64).

239. **fine** clever, ingenious, cunning.

240. **broad** outspoken.

241. On *parrhesia*, see Susenbrotus 64–65; see also *Ad Herennium* 4.36.48–37.50; Quintilian 9.2.27–29; Wilson 223.31–224.4 and note; Peacham (1577) M2v–3v, (1593) 113–15; Day 90.

242. Puttenham versifies an example in

Susenbrotus (64).

243. On *anachinosis*, see Susenbrotus 63; see also Cicero, *De oratore* 3.53.204 (cited in Quintilian 9.1.30); Quintilian 9.2.20; Sherry 55; Wilson 212.13–20; Peacham (1577) M2r, (1593) 110.

244. Puttenham's example may be based on one in Susenbrotus (63).

245. These are lines 27–28 of Sir Arthur Gorges's poem "But this and then no more" (discussed in note 99). (Cf. Gorges no. 25.53–56.)

246. **avoid** make void, invalidate.

matter is so plain that it cannot be denied or traversed,[247] it is good that it be justified by confessal and avoidance. I call it the Figure of Admittance.[248] As we once wrote to the reproof of a lady's fair but cruelty[249]:

I know your wit,° I know your pleasant tongue,
Your some sweet smiles, your some but lovely lours[250]*:*
A beauty to enamor old and young.
Those chaste desires, that noble mind of yours,
And that chief part whence all your honor springs,
A grace to entertain the greatest kings:
All this I know, but sin it is to see,
So fair parts spilt[251] *by too much cruelty.**

In many cases we are driven for better persuasion to tell the cause that moves us to say thus or thus, or else when we would fortify our allegations by rendering reasons to every one; this assignation of cause the Greeks called *etiologia*, which, if we might without scorn of a new invented° term call Tell-Cause, it were right according to the Greek original.[252] And I pray you why should we not, and with as good authority as the Greeks? Sir Thomas Smith, her Majesty's principal secretary and a man of great learning and gravity, seeking to give an English word to this Greek word αγαμοσ, called it Spitewed, or Wedspite.[253] Master Secretary Wilson, giving an English name to his *Art of Logic*, called it *Witcraft*.[254] Methink I may be bold with like liberty to call the figure *etiologia* Tell-Cause. And this manner of speech is always continued[255] with these words: "for," "because," and such other confirmatives. The Latins, having no fit name to give it in one single word, gave it no name at all but by circumlocution. We also call him the Reason-Renderer and leave[256] the right English word Tell-Cause much better

Etiologia,
or the Reason-
Renderer, or the
Tell-Cause

247. **traversed** contradicted formally (in law, it refers to denying a fact alleged in a previous statement).

248. On *paramologia*, see Susenbrotus 81–82; see also Quintilian 9.2.17, 51; Day 96.

249. **lady's fair but cruelty.** The incoherence of the word forms seemingly preserves either a fossil of partly revised text or a printer's error.

250. **lours** frowns.

251. **spilt** spoiled.

252. On *etiologia*, see Susenbrotus 81; see also *Ad Herennium* 4.16.23–24; Quintilian 9.3.93; Wilson 229.23–26 and note; Peacham (1577) S4r–v, (1593) 184–85; Day 95. *Etiologia*, or more accurately, *aetiologia*, means in Greek precisely what Puttenham says it does (from *aetio*, "to ask or inquire into," and *logos*, "reason or cause").

253. agamos . . . **Wedspite** *Agamos* is Greek for "unmarried," whether single or widowed.

Smith uses its Latinate form "Agamus" in his 1561 work concerning the queen's marriage (unpublished until Strype's *Life* of Smith [1820], but widely read in manuscript): the first part is titled "Agamus, or Wedspite's oration for the Queen's single life."

254. Apparently a confusion of Thomas Wilson's *The Rule of Reason* (1552) with Ralph Lever's *The Arte of Reason, rightly termed witcraft, teaching a perfect way to argue and dispute* (1573).

255. **continued** *1589* clearly reads "contemned," which Willcock and Walker retain. This word's meaning in context is opaque, however: we prefer to emend to "continued," with the following sense: "This manner of speech [the Tell-Cause or *etiologia*] is always continued with [i.e., followed by] 'confirmatives' such as 'for,' 'because,' etc." Alexander emends to "confirmed."

256. **leave** meaning obscure.

answering the Greek original. Aristotle was most excellent in use of this figure, for he never propones[257] any allegation or makes any surmise but he yields a reason or cause to fortify and prove it, which gives it great credit. For example ye may take these verses, first pointing, then confirming by similitudes:

> *When fortune shall have spit out all her gall,*
> *I trust good luck shall be to me allowed,*
> *For I have seen a ship in haven fall,*
> *After the storm had broke both mast and shroud.*[258]

And this:

> *Good is the thing that moves us to desire,*
> *That is to joy[259] the beauty we behold,*
> *Else were we lovers as in an endless fire,*
> *Always burning and ever chill a-cold.*[†]

And in these verses:

> *Accused though I be without desert,*
> *Sith[260] none can prove, believe it not for true,*
> *For never yet since first ye had my heart,*
> *Entended I to false or be untrue.*[261]

And in this distich°:

> *And for her beauty's praise, no wight° that with her wars[262]:*
> *For where she comes, she shows herself like sun among the stars.*[263]

And in this other ditty, of ours, where the lover complains of his lady's cruelty, rendering for every surmise a reason, and by telling the cause seeketh (as it were) to get credit, thus:

---

257. **propones** proposes.

258. **shroud** rigging. See Wyatt, "He is not dead, that somtime had a fall" (*Tottel* no. 72.30–33, Rebholz no. 42.3–6); translated from Serafino's *strambotto* "Sio son caduto in terra non son morto" (*Opere* [1516], f. 120: *Tottel* 2.184). Editors have speculated that these lines refer to one of Wyatt's imprisonments (in 1536 and 1541).

259. **joy** enjoy.

260. **Sith** since.

261. See Wyatt, *Tottel* no. 74.16–19 (Rebholz no. 66.1–4). Rollins suggested that the poem was originally a sonnet, now with two lines omitted after his line 25. Rebholz, however, established that in the Blage MS (Trinity College, Dublin, MS.2.7, pts. 2 and 3) the lines are the first four lines of a twelve-line acrostic, the first letter of each line spelling out "Anne Stanhope." (The Blage MS lead words are Accused / None / Nor / Entended.) Puttenham's version and *Tottel*'s depart from this pattern, but the *Art*'s old spelling of "Entended" (i.e., intended) is retained here in respect of the obscured pattern. Anne Stanhope was either (1) the lady-in-waiting to Anne Boleyn who eventually married Edward Seymour, duke of Somerset and Lord Protector to Edward VI; or (2) the lady-in-waiting's half-brother's wife, also named Anne Stanhope.

262. This obscure line may mean either that as far as her beauty is concerned, no one disputes ("wars") that with her, namely, that she is beautiful; or that as far as her beauty is concerned, no one disputes that it is worthy of praise.

263. See *Tottel* no. 168.15–16 (the first of *Tottel*'s "Poems by Uncertain Authors").

Cruel you be who can say nay,
Since ye delight in others' woe;
Unwise am I, ye may well say,
For that I have honored you so.
But blameless I, who could not choose,
To be enchanted by your eye,
But ye to blame, thus to refuse
*My service and to let me die.**

Sometimes our error is so manifest, or we be so hardly pressed with *Dicaeologia,* our adversaries, as we cannot deny the fault laid unto our charge; in *or the Figure* which case it is good policy° to excuse it by some allowable pretext.[264] *of Excuse* As did one whom his mistress burdened[265] with some unkind speeches which he had passed[266] of her, thus:

I said it, but by lapse of lying tongue,
When fury and just grief my heart oppressed;
I said it, as ye see, both frail and young,
When your rigor had rankled[267] in my breast
The cruel wound that smarted me so sore;
Pardon therefore (sweet sorrow), or at least
Bear with mine youth that never fell before,
Lest your offense increase my grief the more.†

And again in these:

I spake amiss, I cannot it deny,
But caused by your great discourtesy,
And if I said that which I now repent,
And said it not but by misgovernment
Of youthful years, yourself that are so young
Pardon for once this error of my tongue,
And think amends° can never come too late:
Love may be curst,[268] but love can never hate.[269]

Speaking before[270] of the figure *synecdoche,* we call him Quick° Con- *Noema, or the* ceit° because he inured[271] in a single word only by way of intendment° *Figure Close* or large meaning, but such as was speedily discovered° by every quick° *Conceit°* wit,°[272] as by the half to understand the whole, and many other ways

264. On *dicaeologia,* see Susenbrotus 82; see also Rutilius Lupus 2.3; Peacham (1577) M4v, (1593) 115–16; Day 96–97.

265. **burdened** reproached.

266. **passed** put into circulation (a metaphor from coining); perhaps also "let pass his lips."

267. **rankled** caused to fester.

268. **curst** fierce, cross, shrewish.

269. These verses may be based on an example in Susenbrotus (82).

270. See 3.17.270.

271. **inured** operated.

272. **we call ... quick wit** i.e., we call this trope the Quick Conceit because it conveys by a single word a signification that, despite the trope's concision or terseness, is quickly perceived by every vigorous mind (?).

appearing by the examples. But by this figure *noema*[273] the obscurity of the sense lieth not in a single word, but in an entire speech whereof we do not so easily conceive the meaning but as it were by conjecture, because it is witty° and subtle or dark,° which makes me therefore call him in our vulgar° the Close Conceit.° As he that said by° himself and his wife, "I thank God, in forty winters that we have lived together never any of our neighbors set us at one," meaning that they never fell out in all that space, which had been the directer speech and more apert,[274] and yet by intendment° amounts all to one, being nevertheless dissemblable[275] and in effect contrary. Paulet, Lord Treasurer of England and first Marquess of Winchester, with the like subtle speech gave a quip to Sir William Gifford, who had married the Marquess's sister and all her lifetime could never love her nor like of her company, but when she was dead made the greatest moan for her in the world, and with tears and much lamentation uttered his grief to the Lord Treasurer: "O good brother," quoth the Marquess, "I am right sorry to see you now love my sister so well," meaning that he showed his love too late and should have done it while she was alive.[276]

A great counselor, somewhat forgetting his modesty, used these words: "Gods, lady, I reckon myself as good a man as he you talk of, and yet I am not able to do so."[277] "Yea sir," quoth the party, "your Lordship is too good to be a man, I would ye were a saint"—meaning she would he were dead, for none are shrined for saints before they be dead.[278]

Orismus,
or the
Definer of
Difference

The logician useth a definition to express the truth or nature of every thing by his true kind and difference, as to say wisdom is a prudent and witty° foresight and consideration of human° or worldly actions with their events.[279] This definition is logical. The orator useth another manner of definition, thus: "Is this wisdom? No, it is a certain subtle knavish crafty wit.° It is no industry as ye call it, but a certain busy° brainsickness, for industry is a lively and unwearied search and occupation in honest things, eagerness[280] is an appetite in base and small matters."

---

273. On *noema*, see Susenbrotus 93; see also Peacham (1577) V4r, (1593) 180–81.

274. **apert** open.

275. **dissemblable** dissimilar.

276. Paulet's sister Eleanor married Sir William Gifford of Itchell in Southamptonshire. Her death date is uncertain, but Gifford died in 1549 (see Franklyn 67–69). The event described in the tale of the *noema* would thus predate the *Art*'s publication by at least some forty years. (Winchester would then have been in his late sixties, Puttenham in his late teens.) Winchester lived into his late eighties (d. 1572), however, and prided himself on his long memory. Puttenham knew Winchester personally: a legal deposition by John Paulet,

Puttenham's stepson by his estranged wife, specifies that "the said Puttenhm did seale and as his deede deliuer vnto the said late Lo. Marques of winton" a £200 bond for his alimony for Lady Windsor, Winchester's granddaughter (1576; PRO, STAC 5 P1/8).

277. **do so** i.e., do what befits a man.

278. **shrined for** venerated as. The reference to modesty suggests a sexual content to this elliptical story, but why the lady wishes the gentleman dead, as Puttenham explains her remark, remains unclear.

279. **events** outcomes. On *orismus*, see Susenbrotus 82; see also *Ad Herennium* 4.25.35; Sherry 58–59; Day 97.

280. **eagerness** impatient haste.

It serveth many times to great purpose to prevent[281] our adversaries' arguments, and take upon us to know before what our judge or adversary or hearer thinketh, and that we will seem to utter it before it be spoken or alleged by them; in respect of which boldness, to enter so deeply into another man's conceit° or conscience, and to be so privy of another man's mind, gave cause that this figure was called the Presumptuous.[282] I will also call him the Figure of Presupposal or the Preventer, for by reason we suppose before what may be said or perchance would be said by our adversary or any other; we do prevent them of their advantage, and do catch the ball (as they are wont to say) before it come to the ground.[283]

Procatalepsis, or the Presumptuous; otherwise, the Figure of Presupposal

It is also very many times used for a good policy° in pleading or persuasion to make wise[284] as if we set but light of the matter, and that therefore we do pass it over slightly, when indeed we do then intend most effectually[285]—and despitefully,[286] if it be invective—to remember it; it is also when we will not seem to know a thing, and yet we know it well enough, and may be likened to the manner of women, who, as the common saying is, will say nay and take it.[287]

Paralepsis, or the Passager

> I hold my peace and will not say for shame
> The much untruth of that uncivil dame:
> For if I should her colors kindly° blaze,[288]
> It would so make the chaste ears amaze, etc.[289]

It is said by manner of a proverbial speech that he who finds himself well should not wag;[290] even so, the persuader, finding a substantial point in his matter to serve his purpose, should dwell upon that point longer than upon any other less assured, and use all endeavor to maintain that one, and as it were to make his chief abode thereupon, for which cause I name him the Figure of Abode, according to the Latin

Commoratio, or the Figure of Abode

---

281. **prevent** anticipate.

282. On *procatalepsis*, see Susenbrotus 80; see also Quintilian 9.2.16–17; Wilson 213.12–25 and note; Peacham (1577) S3v, (1593) 183–84; Day 95.

283. Puttenham plays here on the etymology of *presumptuous*. The word comes from *presume*, which means to "come before." Hence *presumptuous* means both "bold" and "anticipating," this latter sense also being the meaning of "prevent" in this passage.

284. **make wise** pretend.

285. **effectually** earnestly, explicitly.

286. **despitefully** scornfully.

287. **say nay and take it** i.e., say no but mean yes. Cf. Greene and Lodge, *A Looking Glass for London and England* (1592?) (2.1.46–47). Puttenham's casual reference to a

"common saying" is consistent with the predatory misogyny he displayed throughout his life. On *paralepsis*, see Susenbrotus 79–80; see also *Ad Herennium* 4.27.37; Sherry 59; Peacham (1577) S2v, (1593) 130–31; Day 95.

288. **her colors kindly blaze** paint her to the life ("emblazon").

289. Puttenham's example of *paralepsis* may be an expansion of a brief example in Susenbrotus: *Pudet me dicere, quod istos non pudet facere* (80: "It shames me to say what it doesn't shame them to do"). Puttenham's transformation of Susenbrotus's gender-neutral example (the masculine plural *istos*) is a familiar piece of courtly misogyny.

290. **wag** to move or budge from a place. (We have not located other records of this proverbial expression.)

name.[291] Some take it not but for a course of argument and therefore hardly may one give any examples thereof.[292]

Metastasis,
or the Flitting
Figure, or the
Remove

Now as art and good policy° in persuasion bids us to abide and not to stir from the point of our most advantage, but the same to enforce and tarry upon with all possible argument, so doth discretion will us sometimes to flit from one matter to another, as a thing meet to be forsaken, and another entered upon; I call him therefore the Flitting Figure, or Figure of Remove, like as the other before was called the Figure of Abode.[293]

Parecbasis, or the
Straggler

Even so again, as it is wisdom for a persuader to tarry and make his abode as long as he may conveniently,° without tediousness to the hearer, upon his chief proofs or points of the cause tending to his advantage, and likewise to depart again when time serves, and go to a new matter serving the purpose as well. So is it requisite many times for him to talk far from the principal matter, and as it were to range aside, to the intent by such extraordinary mean to induce or infer other matter as well or better serving the principal purpose, and nevertheless in season to return home where he first strayed out. This manner of speech is termed the Figure of Digression by the Latins; following the Greek original, we also call him the Straggler, by allusion to the soldier that marches out of his array, or by those that keep no order in their march, as the battles[294] well ranged do; of this figure there need be given no example.[295]

Expeditio, or
the Speedy
Dispatcher

Occasion offers many times that our maker as an orator, or persuader, or pleader should go roundly[296] to work, and by a quick and swift argument dispatch his persuasion, and, as they are wont to say, not to stand all day trifling to no purpose, but to rid it out of the way quickly. This is done by a manner of speech both figurative and argumentative, when we do briefly set down all our best reasons serving the purpose, and reject all of them saving one, which we accept to satisfy the cause.[297] As he that in a litigious case for land would prove it not the adversary's, but his client's:

> *No man can say it's his by heritage,*
> *Nor by legacy, or testator's device,°*

291. On *commoratio*, see Susenbrotus 95; see also *Ad Herennium* 4.45.58; Cicero *De oratore* 3.53.202 (cited in Quintilian 9.1.28); Quintilian 9.2.4; Wilson 203.13–20 and note; Peacham (1577) T4r–v, (1593) 152–53; Day 98. *Commoratio* is derived from *commoror*, meaning "to stop, tarry, or reside [in a place]."

292. Puttenham is following Susenbrotus and Cicero here in suggesting that one cannot give examples of *commoratio* because it is not so much an independent figure as a way of writing that flows through an entire speech or portion of a speech ("course of argument") and is thus inseparable from the whole.

293. On *metastasis*, see Susenbrotus 80–81; see also Quintilian 4.2.50; Wilson 207.9–15 and note; Peacham (1577) T3r, (1593) 181–82.

294. **battles** soldiers arranged in battle array.

295. On *parecbasis*, see Susenbrotus 99–100; see also Quintilian 4.3.12–17, 9.1.28 (citing Cicero, *De oratore* 3.53.203); Wilson 206.28–207.8; Day 100.

296. **roundly** directly, briskly.

297. On *expeditio*, see Susenbrotus 94; see also *Ad Herennium* 4.29.40–41; Peacham (1577) T4r, (1593) 186; Day 98.

Nor that it came by purchase or engage,[298]
Nor from his prince for any good service.
Then needs must it be his by very wrong,
Which he hath offered this poor plaintiff so long.[299]

Though we might call this figure very well and properly the Paragon,[300] yet dare I not so to do for fear of the courtier's envy,° who will have no man use that term but after a courtly manner—that is, in praising of horses, hawks, hounds, pearls, diamonds, rubies, emeralds, and other precious stones; especially of fair women whose excellence is discovered° by paragonizing or setting one to another, which moved the zealous poet, speaking of the Maiden Queen, to call her the Paragon of Queens.[301] This considered, I will let our figure enjoy his best beknown name, and call him still° in all ordinary cases the Figure of Comparison,[302] as when a man will seem to make things appear good or bad, or better or worse, or more or less excellent, either upon spite or for pleasure, or any other good affection,° then he sets the less by the greater, or the greater to the less, the equal to his equal, and by such confronting of them together, drives out the true odds that is betwixt them, and makes it better appear. As when we sang of our Sovereign Lady thus, in the twentieth Partheniade:

As falcon fares to buzzard's flight,
As eagle's eyes to owlet's sight,
As fierce saker[303] *to coward kite,*
As brightest noon to darkest night,
As summer sun exceedeth far
The moon and every other star:
So far my Princess's praise doth pass
The famoust[304] *Queen that ever was.*[305]

298. **engage** engagement, bargain.

299. The example in these verses appears to have been inspired by a similar example in *Ad Herennium* 4.29.40, which Puttenham probably took from Susenbrotus (94).

300. Something appears to have been omitted from the text after the last quoted passage. Up to the end of the quotation the text is exemplifying *expeditio*. The next sentence speaks of "this figure" as "properly" called "the Paragon," a quite different figure. Furthermore, the claimed fitness of the English translation points to a criterion derived from a definition or example not given. Finally, the "Figure of Comparison" has no marginal label, nor does it appear in the chart at the end of the *Art* that lists "the names of your Figures Auricular," which goes directly from *expeditio* to *dialogismus*. Material on Paragon seems to be missing, and perhaps more on *expeditio* as well, since the text often provides several examples of a figure.

301. Puttenham is the "zealous poet." He so refers to himself when citing *Partheniades* 12 (3.19.308), and also says that "her Maiestie is the onlye paragon of princes in this oure age" (prose headnote to *Partheniades* 15).

302. Puttenham's "Figure of Comparison" is *comparatio*, for which see Susenbrotus 70–72; see also Quintilian 9.2.100; Sherry 75, 90; Peacham (1577) Q3v.

303. **saker** large female lanner falcon (*Falco sacer*), used in falconry. It may be relevant that the Spanish, Portuguese, and Italian word *sacro*, like the Latin adjective *sacer* from which it is derived, means "sacred." The name has in consequence sometimes been thought to mean "sacred falcon."

304. **famoust** famousest.

305. These lines are actually in *Partheniades* 16 ("Euterpe"): 436–45, omitting 440–41.

And in the eighteenth Partheniade thus[306]:

> Set rich ruby to red esmayle,[307]
> The raven's plume to peacock's tail,
> Lay me the lark's to lizard's eye,[308]
> The dusky cloud to azure sky,
> Set shallow brooks to surging seas,
> An orient pearl to a white pease,[309] etc.

Concluding:

> There shall no less an odds be seen
> In mine from every other queen.

Dialogismus, or the Right Reasoner
We are sometimes occasioned in our tale to report some speech from another man's mouth, as what a king said to his Privy Council or subject, a captain to his soldier, a soldier to his captain, a man to a woman, and contrariwise, in which report we must always give to every person his fit and natural,[310] and that which best becometh him.[311] For that speech becometh a king which doth not a carter,° and a young man that doth not an old, and so in every sort and degree.° Vergil, speaking in the person of Aeneas, Turnus, and many other great princes, and sometimes of meaner° men, ye shall see what decency° every of their speeches holdeth with the quality,[312] degree,° and years of the speaker. To which examples I will for this time refer you.

So if by way of fiction we will seem to speak in another man's person, as if King Henry VIII were alive, and should say of the town of Boulogne, "What we by war to the hazard of our person hardly[313] obtained, our young son without any peril at all, for little money delivered up again."[314] Or if we should feign King Edward III, understanding how his successor Queen Mary had lost the town of Calais by negligence, should say, "That which the sword won, the distaff hath

---

306. Actually in *Partheniades* 15 (which appears in the Morfill edition without ascription to a muse), 422–29, 434–35.

307. **esmayle** enamel (Fr. *émaille*, spelled *esmaille* in the period).

308. **eye** *1589* prints *eyes*, but *Partheniades* (15.426) prints *eye*, which we here adopt to stabilize the rhyme.

309. **pease** not a plural. About 1600 a back-formation from *pease* taken to be plural led to *pea* as singular.

310. **fit and natural** appropriate and natural voice.

311. On *dialogismus*, see Susenbrotus 89–90; see also Rufinianus, *De figuris* 20; Sherry 69; Day 97. Quintilian says (9.2.31), when discussing the figure *prosopopeia* (im-

personation), that some writers prefer to call an imaginary conversation *dialogos* in Greek, or *sermocinatio* in Latin. Why Puttenham translates the figure as "the Right Reasoner" is obscure.

312. **quality** character, disposition.

313. **hardly** with difficulty.

314. Boulogne surrendered to Henry VIII's forces on September 14, 1544. Six years later the Anglo-French hostilities had become extremely unpopular in England; the treasury was drained, and there was near-disabling unrest among the people. On March 24, 1550, the thirteen-year-old King Edward's commissioners relinquished the town to the French for a payment of 400,000 crowns.

lost."[315] This manner of speech is by[316] the figure *dialogismus*, or the Right Reasoner.

In weighty causes and for great purposes, wise persuaders use grave and weighty speeches, especially in matter of advice or counsel, for which purpose there is a manner of speech to allege texts or authorities of witty° sentence,° such as smatch[317] moral doctrine° and teach wisdom and good behavior. By the Greek original we call him the Director; by the Latin he is called *sententia*;[318] we may call him the Sage Sayer.[319] Thus:

Gnome, or the Director

> *Nature bids us as a loving mother*
> *To love ourselves first and next to love another.*

Sententia, or the Sage Sayer

> *The prince that covets all to know and see*
> *Had need full mild and patient to be.*

> *Nothing sticks faster by us as appears*
> *Than that which we learn in our tender years.*[320]

And that which our Sovereign Lady wrote in defiance of fortune:

> *Never think you fortune can bear the sway,*
> *Where virtue's force can cause her to obey.*[321]

Heed must be taken that such rules or sentences° be choicely made and not often used, lest excess breed loathsomeness.

Art and good policy° moves us many times to be earnest in our speech, and then we lay on such load and so go to it by heaps as if we would win the game by multitude of words and speeches, not all of one but of divers matter and sense, for which cause the Latins called it *congeries* and we the Heaping Figure,[322] as he that said:

Sinathrismus, or the Heaping Figure

315. Calais surrendered to Edward III on August 3, 1347, a year after the famous battle of Crécy. Of all his conquests Calais was the only abiding acquisition, remaining an English possession until its surrender to the forces of the duke of Guise on January 7, 1558, some eleven months before the death of Mary I on November 16 of that year.

316. **by** i.e., called by.

317. **smatch** taste of.

318. **sententia** idea, opinion, saying, maxim.

319. On *gnome* and *sententia* (Greek and Latin equivalents: the two side notes refer to the same figure), see Susenbrotus 90–91; see also Aristotle, *Rhetoric* 2.21.2–8 (1394a–1395a); *Ad Herennium* 4.17.24–25; Quintilian 8.5.2–7; Peacham (1577) V3r–v, (1593) 189–91. Puttenham is translating the Greek *gnome* (maxim) as "the Director," most likely because he sees such sayings as giving directions for living.

320. Puttenham's examples here are most likely derived from Susenbrotus (91). The first saying ultimately comes from Terence, *Andria* 2.5.427, probably via Erasmus, *Adagia* 1.3.91 (LB 2.146E, *CWE* 31.310). The second saying Quintilian (8.5.3) attributes to Domitius Afer. Cf. *Qui nescit dissimulare nescit regnare* above (3.18.271). The earliest version of this third saying can be found in Plato, *Timaeus* 26b; cf. Erasmus, *Adagia* 2.4.20 (LB 2.529C, *CWE* 33.200); Quintilian 1.1.19.

321. Though these lines indeed seem a sententious unit, they appear as lines 15–16 of poem 1 in the poems of Queen Elizabeth printed in May, *Elizabethan Courtier Poets*, as "An nanswer [sic]" ("Ah silly pugg, wert thou so sore afrayed?"), a reply to Ralegh's "Fortune hath taken thee away, my Love," cited there as poem 1a (see May 316–21). See also Ralegh 15A–D and commentary, cited twice above, at 3.19.282 and 285.

322. On *sinathrismus*, see Susenbrotus 69; see also Quintilian 8.4.26–27; Peacham (1577) T3v–4r, (1593) 151–52; Sherry 50; Day 92.

> *To muse in mind how fair, how wise, how good,*
> *How brave, how free, how courteous, and how true*
> *My lady is doth but inflame my blood.*

Or thus:

> *I deem, I dream, I do, I taste, I touch,*
> *Nothing at all but smells of perfect bliss.*[323]

And thus by Master Edward Dyer, vehement, swift, and passionately:

> *But if my faith, my hope, my love, my true intent,*
> *My liberty, my service vowed, my time and all be spent*
> *In vain, etc.*[324]

But if such earnest and hasty heaping up of speeches be made by way of recapitulation, which commonly is in the end of every long tale and oration, because the speaker seems to make a collection[325] of all the former material points, to bind them as it were in a bundle and lay them forth to enforce the cause and renew the hearers' memory, then ye may give him more properly the name of the Collector or Recapitulator, and serveth to very great purpose, as in a hymn written by us to the Queen's Majesty entitled "Minerva," wherein, speaking of the mutability of fortune in the case of all princes generally, we seemed to exempt her Majesty of all such casualty,[326] by reason she was, by her destiny and many divine parts in her, ordained to a most long and constant prosperity in this world, concluding with this recapitulation:

> *But thou art free; but were thou not indeed,*
> *But were thou not come of immortal seed;*
> *Never yborn, and thy mind made to bliss,*
> *Heaven's metal*[327] *that everlasting is;*
> *Were not thy wit,° and that thy virtues shall,*
> *Be deemed divine, thy favor,*[328] *face, and all;*
> *And that thy lose*[329] *nor name may never die,*
> *Nor thy state*[330] *turn, stayed by destiny;*
> *Dread were lest once thy noble heart may feel*
> *Some rueful turn of her unsteady wheel.**

323. See Gascoigne, Additions from *The Posies, Dan Bartholomew of Bath* 26, "Dan Bartholomew his second Triumphe" 25–27 (387) and 4–5 (386).

324. These are lines 5–7 of the Gorges poem "But this and then no more," discussed in note 99.

325. **collection** summary.

326. **casualty** uncertainty.

327. **metal** Early modern English did not distinguish by spelling between *metal* and *mettle*. We print "metal" to mark the probable meanings of gold ("heaven's metal") and metal as durable ("everlasting"). However, *mettle* (originally a figurative use of *metal*), meaning "quality of disposition or temperament," lies close behind *metal* here.

328. **favor** appearance.

329. **lose** fame, reputation (Old Fr. *los*, Lat. *laus*).

330. **state** i.e., state of her fortune.

Many times when we have run a long race in our tale spoken to the hearers, we do suddenly fly out and either speak or exclaim at some other person or thing, and therefore the Greeks call such figure (as we do) the Turn-Way or Turn-Tale, and breedeth by such exchange a certain recreation to the hearers' minds.[331] As this used by a lover to his unkind mistress:

Apostrophe, or the Turn-Tale

> *And as for you, fair one, say now by proof ye find*
> *That rigor and ingratitude soon kill a gentle mind.*[332]

And as we in our *Triumphals*, speaking long to the Queen's Majesty, upon the sudden we burst out in an exclamation to Phoebus, seeming to draw in a new matter, thus:

> *But O Phoebus,*
> *All glistering in thy gorgeous gown,*
> *Wouldst thou wit*[333] *safe to slide a-down*
> *And dwell with us*
>
> *But for a day,*
> *I could tell thee close in thine ear*
> *A tale that thou hadst liever*[334] *hear,*
> *I dare well say,*
>
> *Than ere thou wert*
> *To kiss that unkind runaway*
> *Who was transformed to boughs of bay*[335]
> *For her curst*[336] *heart . . . etc.* *

And so returned again to the first matter.

The matter and occasion leadeth us many times to describe and set forth many things in such sort as it should appear they were truly before our eyes though they were not present, which to do it requireth cunning,° for nothing can be kindly° counterfeit° or represented in his absence, but by great discretion in the doer.[337] And if the things we covet to describe be not natural or not veritable, then yet the same asketh more cunning° to do it, because to feign a thing that never was nor is like to be proceedeth of a greater wit° and sharper invention° than to describe things that be true.

Hypotyposis, or the Counterfeit° Representation

And these be things that a poet or maker is wont to describe sometimes as true or natural, and sometimes to feign as artificial° and not

Prosopographia

---

331. On *apostrophe*, see Susenbrotus 65; see also *Ad Herennium* 4.15.22; Quintilian 9.2.38–39; Sherry 60; Wilson 229.15–18 and note; Peacham (1577) M4v–N1r, (1593) 116–17; Day 90.

332. These are lines 29–30 of the Gorges poem "But this and then no more" discussed in note 99. "Proof" means "experience."

333. **wit** think (it).

334. **liever** rather.

335. **A tale . . . bay** i.e, you'd be gladder to hear this tale than ever you were glad to kiss Daphne.

336. **curst** unaccommodating, shrewish.

337. On *hypotyposis*, see Susenbrotus 83; see also *Ad Herennium* 4.55.68; Quintilian 9.2.40–44; Wilson 212.21–32; Peacham (1577) O2r, (1593) 134–35; Day 97.

true, *videl.*,° the visage, speech, and countenance of any person absent or dead. And this kind of representation is called the Counterfeit° Countenance.[338] As Homer doth in his *Iliad*, diverse personages—namely Achilles and Thersites—according to the truth and not by fiction;[339] and as our poet Chaucer doth in his *Canterbury Tales* set forth the Summoner, Pardoner, Manciple, and the rest of the pilgrims most naturally and pleasantly.

Prosopopeia,
or the
Counterfeit°
Impersonation

But if ye will feign any person with such features, qualities, and conditions, or if ye will attribute any human° quality, as reason or speech, to dumb creatures or other insensible things, and do study (as one may say) to give them a human° person, it is not *prosopographia* but *prosopopeia*, because it is by way of fiction.[340] And no prettier examples can be given to you thereof than in the *Romaunt of the Rose*, translated out of French by Chaucer, describing the persons of Avarice, Envy,° Old Age, and many others, whereby much morality is taught.[341]

Chronographia,
or the Counter-
feit° Time

So if we describe the time or season of the year, as winter, summer, harvest, day, midnight, noon, evening, or such like, we call such description the Counterfeit° Time, *chronographia*.[342] Examples are everywhere to be found.

Topographia, or
the Counterfeit°
Place

And if this description be of any true place, city, castle, hill, valley, or sea, and such like, we call it the Counterfeit° Place, *topographia*, or if ye feign places untrue, as heaven, hell, paradise, the house of fame, the palace of the sun, the den of sleep, and such like which ye shall see in poets.[343]

---

338. On *prosopographia*, see Susenbrotus 83; see also *Ad Herennium* 4.49.63; Sherry 66–68; Peacham (1577) O2r–3r, (1593) 135–36.

339. Puttenham's grounds for regarding these particular characters as historical are unclear. In 1.19 he speaks of the *Iliad* and *Odyssey* as "histories" of "fabulous or mixed report" (130). As late as Sandys's translation of Ovid's *Metamorphoses* (1626), some serious Renaissance readers thought the *Iliad* to some degree historical: Sandys's commentary discusses the location of Achilles' tomb "on the promontory of Sigaeum" (568), and cites Homer and Tacitus in tandem to elucidate the fight over Achilles' arms. (More common is the resort to euhemerism to argue that the pagan *gods* were historically notable humans, as Puttenham argues in 1.16; on this, see Seznec and Ferguson.) Milton has begun to doubt it wholesale by the time he writes *The History of Britain* (published 1670): "[T]o examine these things with diligence, were but to confute the fables of Britain, with the fables of Greece or Italy: for of this age, what we have to say, as well concerning

most other countries, as this island, is equally under question" (*Complete Prose Works* 5.11).

340. On *prosopopeia*, see Susenbrotus 83–84; see also Quintilian 9.2.29–37; Peacham (1577) O3r–v, (1593) 9, 136–37; Day 90–91.

341. Chaucer produced a fragmentary translation of this famous thirteenth-century allegory by Guillaume de Lorris and Jean de Meun. A Middle English text was first printed as Chaucer's in the Thynne edition of 1532 (though the larger part of it—the so-called Fragment B, written in a northern dialect—is now rejected by scholars as non-Chaucerian). Puttenham might also have read it in Stow's edition of 1561. It may be significant that a major character in the poem is Faus-Semblant, of which Puttenham has much to say at 3.18.270–71. Puttenham also mentions this book at 1.31.149.

342. On *chronographia*, see Susenbrotus 85–86; Peacham (1577) P1v–P3r, (1593) 142–43.

343. On *topographia*, see Susenbrotus 85; see also Quintilian 9.2.44; Peacham (1577) P1r, (1593) 141.

So did Chaucer very well describe the country of Saluces in Italy, which ye may see, in his report of the Lady Grysyll.[344]

But if such description be made to represent the handling of any busi- *Pragmatographia,* ness, with the circumstances° belonging thereunto, as the manner of a *or the Counter-* battle, a feast, a marriage, a burial, or any other matter that lieth in feat *feit° Action* and activity, we call it then the Counterfeit° Action, *pragmatographia.*[345] In this figure the Lord Nicholas Vaux,[346] a noble gentleman, and much delighted in vulgar° making, and a man otherwise of no great learning but having herein a marvelous facility, made a ditty representing the battle and assault of Cupid so excellently well as for the gallant and proper application of his fiction in every part, I cannot choose but set down the greatest part of his ditty, for in truth it cannot be amended°:

> When Cupid scaled first the fort
> Wherein my heart lay wounded sore,
> The battery[347] was of such a sort
> That I must yield or die therefore.
> There saw I love upon the wall,
> How he his banner did display:
> "Alarm, alarm," he gan[348] to call,
> And bade his soldiers keep array.[349]
> The arms the which that Cupid bare[350]
> Were pierced hearts with tears besprent,[351]
> In silver and sable[352] to declare
> The steadfast love he always meant.
> There might you see his band all dressed
> In colors like to white and black,
> With powder and with pellets prest,[353]
> To bring them forth to spoil and sack.
> Good Will, the master of the shot,
> Stood in the rampire,[354] brave and proud;
> For expense of powder he spared not
> "Assault! assault!" to cry aloud.
> There might you hear the cannons roar,
> Each piece discharging a lover's look, etc.[355]

344. In the "Clerk's Tale," in the *Canterbury Tales*, derived from Petrarch's *De obedientia ac fide uxoria mythologia* (A Fable of Wifely Obedience and Faithfulness), itself a version of Boccaccio's story in the *Decameron* (10.10). "Saluces" is Saluzzo, a region and town in northern Italy. Grysyll is Chaucer's Grisilde.

345. On *pragmatographia*, see Susenbrotus 84; see also Wilson 203.21–205.14 and note; Peacham (1577) O4v, (1593) 139–41.

346. Actually Thomas Vaux, eldest son of Nicholas.

347. **battery** bombardment.

348. **gan** began.

349. **keep array** stay in rank.

350. **bare** bore.

351. **besprent** sprinkled.

352. **sable** black (a term from heraldry).

353. **prest** ready (the anglicized Fr. *prêt*).

354. **rampire** rampart.

355. *Tottel* no. 211.2–23, Anonymous; cf. poem 14 in the Grosart edition of Vaux (386–87). Puttenham was not alone in finding the poem noteworthy: Rollins reports that it was moralized as "The Cruel Assault of Gods

As well to a good maker and poet as to an excellent persuader in
prose, the Figure of Similitude is very necessary, by which we not only
beautify our tale but also very much enforce and enlarge it.[356] I say enforce because no one thing more prevaileth with all ordinary judgments
than persuasion by similitude. Now because there are sundry sorts of
them, which also do work after diverse fashions in the hearers' conceits,° I will set them all forth by a triple division, exempting[357] the
general Similitude as their common ancestor, and I will call him by the
name of Resemblance without any addition, from which I derive three
other sorts, and give every one his particular name, as Resemblance by
Portrait or Imagery, which the Greeks call *icon*; Resemblance Moral or
Mystical, which they call *parabola*; and Resemblance by Example,
which they call *paradigma*.[358]

And first we will speak of the general Resemblance, or bare Similitude, which may be thus spoken:

> But as the wat'ry show'rs delay the raging wind,
> So doth good hope clean put away despair out of my mind.[359]

And in this other likening the forlorn lover to a stricken deer:

> Then as the stricken deer withdraws himself alone,
> So do I seek some secret place, where I may make my moan.[360]

And in this of ours where we liken glory to a shadow:

> As the shadow (his nature being such)
> Followeth the body, whether it will or no,
> So doth glory, refuse it ne'er so much,
> Wait on virtue, be it in weal[361] or woe.
> And even as the shadow in his kind,°
> What time it bears the carcass company,
> Go'th oft before, and often comes behind,
> So doth renown, that raiseth us so high,
> Come to us quick,° sometime not till we die.
> But the glory that grow'th not overfast
> Is ever great, and likeliest long to last. *[362]

Fort" (ca. 1560), registered for publication as a
ballad in 1565–66, and as such was popular
enough to be noted as providing the tune for
another ballad-poem in 1578 (see *Tottel* 2.283).

356. **enforce and enlarge it** strengthen and
magnify it. On *omiosis* (or *homiosis*), see
Susenbrotus 95–97; see also *Ad Herennium*
4.45.59; Quintilian 8.3.72–81; Wilson
213.31–218.35; Day 99.

357. **exempting** setting off.

358. In identifying three derivatives of

Similitude as *icon, parabola*, and *paradigma*,
Puttenham follows Susenbrotus 97–99.

359. See Surrey, *Tottel* no. 265 (1.210.24–
25) (Jones no. 14).

360. See Surrey, *Tottel* no. 265 (1.209.35–
36) (Jones no. 14).

361. **weal** well-being.

362. For the saying in the last two lines,
see Erasmus, *Parabolae* (LB 594C–D, *CWE*
23.213.25–27); for its original, see Seneca,
Epistolae 79.13.

Again, in a ditty to a mistress of ours, where we likened the cure of love to Achilles' lance:

> *The lance so bright, that made Telephus' wound—*
> *The same, rusty, salved the sore again.*[363]
> *So may my meed*[364] *(Madam) of you redound,*
> *Whose rigor was first author of my pain.**

The Tuscan poet useth this Resemblance, inuring[365] as well by Dissimilitude as Similitude, likening himself (by implication) to the fly, and neither to the eagle nor to the owl; very well Englished by Sir Thomas Wyatt after his fashion,[366] and by myself thus:

> *There be some fowls of sight so proud and stark,*[367]
> *As can behold the sun and never shrink;*
> *Some so feeble, as they are fain to wink,*
> *Or never come abroad till it be dark.*
> *Others there be so simple,° as*[368] *they think,*
> *Because it shines, to sport° them in the fire,*
> *And feel un'ware, the wrong of their desire,*
> *Fluttering amidst the flame that doth them burn.*
> *Of this last rank (alas) am I aright,*
> *For in my lady's looks to stand or turn*
> *I have no power, nor find place to retire*
> *Where any dark may shade me from her sight,*
> *But to her beams so bright whilst I aspire,*
> *I perish by the bane of my delight.**

Again in these, likening a wise man to the true lover:

> *As true love is content with his enjoy,*
> *And asketh no witness nor no record;*
> *And as faint love is evermore most coy*[369]
> *To boast and brag his troth° at every word;*
> *Even so the wise withouten other meed*[370]
> *Contents him with the guilt*[371] *of his good deed.*[372]

---

363. For Puttenham's likely source for the saying about Telephus' wound, see Erasmus, *Parabolae* (LB 1.579E, 584A, *CWE* 23.180.67, 190.7–13), who probably derived it from Plutarch, "On Listening to Lectures" 16 (*Moralia* 46F). For the story behind the saying, see Pseudo-Apollodorus E.3.20.

364. **meed** recompense.

365. **inuring** operating.

366. See *Tottel* no. 47 (Rebholz no. 15), after Petrarch, *Canzoniere* 19; Rollins also records another period translation (2.166).

367. **stark** strong.

368. **as** that.

369. **coy** reluctant.

370. **meed** recompense.

371. **guilt** gilt, gold. Puttenham may also mean to suggest a kind of conceptual pun on guilt = responsibility = credit, reputation.

372. This poem begins a string of six examples taken from Erasmus's *Parabolae*. See LB 1.582C, *CWE* 23.186.16–19; for the original, see Plutarch, "Progress in Virtue" 9 (*Moralia* 80E).

And in this, resembling the learning of an evil man to the seeds sown in barren ground:

> As the good seeds sown in fruitful soil
> Bring forth foison[373] when barren doth them spoil,
> So doth it fare when much good learning hits
> Upon shrewd° wills and ill-disposed wits.[374]

And in these likening the wise man to an idiot:

> A sage man said, many of those that come
> To Athens' school for wisdom, ere they went,
> They first seem'd wise, then lovers of wisdom,
> Then orators, then idiots, which is meant
> That in wisdom all such as profit most
> Are least surly,[375] and little apt to boast.[376]

Again, for a lover whose credit upon some report had been shaken, he prayeth better opinion by similitude:

> After ill crop the soil must eft[377] be sown,
> And from shipwreck we sail to seas again;
> Then God forbid, whose fault hath once been known
> Should forever a spotted wight° remain.[378]

And in this working by resemblance in a kind of dissimilitude between a father and a master:

> It fares not by fathers as by masters it doth fare,
> For a foolish father may get[379] a wise son,
> But of a foolish master it haps very rare
> Is bred a wise servant wherever he won.[380]

373. **foison** abundance.

374. See Erasmus, *Parabolae* (LB 1.593E, CWE 23.212.4–6); for the original, see Seneca, *Epistolae* 38.2 (or a related passage in 73.16). Cf. the parable of the tares and the wheat (Matthew 13:24–30).

375. **surly** arrogant.

376. **idiot** an ordinary person or citizen. Although in the Renaissance this word could designate someone mentally deficient, as it does now, Puttenham appears to use it in its original Greek sense of "ordinary person." (Because such persons were uneducated, the meaning of "mentally deficient" later became central in Latin and English versions of the word.) Puttenham here translates a saying attributed to the Greek philosopher Menedemus of Eretria (ca. 339–ca. 265 BCE) that appears in Erasmus's *Parabolae* (LB 1.582D–E, CWE 23.187.3–7) and in his *Apophthegmata* 7, "Menedemus Eretriensis" 9 (LB 4.333B–C).

It comes originally from Plutarch, "Progress in Virtue" (*Moralia* 81F), where what is said is clearer than Puttenham's version: "Menedemus . . . said that the multitudes who came to Athens to school were, at the outset, wise; later they became lovers of wisdom, later still orators, and, as time went by, just ordinary persons [*idiotas*], and the more they laid hold on reason the more they laid aside their self-opinion and conceit." In other words, as men became better philosophers, they used less inflated names for themselves, going from "wise" through "lovers of wisdom" and "orators," down to "ordinary persons."

377. **eft** again.

378. See Erasmus, *Parabolae* (LB 1.594C, CWE 23.213.17–20); for the original, see Seneca, *Epistolae* 81.1–2.

379. **get** beget.

380. **won** dwell. See Erasmus, *Parabolae* (LB 1.624A, CWE 23.274.23–25).

And in these, likening the wise man to the giant, the fool to the dwarf:

> *Set the giant deep in a dale, the dwarf upon a hill:*
> *Yet will the one be but a dwarf, th'other a giant still.*°
> *So will the wise be great and high, even in the lowest place;*
> *The fool, when he is most aloft, will seem but low and base.*[381]

But when we liken a human° person to another in countenance, stature, speech, or other quality, it is not called bare Resemblance but Resemblance by Imagery or Portrait, alluding to the painter's term, who yieldeth to the eye a visible representation of the thing he describes and painteth in his table.°[382] So we, commending her Majesty for wisdom, beauty, and magnanimity, likened her to the serpent, the lion, and the angel, because by common usurpation,[383] nothing is wiser than the serpent, more courageous than the lion, more beautiful than the angel. These are our verses in the end of the seventh Partheniade:

Icon, or Resemblance by Imagery

> *Nature that seldom works amiss,*
> *In woman's breast by passing*[384] *art*
> *Hath lodged safe*[385] *the lion's heart,*
> *And featly*[386] *fixed with all good grace*
> *To serpent's head an angel's face.*[387]

And this manner of Resemblance is not only performed by likening of lively[388] creatures one to another, but also of any other natural thing bearing a proportion° of similitude, as to liken yellow to gold, white to silver, red to the rose, soft to silk, hard to the stone, and such like. Sir Philip Sidney in the description of his mistress excellently well handled this Figure of Resemblance by Imagery, as ye may see in his book of *Arcadia*.[389] And ye may see the like of our doings in a Partheniade written of our Sovereign Lady, wherein we resemble every part of her body to some natural thing of excellent perfection in his kind, as of her forehead, brows, and hair, thus:

> *Of silver was her forehead high,*
> *Her brows two bows of ebony,*
> *Her tresses trussed were to behold*
> *Frizzled and fine as fringe of gold.*

381. See Erasmus, *Parabolae* (LB 1.594B, CWE 23.213.4–6); for the original, see Seneca, *Epistolae* 76.32.

382. On *icon*, see Susenbrotus 97; see also Bede 618; Sherry 91–92; Wilson 231.30–232.5 and note; Peacham (1577) V2r–v, (1593) 145–46; Day 99–100.

383. **usurpation** accepted usage.

384. **passing** surpassing.

385. **safe** securely.

386. **featly** fitly, gracefully, cleverly.

387. Actually in *Partheniades* 4 ("Thalia"): 72–76.

388. **lively** living.°

389. Sidney did not write of "his" mistress in the *Old Arcadia*, but the blazon sung by Philisides for Mira, then recalled by Pyrocles (no. 62), became Sidney's most famous poem, copied or quoted more than any other (Ringler 85–90, 410). Cf. also no. 3 (Alethes's mock-blazon of Mopsa: 12).

And of her lips:

> *Two lips wrought out of ruby rock,*
> *Like leaves to shut and to unlock.*
> *As portal door in prince's chamber:*
> *A golden tongue in mouth of amber. . . .*

And of her eyes:

> *Her eyes, God wot° what stuff they are,*
> *I durst[390] be sworn each is a star:*
> *As clear and bright as wont to guide*
> *The pilot in his winter tide.*

And of her breasts:

> *Her bosom sleek as Paris plaster,*
> *Held up two balls of alabaster;*
> *Each bias[391] was a little cherry,*
> *Or else I think a strawberry.[392]*

And all the rest that followeth, which may suffice to exemplify your figure of *icon*, or Resemblance by Imagery and Portrait.

Parabola, or Resemblance Mystical

But whensoever by your similitude ye will seem to teach any morality or good lesson by speeches mystical and dark,° or far-fetched, under a sense metaphorical, applying one natural thing to another or one case to another, inferring by them a like consequence in other cases, the Greeks call it *parabola*, which term is also by custom accepted of us.[393] Nevertheless, we may call him in English the Resemblance Mystical, as when we liken a young child to a green twig, which ye may easily bend every way ye list,° or an old man who laboreth with continual infirmities to a dry and drixy[394] oak. Such parables were all the preachings of Christ in the Gospel, as those of the wise and foolish virgins, of the evil steward, of the laborers in the vineyard, and a number more. And they may be feigned as well as true, as those fables of Aesop, and other apologues[395] invented° for doctrine's° sake by wise and grave men.

Paradigma, or a Resemblance by Example

Finally, if in matter of counsel or persuasion we will seem to liken one case to another, such as pass ordinarily in man's affairs, and do compare the past with the present, gathering probability of like success° to come in the things we have presently in hand; or if ye will draw the judgments precedent and authorized by antiquity as veritable, and peradventure°

---

390. **durst** dare.

391. **bias** nipple. This is a figurative use, derived, says *OED*, from the asymmetrical shape of an early modern bowling ball; here, from the protuberant side.

392. All four passages on the queen's body are from *Partheniades* 7 ("Uterpe"): 129–32, 137–40, 133–36, and 149–52.

393. On *parabola*, see Susenbrotus 97–98; see also Quintilian 5.11.23; Sherry 90; Peacham (1577) V2r.

394. **drixy** decayed.

395. **apologues** moral fables, especially beast fables and others drawn from natural history.

feigned and imagined for some purpose, into similitude or dissimilitude with our present actions and affairs, it is called Resemblance by Example.[396] As if one should say thus: Alexander the Great in his expedition to Asia did thus, so did Hannibal coming into Spain, so did Caesar in Egypt; therefore, all great captains and generals ought to do it.

[*The next paragraph contains the anti-Flemish passage that appears in some copies of the 1589 text. The pro-Flemish passage found in other copies appears in the bracketed paragraph that follows after.*][397]

And consulting upon the affairs of the Low Countries at this day, peradventure° her Majesty might be thus advised: the Flemings[398] are a people very unthankful and mutable, and rebellious against their princes,[399] for they did rise against Maximilian, Archduke of Austria, who had married the daughter and heir of the house of Burgundy, and took him prisoner, till by the Emperor Frederick III, his father, he was set at liberty. They rebelled against Charles V, Emperor, their natural prince. They have falsed their faith to his son Philip, King of Spain, their sovereign lord; and since to Archduke Matthias, whom they elected[400] for their governor; after to their adopted Lord Monsieur of France, Duke of Anjou. I pray you what likelihood is there they should be more assured to the Queen of England than they have been to all these princes and governors, longer than their distress continueth and is to be relieved by her goodness and puissance?[401]

396. On *paradigma*, see Susenbrotus 98–99; see also Quintilian 5.11.1–5; Wilson 215.17–218.35; Peacham (1577) V2v–r, (1593) 186–89; Day 100.

397. At this point some copies of the *Art* print this anti-Flemish passage to exemplify Puttenham's treatment of *paradigma*, and others substitute the pro-Flemish passage that follows it. The content of both versions is of considerable interest as an *argumentum in utramque partem* demonstration of politically subtle *paradigma*. We have therefore printed both passages serially in the text proper, rather than relegate the earlier one to an appendix (as Willcock and Walker do). The first passage, beginning here, must have been written between the Flemish rebellion against Anjou in early 1583 (the latest rebellion Puttenham cites) and late summer 1585. On August 17 of that year Antwerp fell to the Spanish forces. In response, Elizabeth decided to set aside her long-standing policy of nonintervention and to aid the Flemish against Spain. She signed the Treaty of Nonsuch on August 20. Troops under the earl of Leicester landed at Flushing on December 9. Puttenham's second paragraph surely dates from these events. (The text announcing the new policy, *A Declaration of the Causes to Give aide in the lowe Countries,*

can be found in Kinney, *Elizabethan Backgrounds* 188–96.) Sources for this historical material have not been sought: the material would have seemed "current events." For details on the events listed, see LN 14.

398. **Flemings** the inhabitants of the southern provinces of the Netherlands, today the Flemish-speaking western half of Belgium.

399. It should be observed generally about Puttenham's list of unthankful "rebellions" that throughout the period from the reign of Archduke Maximilian of Austria in 1477 to the tempestuous events of the author's own day, the Low Countries were continuously subjected to foreign rule, mostly Habsburg, by parties whose geopolitical interests were notoriously different from those of the inhabitants of the seventeen provinces. Whether this citation of "rebellions" against foreign domination is a straightforward rhetorical deployment of *paradigma*, or a clue to Puttenham's own political views, inculcated perhaps by his now shadowy experience residing on the continent, is impossible to determine.

400. **elected** chose.

401. **puissance** power. The text for this earlier passage follows the Da Capo facsimile, which matches Willcock and Walker's use of BM, C. 71, c. 16.

[And thus again, it hath been always usual among great and magnanimous princes in all ages not only to repulse any injury and invasion from their own realms and dominions, but also with a charitable and princely compassion to defend their good neighbors, princes and potentates, from all oppression of tyrants and usurpers. So did the Romans by their arms restore many kings of Asia and Africa expulsed out of their kingdoms.[402] So did King Edward I reestablish Balliol, rightful owner of the crown of Scotland, against Robert le Bruce no lawful king.[403] So did King Edward III aid Don Peter, King of Spain, against Henry, bastard and usurper.[404] So have many English princes helped with their forces the poor dukes of Brittany, their ancient friends and allies, against the outrages of the French kings.[405] And why may not the Queen our Sovereign Lady with like honor and godly zeal yield protection to the people of the Low Countries, her nearest neighbors, to rescue them, a free people, from the Spanish servitude?][406]

And as this Resemblance is of one man's action to another, so may it be made by examples of brute beasts aptly corresponding in quality or event, as one that wrote certain pretty verses of the Emperor Maximinus, to warn him that he should not glory too much in his own strength—for so he did in very deed, and would take any common soldier to task at wrestling, or weapon, or in any other activity and feats of arms, which was by the wiser sort misliked. These were the verses:

> The elephant is strong, yet death doth it subdue;
> The bull is strong, yet cannot death eschew.

402. Puttenham is thinking of many an instance familiar to readers of Plutarch, Livy, Suetonius, and Tacitus on the Romans' relations with the African kingdoms of Numidia and Mauretania, Ptolemaic Egypt, and the kingdoms of Armenia and Parthia.

403. Edward I adjudged John de Balliol king of Scotland in 1292.

404. This king is Pedro I (ruled as king of Castile and Leon 1350–69), known by contemporary enemies as Peter the Cruel. Puttenham names him "Dampeter" (1589: "Dampecter"), deriving the odd form of his name from Sir John Bourchier, Lord Berners's translation of the *Chronicle* of Froissart (see the Tudor Translation version, 3.251ff.). The French original refers to "damps Pieres" and "dans Pieres" (364), "dan Piere" (365), and "dan Piere" and "damps Pieres" (366). These variants are probably attempts to reproduce the Spanish *don* (from Lat. *dominus*) but nasalized in French with the "an" rather than the "on" sound. Berners consistently uses the form "Dampeter," so it seems likely that the volume of Froissart that Puttenham owned was Berners's version. (Berners's first

sentence describes Pedro as "full of marveylous opinyons, and he was rude and rebell agaynst the commaundementes of holy churche," raising the dim possibility that Puttenham's use of the form partly encodes a hostile English byname, "Damn Peter.") The relevant historical events are these: challenging Pedro's right to rule, his half-brother Henry of Trastámara expelled him from the kingdom in 1366. In order to recover his throne, the king enlisted the help of Edward, Prince of Wales (the "Black Prince," son of Edward III), and a combined Anglo-Castilian army defeated Henry at Nájera in 1367.

405. Probably a reference to the intermittent role played by England during the late fourteenth century in the War of the Breton Succession (concluded in 1364) and events following, known more generally as the Hundred Years' War. Brittany remained independent of France until 1532. Puttenham could have read about these events in Holinshed (see 2.621–24, 675, 723, 729, 732, 761).

406. This paragraph is taken from the Ben Jonson copy of the *Art*, BM, G. 11548 (see the Scolar Press facsimile).

The lion strong, and slain for all his strength;
The tiger strong, yet killed is at the length.
Dread thou many, that dreadest not any one;
Many can kill, that cannot kill alone.[407]

And so it fell out, for Maximinus was slain in a mutiny of his soldiers, taking no warning by these examples written for his admonition.

407. See Erasmus, *Apophthegmata* 6, "Maximinus" 3 (LB 4.285F); for the original, see the life of the elder Maximinus, attributed to Julius Capitolinus, in the *Scriptores Historiae Augustae* 9.4 (2.333). Note that Puttenham's second line, concerning the bull, is not in the original; he seems to have added it in order to be able to turn the five verses of the original into three couplets. The poem in question was recited by Maximinus to those who seemed overconfident in the gladiatorial games.

CHAPTER 20

The last and principal figure of our poetical ornament

For the glorious luster it setteth upon our speech and language, the Greeks call it *exergasia*, the Latin *expolitio*, a term transferred[1] from these polishers of marble or porphyrite,[2] who, after it is rough hewn and reduced° to that fashion they will, do set upon it a goodly glass,[3] so smooth and clear as° ye may see your face in it; or otherwise as it fareth by the bare and naked body, which, being attired in rich and gorgeous apparel, seemeth to the common usage of the eye much more comely and beautiful than the natural.[4] So doth this figure (which therefore I call the Gorgeous) polish our speech and as it were attire it with copious and pleasant amplifications and much variety of sentences° all running upon one point and to one intent, so as° I doubt whether I may term it a figure, or rather a mass of many figurative speeches, applied to the beautifying of our tale or argument. In a work of ours entitled *Philocalia* we have strained to show the use and

Exergasia, or the Gorgeous

1. Here begins the third of Puttenham's substantial revisions in the text of the *Art* (along with the "Ben Jonson" pages added to 2.12 and the alternative discussion of the Flemish in 3.19). Puttenham's revisions of this passage are intermittent and minor; for discussion, see Willcock and Walker ciiiff. We print here the later passage, from the Scolar Press facsimile of BM, G. 11548; the earlier version (printed from the Da Capo Press facsimile) appears at pages 395–96.

2. **porphyrite** a red or purple precious stone mined in Egypt, according to Pliny (*Natural History* 36.11.57).

3. **glass** gloss.

4. On *exergasia*, see Susenbrotus 86–87; see also *Ad Herennium* 4.42.54–44.57; Quintilian 8.3.88; Sherry 93; Peacham (1577) P4v–r, (1593) 193–96. The Greek and Latin terms mean "polishing, adorning." Although both Susenbrotus and Puttenham classify *exergasia* as a figure, the term refers to a general polishing or refining of one's style rather than identifying a single rhetorical figure such as *icon* or *parabola*. Puttenham himself acknowledges this later in this paragraph.

application of this figure and all others mentioned in this book, to which we refer you.[5]

I find none example in English meter° so well maintaining this figure as that ditty of her Majesty's own making, passing[6] sweet and harmonical, which figure being, as his very original name purporteth, the most beautiful and gorgeous of all others, it asketh in reason to be reserved for a last complement,[7] and deciphered[8] by the art of a lady's pen, herself being the most beautiful, or rather beauty, of queens. And this was the occasion: our Sovereign Lady, perceiving how by the Sc. Q.[9] residence within this realm at so great liberty and ease (as were scarce meet for so great and dangerous a prisoner) bred secret factions among her people, and made many of the nobility incline to favor her party—some of them desirous of innovation in the state, others aspiring to greater fortunes by her liberty and life. The Queen, our Sovereign Lady, to declare that she was nothing ignorant of those secret practices, though she had long with great wisdom and patience dissembled it, writeth this ditty most sweet and sententious,° not hiding from all such aspiring minds the danger of their ambition and disloyalty; which afterward fell out most truly by the exemplary chastisement of sundry persons, who, in favor of the said Sc. Q. declining[10] from her Majesty, sought to interrupt the quiet of the realm by many evil and undutiful practices. The ditty is as followeth.[11]

> *The doubt[12] of future foes exiles my present joy,*
> *And wit° me warns to shun such snares as threaten mine annoy.*
> *For falsehood now doth flow, and subjects' faith doth ebb,*
> *Which would not be, if reason rul'd or wisdom weav'd the web.*
> *But clouds of toys° untried do cloak aspiring minds,*
> *Which turn to reign[13] of late repent by course of changed winds.*
> *The top of hope supposed, the root of ruth will be,*

5. This sentence referring to Puttenham's *Philocalia* matches quite closely the final sentence of this chapter. The occurrence here, less detailed in its description of *Philocalia* than the later one, may be an unrevised fossil. Yet its final words ("mentioned in this book, to which we refer you") might seem to fit better in the closing passage, as a summary statement. (The work is also cited at 2.12.186.) *Philocalia* means "lover of beauty."

6. **passing** surpassingly.

7. **complement** consummating feature.

8. **deciphered** put into writing.

9. **Sc. Q.** Scottish Queen's. Puttenham is referring to Mary, Queen of Scots, imprisoned in England since 1568 and executed on February 8, 1587. We retain Puttenham's abbreviation here, probably a form of verbal tiptoeing, signaling his reticence and care in

mentioning such a risky matter. Shortly before his death Puttenham wrote his *Justification of Queen Elizabeth in relation to the Affair of Mary Queen of Scots* (see Introduction 16–17), which parallels the ideas stated here in many particulars, especially in these words: "Yea, though her Majestie were not uninformed of manie undue meanes which the said Ladie being restrained practized from tyme to tyme to her Majesties great danger, but winked at them, and for her princelie lenitie would not seeme to perceave or be acknowen thereof" (80).

10. **declining** swerving away (in duty or allegiance).

11. The revised page ends at "followeth."

12. **doubt** fear.

13. **reign** with a pun on "rain," presumably.

And fruitless all their grafted guiles, as shortly ye shall see.
Then dazzled eyes with pride, which great ambition blinds,
Shall be unseeled[14] by worthy wights[15] whose foresight falsehood finds.
The daughter of debate, that eke[16] discord doth sow,
Shall reap no gain where former rule hath taught still peace to grow.
No foreign banished wight shall anchor in this port:
Our realm it brooks no strangers'° force; let them elsewhere resort.
Our rusty sword with rest shall first his edge employ
To poll their tops[17] that seek such change and gape for joy.[18]

In a work of ours entitled *Philocalia*, where we entreat° of the loves between Prince Philo and Lady Calia in their mutual letters, messages, and speeches, we have strained our muse to show the use and application of this figure, and of all others.

14. **unseeled** not stitched up: a term from falconry referring to the sewing shut ("seeling") of a bird's eyes during its taming.

15. **wights** persons.

16. **eke** also.

17. **poll their tops** behead them.

18. This famous poem is extant in many manuscripts; for an account of its variations, see Elizabeth 133 and notes. Puttenham's version ends not with poulter's measure (its ongoing form) but with an alexandrine couplet, which other versions of the poem regularize by adding "future" before "joy." The poem first appears in print here; for its manuscript history and numerous corrupt departures from the best sources, see May, "Queen Elizabeth's 'Future Foes.'"

CHAPTER 21

Of the vices or deformities in speech and writing principally noted by ancient poets

It hath been said before how, by ignorance of the maker, a good figure may become a vice, and, by his good discretion, a vicious° speech go for a virtue in the poetical science.°[1] This saying is to be explained and qualified, for some manner of speeches are always intolerable and such as cannot be used with any decency,° but are ever indecent°: namely barbarousness,° incongruity, ill disposition,[2] fond[3] affectation, rusticity, and all extreme darkness° such as it is not possible for a man to understand the matter without an interpreter; all which parts are generally to be banished out of every language, unless it may appear that the maker or poet do it for the nonce,° as it was reported by° the philosopher Heraclitus that he wrote in obscure and dark° terms of purpose not to be understood, whence he merited the nickname *Scotinus*.[4]

1. See 3.7.239.

2. **disposition** arrangement.

3. **fond** foolish.

4. In his history of Rome, Livy mentions Heraclitus, "whose surname was Scotinus" (23.39.3), a Latinized version of the Greek *skoteinos* (dark, obscure). See also Seneca, *Epistulae* 12.5, and Cicero, *De finibus* 2.5.15.

Otherwise I see not but the rest of the common faults may be borne with sometimes, or pass without any great reproof, not being used overmuch or out of season as I said before; so as° every surplusage° or preposterous° placing or undue iteration or dark° word or doubtful° speech are not so narrowly to be looked upon in a large poem, nor especially in the pretty poesies and devices° of ladies and gentlewomen makers, whom we would not have too precise[5] poets, lest, with their shrewd° wits, when they were married they might become a little too fantastical° wives. Nevertheless, because we seem to promise an art, which doth not justly admit any willful error in the teacher, and to the end we may not be carped at by these methodical men that we have omitted any necessary point in this business to be regarded,[6] I will speak somewhat touching these viciosities° of language particularly and briefly, leaving no little to the grammarians for maintenance of the scholastical° war and altercations[7]—we for our part condescending in this device° of ours to[8] the appetite of princely personages and other so tender and queasy complexions[9] in court as are annoyed with nothing more than long lessons and overmuch good order.

5. **precise** over-strict.
6. Puttenham appears to say that although he shuns obsessive precision (supposedly because of its effects as a model on the "gentlewomen makers"), he must nonetheless, since he promises an *art* (a systematic account or theory), be technically, if wearisomely, precise regarding the "viciosities of language" to be discussed next (in 3.22).
7. Puttenham's statement that the stylistic faults he will discuss also concern the grammarian follows *Ad Herennium* 4.12.17 and Quintilian 8.1.2.
8. **condescending . . . to** complying with, acceding to (deferentially).
9. **complexions** temperaments.

CHAPTER 22

Some vices in speeches and writing are always intolerable, some others now and then borne withal° by license of approved authors and custom

Barbarismus, or Foreign Speech The foulest vice in language is to speak barbarously.°[1] This term grew by the great pride of the Greeks and Latins when they were dominators of the world, reckoning no language so sweet and civil as their own, and that all nations beside themselves were rude° and uncivil, which they called barbarous;° so as° when any strange word not of the natural Greek or Latin was spoken, in the old time they called it *barbarism*; or when any of their own natural words were sounded and pronounced with strange and ill-shaped accents, or written by wrong

1. On *barbarismus*, see Mosellanus B2v–B3r; see also *Ad Herennium* 4.12.17; Quintilian 1.5.5–17; Sherry 36.

orthography, as he that would say with us in England, a "dousand" for a "thousand," "isterday" for "yesterday" as commonly the Dutch and French people do, they said it was barbarously° spoken. The Italian at this day by like arrogance calleth the Frenchman, Spaniard, Dutch, English, and all other bred behither[2] their mountains Apennines, *Tramontani*, as who would say "barbarous."°[3]

This term being then so used by the ancient Greeks, there have been since, notwithstanding, who[4] have digged for the etymology somewhat deeper, and many of them have said[†] that it was spoken by° the rude° and barking language of the Africans now called Barbarians, who had great traffic° with the Greeks and Romans; but that cannot be so, for that part of Africa hath but of late received the name of Barbary, and some others rather think that of this word "barbarous,"° that country came to be called Barbaria and but few years in respect ago. Others, among whom is Juan Leon, a Moor of Granada, will seem to derive Barbaria from this word *Bar*, twice iterated—thus, *Barbar*—as much to say as,° "fly, fly," which chanced in a persecution of the Arabians by some seditious Mohammedans in the time of their pontiff[5] Habdul Mumi, when they were had in the chase, and driven out of Arabia westward into the countries of Mauritania,[6] and during the pursuit cried one upon another, "fly away, fly away," or "pass, pass"; by which occasion they say, when the Arabians which were had in chase came to stay and settle themselves in that part of Africa, they called it Barbar, as much to say,° the "region of their flight or pursuit."[7] Thus much for the term, though not greatly pertinent to the matter, yet not unpleasant to know for them that delight in such niceties.°

Your next intolerable vice is *solecismus* or Incongruity.[8] As when we speak false English, that is, by misusing the grammatical rules to be observed in cases, genders, tenses, and such like; every poor scholar° knows the fault, and calls it "the breaking of Priscian's head,"[9] for he was among the Latins a principal grammarian.

Solecismus, or Incongruity

Ye have another intolerable ill manner of speech, which by the Greeks' original we may call Fond Affectation.°[10] And is when we affect

Cacozelia, or Fond Affectation°

---

2. **behither** on this side of.

3. *Tramontani* literally means "those who live beyond the mountains."

4. **who** i.e., those who.

5. **pontiff** chief priest.

6. In Roman times, Mauritania was the region west of Egypt, called Mauritania Caesariensis, where modern Libya is to be found; not to be confused with Mauritania Tingitana, on the Atlantic coast of northwest Africa, now roughly the modern country of Mauritania.

7. This etymological tale derives from the *Descrittione dell'Africa* (1550) of Juan Leon (now commonly known as Leo Africanus),

which was not translated into English until 1600 by John Pory, as *A Geographical Historie of Africa*; the tale appears there at A3r–4v. Puttenham could have consulted this work in the original Italian or perhaps in French or Latin translation.

8. On *solecismus*, see Mosellanus B3r–v; see also Aristotle, *Rhetoric* 3.5.7 (1407b); *Ad Herennium* 4.12.17; Sherry 36.

9. Cf. *Love's Labor's Lost* 5.1.28–29: "Priscian a little scratched."

10. **Fond** foolish. On *cacozelia*, see Quintilian 8.3.56–58; Sherry 34–35; Peacham (1577) G2v.

new words and phrases other than the good speakers and writers in any language, or than custom, hath allowed; and is the common fault of young scholars° not half well-studied before they come from the university or schools, and when they come to their friends, or happen to get some benefice[11] or other promotion in their countries,[12] will seem to coin fine words out of the Latin and to use newfangled speeches, thereby to show themselves among the ignorant the better learned.

Soraismus,
or the
Mingle-Mangle

Another of your intolerable vices is that which the Greeks call *soraismus*, and we may call the Mingle-Mangle,[13] as when we make our speech or writings of sundry languages, using some Italian word, or French, or Spanish, or Dutch, or Scottish, not for the nonce° or for any purpose (which were in part excusable) but ignorantly and affectedly. As one that said, using this French word *roy* to make rhyme with another verse, thus:

> O mighty Lord of Love, dame Venus' only joy,
>   Whose princely power exceeds each other heavenly roy.[14]

The verse is good but the term peevishly[15] affected.

Another[16] of reasonable good facility in translation, finding certain of the hymns of Pindar and of Anacreon's odes and other lyrics among the Greeks very well translated by Ronsard the French poet, and applied to the honor of a great prince[17] in France, comes our minion[18] and translates the same out of French into English, and applieth them to the honor of a great nobleman in England (wherein I commend his reverent mind and duty); but doth so impudently rob the French poet, both of his praise and also of his French terms, that I cannot so much pity him as be angry with him for his injurious dealing, our said maker not being ashamed to use these French words—*freddon, egar, superbous, filanding, celest, calabrois, thebanois*,[19] and a number of others—for English

---

11. **benefice** ecclesiastical living.

12. **their countries** their own regions, perhaps esp. those away from cultural centers. The tendency among the newly educated to use ostentatiously "newfangled" language among their former peers may suggest that the latter are rural "country bumpkins."

13. On *soraismus*, see Mosellanus B2v; see also Quintilian 8.3.59; Sherry 35; Peacham (1577) G4r.

14. See Turberville, "The Louer to Cupid for mercie" (EE, leaves 45r-v: 1–4).

15. **peevishly** foolishly.

16. This poet is John Southern, author of *Pandora* (1584), dedicated to Edward de Vere, seventeenth earl of Oxford.

17. Henry II.

18. **minion** in a positive sense, "darling" or "favorite," particularly the favorite of a powerful political figure; in a negative sense,

"servile agent" or "slave." The word comes from Fr. *mignon*, which has roughly the same meanings.

19. All these terms but *celest* appear in Southern's *Pandora*, Ode 1: *freddon* in Strophe 2.3, *egar* in Strophe 3.12, *superbous* in Epode [2].42 (as well as in Ode 2, Antistrophe 17), *filanding* in Epode [3].46, *calabrois* in Strophe 2.10 and Epode [2].50, and *thebanois* in Strophe 2.11 and Epode [2].50. (References are to the LION text, which omits some section numbers, here supplied in brackets.) *Celest* appears four times in *Pandora*, in sonnets 4.11, 5.12, and 9.4, and in Elegia 16. The meanings of the words are as follows: *freddon* (or, more correctly, *fredon*) from *fredonner*, "to hum or trill"; *egar*, from *égarer*, "to mislead," reflexive "to wander"; *superbous*, from *superbe*, "proud, lofty" (the form of the word really points to the Latin *superbus*); *filanding*, from the present participle

words, which have no manner of conformity with our language, either by custom or derivation, which may make them tolerable. And in the end (which is worst of all) makes his vaunt that never English finger but his hath touched Pindar's string, which was nevertheless word by word as Ronsard had said before by like braggery.[20] These be his verses:

> *And of an ingenious invention,° infanted[21] with pleasant travail.°[22]*

Whereas the French word is *enfante,* as much to say born as a child. In another verse he saith:

> *I will freddon in thine honor.[23]*

For I will shake or quiver my fingers, for so in French is *freddon.*[24] And in another verse:

> *But if I will thus like Pindar,*
> *In many discourses egar.[25]*

This word *egar* is as much to say as° "to wander or stray out of the way," which in our English is not received, nor these words *calabrois, thebanois,* but rather *Calabrian, Theban,* "filanding sisters" for the "spinning sisters." This man deserves to be indicted of petty larceny for pilfering other men's devices° from them and converting them to his own use, for indeed, as I would wish every inventor° which is the very poet to receive the praises of his invention,° so would I not have a translator be ashamed to be acknown of[26] his translation.

Another of your intolerable vices is ill disposition or placing of your words in a clause or sentence,[27] as when you will place your adjective after your substantive, thus: "maid fair," "widow rich," "priest holy," and such like, which, though the Latins did admit, yet our English did not, as one that said ridiculously:

Cacosyntheton, or the Misplacer

> *In my years lusty, many a deed doughty did I.†*

(*filant*) of *filer,* "to spin"; *celest,* from *celeste,* "heavenly"; *calabrois,* Calabrian; *thebanois,* Theban. According to LION, *freddon, egar* (in this sense), *superbous, filanding, calabrois,* and *thebanois* seem to have been used only by Southern among contemporary English poets. *Celest* and *infanted,* however, do appear, if infrequently, in the works of others.

20. This claim appears at the end of Ode 1 of *Pandora:* addressing Oxford, Southern says, "neuer man before, / Now in England, knewe Pindars string" (52).

21. **infanted** brought forth as a child (from Fr. *enfanter*).

22. From *Pandora* (1584), Ode 1, Epode [1].44–45.

23. From *Pandora* (1584), Ode 1, Strophe 2.3.

24. For this meaning of *freddon* (or *fredon*), see Cotgrave's *Dictionarie:* "To shake, diuide, warble, quauer in singing, or playing on an instrument." What is shaken when one trills on a musical instrument is one's fingers; hence, Puttenham's definition. In the poem, however, the word might best be translated as "warbled."

25. From *Pandora* (1584), Ode 1, Strophe 3.12.

26. **acknown of** known for.

27. On *cacosyntheton,* see Mosellanus B2v; see also Susenbrotus 36; Quintilian 8.3.59; Sherry 35; Gascoigne, *Certayne Notes* 459; Peacham (1577) G4r. See LN 15.

Cacemphaton,
or the Figure of
Foul Speech

All these remembered faults be intolerable and ever indecent.°

Now have ye other vicious° manners of speech, but sometimes and in some cases tolerable, and chiefly to the intent to move laughter and to make sport,° or to give it some pretty strange° grace; and is when we use such words as may be drawn to a foul and unshamefast sense.[28] As one that would say to a young woman, "I pray you let me jape with you," which indeed is no more but "let me sport° with you." Yea, and though it were not altogether so directly spoken, the very sounding of the word were not commendable, as he that in the presence of ladies would use this common proverb:

> Jape with me but hurt me not,
> Bourd[29] with me but shame me not.[30]

For it may be taken in another perverser sense by that sort of persons that hear it, in whose ears no such matter ought almost to be called in memory. This vice is called by the Greeks *cacemphaton*; we call it the Unshamefast or Figure of Foul Speech, which our courtly maker shall in any case shun, lest of a poet he become a buffoon or railing companion—the Latins called him *scurra*.[31] There is also another sort of ill-favored speech subject to this vice, but resting more in the manner of the ill-shaped sound and accent, than for the matter itself, which may easily be avoided in choosing your words those that be of the pleasantest orthography, and not to rhyme too many like-sounding words together.

Tautologia,
or the Figure of
Self-Saying

Ye have another manner of composing your meter° nothing commendable, especially if it be too much used, and is when our maker takes too much delight to fill his verse with words beginning all with a letter.[32] As an English rhymer that said:

> The deadly drops of dark disdain
> Do daily drench my due deserts.[33]

And as the monk we spake of before wrote a whole poem to the honor of Carolus Calvus, every word in his verse beginning with C, thus:

---

28. On *cacemphaton*, see Mosellanus B2r; see also Susenbrotus 36; Quintilian 8.3.44–47; Sherry 34. See LN 15.

29. **Bourd** jest. The unshamefast sense that Puttenham remarks is the potentially sexual pun on *board*, as "accost" or (more physically) "enter." See, for example, John Lyly, *Euphues and His England* (1580) 2.105: "Ladyes pretende a great skyrmishe at the first, yet are boorded willinglye at the last"; cf. *Othello* 1.2.50.

30. This proverb does not appear in Tilley or Whiting, but it does in Harvey's *Marginalia* (188), slightly varied.

31. In ancient Rome *scurra* originally meant a witty, urbane gentleman, but by Plautus' time had come to designate a person whose clowning and clever language enabled him to gain a place in the entourage of a wealthy patron; the word thus became synonymous with "parasite." It also served to identify the clown who appeared in Roman pantomimes.

32. The device discussed here is not *tautologia*, as the side note says, but excessive alliteration. See LN 16.

33. Cf. Gascoigne, *The Devises of Sundrie Gentlemen* 36 (248.1–2).

Carmina clarisonae Calvis cantate camenae.[34]

Many of our English makers use it too much, yet we confess it doth not ill but prettily becomes the meter,° if ye pass not two or three words in one verse, and use it not very much, as he that said by way of epithet:

The smoky sighs, the trickling tears.[35]

And such like. For such composition makes the meter° run away smoother, and passeth from the lips with more facility by iteration of a letter than by alteration, which alteration of a letter requires an exchange of ministry and office[36] in the lips, teeth, or palate, and so doth not the iteration.

Your misplacing and preposterous° placing is not all one in behavior of language, for the misplacing is always intolerable, but the Preposterous° is a pardonable fault, and many times gives a pretty grace unto the speech.[37] We call it by a common saying to "set the cart before the horse,"[38] and it may be done either by a single word or by a clause of speech. By a single word thus:

Hysteron, Proteron, or the Preposterous°

And if I not perform, God let me never thrive.[39]

For "perform not." And this vice is sometime tolerable enough, but if the word carry any notable sense, it is a vice not tolerable,[40] as he that said, praising a woman for her red lips, thus:

A coral lip of hue.[41]

Which is no good speech, because either he should have said no more but "a coral lip," which had been enough to declare the redness, or else he should have said, "a lip of coral hue," and not "a coral lip of hue."

---

34. "Clear-sounding Muses, sing your songs about the bald." Hucbaldus, *Ecloga de laudibus calvitii* 1. Carolus Calvus was the French king Charles II, known as Charles the Bald. Cf. 1.7.105.

35. *Tottel* no. 214 (Anonymous), cited at length at 2.4.161.

36. **ministry and office** function and service.

37. On *hysteron proteron*, see Mosellanus B8r; see also Susenbrotus 32–33; Bede 614; Sherry 31; Peacham (1577) F4r–v, (1593) 119, 141; Day 83. Puttenham has discussed this figure before; see 3.13.253.

38. Tilley C103.

39. Gascoigne, *The Adventures of Master F. J.* 175.21.

40. Puttenham's examination of misplacing and preposterous placing is confusing because it intermixes—while attempting to distinguish—"misplacement" (always a vice) and "preposterous" phrasing (often a "pardonable fault," sometimes even a "pretty grace"). He appears to grade the faultiness of "misplacement" as somehow proportional to both the distance of relocation of the semantic unit in question (from its expected placement) and its comparative semantic weight ("notable sense," "sentence"). In the examples, Puttenham thus seems to be less troubled by the transpositions of "not" (an adverb which would normally follow rather than precede the verb "perform," but which still functions as a negation) than he is by what happens with "coral." When this word is moved from its normal place in the prepositional phrase "of [coral] hue," it may still occupy a grammatically correct place, namely before the noun "lip," but the prepositional phrase following "lip" then becomes incomprehensible.

41. From Turberville, "Praise of his Loue" (EE, leaf 129v: 34).

Now if this disorder be in a whole clause, which carrieth more sen-
tence° than a word, it is then worst of all.

Ye have another vicious° speech which the Greeks call *acyron*—we
call it the Uncouth—and is when we use an obscure and dark° word,
and utterly repugnant to that we would express, if it be not by virtue of
the figures *metaphor*, *allegory*, *abusion*, or such other laudable figure
before remembered.[42] As he that said by way of epithet:

> *A dungeon deep, a damp as dark as hell.*[43]

Where it is evident that a damp, being but a breath or vapor and not to
be discerned by the eye, ought not to have this epithet *dark*, no more
than another that praising his mistress for her beautiful hair, said very
improperly and with an uncouth term:

> *Her hair surmounts Apollo's pride,*
> *In it such beauty reigns.*[44]

Whereas this word *reign* is ill applied to the beauty of a woman's hair,
and might better have been spoken of her whole person, in which beauty,
favor, and good grace may perhaps in some sort be said to reign, as ourselves wrote, in a Partheniade praising her Majesty's countenance, thus:

> *A cheer*[45] *where love and majesty do reign,*
> *Both mild and stern, etc.*[46]

Because this word *majesty* is a word expressing a certain sovereign dignity, as well as a quality of countenance, and therefore may properly be
said to "reign," and requires no meaner° a word to set him forth by. So
it is not of the beauty that remains in a woman's hair, or in her hand or
any other member: therefore when ye see all these improper or hard epithets used, ye may put them in the number of Uncouths, as one that
said, "the floods of graces."[47] I have heard of "the floods of tears" and
"the floods of eloquence," or of any thing that may resemble the nature
of a water-course, and in that respect we say also, "the streams of tears"
and "the streams of utterance," but not "the streams of graces," or "of
beauty." Such manner of uncouth speech did the Tanner of Tamworth
use to King Edward IV, which Tanner, having a great while mistaken
him and used very broad talk with him, at length perceiving by his
train that it was the king, was afraid he should be punished for it, said
thus with a certain rude° repentance:

---

42. On *acyron*, see Mosellanus B1r; see
also Susenbrotus 11–12; Quintilian 8.2.3–4;
Sherry 32.

43. From Turberville, "The Louer whose
Lady dwelt fast by a Prison" (EE, leaf 120v:
14).

44. Not from "another," but also from

Turberville, "Praise of his Loue" (EE, leaf
129v: 29–30).

45. **cheer** face or expression.

46. Puttenham, *Partheniades* 8 ("Thalia"):
187–88.

47. From Turberville, "Praise of his
Loue" (EE, leaf 129v: 20).

I hope I shall be hanged tomorrow.[48]

For "(I fear me) I shall be hanged," whereat the king laughed a good,[49] not only to see the Tanner's vain fear, but also to hear his ill-shaped term, and gave him for recompense of his good sport° the inheritance of Plumton Park. I am afraid the poets of our time that speak more finely and correctly will come too short of such a reward.

Also the poet or maker's speech becomes vicious° and unpleasant by nothing more than by using too much Surplusage,° and this lieth not only in a word or two more than ordinary, but in whole clauses, and peradventure° large sentences impertinently° spoken, or with more labor and curiosity° than is requisite. The first Surplusage° the Greeks call *pleonasm*—I call him Too Full Speech—and is no great fault.[50] As if one should say, "I heard it with mine ears, and saw it with mine eyes," as if a man could hear with his heels, or see with his nose. We ourselves used this superfluous speech in a verse written of our mistress, nevertheless not much to be misliked, for even a vice, sometime being seasonably used, hath a pretty grace:

The Vice of Surplusage°

> *Forever may my true love live and never die*
> *And that mine eyes may see her crowned a queen.*°

Pleonasm, or Too Full Speech

As, if she lived ever she could ever die,[51] or that one might see her crowned without his eyes.

Another part of Surplusage° is called *macrologia*, or Long Language, when we use large clauses or sentences more than is requisite to the matter; it is also named by the Greeks *perissologia*.[52] As he that said, "The ambassadors after they had received this answer at the king's hands, they took their leave and returned home into their country from whence they came."[†] So said another of our rhymers, meaning to show the great annoy and difficulty of those wars of Troy, caused for Helen's sake:

Macrologia, or Long-Language

> *Nor Menelaus was unwise,*
> *Or troop of Trojans mad,*
> *When he with them and they with him,*
> *For her such combat had.*[53]

---

48. There seems to be no surviving form of the ballad that is the probable source for this tale ("King Edward IV and the Tanner of Tamworth") which contains the substitution of "hope" for "fear." (For surviving forms of the ballad, see Percy's *Reliques* 2.92–100; Percy cites another ballad containing this construction, however, at 2.93.) Latin sometimes uses *spero* for *timeo* with something like the sense of "expect": see Vergil, *Aeneid* 4.419 (cited by Quintilian at 8.2.4 as an example of *acyron*), and Juvenal 4.57. For a related example of *acyrologia*, see Sherry 32.

49. **a good** abundantly.
50. On *pleonasm*, see Mosellanus B11; see also Susenbrotus 29–30; Quintilian 1.5.40, 8.3.53, 9.3.46–47; Sherry 32; Peacham (1577) F21; Day 82.
51. I.e., (it is absurd to say) she could ever die if she lived (for)ever.
52. On *macrologia*, see Mosellanus A81; see also Susenbrotus 30; Quintilian 8.3.53; Sherry 34; Peacham (1577) F2v; Day 82. *Perissologia* means "wordiness."
53. From Turberville, "In praise of Ladie P." (EE, leaf 138v: 53–56).

These clauses ("he with them and they with him") are Surplusage,° and one of them very impertinent,° because it could not otherwise be intended, but that Menelaus, fighting with the Trojans, the Trojans must of necessity fight with him.

Another point of Surplusage° lieth not so much in superfluity of your words, as of your travail° to describe the matter which ye take in hand, and that ye over-labor yourself in your business. And therefore the

Periergia, or Over-Labor; otherwise called the Curious°

Greeks call it *periergia*.[54] We call it Over-Labor, jump[55] with the original, or rather, the Curious,° for his overmuch curiosity° and study to show himself fine in a light matter. As one of our late makers, who in most of his things wrote very well, in this (to mine opinion) more curiously° than needed, the matter being ripely considered; yet is his verse very good, and his meter° cleanly.° His intent was to declare how upon the tenth day of March he crossed the river of Thames, to walk in Saint George's field—the matter was not great as ye may suppose:

> *The tenth of March when Aries received*
> *Dan Phoebus'[56] rays into his horned head,*
> *And I myself by learned lore perceived*
> *That Ver[57] approached and frosty winter fled,*
> *I crossed the Thames to take the cheerful air*
> *In open fields, the weather was so fair.*[58]

First, the whole matter is not worth all this solemn circumstance to describe the tenth day of March, but if he had left at the two first verses, it had been enough. But when he comes with two other verses to enlarge his description, it is not only more than needs, but also very ridiculous, for he makes wise[59] as if he had not been[60] a man learned in some of the mathematics (by learned lore) that he could not have told that the tenth of March had fallen in the spring of the year, which every carter° and also every child knoweth without any learning. Then also, when he saith "Ver approached, and frosty winter fled," though it were a Surplusage° (because one season must needs give place to the other), yet doth it well enough pass without blame in the maker. These and a hundred more of such faulty and impertinent° speeches may ye find amongst us vulgar° poets, when we be careless of our doings.

Tapinosis, or the Abaser

It is no small fault in a maker to use such words and terms as do diminish and abase the matter he would seem to set forth, by impairing

---

54. On *periergia*, see Mosellanus BIV; see also Sherry 33–34; Peacham (1577) G3v.
55. **jump** coinciding.
56. **Dan Phoebus'** Apollo's (the sun's). "Dan," meaning "Lord" or "Master" (from Lat. *dominus*), was applied to members of religious orders and extended to knights,

squires, and distinguished men generally as an honorific title.
57. **Ver** (Lat.) Spring.
58. See Gascoigne, *The Devises of Sundrie Gentlemen* 25 (237.1–6). Puttenham also cites the first two of these lines in 3.18.278.
59. **makes wise** pretends.
60. I.e., had he not been.

the dignity, height, vigor, or majesty of the cause he takes in hand.[61] As one that would say King Philip shrewdly° harmed the town of St. Quentin when indeed he won it and put it to the sack, and that King Henry VIII made spoils in Turwin, when as indeed he did more than spoil it, for he caused it to be defaced and razed flat to the earth, and made it inhabitable.[62] Therefore the historiographer that should by such words report of these two kings' gests° in that behalf, should greatly blemish the honor of their doings and almost speak untruly and injuriously by way of abasement, as another of our bad rhymers that very indecently° said:

> *A miser's mind thou hast, thou hast a prince's pelf.*[63]

A lewd° term to be given to a prince's treasure ("pelf") and was a little more mannerly spoken by Sergeant Bendlowes, when in a progress time coming to salute the Queen in Huntingtonshire he said to her coachman, "Stay thy cart, good fellow, stay thy cart, that I may speak to the Queen," whereat her Majesty laughed as she had been tickled, and[64] all the rest of the company, although very graciously (as her manner is) she gave him great thanks and her hand to kiss.[65] These and such other base words do greatly disgrace° the thing and the speaker or writer: the Greeks call it *tapinosis*; we the Abaser.

Others there be that fall into the contrary vice by using such bombasted[66] words, as seem altogether farced[67] full of wind, being a great deal too high and lofty for the matter, whereof ye may find too many in all popular rhymers.[68]   *Bomphiologia, or Pompous Speech*

Then have ye one other vicious° speech with which we will finish this chapter, and is when we speak or write doubtfully° and that the sense may be taken two ways. Such ambiguous terms they call *amphibologia*;   *Amphibologia, or the Ambiguous*

61. On *tapinosis*, see Mosellanus B2r; see also Susenbrotus 35; Quintilian 8.3.48; Sherry 34; Peacham (1577) G2r, (1593) 33, 168.

62. **inhabitable** i.e., uninhabitable. On the battle of St. Quentin, see 3.18, note 80. Turwin (Thérouanne) is a town in northern France which Henry captured on August 4, 1513.

63. From Turberville, "Of a Ritch Miser" (EE, leaf 119v: 1–2).

64. **and** i.e., as did.

65. Willcock and Walker (xxx) cite in regard to this tale a notation from Stow's *Annales* of 1615 that "[i]n the year 1564 Guylliam Boonen, a Dutchman, became the Queenes Coachmanne and was the first that brought the use of Coaches into England" (867). Ward (288) locates the event as taking place on the progress of 1564 ("the only progress undertaken by the Queen to Huntingdonshire before 1588," i.e., before the *Art* went to press), and the Cambridge editors suggest that the novelty of coaches might have made the story unusually piquant. Interestingly, Peacham (1577) illustrates this trope by saying, "as to call . . . a Ladyes Coutch a Carte" (G2r); he may be recalling the same news item.

66. **bombasted** stuffed, as with padding.

67. **farced** stuffed (a cooking term).

68. On *bomphiologia*, see Sherry 61. Sherry appears to be coining this term, which he also calls *verborum bombus* (booming words) and exemplifies by reference to Terence's braggart soldier. This is probably a slip for Plautus' Pyrgopolynices, the title character in the *Miles gloriosus*, who refers to a commander of his named Bombomachides ("booming fighter," 1.14).

we call it the Ambiguous, or Figure of Sense Uncertain.[69] As if one should say Thomas Tayler saw William Tyler drunk, it is indifferent° to think either the one or the other drunk. Thus said a gentleman in our vulgar° prettily notwithstanding because he did it not ignorantly, but for the nonce°:

> *I sat by my lady soundly sleeping;*
> *My mistress lay by me bitterly weeping.*[†]

No man can tell by this whether the mistress or the man slept or wept. These doubtful° speeches were used much in the old times by their false prophets as appeareth by the oracles of Delphos and of the Sibyls' prophecies[70] devised by the religious persons of those days to abuse° the superstitious people, and to encumber their busy° brains with vain hope or vain fear.

Lucian, the merry Greek, reciteth a great number of them, devised by a cozening companion, one Alexander, to get himself the name and reputation of the god Aesculapius.[71] And in effect all our old British and Saxon prophecies be of the same sort, that turn them on which side ye will, the matter of them may be verified, nevertheless carrieth generally such force in the heads of fond[72] people, that by the comfort[73] of those blind prophecies many insurrections and rebellions have been stirred up in this realm—as that of Jack Straw and Jack Cade in Richard II's time, and in our time by a seditious fellow in Norfolk calling himself Captain Ket, and others in other places of the realm—led altogether by certain prophetical rhymes, which might be construed two or three ways as well as to that one whereunto the rebels applied it.[74] Our maker shall therefore avoid all such ambiguous speeches unless it be when he doth it for the nonce° and for some purpose.

---

69. On *amphibologia*, see Mosellanus B1v; see also *Ad Herennium* 2.11.16; Quintilian 7.9.1–15; Sherry 33; Peacham (1577) G1r–v.

70. The oracle of Apollo at Delphos (or, more correctly, Delphi), dating from the end of the ninth century BCE, gave the Greeks religious guidance, though that guidance was characteristically ambiguous. There was originally just one Sibyl, but the name was eventually applied to more than ten figures (most famously the Sibyl of Cumae). The Romans possessed a collection of sibylline prophecies to which they turned in times of doubt. The original collection was destroyed in 83 BCE, but there were copies that the early Christians also consulted. They felt that the prophecies anticipated various aspects of their religion.

71. In his satire *Alexander*, Lucian attacks the charlatan Alexander the Paphlagonian, discussing the hoaxes by which he enriched himself as a priest of Aesculapius.

72. **fond** foolish.

73. **comfort** encouragement.

74. Such texts survive, mutatis mutandis, for many of the popular rebellions to which Puttenham refers, though they are not always ambiguous or in verse. See LN 17.

CHAPTER 23

*What it is that generally makes our speech well
pleasing and commendable, and of
that which the Latins call decorum*[1]

In all things to use decency° is it only that giveth everything his good
grace and without which nothing in man's speech could seem good
or gracious, insomuch as° many times it makes a beautiful figure fall
into a deformity, and on the other side, a vicious° speech seem pleasant and beautiful; this decency° is therefore the line and level[2] for all
good makers to do their business by. But herein resteth the difficulty:
to know what this good grace is and wherein it consisteth, for perad-
venture° it be easier to conceive than to express. We will therefore examine it to the bottom and say that everything which pleaseth the
mind or senses, and the mind by the senses as by means instrumental,
doth it for some amiable° point or quality that is in it, which draweth
them to a good liking and contentment with their proper[3] objects.
But that cannot be if they discover° any ill-favoredness or disproportion to the parts apprehensive,[4] as, for example, when a sound is either
too loud or too low or otherwise confused, the ear is ill-affected;[5] so
is the eye if the color be sad° or not luminous and recreative, or the
shape of a membered[6] body without his due measures and symmetry,
and the like of every other sense in his proper function. These excesses
or defects° or confusions and disorders in the sensible° objects are deformities and unseemly to the sense. In like sort the mind for the
things that be his mental objects hath his good graces and his bad,
whereof the one contents him wondrous well, the other displeaseth
him continually, no more nor no less than ye see the discords of music
do to a well-tuned ear.

The Greeks call this good grace of everything in his kind *το πρεπον*,
the Latins *decorum*; we in our vulgar° call it by a scholastical° term

---

1. This chapter probably contains ideas
from Puttenham's lost treatise *De decoro*,
mentioned at 3.24.360. Despite its enormous
importance, decorum is treated only in passing by most rhetoricians, both in antiquity
and in the Renaissance, and when they do
define it, they usually do so by citing instances of decorous (or, more typically, indecorous) language or behavior, just as
Puttenham does. For some ancient examples,
see Aristotle, *Rhetoric* 3.2 (1404b–1405b);
Cicero, *Orator* 21.70–22.74 and *De oratore*
3.55.210–12; and Quintilian 11.1.31–42.
Juan Luis Vives has an extended treatment

of the concept (753–72). Among English Renaissance writers, see Gascoigne, *Certayne
Notes* 455; Whetstone 172–74; E. K.'s Epistle
to Gabriel Harvey introducing Spenser's
Shepheardes Calender 13–20; Stanyhurst
(Smith, *Essays* 1.137); Sidney, *Defence*
242–46; and Webbe 1.263, 294.

2. **line and level** (carpenter's) plumb line
and level; hence, measure or criterion.

3. **proper** own, appropriate.

4. **parts apprehensive** perceptual or sensory apparatus.

5. **is ill-affected** dislikes it.

6. **membered** having members or limbs.

decency.°⁷ Our own Saxon English term is *seemliness*, that is to say, for his good shape and utter⁸ appearance well pleasing the eye. We call it also *comeliness* for the delight it bringeth coming towards us, and to that purpose may be called *pleasant approach*, so as° every way seeking to express this πρεπον of the Greeks and *decorum* of the Latins, we are fain in our vulgar° tongue to borrow the term which our eye only for his noble prerogative over all the rest of the senses doth usurp, and to apply the same to all good, comely, pleasant, and honest things, even to the spiritual⁹ objects of the mind, which stand no less in¹⁰ the due proportion° of reason and discourse¹¹ than any other material thing doth in his sensible° beauty, proportion,° and comeliness.

Now because this comeliness resteth in the good conformity of many things and their sundry circumstances° with respect one to another, so as° there be found a just correspondence between them by this or that relation, the Greeks call it *analogy*,¹² or a convenient° proportion.° This lovely conformity, or proportion,° or convenience° between the sense and the sensible° hath nature herself first most carefully observed in all her own works, then also by kind° grafted it in the appetites of every creature working by intelligence to covet and desire and in their actions to imitate and perform, and of man chiefly before any other creature, as well in his speeches as in every other part of his behavior. And this in generality and by a usual term is that which the Latins call *decorum*. So, albeit we before alleged that all our figures be but transgressions of our daily speech, yet if they fall out decently° to the good liking of the mind or ear and to the beautifying of the matter or language, all is well; if indecently° and to the ear's and mind's misliking (be the figure of itself never so commendable), all is amiss: the election is the writer's, the judgment is the world's, as theirs to whom the reading appertaineth.

But since the actions of man with their circumstances° be infinite, and the world likewise replenished¹³ with many judgments, it may be a question who shall have the determination of such controversy as may arise whether this or that action or speech be decent° or indecent.° And verily, it seems to go all by discretion, not perchance of everyone, but by a learned and experienced discretion. For otherwise seems the *decorum* to a weak and ignorant judgment than it doth to one of better knowledge

---

7. *Tò prepón* comes from the Greek verb *prépo*, which originally meant a striking visual aspect of something or someone; later, what was characteristic (what was "fitting") of the object or person; and finally, used in the impersonal form, what was apt, appropriate, fitting, or seemly in aesthetic, ethical, or rhetorical terms. In his *Orator*, Cicero says the Latin *decorum* is a direct translation of the Greek *tò prepón* (21.70). *Decorum* derives from the verb *decere*, meaning "to be fitting, appropriate," from which English

took the word *decency*. Both *decorum* and *decency* entered the language only in the mid-sixteenth century; Puttenham's uses of the terms are among the earliest in the language.

8. **utter** outward.

9. **spiritual** intellectual, religious.

10. **stand . . . in** consist of.

11. **discourse** discursive understanding.

12. *Analogía* in Greek means "mathematical proportion."

13. **replenished** filled.

and experience, which showeth that it resteth in the discerning part of the mind, so as° he who can make the best and most differences of things by reasonable and witty° distinction is to be the fittest judge or sentencer of decency.° Such generally is the discreetest man, particularly in any art the most skillful° and discreetest, and in all other things for the more part those that be of much observation and greatest experience.

The case then standing that discretion must chiefly guide all those businesses, since there be sundry sorts of discretion all unlike, even as there be men of action or art, I see no way so fit to enable a man truly to estimate of decency° as example, by whose verity we may deem the differences of things and their proportions,° and by particular discussions come at length to sentence° of it generally, and also in our behaviors the more easily to put it in execution. But by reason of the sundry circumstances° that man's affairs are, as it were, wrapped in, this decency° comes to be very much alterable and subject to variety, insomuch as° our speech asketh one manner of decency° in respect of the person who speaks, another of him to whom it is spoken, another of whom we speak, another of what we speak, and in what place and time and to what purpose. And as it is of speech, so of all other our behaviors. We will therefore set you down some few examples of every circumstance how it alters the decency° of speech or action. And by these few shall ye be able to gather a number more to confirm and establish your judgment by a perfect° discretion.

This decency,° so far forth[14] as appertaineth to the consideration of our art, resteth in writing, speech, and behavior. But because writing is no more than the image or character of speech, they shall go together in these our observations. And first we will sort you out divers points, in which the wise and learned men of times past have noted much decency° or indecency,° every man according to his discretion, as it hath been said afore, but wherein for the most part all discreet men do generally agree and vary not in opinion, whereof the examples I will give you be worthy of remembrance. And though they brought with them no doctrine° or institution[15] at all, yet for the solace they may give the readers, after such a rabble of scholastical° precepts, which be tedious, these reports being of the nature of matters historical, they are to be embraced. But old memories are very profitable to the mind, and serve as a glass[16] to look upon and behold the events of time, and more exactly to scan[17] the truth of every case that shall happen in the affairs of man. And many there be that haply do not observe every particularity in matters of decency° or indecency,° and yet when the case is told them by another man, they commonly give the same sentence° upon it. But yet whosoever observeth much shall be counted the wisest and discreetest man, and whosoever

14. **so far forth** insofar.
15. **institution** instruction.

16. **glass** mirror, lens.
17. **scan** examine.

spends all his life in his own vain actions and conceits,° and observes no man's else, he shall in the end prove but a simple° man. In which respect it is always said, one man of experience is wiser than ten learned men, because of his long and studious observation and often trial.°

And your decencies° are of sundry sorts, according to the many circumstances° accompanying our writing, speech, or behavior, so as° in the very sound or voice of him that speaketh, there is a decency° that becometh, and an indecency° that misbecometh us, which the Emperor Antoninus marked well in the orator Philiscus, who spake before him with so small and shrill a voice as the Emperor was greatly annoyed therewith, and to make him shorten his tale, said, "By thy beard thou shouldst be a man, but by thy voice a woman."[18]

Favorinus the philosopher was counted very wise and well learned, but a little too talkative and full of words, for the which Timocrates reproved him in the hearing of one Polemon.[19] "That is no wonder," quoth Polemon, "for so be all women." And besides, Favorinus being known for a eunuch or gelded man came by the same nip to be noted as an effeminate and degenerate person.[20]

And there is a measure to be used in a man's speech or tale, so as° it be neither for shortness too dark,° nor for length too tedious. Which made Cleomenes, King of the Lacedaemonians, give this unpleasant answer to the ambassadors of the Samians, who had told him a long message from their city and desired to know his pleasure in it. "My masters," saith he, "the first part of your tale was so long that I remember it not, which made that the second I understood not, and as for the third part, I do nothing well allow of."[21] Great princes and grave counselors who have little spare leisure to hearken would have speeches used to them such as be short and sweet. And if they be spoken by a man of account, or one who for his years, profession, or dignity should be thought wise and reverend, his speeches and words should also be grave, pithy, and sententious,° which was well noted by King Antiochus, who likened Hermogenes, the famous orator of Greece, unto these fowls in their moulting time, when their feathers be sick, and be so loose in the flesh that at any little rouse they can easily shake them off. "So," saith he, "can Hermogenes of all the men that ever I knew, as easily deliver from him his vain and impertinent° speeches and words."[22]

18. Cf. Philostratus, *Lives of the Sophists* 2.30.621–23. Antoninus is the emperor Caracalla, who says in Philostratus that Philiscus' hair, which was curled, showed what sort of man he was, and his voice what sort of orator.

19. Puttenham uses this name in his lost comedy *Ginecocratia*, discussed at 2.18.218–19.

20. Cf. Philostratus, *Lives of the Sophists* 1.25.541. Like Favorinus, Timocrates was a Sophist and the teacher of Polemon.

21. See Erasmus, *Apophthegmata* 1, "Cleomenes" 16 (LB 4.120D–E); for the original, see Plutarch, *Sayings of the Spartans* ("Cleomenes," Son of Anaxandridas") 7 (*Moralia* 223D). The Samian ambassador has not been identified.

22. Cf. Philostratus, *Lives of the Sophists* 2.7.577–78. This Antiochus was not a king but a Sophist.

And there is a decency,° that every speech should be to the appetite and delight, or dignity of the hearer, and not for any respect arrogant or undutiful, as was that of Alexander sent ambassador from the Athenians to the Emperor Marcus. This man, seeing the Emperor not so attentive to his tale as he would have had him, said by way of interruption, "Caesar, I pray thee, give me better ear; it seemest thou knowest me not, nor from whom I came." The Emperor, nothing well liking his bold, malapert[23] speech, said, "Thou art deceived, for I hear thee and know well enough that thou art that fine, foolish, curious,° saucy Alexander that tendest to nothing but to comb and curry thy hair, to pare thy nails, to pick thy teeth, and to perfume thyself with sweet oils, that no man may abide the scent of thee."[24] Proud speeches and too much finesse[25] and curiosity° is not commendable in an ambassador. And I have known in my time such of them as studied more upon what apparel they should wear, and what countenances they should keep at the times of their audience, than they did upon the effect of their errand or commission.

And there is decency° in that every man should talk of the things they have best skill° of, and not in that their knowledge and learning serveth them not to do—as we are wont to say, he speaketh of Robin Hood that never shot in his bow.[26] There came a great orator before Cleomenes, King of Lacedaemonia, and uttered much matter to him touching fortitude and valiancy in the wars. The King laughed. "Why laughest thou," quoth the learned man, "since thou art a king thyself, and one whom fortitude best becometh?" "Why," said Cleomenes, "would it not make anybody laugh to hear the swallow, who feeds only upon flies, to boast of his great prey, and see the eagle stand by and say nothing? If thou wert a man of war or ever hadst been day of thy life, I would not laugh to hear thee speak of valiancy, but never being so, and speaking before an old captain, I cannot choose but laugh."[27]

And some things and speeches are decent° or indecent° in respect of the time they be spoken or done in. As when a great clerk° presented King Antiochus with a book treating all of justice, the King that time lying at the siege of a town, who looked upon the title of the book, and cast it to him again, saying, "What a devil tellest thou to me of justice, now thou seest me use force and do the best I can to bereave mine enemy of his town?"[28] Everything hath his season, which is called

---

23. **malapert** saucy.

24. For this story about Alexander (Peloplaton), see Philostratus, *Lives of the Sophists* 2.5.570–71.

25. **finesse** i.e., fineness: conspicuous elegance.

26. Tilley R148, Whiting R156.

27. See Erasmus, *Apophthegmata* 1, "Cleomenes" 21 (LB 4.121A–B); for the original, see Plutarch, *Sayings of the Spartans* ("Cleomenes, Son of Anaxandridas") 12

(*Moralia*, 223F). What Cleomenes says in Erasmus and Plutarch is that he would have laughed if a swallow had spoken thus, but not if it had been an eagle. Cleomenes' interlocutor has not been identified; in both Plutarch and Erasmus, he is called a Sophist.

28. Puttenham mistakenly calls Antigonus I "Antiochus" here: see Erasmus, *Apophthegmata* 4, "Antigonus Rex Macedonum" 24 (LB 4.205A, Udall 248).

opportunity, and the unfitness or indecency° of the time is called importunity.[29]

Sometime the indecency° ariseth by the indignity of the word in respect of the speaker himself, as when a daughter of France and next heir general to the crown (if the law Salic had not barred her), being set in a great chafe[30] by some hard words given her by another prince of the blood, said in her anger, "Thou durst not have said thus much to me if God had given me a pair of, etc.," and told all out, meaning if God had made her a man and not a woman, she had been king of France.[31] The word became not the greatness of her person, and much less her sex, whose chief virtue is shamefastness, which the Latins call *verecundia*, that is, a natural fear to be noted with any impudicity,[32] so as° when they hear or see anything tending that way, they commonly blush, and is a part greatly praised in all women.

Yet will ye see in many cases how pleasant speeches and savoring some scurrility and unshamefastness have now and then a certain decency,° and well become both the speaker to say, and the hearer to abide, but that is by reason of some other circumstance, as when the speaker himself is known to be a common jester or buffoon, such as take upon them to make princes merry, or when some occasion is given by the hearer to induce such a pleasant speech, and in many other cases whereof no general rule can be given, but are best known by example. As when Sir Andrew Flamock, King Henry VIII's standard-bearer, a merry, conceited° man and apt to scoff, waiting one day at the King's heels when he entered the park at Greenwich, the King blew his horn, Flamock, having his belly full and his tail at commandment, gave out a rap nothing faintly, that the King turned him about and said, "How now, sirrah?" Flamock, not well knowing how to excuse his unmannerly act, "If it please you, Sir," quoth he, "your Majesty blew one blast for the keeper, and I another for his man." The King laughed heartily and took it nothing offensively: for indeed, as the case fell out, it was not indecently° spoken by Sir Andrew Flamock, for it was the cleanliest[33] excuse he could make, and a merry implicative[34] in terms nothing odious, and therefore a sporting° satisfaction to the King's mind, in a matter which without some such merry answer could not have been

---

29. **importunity** the condition of being inopportune.

30. **chafe** anger.

31. Corrozet (42v) attributes these words to Blanche, the duchess of Orleans, the daughter of Charles IV (1294–1328), who was responding to something said to her by Philippe VI (1293–1350), who, as a male, had succeeded his cousin Charles on the throne. In Corrozet's text, Blanche's comment is less censored than it is in the *Art*. She tells

Philippe, *Si i'avois des couillons, vous n'oseriez m'avoir dit les parolles que vous auez proferees, que ce ne fust à vostre dommage* (If I had balls, you would never have uttered those words you said to me except to your harm).

32. **impudicity** immodesty.

33. **cleanliest** wittiest (with a pun on the modern sense of the word).

34. **implicative** a statement implying more than it expressly states.

well taken. So was Flamock's action most uncomely, but his speech excellently well becoming the occasion.

But at another time and in another like case, the same scurrility of Flamock was more offensive, because it was more indecent.°35 As when the King, having Flamock with him in his barge, passing from Westminster to Greenwich to visit a fair lady whom the King loved and was lodged in the tower of the Park,36 the King, coming within sight of the tower, and being disposed to be merry, said, "Flamock, let us rhyme." "As well as I can," said Flamock, "if it please your Grace." The King began thus:

> *Within this tower,*
> *There lieth a flower,*
> *That hath my heart.*

Flamock for answer: "Within this hour, she will, etc.," with the rest in so uncleanly terms, as might not now become me by the rule of *decorum* to utter, writing to so great a Majesty, but the King took them in so evil part, as he bid Flamock, "Avaunt37 varlet," and that he should no more be so near unto him.38 And wherein, I would fain learn, lay this indecency?° In the scurrilous and filthy terms not meet for a king's ear? Perchance so. For the King was a wise and grave man, and though he hated not a fair woman, yet liked he nothing well to hear speeches of ribaldry, as they report of the Emperor Octavian: *Licet fuerit ipse incontinentissimus, fuit tamen incontinente severissimus ultor.*†39 But the very cause indeed was for that Flamock's reply answered not the

35. The suppressed rhyme word in the poem now quoted is clearly "fart." For reasons obscure, Puttenham associates Flamock with flatulence. A generic element may be at work: the ballad of the Tanner of Tamworth, cited (see 3.22, note 48) as a possible source for another example Puttenham examines, also contains a passage in which a man of low status farts before a king: "The kinge he took him up by the legge [to help him mount his horse]; / The tanner a f˙˙ let fall. / Nowe marrye, good fellow, sayd the kyng, / Thy courtesy is but small" (Percy 2.98). Another such Percy ballad, "The King and the Miller of Mansfield," also contains such a scatological reference (3.186).

36. Puttenham possibly refers here to Katherine Howard, queen from July 28, 1540. Richard Hilles wrote to Heinrich Bullinger in 1541 that although Henry married Anne of Cleves at the Feast of Epiphany (January 6) of 1540, by June 24 courtiers had "observed the king to be much taken with another young lady . . . [and] about the same time many citizens of London saw the king very frequently in the day-time, and sometimes at midnight,

pass over to her on the river Thames in a little boat" (translated from the Lat. in *Original Letters relative to the English Reformation*, no. 105: 1.201–2). A contemporary (1544) drawing showing the tower in Greenwich Park, demolished in 1662, can be found in Wyngaerde's *Panorama*, as drawing XIII (41).

37. **avaunt** away, hence.

38. A tradition stating the full immodest answer to the king's rhyme is recorded at least as early as Samuel Rowley's *When You See Me, You Know Me* (1605). There Henry so challenges not Flamock but Henry's famous court fool Will Summers (before, hilariously, a visiting Charles V, Holy Roman Emperor, and Queen Catherine of Aragon). Summers replies, "Within this houre, she pist full sower, & let a fart" (2929, from the LION text). Summers and the historical king frequently indulged in rhyming contests, and Summers was famously given to excremental humor. See LN 18.

39. "Although he might have been most incontinent himself, he was nevertheless the harshest punisher of incontinence." *Incontinente* in the quotation is probably a slip for

King's expectation, for the King's rhyme, commencing with a pleasant and amorous proposition, Sir Andrew Flamock to finish it not with love but with loathsomeness, by terms very rude° and uncivil, and seeing the King greatly favored that lady for her much beauty belike or some other good parts, by his fastidious[40] answer to make her seem odious[41] to him, it held a great disproportion to the King's appetite. For nothing is so unpleasant to a man as to be encountered[42] in his chief affection,° and especially in his loves. And whom we honor, we should also reverence their appetites, or at the least bear with them (not being wicked and utterly evil), and whatsoever they do affect, we do not as becometh us if we make it seem to them horrible. This in mine opinion was the chief cause of the indecency° and also of the King's offense. Aristotle, the great philosopher, knowing this very well, what time he put Callisthenes to King Alexander the Great's service, gave him this lesson. "Sirrah," quoth he, "ye go now from a scholar° to be a courtier; see ye speak to the King your master either nothing at all, or else that which pleaseth him." Which rule if Callisthenes had followed and forborne to cross the King's appetite in divers speeches, it had not cost him so deeply as afterward it did.[43]

A like matter of offense fell out between the Emperor Charles V and an ambassador of King Henry VIII whom I could name but will not for the great opinion the world had of his wisdom and sufficiency in that behalf, and all for misusing of a term.[44] The King in the matter of con-

---

incontinentie or incontinentiae (of incontinence). Although we have not found a source for this statement, it does echo some of the language used about Augustus by Sextus Aurelius Victor in his *De vita et moribus imperatorum romanorum* (also called *Epitome de Caesaribus*): *Cumque esset luxuriae seruiens, erat tamen eiusdem uitii seuerissimus ultor* (1.24: "Although he was subject to lust, he was nevertheless the harshest punisher of this vice").

40. **fastidious** causing disgust, disagreeable, distasteful. This is the common sense of the word in the writings of Sir Thomas Elyot, Puttenham's uncle. In *The Governour* Elyot warns against tutors who beat their charges, for "that thing for the which children be often times beaten is to them ever after fastidious" (27).

41. **odious** Puttenham's typically sly pun looks forward to Dogberry's observation that "[c]omparisons are odorous" (*Much Ado About Nothing* 3.5.15).

42. **encountered** opposed, thwarted.

43. An account of the warning Aristotle gave to his nephew, the historian Callisthenes of Olynthus (d. 327 BCE), can be found in Diogenes Laertius' *Aristotle*, in *Lives of Eminent*

Philosophers 5.5. In his life of Alexander, Plutarch recounts how Callisthenes fell out of favor with Alexander and was put to death as a result (*Alexander* 52–55); he also says that when informed of Callisthenes' behavior at Alexander's court, Aristotle said his kinsman lacked common sense (54). Neither writer, however, says specifically that Aristotle told Callisthenes he was going to Alexander as a courtier, nor does either one say anything like the words Puttenham is citing. In Lydgate's *Fall of Princes* (printed 1527), Callisthenes proceeds to critique Alexander's tyrannical vices in a manner "Voyde of dissymulyng and dylacions," and is tortured and mutilated for his pains. He who would be valued by tyrants, the tale says, must "kunne [con, practice] flatre & fage [coax, flatter] doutles, / Be double of herte, with feyned contenaunce, / [and] With cheer contreued doon his obseruaunce" (4.8; T2v). Erasmus, relying on Plutarch's *Alexander* (53), also records a condemnatory remark made by Alexander the Great about Callisthenes in *Apophthegmata* 4, "Alexander Magnus" 48 (LB 4.201A, Udall 227).

44. For the possible identity of this ambassador, see LN 19.

troversy betwixt him and Lady Catherine of Castile, the Emperor's aunt, found himself grieved that the Emperor should take her part and work underhand with the Pope to hinder the divorce, and gave his ambassador commission in good terms to open his griefs to the Emperor, and to expostulate with his majesty, for that he seemed to forget the King's great kindness and friendship beforetimes used with the Emperor, as well by disbursing for him sundry great sums of money, which were not all yet repaid, as also by furnishing him at his need with store° of men and munition to his wars—and now to be thus used, he thought it a very evil requital. The ambassador, for too much animosity and more than needed in the case, or perchance by ignorance of the propriety[45] of the Spanish tongue, told the Emperor, among other words, that he was *Hombre el mas ingrato en el mondo*, "the ingratest person in the world,"[46] to use his master so. The Emperor took him suddenly with the word, and said, "Callest thou me *ingrato*? I tell thee, learn better terms, or else I will teach them thee." The ambassador excused it by his commission, and said, they were the King his master's words, and not his own. "Nay," quoth the Emperor, "thy master durst not have sent me these words, were it not for that broad ditch between him and me," meaning the sea, which is hard to pass with an army of revenge. The ambassador was commanded away and no more heard by the Emperor, till by some other means afterward the grief was either pacified or forgotten. And all this inconvenience° grew by misuse of one word, which being otherwise spoken and in some sort qualified, had easily helped all, and yet the ambassador might sufficiently have satisfied his commission and much better advanced his purpose, as to have said for this word "Ye are ingrate," "Ye have not used such gratitude towards him as he hath deserved." So ye may see how a word spoken indecently,° not knowing the phrase or propriety of a language, maketh a whole matter many times miscarry.[47]

In which respect it is to be wished, that none ambassador speak his principal commandments[48] but in his own language, or in another as natural to him as his own, and so it is used in all places of the world saving in England.[49] The princes and their commissioners, fearing lest otherwise they might utter anything to their disadvantage, or else to

---

45. **propriety** particular character.

46. For what it is worth, the grammatical construction (whether Elyot's or Puttenham's) is not quite right; it should be *el hombre mas ingrato del mundo*.

47. In the *Justification* Puttenham reproaches Mary, Queen of Scots, in terms that suggest the fierce potency of this social sin (which has become a milder matter in modern times): "I speake nothinge of her ingratitude toward her Majestie, soo beynge a protectour,

the most haynous offence of anie other, and for which no sufficient and worthye retrybucion could be made or invented" (123).

48. **commandments** i.e., what he was commanded to say.

49. Although during the early part of the sixteenth century diplomacy was ordinarily conducted in Latin, by mid-century negotiation through interpreters had become common in the main royal councils (see Mattingly 236–37).

their disgrace—and I myself, having seen the courts of France, Spain, Italy, and that of the Empire, with many inferior courts, could never perceive that the most noble personages, though they knew very well how to speak many foreign languages, would at any times that they had been spoken unto, answer but in their own, the Frenchman in French, the Spaniard in Spanish, the Italian in Italian, and the very Dutch Prince[50] in the Dutch language: whether it were more for pride, or for fear of any lapse, I cannot tell. And Henry, Earl of Arundel, being an old courtier and a very princely man in all his actions, kept that rule always. For on a time passing from England towards Italy by her Majesty's license,[51] he was very honorably entertained at the Court of Brussels by the Lady Duchess of Parma, Regent there, and sitting at a banquet with her, where also was the Prince of Orange, with all the greatest princes of the state, the Earl, though he could reasonably well speak French, would not speak one French word, but all English, whether he asked any question, or answered it, but all was done by truchmen.[52] Insomuch as° the Prince of Orange, marveling at it, looked aside on that part where I stood a beholder of the feast, and said, "I marvel your noblemen of England do not desire to be better languaged in the foreign languages." This word was by and by[53] reported to the Earl. Quoth the Earl again, "Tell my Lord the Prince that I love to speak in that language in which I can best utter my mind and not mistake."[54]

Another ambassador used the like oversight[55] by overweening[56] himself that he could naturally speak the French tongue, whereas in troth° he was not skillful° in their terms. This ambassador, being a Bohemian, sent from the Emperor to the French court, where after his first audience, he was highly feasted and banqueted. On a time, among other, a great princess, sitting at the table, by way of talk asked the ambassador whether the Empress his mistress, when she went a-hunting, or otherwise travailed° abroad for her solace, did ride a-horseback or go in her coach. To which the ambassador answered, unwares and not knowing the French term, *Par ma foy elle chevauche fort bien, et si en prend grand plaisir.* "She rides," saith he, "very well, and takes great pleasure in it."[57] There was good smiling one upon another of the ladies and lords, the ambassador wist° not whereat, but laughed himself for com-

---

50. William of Orange.

51. The necessity for official approval of such travel dates to 1381 (see 5 Richard II, stat. 1, c.2). For the history and uneven enforcement of this statute, which gained new importance with the religious hostilities of Puttenham's time, see Ghazvinian.

52. **truchmen** intermediaries (an Anglicized French word).

53. **by and by** directly.

54. The Lady Duchess of Parma is Margaret of Parma, the Regent of the Netherlands. The Prince of Orange is William I. On the probable date of this meeting (late summer 1566), see LN 20.

55. **used ... oversight** made a similar mistake by inadvertence.

56. **overweening** overestimating.

57. A more complete translation would be: "By my faith, she rides really well and truly takes great pleasure in it."

pany.† This word *chevaucher* in the French tongue hath a reprobate sense, especially being spoken of a woman's riding.

And as rude° and uncivil speeches carry a marvelous great indecency,° so do sometimes those that be overmuch affected and nice,° or that do savor of ignorance or adulation, and be in the ear of grave and wise persons no less offensive than the other. As when a suitor in Rome came to Tiberius the Emperor and said, "I would open my case to your Majesty, if it were not to trouble your sacred business," *sacras vestras occupationes*, as the historiographer reporteth. "What meanest thou by that term?" quoth the Emperor; "say *laboriosas*, I pray thee, and so thou mayst truly say"—and bid him leave off such affected, flattering terms.[58]

The like indecency° used a herald at arms sent by Charles V, Emperor, to Francis I, French King, bringing him a message of defiance, and thinking to qualify the bitterness of his message with words pompous and magnificent for the King's honor, used much this term "sacred majesty," which was not usually given to the French King, but to say for the most part *sire*. The French King, neither liking of his errand, nor yet of his pompous speech, said somewhat sharply, "I pray thee, good fellow, claw me not where I itch not with thy 'sacred majesty,' but go to thy business, and tell thine errand in such terms as are decent° betwixt enemies, for thy master is not my friend"—and turned him to a prince of the blood who stood by, saying, "Methinks this fellow speaks like Bishop Nicholas." For on Saint Nicholas's night commonly the scholars° of the country make them a bishop, who like a foolish boy goeth about blessing and preaching with so childish terms as maketh the people laugh at his foolish counterfeit° speeches.[59]

And yet in speaking or writing of a prince's affairs and fortunes there is a certain *decorum*, that we may not use the same terms in their business as we might very well do in a meaner° person's; the case being all one, such reverence is due to their estates.° As for example, if a historiographer shall write of an emperor or king, how such a day he joined battle with his enemy, and being overlaid,[60] ran out of the field and took his heels, or put spur to his horse and fled as fast as he could, the terms be not decent,° but of a mean° soldier or captain, it were not indecently° spoken. And as one who, translating certain books of Vergil's

---

58. See Erasmus, *Apophthegmata* 6, "Tiberius Caesar" 3 (LB 4.273A); for the original, see Suetonius, *Tiberius* 3.27.

59. Puttenham inaccurately conflates English and continental practices when speaking of a popular folk festivity in which boys in a given locality would take over a local cathedral, elect a Boy Bishop, and fulfill most clerical functions there except for saying Mass. On the continent this festivity took place on December 28 (the eve of the Feast of the Holy Innocents), but in England it was observed on December 6 (the eve of the Feast of Saint Nicholas, the patron of children).

60. **overlaid** overwhelmed

Aeneid into English meter,° said that Aeneas was fain to trudge out of Troy, which term became better to be spoken of a beggar, or of a rogue, or a lackey, for so we use to say to such manner of people, "Be trudging hence."[61]

Another Englishing this word of Vergil, *fato profugus*, called Aeneas "by fate a fugitive," which was indecently° spoken, and not to the author's intent in the same word: for whom he studied by all means to advance above all other men of the world for virtue and magnanimity, he meant not to make him a fugitive.[62] But by occasion of his great distresses, and of the hardness of his destinies, he would have it appear that Aeneas was enforced to fly out of Troy, and for many years to be a roamer and a wanderer about the world both by land and sea (*fato profugus*), and never to find any resting place till he came into Italy, so as° ye may evidently perceive in this term "fugitive" a notable indignity offered to that princely person, and by the other word, "a wanderer," none indignity at all, but rather a term of much love and commiseration. The same translator, when he came to these words, *Insignem pietate virum, tot volvere casus tot adire labores compulit*, he turned it thus, "What moved Juno to tug so great a captain as Aeneas"[63]—which word "tug," spoken in this case, is so indecent° as none other[64] could have been devised, and took his first original from the cart, because it signifieth the pull or draught of the oxen or horses, and therefore the leathers that bear the chief stress of the draught—the carters° call them tugs—and so we use to say that shrewd° boys "tug" each other by the ears, for "pull."

Another of our vulgar° makers spoke as ill-faringly in this verse written to the dispraise of a rich man and covetous: "Thou hast a miser's mind, thou hast a prince's pelf"—a lewd° term to be spoken of a prince's treasure, which in no respect nor for any cause is to be called "pelf," though it were never so mean,° for "pelf" is properly the scraps or shreds of tailors and of skinners, which are accounted of so vile price as they be commonly cast out of doors, or otherwise bestowed upon base purposes; and carrieth not the like reason or decency,° as when we say in reproach of a niggard, or usurer, or worldly, covetous man, that he setteth more by a little pelf of the world, than by his credit, or

---

61. The text here alludes to Richard Stanyhurst's translation of the *The First Four Books of Virgil His Aeneis* (1582): "Lyke wandring pilgrim too famosed Italie trudging" (1.7).

62. **fugitive** Although this word could simply mean "exile" in the sixteenth century, it was also applied to someone who had run away from battle, was shifty and vagrant, or had taken flight from duty, justice, or a master. Vergil's *profugus* generally lacks these negative meanings. The other Englishing of

Vergil's words is from Gavin Douglas's *Eneados* (1553), which says that Aeneas is "that fugitive / By fate to Ytal come" (1.2–3).

63. The translation Puttenham cites from Stanyhurst covers only a portion of Vergil's Latin (1.9–11: "[Juno] forced a man, renowned for piety, to undergo so many experiences and to undertake so many labors"). Puttenham slightly misquotes Stanyhurst, who does, however, use "tugge" (1.11).

64. **none other** i.e., no other more indecent.

health, or conscience.[65] For in comparison of these treasures, all the gold or silver in the world may by a scornful term be called "pelf," and so ye see that the reason of the decency° holdeth not alike in both cases. Now let us pass from these examples to treat of those that concern the comeliness and decency° of man's behavior.[66]

And some speech may be when it is spoken very indecent,° and yet the same, having afterward somewhat added to it, may become pretty and decent,° as was the stout word used by a captain in France, who, sitting at the lower end of the Duke of Guise's table among many, the day after there had been a great battle fought, the Duke, finding that this captain was not seen that day to do anything in the field, taxed him privily[67] thus in all the hearings: "Where were you, Sir, the day of the battle, for I saw ye not?" The captain answered promptly, "Where ye durst not have been." And the Duke began to kindle with the word, which the gentleman perceiving said speedily, "I was that day among the carriages, where your Excellency would not for a thousand crowns have been seen."[68] Thus from indecent° it came by a witty° reformation[69] to be made decent° again.

The like happened on a time at the Duke of Northumberland's board,° where merry John Heywood was allowed to sit at the table's end. The Duke had a very noble and honorable mind always to pay his debts well, and when he lacked money, would not stick° to sell the greatest part of his plate: so had he done few days before. Heywood, being loath to call for his drink so oft as he was dry, turned his eye toward the cupboard and said, "I find great miss of your Grace's standing[70] cups." The Duke, thinking he had spoken it of some knowledge that his plate was lately sold, said somewhat sharply, "Why, Sir, will not those cups serve as good a man as yourself?" Heywood readily replied, "Yes, if it please your Grace, but I would have one of them stand still° at mine elbow full of drink that I might not be driven to trouble your men so often to call for it." This pleasant and speedy reverse of the former words helped all the matter again, whereupon the Duke became very pleasant and drank a bowl of wine to Heywood, and bid a cup should always be standing by him.†

It were too busy° a piece of work for me to tell you of all the parts of decency° and indecency° which have been observed in the speeches of

---

65. Puttenham's sense that *pelf* "properly" means the "scraps and shreds of tailors and of skinners" is misleading. The word is probably derived from the Latin *pilare*, "to pillage," and identifies goods or booty so obtained. Puttenham limits the word to one of its more specialized meanings.

66. Although Puttenham here announces the subject of his next chapter, he adds three more examples of indecorum in speech.

67. **privily** privately, in the sense of individually; personally; in a private, as opposed to a public or official, capacity (?). (The word certainly does not mean "privately" in its modern sense, that is, "in private," just between the duke and the captain alone, since other people are able to hear what is being said.)

68. For a version of this anecdote, see Corrozet 116r–v. According to Corrozet, the incident occurred during the reign of Francis I (1515–47).

69. **reformation** transformation.

70. **standing** having a stem.

man and in his writings, and this that I tell you is rather to solace your
ears with pretty conceits° after a sort[71] of long scholastical° precepts
which may happen have doubled them,[72] rather than for any other purpose of institution[73] or doctrine,° which to any courtier of experience is
not necessary in this behalf. And as they appear by the former examples
to rest in our speech and writing, so do the same by like proportion°
consist in the whole behavior of man, and that which he doth well and
commendably is ever decent,° and the contrary indecent,° not in every
man's judgment always one, but after[74] their several discretion and by
circumstance diversely, as by the next chapter shall be shown.

71. **sort** quantity.
72. **happen ... doubled them** happen to
have doubled up the ears, as if clenched; i.e.,
closed them.

73. **institution** instruction.
74. **after** according to.

Chapter 24

*Of decency° in behavior which also belongs to the
consideration of the poet or maker*

And there is a decency° to be observed in every man's action and behavior as well as in his speech and writing, which some peradven-
ture° would think impertinent° to be treated of in this book, where we
do but inform° the commendable fashions of language and style. But
that is otherwise, for the good maker or poet, who is, in decent° speech
and good terms, to describe all things and with praise or dispraise to report every man's behavior, ought to know the comeliness of an action
as well as of a word and thereby to direct himself both in praise and persuasion or any other point that pertains to the orator's art. Wherefore
some examples we will set down of this manner of decency° in behavior, leaving you for the rest to our book which we have written, *De
decoro*, where ye shall see both parts[1] handled more exactly.[2] And this
decency° of man's behavior as well as of his speech must also be
deemed[3] by discretion, in which regard the thing that may well become
one man to do may not become another, and that which is seemly to be
done in this place is not so seemly in that, and at such a time decent,°
but at another time indecent,° and in such a case and for such a purpose, and to this and that end, and by this and that event,[4] perusing all
the circumstances° with like consideration. Therefore, we say that it
might become King Alexander to give a hundred talents to Anaxagoras

1. **parts** i.e., speech and behavior.
2. Puttenham's treatise is no longer extant.

3. **deemed** judged.
4. **event** outcome.

the philosopher, but not for a beggarly philosopher to accept so great a gift, for such a prince could not be so impoverished by that expense, but the philosopher was by it excessively to be enriched, so was the King's action proportionable to his estate° and therefore decent,° the philosopher's, disproportionable both to his profession and calling and therefore indecent.°[5]

And yet if we shall examine the same point with a clearer discretion, it may be said that whatsoever it might become King Alexander of his regal largesse to bestow upon a poor philosopher unasked, that might as well become the philosopher to receive at his hands without refusal, and had otherwise been some impeachment of the King's ability or wisdom, which had not been decent° in the philosopher, nor the immoderateness of the King's gift in respect of the philosopher's mean° estate° made his acceptance the less decent,° since princes' liberalities are not measured by merit nor by other men's estimations, but by their own appetites and according to their greatness.[6] So said King Alexander, very like himself, to one Perillus to whom he had given a very great gift, which he made courtesy[7] to accept, saying it was too much for such a mean person. "What," quoth the King, "if it be too much for thyself, hast thou never a friend or kinsman that may fare the better by it?"[8] But peradventure° if any such immoderate gift had been craved by the philosopher and not voluntarily offered by the King, it had been indecent° to have taken it.

Even so, if one that standeth upon his merit and spares to crave[9] the prince's liberality in that which is moderate and fit for him, doth as indecently.° For men should not expect[10] till the prince remembered it of himself and began, as it were, the gratification, but ought to be put in remembrance by humble solicitations, and that is dutiful and decent.° Which made King Henry VIII, her Majesty's most noble father—and for liberality nothing inferior to King Alexander the Great—answer one of his privy chamber, who prayed him to be good and gracious to a certain

---

5. Puttenham garbles data from Erasmus in this and the next paragraph. His "Anaxagoras" is a slip for Anaxarchus (mid- to late 4th c. BCE) who was a coeval of Alexander (356–323 BCE), unlike Anaxagoras (500–ca. 428 BCE). Erasmus uses the correct name at *Apophthegmata* 4, "Alexander Magnus" 7 (LB 4.196F–197A, Udall 207); for the original, see Plutarch, *Sayings of Kings*, "Alexander" 7 (*Moralia* 179F). Erasmus's story is not identical to the one Puttenham rehearses. The immediately preceding apophthegm (6, LB 4.196F), recording a similar tale concerning Perillus, a friend of Alexander's, ends, in Udall's translation (243): "Yea (quoth Alexander) so much [i.e., fifty talents] is enough for thee to take, but

the same is not enough for me to geue." A similar story with different personnel occurs at *Apophthegmata* 4, "Antigonus" 15 (LB 4.204B, Udall 243).

6. Cf. Elyot, *The Governour* 130.

7. **made courtesy** scrupled.

8. Here Puttenham cites from Erasmus a similar tale, not of Perillus (as he erroneously says) but of "Xenocrates the Philosophier," who declined a gift from Alexander, who then, in Udall's translation (219), "demaunded whether he had not so much as any one frende neither, that had nede" (see Erasmus, *Apophthegmata* 4, "Alexander Magnus" 30 [LB 4.199C–D]).

9. **spares to crave** refrains from seeking.

10. **expect** wait.

old knight, being his servant, for that he was but an ill beggar: "If he be ashamed to beg, we will think scorn to give."[11] And yet peradventure° in both these cases, the indecency° for too much craving or sparing to crave might be easily helped by a decent° magnificence[12] in the prince, as Amasis, King of Egypt, very honorably considered, who asking one day for one Diopithes, a nobleman of his court, what was become of him for that he had not seen him wait[13] of long time, one about the King told him that he heard say he was sick and of some conceit° he had taken[14] that his majesty had but slenderly[15] looked to him, using many others very bountifully. "I beshrew his fool's head," quoth the King, "Why had he not sued unto us and made us privy of his want?";° then added, "But in truth we are most to blame ourselves, who by a mindful beneficence without suit should have supplied[16] his bashfulness"—and forthwith commanded a great reward in money and pension to be sent unto him. But it happened that when the King's messengers entered the chamber of Diopithes, he had newly given up the ghost. The messengers sorrowed the case, and Diopithes' friends sat by and wept, not so much for Diopithes' death, as for pity that he overlived not the coming of the King's reward. Thereupon it came ever after to be used for a proverb that when any good turn cometh too late to be used, to call it Diopithes' reward.[17]

In Italy and France I have known it used for common policy,° the princes to defer the bestowing of their great liberalities, as[18] cardinalships and other high dignities and offices of gain, till the parties whom they should seem to gratify be so old or so sick as it is not likely they should long enjoy them. In the time of Charles IX, French King, I being at the Spa waters, there lay a Marshall of France, called Monsieur de Sipier, to use those waters for his health, but when the physicians had all given him up, and that there was no hope of life in him, came from the King to him a letters patent[19] of six thousand crowns yearly pension during his life with many comfortable words. The man was not so much past remembrance, but he could say to the messenger, "*Trop tard, trop tard,*[20] it should have come before," for indeed it had been promised long and came not till now that he could not fare the better by it.[21]

---

11. Puttenham tells this story of the duke of Norfolk and Sir Anthony Rous earlier, at 3.18.274, and again at 3.24.375–76.

12. **magnificence** liberality, munificence; one of the moral virtues according to Aristotle; see *Nicomachean Ethics* 4.2.1–19 (1122a–b).

13. **wait** be in attendance (upon a superior).

14. Cf. 3.25.379–80.

15. **slenderly** to a small extent.

16. **supplied** compensated for.

17. See Aristotle, *Rhetoric* 2.8.11 (1386a). See also LN 21.

18. **as** i.e., such as.

19. **letters patent** (Lat. *litterae patentes,* "open letter") a letter from a sovereign or some person in authority issued for various purposes, often conferring benefits, rights, and privileges.

20. "Too late, too late."

21. There are two claimants for "Monsieur de Sipier." He may be François de Scépeaux (ca. 1510–1571), a successful soldier and diplomat who helped to negotiate the Treaty of Cateau-Cambrésis in 1559, for which he was made Maréchal (Marshall) de France in that year, and who did in fact receive a pension of ten thousand écus from

And it became King Antiochus better to bestow the fair Lady Stratonice his wife upon his son Demetrius, who lay sick for her love and would else have perished, as the physicians cunningly° discovered by the beating of his pulse, than it could become Demetrius to be enamored with his father's wife, or to enjoy her of his gift, because the father's act was led by discretion and of a fatherly compassion, not grudging to depart from his dearest possession to save his child's life, whereas the son in his appetite had no reason to lead him to love unlawfully, for whom it had rather been decent° to die than to have violated his father's bed with safety of his life.[22]

No more would it be seemly for an aged man to play the wanton° like a child, for it stands not with the conveniency° of nature. Yet when King Agesilaus, having a great sort[23] of little children, was one day disposed to solace himself among them in a gallery where they played, and took a little hobbyhorse of wood and bestrode it to keep them in play, one of his friends seemed to mislike his lightness. "O good friend," quoth Agesilaus, "rebuke me not for this fault till thou have children of thine own," showing indeed that it came not of vanity, but of a fatherly affection, joying in the sport° and company of his little children, in which respect and as that place and time served, it was dispensable[24] in him and not indecent.°[25]

And in the choice of a man's delights and manner of his life, there is a decency,° and so we say the old man generally is no fit companion for the young man, nor the rich for the poor, nor the wise for the foolish. Yet in some respects and by discretion it may be otherwise, as when the old man hath the government of the young, the wise teaches the foolish, the rich is waited on by the poor for their relief, in which regard the conversation° is not indecent.°

And Proclus the philosopher, knowing how every indecency° is unpleasant to nature, and namely, how uncomely a thing it is for young men to do as old men do (at leastwise as young men for the most part do take it), applied it very wittily to his purpose: for having his son and heir

---

the king just before his death. "Sipier" may instead be Philibert de Marcilly, seigneur de Cipièrre, another distinguished soldier who died at Liège in 1566. Willcock and Walker canvass the claims at xxvii, opting for de Scépeaux. The city of Spa is a famous health resort in eastern Belgium, known since Roman times for its curative waters. If Puttenham was present at the dinner in Brussels with Margaret of Parma in 1566 (when Arundel was on the way to Padua's waters for the gout; see 3.23.356 and LN 20), he may have visited Spa on that same trip. It is on the route from Brussels to Padua, and Arundel might have wished to try Spa's waters as well. The Sipier event took place in 1571,

however; possibly Puttenham returned for another visit.

22. **with safety ... life** i.e., while preserving his own life. Puttenham garbles the names. Plutarch (*Demetrius* 38), says Antiochus I Soter (the son) was dying of lovesickness for her until his physician Erasistratus discovered the cause and revealed it to Seleucus I Nicator (the father), whereupon the latter gave her to his son as his wife.

23. **sort** quantity.

24. **dispensable** excusable.

25. See Erasmus, *Apophthegmata* 1, "Agesilaus" 68 (LB 4.103A–B); for the original, see Plutarch, *Sayings of the Spartans*, "Agesilaos the Great" 70 (*Moralia* 213D).

a notable unthrift, and delighting in nothing but in hawks and hounds and gay apparel and such like vanities, which neither by gentle nor sharp admonitions of his father could make him leave, Proclus himself not only bore with his son, but also used it[26] himself for company, which some of his friends greatly rebuked him for, saying, "O Proclus, an old man and a philosopher to play the fool and lascivious[27] more than the son!" "Marry,"[28] quoth Proclus, "and therefore I do it, for it is the next[29] way to make my son change his life, when he shall see how indecent° it is in me to lead such a life, and for him being a young man to keep company with me, being an old man, and to do that which I do."[30]

So is it not unseemly for any ordinary captain to win the victory or any other advantage in war by fraud and breach of faith, as Hannibal with the Romans, but it could not well become the Romans, managing so great an empire by examples of honor and justice, to do as Hannibal did. And when Parmenio in a like case persuaded King Alexander to break the day of his appointment and to set upon Darius at the sudden, which Alexander refused to do, Parmenio saying, "I would do it if I were Alexander." "And I too," quoth Alexander, "if I were Parmenio, but it behooveth me in honor to fight liberally[31] with mine enemies and justly to overcome." And thus ye see that was decent° in Parmenio's action, which was not in the King his master's.[32]

A great nobleman and counselor in this realm was secretly advised by his friend not to use so much writing his letters in favor of every man that asked[33] them, especially to the judges of the realm in cases of justice. To whom the nobleman answered, "It becomes us counselors better to use instance[34] for our friend, than for the judges to sentence at instance: for whatsoever we do require them, it is in their choice to refuse to do."† But for all that, the example was ill and dangerous.

And there is a decency° in choosing the times of a man's business, and as the Spaniard says, *es tiempo de negotiar*, "there is a fit time for every man to perform his business in and to attend his affairs," which out of that time would be indecent°: as to sleep all day and wake all night, and to go a-hunting by torchlight, as an old Earl of Arundel[35]

---

26. **it** i.e., his son's debauched way of life.

27. **lascivious** i.e., (be) lascivious (licentious or wanton).

28. **Marry** By Mary (a mild oath).

29. **next** nearest.

30. See Erasmus, *Apophthegmata* 8, "Proclus" 44 (LB 4.355B); for the original, see Philostratus, *Lives of the Sophists* 2.21.603.

31. **liberally** as a person of superior station, a gentleman (from Lat. *liberus*, a free man, as opposed to a slave).

32. See Erasmus, *Apophthegmata* 4, "Alexander Magnus" 11 (LB 4.197C, Udall 209); for the original, see Plutarch, *Sayings of*

Kings and Commanders, "Alexander" 11 (*Moralia* 180B).

33. **asked** i.e., asked for.

34. **instance** importunity.

35. Perhaps Henry Fitzalan, twelfth earl of Arundel (1511?–1580; earl from 1544), mentioned at 3.23.356 as dining with Margaret of Parma, when Puttenham might have been present. His father, William Fitzalan (1483–1544), the eleventh earl, is also possible: he died at age sixty-one, when Puttenham was about fourteen. A. L. Boyle, biographer of the twelfth earl, believes this reference to be to the eleventh earl (personal communication).

used to do, or for any occasion of little importance to wake a man out of his sleep, or to make him rise from his dinner to talk with him, or such like importunities, for so we call every unseasonable[36] action, and the indecency° of the time.

Callicratidas, being sent ambassador by the Lacedaemonians to Cyrus, the young King of Persia, to contract with him for money and men toward their wars against the Athenians, came to the court at such unseasonable time as the King was yet in the midst of his dinner, and went away again, saying, "It is now no time to interrupt the King's mirth." He came again another day in the afternoon, and finding the King at a rear-banquet[37] and to have taken the wine somewhat plentifully, turned back again, saying, "I think there is no hour fit to deal with Cyrus, for he is ever in his banquets; I will rather leave all the business undone than do anything that shall not become the Lacedaemonians"—meaning to offer conference of so great importance to his country[38] with a man so distempered° by surfeit, as he was not likely to give him any reasonable resolution in the cause.[39]

One Eudamidas, brother to King Agis of Lacedaemonia, coming by Xenocrates' school and looking in, saw him sit in his chair, disputing with a long hoary beard, asked who it was; one answered, "Sir, it is a wise man, and one of them that searches after virtue." "And if he have not yet found it," quoth Eudamidas, "when will he use it, that now at these years is seeking after it"—as who would say it is not time to talk of matters when they should be put in execution, nor for an old man to be to seek what virtue is, which all his youth he should have had in exercise.[40] Another time coming to hear a notable philosopher dispute, it happened that all was ended even as he came, and one of his familiars would have had him request the philosopher to begin again. "That were indecent° and nothing civil," quoth Eudamidas, "for if he should come to me supperless when I had supped before, were it seemly for him to pray me to sup again for his company?"[41]

And the place makes a thing decent° or indecent,° in which consideration one Euboedas, being sent ambassador into a foreign realm, some of his familiars took occasion at the table to praise the wives and

---

36. **unseasonable** untimely.

37. **rear-banquet** small meal after dining; dessert.

38. This word appears thirteen times in this chapter, perhaps because decorum is so context-specific. Sometimes it means (as here) "nation," or (adjectivally, where we would expect a genitive) "national"; on other occasions (usually in an English context) it refers to "the parts of a region distant from cities or courts"; sometimes it appears to mean simply "regional."

39. See Erasmus, *Apophthegmata* 1,

"Callicratidas" 5 (LB 4.119A–D); for the original, see Plutarch, *Sayings of Spartans*, "Callicratidas" 2 (*Moralia* 222C–D). See also Xenophon, *Hellenica* 1.6.1–33. The Cyrus mentioned here is Cyrus the Younger.

40. See Erasmus, *Apophthegmata* 1, "Eudamidas" 78 (LB 4.115E–F); for the original, see Plutarch, *Sayings of Spartans*, "Eudamidas, Son of Archidamus" 1 (*Moralia* 220D).

41. See Erasmus, *Apophthegmata* 1, "Eudamidas" 80 (LB 4.116A–B); for the original, see Plutarch, *Sayings of Spartans*, "Eudamidas, Son of Archidamus" 3 (*Moralia* 220D).

women of that country in presence of their own husbands, which the ambassador misliked, and when supper was ended and the guests departed, took his familiars aside and told them that it was nothing decent° in a strange° country to praise the women, nor especially a wife before her husband's face, for inconvenience° that might rise thereby, as well to the praiser as to the woman, and that the chief commendation of a chaste matron was to be known only to her husband, and not to be observed[42] by strangers° and guests.[43]

And in the use of apparel there is no little decency° and indecency° to be perceived, as well for the fashion as the stuff, for it is comely that every estate° and vocation should be known by the differences of their habit: a clerk° from a lay man, a gentleman from a yeoman, a soldier from a citizen, and the chief of every degree° from their inferiors, because in confusion and disorder there is no manner of decency.° The Romans, of any other people most severe censurers[44] of decency,° thought no upper garment so comely for a civil man as a long, pleated gown, because it showeth much gravity and also pudicity,[45] hiding every member of the body which had not been pleasant to behold. Insomuch as° a certain *proconsul* or legate of theirs, dealing one day with Ptolemy, King of Egypt, seeing him clad in a strait[46] narrow garment very lasciviously, discovering° every part of his body, gave him a great check for it, and said that unless he used more sad° and comely garments, the Romans would take no pleasure to hold amity with him, for by the wantonness° of his garment they would judge the vanity of his mind, not to be worthy of their constant friendship.† A pleasant old courtier wearing one day in the sight of a great counselor, after the new guise, a French cloak scarce reaching to the waist, a long beaked doublet hanging down to his thighs, and a high pair of silk netherstocks[47] that covered all his buttocks and loins, the counselor marveled to see him in that sort disguised[48] and otherwise than he had been wont to be. "Sir," quoth the gentleman to excuse it, "if I should not be able, when I had need, to piss out of my doublet, and to do the rest in my netherstocks (using the plain term), all men would say I were but a lout." The counselor laughed heartily at the absurdity of the speech.† But what would those sour[49] fellows of Rome have said, trow ye?[50] Truly, in mine

---

42. **observed** regarded with attention or courteously.

43. See Erasmus, *Apophthegmata* 1, "Euboidas" 77 (LB 4.115E); for the original, see Plutarch, *Sayings of Spartans*, "Euboedas" (*Moralia* 220D). Euboedas is otherwise unknown.

44. **censurers** judges.

45. **pudicity** modesty.

46. **strait** tight-fitting.

47. **netherstocks** stockings.

48. **disguised** dressed strangely or in a manner other than customary.

49. **sour** austere. The "sour fellows" are probably the Roman Stoics (or perhaps the Romans in general), so described because of their scorn for the pleasures of the flesh, their emphasis on self-discipline and the postponement of gratification, and their hostility to lavish dress and bodily adornment, which they associated with Greeks and Asiatics.

50. **trow ye** do you think.

opinion, that all such persons as take pleasure to show their limbs, especially those that nature hath commanded out of sight, should be enjoined either to go stark naked, or else to resort back to the comely and modest fashion of their own country apparel used by their old, honorable ancestors.

And there is a decency° of apparel in respect of the place where it is to be used, as: in the court to be richly appareled; in the country to wear more plain and homely garments. For who would not think it a ridiculous thing to see a lady in her milk-house[51] with a velvet gown, and at a bridal in her cassock of mockado;[52] a gentleman of the country among the bushes and briars go in a pounced[53] doublet and a pair of embroidered hose, in the city to wear a frieze[54] jerkin and a pair of leather breeches? Yet some such fantasticals[55] have I known, and one a certain knight, of all other the most vain, who commonly would come to the sessions and other ordinary meetings and commissions in the country, so bedecked with buttons and aglets[56] of gold and such costly embroideries, as the poor, plain men of the country called him (for his gayness)[57] "the golden knight."[†] Another for the like cause was called "Saint Sunday."[†] I think at this day they be so far spent,[58] as either of them would be content with a good cloth cloak. And this came by want° of discretion, to discern and deem right of decency,° which many gentlemen do wholly limit by the person or degree,° where reason doth it by the place and presence, which may be such as it might very well become a great prince to wear coarser apparel than, in another place or presence, a meaner° person.

Nevertheless, in the use of a garment many occasions alter the decency°: sometimes the quality of the person, sometimes of the case, otherwhiles the country custom, and often the constitution of laws, and the very nature of use itself. As, for example, a king and prince may use rich and gorgeous apparel decently,° so cannot a mean° person do, yet if a herald of arms to whom a king giveth his gown of cloth of gold, or to whom it was incident[59] as a fee of his office, do wear the same, he doth it decently,° because such hath always been the allowances of heralds. But if such herald have worn out, or sold, or lost that gown, to buy him a new of the like stuff with his own money and to wear it, is not decent° in the eye and judgment of them that know it.

And the country custom maketh things decent° in use, as: in Asia for all men to wear long gowns both afoot and horseback; in Europe short

---

51. **milk-house** dairy.

52. **cassock of mockado** loose coat or gown made of inferior wool.

53. **pounced** perforated or lacerated ornamentally.

54. **frieze** coarse woolen cloth.

55. **fantasticals** persons subject to fanciful ideas (pejorative).

56. **aglets** metal tips on laces for threading through eyelets (from Fr. *aiguillette*, "little needle").

57. **gayness** dressiness.

58. **spent** exhausted; i.e., their fortunes were used up.

59. **incident** attached.

gabardines, or cloaks, or jackets, even for their upper garments. The Turk and Persian to wear great turbans of ten, fifteen, and twenty ells of linen apiece upon their heads, which cannot be removed; in Europe to wear caps or hats, which upon every occasion of salutation we use to put off as a sign of reverence. In the east parts the men to make water cowering[60] like women; with us, standing at a wall.[61] With them to congratulate[62] and salute by giving a beck[63] with the head or a bend of the body; with us here in England, and in Germany, and all other northern parts of the world to shake hands; in France, Italy, and Spain to embrace over the shoulder, under the arms, at the very knees, according [to] the superior's degree.°[64] With us the women give their mouth to be kissed, in other places their cheek, in many places their hand, or instead of an offer to the hand, to say these words *Beso los manos*; and yet some others, surmounting[65] in all courtly civility, will say, *Los manos y los piedes*;[66] and above that reach too, there be that will say to the ladies, *L'ombra de sus pisadas*, "the shadow of your steps." Which I recite unto you to show the phrase of those courtly servitors in yielding the mistresses honor and reverence.

And it is seen that very particular use[67] of itself makes a matter of much decency° and indecency,° without any country custom or allowance, as if one that hath many years worn a gown shall come to be seen wearing a jacket or jerkin, or he that hath many years worn a beard or long hair among those that had done the contrary, and come suddenly to be polled or shaven, it will seem [not][68] only to himself a desight[69] and very indecent,° but also to all others that never used to go so, until the time and custom have abrogated that mislike. So was it here in England till her Majesty's most noble father, for divers good respects,[70] caused his own head and all his courtiers' to be polled and his beard to be cut short.[71] Before that time it was thought more decent° both for old men and young to be all shaven and to wear long hair either rounded or square. Now again at this time, the young gentlemen of the court have taken up the long hair trailing on their shoulders and think it more decent°—for what respect I would be glad to know.

The Lacedaemonians, bearing long bushes of hair finely kept and curled up, used this civil argument to maintain that custom. "Hair,"

60. **cowering** crouching.
61. On this last custom, see LN 22.
62. **congratulate** greet.
63. **beck** gesture, bow.
64. "To" has been added after "according" since Renaissance English, according to *OED*, always uses the preposition with the adjective.
65. **surmounting** excelling.
66. *Beso los manos … Los manos y los piedes* (Sp.) "I kiss your hands"; "Your hands and feet." (It should be *las manos*, of course.)

67. **particular** pertaining to a single individual.
68. "Not" has been added here, without which this sentence is unintelligible.
69. **desight** eyesore; *OED* cites this passage as the first usage of the term, but speculates that Puttenham's "desight" may be a misprint for "despight."
70. **respects** reasons.
71. On haircuts at the Henrician court, see LN 23.

say they, "is the very ornament of nature appointed for the head, which therefore to use[72] in his most sumptuous degree is comely, especially for them that be lords, masters of men, and of a free life, having ability and leisure enough to keep it clean"—and so, for a sign of seignory,[73] riches, and liberty, the masters of the Lacedaemonians used long hair. But their vassals, servants, and slaves used it short or shaven in sign of servitude and because they had no mean nor leisure to comb and keep it cleanly. It was, besides, cumbersome[74] to them, having many businesses to attend; in some services[75] there might no manner of filth be falling from their heads.† And to all soldiers it is very noisome[76] and a dangerous disadvantage in the wars or in any particular combat,[77] which being the most comely profession of every noble, young gentleman, it ought to persuade them greatly from wearing long hair. If there be any that seek by long hair to help or to hide an ill-featured face, it is in them allowable so to do, because every man may decently° reform by art the faults and imperfections° that nature hath wrought in them.

And all singularities or affected parts of a man's behavior seem indecent,° as for one man to march or jet[78] in the street more stately, or to look more solemnly, or to go more gaily[79] and in other colors or fashioned garments than another of the same degree° and estate.° Yet such singularities have had many times both good liking and good success, otherwise than many would have looked for. As when Dinocrates, the famous architect, desirous to be known to King Alexander the Great, and having none acquaintance to bring him to the King's speech, he came one day to the court very strangely° appareled in long scarlet robes, his head compassed° with a garland of laurel, and his face all tobeslicked with sweet oil, and stood in the King's chamber, motioning nothing to any man. News of this stranger° came to the King, who caused him to be brought to his presence, and asked his name, and the cause of his repair[80] to the court. He answered, his name was Dinocrates the architect, who came to present his Majesty with a platform of his own devising, how his Majesty might build a city upon the mountain Athos in Macedonia, which should bear the figure of a man's body, and told him all how. Forsooth, the breast and bulk of his body should rest upon such a flat;[81] that hill should be his head, all set with forgrown[82] woods like hair; his right arm should stretch out to such a hollow bottom as might be like his hand, holding a dish containing all the waters that should serve that city; the left arm with his hand should

---

72. **use** wear.
73. **seignory** lordship, dominion.
74. **cumbersome** troublesome.
75. **services** public duties; work done for a superior.
76. **noisome** troublesome.
77. Erasmus cites Alexander on this piece

of wisdom in *Apophthegmata* 4, "Alexander Magnus" 10 (LB 4.197B–C, Udall 209).
78. **jet** strut.
79. **gaily** (in reference to dress) showily.
80. **repair** resort.
81. **flat** level expanse of ground.
82. **forgrown** overgrown.

hold a valley of all the orchards and gardens of pleasure pertaining thereunto; and either leg should lie upon a ridge of rock very gallantly to behold—and so should accomplish the full figure of a man. The King asked him what commodity of soil, or sea, or navigable river lay near unto it, to be able to sustain so great a number of inhabitants. "Truly, Sir," quoth Dinocrates, "I have not yet considered thereof, for in truth it is the barest part of all the country of Macedonia." The King smiled at it and said very honorably, "We like your device° well and mean to use your service in the building of a city, but we will choose out a more commodious situation°"—and made him attend in that voyage in which he conquered Asia and Egypt, and there made him chief surveyor of his new city of Alexandria. Thus did Dinocrates' singularity in attire greatly further him to his advancement.[83]

Yet are generally all rare things and such as breed marvel and admiration° somewhat holding of the indecent,° as when a man is bigger and exceeding the ordinary stature of a man, like a giant, or far under the reasonable and common size of men, as a dwarf, and such indecencies° do not anger us, but either we pity them or scorn at them. But at all insolent[84] and unwonted parts of a man's behavior, we find many times cause to mislike or to be mistrustful, which proceedeth of some indecency° that is in it, as when a man that hath always been strange° and unacquainted with us, will suddenly become our familiar and domestic;[85] and another that hath been always stern and churlish will be upon the sudden affable and courteous—it is neither a comely sight, nor a sign of any good towards us. Which the subtle Italian[86] well observed by the successes° thereof, saying in proverb:

> *Chi me fa meglio che non suole,*
> *Traditio me ha o tradir me vuole.*[†][87]
>
> *He that speaks me fairer than his wont was to*
> *Hath done me harm, or means for to do.*

Now again, all manner of conceits° that stir up any vehement passion in a man do it by some turpitude or evil and indecency° that is in them, as: to make a man angry, there must be some injury or contempt offered; to make him envy,° there must proceed some undeserved prosperity of his equal or inferior; to make him pity, some miserable fortune or spectacle to behold. And yet in every of these passions being, as it were, indecencies,° there is a comeliness to be discerned, which some men can keep and some men cannot, as to be angry, or to envy,° or to hate, or to

83. See Vitruvius 2.Preface.5–7. Puttenham appears to have owned more than one copy of Vitruvius.

84. **insolent** unaccustomed.

85. **domestic** intimate.

86. Although the Italian proverb cited

does not come from any of Machiavelli's works, he is the likeliest candidate for the "subtle Italian."

87. Puttenham's Italian is not quite accurate; his translation of the first line should begin: "He who treats me better. . . ."

pity, or to be ashamed, decently°—that is, none otherwise than reason requireth. This surmise appeareth to be true, for Homer, the father of poets, writing that famous and most honorable poem called the *Iliad*, or wars of Troy, made his commencement the magnanimous wrath and anger of Achilles in his first verse thus: μενιν αιδε θεα πιλιαδεω αχιλειουσ, "Sing forth, my muse, the wrath of Achilles, Peleus' son"—which the poet would never have done if the wrath of a prince had not been in some sort comely and allowable. But when Arrian and Curtius, historiographers that wrote the noble gests° of King Alexander the Great, came to praise him for many things, yet for his wrath and anger they reproached him, because it proceeded not of any magnanimity, but upon surfeit and distemper° in his diet, nor growing of any just causes, was exercised to the destruction of his dearest friends and familiars, and not of his enemies, nor any other ways so honorably as the other's was, and so could not be reputed a decent° and comely anger.[88]

So may all your other passions be used decently° though the very matter of their original[89] be grounded upon some indecency,° as it is written by a certain king of Egypt, who, looking out of his window and seeing his own son for some grievous offense carried by the officers of his justice to the place of execution, he never once changed his countenance at the matter, though the sight were never so full of ruth and atrocity.[90] And it was thought a decent° countenance and constant animosity[91] in the king to be so affected, the case concerning so high and rare a piece of his own justice. But within few days after, when he beheld out of the same window an old friend and familiar of his stand begging an alms in the street, he wept tenderly, remembering their old familiarity and considering how by the mutability of fortune and frailty of man's estate,° it might one day come to pass that he himself should fall into the like miserable estate.° He therefore had a remorse very comely for a king in that behalf, which also caused him to give order for his poor friend's plentiful relief.[92]

But generally to weep for any sorrow (as one may do for pity) is not so decent° in a man, and therefore all high-minded persons, when they cannot choose but shed tears, will turn away their face as a countenance indecent° for a man to show, and so will the standers-by till they have suppressed such passion, thinking it nothing decent° to behold such an uncomely countenance. But for ladies and women to weep and shed tears at every little grief, it is nothing uncomely, but rather a sign of much good nature and meekness of mind, a most decent° property[93]

---

88. For examples of the reproaches directed at Alexander by Arrian and Curtius, see Arrian, *Anabasis* 4.9.1, 7.8.3, and Curtius Rufus, *De rebus gestis Alexandri magni* 3.12.18–19.

89. **original** source, cause.

90. **atrocity** horror.

91. **animosity** spirits.

92. This story concerns Psammenitus, son of Amasis; see Herodotus 3.14. It is retold (as of Amasis) in Aristotle, *Rhetoric* 2.8.12 (1386a); cf. LN 21.

93. **property** attribute.

for that sex. And therefore they be for the more part more devout and charitable, and greater givers of alms than men, and zealous relievers of prisoners, and beseechers of pardons, and such like parts of commiseration. Yea, they be more than so too, for by the common proverb, a woman will weep for pity to see a gosling go barefoot.[94]

But most certainly, all things that move a man to laughter, as do these scurrilities and other ridiculous behaviors, it is for some indecency° that is found in them, which maketh it decent° for every man to laugh at them. And therefore when we see or hear a natural fool and idiot do or say anything foolishly, we laugh not at him but when he doth or speaketh wisely, because that is unlike himself. And a buffoon or counterfeit° fool, to hear him speak wisely, which is like himself, it is no sport° at all, but for such a counterfeit° to talk and look foolishly, it maketh us laugh, because it is no part of his natural, for in every uncomeliness there must be a certain absurdity and disproportion° to nature and the opinion of the hearer or beholder to make the thing ridiculous. But for a fool to talk foolishly or a wise man wisely, there is no such absurdity or disproportion.° And though at all absurdities we may decently° laugh, and when they be no absurdities not decently,° yet in laughing is there an indecency° for other respects sometime than of the matter itself. Which made Philippus, son to the first Christian emperor, Philippus Arabicus, sitting with his father one day in the theater to behold the sports,° give his father a great rebuke because he laughed, saying that it was no comely countenance for an emperor to bewray° in such a public place, nor especially to laugh at every foolish toy.° The posterity gave the son for that cause the name of Philippus Agelastos, or "without laughter."[95]

I have seen foreign ambassadors in the Queen's presence laugh so dissolutely[96] at some rare pastime or sport° that hath been made there, that nothing in the world could worse have become them, and others, very wise men, whether it have been of some pleasant humor and complexion, or for other default in the spleen, or for ill education or custom, that could not utter any grave and earnest speech without laughter, which part was greatly discommended in them. And Cicero, the wisest of any Roman writers, thought it uncomely for a man to dance, saying, *Saltantem sobrium vidi neminem*: "I never saw any man dance that was sober and in his right wits."[97] But there, by your leave, he failed, nor our young courtiers will allow it, besides that it is the most decent° and comely demeanor[98] of all exultations and rejoicements of the heart, which is no less natural to man than to be wise, or well-learned, or sober.[99]

94. Tilley P365. Cf. Heywood 209.
95. Cf. Victor 28.3.
96. **dissolutely** unrestrainedly.
97. Puttenham paraphrases Cicero, *Pro Murena* 13.

98. **demeanor** behavior.
99. Elyot presents a lengthy defense of dancing in *The Governour* 1.19–26, 69–88.

To tell you the decencies° of a number of other behaviors, one might do it to please you with pretty reports, but to the skillful° courtiers it shall be nothing necessary, for they know all by experience without learning. Yet some few remembrances we will make you of the most material, which ourselves have observed, and so make an end.

It is decent° to be affable and courteous at meals and meetings, in open assemblies more solemn and strange,° in place of authority and judgment not familiar nor pleasant, in counsel secret and sad,° in ordinary conferences easy and apert,[100] in conversation° simple,° in capitulation[101] subtle and mistrustful, at mournings and burials sad° and sorrowful, in feasts and banquets merry and joyful, in household expense pinching and sparing, in public entertainment spending and pompous.[102] The prince to be sumptuous and magnificent, the private man liberal with moderation, a man to be in giving free, in asking spare, in promise slow, in performance speedy, in contract circumspect but just, in amity sincere, in enmity wily and cautelous[103]—*dolus an virtus quis in hoste requirit*, saith the Poet[104]—and after the same rate° every sort and manner of business or affair or action hath his decency° and indecency,° either for the time or place or person or some other circumstance, as priests to be sober and sad,° a preacher by his life to give good example, a judge to be uncorrupted, solitary, and unacquainted with courtiers or courtly entertainments, and as the Philosopher saith, *Oportet iudicem esse rudem et simplicem*,†[105] without plait or wrinkle, sour in look and churlish in speech. Contrariwise, a courtly gentleman to be lofty and curious in countenance,[106] yet sometimes a creeper and a curry-favel[107] with his superiors.

And touching the person, we say it is comely for a man to be a lamb in the house and a lion in the field,[108] appointing the decency° of his quality by the place, by which reason also we limit the comely parts of a woman to consist in four points, that is, to be a shrew in the kitchen, a saint in the church, an angel at the board,° and an ape in the bed,[109] as the chronicle reports by Mistress Shore, paramour to King Edward IV.†

Then also there is a decency° in respect of the persons with whom we do negotiate, as with the great personages his equals to be solemn and surly,[110] with meaner° men pleasant and popular,° stout with the sturdy[111]

---

100. **apert** open.
101. **capitulation** bargaining.
102. **pompous** magnificent.
103. **cautelous** crafty, wary.
104. Vergil, *Aeneid* 2.390: "Trickery or courage, what does it matter against an enemy?"
105. "A judge should be artless and frank" (presumably from Aristotle).
106. **curious in countenance** artful in demeanor.

107. **curry-favell** flatterer. "Curry-favell" is identified as a rhetorical figure at 3.17.269.
108. Tilley L311.
109. Shakespeare's Iago addresses such words to Desdemona in *Othello* (2.1.111–14).
110. **surly** haughty.
111. **stout ... sturdy** formidable, menacing ... stalwart, fierce.

and mild with the meek, which is a most decent° conversation° and not reproachful[112] or unseemly, as the proverb goeth, by those that use the contrary, a lion among sheep and a sheep among lions.

Right so,[113] in negotiating with princes we ought to seek their favor by humility and not by sternness, nor to traffic° with them by way of indent[114] or condition, but frankly and by manner of submission to their wills, for princes may be led but not driven, nor they are to be vanquished by allegation,[115] but must be suffered to have the victory and be relented unto. Nor they are not to be challenged for right or justice, for that is a manner of accusation, nor to be charged with their promises, for that is a kind of condemnation. And at their request we ought not to be hardly[116] entreated but easily, for that is a sign of diffidence[117] and mistrust in their bounty and gratitude; nor to recite the good services which they have received at our hands, for that is but a kind of exprobation,[118] but in craving their bounty or largesse to remember unto them all their former beneficences, making no mention of our own merits, and so it is thankful;[119] and in praising them to their faces to do it very modestly; and in their commendations not to be excessive, for that is tedious and always savors of subtlety[120] more than of sincere love.

And in speaking to a prince the voice ought to be low and not loud nor shrill, for the one is a sign of humility, the other of too much audacity and presumption. Nor in looking on them seem to overlook[121] them, nor yet behold them too steadfastly, for that is a sign of impudence or little reverence. And therefore to the great princes oriental, their servitors speaking or being spoken unto, abase their eyes in token of lowliness—which behavior we do not observe to our princes with so good a discretion as they do—and such as retire from the prince's presence do not by and by[122] turn tail to them, as we do, but go backward or sideling[123] for a reasonable space, till they be at the wall or chamber door, passing out of sight, and is thought a most decent° behavior to their sovereigns. I have heard that King Henry VIII, her Majesty's father, though otherwise the most gentle and affable prince of the world, could not abide to have any man stare in his face or to fix his eye too steadily upon him when he talked with them;† nor for a common suitor to exclaim or cry out for justice, for that is offensive and, as it were, a secret impeachment[124] of his[125] wrong-doing, as happened once to a knight in this realm of great worship speaking to the King.† Nor in speeches with them to be too long, or too much affected, for the one is

---

112. **reproachful** deserving reproach.
113. **Right so** in the same way.
114. **indent** indenture (a contract between two parties).
115. **allegation** assertive argument.
116. **hardly** forcefully.
117. **diffidence** lack of confidence.
118. **exprobation** reproach.

119. **thankful** expressive of thanks.
120. **subtlety** craftiness.
121. **overlook** regard haughtily.
122. **by and by** immediately.
123. **sideling** sideways.
124. **impeachment** accusation.
125. **his** i.e., Henry's.

tedious, the other is irksome; nor with loud acclamations to applaud them, for that is too popular° and rude° and betokens either ignorance, or seldom access to their presence, or little frequenting their courts; nor to show too merry or light a countenance, for that is a sign of little reverence and is a piece of a contempt.

And in gaming with a prince it is decent° to let him sometimes win of purpose, to keep him pleasant, and never to refuse his gift, for that is undutiful; nor to forgive him his losses, for that is arrogant; nor to give him great gifts, for that is either insolence or folly; nor to feast him with excessive charge,[126] for that is both vain and envious.° And therefore the wise prince King Henry VII, her Majesty's grandfather, if his chance had been to lie at any of his subject's houses, or to pass more meals than one, he that would take upon him to defray the charge of his diet, or of his officers and household, he would be marvelously offended with it, saying, "What private subject dare undertake a prince's charge, or look into the secret of his expense?"[127] Her Majesty hath been known oftentimes to mislike the superfluous expense of her subjects bestowed upon her in times of her progresses.[128] Likewise, in matter of advice it is neither decent° to flatter him, for that is servile, neither to be too rough or plain with him, for that is dangerous, but truly to counsel and to admonish, gravely not grievously, sincerely not sourly—which was the part that so greatly commended Cineas, counselor to King Pyrrhus, who kept that decency° in all his persuasions, that he ever prevailed in advice, and carried the King which way he would.[129]

And in a prince it is comely to give unasked, but in a subject to ask unbidden, for that first is sign of a bountiful mind, this of a loyal and confident. But the subject that craves not at his prince's hand, either he is of no desert, or proud, or mistrustful of his prince's goodness. Therefore, King Henry VIII to one that entreated him to remember one Sir Anthony Rous with some reward for that he had spent much and was an ill beggar, the King answered (noting his insolence),[130] "If he be

---

126. **charge** expense.

127. Given Henry VII's reputation for parsimony, the tale seems unlikely. However, Puttenham may have had some kind of access to a tale reported by Francis Bacon in 1622, wherein, on progress in 1498, Henry rebuked John de Vere, thirteenth earl of Oxford, for entertaining him "nobly and sumptuously" with a display of prohibited liveried retainers, using these words: "My lord, I have heard much of your hospitality, but I see it is greater than the speech. . . . My attorney must speak with you." Bacon continues, "[I]t is part of the report, that the Earl compounded for no less than fifteen thousand marks" (*Henry VII* 223–24). The

king's unhappiness with Oxford rests on worries about overmighty subjects and private armies, not on a mere error of manners. The vanity and envy of which Puttenham speaks can easily constitute large-scale insolence. Cf. also Elyot, *The Governour* 161–62.

128. A fig-leaf gesture: the queen's subjects much more often privately bemoaned the great expense of entertaining her and her train on progress, and often sought to avoid the "honor." See Cole, esp. 85–97.

129. For Cineas and Pyrrhus, see Plutarch, *Pyrrhus* 14.2.

130. **insolence** i.e., disrespect for his king's presumptive royal munificence.

ashamed to beg, we are ashamed to give"—and was nevertheless one of the most liberal princes of the world.[131] And yet in some courts it is otherwise used, for in Spain it is thought very indecent° for a courtier to crave, supposing that it is the part of an importune. Therefore, the king of ordinary[132] calleth every second, third, or fourth year for his Chequer-roll,[133] and bestoweth his *mercedes*[134] of his own mere motion[135] and by discretion, according to every man's merit and condition.

And in their commendable delights to be apt and accommodate, as, if the prince be given to hawking, hunting, riding of horses, or playing upon instruments, or any like exercise, the servitor to be the same. And in their other appetites wherein the prince would seem an example of virtue and would not mislike° to be equaled by others: in such cases it is decent° their servitors and subjects study to be like to them by imitation, as in wearing their hair long or short, or in this or that sort of apparel, such excepted as be only fit for princes and none else, which were indecent° for a meaner° person to imitate or counterfeit.° So is it not comely to counterfeit° their voice, or look, or any other gestures that be not ordinary and natural in every common person, and therefore to go upright,[136] or speak, or look assuredly, it is decent° in every man. But if the prince have an extraordinary countenance, or manner of speech, or bearing of his body, that for a common servitor to counterfeit° is not decent,° and therefore it was misliked in the Emperor Nero, and thought uncomely for him to counterfeit° Alexander the Great by holding his head a little awry and nearer toward the one[137] shoulder, because it was not his own natural.[138]

And in a prince it is decent° to go[139] slowly, and to march with leisure and with a certain grandity[140] rather than gravity, as our Sovereign Lady and Mistress, the very image of majesty and magnificence, is accustomed to do generally, unless it be when she walketh apace[141] for her pleasure or to catch her a heat in the cold mornings. Nevertheless, it is not so decent° in a meaner° person, as I have observed in some counterfeit° ladies of the country,[142] which use it much to their own derision. This comeliness was

---

131. This is the third report of this tale in the *Art*, after 3.18.274 and 3.24.361–62. Since the point of the anecdote does not vary in its use here, the repetition may be a failure of editing on Puttenham's part. It may also, however, evidence his obsession with patronage.

132. **of ordinary** ordinarily.

133. **Chequer-roll** a list of individuals paid out of the king's revenues; the Chequer was the Exchequer, the department charged with managing royal revenues.

134. *mercedes* rewards (lit. mercies or graces).

135. **mere motion** sole prompting.

136. **upright** with an erect carriage (with the implication, perhaps, that one has personal integrity or moral rectitude).

137. **one** *1589* prints "tone," i.e., t'one, the one.

138. The story derives from Plutarch, *Alexander* 4.1. Elyot cites it in *The Governour* (155–56), omitting the reference to Nero. In light of the story Puttenham tells above about Henry VIII requiring specific haircut styles from his courtiers (see 368), perhaps Elyot sought to avoid suggesting an unpalatable link between Henry VIII and Nero.

139. **go** walk.

140. **grandity** grandeur. The contrast with "gravity" is obscure.

141. **apace** at a (goodly) pace.

142. Whether this criticism refers to rural or socially mobile ladies is not clear; perhaps both.

wanting° in Queen Mary,[†] otherwise a very good and honorable princess. And was some blemish to the Emperor Ferdinand, a most noble-minded man, yet so careless and forgetful of himself in that behalf, as I have seen him run up a pair of stairs so swift and nimble apace, as almost had not become a very mean° man, who had not gone in some hasty business.[†143]

And in a noble prince nothing is more decent° and well-beseeming his greatness than to spare foul speeches, for that breeds hatred, and to let none humble suitors depart out of their presence (as near as may be) miscontented. Wherein her Majesty hath of all others a most regal gift, and nothing inferior to the good prince Titus Vespasian's in that point.[144] Also, not to be passionate[145] for small detriments or offenses, nor to be a revenger of them but in cases of great injury, and especially of dishonors, and therein to be very stern and vindictive, for that savors of princely magnanimity. Nor to seek revenge upon base and obscure persons, over whom the conquest is not glorious, nor the victory honorable, which respect moved our Sovereign Lady (keeping always the decorum of a princely person) at her first coming to the crown, when a knight of this realm, who had very insolently behaved himself toward her when she was Lady Elizabeth, fell upon his knee to her and besought her pardon, suspecting (as there was good cause) that he should have been sent to the Tower. She said unto him most mildly, "Do you not know that we are descended of the lion, whose nature is not to harm or prey upon the mouse, or any other such small vermin?"[146]

And with these examples I think sufficient to leave,[147] giving you information of this one point, that all your figures poetical or rhetorical

---

143. Such a judgment may seem alien, but Udall writes: "*Seneca* in his Epistles beareth witness: of all thinges (saieth he) if thei be well marked, there hath been priuie tokens, yea, and of the lest thinges that bee, maie a man gather arguments and presumpcions of mennes maners & conditions. An vnchast person, or a vicious man of his bodie, both pace of going [walking] doeth shewe, and [other behaviors]" (360; see Seneca, *Epistulae* 3.114.3). And in *Apophthegmata* 4, "M. Tullius Cicero" 28 (LB 4.223E; Udall 349), Cicero rebukes his daughter Tullia, who "went [walked] with a more stieryng and faste passe then was comely for a woman," and likewise her husband, Piso, who walked "with a more still passe then beseemed a man to do."

144. On Titus' munificence, see Suetonius, *The Deified Titus* 7.3. If the point of the comparison Puttenham is making between Elizabeth and Titus Vespasian also involves the notion that both used chaste language, then there is nothing in Sueto-

nius' biography to support such a claim about the latter.

145. **passionate** angry.

146. Cf. George Cavendish, *The Life and Death of Cardinal Wolsey* (1558): *Parcere prostrates| Scit nobilis Ira leonis| / Tu quoque fac Simile| quisquis regnabis in orbem|* (115: "The lion in his noble anger knows how to spare those who prostrate themselves before him; you, too, should do likewise, you who will rule over the earth"). Though Wolsey is said to have spoken these words at the time of his fall (1529–30), to the duke of Norfolk, Cavendish cites the saying just when Puttenham has Elizabeth using it: his flyleaf note dates his book's completion on June 24, 1558. Wolsey utters the words from below, seeking mercy; Elizabeth from above, with smiling disdain. Later, in another variation, Marlowe's Pembroke says to Edward, "Can kingly lions fawn on creeping ants?" (*Edward II* 1.4.15). For discussion of possible sources, see Sylvester's note (238–39).

147. **leave** stop.

are but observations[148] of strange° speeches and such as without any art at all we should use, and commonly do, even by very nature without discipline.° But more or less aptly and decently,° or scarcely, or abundantly, or of this or that kind of figure, and one of us more than another, according to the disposition of our nature, constitution of the heart, and facility of each man's utterance. So as° we may conclude that nature herself suggesteth the figure in this or that form, but art aideth the judgment of his use and application, which gives me occasion finally and for a full conclusion to this whole treatise to inform° you in the next chapter how art should be used in all respects, and especially in this behalf of language, and when the natural is more commendable than the artificial,° and contrariwise.

148. **observations** employments.

Chapter 25

That the good poet or maker ought to dissemble his art, and in what cases the artificial° is more commended than the natural, and contrariwise

And now, most excellent Queen, having largely° said of poets and poesy and about what matters they be employed, then of all the commended forms of poems, thirdly of metrical proportions,° such as do appertain to our vulgar° art, and last of all set forth the poetical ornament consisting chiefly in the beauty and gallantness[1] of his language and style, and so have appareled him to our seeming[2] in all his gorgeous habiliments,[3] and pulling him first from the cart to the school, and from thence to the court, and preferred[4] him to your Majesty's service, in that place of great honor and magnificence to give entertainment to princes, ladies of honor, gentlewomen, and gentlemen, and by his many modes of skill° to serve the many humors of men thither haunting and resorting, some by way of solace, some of serious advice, and in matters as well profitable as pleasant and honest—we have in our humble conceit° sufficiently performed our promise, or rather duty, to your Majesty in the description of this art, so always as we leave him not unfurnished of one piece that best beseems that place of any other and may serve as a principal good lesson for all good makers to bear continually in mind in the usage of this science°: which is, that being now lately become a courtier, he show not himself a crafts-

1. **gallantness** gorgeousness, ornateness.
2. **to our seeming** in our opinion.
3. **habiliments** attire.
4. **preferred** advanced.

man, and merit to be disgraded,[5] and with scorn sent back again to the shop or other place of his first faculty[6] and calling, but that so wisely and discreetly he behave himself as he may worthily retain the credit of his place and profession of a very courtier, which is, in plain terms, cunningly° to be able to dissemble.

But (if it please your Majesty) may it not seem enough for a courtier to know how to wear a feather, and set his cap aflaunt, his chain *en echarpe*, a strait buskin *al inglesse*, a loose *alo Turquesque*, the cape *alla Spaniola*, the breech *a la Françoise*,[7] and by twenty manner of newfashioned garments to disguise his body, and his face with as many countenances, whereof it seems there be many that make a very art and study who can show himself most fine, I will not say most foolish and ridiculous? Or perhaps, rather that he could dissemble his conceits° as well as his countenances, so as he never speak as he thinks, or think as he speaks, and that in any matter of importance his words and his meaning very seldom meet. For so, as I remember, it was concluded by us setting forth the figure *allegoria*, which therefore not impertinently° we call the Courtier or Figure of Fair Semblant.[8] Or is it not perchance more requisite our courtly poet do dissemble not only his countenances and conceits,° but also all his ordinary actions of behavior, or the most part of them, whereby the better to win his purposes and good advantages? As now and then to have a journey or sickness in his sleeve, thereby to shake off other importunities of greater consequence, as they use their pilgrimages in France, the Diet[9] in Spain, the bains[10] in Italy? And when a man is whole,[11] to feign himself sick to shun the business in court;[12] to entertain[13] time and ease at home; to salve offenses without discredit; to win purposes by mediation in absence which their presence would either impeach[14] or not greatly prefer;[15] to hearken after the popular° opinions and speech; to intend° to their more private solaces; to practice[16] more deeply both at leisure and liberty; and when any public affair or other attempt and counsel of theirs hath not received good success,° to avoid thereby the prince's present reproof; to cool

---

5. **disgraded** deprived of rank and status.

6. **faculty** occupation, profession.

7. **en echarpe** in the manner of a scarf or sash, i.e., worn obliquely across the breast from shoulder to waist (modern Fr.: *en écharpe*); **strait buskin *al inglesse*** close-fitting half-boot in the English style or manner (modern It.: *all'inglese*); **loose *alo Turquesque*** loose-fitting [buskin] in the Turkish style or manner (modern form: either *alla turca* [It.] or *à la turque* [Fr.]); **alla Spaniola** in the Spanish style or manner (modern It.: *alla spagnola*); **a la Françoise** in the French manner (modern Fr.: *à la française*).

8. **Fair Semblant** fair appearance. In the definition he gave of *allegoria* earlier, Puttenham called it the "Figure of False Semblant" (see 3.18.270–72). This alternative reflects an ambiguity concerning the moral status of the courtly poet that runs throughout his work.

9. **Diet** courtly or administrative session.

10. **bains** baths (Fr. *bains*; It. *bagni*).

11. **whole** healthy.

12. Cf. the case of the earl of Arundel (LN 20).

13. **entertain** obtain; enjoy.

14. **impeach** hinder.

15. **prefer** advance.

16. **practice** plot, scheme; perhaps, hone some skill.

their cholers[17] by absence; to win remorse by lamentable[18] reports and reconciliation by friends' entreaty? Finally, by sequestering themselves for a time from the court, to be able the freelier and clearer to discern the factions and state of the court and of all the world besides, no less than doth the looker-on or beholder of a game better see into all points of advantage, than the player himself?[19]

And in dissembling of diseases, which, I pray you? For I have observed it in the court of France, not a burning fever or a pleurisy, or a palsy, or the hydropic[20] and swelling gout, or any other like disease, for if they may be such as may be either easily discerned or quickly cured, they be ill to dissemble and do half-handsomely serve the turn. But it must be either a dry dropsy, or a megrim,[21] or lethargy, or a fistula *in ano*,[22] or some such other secret disease, as the common conversant can hardly discover, and the physician either not speedily heal, or not honestly bewray?[23] Of which infirmities the scoffing Pasquil wrote, *Ulcus vesicae, renum dolor, in pene scirrus.*[†24] Or as I have seen in divers places where many make themselves heart-whole,[25] when indeed they are full sick, bearing it stoutly out to the hazard of their health, rather than they would be suspected of any loathsome infirmity which might inhibit them from the prince's presence or entertainment of the ladies. Or as some other do, to bear a port of state[26] and plenty when they have neither penny nor possession, that they may not seem to droop and be rejected as unworthy or insufficient for the greater services, or be pitied for their poverty, which they hold for a marvelous disgrace, as did the poor squire of Castile, who had rather dine with a sheep's head at home and drink a cruse[27] of water to it, than to have a good dinner given him by his friend who was nothing

---

17. **cholers** angers.

18. **lamentable** provoking lamentation.

19. Puttenham's list may seem overelaborate, but we may compare it with John Hayward's account (from ca. 1611–20) of suspicions about the illness of John Dudley, earl of Warwick, during negotiations with the French over the fate of Boulogne in 1550: "These matters [of negotiation] aduertised into England much troubled the counsaile, and the rather for that the Earle of Warwicke was at that time retired, pretending much infirmity in his health. Hereupon many sinister surmises began to spring vp among some of the counsaile, partly probable and parte happily deuised, for as they knew not whether hee were more dangerous present or away; so as the nature of all feare is they suspected that which happened to be the worst. From hence diuerse of the counsaile began to murmur against him. What said they is he neuer sicke, but when affaires of greatest weight are in de-

bating? Or wherefore else doth hee withdraw himselfe from the company of those who are not well assured of his loue? Wherefore doth he not now come forth and openly ouerrule, as in other matters hee is accustomed? Would he haue vs imagine by his absence that he acteth nothing? Or knowing that all moueth from him, shall wee not thinke that he seeketh to enjoy his owne ends, which bearing blame for any euent [sic]?" (Hayward 122–23).

20. **hydropic** dropsical (swollen with fluid).

21. **megrim** migraine.

22. **fistula *in ano*** anal fistula.

23. **honestly bewray** reveal with propriety.

24. "An ulcer of the bladder, a pain in the kidneys, a tumor on the penis." On Pasquil, who is presumably mocking such false excuses, see 1.27.142 and LN 4.

25. **heart-whole** completely well.

26. **port of state** lifestyle displaying one's high status.

27. **cruse** small pot or jar.

ignorant of his poverty.[28] Or as others do, to make wise[29] they be poor when they be rich, to shun thereby the public charges and vocations,[30] for men are not nowadays (especially in states of oligarchy, as the most in our age) called so much for their wisdom as for their wealth; also to avoid envy° of neighbors or bounty in conversation,[31] for whosoever is reputed rich cannot without reproach but be either a lender or a spender. Or as others do, to seem very busy when they have nothing to do, and yet will make themselves so occupied and overladen in the prince's affairs as it is a great matter to have a couple of words with them, when notwithstanding they lie sleeping on their beds all an afternoon, or sit solemnly at cards in their chambers, or entertaining of the dames, or laughing and gibing with their familiars four hours by the clock, while the poor suitor desirous of his dispatch[32] is answered by some secretary or page, "*Il fault attendre; Monsieur*[33] is dispatching the king's business into Languedoc, Provence, Piedmont"—a common phrase with the secretaries of France. Or as I have observed in many of the princes' courts of Italy, to seem idle when they be earnestly occupied and intend° to nothing but mischievous practices, and do busily negotiate by color° of otiation.[34] Or as others of them that go ordinarily to church and never pray, to win an opinion of holiness; or pray still° apace, but never do good deed; and give a beggar a penny and spend a pound on a harlot; to speak fair to a man's face and foul behind his back; to set him at his trencher and yet sit on his skirts, for so we use to say by[35] a feigned friend; then also to be rough and churlish in speech and appearance, but inwardly[36] affectionate° and favoring, as I have seen of the greatest podestates[37] and gravest judges and presidents of parliament in France.[38]

These and many such like disguisings do we find in man's behavior, and especially in the courtiers of foreign countries, where in my youth I was brought up and very well observed their manner of life and conversation,° for of mine own country I have not made so great experience.

---

28. This may be an allusion to the squire (*escudero*) who appears in the third chapter of the first Spanish picaresque novel, *Lazarillo de Tormes* (1554). Judging from Puttenham's occasional use of Spanish in the *Art*, from the fact that he had a volume in his library marked "Hispanice" (in Spanish), and from the fact that he was clearly conversant with Italian, which was—and is—quite close to Spanish, he may have read *Lazarillo* in that language, although he could have read a French translation that appeared in 1561.

29. **make wise** pretend.

30. **vocations** calls to a public position or activity. For such aversion among Elizabeth's courtiers, see Cole, esp. 85–97.

31. **bounty in conversation** i.e., the expectation of public generosity.

32. **his dispatch** the settling of his business.

33. "You must wait; my Lord" (*Monsieur* is the subject of "is dispatching").

34. **negotiate . . . otiation** deal with affairs while pretending to be at one's ease. Puttenham is playing on the Latin words *otium* (leisure, idleness) and *negotium* (business, affairs).

35. **by** of.

36. **inwardly** at heart.

37. **podestates** the powerful (more accurately, *potestates*).

38. French parliaments (*parlements*) were not legislative bodies but judicial ones, located in principal cities such as Paris and Bordeaux.

Which parts, nevertheless, we allow not now in our English maker, because we have given him the name of an honest man and not of a hypocrite. And therefore, leaving these manner of dissimulations to all base-minded men and of vile[39] nature or mystery,[40] we do allow our courtly poet to be a dissembler only in the subtleties of his art; that is, when he is most artificial,° so to disguise and cloak it as it may not appear, nor seem to proceed from him by any study or trade[41] of rules, but to be his natural; nor so evidently to be descried, as every lad that reads him shall say he is a good scholar,° but will rather have him to know his art well and little to use it.[42]

And yet peradventure° in all points it may not be so taken, but in such only as may discover° his grossness[43] or his ignorance by some scholarly° affectation, which thing is very irksome to all men of good training, and especially to courtiers. And yet for all that, our maker may not be in all cases restrained, but that he may both use and also manifest his art to his great praise, and need no more be ashamed thereof than a shoemaker to have made a cleanly° shoe, or a carpenter to have built a fair house. Therefore, to discuss and make this point somewhat clearer—to wit, where art ought to appear and where not—and when the natural is more commendable than the artificial° in any human° action or workmanship, we will examine it further by this distinction.

In some cases we say art is an aid and coadjutor[44] to nature, and a furtherer of her actions to a good effect, or peradventure° a mean to supply her wants° by reinforcing the causes wherein she is impotent and defective, as doth the art of physic[45] by helping the natural concoction,[46] retention, distribution, expulsion, and other virtues° in a weak and unhealthy body. Or as the good gardener seasons his soil by sundry sorts of compost, as° muck or marl,[47] clay or sand, and many times by blood, or lees of oil or wine, or stale,[48] or perchance° with

---

39. **vile** base, low.

40. **mystery** craft, occupation.

41. **trade** practice, application.

42. Cf. Castiglione 1.25–26, a passage based on ideas presented throughout the first book of Cicero's *De oratore*. Castiglione labels his key principle in this passage with the neologism *sprezzatura* (1.26.124: nonchalance), signifying an effortlessness of manner in courtly conduct that implies a certain superiority to, even scorn (It. *disprezza*) for, the social rules by which others are normally bound. As Thomas Hoby's 1561 translation puts it, this artful hiding of social art is the "one rule that is most generall, [and] taketh place in all things belonging to a man in word or deede, above all other: . . . to eschue as much as a man may, and as a sharpe and daungerous rocke, too much curiousnesse,

and (to speake a new word) to use in everye thing a certaine disgracing [*sprezzatura*] to cover arte withall, and seeme whatsoever he doth and saith, to doe it without paine, and (as it were) not minding it" (45–46). Sidney also writes about using art to hide art; see *Defence* 246–47.

43. **grossness** lack of instruction or refinement.

44. **coadjutor** one who works with and helps another.

45. **physic** medicine.

46. **concoction** digestion (lit., the cooking together of materials in the body during the digestive process).

47. **as . . . marl** such as dung or soil (consisting of clay mixed with lime); both muck and marl were used as soil amendment.

48. **stale** urine, usually of horses or cattle.

more costly drugs;[49] and waters his plants, and weeds his herbs and flowers, and prunes his branches, and unleaves his boughs to let in the sun; and twenty other ways cherisheth them, and cureth their infirmities, and so makes that never, or very seldom, any of them miscarry, but bring forth their flowers and fruits in season. And in both these cases it is no small praise for the physician and gardener to be called good and cunning° artificers.

In another respect art is not only an aid and coadjutor to nature in all her actions, but an alterer of them, and in some sort a surmounter of her skill,° so as° by means of it her own effects shall appear more beautiful or strange° and miraculous, as in both cases before remembered. The physician by the cordials[50] he will give his patient shall be able not only to restore the decayed spirits of man and render him health, but also to prolong the term of his life many years over and above the stint[51] of his first and natural constitution. And the gardener by his art will not only make an herb, or flower, or fruit come forth in his season without impediment, but also will embellish the same in virtue,° shape, odor, and taste, that nature of herself would never have done, as to make the single gillyflower, or marigold, or daisy, double, and the white rose, red, yellow, or carnation;[52] a bitter melon, sweet; a sweet apple, sour; a plum or cherry without a stone; a pear without core or kernel; a gourd or cucumber like to a horn or any other figure he will—any of which things nature could not do without man's help and art.[53] These actions also are most singular, when they be most artificial.°

In another respect, we say art is neither an aider nor a surmounter, but only a bare imitator of nature's works, following and counterfeiting° her actions and effects, as the marmoset doth many countenances and gestures of man, of which sort are the arts of painting and carving, whereof one represents the natural by light, color, and shadow in the superficial or flat, the other in a body massive,[54] expressing the full and empty, even, extant,[55] rabated,° hollow, or whatsoever other figure and passion of quantity.[56] So also the alchemist counterfeits° gold, silver, and all other metals; the lapidary, pearls and precious stones, by glass and other substances falsified and sophisticated[57] by art. These men also be praised for their craft, and their credit is nothing impaired to say that their conclusions and effects are very artificial.°

---

49. **drugs** ingredients used in chemistry, pharmacy, and the arts generally.

50. **cordials** medicinal liqueurs thought to affect the heart (from Lat. *cor, cordis,* "heart").

51. **stint** customary limit of time.

52. **carnation** deep crimson.

53. Cf. *The Winter's Tale* 4.4.79–108.

Shakespeare may recall parts of Puttenham's passage here.

54. **massive** three-dimensional.

55. **extant** projecting or protruding.

56. **passion of quantity** property of (its) size, specifically of its magnitude in three dimensions.

57. **sophisticated** altered deceptively.

Finally, in another respect art is, as it were, an encounterer[58] and contrary to nature, producing effects neither like to hers, nor by participation with her operations, nor by imitation of her patterns, but makes things and produceth effects altogether strange° and diverse, and of such form and quality (nature always supplying stuff) as she never would nor could have done of herself, as the carpenter that builds a house, the joiner[59] that makes a table or a bedstead, the tailor a garment, the smith a lock or a key, and a number of like, in which case the workman gaineth reputation by his art, and praise when it is best expressed and most apparent and most studiously.[60] Man also in all his actions that be not altogether natural, but are gotten by study and discipline° or exercise, as to dance by measures, to sing by note, to play on the lute, and such like, it is a praise to be said an artificial° dancer, singer, and player on instruments, because they be not exactly known or done, but by rules and precepts or teaching of schoolmasters. But in such actions as be so natural and proper to man, as he may become excellent therein without any art or imitation at all (custom and exercise excepted, which are requisite to every action not numbered among the vital or animal),[61] and wherein nature should seem to do amiss and man suffer reproach to be found destitute of them: in those to show himself rather artificial° than natural were no less to be laughed at, than for one that can see well enough to use a pair of spectacles, or not to hear but by a trunk[62] put to his ear, nor feel without a pair of annealed[63] gloves, which things indeed help an infirm sense, but annoy[64] the perfect, and therefore showing a disability natural move rather to scorn than commendation and to pity sooner than to praise.

But what else is language and utterance, and discourse and persuasion, and argument in man than the virtues° of a well-constituted body and mind, little less natural than his very sensual[65] actions, saving that the one is perfected° by nature at once, the other not without exercise and iteration? Peradventure° also it will be granted that a man sees better and discerns more bremely[66] his colors, and hears and feels more exactly by use and often hearing and feeling and seeing, and though it be better to see with spectacles than not to see at all, yet is their praise not equal nor in any man's judgment comparable. No more is that which a poet makes by art and precepts rather than by natural instinct, and that which he doth by long meditation rather than by a sudden inspiration,

---

58. **encounterer** opponent, opposite.
59. **joiner** cabinetmaker, furniture maker.
60. **studiously** carefully, deliberately. In this sentence Puttenham is rehearsing Aristotle's opposition of form and matter ("stuff"); see *Physics* 2.1.192b–2.2.194b and *Metaphysics* 7.1–4 (1028a–b) and Books 7 and 8 of that work generally.
61. **vital or animal** vital "spirits" (actually,

a fluid) were thought responsible for the fundamental life processes of the body, such as being, whereas animal spirits were thought responsible for sensation and voluntary motion.
62. **trunk** ear trumpet.
63. **annealed** toughened (by heat).
64. **annoy** impair.
65. **sensual** pertaining to the senses.
66. **bremely** clearly, distinctly.

or with great pleasure and facility than hardly[67] and (as they are wont to say) in spite of nature or Minerva,[68] than which nothing can be more irksome or ridiculous.

And yet I am not ignorant that there be arts and methods both to speak and to persuade and also to dispute, and by which the natural is in some sort relieved,[69] as the eye by his spectacles—I say relieved in his imperfection,° but not made more perfect° than the natural, in which respect I call those arts of grammar, logic, and rhetoric not bare imitations, as the painter or carver's craft and work in a foreign[70] subject, *videl.*,° a lively portrait in his table° or wood, but by long and studious observation rather a repetition or reminiscence natural, reduced° into perfection,° and made prompt by use and exercise.[71] And so, whatsoever a man speaks or persuades, he doth it not by imitation artificially,° but by observation naturally (though one follow another), because it is both the same and the like that nature doth suggest. But if a popinjay speak, she doth it by imitation of man's voice artificially° and not naturally, being the like, but not the same that nature doth suggest to man.

But now because our maker or poet is to play many parts and not one alone, as first to devise his plat[72] or subject, then to fashion his poem, thirdly to use his metrical proportions,° and last of all to utter with pleasure and delight, which rests in his manner of language and style, as hath been said, whereof the many modes and strange° phrases are called figures, it is not altogether with him as with the craftsman, nor altogether otherwise than with the craftsman. For in that he useth his metrical proportions° by appointed and harmonical measures and distances, he is like the carpenter or joiner, for, borrowing their timber and stuff of nature, they appoint and order it by art otherwise than nature would do, and work effects in appearance contrary to hers. Also in that which the poet speaks or reports of another man's tale or doings, as Homer of Priam or Ulysses, he is as the painter or carver that work by imitation and representation in a foreign[73] subject. In that he speaks figuratively, or argues subtly, or persuades copiously and vehemently, he doth as the cunning° gardener that, using nature as a coadjutor, furthers her conclusions and many times makes her effects more absolute[74] and strange.° But for that in our maker or poet, which rests

---

67. **hardly** with difficulty.

68. **in spite of ... Minerva** Puttenham here translates the Latin saying *invita Minerva*, which means to do something against one's natural bent; cf. Horace, *Ars poetica* 385; Cicero, *De officiis* 1.31.110. At the start of Adage 1.1.37: *Crassa Minerva, Pingui Minerva, Crassiore Minerva* (LB 2.42A; CWE 31.85–86: "Without Art or Skill"), Erasmus suggests why Minerva's name is being used: "Minerva, according to the fables of the po-

ets, watches over arts and talents [*ingeniis*]." *Ingenium* can mean natural inclination, talents, or genius.

69. **relieved** assisted.

70. **foreign** external.

71. Cf. the three things requisite for the mastery of oratory: art, imitation, and practice (see *Ad Herennium* 1.2.3).

72. **plat** plan or scheme; plot.

73. **foreign** not his own.

74. **absolute** finished, consummate.

only in device[75] and issues from an excellent, sharp, and quick° invention,° helped by a clear and bright fantasy and imagination, he is not
as the painter to counterfeit° the natural by the like effects and not
the same, nor as the gardener aiding nature to work both the same and
the like, nor as the carpenter to work effects utterly unlike, but even
as nature herself, working by her own peculiar virtue° and proper[76] instinct and not by example or meditation or exercise as all other artificers do, is[77] then most admired° when he is most natural and least
artificial.° And in the feats of his language and utterance, because
they hold as well of nature to be suggested and uttered as by art to be
polished and reformed, therefore shall our poet receive praise for both,
but more by knowing of his art than by unseasonable[78] using it, and be
more commended for his natural eloquence than for his artificial,°
and more for his artificial° well dissembled than for the same overmuch affected and grossly or indiscreetly bewrayed,° as many makers
and orators do.

75. **rests … device** subsists purely as a
mental form.
76. **proper** inherent.

77. **is** i.e., he is.
78. **unseasonable** untimely.

The Conclusion

And with this, my most gracious Sovereign Lady, I make an end,
humbly beseeching your pardon, in that I have presumed to hold your
ears so long annoyed with a tedious trifle, so as° unless it proceed more
of your own princely and natural mansuetude[1] than of my merit, I fear
greatly lest you may think of me as the philosopher Plato did of Anniceris, an inhabitant of the city Cyrene, who being in troth° a very active and artificial° man in driving of a prince's chariot or coach (as your
Majesty might be)[2] and knowing it himself well enough, coming one day
into Plato's school, and having heard him largely° dispute in matters
philosophical, "I pray you," quoth he, "give me leave also to say somewhat of mine art"—and indeed showed so many tricks of his cunning,°
how to launch forth and stay, and change pace, and turn and wind[3] his
coach this way and that way, uphill downhill, and also in even or rough
ground, that he made the whole assembly wonder at him.[4] Quoth Plato,
being a grave personage, "Verily in mine opinion, this man should be utterly unfit for any service of greater importance than to drive a coach. It

1. **mansuetude** mildness.
2. **might be** i.e., driven in.
3. **wind** move in a curve.
4. See Aelian, *Varia historia* 2.27. This is
the only reference in antiquity to Anniceris

the charioteer, who is otherwise unidentified. He should not be confused with Anniceris the Cyrenaic, a hedonist philosopher
mentioned by Diogenes Laertius (2.85–86,
96, and 3.20).

is great pity that so pretty[5] a fellow had not occupied his brains in studies of more consequence." Now I pray God it be not thought so of me in describing the toys° of this our vulgar° art.[6] But when I consider how everything hath his estimation by opportunity,[7] and that it was but the study of my younger years in which vanity reigned; also that I write to the pleasure of a Lady and a most gracious Queen, and neither to priests nor to prophets or philosophers; besides, finding by experience that many times idleness° is less harmful than unprofitable occupation, daily seeing how these great aspiring minds and ambitious heads of the world,[8] seriously searching to deal in matters of state, be oftentimes so busy and earnest that they were better be unoccupied, and peradventure° altogether idle°: I presume so much upon your Majesty's most mild and gracious judgment, howsoever you conceive of mine ability to any better or greater service, that yet in this attempt ye will allow of my loyal and good intent, always endeavoring to do your Majesty the best and greatest of those services I can.

5. **pretty** crafty, artful (ironic).

6. Puttenham's slighting reference to his work as idle "toys" and "trifles" exhibits the *sprezzatura* or nonchalance that Castiglione and Puttenham himself recommended for courtiers. The *apologia* ends his weighty book with a most ironic, nonchalant, and disenchanting illustration of its subject: despite the dissociative allegation of vain and trivial youth, he has shown throughout that he and his courtly fellows know well that poetic tools help rulers rule and courtiers court. Such modesty is, as Francis Bacon said, an art of ostentation (see "Of Vain-Glory," *Essays* 159).

7. **everything . . . opportunity** everything is judged (or valued) according to circumstances (such as by whom, when, and how it is produced).

8. **heads of the world** worldly persons, worldlings (cf. "Wily worldling," 3.19.289).

A Table of the Chapters in This Book and Everything in Them Contained

The arrangement of data in this "Table" from 1589 is problematic. The chapter titles here do not entirely correspond to those in the text. One title and several names for figures of speech are omitted. The "Table" provides separate headings for Books 2 and 3, but none for Book 1. Finally, it interrupts the sequence of chapters in Book 3 with a new title (in the running header) when it begins listing the figures, and among them new chapter titles then appear. We have transcribed the "Table" as 1589 presents it without annotating it. We have, however, added, in brackets, the following: a title for Book 1; chapter numbers before each of the chapters; page numbers (keyed to the pages in this edition) after each entry; and the missing chapter title as well as the names of missing figures. Note: we have not corrected the chapter titles supplied in the "Table."

The Table of the Second Book

THE TABLE OF THE THIRD BOOK

THE NAMES OF YOUR FIGURES AURICULAR

The uncorrected state of *1589* p. 207, sig. Ee2r (see 3.20.333–34)

This (modernized) text is taken from the Da Capo Press facsimile of Douce PP 206.

transferred from these polishers of marble or porphicite, who after it is rough hewn and reduced to that fashion, they will set upon it a goodly glass, so smooth and clear as ye may see your face in it; or otherwise as it fareth by the bare and naked body, which, being attired in rich and gorgeous apparel, seemeth to the common usage of the eye much more comely and beautiful than the natural. So doth this figure (which therefore I call the Gorgeous) polish our speech and as it were attire it with copious and pleasant amplifications and much variety of sentences all running upon one point and to one intent, so as I doubt whether I may term it a figure, or rather a mass of many figurative speeches, applied to the beautifying of our tale or argument. In a work of ours entitled *Philocalia* we have strained to show the use and application of this figure and all others mentioned in this book, to which we refer you.

I find none example that ever I could see so well maintaining this figure in English meter of the Gorgeous as that ditty of her Majesty's own making, passing sweet and harmonical, which figure being, as his very original name purporteth, the most beautiful of all others, it asketh in reason to be reserved for a last complement, and deciphered by the art of a lady's pen, herself being the most gorgeous and beautiful, or rather beauty, of queens. And this was the action: our Sovereign Lady, perceiving how by the Sc. Q. residence within this realm at so great liberty and ease (as were scarce worthy of so great and dangerous a prisoner) bred secret factions among her people, and made many of her nobility incline to favor her party—many of them desirous of innovation in the state, some of them aspiring to greater fortunes by her liberty and life. The Queen, our Sovereign Lady, to declare that she was nothing ignorant in those secret favors, though she had long with great wisdom and patience dissembled it, writeth this ditty most sweet and sententious, not hiding from all such aspiring minds the danger of their ambition and disloyalty; which afterward fell out most truly by the exemplary chastisement of sundry persons, who, in favor of the said Sc. Q. derogating from her Majesty, sought to interrupt the quiet of the realm by many evil and undutiful practices. The ditty is as followeth.

Emendations

We have silently corrected turned letters (u/n), parentheses, and brackets in Field's text, as well as confusions of "long s" and f. The following list of remaining corrections follows this protocol: book.chapter.page.line number of this edition; **1589 text] this text**; *1589* page number or signature (BM, G. 11548 unless otherwise noted). Note that line numbers include the lines in chapter headings and titles but not those in footnotes, and that when a chapter begins mid-page, line numbers for emendations in that chapter on that page count down from the first line of the chapter title. When appropriate, the modernized form of the corrected text (e.g., *than* for *then*) appears in parentheses following the corrected text.

Longer Notes

I

1.5.99–100 [note 2, on Hebrew verse]   Ever since Jerome it had been assumed that portions of the Old Testament were in verse form, although, as Sidney observed, "the rules be not yet fully found" (*Defence* 215). Philo and Josephus had judged this Hebrew poetry to obey the rules of quantity, but much was obscure. The subject had received considerable recent discussion resulting from the publication in Frankfurt (1575–79) of the translation of the Old Testament from Hebrew into Latin by Immanuel Tremellius, who had worked on the Book of Common Prayer with Archbishop Thomas Cranmer and was appointed to the chair of Hebrew at Cambridge in 1549. (He fled the country in 1553 with many other Marian exiles.) He dedicated his grammar of Chaldean and Syriac to Archbishop Matthew Parker in 1568 and his New Testament to Elizabeth in 1569. The preface to the third division of his Old Testament identifies it specifically as verse: *hos libros omneis communiter vocamus Psalmos, quia sunt rythmici; non prosa orationae scripi, ut omnes alii . . . sed numeris adstricti ad commoditatem memoriae & cantus* (we generally call all those books Psalms, since they are rhythmical; [they are] not written in formal prose, as all the others [are], but are put under the constraints of meter and song for the benefit of the memory). His work was well known and much admired in the Protestant world; Sidney refers to him by name in the *Defence* (217). Puttenham may also be thinking here of other noted Hebraists such as the scholars Joannes Mercerus and Augustinus Steuchus. Steuchus in particular argued for an accentual rhymed Biblical poetry: *Hebraicum nulla tempora; sed numerum duntaxat atque similitudinem cadentium syllabarum* (the Hebrew does not observe the quantity but only the number and the likeness of the ends of the syllables). (This passage is cited from a discussion in the seventeenth-century literary theorist Gomarus by Israel Baroway, whose series of essays from 1933 to 1950 trace this and related matters in detail. For the quotation from Tremellius, see "Tremellius" 146; for that from Steuchus [in Gomarus], see "Accentual Theory" 124.)

2

1.7.105 [note 31, on leonine verse]   Verse lion is Latin or French verse in which the last word in a line was rhymed with the word occurring just before the caesura in the middle of the line. It was referred to as "rime leonine" in the anonymous twelfth-century romance *Guillaume d'Angleterre*. A later tradition attributes the invention of this form to a twelfth-century Parisian canon and Latin poet named Leonius or Leoninus. Puttenham appears to confuse the formal feature of a species of palindrome that the Latins called *versus retrogradi* (backward verses) or *carmen retrogradum* or *reciprocum* (backward poem) in his example with the internal rhyme feature of leonine verse. He may have been led into this confusion because of what he found in Scaliger, who discusses *versus Leoninus* at the end of 2.29, declaring that he does not know why it is called thus, but clearly showing that he knows it involves the sort of internal rhyme described above. In the next chapter Scaliger talks generally about how the arrangement (*dispositio*) of a line (or lines) of verse affects its meaning. A bit into the chapter he writes about that ingenious kind of verse which can have the same meaning whether you read it backward or forward—or that can have exactly contrary meanings when you read it in the two different directions, what he calls *versus reciproci* (backward verses). The example he then gives for the latter is (almost) Puttenham's: "Laus tua, non tua fraus: virtus, non copia rerum / Scandere te fecit hoc decus Omnipotens." Scaliger explains neither to whom these lines refer nor how the meaning changes when one reads them backward. Puttenham may be confusing "verse lion" and *versus retrogradi* here simply because of the placement of the two discussions in Scaliger's book, where they appear adjacent to each other in parallel columns, and also because in the left-hand margin next to the discussion of the "verse lion," Scaliger has written "Leoninus," which Puttenham may have taken as applying to everything across the page. Or perhaps his attention simply wandered.

3

1.8.107 [note 15, on Gray of Reading and "The hunt is up"]   The ballad's title became a common noun meaning "morning song," seen in *Romeo and Juliet*, where Juliet complains to Romeo that the lark's "voice doth us affray, / Hunting thee hence with hunt's-up to the day" (3.5.33–34). Soon after, directly erotic "aubade" uses of the term appear; several (dating from 1594 to 1617) are quoted in H. Ellis Wooldridge's notes to Chappell, *Old English Popular Music* 86–89 (where one version of the music also appears). Wooldridge also cites religious adaptations: one (undated) runs, "For Christ our Kyng is cum a hunting, / And browght his deare to staye" (88); the other (dating in print probably from 1590) refers to the pope, who never ceased "under dispence, to get our pence" (88). Gray had in his own time earned something of a name as a Reformation controversialist, and these words may preserve another strand of his writing.

  Despite the supposedly original "bluff King Harry" text and Puttenham's own deployment of Gray's example, the ballad was not always sung in service to royal preeminence and the reflected honor of educated persons. Indeed, the earliest surviving reference to the ballad presents just the opposite view. During the northern risings of 1536 (known generally as the Pilgrimage of Grace) against Cromwell, the Dissolution of the Monasteries, and increased government control, one John Hogon, a wandering minstrel, is reported to have sung it with the following words: "The masters of art and doctors of divinity have brought this realm out of good unity. Three noble men have take this to stay; my lord of Norfolk, lord Surrey, and my lord of Shrewsbury. The duke of Suffolk might a made England merry" (L&P 1537: XII.1, no. 424; February 15). (The L&P record preserves something of the auditors' fascinating discussion with Hogon about how to interpret his words. By "the hunt is up" he meant "the Northern men are up.") Hogon claimed to have sung the song twice as such before the poet earl of Surrey, at Cambridge and at Thetford Abbey. This claim was disputed by one of Hogon's interrogators, who said that if he had sung it before Surrey, the latter would have "set him by the feet" (in the stocks) for slandering him. The date of this L&P record reporting Hogon to the authorities coincides exactly with the barrage of executions that followed the rebellion: he may have been one of the 250 or so who then lost their lives.

Puttenham's explicit reference to Gray's standing as poet to Somerset (a self-commending one, it turns out) can be notably documented. Two poems by Gray are extant that were given to Somerset as New Year's gifts. (They are preserved in Furnivall's *Ballads from Manuscripts*, vol. 1.) The first, for 1550 (possibly composed in prison; a William Gray was imprisoned with Somerset at this time; see Loades, *John Dudley* 140, 150), finds Somerset in the Tower, and, after counseling patience, advises: "Be liberall hencefurthe booeth of pursse and tongue . . . / Beware of all flatterers, wherof you had store; / Revenge not, Rewarde them, but truste them no more!" (1.417: 7, 9–10). The second, for 1551, observes: "The Laste newey[e]res gefte that I to yow gaue, / parchance ye fforgott, though stell yow yt have; / ffor Lyke as olde ffrwtt in time well be Rotton, / yeven so maye olde geftes in tyme be fforgotton" (1.418: 11–14). Gray then goes on to exhort Somerset's generosity in hilariously direct terms (1.420–22: 57–60, 63–70):

> yf yow be mynded to do good in dede,
> to them that yow do it, do yt with spede;
> yt grevethe the hart of him that desarveth,
> to se the gress grow whyle the hors starvethe.
> . . .
>
> A Dwke to be hard, is as mette a thenge
> As ffor a hogghs nose to wayre a golde Rynge.
> yf Lacke were the Lett of yower lybrall hande,
> why sholde yow nott sell part of yower Lande?
> the doynge wher-of cowlde nott sett yow backe;
> ye have [e]nought, and we['re] Lyke to Lacke;
> This is pore cownsell, as yt sholde apere,
> bwtt to a kynges vnkell what can be dere? . . .

Gray's New Year's poems fit very closely with Puttenham's agenda in the text. Along with his own claim at 3.13.253 to have dedicated his lost eclogue

Elpine, "which [he] made being but eighteen years old [in about 1547], to king Edward VI a prince of great hope," they make it tempting to imagine Puttenham in attendance at the presentation of such gifts during the royal celebration of the New Year (so often later used by Elizabeth as an occasion for calibration of courtiers' standing, the gifts exchanged being logged in great detail: see Whigham, *Ambition and Privilege* 68–70). Puttenham might well have included Gray among his list of court poets by personal knowledge of these poems and their acceptance. (For further data, see Dormer, *Gray of Reading.*

4

1.27.142 [note 7, on Pasquil and Marphorius] Pasquil (or, more accurately, Pasquin; in Italian, *Pasquino*), and Marphorius (in Italian, *Marforio;* from Latin, *Martis forum,* the "forum of Mars") were two "talking statues" in Renaissance Rome. Pasquin was a ruined Roman statue discovered in 1501 that was set up in the Piazza Navona and according to different accounts was named after a local tailor, barber, or pedagogue. Initially it was dressed up as an ancient deity or famous person on Saint Mark's Day (April 25) and festooned with Latin verses saluting it written by students and professors. During the papacy of Leo X (1513–21), people began placing satirical pieces about local persons and events on the statue at various times (not just when the pope had died, that is, when his seat was empty: *sede vacante,* as the text puts it). The Marphorius was a colossal Roman statue of a river god, possibly the Tiber, located in front of the church of San Pietro in Carcere (moved to the Piazza San Marco in 1587 and the Campidoglio in 1592). People would place verses on it in response to those on the Pasquin. Many of these poems, called *pasquinate* in Italian (pasquinades), were collected and published during the first half of the sixteenth century. The text identifies Pasquin and Marphorius as satyrs, relying on the traditional etymology of *satire* that linked it to *satyr* and that justified its harshness by stressing the roughness and savagery of the satyr.

Puttenham's uncle Sir Thomas Elyot published (anonymously) the first English pasquinade, an English dialogue called *Pasquil the Playne* (1533), which Puttenham probably knew. This work consists of a discussion among Pasquil, the talkative and self-seeking courtier Gnatho, and the silent Harpocrates, concerning flattery, success at court, and how and when to give potentially unwelcome advice. The introductory letter "to gentile reders" identifies this Pasquil as the "image of stone sitting in the cittie of Rome openly." Elyot clearly refers to the satiric tradition but adapts his character so that "he vseth suche a temperaunce, that he notith not any particular persone or Countrey" (*Four Political Treatises* 42). That is, in order to discuss plain speaking generically, Elyot forgoes the Pasquil tradition's edge. (He later published a second edition of the work in 1540 under his own name.) Elyot may have learned of the tradition during his travels on the continent; various collections of Roman pasquinade verses were published. A woodcut of the Pasquino statue is preserved in "an anonymous collection of verses affixed to the statue," dated 1512, in the University Library, Cambridge (class mark F.151.2.24); reprinted in Lehmberg, *Sir Thomas Elyot* (facing page

136; see 117 note 8 for the quotation). Hogrefe suggests that Elyot may also have seen a dialogue concerning Pasquil and Marphorius that Edmund Bonner sent to Thomas Cromwell, Elyot's patron (see *L&P* 1532: V, no. 1658). Any of these data may have influenced Puttenham's reference.

5

2.2.155 [note 8, on band, rhyme royal, and *ottava rima*] A clue to Puttenham's reasoning about eight and seven appears in Michael Drayton's revision of his rhyme-royal *Mortimeriados* (1596) into *ottava rima* (as *The Barons' Wars*, 1603), marking the end of rhyme royal's dominance as the great heroic measure. In the 1603 explanatory letter to the Reader, Drayton says that "the often harmony" of the rhyme-royal stanza "softened the verse more than the Majesty of the subject would permit," and that shorter forms than that of eight lines "detain not the music nor the Close . . . long enough for an epic poem. . . . This of eight both holds the tune clean through [by means of "six interwoven" lines] to the base of the column (which is the couplet, the foot or bottom) and closeth not but with a full satisfaction to the ear for so long detention." The stanza resembles, he says, "the pillar which in architecture is called the Tuscan, whose shaft is of six diameters, and Bases of two" (II.3–4). This contrast between rhyme-royal "softness" and the strong and architecturally extended detention and closure of *ottava rima* helps explain why Puttenham thought the latter stanza superior in "band."

6

2.2.156 [note 11, on the carol, ballad, song, round, and virelay] Puttenham's categories are not always clearly identifiable. (1) The *carol* was a medieval form, originally a festive song that accompanied a ring dance. It usually had a uniform stanza (often a quatrain) and a refrain or burden. The carol was often erotic and thus was violently denounced by medieval clerics as a pagan survival. Carols that focused on Christmas and Easter (more common after the Reformation, and the majority now) were probably designed to help supplant such forebears, but political, moral, and satirical carols were also abundant. Puttenham calls the *encomium* a carol "of honor" (1.23.135). (2) The *ballad*, originally a popular oral form, had by Puttenham's time been adapted to the somewhat more literate and urban forms of the street broadside (often political or "news" oriented) and the hymnal form found in Sternhold and Hopkins (see Puttenham's mention at 1.8.107), which gave rise to the term "ballad meter." Puttenham may also have been familiar with the French *ballade*, the dominant poetic form in that language during the fourteenth and fifteenth centuries; it consisted of three eight-line stanzas of complexly rhymed octosyllabic verse and a four-line *envoi*. (3) The *song* is presumably the totally generic term familiar today. (4) Puttenham's *round* may refer to the French forms called *rondeau* and *rondel*, terms often used interchangeably but which also often denote different forms. The former, identified with the poet Clément Marot, most commonly consisted of three stanzas of five, three, and five lines of partly rhymed octosyllables. The latter was a complex fixed form which nonetheless underwent much variation over time. The *rondeau* was notably Englished by Wyatt (Rebholz nos. 1–8; nos. 1, 3, and 4 in *Tottel*). Puttenham perhaps instead refers here to the traditional form Webbe defines as the "round," "being mutuallie sung betweene two: one singeth one verse, the other the next; eche rymeth with himselfe" (1.261). Puttenham also discusses (obscurely) a shaped form he calls the *roundel* or *sphere*, at 2.12.187. (5) The *virelay* was another fixed form, originating in France in the thirteenth century. It usually consisted of lines in three-line groupings in several stanzas, each of which has just two rhymes, one of which can serve as the initial rhyme of the next stanza. The form was, however, subject to considerable variation.

7

2.12.180 [note 2, on Anacreon's egg and the Greek Anthology] The *Greek Anthology* was originally compiled in the very late Hellenistic period, then edited by the Byzantine Greek Constantine Cephalas in the ninth century. The *Palatine Anthology*, a revised and expanded version of Cephalas's work, was made in 980 but disappeared until it was rediscovered in 1606. (Not printed until the nineteenth century, it remained largely unknown to poets and readers until then.) Another, somewhat shorter version of the anthology, called the *Planudean Anthology*, was also compiled on the basis of Cephalas's work in 1301 by the Italian scholar Maximus Planudes. Many manuscript copies were made of his collection, especially after it was brought to Italy from Byzantium after 1453. The collection was printed in 1494 and had an enormous influence on the Renaissance after that as a result. Puttenham's allusion to "Anacreon's egg" suggests he may have known of this collection, although it cannot be certain that he had actually read it. In his *Letter-Book* (1573–80), in the draft material for letters to Spenser, Gabriel Harvey writes that the practice of shaped poetry, which he thinks contemptible, has been "of late foolishely revivid by sum, otherwise not unlernid, as Pierus, Scaliger, Crispin, and the rest of that crue" (100).

8

3.2.223 [note 3, on the old knight of Yorkshire] The identity of the old knight of Yorkshire is problematic. The Speaker of the first session of the House of Commons under Mary, in 1553–55, was Sir John Pollard (1508?–1557). He was about forty-five in 1553, but was not knighted until sometime between October 1555 and April 1557. Furthermore, although a branch of the Pollard family was established in Yorkshire, Sir John was born in Devonshire and was elected as a member of the House first for Plymouth and then for many years thereafter for Oxfordshire. In 1553, then, he would perhaps not have been thought old, a knight, or from Yorkshire. Gregory Smith, however, suggests (2.418–19) that the reference is to Sir Thomas Gargrave of Yorkshire (1495–1579; knighted 1549), the Speaker for *Elizabeth's* first parliament in 1559: he would then have been arguably old (about sixty-five), a knight, and both from and representing Yorkshire. Gargrave wrote to Burghley in 1572, however, complaining about the lack of legal expertise on the Council of the North (on which he served): "for that little I had is forgotten, because it is 28 years since I left the study of the law" (Hasler 167). Perhaps, however, this does not fully contradict Puttenham's "not unlearned in the laws of the Realm." In any case, both speakers are recorded to have delivered "excellent" or "notable" and "learned" orations during the parliaments in question (Bindoff, *The House of Commons, 1509–1558* 3.120; Hasler, *The House of Commons, 1558–1603* 2.167). We may be faced with the use of deliberate alterations by Puttenham in order to avoid offense: Gargrave survived till 1579, and if this part of the *Art* dates from the 1560s, as much of it seems to, Pollard's memory (or family) might still have required propitiation.

9

3.2.223 [note 11, on Lord Chancellor and Lord Keeper] The Lord Chancellorship, a more ancient office, generally entailed the following duties: (1) executing justice in the Court of Chancery, especially with regard to questions of equity; (2) authenticating grants of honor and property via the Great Seal; (3) serving (at the pleasure of the prince) as a Privy Councilor; (4) serving as Speaker of the House of Lords; (5) presiding over Star Chamber proceedings. Such duties being onerous, the Chancellors sometimes deputed the Great Seal to a lieutenant. It also happened that the Great Seal was sometimes entrusted by the monarch to a deputy while the office of Chancellor was vacant or in transition, either with limited powers or all the powers but not the rank of Chancellor. Eventually the practice arose of appointing someone as "Keeper" permanently, holding the office in his own right and discharging its full duties. When Elizabeth, ever parsimonious in conferring honors, appointed Sir Nicholas Bacon Keeper in 1558, questions arose as to the legality of some of his acts. A statute was then passed (5 Eliz. c. 18) that specified that the Lord Keeper had "the same place, pre-eminence, and jurisdiction" as a Chancellor would. Since that time there has never been a Chancellor and a Keeper concurrently. The only difference between the two titles, then, is that the former is often seen as a mark of higher royal favor.

10

3.2.225 [note 24, on the litigious wife] There are at least two candidates for the litigious wife in Puttenham's own life: (1) George Puttenham's wife, Elizabeth, who, with her Paulet relatives, especially Katherine Paulet, went to law with her husband. In SP 12 126/16, ff. 30–35, George writes to the Privy Council blaming his problems in part on "a cowple of wemen voyde of all shamefastnes and regarde how they abvse your authoritee by falce and slaunderows suggestions"; he complains further of persecution by "my wyves chyllderne" and speaks of "a complaynt my wyfe exhibiteth withowt iuste cawse." He returns later to "a cowple of shameles wemen who neuer knowe tyme to make an ende." In SP 12 126/17, ff. 36–37v, a letter from about 1580 to Sir John Throckmorton (George's brother-in-law, referred to in 3.17 and perhaps in 3.16), he asserts that he has "ben putt in danger to be murdred ... twyse or thrise other tymes by mrs pawlets sarvants." Her brother-in-law Thomas Paulet admitted in 1562 that he confronted Puttenham at his home, wounded him in the head with his dagger, and "then

agayne with the blade of the said dagger gave unto the said complainant one
other litle Stroke" (PRO STAC 5, P66/2). (2) Mary, the wife of George's elder
brother, Richard, whose conflicts at law were witnessed by George. Richard
argued (unsuccessfully) that he should not have to pay "to mainteine A
proude stubborne woman his wief in unbrydled libertie from him"; she was,
he said, a "clamorous strumpet" who "impudently craveth twise or thrise so
much to lyve on alone . . . as her father, mother, brothers, systers and her-
selfe were wonte and fayne to lyve on all together" (PRO Req [1]14, fols.
279r–v: quoted in Stretton, *Women Waging Law* 143, 191–92).

11

3.8.240 [note 5, on *tasis*]   Brian Vickers has emended *tasis* to *taxis*, which
means "arrangement," and which can be found in Aristotle, *Rhetoric* 3.12.6
(1414a). This suggestion makes some sense: Puttenham is talking about the
general principles of style; the next two principles identified also involve the
way speeches are constructed (rather than how they sound); and in the next
paragraph he refers to what he has just said here as "proportion, volubility,
good construction, and the rest," thus putting "good construction" more or
less in the same place as "tunable to the ear." In the later sentence, however,
"volubility" might be meant to refer to both "voluble upon the tongue" and
"tunable to the ear," in which case "good construction" would be synonymous with "not tediously long, but brief and compendious." Moreover, the
OED lists no occurrence of *taxis* before 1759 and none at all for it as meaning
the rhetorical principle of arrangement.
    That Puttenham meant *tasis* and not *taxis* is suggested most directly by
the likeliest source for this chapter, namely, Petrus Mosellanus's *Tabulae de
schematibus et tropis* (1527), which was the basis for Richard Sherry's *Treatise of Schemes and Tropes* (1550), which Puttenham also used. In the relevant passage in the *Tabulae*, Mosellanus is speaking of *Virtus* (excellence),
his third subdivision of schemes (beyond those of thoughts and words) which
lift speech up above the common level, and which he divides into two kinds:
Proprietas (propriety) and *Ornatus* (adornment). Mosellanus subdivides *Proprietas* into *analogia, tasis,* and *syntomia,* and *Ornatus* into *synthesis, cyriologia,* and *tropus,* precisely the six qualities of style that Puttenham lists in
3.8.

12

3.18.271 [note 4, on *Qui nescit dissimulare nescit regnare*]   Although
the expression *Qui nescit dissimulare, nescit regnare* (Who does not know
how to dissimulate, does not know how to rule) is consistent with sentiments expressed in the works of Seneca, it does not occur there, nor have we
found it in any database of classical literature. Quintilian attributes a similar saying to Domitius Afer, an orator and consul during the reign of
Tiberius: *Princeps, qui vult omnia scire, necesse habet multa ignoscere*
(8.5.3), which Puttenham translates at 3.19.321: "The Prince that covets all
to know and see / Had need full mild and patient to be." Most modern collections of proverbs and sayings, however, attribute it to the French king

Louis XI (b. 1423, ruled 1461–83), although the saying has also been identified as a medieval proverb by Hans Walther, in his *Lateinische Sprichwörter und Sentenzen des Mittelalters*, 4, no. 24329. Nevertheless, starting in the Renaissance, it seems to have been assigned to Louis XI pretty consistently, no matter what its origin. Thus, Gilles Corrozet attributes it to him, citing it in French as "Qui ne sçait dissimuler, il ne sçait regner" in *Les divers propos memorables des nobles & illustres hommes de la Chrestienté*, 49r. The earliest use of the phrase in early modern English that we have found occurs in Thomas Danett's continuation of *The History of Commines* (the memoirs of Philippe de Commines [1445–1509], counselor to Charles, duke of Burgundy, and Louis XI). Danett's translation and continuation were not published in full until 1596, but his dedication says that he first submitted the work to Burghley and Leicester "thirty yeeres since." In the initial paragraph of the continuation, which picks up the French narrative immediately after Louis XI's death, Danett speaks of how Louis educated his son, the future Charles VIII, supposedly not allowing him "to learne any more Latine than this one sentence: He that cannot dissemble cannot raigne' " (de Commines 2.129). It is also possible, of course, that Puttenham read Commines's text in the original French: a text of some version of the *Memoires* appears in his 1576 library inventory. Whether it contained what Danett translated as the continuation is unknown; modern editions of the *Memoires* do not, and do not quote the famous phrase. Another early modern English ascription appears in Justus Lipsius, *Politicorum . . . libri sex* (1589), where one side note to the phrase suggests, *Fridericus siue* [or] *Sigismundus. Nam variant* [for they vary], and another says, *Cuius late vsus* [a widely known saying] (4.14.131). These references are probably to Frederick III (b. 1415, Holy Roman Emperor 1452–93) and Sigismund (b. 1368, Holy Roman Emperor 1433–37). The expression seems generally to have been thought a mid- to late-fifteenth-century one. (The first side note is reproduced in William Jones's 1594 translation of Lipsius; see 117.) The phrase also sometimes serves, unsurprisingly, as a critique of corrupt rule. See, for instance, Whetstone, *The English Myrrour* 148–49; it is also the title-page epigraph to Sir Anthony Weldon's sulfurous *Court and Character of King James* (printed 1650).

13

3.18.273 [note 28, on "Totnes is turned French"] This proverb appears in two alliterating forms (with "Totnes" and "Tottenham"), both of which xenophobically contrast fundamentalist Englishry to offensive foreign corruption. (1) Totnes is a small Devonshire port on the river Dart, facing the English Channel (and France, presumably in a competitive posture). It was famed in originary myth (in Geoffrey of Monmouth's *Historia Regum Brittaniae* [1136] and derivative texts) as the place where the eponymous Brutus first landed with his followers to expel the giants and "found" Britain. (In fact the founding is an invasion.) According to Tilley (T444) the first recorded instance of this version is Puttenham's. (2) Tottenham was in the early modern period a village about five miles north of London (not to be confused with Tottenham Court, a fashionable and perhaps "Frenchified" London eatery of the seventeenth century). The earliest recorded use of this form, presumably unknown to Puttenham, appears in a letter from the duke of Norfolk to Cromwell (*L&P* XI [1536], no. 233). In his *History of the Worthies of England* (1662), Thomas Fuller derived this form of the proverb from the civil disturbances of "Evil May Day" 1517, partly provoked by the invasive presence in London of supposed French insolence and economic competition: "Nor was the city only, but country villages for four miles about, filled with French fashions and infections" (2.315). Fuller is not always reliable, but such French insolence in London in 1516–17—and similar behavior by Frenchified young Englishmen in 1520—is documented in Hall's *Union* (1548; 1809 ed., 586–91, 597). (Among these latter appears Sir Francis Bryan, principal figure in Wyatt's satire "A Spending Hand," Rebholz no. 151.) Hall's recording of the case of these Frenchified young men, like Ascham's outcry against their Italianate equivalents of a generation later, suggests that the proverb may contain a suggestion of the perversion of the English *becoming* French, not just being overcome by them: that is, that it registers not just impossibility (the usual supposed meaning of the proverb) but all-too-real possibility.

14

3.19.331 [note 397, on Puttenham and Anglo-Flemish politics]   The modern sense of the historical record on Anglo-Flemish politics at this time departs in a variety of ways from Puttenham's highly rhetorical report. The glosses that follow attempt to situate Puttenham's descriptions within this modern perspective.

A word on terminology.   Around this time the people of the northern Netherlands began to be distinguished from the inhabitants of the southern provinces (to whom the name "Flemings" continued to cling) by the appellation "Hollanders," after their principal province. The English, however, came to apply exclusively to the Hollanders the term "Dutch," which previously they had applied to all German speakers (from German *Deutsch*, Dutch *Duits*). The name "Netherlanders," which remained in use in the Low Countries for the inhabitants of the United Provinces specifically and for all those, north or south, who spoke Dutch (*Nederlands*), passed out of currency in most foreign countries or came to be restricted to the northerners.

On the rebellion against Maximilian.   After the death of Charles the Bold, duke of Burgundy, in 1477, his daughter Mary of Burgundy (1457–1482) became duchess of Burgundy (1477–82) and on August 18, 1477, married the Austrian archduke Maximilian of Habsburg (later Holy Roman Emperor). Meanwhile, French pressures on Burgundy enabled the States-General (the representative assembly of the Low Countries) to obtain the first written constitution for the whole of the principalities in the Low Countries, the "magna carta" of Holland. It recognized extensive rights to the States-General, such as control over the waging of war, currency, taxation, and tolls. When Mary died in 1482, her husband, Maximilian, became regent (for their son Philip), and worked to undo the advances of the States-General. His political strategy aimed to recover the territorial and institutional losses since 1477, but his policy of high taxation, warfare, and violation of privileges, during a period of deep general economic crisis, provoked opposition and revolt, first in Flanders but also later in Holland, Brabant, and Utrecht. In 1488 the archduke attempted to subdue the important Flemish city of Bruges but was himself captured. He negotiated his release, signing away his authority over Flanders but retaining his regency over the other provinces. Once he was freed, his father, the emperor Frederick III, sent him an army, and after a year of struggle Flanders was subjugated in 1489.

On the rebellion against Charles V. Charles V was the grandson of Maximilian I and Mary of Burgundy. After the death of his father, Philip I ("the Handsome"), in 1506, Charles was raised by his paternal aunt Margaret of Austria, regent of the Netherlands. When Charles attempted to force a large subsidy from Flanders, Ghent refused and openly rebelled, seeking aid from Francis I of France. The latter reported the overtures to Charles, who then came to Ghent, executed the rebellious leaders, and annulled all charters, privileges, and laws of Ghent (1540).

On the rebellion against Philip II. Under Charles's son Philip II, who in 1555–56 succeeded as king of Spain and prince of the Netherlands, the policy of centralization was continued. It culminated in the introduction of a new Catholic ecclesiastical hierarchy, which occasioned vigorous Protestant resistance. The so-called Breaking of the Images in 1566 resulted in the appointment of the duke of Alva as governor general in 1567, whose harsh measures triggered a resistance to the government (often referred to as the "Revolt") that led to the Eighty Years' War (1568–1648).

On the rebellion against the archduke Matthias. In 1577 the archduke, a nephew of Philip II, was invited by the Catholic nobility of the Spanish Netherlands to become governor general and save the country for the Habsburgs and Catholicism. He was unable to arrange a compromise peace between Spain and the Protestant faction headed (but barely controlled) by Prince William of Orange. Calvinist resistance flared up in a variety of ways, despite Orange's efforts to promote tolerance, and Matthias returned to Germany in 1581 to make room for Anjou.

On the rebellion against the duke of Anjou. Prince William of Orange, pursuing a policy of collaboration between Roman Catholics and Calvinists throughout the Low Countries in resistance to the Spanish domination, managed to get the duke of Anjou appointed to administer the constitutionally prescribed "lordship" of the Low Countries in 1580. (This duke is better known to students of English literature as Alençon, the French suitor to Elizabeth, familiarly called Monsieur.) Smarting under his positional inferiority to the prince, Anjou attempted to seize total control of the region, invading Antwerp (and numerous other cities surprised on the same day) in the so-called French Fury of January 17, 1583. Incensed at his betrayal of the articles, the burghers of Antwerp defended themselves well and crushed the invaders. Anjou's coup failed humiliatingly, and, after some self-righteous blame-shifting, he returned to France, and died soon after (in June 1584).

15

3.22.339–40 [notes 27 and 28, on *cacosyntheton* and *cacemphaton*] There is some real confusion in Puttenham's text about these two terms. Quintilian defines *cacosyntheton* as words badly joined together (*male collocatum*), and in a completely different passage (8.3.44–47) he defines *cacemphaton* as using words that could be assigned an obscene meaning (really, obscene double entendres). Mosellanus, who was one of Puttenham's sources in Book 3 of the *Art*, especially for the "vices" of speech described in 3.22, follows Quintilian closely, defining *cacemphaton* as speech that can be twisted into having an "obscene sense" (A8v: *obscoenum intellectum*). He nevertheless opens the door to a misunderstanding that occurs in Susenbrotus because he also defines it as an "ill-sounding arrangement of words" (B1r: *iunctura deformiter sonat*), which is essentially how he later defines *cacosyntheton*, that is, as words out of place (B1r: *male collocatum*). Part of Puttenham's problem is that Susenbrotus takes a step beyond Mosellanus: he misunderstands the first of the terms (by limiting its meaning) and then runs the two figures and their definitions together. Starting with *cacemphaton*, Susenbrotus drops its meaning as obscene double entendre, calling it simply a crude composition of words (36: *illepida ac inconcinna verborum compositio*), and illustrating it three different ways: using a word starting with *n* after *cum*, using a word that starts with the same syllable as the syllable at the end of the preceding word, and using a series of words all starting with the same letter. Susenbrotus seems to have misunderstood both Mosellanus and his source, Quintilian, or to have censored his response to what he read. A bit of Quintilian and Mosellanus does survive, albeit disguised, when Susenbrotus speaks of avoiding words that start with *n* after *cum*. In one of his examples, Quintilian explains that one should always write *cum hominibus notis* (with well-known men) in order to avoid avoid the obscene double entendre that results from *cum notis hominibus*, which is pronounced as though it were *cunnotis hominibus* (with cunty men). Having thus defined *cacemphaton* as a matter of badly structured phrasing, Susenbrotus goes on to say that the last form it takes—a series of words all starting with the same letter, or what we would call excessive alliteration—is also called *cacosyntheton*, which he then, possibly following the lead of Mosellanus, defines in almost the same terms (*Compositura mala est vocum*) he used for his original definition of *cacemphaton*. Thus, the two figures confusingly overlap. (Sherry does not help the situation when he defines *cacosyntheton* as *male collocatum*, but then goes on to say it occurs "when wordes be naughtelye ioyned together, or set in a place wher they shuld not be" [35], for he thus includes in the meaning of the word a hint of what Quintilian defines as *cacemphaton*.)

It would seem that Puttenham starts out by restoring Quintilian's definitions. He thus defines *cacosyntheton* as the awkward joining together of words (though he strangely limits it just to the faulty placement of adjectives after nouns). Then he defines *cacemphaton* in Quintilian's manner as a matter of obscene double entendres. (Note that he is reversing the sequence in which the two figures appear in Quintilian, Mosellanus, and Susenbrotus.) Puttenham then muddies the waters considerably, however, by continuing his definition of *cacemphaton* with what may be a response to Susenbrotus's (faulty) definition of the word by saying it can also be defined as an awkward composition of words.

16

3.22.340–41 [note 32, on *tautologia*] Since *tautologia* in ancient Greek meant something very much like what "tautology" means now (i.e., the repetition of the same idea in different words, often in a way that is wearisome or unnecessary), Puttenham's choice of it to mean what we would call alliteration is mysterious. This last term was not available to him in either English or Latin, having been coined in the former language only in the mid-seventeenth century. Puttenham may have chosen *tautologia*, however, because of the way Quintilian and Mosellanus define it. Quintilian says not that it is the needless repetition of an idea (i.e., the use of different words to say exactly the same thing), but rather that it is the repetition of the same word or phrase (8.3.50: *eiusdem verbi aut sermonis iteratio*); Mosellanus repeats this definition verbatim (A8r). More important, the example Quintilian gives at 8.3.51 (again, Mosellanus follows suit) of this fault is this one, which he takes from Cicero: *Non solum igitur illud iudicium iudicii simile, iudices, non fuit* ("Not only was that judgment not like a judgment, Judges"; see *Pro Cluente* 35.96). Thus, Puttenham may be defining what we would call alliteration as *tautologia* because he is reacting to the idea of repetition contained in Quintilian's and Mosellanus's definition of the term as well as to the repetition not only of different forms of the word *iudicium* in the example from Cicero, but also the alliteration of those words with *iudices* as well as with all the other words in the example starting with *i*. That Puttenham's use of *tautologia* to define excessive alliteration is not some casual mistake is demonstrated by what he says earlier, in chapter 16, when discussing *paroemion*, which he defines as the "figure of like letter" (i.e., alliteration), for he says that if it is overdone, it becomes the vice called *tautologia*, which he says he will discuss in a later chapter (i.e., in this one). For other early modern English discussions of *tautologia*, see Sherry 33 ("inutilis repelicio [=repeticio?] eiusdem"); Peacham (1577) F3r–v, (1593) 42, 49, 193, 196.

17

3.22.346 [note 74, on rebellious verse prophecies]   Such ambiguous verse prophecies form a subset of the larger category of popular political writings of which I. M. W. Harvey writes as follows (speaking of the Jack Cade rebellion):

> Such political poetry or doggerel as remains from this period is now a close gauge of how events were popularly viewed there and then. In some cases this can be detected month by month, since these unliterary productions came out in quick succession, soon to be superseded.... Whether they were an appeal to popular opinion rather than its expression it is hard to say. Certainly this was a recognized way of moving opinion. (*Jack Cade's Rebellion* 77)

Such texts survive, *mutatis mutandis*, for many of the popular rebellions to which Puttenham refers, though not always ambiguous or in verse. (Whether such rhymes should be thought to be of "popular" origin, or to be the work of "leaders" of popular rebellion, members of the elite seeking mass support, depends greatly on definitions that are themselves ideological.) For a related early example, see Puttenham's own citation of the "long beards" rhyme from 1327, at 3.16.258.

Jack Straw was the name or pseudonym of a leading participant in the Peasants' Revolt of 1381, the first great popular rebellion in English history, protesting harsh taxation of the poor; it is also called Wat Tyler's Rebellion, after its principal leader (sometimes identified with Jack Straw). Holinshed records that immediately after, in 1382, when the radical priest John Ball (who preached famously on the old text, "When Adam delu'd, and Eva span,/Who was then a gentleman") was imprisoned, "he prophesied that he should be delivered with the force of twentie thousand men, and euen so it came to passe in time of the rebellion of the commons" (2.749). Holinshed also preserves (at 2.749) a letter containing an ambiguous prophecy that Ball supposedly wrote to "the captaine of the Essex rebels":

> Iohn scheepe S. Marie preest of Yorke, and now of Colchester, greeteth well Iohn nameless, and Iohn the Miller, and Iohn Carter, & biddeth them that they beware of guile in Burrough, & stand togither in Gods name, & biddeth Piers ploughman go to his worke, and chastise well Hob the robber, & take with you Iohn Trewman and all his fellows, and no mo. Iohn the Miller Y ground small, small small, the kings sonne of heauen shall paie for all.

These records, which survive in several sources, mark the first occasion on which an English popular rebel set his ideological views to paper, according to Alastair Dunn (*The Great Rising* 60). For related and alternative texts, see *Medieval English Political Writings*, edited by James M. Dean.

Jack Cade was the leader of a major popular rebellion in Kent, not in Richard II's time (1377–99) but against Henry VI in 1450. (Puttenham has switched Jack Cade's king with Jack Straw's.) High taxes and prices were at issue. We have not recovered ambiguous verse prophecies for this rebellion, but Shakespeare interestingly inserts doubtful prophecies, apparently of his own invention, into his Jack Cade play, *Henry VI, Part Two*. He does not attach them to the popular rebels, however, imputing them instead to the demonic spirit Asmath, summoned by a witch and a conjurer for the duchess of Gloucester, who will use them to "move opinion," as Harvey puts it. (For an example appearing very close in time to the Shakespeare play, also located in the aristocratic orbit, see the ambiguous letter that leads to Edward II's assassination in Marlowe's *Edward II* 5.4.8, based on Holinshed 2.586. The prophecies of Macbeth's witches combine the supernatural and the popular, but are addressed to a leader.)

"Captain" Robert Ket was leader of the Norfolk rising of 1549 (afterward called Ket's Rebellion), which arose from complaints about enclosure. John Hayward documents such an equivocal prophecy in his *Life and Raigne of King Edward the Sixt* (1630). After running out of provisions, he reports, some of Ket's rebels fired their cabins and left the hill where they had been positioned, entrenching themselves at its foot in a valley called Duffendale:

> [A]nd as there hath seldome hapned any sedition within this realm, but the chief actors therein haue been abused with some prophecies of doubtfull construction, so the seditious were moued to remoue to this place vpon a prophecy much credited among them, that they should fill it with slaughtered bodies, but whether of their enemies or of their owne it was left vncertaine, the words of the prophecy were these. The country Knuffes [churls] Hob, Dicke and Hick, with clubbes and clouted shoone: Shall fill vp Duffendale, with slaughtered bodies soone. (75–76)

Hayward also reports another prophecy (though not one in verse) that played a role in the Northriding rebellion in Yorkshire right after Ket's Rebellion (78).

As an effect of these turmoils, a law was passed (3 & 4 Edward VI c. 15) that criminalized such prophecies. It reads in part:

> [W]here nowe of late ... divers evill disposed parsons ... have of their perverse mynde feyned ymagined invented published and practised dyvers fantasticall and fonde Prophesyes ... [if any such] doe sett forth in writing printing singing speaking, and publish or otherwise declare ... any phantasticall or falce prophesye, apon occasion of any armes fildes [fields of battle? an enclosure reference?] beastes fowles badges and such other lyke things accustomed in armes conysances or sygnets [three forms of aristocratic insignia], or by reason of any tyme yere or daye name bludshed or warr, ...

then every such person shall suffer a year's imprisonment for a first offense and life imprisonment for a second. (See *Statutes of the Realm* for the full text.)

For a detailed treatment of another abundant body of obscure verse prophecy also probably on Puttenham's mind, one of the "others" (that is, the other sets of prophecies) he refers to, namely those prophecies concerning the Pilgrimage of Grace (1536–37), see Sharon L. Jansen's *Political Protest and Prophecy under Henry VIII* and her *Dangerous Talk and Strange Behavior.* See also Fox, *Oral and Literate Culture in England, 1500–1700.*

18

3.23.352–53 [note 38, on Flamock and excremental humor] Will Summers was famously given to excremental humor. (Cf. his role in Deloney's *Jack of Newbury,* from 1597, and in the thirty-two-page anonymous pamphlet *The Pleasant History of the Life and Death of Will Summers,* from 1676, which records five such stories.) Henry might have expected such a rejoinder, which, indeed, in the 1676 text "the king laughed at exceedingly" (15). In the Rowley play the king is silent; his companion Empson comments, "Hees too hard for you my Lord" (2930). Rowley's contest presents two other rhyming jokes about the king's sexuality: "*King*: The bud is spread the Rose is red, the leafe is greene, / *Wil*: A wench t'is sed, was found in you[r] bed, besides the Queene" (2919–20); and "*Emp*: A ruddy lip, with a cherry tip, is fit for a King. / *Wil*: I [aye], so he may dip, about her hip, i'th tother thing" (2936–37).

What to make of the substitution of Summers for Flamock in these later versions is not clear. Perhaps the story did originally involve Summers, and Puttenham substituted Flamock. If Henry's erotic life was such fair game as these low-comic examples suggest, perhaps Puttenham wanted a courtier, a *non*-official court entertainer, to fail with Henry so that Puttenham's own ostentatious modesty might succeed with Henry's daughter Elizabeth. Since Puttenham may have known Flamock through his father, perhaps a buried personal joke is at work; maybe Flamock claimed it, and Puttenham knew no better. Alternatively, perhaps Flamock was the historical originator, but Will Summers was funnier than Flamock, or just more well known, and more likely to attract such tales. Perhaps Henry even administered this challenge repeatedly, to all comers.

19

3.23.354 [note 44, on Henry's ambassador, Charles V, and *ingrato*] There are two possible candidates for Puttenham's unnamed ambassador to Charles V: Sir Thomas Elyot and Sir Thomas Wyatt. Elyot (Puttenham's uncle) was in 1531 appointed Henry VIII's ambassador to the peripatetic imperial court of Charles V at Tournai and Regensburg (Ratisbon) in modern-day Belgium and Germany. (Puttenham was then a toddler, but the tale might well have become family lore.) (1) His instructions, which survive in some detail (printed by Croft, 1.lxxii–lxxv), deal exactly with Charles and Pope Clement VII's resistance to Henry's divorce from Charles's aunt, Catherine of Aragon (whom Puttenham here calls Catherine of Castile). These instructions do not refer specifically to funds, men, and munitions, but he would also have received oral directives. Issues of indebtedness were central to England's diplomatic relations during this period, and such challenges were often quite direct. In 1526, for example, Edward Lee, Elyot's predecessor, said to Charles that "he had no excuse for not paying the King [Henry], who had waited so long a time" (*L&P* 1529–30: IV.3, Appendix no. 69 [Brewer's summary], dated 1526).

Most likely the aggressive language attributed to Elyot here is fairly accurately reported, if insufficiently polite. Charles presumably chose to take strategic offense at the language of the sentence as a way of evading its content. (2) In the prologue to his *Dictionary* (1538), Elyot says of the prior dictionary composed by the Spanish humanist Antonio de Nebrija that it contains some "wordes . . . [expounded] in the spainysh tunge, which I do not understand" (see *Letters* 63). Whether only these difficult words defeated him or the language in general, we cannot tell, but he was presumably not fluent. (3) Elyot had thought a good deal about ingratitude. He devoted a specific chapter to the subject in his *Governour* (2.13: 152–54), published just before the September 1531 embassy. This chapter, along with the oft-repeated critique of flatterers (2.14: 154–58 and passim), seems to Lehmberg evidence of Elyot's personal resentment of his insufficient reward for six years' prior service as clerk of the King's Council, his last position before the embassy, for which he remained entirely unpaid (see Lehmberg, *Sir Thomas Elyot* 68–69; Elyot, *Letters* 13). The book was Elyot's first. The embassy to Charles V was perhaps a reward for its praise of strong monarchy (possibly suborned by Cromwell; see Lehmberg *Sir Thomas Elyot* 46, 49–51). Such propaganda would have been especially welcome to Henry in 1531, when he was struggling to break free of Queen Catherine (the embassy's central subject). (4) His faux pas (if it is his) is the more interesting in view of his sense (reported by him to Cromwell after his return) of his unusual rapport with the emperor, owing to his deployment of "silken wordes" (*Letters* 9).

Sir Thomas Wyatt was Henry's ambassador to Charles's court in France and Flanders from November 1539 until May 1540 (when Puttenham was about ten). Catherine of Aragon had died on January 7, 1536, and political matters had moved well on from the issue Puttenham cites as the occasion for the embassy. Among other things current in 1539, Wyatt was to require at the emperor's hands the seizure of one Robert Brancetour, an Englishman formerly in the emperor's service who was suspected by Henry of illicit workings with Cardinal Pole, an English agent of the pope. Wyatt wrote to Henry recounting his audience with Charles on February 3, when he asked that Brancetour be handed over. He had apparently reproached Charles in Henry's name with ingratitude over the affair (Brancetour having now come under the emperor's protection). Charles took immediate offense, and Wyatt records in detail for Henry a fascinating account of their bristling debate about the proper use of the term (Muir, *Life and Letters* 134–37). The letter makes clear that the conversation took place in French: "I can not render that terme in my tong," Wyatt said to Charles, "in to the French tong by eny other terme wiche I know also to discend owt off the latyn" (135). French was the only language in which, Mattingly tells us, Charles could "converse freely" (*Renaissance Diplomacy* 236). (He was born in Ghent in 1500 and raised in southern Flanders till 1517 in the French and Dutch tongues, though he later added Spanish, and was noted as multilingual.)

There is no clear way to make sure which ambassador Puttenham meant. Elyot was dispatched to deal with the divorce issue when it was pending, and probably spoke no Spanish. Wyatt's embassy took place nearly a decade later, well after Catherine's death, and dealt in French, but documents the unfortunate use of the term. Charles is unlikely to have spoken Spanish to any English ambassador. English reproaches for "ingratitude" and imperial sensitivity to dishonor were likely at both times, for different reasons. Shyness about naming the ambassador might attach with somewhat more likelihood to Puttenham's uncle than to a poet he quotes frequently with admiration. Perhaps Puttenham, having heard the story (or stories) long before, confused one episode with the other; perhaps it happened twice; perhaps he changed the details intentionally, for reasons of tact.

20

3.23.356 [note 54, on Arundel's dinner with Margaret and Orange]   Arundel had been mentioned as a possible suitor for Elizabeth's hand, and the fourteen-month trip to Italy he embarked upon in 1566 (his only recorded trip to the continent) was "to mitigate his Grief" over not winning it, according to Camden (82), though it was described in the anonymous "Life" of Arundel (probably written by one of his servants about 1580) as a venture to the baths of Padua for cure of the gout (211). (It may also be relevant that his only son, Maltravers, was buried in Brussels in 1556.) Retirement from court for supposed illness was a common aristocratic ploy in the period (see 3.25.379–80), but Arundel's contemporary biographer writes of the earl as "sore troubled with the goute" (214) in his final days. Despite these various sufferings, the author of the "Life" remarks that "in [this] jorney his greate intertainment wch he received of forren Princes was much to be noted" (211). The Regent (whose confessor was Ignatius Loyola, founder of the counterrevolutionary Jesuit order) was a vigorous anti-Protestant, and the dinner in Brussels with Orange, the eventual leader of the Netherlandish rebellion against Philip II, almost surely took place before August 10, 1566. On that date began a widespread and violently iconoclastic Protestant uprising that decisively divided Orange from Margaret. Arundel was certainly traveling in a politically volatile year.

21

3.24.362 [note 17, on Diopithes' reward]   Diopithes (mid-4th c. BCE), the father of the poet Menander, was an Athenian general who was a fierce opponent of Philip of Macedonia. We have found no sure historical record for the incident Puttenham recounts, but it seems likely that Diopithes' opposition to Philip endeared him to the Persian king Artaxerxes III, who sent him presents that did not arrive until after his death. Puttenham's probable source for this information was Aristotle's *Rhetoric*, which merely says that pity is aroused when good things come too late and then illustrates this notion with the example of Diopithes, to whom an unspecified "king" sent presents that only arrived after his death (2.8.11). Possibly Puttenham conflates this king with Amasis, because the latter is mentioned in the very next paragraph of the *Rhetoric*, where Aristotle recounts an anecdote about Amasis, saying that he did not weep when his son was led to execution but did do so when an old friend was reduced to begging (2.8.12). A version of this anecdote appears later in this chapter (371), although there Puttenham simply speaks of "a certain king of Egypt." Both here and in this later case, Puttenham embroiders the anecdotes he found in Aristotle considerably, turning Diopithes into Amasis' courtier, for example, and having the king of Egypt actually see his son being led to execution. The proverbial status of the idea that a reward coming too late is called "Diopithes' reward" may well be Puttenham's invention; the notion is certainly not found in Aristotle.

22

3.24.368 [note 61, on the Turks] In 1554 the Flemish writer and diplomat Ogier Ghislain de Busbecq (1520/21–1592) came to England to represent the Austrian monarch Ferdinand I at the wedding of Mary I and Philip II of Spain. Two years later Ferdinand sent Busbecq to Istanbul as ambassador to the Ottoman Empire of the Sultan Suleiman, where he served till 1562. While in Turkey, Busbecq composed his *Itinera Constantinopolitanum et Amasianum* (1581), later published as *A. G. Busbequii D. legationis Turcicae epistolae quattor* (1595). This work was translated into English in 1694 as *The four epistles of A. G. Busbequius concerning his embassy into Turkey*. In this English translation Busbecq observes that "the Turks count it profane either to Eat, Drink, or Piss, in a standing posture, unless in case of necessity; but they do it bending their Bodies; as Women do with us when they make Water" (246).

Puttenham may have heard of the practice from Busbecq himself, having had opportunity as a hopeful young man (Busbecq was ten years his senior) to make contact with him in 1554, and perhaps later at one of the imperial courts (Charles V abdicated in 1556, and Ferdinand officially became Holy Roman Emperor in 1558). Puttenham tells us at 3.18.275 of having heard (or heard about) the emperor Charles V interacting with "King Ferdinand" (before 1556?), of being present at the imperial court (3.23.356), and of having witnessed "the Emperor Ferdinand" un-self-consciously climbing stairs (3.19.377). Busbecq returned from Turkey to Vienna in 1562 to serve as a counselor to Ferdinand, who died in 1564. We know independently that Puttenham was on the continent in February 1563 (see Introduction 7). These last two years are thus the most likely for a personal conversation about Turkish customs between Busbecq and Puttenham. He may instead, of course, have read the 1581 work years later.

23

3.24.368 [note 71, on Henry VIII's haircuts] Puttenham is probably referring to an occasion during the Lord Mayoralty of Sir John Champness, mayor from 1534, recorded with variations in several London chronicles. The first of the *Two London Chronicles*, ed. Kingsford, describes such a royal polling on May 8, 1535, following a record of the execution of four Carthusian monks and a priest for treason (for denying that Henry was Supreme Head of the Church in England) four days prior: "the kynge comaundyd all about his court to powl theyr hedes, & to gyve them ensample he dyd cawse his owne hed to be powellyed lykewyse" (10). A third chronicle, the so-called *London Chronicle*, ed. Hopper, reports the same or a similar event on or following July 6 of that year: "sir Thomas Moore, knyght, and Chauncelar of Inglond, [was] beheded at Towr hille on saynte Thomas eve after mydsomer, and was beryid wtin the Tour of London. Then the kyng made his owne hed to be pold, and many lordes and knyghtes, and all the corte" (9–10). More also died for his nominally treasonous refusal to accept the Royal Supremacy. How the polling of hair is linked to the polling of heads is not absolutely clear. However, given that, when Catherine of Aragon died six months later, Henry raucously celebrated her death with "a banquet, dancing and jousting," "dressed from head to toe in exultant yellow," as Scarisbrick has it (335), it seems probable that the courtly haircuts were also exhibitions of defiant celebration. *Requiring* such mimicry (as here) was often thought a feature of the tyrant's psychology; see Whigham, *Seizures of the Will* 195 and note 21. However, Puttenham judges below that at least on some occasions "it is decent [princes'] servitors and subjects study to be like to them by imitation, as in wearing their hair long or short" (3.24.376).

Name Glossary

'Abd al-Mu'min ibn 'Ali (b. 1094, ruled 1130–63). Berber caliph of the Almohad dynasty who conquered the North African Maghrib from the Almoravids and brought all the Berbers under one rule. He was known by some in early modern England as King Iphricus.

Adam Bell. See Bell, Adam.

Aeolus. In Greek legend, the king of Aeolia and keeper of the winds.

Aerschot, duke of. See Philip III, 3rd duke of Aerschot.

Agesilaus II (b. ca. 445 BCE, ruled 400–359 BCE). Spartan king who was a charismatic figure at home but not a particularly effective military leader abroad. He could not prevent the decline of Sparta's power and the rise of Thebes to prominence during the decade prior to his death.

Agis II (ruled 427?–400 BCE). Spartan king who led the invasion of Attica in 425 and then fought a series of battles against the Argives and the Athenians until the fall of Athens in 404.

Alexander VI, Pope (Rodrigo Borgia, b. 1434, pope 1492–1503). Corrupt, worldly, and ambitious pope, whose neglect of the spiritual inheritance of the Church contributed to the development of the Protestant Reformation.

Alexander of Aphrodisias (b. 200 CE). Commentator on Aristotle, and author of On Fate (in which he defends free will against the Stoic doctrine of necessity, or predetermined human action) and On the Soul, which figured substantially in thirteenth-century Scholastic debates about Aristotle.

Alexander Peloplaton ("Clay-Plato") (late 2nd to early 3rd c. CE). A rhetorician born in Seleucia, he was sent for unknown reasons as an ambassador to the emperor Antoninus Pius in Rome, who mocked him for the extravagant care he bestowed on his appearance. He received his surname from a Corinthian named Sceptes who said he found in Alexander the "clay (pelos), but not Plato." Alexander spent most of his life away from his native city.

Alfonso V (b. 1396, king of Aragon 1416–58, king of Naples [as Alfonso I] 1442–58). Famous military figure who moved his court permanently to Naples after conquering it in 1443, and studied there with the Italian humanist Lorenzo Valla. His court became a famous center of art and culture.

Alfonso X (b. 1221, king of León and Castile 1252–84). Writer, intellectual, and lawgiver who had the Alfonsine Tables of planetary motion prepared by his court scholars.

Almansor, king of Morocco (probably Abu Yusuf Ya'qub Ibn 'abd Al-mu'min Al-mansur) (b. 1160?, ruled 1184–99). Third ruler of the Mu'minid dynasty of

Spain and North Africa, who brought the power of his dynasty to its zenith. Averroës produced his famous commentaries on Aristotle at the court of Al-mansur's predecessor Abu Ya'qub Yusuf (1163–84).

Amasis (ruled 570–ca. 525 BCE). Egyptian pharaoh who allied himself with vari-ous Greek city-states in order to meet the growing threat from Persia, which conquered Egypt in 525 shortly after Amasis' death.

Amyntas, king of Macedonia. No king named Amyntas ruled Macedonia during Euripides' residence there, but such kings did rule before and after this time. Euripides moved there in 408 BCE (two years before his death) at the invitation of King Archelaus (ruled 413–399). The source of the *Art*'s error is unknown.

Anacreon (582?–485? BCE). Greek poet who was, after Archilochus, the most im-portant writer of personal lyric in the Ionic dialect. Only fragments of his verse survive.

Anaxagoras (ca. 500–ca. 428 BCE). Greek philosopher, mentor of Pericles, and au-thor of *On Nature*. Only fragments of his works survive.

Anaxarchus (mid- to late 4th c. BCE). Greek philosopher who followed Democri-tus' teachings and leaned toward skepticism. He accompanied Alexander the Great to Asia and wrote a book on kingship.

Anne of Brittany (1477–1514). Twice Queen Consort of France, first to Charles VIII (m. 1491) and then to Louis XII (m. 1499). Born forty-four years after the death of Alain Chartier, with whom the *Art* associates her.

Anne, duke of Montmorency (b. 1493, Constable of France 1538, duke 1551–67). French statesman and military commander during the reigns of Francis I, Henry II, and Charles IX. He was named after his godmother, Queen Anne of Brittany.

Antimenides. Aristotle observed that the people of Mitylene once elected Pitta-cus to resist a band of the exiles under the leadership of Antimenides and his brother the poet Alcaeus (ca. 620– ca. 580 BCE); see *Politics* 3.9.1285a.

Antiochus I Soter, Seleucid king of Babylonia (b. ca. 324, ruled 281–61 BCE). Son of Seleucus I Nicator (ca. 358–281 BCE), who in the 290s married a second wife Stra-tonice (daughter of Demetrius Poliorcites of Macedonia) for political considera-tions. Seleucus afterward gave her to Antiochus to strengthen the succession. Hellenistic authors later constructed a court drama (based on Euripides' *Hippoly-tus*) in which the son, pining for his father's young wife, was saved by the inter-vention of his physician Erasistratus, who engineered the gift from father to son.

Antiochus of Athens (2nd c. CE). Greek Sophist who composed historical and philosophical works and was known for the sharpness of his wit.

Antoninus, Marcus Aurelianus. See **Caracalla**.

Aratus (315?–245? BCE). Greek poet who was the author of *Phaenomena*, a long poem on astronomy.

Arcadia. Region in ancient Greece in the middle of the Peloponnesus inhabited by shepherds and used as a setting in pastoral poetry to suggest primal inno-cence and simplicity.

Ariosto, Ludovico (1474–1533). Italian poet who produced an array of works, in-cluding verse satires and comedies, and whose masterpiece, the epic poem *Or-lando furioso*, was known and imitated throughout Europe.

Arrian (Lucius Flavius Arrianus) (ca. 86–160 CE). Greek writer who enjoyed the political patronage of the Roman emperor Hadrian, published philosophical works, and, representing himself as a second Xenophon, wrote a series of his-torical works, the most famous of which was the so-called *Anabasis of Alexan-der*, a seven–volume history of Alexander the Great.

Arsinoë II Philadelphus, queen of Egypt (ca. 316–270 BCE). The daughter of Ptolemy I, she who was married initially to Lysimachus of Macedonia, then to her half-brother Ptolemy Ceraunus, and finally to her brother Ptolemy II in the mid-270s. She had great influence on her brother, who made her and himself deities in a religious cult.

Arundel, Henry Fitzalan, 12th earl of (1512–1580). A godson of Henry VIII who remained a religious conservative after the English break with the Church of Rome and rose to become Lord Steward under Mary. He retained this position under Elizabeth (and was rumored to have been her suitor during the 1550s), but eventually resigned in 1564 because of suspicions about his loyalty. He was implicated in several Catholic plots against Elizabeth, but was never brought to trial for lack of sufficient evidence.

Attila, king of the Huns (ruled 434–453 CE). One of the greatest of the barbarian rulers who assailed the Roman Empire, invading the southern Balkan provinces and Greece and then Gaul and Italy.

Aurelius, Marcus. See **Marcus Aurelius**.

Avicenna (980–1037). Not a prince, but an Iranian physician, the most famous and influential of the philosopher–scientists of Islam.

Bacon, Sir Nicholas (1509–1579). Elizabethan courtier and politician, Lord Keeper of the Great Seal after 1558, and father of Sir Francis Bacon. Together with William Cecil, Lord Burghley, he worked to retain the moderate Protestantism of the English Church, sought to undermine Catholic power elsewhere in Europe, and was one of the chief opponents to reinstating Mary Stuart on the throne of Scotland after 1570.

Balliol, John de, king of Scotland (1250–1313, ruled 1292–96). Having married Margaret, the Maid of Norway and heiress to the Scottish throne, in 1290, John named himself the rightful heir. Edward I of England asserted his feudal superiority over Scotland and approved John's claim to be king in 1292. John, however, soon began resisting English authority, was defeated in battle by Edward's forces, and was forced to resign the throne in 1296.

Bell, Adam. Like Clym of the Clough, Adam Bell was a legendary outlaw and skilled archer who was said to have lived in the forest of Englewood during the time of Robin Hood's father. Both men were the subject of popular ballads that were printed by William Copland in a collection titled *Adam Bell, Clym of the Cloughe and Wyllyam of Cloudslee* (ca. 1550).

Berenice (fl. 317?–272? BCE). The name of several different queens of the Ptolemaic rulers of Egypt. No Queen Berenice was married to the Ptolemy who patronized Theocritus, as the *Art* says. Berenice I was the mother of that Ptolemy (Ptolemy II Philadelphus); another Berenice (unnumbered) was the daughter of that king and his sister Arsinoë II of Egypt; and that Ptolemy arranged the marriage of his son and eventual successor Ptolemy III Euergetes to Berenice II, daughter of King Magas of Cyrene. The source for the *Art*'s error is unidentified.

Bevis of Southampton. A mistake for Bevis of Hampton, the subject of a medieval English romance named after him, in which he is sold into slavery after his father's death, distinguishes himself as a knight, and eventually regains his father's realm.

Blackfriars. An ensemble of buildings and grounds in London, until 1538 housing a convent of the Dominican order (the "black friars"). The precinct or "liberty" of its grounds constituted a zone in but not under the authority of the City of

London, and after its "nationalization" with the break from the Church of Rome, the central government used its environs for many official and court purposes and protected it from meddlesome City authorities. Later in the century it was much used for residential purposes, and its freedom from City supervision gave it a racy reputation for borderline activities such as bowling and what would become "the arts."

Breton, Nicholas (1553?–1625?). English writer of lyrical poems, satires, dialogues, essays, and pastoral poetry, who also wrote books of characters modeled on the *Characters* of the Greek philosopher Theophrastus (382?–287? BCE).

Buckhurst, Thomas, Lord. See **Sackville, Thomas**.

Budaeus (Guillaume Budé) (1467–1540). An associate of Erasmus and a French humanist important not only for his historical and philological studies but also for his having influenced Francis I to establish the Collège de France and a humanist library in his château at Fontainebleau.

Burghley, Lord. See **Cecil, Sir William**.

Cade, Jack (d. 1450). English rebel leader of a popular revolt in Kent in 1450, deriving from complaints of the poor concerning crown insolvency, taxation, corruption among courtly favorites, and the loss of Normandy to the French. His army looted London, and Cade escaped with considerable booty, but he was captured in Sussex as a traitor. He died of his wounds while being taken to London, where his body was quartered and his head placed on London Bridge.

Caelus. The Roman divinity equated with the Greek Uranus (Heaven), who was husband of Gaea (Earth) and father of Saturn.

Caligula (Gaius Caesar Germanicus), Roman emperor (b. 12 CE, ruled 37–41). Famous for his great cruelty, pretensions to divinity, and despotic caprice, he died at the hands of an assassin.

Calixtus II, Pope (pope 1119–24). Convoked the First Lateran Council (1123), which passed several decrees against clerical abuses such as simony and concubinage.

Callicratidas (d. 406 BCE). Spartan admiral who impulsively led a fleet against the Athenians, but after an initial success was defeated and drowned off the Arginusae islands.

Callimachus (fl. ca. 260 BCE). Greek poet who lived in Alexandria and wrote *Aetia (Causes)*, a collection of tales from Greek mythology and history, as well as other polished, witty short poems.

Callisthenes (360–327 BCE). Greek philosopher, nephew of Aristotle, and follower of Alexander, whose exploits he recorded, but who had him put to death when he criticized Alexander's taste for oriental luxury and his pretensions to divinity.

Callisto. In Greek mythology, a nymph, and one of the goddess Artemis' huntress companions. She swore to remain chaste, but she copulated with Zeus and was turned into a she-bear, either by Zeus (to conceal the deed from his wife, Hera) or by Artemis or Hera (who were enraged at her unchastity).

Cannibal. Originally one of the forms of the ethnic name "Carib" or "Caribes," a fierce nation of the West Indies, who are recorded to have been anthropophagi, and from whom the name was subsequently extended as a descriptive term.

Capua. In ancient times, the chief city of the Campania region of Italy, located about one hundred miles southeast of Rome and sixteen miles north of Neapolis (Naples).

Caracalla (Marcus Aurelianus Antoninus), Roman emperor (b. 188 CE, ruled with his father, Septimius Severus, 198–211 and then alone 211–17). His major accomplishments were the baths named after him and the extension of Roman citizenship to all free men in the empire in 212. Cruel and domineering, he was assassinated while on a campaign against the Medes.

Carolus Calvus. See **Charles II**.

Catherine of Aragon, queen of England (1485–1536, queen 1509–1531). Youngest daughter of Ferdinand V of Aragon and Isabella of Castile and aunt of the Holy Roman Emperor Charles V, she married the English king Henry VII's eldest son, Arthur, in 1501, who died the next year, then married Henry VIII when he came to the throne in 1509. Although she gave birth to several children, only her daughter Mary survived. In quest of a male heir through Anne Boleyn, Henry had his marriage to Catherine declared null and void in 1533 while he was breaking with the Church of Rome.

Catherine of Castile. See **Catherine of Aragon.**

Cato the Censor (Marcus Porcius Cato, also called Cato the Elder), (234–149 BCE). Roman statesman and author of *De re rustica (On Agriculture)* who was known for his eloquence and his moral severity.

Cecil, Sir William, Lord Burghley (1520–1598). Lord Treasurer from 1572 on who was principal adviser to Elizabeth I and renowned for his gravity.

Chaldees. Inhabitants of the Middle Eastern region of Shinar, of which Babylon was capital; later (beginning with Daniel 2:10, ca. 165 BCE) the term became synonymous with "astrologer" or "magician," apparently denoting a priestly class.

Chaloner, Sir Thomas (1515?–1565). English knight, diplomat, and writer who served Elizabeth and wrote tracts and a variety of poems as well as translating the works of Saint John Chrysostom and, most famously, Erasmus's *Praise of Folly.*

Chancery, Court of. The court of the Lord Chancellor, the highest court in Great Britain under the House of Lords.

Charlemagne (b. 742, king of the Franks 768–814, king of the Lombards 774–814, and Holy Roman Emperor 800–814; reckoned as Charles I of France). With the exceptions of the kingdom of Asturias in Spain, southern Italy, and the British Isles, he united in one superstate practically all the Christian lands of western Europe.

Charles II (b. 823, king of France 843–877, Holy Roman Emperor 875–877). Known as Charles the Bald (Lat. *calvus*; hence Carolus Calvus).

Charles V (1500–1558, king of Spain 1516–56, Holy Roman Emperor 1519–56). Ruling an empire that included Spain, the kingdom of Naples, Austria, and the Netherlands in Europe as well as the Spanish possessions in the Americas, Charles was one of the chief opponents of Protestantism. While holding off the Turks, he battled France for hegemony in western Europe, defeated and captured the French king, Francis I, at Pavia in 1525, thereby assuring the Spanish dominance of the Italian peninsula. At the end of his life Charles abdicated, making his brother Maximilian the new emperor and his son Philip II the new king of Spain and the Netherlands.

Charles VIII, king of France (b. 1470, ruled 1483–98). First husband of Anne of Brittany. Initiating the Italian Wars, he invaded Italy in 1494 in order to capture the Kingdom of Naples, to which he had a vague dynastic claim; he was defeated and returned to France the following year.

Charles IX, king of France (b. 1550, ruled 1563–74). Made king in his minority when his brother Henry II was killed, Charles was dominated by his mother,

Catherine de Médicis, who persuaded him to order the massacre of Protestants on Saint Bartholomew's Day (August 23–24, 1572).

Charles the Great. See **Charlemagne**.

Chartier, Alain (1385–1433?). Medieval French poet and political writer, dead for forty-four years before the birth of Anne of Brittany, with whom the *Art* associates him. He was celebrated as a predecessor by French Renaissance poets, and Keats used the title of one of his poems for *La Belle Dame sans Merci*.

Chimera. In Greek mythology, a fire–breathing female monster resembling a lion in the forepart, a goat in the middle, and a dragon behind.

Choerilus (fl. 4th c. BCE). According to Horace, a bad epic poet of Iasos in Asia Minor whom Alexander the Great patronized (Horace, *Epistles* 2.1.233; *Ars poetica* 357).

Cineas (d. ca. 277 BCE). Greek orator trained by Demosthenes who served King Pyrrhus of Epirus and was celebrated for his rhetorical power.

Cleomenes I, king of Sparta (ruled ca. 520–490 BCE). He consolidated the position of his city as the major power in the Peloponnesus; he refused to engage in wars overseas but frequently intervened in the affairs of Athens. He supposedly went mad and met a violent end, probably at his own hand.

Clym of the Clough. See **Bell, Adam**.

Constable of France. See **Anne, duke of Montmorency**.

Constantinus Cepronimus. See **Constantine V Copronymus**.

Constantine V Copronymus, emperor of Byzantium (b. 718, ruled 740–775). Son of the Iconoclast emperor Leo III the Isaurian, he shared his father's heresy. The malice of the Orthodox Iconodules (venerators of icons) led them to give him the byname "Copronymus" (He whose name is dung), and the story of his baptism was further invented to explain it.

Cornelius Gallus. See **Gallus, Gaius Cornelius**.

Corydon. A shepherd who appears in the second and seventh of Vergil's *Eclogues*.

Crates (fl. 4th c. BCE). Cynic philosopher and pupil of Diogenes who authored parodies in which he mocked other philosophers and praised the Cynic way of living.

Curtius Rufus, Quintus (fl. late 1st or early 2nd c. CE). Roman rhetorician and historian who wrote a highly rhetorical ten-book life of Alexander the Great.

Cynthia. In Greek mythology, a name for the moon goddess Artemis or Diana, derived from Mount Cynthus in Delos, her birthplace. "Cynthia" was a common epithet for Elizabeth I as Virgin Queen.

Cyrus II, king of Persia (d. 401 BCE). Second son of Darius II of Persia who attempted a coup d'état against his elder brother Artaxerxes, but was defeated and killed at the battle of Cunaxa.

Danaë. In Greek mythology, the mother of Perseus by Zeus, who visited her as a shower of gold.

Darius III, king of Persia (b. d. unknown, ruled 336–330 BCE). Defeated by Alexander the Great at Gaugamela (in Mesopotamia) in 331.

Demetrius. See **Antiochus I Soter**.

Democritus of Abdera (b. ca. 460–457 BCE). Greek philosopher who was credited in antiquity with the creation of the atomic theory, and in later times became known as "the laughing philosopher," probably because he held that cheerfulness was the goal to pursue in life.

De Vere, Edward, 17th earl of Oxford (1550–1604). Narcissistic and extravagant English nobleman, poet, "Italianate Englishman," and favorite of Elizabeth I. He insulted Sir Philip Sidney on the tennis court, who then challenged him, but

Elizabeth forced Sidney to defer to Oxford's superior rank. About twenty of his poems, some doubtful, survive. Though Puttenham cites him as a writer of comedy, no dramatic texts are extant. Many literary works were dedicated to him by Lyly, Watson, Golding, Day, and others; Spenser wrote a dedicatory sonnet to him (one of 17 addressed to various worthies) in the 1590 *Faerie Queene*.

Dinocrates (fl. 4th c. BCE). Greek architect who served Alexander the Great and designed the city of Alexandria for him using a regular gridwork plan.

Domitian (Titus Flavius Domitianus), Roman emperor (b. 51 CE, ruled 81–96). Known chiefly for the reign of terror under which prominent members of the Senate lived during his last years; he was murdered in 96.

Don Peter, king of Spain. See **Peter I.**

Drake, Sir Francis (1540?–1596). Famous Elizabethan pirate and naval commander who circumnavigated the globe (1577–80) and warred on Spain for Elizabeth, sacking Cartagena and Santo Domingo in 1585–86, attacking Cadiz in 1587, and serving as second in command of the English fleet that fought with the Spanish Armada. He died of dysentery on another voyage, in Panama in 1596.

Dudley, John, duke of Northumberland (1502?–1553). Court magnate under Henry VIII and Edward VI, and father of Robert, earl of Leicester, who became Elizabeth's principal favorite. Celebrated for martial prowess, he became a Privy Councillor to Henry VIII in 1543. Upon Henry's death in 1547, he was appointed a joint regent for the boy king with fifteen others, was created earl of Warwick in that year, and put down Ket's Rebellion in 1549. He remained subordinate to the Lord Protector Somerset, however, until the latter's fall in 1549, when Dudley took control, becoming duke of Northumberland in 1551. Upon Edward's death in 1553, he attempted to put Lady Jane Grey on the throne but failed, and was tried and executed for high treason against Mary I.

Dyer, Sir Edward (1543–1607). English courtier-poet, friend to Sir Philip Sidney, and client of the earl of Leicester; only a few of his occasional lyrics survive.

Edmund II, king of England (b. ca. 993, ruled April 23–November 30, 1016). Was called "Edmund Ironside" for his staunch resistance to a massive invasion led by the Danish king Canute. The son of King Ethelred II the Unready (ruled 978–1016), Edmund was proclaimed king by a body of counselors and citizens of London upon his father's death, but a larger body of nobles at Southampton declared for Canute. Edmund was decisively defeated by Canute at Ashington, Essex, on October 18, 1016. He retained the rule of Wessex in the peace settlement, but after he died Canute became sole ruler of England.

Edmund Ironside. See **Edmund II.**

Edward I, king of England (b. 1239, ruled 1272–1307). Called "Edward Longshanks" because of his height, he was also known as the "Hammer of the Scots." During his reign he kept the Scots under English rule and conquered Wales as well.

Edward III, king of England (b. 1312, ruled 1327–77). Began the Hundred Years' War with France and instituted the Order of the Garter.

Edward IV, king of England (b. 1442, ruled 1461–70 and 1471–83). A leading Yorkist participant in the Wars of the Roses.

Edward VI, king of England (b. 1537, ruled 1547–53). Son of Henry VIII and his third queen, Jane Seymour, half-brother to Mary I and Elizabeth I. In his short reign he was dominated by two magnates, Somerset (his Seymour uncle) and Northumberland, who supervised the full Protestantization of the English Church.

Edward, earl of Oxford. See **De Vere, Edward**.

Edwards, Richard (1523?–1566). English poet and playwright who was made Master of the Children of the Chapel Royal and composed plays for them which were acted before Queen Elizabeth; only his *Damon and Pythias* survives.

Endymion. In Greek mythology, a beautiful youth who spent much of his life in perpetual sleep, and who was beloved by the moon goddess Selene, often identified with Artemis.

Ennius, Quintus (239–169 BCE). Epic poet, dramatist, and satirist, who was the most influential of the early Latin poets and considered the founder of Roman literature.

Erasmus, Desiderius (1469–1536). Greatest scholar of the northern Renaissance and the first editor of the Greek New Testament. By criticizing ecclesiastical abuses while pointing to a better age in the distant past, he encouraged the growing urge for reform, which found expression both in the Protestant Reformation and in the Catholic Counter-Reformation. His independent stance in an age of fierce confessional controversy—he rejected both Luther's doctrine of predestination and the powers that were claimed for the papacy—made him a target of suspicion for loyal partisans on both sides.

Eudamidas I (late 4th c. BCE). Son of Archidamas III and brother of Agis II, Eudamidas began ruling as the king of Sparta in 331.

Europa. In Greek mythology, the beauty of Europa inspired the love of Zeus, who approached her in the form of a white bull and carried her away from Phoenicia to Crete.

Evax, king of Arabia. An imaginary Eastern monarch, supposed author of a letter of introduction addressed to Tiberius extolling his virtues and liberality, and offering in return the occult knowledge contained in the book of jewels the letter accompanied. Versions of and allusions to this letter appear in many medieval lapidary texts.

Ewelme. Manor in Oxfordshire that belonged to Thomas Chaucer (1367?–1434), the poet Geoffrey's elder son, to whom it came with other estates by his marriage to Matilda, second daughter of Sir John Burghersh, nephew of Henry Burghersh, bishop of Lincoln, treasurer and chancellor of the kingdom. Though it had no real connection with the poet, it was thought in the sixteenth century to be his, as in Puttenham's tale. The source for the spurious link may well be John Stow, famous for disseminating such misinformation.

Favorinus (ca. 85–155). Roman Sophist who was a Stoic inclining toward mild skepticism and engaged in a bitter feud in Athens with his fellow Sophist Polemon. He is credited with an extensive array of histories, declamations, and philosophical works as well as a mock oration in praise of the quartan fever (malaria).

Ferdinand I (b. 1503, king of Bohemia and Hungary 1526–64, Holy Roman Emperor 1558–64). Younger brother of Charles V, Holy Roman Emperor (1519–56), he was noted for signing the Peace of Augsburg, which concluded the era of religious strife in Germany that followed the rise of Lutheranism by recognizing the right of territorial princes to determine the religion of their subjects.

Ferrers, Edward (d. 1564). English dramatist, educated at Oxford. The details of his life are uncertain, and some of the works attributed to him during the Renaissance are now ascribed to George Ferrers (1500?–1579?). He wrote various verses that were part of the celebrations of the queen at the earl of Leicester's famous 1575 progress entertainment at Kenilworth.

Field, Richard (fl. 1579–1624). Printer of Puttenham's *Art* who was a fellow Stratford native and perhaps personal friend of Shakespeare, whose *Venus and Adonis* and *Rape of Lucrece* he printed (1593–96). Among his other important productions were Harington's English translation of Ariosto's *Orlando furioso* (1592), North's *Plutarch* (1603, 1610–12), and a French translation of Camden's *Annales* (1624).

Flamock, Sir Andrew. Minor courtier to Henry VIII with an unusual set of links to figures in literary history. In 1536 he served as one of fifty squires in a procession for the reception of Anne of Cleves; among the other squires were Robert Puttenham (Puttenham's father), John Poyntz (possibly the man from Wyatt's satire), "Ant. Rous" (the man identified in 3.18), "John Chek" (the famous humanist), and "Fulk Grevell" (the grandfather of Sidney's biographer). In 1540 Flamock and his son visited Sir John Dudley (Leicester's father), carrying the plague to the house. (The next day the son died.) Dudley reports to Cromwell that they "came out of Gloucestershire from Mr. Poyntz": Wyatt's John Poyntz was from Gloucestershire. In 1542 the Privy Council wrote to Flamock and "Fowke Grivell" about "inordinate hunting" on the king's lands. Finally, the earl of Surrey wrote in 1546 from France (where he served as Field Marshal of France and Flamock served as Porter of Boulogne) to William Paget, secretary of state, of "poor Sir Andrew Flamock who, by service in town and field, has deserved to be defended from poverty now in his old days." Probably as a result, we hear in a later record the same year that "the king" decided to employ Flamock on the English side of the Channel, and soon after, Olufton manor was licensed to be transferred to him and his wife, Elizabeth. This last material may document the personal acquaintance with Henry that Puttenham records in 3.23.

Francis I, king of France (b. 1494, ruled 1515–47). Taught by humanists, he founded the Collège de France to advance humanistic studies and patronized leading French writers such as Clément Marot. He fought Charles V, king of Spain and Holy Roman Emperor, for dominance in Europe and was captured and imprisoned by the Spanish at the battle of Pavia (1525), the result of which was that France lost its position as a rival to Spain for dominance in the Italian peninsula.

Frederick III, Holy Roman Emperor (b. 1415, ruled 1452–93). Father of Maximilian, archduke of Austria, who made his family, the Habsburgs, dominant in sixteenth-century Europe.

Galen of Paramus (129–216? CE). Greek physician, philosopher, and writer who believed in humoral medicine (the notion that the body contains four humors whose balance meant health and whose imbalance meant sickness) and whose works dominated medicine up until the seventeenth century.

Gallus, Gaius Cornelius (70?–26 BCE). Friend of Augustus and Vergil and one of the great Roman elegiac poets (along with Tibullus, Propertius, and Ovid, according to Quintilian); when Augustus conquered Antony and Cleopatra at the battle of Actium and brought the Ptolemaic rule of Egypt to an end, he appointed Gallus the first Roman viceroy of Egypt (30–26).

Gascoigne, George (1525?–1577). English lawyer, courtier, soldier, and writer whose work foreshadowed the English sonnet sequence, Elizabethan courtly fiction, early modern drama, and literary theory. His most important work, *The*

Adventures of Master F. J., is a series of love poems set in a narrative of transgressive eroticism and courtly wit and framed by an elaborate set of nested letters of apology and justification. His *Certayne Notes* (1575) is the first English treatise on prosody.

Gifford, Sir William (d. 1549), of Itchell in Southamptonshire. Husband of Sir William Paulet's sister Eleanor.

Golding, Arthur (1536?–1605?). English writer and translator who enjoyed the patronage of many courtiers in Elizabeth's court and translated works by Julius Caesar, Calvin, and Theodore Beza; he was and is best known for his translation of Ovid's *Metamorphoses*.

Gower, John (d. 1408). English poet considered second to Chaucer among medieval writers whose best-known work was the *Confessio amantis* (*The Lover's Confession*).

Gratian (Flavius Gratianus Augustus), Roman emperor (b. 359 CE, co-ruled with his father and then his uncle 367–383). He spent most of his reign in Gaul repelling the tribes that were invading from across the Rhine.

Gray, William (before 1514–1551). Client of Henry VIII and Cromwell, and later Edward Seymour, duke of Somerset and Lord Protector under Edward VI. Gray attracted the notice of Henry as author of the ballad "The Hunt is Up" (known by 1537). He took part in a ballad controversy over reformist Church issues, for which he was committed to the Fleet by the Privy Council in 1541. He served as member of Parliament for Reading in 1547, received various awards of land from the Court of Augmentations, and wrote two surviving New Year's poems to Somerset.

Greenwich. The name of a royal palace that was located in the London suburb of the same name. It began as a manor which originally belonged to the Church, but it came into the possession of Henry IV, who granted it to Humphrey, duke of Gloucester, who began to enclose the grounds (the "park"). On his death it reverted to the crown, and Edward IV later began beautifying and extending the palace. Henry VII bestowed it upon his wife, who gave birth to Henry VIII there. Henry VIII was married to Catherine of Aragon at Greenwich Palace, in which Mary, Elizabeth, and Edward VI were also born. It was demolished by Charles II.

Greville, Fulke, 1st Baron Brooke (1554–1628). English courtier, officeholder, and poet, and one of Elizabeth's favorites, who rose to become Chancellor of the Exchequer under James. An intimate of Sir Philip Sidney's, he wrote a biography about his friend, three tragedies—*Mustapha, Alaham,* and a treatment of Antony and Cleopatra (which he destroyed after the Essex rebellion)—and a sonnet sequence, *Caelica.*

Guillaume de Lorris (fl. 13th c.). French author of the first and more poetic part of the medieval verse allegory the *Roman de la rose* (*The Romance of the Rose*), begun sometime around 1230–40.

Guise, duke of (Henry I de Lorraine) (1550–1588). Leader of the extreme Catholic Party in France during the Wars of Religion (1562–89). He was assassinated by members of the bodyguard of Henry III in 1588. (Henry III also died that same year, and Henry of Navarre, who converted to Catholicism, then ascended the throne as Henry IV).

Guy of Warwick. Knight who is the subject of a medieval romance named after him in which he falls in love with his master's daughter, earns her hand by becoming the foremost knight in the world, but then feels remorse over having killed many knights and ends his life as a penitent pilgrim.

Habdul mumi. See ʿAbd al-Muʾmin ibn ʿAli.

Hannibal (247–183 BCE). Carthaginian general who led an invasion into Italy across the Alps and won a series of battles against the Romans, but was finally defeated by Scipio Africanus at the battle of Zama in 202.

Hardyng, John (1378–1465?). English soldier, officeholder, and historian who composed a *Chronicle* in rhyme royal that unfolds the history of England from the time of its legendary founder Brute up to events of 1463.

Hegesias (fl. ca. 290 BCE). Greek philosopher and head of the Cyrenaic school at the time of Ptolemy I Soter who was called the "Death-persuader" because his emphasis on the wretchedness of the human condition apparently encouraged people to commit suicide; he was expelled from Alexandria because of the scandal caused by his lectures.

Heliogabalus (Caesar Marcus Aurelius Antoninus Augustus, original name **Varius Avitus Bassianus**), Roman emperor (b. 204 CE, ruled 218–22). He imposed the worship of Baal upon the Roman world, promoted many favorites distinguished by personal beauty and humble and alien origins, and otherwise outraged Roman opinion by openly holding homosexual orgies.

Henry I Beauclerk, king of England (b. ca. 1068, ruled 1100–1135). The fourth son of William the Conqueror, Henry succeeded William's second son as king and defeated William's eldest son in 1106, so that he controlled Normandy as well. He was a successful administrator and was (by a 14th-century tradition) nicknamed "Beauclerk" or "Beauclerc" (the "lovely scholar") for his unusual education.

Henry II, king of France (b. 1519, ruled 1547–59). A competent administrator who was married to Catherine de Médicis and vigorously attempted to suppress Protestantism within his kingdom. He continued his father's warfare against the Holy Roman Emperor Charles V and the Spanish king Philip II until the Treaty of Cateau-Cambrésis was signed in 1559 ceding control of Italy to Spain. He died from a wound received in jousting at the celebration of the marriages of his sister and daughter, which were to cement the treaty.

Henry IV, king of England (b. 1366?, ruled 1399–1413). Usurped the throne from Richard II, and was the father of the celebrated Henry V.

Henry VII, king of England (b. 1457, ruled 1485–1509). Founder of the Tudor dynasty who ended the War of the Roses by defeating Richard III at Bosworth Field and by uniting his House of Lancaster with that of York by marrying Edward IV's eldest daughter, Elizabeth. During his reign he defeated a series of rebellions and successfully strengthened the monarchy by amassing considerable wealth through a variety of domestic taxes and the like as well as by avoiding costly foreign wars.

Henry VIII, king of England (b. 1491, ruled 1509–47). Son of Henry VII who broke with the Catholic Church, married six times in an effort to produce a male heir, patronized humanist learning and the arts, and was himself a poet and musician.

Heraclitus (ca. 540–450 BCE). Greek philosopher remembered for his cosmology, in which fire forms the basic material principle of an orderly universe, as well as for his obscurity. His views survive in short fragments quoted and attributed to him by later authors.

Hermes Trismegistus. Putative author of certain ancient metaphysical works dealing with the harmony of all beings and things in the universe. These works were attributed to the Egyptian god Thoth, who was identified with the Greek god Hermes and was called Hermes Trismegistus (Hermes the Thrice Great).

The books were influential on Neoplatonic philosophers in the third century CE and on a variety of Renaissance thinkers.

Hermogenes (b. ca. 161). Greek rhetor and Sophist who authored treatises and handbooks, including one on rhetorical topics and another titled *On Different Styles*, a standard stylistic manual in the Byzantine Empire and during the Renaissance that identifies seven types of style, all of which are to be found in the orations of Demosthenes.

Hesiod (8th c. BCE; after Homer). Greek poet who wrote *Works and Days* and *The Theogony*.

Heywood, John (1497?–1575). English writer who was active at the courts of Henry VIII, Edward VI, and Mary, and who wrote a variety of works, the most important of which were his interludes, witty dialogues for the stage on set subjects that are moralistic but contain elements of farce. A Roman Catholic, he fled to Belgium in 1564, where he remained until his death.

Howard, Henry, earl of Surrey (1517–1547). English poet who, with Thomas Wyatt, introduced Italian forms into English poetry. A participant in the political intrigues of Henry VIII's court, he was executed because he and his family were supposedly plotting to set aside Henry's son, Edward, and assume the throne.

Hugobald the Monk (Hucbald de Saint-Amand) (840?–930). Medieval abbot and musical theorist of great importance.

Huns. A nomadic pastoral people who invaded southeastern Europe ca. 370 CE and during the next seven decades built up an enormous empire there and in central Europe.

Irus. A beggar in Ithaca who ran errands for Penelope's suitors, attempted to throw Odysseus out of his house, and was knocked out by him with one blow; see *Odyssey* 17.1–110.

Isocrates (436–338 BCE). Greek rhetorician and teacher who was influenced by the Sophist Gorgias and was more concerned in his teachings with polished language than philosophical complexity. He was identified politically with the cause of Panhellenic opposition to Persia and the project of colonialism as a solution to Athenian poverty.

Jason. Mythological Greek hero who was tutored by the centaur Chiron and later led the Argonauts in quest of the Golden Fleece, which he obtained with the aid of the Colchian princess Medea. Jason and Medea then went to Corinth, and when he decided to marry the daughter of King Creon, Medea slew the children they had had together. There are various accounts of Jason's death.

Jean de Meun (1240?–1305?). Most likely the archdeacon of Beauce, who wrote satirical poems and was most famous for his continuation of *La Roman de la rose* (*The Romance of the Rose* [ca. 1280]), an allegorical poem in the courtly love tradition begun by Guillaume de Lorris between 1230 and 1240. The fragments that remain of the translation ascribed to Chaucer come from parts of the poem written by both French authors.

Joannes Secundus. See **Secundus, Joannes**.

John Frederick, duke of Saxony (b. 1503, ruled 1532–47; d. 1554). Last Elector of the Ernestine branch of the Saxon House of Wettin and leader of the Protestant Schmalkaldic League. His wars against the Holy Roman Emperor Charles V and his fellow princes caused him to lose both the electoral rank and much of his territory.

Juan Leon, a Moor of Granada. See **Leo Africanus**.

Ket, Robert ("Captain Ket") (d. 1549). A tanner or, more likely, a small landowner who was the leader of the Norfolk Rebellion of 1549 (afterward called Ket's Rebellion). It began at a feast in June 1549 as a protest against the enclosure of common land, then grew to an armed rebellion of sixteen thousand men who took the town of Norwich on August 1. They were defeated four weeks later, and Ket was sent to London, where he was executed for treason in December.

Lacedaemonians. Inhabitants of ancient Sparta, ruled by military oligarchy from the sixth to the second century BCE.

Landgrave of Hesse, Philip (1504–1567). Called "the Magnanimous" because of his concern for his state and his religious tolerance, he was one of the great figures of German Protestantism, forming the Schmalkaldic League in 1531 to champion the independence of German Protestant princes from the Holy Roman Emperor Charles V. The league was defeated in 1547, and when Philip submitted to the emperor, he was imprisoned in the Spanish Netherlands, only gaining his release in 1562 after German Protestants defeated Charles and were granted positions of equality with Catholic princes in the Empire.

Langland, William (1330?–1400?). Presumed author of *Piers Plowman*, a long allegorical poem narrating a dream vision presenting a complex variety of Christian themes. He was regarded by many Renaissance Protestants as a Reformation writer *avant la lettre*.

Law Salic. See **Salic law**.

Leda. In Greek mythology (in extremely varied forms), a woman believed to have been the mother (by Zeus, who approached her in the form of a swan, or by other divine and human fathers) of the twins Castor and Pollux, Clytemnestra, and/or the Trojan Helen, often but not always supposedly hatched from eggs.

Leo Africanus (Latin byname Johannes Leo, Spanish byname Juan Leon, Italian byname Giovanni Leone, original Arabic name al-Hasan Ibn Muhammad al-Wazzan al-Zayyati, or al-Fasi) (1485–1554). Traveler whose writings remained, for some four hundred years, one of Europe's principal sources of information about Islam. Captured and enslaved in youth by Christian pirates, he was presented as a gift to Pope Leo X. Impressed with his slave's learning, the pontiff freed him after a year and, having persuaded him to profess Christianity, stood sponsor at his baptism in 1520. As Giovanni Leone, the new convert enjoyed favor in scholarly Roman society, learned Latin and Italian, and taught Arabic. Around 1526 he completed his greatest work, *Descrittione dell'Africa* (1550; *A Geographical Historie of Africa* [1600]).

Leon, Juan. See **Leo Africanus**.

Linus. In classical mythology, the name for several figures, one of whom was a musician and poet; when he set himself up as a rival to Apollo, the god destroyed him.

Lord Monsieur of France, duke of Anjou (Hercule-François, duc d'Anjou) (b. 1554, duke of Alençon 1566–76, duke of Anjou 1576–84). Fourth and youngest son of Henry II of France and Catherine de Médicis; each of his three brothers—Francis II, Charles IX, and Henry III—became king of France. He too would have been king had he not died early, at age thirty. He courted Elizabeth I, negotiating a marriage contract in 1579, which was never concluded, though he visited her in London twice to woo her (1579, 1581–82). Seeking to exploit the unsettled conditions in the Netherlands during the Dutch revolt against Spanish rule, he had himself proclaimed duke of Brabant and count of Flanders (1581), but the titles were not recognized.

Louis XII, king of France (b. 1462, ruled 1498–1515). Second husband of Anne of Brittany.

Lucian of Samosate (125–ca. 190 CE). Greek satirical author whose numerous works include *Herakles* (Hercules) and *True Histories*, a cynical parody of contemporary travel and adventure stories.

Lucilius, Gaius (180?–103? BCE). Effectively the inventor of poetical satire who gave to the existing, formless Latin *satura* (meaning "a mixed dish") the distinctive character of critical comment that the word *satire* still implies.

Lucius III, Pope (b. 1097?, pope 1181–85). Lucius's synod implemented the strict decrees of the Third Lateran Council (1179) and founded the medieval Inquisition. He was active in the Church's attack against the Cathars (a heretical sect which held that good and evil had separate creators) and the Waldensians (who sought to follow Christ in poverty and simplicity).

Lucretius (Titus Lucretius Carus) (98?–55? BCE). Latin poet and philosopher, author of *De rerum natura* (*On the Nature of Things*), a poem expounding the physical, ethical, and logical theory of the Greek materialist philosopher Epicurus.

Lycophron of Chalcis (early 3rd c. BCE). Tragic poet, grammarian, and commentator on the comic poets; only fragments of his works survive.

Lydgate, John (1370?–1450?). English poet and Benedictine monk in the monastery of Bury St. Edmund's who was known for long and moralizing devotional works, among them *The Fall of Princes*.

Macrinus, Salmoneus. See **Salmon, Jean.**

Manilius, Marcus (fl. early 1st c. CE). Latin writer, author of *Astronomica*, an unfinished poem about astronomy written in the style of Lucretius, Vergil, and Ovid.

Mantuan (Battista Spagnoli) (1448–1516). Italian humanist and poet, born in Mantua, whose literary reputation rested on his *Eclogues*, ten pastoral poems in Latin, which were widely imitated throughout Europe in both Latin and the vernacular languages.

Marcellus (Marcus Claudius Marcellus) (42–23 BCE). Nephew of the emperor Augustus, son of Octavia, and husband of the emperor's daughter Julia, who was thought to have been chosen as Augustus' heir, though Augustus himself denied it. Marcellus was celebrated by many writers, especially by Vergil in a famous passage in the *Aeneid* (6.1179ff.). He is frequently identified with the wondrous newborn boy whose birth Vergil's *Fourth Eclogue* celebrates.

Marcus Aurelius (Caesar Marcus Aurelius Antoninus Augustus; original name **Marcus Annius Verus)**, Roman emperor (b. 121 CE, ruled 161–180). Best known for his *Meditations*, a collection of maxims written in Greek that express his Stoic philosophy.

Margaret of France, queen of Navarre (1492–1549). Margaret of Angoulême, also called Margaret of Navarre, was Queen Consort of Henry II of Navarre and sister of Francis I of France. A patron of humanists and Reformers, she was an author in her own right, best known for the *Heptameron* (1558). The future Elizabeth I of England later translated her 1531 *Miroir de l'Ame Pécheresse* (Mirror of the Sinful Soul), published in Marburg in 1548.

Margaret of Parma (1527–1586). Illegitimate daughter of the Holy Roman Emperor Charles V, wife of Ottavio Farnese, duke of Parma, and mother of

Alessandro Farnese, a brilliant soldier and diplomat who secured Spanish rule in the southern Dutch provinces. Margaret was made Regent of the Netherlands in 1559, opposed the Dutch rebellion led by William of Orange, but resigned when Philip decided to use force to suppress the rebellion.

Marot, Clément (1496?–1544). Major poet of the French Renaissance and client of Francis I. Marot introduced many developments from Italian poetry into his verse, and produced controversially artful translations of the Psalms.

Mary I, queen of England (b. 1516, ruled 1553–58). Daughter of Henry VIII and Catherine of Aragon who married Philip II of Spain and returned the Church of England to Catholicism, coming to be known as "Bloody Mary" because of her persecution of Protestants (nearly three hundred of whom were burned at the stake during her reign).

Mary, queen of Scots (Mary Stuart) (b. 1542, queen of Scotland 1542–67, Queen Consort of France 1559–60, d. 1587). Only child of King James V of Scotland and his French wife, Mary of Guise; raised from age five at the French court by Henry II and his wife, Catherine de Médicis, she married their son and heir Francis in 1558, but was widowed in 1560. Returning to Scotland as queen in 1561, the Catholic Mary became involved in complex court intrigue and was eventually forced by the Protestant nobles to renounce the throne in favor of her son, James VI. She fled for protection to England in 1567, where she was placed under house arrest. A focus for Catholic plots to depose Elizabeth in her favor, after twenty years of continuing international intrigue, she was executed in 1587 for her supposed role in a plot to assassinate Elizabeth. Puttenham probably wrote the anonymous *Justification of Queen Elizabeth in Relation to the Affair of Mary Queen of Scots* (unpublished in the period; written ca. 1588–90).

Matthias, archduke of Austria, Holy Roman Emperor (b. 1557, ruled 1612–19). Third son of the archduke Maximilian of Austria (later emperor), he received no territories on his father's death. This incompetent and unreliable Habsburg ruler was invited by the Catholic nobility of the Spanish Netherlands to replace Don Juan of Austria as governor general (1577). Unable to arrange a compromise peace between Spain and the Protestant faction headed by William of Orange, he returned to Germany in 1581. In a reversal of the policy of his father, Maximilian II, he sponsored a Catholic revival in the Habsburg domains that, despite his moderating influence, eventually led to the outbreak of the Thirty Years' War.

Maximilian, archduke of Austria, Holy Roman Emperor (b. 1459, archduke 1493, Emperor 1508–19). Son of Emperor Frederick III, father of the archduke Matthias, grandfather of Charles V, he was a German king and Holy Roman Emperor who established the Habsburgs as the dominant political family in sixteenth-century Europe. In 1477 he married Mary, duchess of Burgundy, and by means of her vast Netherlandish holdings became the first of a long series of unwelcome Habsburg (and foreign) rulers of the Low Countries, whose troubles with their subject people continued well beyond Puttenham's time.

Maximinus (Gaius Julius Verus Maximinus), emperor of Rome (b. ca. 173 CE, ruled 235–238). The first soldier to rise from the ranks to become emperor; renowned for his physical strength.

Menander (342?–292? BCE). Athenian dramatist whom ancient critics considered the supreme poet of Greek New Comedy—the last flowering of Athenian stage comedy.

Musaeus (1). In classical mythology, a seer and priest associated with Orpheus; said to have produced poetry even before Homer.

Musaeus (2) (**Musaeus Grammaticus**) (fl. beginning 6th c.). A Latin poet who wrote an account of Hero and Leander.

Musonius (**Gaius Musonius Rufus**) (1st c. CE). Roman Stoic philosopher who taught Pliny the Younger and the Stoic philosopher Epictetus.

Nicander (2nd c. BCE). Greek grammarian, poet, and doctor who composed works on medicine and grammar as well as literature, of which only two survive, including *Alexipharmaca*, a poem about poisons and their antidotes.

Northumberland, duke of. See **Dudley, John**.

Oppianus (2nd c. CE). Greek didactic poet who composed a poem on fishing in five books. He also wrote a work on hunting that has been lost; another extant book on that subject was formerly attributed to him, although it is now attributed to another Oppianus who composed it a century later.

Paget, Henry, 2nd Lord of Beaudesert (1537?–1568). English nobleman, first son and heir of a major officeholder under Henry VIII and 2nd Baron Paget, who was made a Knight of the Bath by Mary in 1553.

Paracelsus (**Philippus Aureolus Theophrastus Bombastus von Hohenheim**) (1493–1541). German-Swiss physician and alchemist who led a revolt against the ancient medical theories of Hippocrates and Galen, established the central role of chemistry in medicine, and believed that people could be cured by giving them small doses of what was causing their sickness, thus anticipating the development of homeopathic medicine.

Parmenio (**Parmenion**) (ca. 400–330 BCE). Macedonian noble and general who served Philip II and his son Alexander the Great. Although he was partly responsible for Alexander's accession to the throne and served as Alexander's loyal second-in-command in Asia, the two were gradually estranged, and when Parmenion's son Philotas was executed for alleged treason in 330, he was himself murdered at Alexander's command.

Paulet, Sir William (1483?–1572). Lord Treasurer of England under Edward, Mary, and Elizabeth (1550–72), who was made 1st marquis of Winchester (1551).

Perseus. In Greek mythology, the son of Zeus and Danaë, the slayer of the Gorgon Medusa, and the rescuer of Andromeda from a sea monster.

Persius (**Antonius Persius Flaccus**) (34–62 CE?). Roman satirical poet who was a Stoic and composed a book of poems, the *Saturae* (Satires), which are characterized by their high moral tone and their bitter denunciations of Roman moral corruption.

Peter I, king of Castile and Leon (b. 1334; ruled 1350–69). Son of Alfonso XI who was known by contemporary enemies as Peter the Cruel.

Petrarch, Francis (**Francesco Petrarca**) (1304–1374). Italian poet and scholar who is considered the father of humanism because of his passionate devotion to classical culture. He wrote numerous works in Latin, including *Secretum meum* (*My Secret*), *De viris illustribus* (*On Famous Men*), and the incomplete epic *Africa*, as well as countless volumes of letters. He is most famous for his vernacular *Trionfi* (*Triumphs*) and, above all, his *Canzoniere* (*Songbook*), a collection of lyrics recounting his love for Laura, which inaugurated the pan-European vogue of the sonnet sequence.

Phaer, Thomas (1510?–1560). English lawyer, physician, and translator who was the author of legal handbooks, a popular medical treatise, occasional poetry, and a partial translation of the *Aeneid*.

Pharnax (Pharnaces II), king of Bosporus (ruled 63–47 BCE). Son of Mithradates IV Eupator who was installed on the throne by Pompey. He rebelled against Roman rule during the civil war between Pompey and Julius Caesar, but was defeated with lightning speed by the latter at the battle of Zela in 47 BCE, prompting the famous boast *Veni, vidi, vici* (I came, I saw, I conquered). He was killed by a rival for the throne later that year upon his return to Bosporus.

Philip II, king of Macedonia (b. 382 BCE, ruled 359–336). Father of Alexander the Great, he conquered the city-states of Greece.

Philip II, king of Spain (b. 1527, ruled 1556–98). During his reign the Spanish Empire attained its greatest power, extent, and influence, though he failed to suppress the revolt of the Netherlands (beginning in 1566) and lost the "Invincible Armada" in an attempted invasion of England (1588).

Philip III, 3rd duke of Aerschot (b. 1526, ruled 1551–95). He was the second son of the Spanish king Philip II; his elder brother Charles was 2nd duke of Aerschot until his assassination in 1551. He became the most powerful person in the Netherlands after William of Orange, but was notorious for his frequent changing of sides in the Low Countries' complex relations with France and Spain.

Philip de Valois, Philip VI, king of France (b. 1293, ruled 1328–50). Ruling at the time of the outbreak of the Hundred Years' War (1337–1453), he left France weak and divided upon his death.

Philippus Agelastos (Marcus Julius Philippus) (237–249 CE). The son of the Roman emperor Philippus Arabicus, he was known for being so serious that he never smiled; he was murdered shortly after his father was killed in battle.

Philippus Arabicus (Marcus Julius Philippus), Roman emperor (ruled 244–249 CE). Born in Arabia; he was only moderately successful as a military leader and was killed in battle by his successor, Decius. The story that he was a Christian is now considered unreliable.

Philiscus (151/157–218/224 CE). Greek rhetorician about whom little is known except that he came from Thessaly, held the chair of rhetoric in Athens, and was disliked by the emperor Caracalla.

***Piers Plowman*.** See **Langland, William**.

Polemon, Marcus Antonius (ca. 88–144). Roman Sophist who was a friend to the emperors Trajan, Hadrian, and Antoninus Pius and was known for his oratory in the grand manner; his most important work was on physiognomy.

Pollio, Gaius Asinius (76 BCE–4 CE). Roman orator, poet, and historian. As Marc Antony's governor of Cisalpine Gaul, he was friendly with Vergil, and in distributing land to veterans he either saved the poet's property from confiscation or got him other lands in compensation. Vergil addressed *Eclogues* 4 and 8 to him.

Pompeius Magnus (106–48 BCE). The Roman general and triumvir called Pompey the Great formed the first Triumvirate with Julius Caesar and Crassus in 60, but broke with Caesar and was defeated by him at the battle of Pharsalia in 48 BCE. He built Rome's first permanent stone theater in 55.

Priscian (Priscianus Caesariensis) (fl. 500 CE). The best known of all the Latin grammarians, author of numerous works, including the *Institutiones grammaticae* (Foundations of Grammar), which had a profound influence on the teaching of Latin and indeed of grammar generally in Europe.

Proclus of Naucratis (ca 140–ca. 230 CE). A Greek born in Egypt who emigrated to Athens, where he became a successful merchant and opened a school in which he taught declamation. Among his pupils was Lucius Flavius Philostratus, who wrote a life of Apollonius of Tyana and the biographical *Lives of the Sophists*.

Propertius, Sextus (b. 55–43 BCE, d. after 16). Greatest elegiac poet of ancient Rome. The first of his four books of elegies, published in 29, is called *Cynthia* after its heroine (his mistress, whose real name was Hostia); it gained him entry into the literary circle centering on Maecenas.

Ptolemy I Soter, king of Egypt (b. ca. 367/66 BCE, ruled 304–283). First Macedonian king of Egypt.

Ptolemy II Philadelphus, king of Egypt (b. 308 BCE, ruled 285–246). Patron of Callimachus and Theocritus who was the brother and husband of Arsinoë II Philadelphus and established a religious cult for himself and her.

Pyrrhus (Pyrrhus II, king of Epirus) (ca. 318–272 BCE). Greek general and ruler who initially fought the Romans successfully, though losing many of his troops (hence the expression "Pyrrhic victory"), but was eventually defeated by them at Argos.

Ralegh, Sir Walter (1554?–1618). English explorer and writer of modest social origins, he was a controversial favorite of Elizabeth, who knighted him in 1585, but was accused of treason after James came to the throne and was imprisoned for many years and eventually executed. Among his works are numerous occasional poems as well as *A Discovery of Guiana* and *The History of the World*.

Rehoboam, King of the Jews (ruled 922–915 BCE). Son of and successor to Solomon.

Richard I, or Richard Coeur de Lion, king of England (Richard the Lion-Hearted) (b. 1157, ruled 1189–99). Duke of Acquitaine from 1168, of Poitiers from 1172, and count of Anjou and king of England from 1189, he was celebrated as the heroic leader of the Third Crusade. He was a ruthless ruler and an accomplished poet, but he earned his nickname from his prowess in battle.

Richard II, king of England (1367–1400, ruled 1377–99). Grandson of Edward III and son of Edward the Black Prince, who predeceased him; he was forced to abdicate by Henry IV and was then murdered at Henry's suggestion.

Robert le Bruce (Robert VIII le Bruce, or the Bruce) (b. 1274, ruled, with the support of Edward I of England, as Robert I of Scotland, 1296–1329). He won Scottish independence from the English by defeating them at the battle of Bannockburn in 1314.

Roscius (Quintus Roscius Gallus) (d. 62 BCE). Roman comic actor of such celebrity that his name became an honorary epithet for any particularly successful actor. He is said to have instructed Cicero in elocution.

Rous, Sir Anthony (ca. 1502–1546). A servant (the treasurer) of the 3rd duke of Norfolk, who rose to a series of high positions under Henry VIII: Comptroller of Calais, Keeper of the King's Jewel House, and finally Treasurer of the Chamber of the 1545 Parliament. He received the abbey of Icklingham from Henry VIII at the time of the Dissolution.

Sackville, Thomas, Lord Buckhurst (1536–1608). English statesman and poet, one of Elizabeth's chief councilors, and author of occasional poems, the "Induction" to the *Mirror for Magistrates*, and the first English tragedy, *Gorboduc* (with Thomas Norton).

Saint-Gelais, Mellin de (1491–1558). A French poet who enjoyed considerable success initially at the court of Francis I, and who opposed, unsuccessfully, the reformation of French poetry undertaken by members of the Pléiade such as Pierre de Ronsard and Joachim Du Bellay.

Salic law. Law of the Salian Franks which supposedly barred women from succeeding to the throne in France; the law actually states that a woman should have no right of succession to Salic land. This issue was used as the basis for the English king Henry V's claim to the French monarchy.

Sallust (Gaius Sallustius Crispus) (86–35/34 BCE). Roman historian who was born in a time of civil war followed by foreign war and political strife, and who wrote the *Bellum Catilinae* (*Conspiracy of Catiline*) and the *Bellum Jugurthinum* (*War of Jugurtha*), both of which are preoccupied with violence.

Salmon, Jean (1490–1557). French humanist and Neo-Latin poet who was known by the sobriquet Macrinus (Skinny), enjoyed the patronage of Cardinal Jean Du Bellay, and published a dozen collections of Neo-Latin poems, including odes, elegies, epigrams, and hymns.

Scipio Africanus the Elder (236–184/183 BCE). Great Roman general (surnamed in honor of his victory over Carthage); friend to the poet Ennius.

Secundus, Joannes (Johan Everaert) (1511–1536). Dutch Neo-Latin poet whose finest work, the *Basia* (*Kisses*), was a set of nineteen poems on the theme of the kiss, much admired by Puttenham.

Selim I (Selim the Grim), Ottoman emperor (b. 1467, ruled 1512–20). Brought the Ottoman Empire to its greatest heights, including within it Syria, Egypt, Palestine, and parts of Arabia and Persia, as well as Turkey and much of the Balkan peninsula.

Seymour, Edward, 1st duke of Somerset (b. ca. 1500–1506, d. 1552). Protector of England during parts of the minority of King Edward VI.

Shore, Jane (d. 1527). A beautiful, charming, and witty woman, the daughter of a merchant and wife of a goldsmith, she became the mistress of Edward IV of England in 1469 and exercised real influence on his policies. At his death in 1483, she became the mistress of the son of Edward's widow and then of William, Lord Hastings. With the latter she opposed Richard, duke of Gloucester, but when Richard became king in 1483, he had her arrested and forced to do public penance as a harlot. She never recovered from this setback and died a beggar.

Sidney, Sir Philip (1554–1586). English soldier, statesman, courtier, poet, and patron of poets and scholars, who wrote numerous works, including *Arcadia*, a long prose romance (in two versions), *The Defence of Poesie*, and *Astrophil and Stella*, a sonnet sequence imitating Petrarch's that gave rise to a host of imitators in English.

Skelton, John (1460?–1529). English poet and priest best known for his satirical verse, which was written in a style of short rhyming lines that have come to be called Skeltonics. In his own time he was considered a "poet laureate" (by virtue of having taken a degree in rhetoric at Oxford), but his reputation was only secured in the twentieth century.

Somerset, 1st duke of. See **Seymour, Edward**.

Stanyhurst, Richard (1547–1618). Accomplished classical scholar and historian who studied at Oxford but converted to Catholicism during a stay in Ireland, moved to the continent, where he became a priest around 1607, and until his death served as the chaplain to Archduke Albert of Austria. He wrote the *Description* and *History of Ireland* that appeared in Holinshed's *Chronicles* (1577), but his chief work was *The First Foure Bookes of Virgil his Aeneis* (1582), in which he tried to demonstrate that classical prosody (quantitative verse) could be applied to English poetry.

Star Chamber. Room in Westminster Palace where the monarch's council met, so called, said Sir Thomas Smith, "either because it is full of windowes, or because at the first all the roofe thereof was decked with images of starres gilted" (*De Republica Anglorum* [1565; printed 1583] 3.4; Dewar ed. 125; not, as *OED* (2nd ed.) has it, the *Discourse of the Commonwealth of England* [1577]). In the fifteenth century it served as a criminal court, but by the reigns of James and Charles its name was regarded by many as shorthand for tyranny.

Sternhold, Thomas (d. 1549). English courtier and writer, author of a translation of the Psalms which was finished by John Hopkins and enjoyed wide popularity throughout England and Scotland, continuing to be used under the name of "Sternhold and Hopkins" for a century and a half.

Stesichorus (632/629–556/553 BCE). Greek lyric poet now known only by fragments. He is credited with having invented the choral lyric and the palinode. According to Plato, Stesichorus was struck blind after having censured Helen of Troy in a poem, but he was cured after composing a poem of recantation, his *Palinodia* (see *Phaedrus* 20.243a–b). The term that he invented for his title, *palinode* (in English usage), derived from the Greek words for "back" and "ode"; it became the standard category label for recantations (usually in poetic contexts).

Stratonice. See **Antiochus I Soter.**

Straw, Jack. A possibly mythical leader of the peasants' revolt of 1381; perhaps instead an alias of Wat Tyler (d. 1381), the most famous of its leaders (along with the Lollard priest John Ball, who famously asked, "When Adam delved and Eve span, who was then the gentleman?").

Surrey. See **Howard, Henry.**

Tamerlane. See **Timur Khan.**

Telephus. A hero of Greek mythology, he was the son of Hercules who was raised in Mysia, a kingdom in the northwestern part of Asia Minor, where he was married to the daughter of the king. When the Greek army that was sailing against Troy disembarked by mistake in Mysia, Telephus led the fight against them. Wounded in battle by Achilles' lance, he languished for years, his wound unhealed, until the Greeks returned, again seeking Troy. In exchange for Telephus' agreeing to lead them to Troy, Achilles healed his wound by applying to it some of the rust from his lance.

Theocritus (b. ca. 310–300, d. 260 BCE). Greek poet born in Syracuse on the island of Sicily who was patronized by Ptolemy II Philadelphus, king of Egypt, and composed the *Idylls*, a work generally considered the first example of pastoral poetry.

Thersites. An ugly malcontent in the Greek army besieging Troy who railed at Agamemnon for leading them there and whom Odysseus rebuked and beat into silence; see *Iliad* 2.211–69.

Theseus. Great hero of Attic legend, central figure in many adventures. Among the most famous are those that concern his wife, Hippolyta, and their son Hippolytus, his exploits with various beasts and monsters such as the Minotaur, and his experiences in the underworld with Pirithous and Persephone.

Thomas, Lord Buckhurst. See **Sackville, Thomas.**

Thrace. The eastern half of the Balkan peninsula; homeland of Orpheus.

Tiberius (Tiberius Julius Caesar Augustus, original name **Tiberius Claudius Nero),** Roman emperor (b. 42 BCE, ruled 14–37 CE). Adopted son of Augustus who in his last years became a tyrannical recluse, inflicting a reign of terror on the major personages of Rome.

Tibullus, Albius (55–19 BCE). Roman poet, the second in the classical sequence of great Latin writers of erotic elegy that begins with Cornelius Gallus and continues through Tibullus and Sextus Propertius to Ovid.

Timocrates (b. ca. 70 CE). Greek Sophist who was the teacher of the Sophist Polemon.

Timur Khan (ca. 1336–1405). Mongol conqueror who was also known as Timur Leng (Timur the Lame) and who claimed descent from Jenghiz Khan. He conquered the area between the Black and Caspian seas, invaded Russia and India, defeated the Ottoman Turks, and finally died while planning an invasion of China. Known for his cruelty, he was the subject of Christopher Marlowe's *Tamburlaine*.

Titus Vespasian. See **Vespasian**.

Tityrus. Shepherd who appears in the first of Vergil's *Eclogues*.

Totila (d. 552 CE). Ostrogoth king who recovered most of central and southern Italy, which had been conquered by the Eastern Roman Empire in 540.

Trajan (**Caesar Divi Nervae Filius Nerva Traianus Optimus Augustus,** original name **Marcus Ulpius Traianus**), Roman emperor (b. 52 CE, ruled 98–117). The first emperor to be born outside Italy, he undertook a vast building program and increased social welfare.

Turberville, George (1540?–1597?). English writer who translated a number of Latin works and was the first in England to publish a book of poems (*Epitaphs, Epigrams, Songs and Sonets*, 1567) dedicated to his "lady," in this case Sir Philip Sidney's aunt, the countess of Warwick.

Twyne, Thomas (1543–1613). English physician who wrote occasional poems and translated a number of Latin works; he finished the translation of the *Aeneid* begun by Thomas Phaer, including with it a translation of Maffeo Vegio's *Supplementum*, the thirteenth book Vegio added to Vergil's work.

Tyrtaeus (fl. 650 BCE). Greek elegiac poet, author of stirring poetry on military themes, which now survives mostly in fragments.

Valentinian (**Flavius Valentinianus**), Roman emperor (b. 321 CE, ruled 364–375). He skillfully and successfully defended the frontiers of the Western Roman Empire against Germanic invasions.

Vandals. Germanic people who maintained a kingdom in North Africa from 429 to 534 CE and who sacked Rome in 455.

Vaux, Thomas, 2nd Baron Vaux of Harrowden (1510–1556). English poet and courtier associated with Wyatt and Surrey and their efforts to employ Italian and French poetic models in English.

Vespasian (**Titus Flavius Vespasianus**) Roman Emperor (b. 9 CE, ruled 69–79). Distinguishing himself as a military commander and administrator under the emperors Claudius and Nero, he became emperor by ending the brief civil war that followed the death of Nero and was the founder of the Flavian dynasty of emperors, including his sons Titus and Domitian.

William I, the Conqueror, king of England (b. 1027?, ruled 1066–87). Illegitimate son of Robert I, duke of Normandy, who succeeded to his father's duchy in 1035, gradually consolidated his rule there, and extracted promises from both Edward of England (Edward the Confessor) and Harold, earl of Wessex, that William should succeed Edward as king. When Harold took the throne in 1066, William invaded England and defeated him at the battle of Hastings. As king, he ruled England with an iron fist until his death from a riding accident in France, which he had invaded in 1087.

William I, Prince of Orange (William the Silent) (1533–1584). Raised in the court of Spain, he was appointed the Stadholder (governor) of Holland by Philip II in 1559, but eventually broke with Spain, converted to Calvinism in 1573, and became one of the principal leaders of the Dutch revolt against the Spanish. Under attack by Spanish forces led by the duke of Parma, he retired from Antwerp to Delft in Holland in 1582, where he was assassinated two years later by the fanatical Catholic Balthasar Gérard.

Wyatt, Sir Thomas (1503–1542). English poet and diplomat who was responsible for introducing various Italian and French forms into English literature; a member of Henry VIII's court, he was knighted by the king in 1537.

Xenocrates of Chalcedon (d. 314 BCE). Greek philosopher who was a disciple of Plato and was made head of the Platonic Academy from 339 until his death. From the fragments of his works that remain, it seems that he was not a particularly original thinker.

Xenophon (427?–355? BCE). A Greek historian, philosopher, and general, the pupil of Socrates and author of many works, including the *Cyropedia*, a life of the Persian king Cyrus, and the *Anabasis*, an account of the retreat of ten thousand Greek troops stranded in Persia.

Word Glossary

Abuse (s. and v.). Improper use of language, misuse, corrupt practice, deceit, injury. Puttenham translates *catachresis*, which involves applying an improper term to something, as "the Figure of Abuse" (3.17.264), and he defines all figures as being "abuses, or rather trespasses, in speech" (3.7.238).

Accident. Event.

Admire (admiration, admirable). Wonder or marvel at, feel awe about.

Affection (s. and v.). Emotion (whether positive or negative); (v.) be moved by.

After the rate. Proportionately, accordingly.

Ambage. Roundabout or indirect speech, periphrasis.

Amend (amends, amendable, amendment). Improve, correct, reform.

Amiable. Worthy of being loved, lovable, lovely.

Artificial (artificially). Artful; the product of art.

As. See **As much to say as, Insomuch as, So as.**

As much to say as. As much as to say.

At large. At length, in general, at liberty, without restraint.

Ballad. A poem, usually intended to be sung and tending to be simple and popular in character.

Band. Connective or unifying force which repetitive structural elements (such as rhyme scheme, refrain, sestina repetition) impart to a stanza of poetry or to entire poems. Puttenham's term is a metaphor from the mason's art, and he consciously notes it as such in 2.11.178, where "band" is defined as that which a mason gives to a wall by alternating bricks laid with the short side showing (called band-stones) and those with the long side showing. This technique strengthened the wall by thickening it, and by making sure that the joints between bricks (weak spots) were not all aligned.

Barbarous (barbarously, barbarousness, barbarian). Non-Hellenic; non-Roman; non-Christian; uncivilized, rude, cruel, savage, primitive, tribal. See Puttenham's consideration of the history of the word in 3.22.336–37.

Bewray. Expose, reveal prejudicially, betray.

Board. Table (usually dining table).

Breach. Act of breaking something up; divisions or units.

Busy. Occupied constantly; actively engaged; involving much work or trouble; elaborate, intricate.

By. Regarding.

Cadence. The falling of the voice, as at the end of a line of verse or song; the rhythmical movement of sound; rhyme.

Carter. One who drives a cart; a poor rural laborer; stereotypically one of low birth or breeding, viewed with condescension as rude and uncultured; hence (as a term of abuse), base fellow, rascal, boor; cf. villain.

Circumstances. Accompanying facts or conditions; in logic and rhetoric, the adjuncts or attributes of a thing.

Cleanly. Artfully; artful.

Clerk (clerkly). Learned man, someone with a university education.

Color (s. and v.). Rhetorical device, ornament of style; (v.) embellish, disguise.

Compass (s. and v.). Circle, circumference, boundary; globe; circumscribed area or space; circular arc, sweep; curved path (as of an arrow); (v.) draw an arc or a circle; encompass, circle round. For Puttenham, the word also designated the tiny arc of the circumflex accent and the little arcs he draws linking rhyme words together in various rhyme schemes.

Conceit. Idea, fanciful notion; elaborate metaphor; conceptual power; mind, imagination; opinion.

Conceited. Witty, clever.

Concord. Rhyme.

Convenient (conveniently, convenience, conveniency). Fitting, appropriate; consonant, congruent.

Conversation (conversant). Social interaction.

Convey. Express, arrange; carry, transfer; communicate; manage cunningly, trick; steal.

Conveyance. Expression; manner of expression, style.

Counterfeit (counterfeiter). Imitate, create, fashion; create fraudulently; (adj.) fashioned, made by art; inflated; miming; would-be; (s.) artist, poet, imitator.

Courage. Spirit, liveliness, mind, feelings, heart, nature, disposition.

Cunning (cunningly). Knowledge, skill; (adj.) knowledgeable, skillful, clever, crafty.

Curious (curiously, curiosity). Skillful, careful, ingenious, subtle, overly subtle, fastidious.

Current (currentness). Flowing, fluent.

Dark (darkness). Obscure, unclear.

Decent (decency, decently, indecent, indecency). Fitting, becoming, appropriate, decorous (from Lat. *decere*, "to be fitting").

Defect (defective). Absence; diminution or reduction; flaw.

Degree. Social rank or station.

Delicate. Delightful, voluptuous, fine, finely made, dainty, effeminate.

Device. Something devised, such as a saying, a figure of speech, or a work of art; an emblem or motto; stratagem, trick; design, conceit. "In device": in fiction, hypothetically.

Discipline (disciplinable). Instruction, teaching; (adj.) teachable.

Discover. Reveal, uncover.

Disgrace (v.). Lose grace, lack decorum, deprive of grace, disparage, shame, disfigure.

Distemper (s. and v.). Improper mixture; disturbance, lack of balance; disorder.

Distich. A pair of lines of verse, usually making complete sense, and often rhyming.

Doctor. Teacher, learned man, minister.
Doctrine. Teaching, instruction.
Doubtful (doubtfully). Ambiguous.

Efficacy. Force, power to produce effects.
Engine. Artifice, contrivance, device, plot, invention.
Enginer. One who contrives, designs, or invents; author; inventor; plotter, layer of snares.
Entreat. Treat.
Envy (envious). Regard with dislike.
Estate. Social status, rank, condition, state.

Fabulous. Pertaining to fables, i.e., exaggerated, ridiculous, untrue; given to fables.
Fantastical (fantastically). Imaginary, fabulous, irrational, capricious, foppish, eccentric, grotesque.
Forasmuch. Insofar.

Gentile. Of or pertaining to any or all of the nations other than the Jewish; heathen, pagan; Greek and Roman.
Gests. Notable deeds or actions; exploits.

Human. (Lat. *humanus*): human; humane; related to literature and the liberal arts (the *studia humanitatis*).

Idle (idly, idleness). Frivolous, trifling; not engaged in work, unemployed, inactive; indolent, lazy; unfruitful, superfluous, useless.
Imperfect. Incomplete, deficient.
Impertinent (impertinently, impertinency). Not pertinent, irrelevant, inappropriate, ill-mannered, absurd.
Inconvenient (inconveniently, inconvenience). Inappropriate, unsuitable.
Indecent (indecently, indecency). Unfitting, inappropriate, unbecoming.
Indifferent. Neutral, impartial, middling.
Inform. Give form or shape to, instruct.
Insomuch as. To such an extent that.
Intend. Direct one's course, mind, or attention; devote oneself; endeavor; mean.
Intendment. Meaning conveyed or intended; signification; import.
Interlude. A stage play, especially of a popular nature, a comedy, a farce. The term derives from the fact that such plays were originally put on between the scenes of medieval mystery and morality plays.
Inveigle. Blind, beguile, deceive.
Invent (invention, inventive, inventor). (Lat. *invenire*) find out, discover (whether by chance or by investigation and effort), contrive, devise.

Kind (kindly). Nature; (adj. and adv.) by nature, naturally.

Large. See **At large**.
Largely. At length.
Laud. Praise, poem of praise.
Lewd. Ignorant, socially base.
List. Desire, wish, choose.
Lusts. Desires, appetites; sexual lusts.

Manners. Customs, habits.

Mean. Socially or otherwise inferior; middling, in between high and low (as in style).

Measure. Meter, metrical unit, foot.

Meter. A particular unit of verse, i.e., a foot; the particular rhythmical pattern of a poem; a piece of metrical composition such as a line of verse or an entire poem.

Nice (niceties). Strange, rare; minute, slight, trivial, subtle; fine, refined; meticulous, attentive.

Nonce. Particular purpose or occasion.

Number. Rhythm, meter; (pl.) metrical units or feet and hence, lines of verse.

Numerosity (numerous). The rhythmical quality possessed by verse; (adj.) measured, rhythmic, harmonious, musical.

Peradventure. Perhaps.

Perfect (perfection). Complete, having all essential characteristics; excellent.

Plausible (plausibly). Acceptable, credible, praiseworthy, pleasing.

Policy. Prudence, sagacity, shrewdness (in general and in political affairs); cunning, dissimulation; prudent procedure; trick or stratagem.

Politician. One versed or interested in the theory of government; a shrewd, crafty schemer (usually negative).

Popular (popularly). In the manner of the common people; designed to appeal to the common people.

Preposterous (preposterously). Inverted, disordered, contrary to reason; literally, backside foremost, i.e., putting what is in front ("pre-") behind ("-posterous"; cf. posterior, posteriors); hence the common Renaissance "translation" of it as *arsy-versy*.

Proportion (proportionable, disproportion, disproportioned). Puttenham thinks of things, from various aspects of a poem to the universe in general (in 2.1), as being arranged in a harmonious, mathematical way so that individual entities are related to others systematically and regularly by what he calls proportion. Proportion thus defines the governing principle of the arrangement, and is synonymous with the qualities of harmony and mathematical regularity. Further, he uses the word to refer to the arrangement itself, so that a poem or the world may have, or even be, (a) proportion. Finally, he uses the word to refer to particular units within an arrangement that are related to one another harmoniously or mathematically, i.e., stanzas and lines within stanzas of poems.

Quick. Live, alive; lively.

Quickness. Liveliness.

Rabate. This term (which Puttenham spells variously in 2.12 [rabates], 3.11 [rabbating, rabbate], and 3.25 [rabbated]) seems to involve one or both of the following senses (both of which derive from the same Old French term): (1) a shortening or diminishing (as in *rebate*); (2) a notch (as in *rabbet*), from the usage in wood and stone work—a channel, usually rectangular, cut out of a piece of wood or stone (designed to receive the like-shaped edge of another piece).

Rate. See **After the rate**.

Recreate (recreative, recreation). Restore to vigor or life, refresh, cheer; engage in pleasurable exercise; give pleasure.

Reduce. Put into order, organize (sometimes by compulsion).
Rude (rudely, rudeness). Uneducated, ignorant, inexperienced, uncivilized, unrefined, unmannerly, disorderly.

Sad. Sober, serious, mournful, dark.
Scholar (scholarly). Student, pupil; learned person.
Scholastical. Academic, relating to the school; unduly formal or subtle, pedantic; pertaining to the Schoolmen, or Scholastic philosophers, such as Thomas Aquinas and Duns Scotus, who were fairly consistently derided by Renaissance humanists.
Science (scientific). Art, branch of knowledge.
Sensible. Capable of being perceived, understood, or felt.
Sentence. Complete thought or grammatical unit, judgment, opinion, meaning, significance, sententious saying; (v.) judge, assess.
Sententious (sententiousness). Meaningful; wise; aphoristic.
Shrewd (shrewdly). Mischievous, wicked, shrewish.
Simple. Guileless, artless; humble, of low rank; insignificant or slight; deficient in knowledge or learning; foolish, silly, stupid.
Situation. Positioning, location.
Skill (skillful, skillfully). Art, knowledge, ability.
Slipper (slippery). Smooth, easily uttered or pronounced.
So as. So that.
Sport (sporting, sportingly) (s. and v.). Amusement, recreation, pastime, jest.
Staff (pl. staves). Stanza.
Stick (v.). Baulk, hesitate; usually complemented by "to," meaning "at."
Still. Always, constantly, on every occasion.
Stir (s.). Poetic beat or stress.
Stir (stirring) (v.). Move both spatially and emotionally. In this latter sense Puttenham sometimes uses the word to translate the Latin *movere* ("to move," and in particular, "to move the emotions"), which identifies one of the three *officia* (offices or functions) of rhetoric, the others being *docere* (to teach) and *delectare* (to delight).
Store. Abundance.
Strange (strangeness). Foreign, unusual; singular, causing wonder; separate, distant; (of persons) distant, cold.
Stranger. Foreigner, non-native.
Success. Outcome, result, termination.
Surplusage. Surplus, excess, superabundance.
Symphony (symphonical). Congruity or harmony of sounds. Puttenham uses it as a synonym for rhyme.

Table (tables). Tablet, whether small (for the pocket) or large (as in funerary monuments); painter's canvas or wooden board; woodcarver's panel; (pl.) the game of backgammon.
Temper (temperament, temperate) (s. and v.). Mixture, composition; character; (v.) mix together; combine together properly or harmoniously; (adj.) properly blended together.
Toy. Trifle, amorous dallying, fantastic trick or notion.
Traffic (s. and v.). Trade, business; (v.) have dealings with a person, carry on negotiations.
Travail. Labor, trouble, exertion; travel.

Trial. Test, experiment, experience of.
Troth. Truth, faithfulness, loyalty.
Tunable (tunably). Tuneful, melodious.
Tune. Sound (as of the human voice), tone, (musical) note; rhythmical succession of sounds forming a melody.

Unskillful. Lacking in art.

Vicious (viciosity). Faulty; given to vice, depraved.
Videl. (abbreviation of *videlicet*). That is to say, namely, to wit.
Virtue (virtuous). Power, efficacy; ability; moral excellence, behavior in conformity with ethical principles.
Voluble (volubility). Fluent; capable of revolving; moving rapidly and easily with an undulating motion.
Vulgar. Vernacular; (s.) vernacular language; uneducated, common people; (adj.) customary, in common use.

Want. Need, lack.
Wanton (wantonly, wantonness). Undisciplined, ungoverned; lawless, violent; lascivious, unchaste, lewd (also, in a milder sense, given to amorous dalliance); frolicsome, sportive; self-indulgent, luxurious; insolent in triumph or prosperity, reckless of justice and humanity, merciless; profuse in growth, luxuriant, rank.
Wist. Knew.
Wit (witty). Intelligence, wisdom, cleverness.
Withal. Also, moreover.
Wot. Know, knows.

Index to First Lines of Illustrative Quotations

This list incorporates the first lines of all exemplary citations of apparent or possible verse in the *Art* (complete lines, parts of lines, longer passages) in English and other languages, as well as some other passages. Puttenham's many analytic interruptions, prosodic rearrangements and rewritings, etc., differentiate the *Art* from ordinary collections of poetry: various adjustments have been made to index such elements of the text.

(1) All inset italicized lines are indexed, as are various passages labeled as verse but not inset, some passages possibly in prose, and some related exemplary cases (mottoes, anagrams, proverbial speech, nicknames).

(2) In shaped poems meant to be read from the bottom up, the final textual line is indexed.

(3) When Puttenham varies a line or phrase for metrical analysis, only the first instance is indexed.

(4) Similarly, if adjacent passages are demonstrably taken from the same poem, interrupted just by prose commentary, only the first line is indexed: e.g., the three passages beginning with "Whom virtue reared, envy hath overthrown" (3.17.263).

(5) However, when two or more consecutive lines appear not to constitute a quotation from a single poem, all are indexed: e.g., the lines starting with "Full many that in presence of thy livelihead" (2.15.211).

(6) The following exemplary elements are *not* indexed: single words examined for meter; patently prose phrases such as "the Western King"; direct discourse passages in the prose tales.

(7) Some labels have been added for clarity.

General Index

Please check the Name Glossary and the Word Glossary for additional information about persons and terms.

the Abaser *(tapinosis)*, 2n5, 58, 269, 344–45
Abode, the Figure of *(commoratio)*, 317–18
abuse of women. *See* rape and abuse of women
Abuse, the Figure of *(catachresis)*, 264–65
acatalectic, 214
accent, time, and stir, 167–68
  auricular figuration of single words by altering, 245–46
  breaking polysyllabic words between feet, 216–17
  cadence and, 169–70
  falsification of, 170–71
  in feet, 158
  Greek and Latin quantitative verse adapted for English use, 157, 200–206
  meter and, 162–63
acclamatio or *epiphonema* (the Surclose or Consenting Close), 199, 302–3
Action, Counterfeit *(pragmatographia)*, 325
acyron (the Uncouth), 342–43
Ad Herennium. See Rhetorica ad Herennium
Adagia (Erasmus). *See* Erasmus, Desiderius; Udall, Nicholas
Adam Bell, 173
Admittance, the Figure of *(paramologia)*, 312–13
the Advancer or Figure of Increase *(auxesis)*, 303–4
Aelian, 386n4
Aeneid (Vergil)
  acyron used in, 343n48
  Augustus Caesar and Marcellus, 112, 235n19
  dissembling in, 373n104
  epiphonema used in, 302

  Erasmus's conflation of two lines in, 300n135
  hysteron proteron example taken from, 254n13
  insultatio used in, 294–95
  onomatopoeia in, 266n26
  spelling, humanist correction of, 205n31
  stress in verse, 205n31
  style of, 234n15
  synonymia used in, 299–300
  translation of, 149, 200, 204, 358
Aeolian mode, 174
Aerschot, Philip III, duke of, 274
Aesculapius, 346
Aesop's fables, 330
affectionate or familiar terms, 305
aged persons
  decorum in conduct and, 363–64
  eloquence in, 226
  patronage of princes and, 362
Agesilaus II (king of Sparta/Lacedaemonia), 363
Agis II (king of Sparta/Lacedaemonia), 365
Alamanni, Luigi, 35
Alarbes (Arabs), 262n41
alchemy and alchemists, 30, 383
Alciati, Andrea, 226n29
ale-house and tavern entertainment, 173
Aleandro, Girolamo, 287n36
Alençon, duke of (Hercule-François, duc d'Anjou), 15, 17, 331, 411–12 (LN 14)
Alexander VI (pope), 105
Alexander of Aphrodisias, 109
Alexander (Athenian ambassador), 351
Alexander the Great, 64n133, 106, 331, 354, 360–61, 364, 369–70, 371, 376
Alexander the Paphlagonian, 346
Alexander, Gavin, 58, 163n15